TRAD 104

S P A R T A

Edited by
Mike Lippman

University of Arizona

First published in the United States of America in 2010 by University Readers

14 13 12 11 10   1 2 3 4 5

Printed in the United States of America

ISBN: 978-1935551-81-2

University Readers™
800.200.3908 I www.universityreaders.com

CONTENTS

THE ILIAD OF HOMER
Book III

Translated by Richmond Lattimore

Now when the men of both sides were set in order by their leaders,
the Trojans came on with clamour and shouting, like wildfowl,
as when the clamour of cranes goes high to the heavens,
when the cranes escape the winter time and the rains unceasing
and clamorously wing their way to the streaming Ocean,   5
bringing to the Pygmaian men bloodshed and destruction:
at daybreak they bring on the baleful battle against them.
But the Achaian men went silently, breathing valour,
stubbornly minded each in his heart to stand by the others.

    As on the peaks of a mountain the south wind scatters the thick mist,   10
no friend to the shepherd, but better than night for the robber,
and a man can see before him only so far as a stone cast,
so beneath their feet the dust drove up in a stormcloud
of men marching, who made their way through the plain in great speed.

    Now as these in their advance had come close together,   15
Alexandros the godlike leapt from the ranks of the Trojans,
as challenger wearing across his shoulders the hide of a leopard,
curved bow and sword; while in his hands shaking two javelins
pointed with bronze, he challenged all the best of the Argives
to fight man to man against him in bitter combat.   20

    Now as soon as Menelaos the warlike caught sight of him
making his way with long strides out in front of the army,
he was glad, like a lion who comes on a mighty carcass,
in his hunger chancing upon the body of a horned stag
or wild goat; who eats it eagerly, although against him   25
are hastening the hounds in their speed and the stalwart young men:
thus Menelaos was happy finding godlike Alexandros
there in front of his eyes, and thinking to punish the robber,
straightway in all his armour he sprang to the ground from his chariot.

Homer, *The Iliad*. Trans. Richmond Lattimore. University of Chicago Press. Copyright © 1961 in the
public domain.

But Alexandros the godlike when he saw Menelaos   30
showing among the champions, the heart was shaken within him;
to avoid death he shrank into the host of his own companions.
As a man who has come on a snake in the mountain valley
suddenly steps back, and the shivers come over his body,
and he draws back and away, cheeks seized with a green pallor;   35
so in terror of Atreus' son godlike Alexandros
lost himself again in the host of the haughty Trojans.
    But Hektor saw him and in words of shame rebuked him:
'Evil Paris, beautiful, woman-crazy, cajoling,
better had you never been born, or killed unwedded.   40
Truly I could have wished it so; it would be far better
than to have you with us to our shame, for others to sneer at.
Surely now the flowing-haired Achaians laugh at us,
thinking you are our bravest champion, only because your
looks are handsome, but there is no strength in your heart, no courage.   45
Were you like this that time when in sea-wandering vessels
assembling oarsmen to help you you sailed over the water,
and mixed with the outlanders, and carried away a fair woman
from a remote land, whose lord's kin were spearmen and fighters,
to your father a big sorrow, and your city, and all your people,   50
to yourself a thing shameful but bringing joy to the enemy?
And now you would not stand up against warlike Menelaos?
Thus you would learn of the man whose blossoming wife you have taken.
The lyre would not help you then, nor the favours of Aphrodite,
nor your locks, when you rolled in the dust, nor all your beauty.   55
No, but the Trojans are cowards in truth, else long before this
you had worn a mantle of flying stones for the wrong you did us.'
    Then in answer Alexandros the godlike spoke to him:
'Hektor, seeing you have scolded me rightly, not beyond measure—
still, your heart forever is weariless, like an axe-blade   60
driven by a man's strength through the timber, one who, well skilled,
hews a piece for a ship, driven on by the force of a man's strength:
such is the heart in your breast, unshakable: yet do not
bring up against me the sweet favours of golden Aphrodite.
Never to be cast away are the gifts of the gods, magnificent,   65
which they give of their own will, no man could have them for wanting them.
Now though, if you wish me to fight it out and do battle,
make the rest of the Trojans sit down, and all the Achaians,
and set me in the middle with Menelaos the warlike
to fight together for the sake of Helen and all her possessions.   70

That one of us who wins and is proved stronger, let him
take the possessions fairly and the woman, and lead her homeward.
But the rest of you, having cut your oaths of faith and friendship,
dwell, you in Troy where the soil is rich, while those others return home
to horse-pasturing Argos, and Achaia the land of fair women.'   75
    So he spoke, and Hektor hearing his word was happy
and went into the space between and forced back the Trojan battalions
holding his spear by the middle until they were all seated.
But the flowing-haired Achaians kept pointing their bows at him
with arrows and with flung stones striving ever to strike him   80
until Agamemnon lord of men cried out in a great voice:
'Argives, hold: cast at him no longer, o sons of the Achaians.
Hektor of the shining helm is trying to tell us something.'
    So he spoke, and they stopped fighting and suddenly all fell
silent; but Hektor between them spoke now to both sides: 85
'Hear from me, Trojans and strong-greaved Achaians, the word
of Alexandros, for whose sake this strife has arisen.
He would have all the rest of the Trojans and all the Achaians
lay aside on the bountiful earth their splendid armour
while he himself in the middle and warlike Menelaos   90
fight alone for the sake of Helen and all her possessions.
That one of them who wins and is proved stronger, let him
take the possessions fairly and the woman, and lead her homeward
while the rest of us cut our oaths of faith and friendship.'
    So he spoke, and all of them stayed stricken to silence;   95
but among them spoke out Menelaos of the great war cry:
'Listen now to me also; since beyond all others this sorrow
comes closest to my heart, and I think the Argives and Trojans
can go free of each other at last. You have suffered much evil
for the sake of this my quarrel since Alexandros began it.   100
As for that one of us two to whom death and doom are given,
let him die: the rest of you be made friends with each other.
Bring two lambs: let one be white and the other black for
Earth and the Sun God, and for Zeus we will bring yet another.
Bring, that he may seal the pledges, the strength of Priam: 105
Priam himself, for his sons are outrageous, not to be trusted;
lest some man overstep Zeus' oaths, and make them be nothing.
Always it is, that the hearts in the younger men are frivolous,
but when an elder man is among them, he looks behind him
and in front, so that all comes out far better for both sides.'   110
    So he spoke, and the Trojans and Achaians were joyful,

hoping now to be rid of all the sorrow of warfare.
They pulled their chariots into line, and themselves dismounted
and stripped off their armour which was laid on the ground beside them,
close together, so there was little ground left between them.   115
Hektor sent away to the citadel two heralds
lightly to bring down the lambs, and to summon Priam;
and powerful Agamemnon in turn sent Talthybios
to go down to the hollow ships, with orders to bring two
lambs: he did not disobey the order of great Agamemnon.   120
    Now to Helen of the white arms came a messenger, Iris,
in the likeness of her sister-in-law, the wife of Antenor's
son, whom strong Helikaon wed, the son of Antenor,
Laodike, loveliest looking of all the daughters of Priam.
She came on Helen in the chamber; she was weaving a great web,   125
a red folding robe, and working into it the numerous struggles
of Trojans, breakers of horses, and bronze-armoured Achaians,
struggles that they endured for her sake at the hands of the war god.
Iris of the swift feet stood beside her and spoke to her:
'Come with me, dear girl, to behold the marvellous things done   130
by Trojans, breakers of horses, and bronze-armoured Achaians,
who just now carried sorrowful war against each other,
in the plain, and all their desire was for deadly fighting;
now they are all seated in silence, the fighting has ended;
they lean on their shields, the tall spears stuck in the ground beside them.   135
But Menelaos the warlike and Alexandros will fight
with long spears against each other for your possession.
You shall be called beloved wife of the man who wins you.'
    Speaking so the goddess left in her heart sweet longing
after her husband of time before, and her city and parents.   140
And at once, wrapping herself about in shimmering garments,
she went forth from the chamber, letting fall a light tear;
not by herself, since two handmaidens went to attend her,
Aithre, Pittheus' daughter, and Klymene of the ox eyes.
Rapidly they came to the place where the Skaian gates stood.   145
Now those who sat with Priam: Panthoös and Thymoites,
Lampos and Klytios, Hiketaon, scion of Ares,
with Antenor and Oukalegon, both men of good counsel:
these were seated by the Skaian gates, elders of the people.
Now through old age these fought no longer, yet were they excellent   150
speakers still, and clear, as cicadas who through the forest
settle on trees, to issue their delicate voice of singing.

Such were they who sat on the tower, chief men of the Trojans.
And these, as they saw Helen along the tower approaching,
murmuring softly to each other uttered their winged words: 155
'Surely there is no blame on Trojans and strong-greaved Achaians
if for long time they suffer hardship for a woman like this one.
Terrible is the likeness of her face to immortal goddesses.
Still, though she be such, let her go away in the ships, lest
she be left behind, a grief to us and our children.'   160
     So they spoke: but Priam aloud called out to Helen:
'Come over where I am, dear child, and sit down beside me,
to look at your husband of time past, your friends and your people.
I am not blaming you: to me the gods are blameworthy
who drove upon me this sorrowful war against the Achaians.   165
So you could tell me the name of this man who is so tremendous;
who is this Achaian man of power and stature?
Though in truth there are others taller by a head than he is,
yet these eyes have never yet looked on a man so splendid
nor so lordly as this: such a man might well be royal.'   170
     Helen, the shining among women, answered and spoke to him:
'Always to me, beloved father, you are feared and respected;
and I wish bitter death had been what I wanted, when I came hither
following your son, forsaking my chamber, my kinsmen,
my grown child, and the loveliness of girls my own age.   175
It did not happen that way: and now I am worn with weeping.
This now I will tell you in answer to the question you asked me.
That man is Atreus' son Agamemnon, widely powerful,
at the same time a good king and a strong spearfighter,
once my kinsman, slut that I am. Did this ever happen?'   180
     This she said, and the old man spoke again, wondering at him:
'O son of Atreus, blessed, child of fortune and favour,
many are these beneath your sway, these sons of the Achaians.
Once before this time I visited Phrygia of the vineyards.
There I looked on the Phrygian men with their swarming horses,   185
so many of them, the people of Otreus and godlike Mygdon,
whose camp was spread at that time along the banks of Sangarios:
and I myself, a helper in war, was marshalled among them
on that day when the Amazon women came, men's equals.
Yet even they were not so many as these glancing-eyed Achaians.'   190
     Next again the old man asked her, seeing Odysseus:
'Tell me of this one also, dear child; what man can he be,
shorter in truth by a head than Atreus' son Agamemnon,

but broader, it would seem, in the chest and across the shoulders.
Now as his armour lies piled on the prospering earth, still he   195
ranges, like some ram, through the marshalled ranks of the fighters.
Truly, to some deep-fleeced ram would I liken him—
who makes his way through the great mass of the shining sheep-flocks.'
    Helen, the daughter descended of Zeus, spoke then in answer:
'This one is Laertes' son, resourceful Odysseus,   200
who grew up in the country, rough though it be, of Ithaka,
to know every manner of shiftiness and crafty counsels.'
In his turn Antenor of the good counsel answered her:
'Surely this word you have spoken, my lady, can be no falsehood.
Once in the days before now brilliant Odysseus came here   205
with warlike Menelaos, and their embassy was for your sake.
To both of these I gave in my halls kind entertainment
and I learned the natural way of both, and their close counsels.
Now when these were set before the Trojans assembled
and stood up, Menelaos was bigger by his broad shoulders   210
but Odysseus was the more lordly when both were seated.
Now before all when both of them spun their speech and their counsels,
Menelaos indeed spoke rapidly, in few words
but exceedingly lucid, since he was no long speaker
nor one who wasted his words though he was only a young man.   215
But when that other drove to his feet, resourceful Odysseus,
he would just stand and stare down, eyes fixed on the ground beneath him,
nor would he gesture with the staff backward and forward, but hold it
clutched hard in front of him, like any man who knows nothing.
Yes, you would call him a sullen man, and a fool likewise.   220
But when he let the great voice go from his chest, and the words came
drifting down like the winter snows, then no other mortal
man beside could stand up against Odysseus. Then we
wondered less beholding Odysseus' outward appearance.'
    Third in order, looking at Aias, the old man asked her: 225
'Who then is this other Achaian of power and stature
towering above the Argives by head and broad shoulders?'
    Helen with the light robes and shining among women answered him:
'That one is gigantic Aias, wall of the Achaians,
and beyond him there is Idomeneus like a god standing   230
among the Kretans, and the lords of Krete are gathered about him.
Many a time warlike Menelaos would entertain him
in our own house when he came over from Krete. And I see them
all now, all the rest of the glancing-eyed Achaians,

all whom I would know well by sight, whose names I could tell you,   235
yet nowhere can I see those two, the marshals of the people,
Kastor, breaker of horses, and the strong boxer, Polydeukes,
my own brothers, born with me of a single mother.
Perhaps these came not with the rest from Lakedaimon the lovely,
or else they did come here in their sea-wandering ships, yet   240
now they are reluctant to go with the men into battle
dreading the words of shame and all the reproach that is on me.'
    So she spoke, but the teeming earth lay already upon them
away in Lakedaimon, the beloved land of their fathers.
    Now through the town the heralds brought the symbols of oaths pledged,   245
two young rams, and cheerful wine, the yield of the tilled land
in a goatskin wine sack, while another carried the shining
mixing bowl (the herald Idaios) and the golden wine-cups.
Standing beside the aged man he spoke words to arouse him:
'Son of Laomedon, rise up: you are called by the chief men   250
of Trojans, breakers of horses, and bronze-armoured Achaians
to come down into the plain that you may seal the oaths pledged.
For warlike Menelaos and Alexandros are to fight
with long spears against each other for the sake of the woman.
Let the woman go to the winner, and all the possessions.   255
Let the rest of them, cutting their oaths of faith and friendship,
dwell, we in Troy where the soil is rich, while those others return home
to horse-pasturing Argos and Achaia the land of fair women.'
    So he spoke, and the old man shuddered, but called his companions
to yoke the horses to the car, and they promptly obeyed him.   260
And Priam mounted into the car and gathered the reins back
as Antenor beside him stepped into the fair-wrought chariot
Through the Skaian gates to the plain they steered the swift horses.
    Now when these had come among the Trojans and Achaians,
they stepped down on the prospering earth from their car with horses   265
and made their way striding among the Achaians and Trojans.
On the other side rose up the lord of men, Agamemnon,
and the resourceful Odysseus rose up. Meanwhile the proud heralds
led up the victims for the gods' oaths, and in a great wine-bowl
mixed the wine, and poured water over the hands of the princes.   270
Atreus' son laid hands upon his work-knife, and drew it
from where it hung ever beside the mighty sheath of his war sword
and cut off hairs from the heads of the lambs; and the heralds thereafter
passed these about to all the princes of the Trojans and Achaians.
Atreus' son uplifting his hands then prayed in a great voice: 275

Father Zeus, watching over us from Ida, most high, most honoured,
and Helios, you who see all things, who listen to all things,
earth, and rivers, and you who under the earth take vengeance
on dead men, whoever among them has sworn to falsehood,
you shall be witnesses, to guard the oaths of fidelity.   280
If it should be that Alexandros slays Menelaos,
let him keep Helen for himself, and all her possessions,
and we in our seafaring ships shall take our way homeward.
But if the fair-haired Menelaos kills Alexandros,
then let the Trojans give back Helen and all her possessions,   285
and pay also a price to the Argives which will be fitting,
which among people yet to come shall be as a standard.
Then if Priam and the sons of Priam are yet unwilling
after Alexandros has fallen to pay me the penalty
I myself shall fight hereafter for the sake of the ransom,   290
here remaining, until I have won to the end of my quarrel.'
     So he spoke, and with pitiless bronze he cut the lambs' throats,
letting them fall gasping again to the ground, the life breath
going away, since the strength of the bronze had taken it from them.
Drawing the wine from the mixing bowls in the cups, they poured it   295
forth, and made their prayer to the gods who live everlasting.
And thus would murmur any man, Achaian or Trojan:
'Zeus, exalted and mightiest, and you other immortals,
let those, whichever side they may be, who do wrong to the oaths sworn
first, let their brains be spilled on the ground as this wine is spilled now,   300
theirs and their sons', and let their wives be the spoil of others.'
     They spoke, but none of this would the son of Kronos accomplish.
Now among them spoke Priam descended of Dardanos also:
'Listen to me, you Trojans and you strong-greaved Achaians.
Now I am going away to windy Ilion, homeward,   305
since I cannot look with these eyes on the sight of my dear son
fighting against warlike Menelaos in single combat.
Zeus knows—maybe he knows—and the rest of the gods immortal
for which of the two death is appointed to end this matter.'
     He spoke, a godlike man, and laid the lambs in the chariot,   310
and mounted into it himself, and pulled the reins backward.
Antenor beside him stepped up into the fair-wrought chariot.
These two took their way backward and made for Ilion.
Hektor now, the son of Priam, and brilliant Odysseus
measured out the distance first, and thereafter picked up   315
two lots, and put them in a brazen helmet, and shook them,

to see which one of the two should be first to cast with his bronze spear,
and the people on each side held up their hands to the gods, and prayed
to them. Thus would murmur any man, Achaian or Trojan:
'Father Zeus, watching over us from Ida, most high, most honoured, 320
whichever man has made what has happened happen to both sides,
grant that he be killed and go down to the house of Hades.
Let the friendship and the sworn faith be true for the rest of us.'
    So they spoke, and tall Hektor of the shining helm shook
the lots, looking backward, and at once Paris' lot was outshaken. 325
All the rest sat down in their ranks on the ground, at the place where
the glittering armour of each was piled by his light-footed horses,
while one of them put about his shoulders his splendid armour,
brilliant Alexandros, the lord of lovely-haired Helen.
First he placed along his legs the fair greaves linked with 330
silver fastenings to hold the greaves at the ankles.
Afterwards he girt on about his chest the corselet
of Lykaon his brother since this fitted him also.
Across his shoulders he slung the sword with the nails of silver,
a bronze sword, and above it the great shield, huge and heavy. 335
Over his powerful head he set the well-fashioned helmet
with the horse-hair crest, and the plumes nodded terribly above it.
He took up a strong-shafted spear that fitted his hand's grip.
In the same way warlike Menelaos put on his armour.
    Now when these two were armed on either side of the battle, 340
they strode into the space between the Achaians and Trojans,
looking terror at each other; and amazement seized the beholders,
Trojans, breakers of horses, and strong-greaved Achaians.
They took their stand in the measured space not far from each other
raging each at the other man and shaking their spearshafts. 345
First of the two Alexandros let go his spear far-shadowing
and struck the shield of Atreus' son on its perfect circle
nor did the bronze point break its way through, but the spearhead bent back
in the strong shield. And after him Atreus' son, Menelaos
was ready to let go the bronze spear, with a prayer to Zeus father: 350
'Zeus, lord, grant me to punish the man who first did me injury,
brilliant Alexandros, and beat him down under my hands' strength
that any one of the men to come may shudder to think of
doing evil to a kindly host, who has given him friendship.'
    So he spoke, and balanced the spear far-shadowed, and threw it 355
and struck the shield of Priam's son on its perfect circle.
All the way through the glittering shield went the heavy spearhead

and smashed its way through the intricately worked corselet;
straight ahead by the flank the spearhead shore through his tunic,
yet he bent away to one side and avoided the dark death. 360
Drawing his sword with the silver nails, the son of Atreus
heaving backward struck at the horn of his helmet; the sword-blade
three times broken and four times broken fell from his hand's grip.
Groaning, the son of Atreus lifted his eyes to the wide sky:
'Father Zeus, no God beside is more baleful than you are. 365
Here I thought to punish Alexandros for his wickedness;
and now my sword is broken in my hands, and the spear flew vainly
out of my hands on the throw before, and I have not hit him.'

He spoke, and flashing forward laid hold of the horse-haired helmet
and spun him about, and dragged him away toward the strong-greaved Achaians, 370
for the broidered strap under the softness of his throat strangled Paris,
fastened under his chin to hold on the horned helmet.
Now he would have dragged him away and won glory forever
had not Aphrodite daughter of Zeus watched sharply.
375 She broke the chinstrap, made from the hide of a slaughtered bullock, 375
and the helmet came away empty in the heavy hand of Atreides.
The hero whirled the helmet about and sent it flying
among the strong-greaved Achaians, and his staunch companions retrieved it.
He turned and made again for his man, determined to kill him
with the bronze spear. But Aphrodite caught up Paris 380
easily, since she was divine, and wrapped him in a thick mist
and set him down again in his own perfumed bedchamber.
She then went away to summon Helen, and found her
on the high tower, with a cluster of Trojan women about her.
She laid her hand upon the robe immortal, and shook it, 385
and spoke to her, likening herself to an aged woman,
a wool-dresser who when she was living in Lakedaimon
made beautiful things out of wool, and loved her beyond all others.
Likening herself to this woman Aphrodite spoke to her:
'Come with me: Alexandros sends for you to come home to him. 390
He is in his chamber now, in the bed with its circled pattern,
shining in his raiment and his own beauty; you would not think
that he came from fighting against a man; you would think he was going
rather to a dance, or rested and had been dancing lately.'
So she spoke, and troubled the spirit in Helen's bosom. 395
She, as she recognized the round, sweet throat of the goddess
and her desirable breasts and her eyes that were full of shining,
she wondered, and spoke a word and called her by name, thus:

'Strange divinity! Why are you still so stubborn to beguile me?
Will you carry me further yet somewhere among cities   400
fairly settled? In Phrygia or in lovely Maionia?
Is there some mortal man there also who is dear to you?
Is it because Menelaos has beaten great Alexandros
and wishes, hateful even as I am, to carry me homeward,
is it for this that you stand in your treachery now beside me?   405
Go yourself and sit beside him, abandon the gods' way,
turn your feet back never again to the path of Olympos
but stay with him forever, and suffer for him, and look after him
until he makes you his wedded wife, or makes you his slave girl.
Not I. I am not going to him. It would be too shameful.   410
I will not serve his bed, since the Trojan women hereafter
would laugh at me, all, and my heart even now is confused with sorrows.'
    Then in anger Aphrodite the shining spoke to her:
'Wretched girl, do not tease me lest in anger I forsake you
and grow to hate you as much as now I terribly love you,   415
lest I encompass you in hard hate, caught between both sides,
Danaans and Trojans alike, and you wretchedly perish.'
    So she spoke, and Helen daughter of Zeus was frightened
and went, shrouding herself about in the luminous spun robe,
silent, unseen by the Trojan women, and led by the goddess.   420
    When they had come to Alexandros' splendidly wrought house,
the rest of them, the handmaidens went speedily to their own work,
but she, shining among women, went to the high-vaulted bedchamber.
Aphrodite the sweetly laughing drew up an armchair,
carrying it, she, a goddess, and set it before Alexandros,   425
and Helen, daughter of Zeus of the aegis, took her place there
turning her eyes away, and spoke to her lord in derision:
'So you came back from fighting. Oh, how I wish you had died there
beaten down by the stronger man, who was once my husband.
There was a time before now you boasted that you were better   430
than warlike Menelaos, in spear and hand and your own strength.
Go forth now and challenge warlike Menelaos
once again to fight you in combat. But no: I advise you
rather to let it be, and fight no longer with fair-haired
Menelaos, strength against strength in single combat   435
recklessly. You might very well go down before his spear.'
    Paris then in turn spoke to her thus and answered her:
'Lady, censure my heart no more in bitter reprovals.
This time Menelaos with Athene's help has beaten me;

another time I shall beat him. We have gods on our side also. 440
Come, then, rather let us go to bed and turn to love-making.
Never before as now has passion enmeshed my senses,
not when I took you the first time from Lakedaimon the lovely
and caught you up and carried you away in seafaring vessels,
and lay with you in the bed of love on the island Kranae, 445
not even then, as now, did I love you and sweet desire seize me.'
    Speaking, he led the way to the bed; and his wife went with him.
So these two were laid in the carven bed. But Atreides
ranged like a wild beast up and down the host, to discover
whether he could find anywhere godlike Alexandros. 450
Yet could none of the Trojans nor any renowned companion
show Alexandros then to warlike Menelaos.
These would not have hidden him for love, if any had seen him,
since he was hated among them all as dark death is hated.
    Now among them spoke forth the lord of men Agamemnon: 455
'Listen to me, o Trojans, Dardanians and companions:
clearly the victory is with warlike Menelaos.
Do you therefore give back, with all her possessions, Helen
of Argos, and pay a price that shall be befitting,
which among people yet to come shall be as a standard.' 460
    So spoke Atreus' son, and the other Achaians applauded him.

THE ODYSSEY OF HOMER
Book IV

Translated by Richmond Lattimore

They came into the cavernous hollow of Lakedaimon
and made their way to the house of glorious Menelaos.
They found him in his own house giving, for many townsmen,
a wedding feast for his son andhis stately daughter. The girl
he was sending to the son of Achilleus, breaker of battalions,   5
for in Troy land first he had nodded his head to it and promised
to give her, and now the gods were bringing to pass their marriage;
so he was sending her on her way, with horses and chariots,
to the famous city of the Myrmidons, where Neoptolemos
was lord, and he brought Alektor's daughter from Sparta, to give   10
powerful Megapenthes, his young grown son born to him
by a slave woman; but the gods gave no more children to Helen
once she had borne her first and only child, the lovely
Hermione, with the beauty of Aphrodite the golden.

   So these neighbors and townsmen of glorious Menelaos   15
were at their feasting all about the great house with the high roof,
 and taking their ease, and among them stepped an inspired singer
playing his lyre, while among the dancers two acrobats
led the measures of song and dance, revolving among them.

   These two now, the hero Telemachos and the shining   20
son of Nestor in the forecourt, themselves and their horses,
stood, while powerful Eteoneus, who was the active
henchman of glorious Menelaos, came forward and saw them
and went with his message through the house to the shepherd of the people.
He came and standing close beside him addressed him in winged words: 25
'Menelaos, dear to Zeus, here are certain strangers,
two men, and they look like the breed of great Zeus. Tell me
then, whether we should unharness their fast horses,
or send them on to somebody else, who can entertain them.'

Homer, *The Odyssey*. Trans. Richmond Lattimore. Harper Collins Publishers, Inc. Copyright © 1999 in the public domain.

Then, deeply vexed, fair-haired Menelaos answered him: 30
'Eteoneus, son of Boëthoös, you were never
a fool before, but now you are babbling nonsense, as a child
would do. Surely we two have eaten much hospitality
from other men before we came back here. May Zeus only
make an end of such misery hereafter. Unharness   35
the strangers' horses then, and bring the men here to be feasted.'
    So he spoke, and the man hurried through the hall, bestirring
the other active henchmen to come on the way along with him.
They set free the sweating horses from under the harness,
and tethered them fast by the reins in front of the horse mangers,   40
and put down fodder before them and mixed white millet into it,
and leaned the chariots up against the glittering inner walls,
and led the men inside the divine house. These marvelled
as they admired the palace of the king whom Zeus loved,
for as the shining of the sun or the moon was the shining   45
all through this high-roofed house of glorious Menelaos.
When with their eyes they had had their pleasure in admiration,
they stepped into the bathtubs smooth-polished and bathed there.
Then when the maids had bathed them and anointed them with oil,
and put cloaks of thick fleece and tunics upon them, they went   50
and sat on chairs beside Menelaos the son of Atreus.
A maidservant brought water for them and poured it from a splendid
and golden pitcher, holding it above a silver basin
for them to wash, and she pulled a polished table before them.
A grave housekeeper brought in the bread and served it to them,   55
adding many good things to it, generous with her provisions,
while a carver lifted platters of all kinds of meat and set them
in front of them, and placed beside them the golden goblets.
Then in greeting fair-haired Menelaos said to them:
'Help yourselves to the food and welcome, and then afterward,   60
when you have tasted dinner, we shall ask you who among
men you are, for the stock of your parents can be no lost one,
but you are of the race of men who are kings, whom Zeus sustains,
who bear scepters; no mean men could have sons such as you are.'
    So he spoke, and taking in his hands the fat beef loin   65
which had been given as his choice portion, he set it before them.
They put their hands to the good things that lay ready before them.
But when they had put away their desire for eating and drinking,
then Telemachos talked to the son of Nestor, leaning
his head close to his, so that none of the others might hear him: 70

'Son of Nestor, you who delight my heart, only look at
the gleaming of the bronze all through these echoing mansions,
and the gleaming of gold and amber, of silver and of ivory.
The court of Zeus on Olympos must be like this on the inside,
such abundance of everything. Wonder takes me as I look on it.'   75
    Menelaos of the fair hair overheard him speaking,
and now he spoke to both of them and addressed them in winged words:
'Dear children, there is no mortal who could rival Zeus, seeing
that his mansions are immortal and his possessions. There may be
some man who could rival me for property, or there may be   80
none. Much did I suffer and wandered much before bringing
all this home in my ships when I came back in the eighth year.
I wandered to Cyprus and Phoenicia, to the Egyptians,
I reached the Aithiopians, Eremboi, Sidonians,
and Libya where the rams grow their horns quickly. Three times   85
in the fulfillment of a year their sheepflocks give birth
and there no lord would ever go wanting, nor would his shepherd,
for cheese or meat, nor for the sweet milk either, but always
the sheep yield a continuous supply for their sucklings.
But while I was wandering those parts and bringing together   90
much property, meanwhile another man killed my brother
secretly, by surprise and by his cursed wife's treachery.
So it is with no pleasure I am lord over all these possessions.
You will have heard all this from your fathers, whoever your fathers
are, for I have suffered much, and destroyed a household   95
that was very strongly settled and held many goods within it.
I wish I lived in my house with only a third part of all
these goods, and that the men were alive who died in those days
in wide Troy land far away from horse-pasturing Argos.
Still and again lamenting all these men and sorrowing   100
many a time when I am sitting here in our palace
I will indulge my heart in sorrow, and then another time
give over, for surfeit of gloomy lamentation comes quickly.
But for none of all these, sorry as I am, do I grieve so much
as for one, who makes hateful for me my food and my sleep, when I   105
remember, since no one of the Achaians labored as much
as Odysseus labored and achieved, and for him the end was
grief for him, and for me a sorrow that is never forgotten
for his sake, how he is gone so long, and we knew nothing
of whether he is alive or dead. The aged Laertes   110
and temperate Penelope must surely be grieving for him,

with Telemachos whom he left behind in his house, a young child.'
     He spoke, and stirred in the other the longing to weep for his father,
and the tears fell from his eyes to the ground when he heard his father's
name, holding with both hands the robe that was stained with purple   115
up before his eyes. And Menelaos perceived it,
and now he pondered two ways within, in mind and in spirit
whether he would leave it to him to name his father,
or whether he should speak first and ask and inquire about everything.
     While he was pondering these things in his heart and his spirit,   120
Helen came out of her fragrant high-roofed bedchamber,
looking like Artemis of the golden distaff. Adreste
followed and set the well-made chair in place for her,
and the coverlet of soft wool was carried in by Alkippe,
and Phylo brought the silver workbasket which had been given   125
by Alkandre, the wife of Polybos, who lived in Egyptian
Thebes, where the greatest number of goods are stored in the houses.
Polybos himself gave Menelaos two silver bathtubs,
and a pair of tripods, and ten talents of gold, and apart from
these his wife gave her own beautiful gifts to Helen.   130
She gave her a golden distaff and a basket, silver,
with wheels underneath, and the edges were done in gold, Phylo,
her maidservant, now brought it in and set it beside her
full of yarn that had been prepared for spinning. The distaff
with the dark-colored wool was laid over the basket. Helen   135
seated herself on the chair, and under her feet was a footstool.
At once she spoke to her husband and questioned him about everything:
'Do we know, Menelaos beloved of Zeus, who these men
announce themselves as being, who have come into our house now?
Shall I be wrong, or am I speaking the truth? My heart tells me   140
to speak, for I think I never saw such a likeness, neither
in man nor woman, and wonder takes me as I look on him,
as this man has a likeness to the son of great-hearted Odysseus,
Telemachos, who was left behind in his house, a young child
by that man when, for the sake of shameless me, the Achaians   145
went beneath Troy, their hearts intent upon reckless warfare.'
     Then in answer fair-haired Menelaos said to her:
'I also see it thus, my wife, the way you compare them,
for Odysseus' feet were like this man's, his hands were like this,
and the glances of his eyes and his head and the hair growing.   150
Now too I was remembering things about Odysseus
and spoke of him, what misery he had in his hard work

for me; and he let fall a heavy tear from under his eyelids,
holding before his eyes the robe that was stained with purple.'

    Now Peisistratos son of Nestor spoke up before him: 155
'Great Menelaos, son of Atreus, leader of the people,
this is in truth the son of that man, just as you are saying;
but he is modest, and his spirit would be shocked at the thought
of coming here and beginning a show of reckless language
in front of you, for we both delight in your voice, as if a god   160
were speaking. The Gerenian horseman Nestor sent me
to go along with him and escort him. He longed to see you
so that youcould advise him somewhat, for word or action.
For a child endures many griefs in his house when his father
is gone away, and no others are there to help him, as now   165
Telemachos' father is gone away, and there are no others
who can defend him against the evil that is in his country.'

    Then in answer fair-haired Menelaos said to him:
See now, this is the son of a man greatly beloved who has come now
'into my house, one who for my sake endured many trials,   170
and I thought he would come, and I would love him beyond all other
Argives, if only Olympian Zeus of the wide brows granted
both of us to come home across the sea in our fast ships.
I would have settled a city in Argos for him, and made him
a home, bringing him from Ithaka with all his possessions,   175
his son, all his people. I would have emptied one city for him
out of those that are settled roundabout and under my lordship.
And, both here, we would have seen much of each other; nothing
would then have separated us two in our friendship and pleasure,
until the darkening cloud of death had shrouded us over.   180
All this must be what the very god himself begrudged him,
who made only him an unhappy man, without a homecoming.'

    He spoke, and started in all of them the desire for weeping.
Helen of Argos, daughter of Zeus, wept, so too Telemachos
wept, as did Menelaos the son of Atreus, nor did   185
Nestor's son, Peisistratos, have eyes altogether tearless,
for he was thinking in his heart of stately Antilochos,
one whom the glorious son of the shining Dawn had cut down.
It was of him he thought as he addressed them in winged words:
'Son of Atreus, the aged Nestor used to say you were   190
thoughtful, surpassing other men, when we spoke about you
there in his own palace, and when we questioned each other.
So now, if it may be, would you do me a favor? For my part

I have no joy in tears after dinnertime. There will always
be a new dawn tomorrow. Yet I can have no objection   195
to tears for any mortal who dies and goes to his destiny.
And this is the only consolation we wretched mortals
can give, to cut our hair and let the tears roll down our faces.
For I myself had a brother who died, he was not the meanest
of the Argives, and you would have known him, but I for my part   200
never met nor saw him. They say he surpassed all others:
Antilochos: surpassingly swift of foot, and a fighter.'
   Then in answer fair-haired Menelaos said to him:
'Dear friend, since you have said all that a man who is thoughtful
could say or do, even one who was older than you are—   205
why, this is the way your father is, so you too speak thoughtfully.
Easily recognized is the line of that man, for whom Kronos'
son weaves good fortune in his marrying and begetting,
as now he has given to Nestor, all his days, for himself
to grow old prosperously in his own palace, and also   210
that his sons should be clever and excellent in the spear's work.
Now we shall let the weeping be, that came to us just now,
and let us think again about dinner, let someone pour us
water for our hands, and there will be time for words tomorrow
at dawn, for Telemachos and me, to talk with each other.'   215
   He spoke, and Asphalion, who was the active henchman
of glorious Menelaos, poured water for them to wash with.
They put their hands to the good things that lay ready before them.
   Now Helen, who was descended of Zeus, thought of the next thing.
Into the wine of which they, were drinking she cast a medicine   220
of heartsease, free of gall, to make one forget all sorrows,
and whoever had drunk it down once it had been mixed in the wine bowl,
for the day that he drank it would have no tear roll down his face,
not if his mother died and his father died, not if men
murdered a brother or a beloved son in his presence   225
with the bronze, and he with his own eyes saw it. Such were
the subtle medicines Zeus' daughter had in her possessions,
good things, and given to her by the wife of Thon, Polydamna
of Egypt, where the fertile earth produces the greatest number
of medicines, many good in mixture, many malignant,   230
and every man is a doctor there and more understanding
than men elsewhere. These people are of the race of Paiëon.
Now when she had put the medicine in, and told them to pour it,
taking up the story again she began to speak to them:

'Son of Atreus, dear to Zeus, Menelaos: and you who   235
are here, children of noble fathers; yet divine Zeus sometimes
gives out good, or sometimes evil; he can do anything.
Sit here now in the palace and take your dinner and listen
to me and be entertained. What I will tell you is plausible.
I could not tell you all the number nor could I name them,   240
all that make up the exploits of enduring Odysseus,
but here is a task such as that strong man endured and accomplished
in the Trojan country where you Achaians suffered miseries.
He flagellated himself with degrading strokes, then threw on
a worthless sheet about his shoulders. He looked like a servant.   245
So he crept into the wide-wayed city of the men he was fighting,
disguising himself in the likeness of somebody else, a beggar,
one who was unlike himself beside the ships of the Achaians,
but in his likeness crept into the Trojans' city, and they all
were taken in. I alone recognized him even in this form,   250
and I questioned him, but he in his craftiness eluded me;
but after I had bathed him and anointed him with olive oil
and put some clothing upon him, after I had sworn a great oath
not to disclose before the Trojans that this was Odysseus
until he had made his way back to the fast ships and the shelters,   255
then at last he told me all the purpose of the Achaians,
and after striking many Trojans down with the thin bronze
edge, he went back to the Argives and brought back much information.
The rest of the Trojan women cried out shrill, but my heart
was happy, my heart had changed by now and was for going back   260
home again, and I grieved for the madness that Aphrodite
bestowed when she led me there away from my own dear country,
forsaking my own daughter, my bedchamber, and my husband,
a man who lacked no endowment either of brains or beauty.'
    Then in answer fair-haired Menelaos said to her: 265
'Yes, my wife, all this that you said is fair and orderly.
In my time I have studied the wit and counsel of many
men who were heroes, and I have been over much of the world, yet
nowhere have I seen with my own eyes anyone like him,
nor known an inward heart like the heart of enduring Odysseus.   270
Here is the way that strong man acted and the way he endured
action, inside the wooden horse, where we who were greatest
of the Argives all were sitting and bringing death and destruction
to the Trojans. Then you came there, Helen; you will have been moved by
some divine spirit who wished to grant glory to the Trojans,   275

and Deïphobos, a godlike man, was with you when you came.
Three times you walked around the hollow ambush, feeling it,
and you called out, naming them by name, to the best of the Danaans,
and made your voice sound like the voice of the wife of each of the Argives.
    Now I myself and the son of Tydeus and great Odysseus   280
were sitting there in the middle of them and we heard you crying
aloud, and Diomedes and I started up, both minded
to go outside, or else to answer your voice from inside,
but Odysseus pulled us back and held us, for all our eagerness.
Then all the other sons of the Achaians were silent: 285
there was only one, it was Antiklos, who was ready to answer,
but Odysseus, brutally squeezing his mouth in the clutch of his powerful
hands, held him, and so saved the lives of all the Achaians
until such time as Pallas Athene led you off from us.'
    Then the thoughtful Telemachos said to him in answer: 290
'Great Menelaos, son of Atreus, leader of the people:
so much the worse; for none of all this kept dismal destruction
from him, not even if he had a heart of iron within him.
But come, take us away to our beds, so that at last now
we can go to bed and enjoy the pleasure of sweet sleep.'   295
    So he spoke, and Helen of Argos told her serving maids
to make up beds in the porch's shelter and to lay upon them
fine underbedding of purple, and spread blankets above it
and fleecy robes to be an over-all covering. The maidservants
went forth from the main house, and in their hands held torches,   300
and they made the beds. The guests were led outside by a herald.
So the hero Telemachos and the glorious son of Nestor
slept in the place outside the house in the porch's shelter,
but the son of Atreus slept in the inner room of the high house,
and by him lay Helen of the light robes, shining among women.   305
    Now when the young Dawn showed again with her rosy fingers,
Menelaos of the great war cry rose from where he was sleeping
and put on his clothes, and slung a sharp sword over his shoulder.
Underneath his shining feet he bound the fair sandals
and went on his way from the chamber, like a god in presence,   310
and sat down by Telemachos and spoke to him and named him:
'What is the need that has brought you here, O hero Telemachos,
to shining Lakedaimon over the sea's wide ridges?
A public or a private matter? Tell me this truly.'
    Then the thoughtful Telemachos said to him in answer: 315
'Great Menelaos, son of Atreus, leader of the people,

I have come to see if you could tell me some news of my father,
for my home is being eaten away, the rich fields are ruined,
and the house is full of hateful men, who now forever
slaughter my crowding sheep and lumbering horn-curved cattle,   320
these suitors of my mother, overbearing in their rapacity.
That is why I come to your knees now, in case you might wish
to tell me of his dismal destruction, whether you saw it
perhaps with your own eyes, or heard the tale from another
who wandered too. His mother bore this man to be wretched.   325
Do not soften it because you pity me and are sorry
for me, but fairly tell me all that your eyes have witnessed,
I implore you, If ever noble Odysseus, my father,
undertook any kind of word or work and fulfilled it
for you, in the land of the Trojans where all you Achaians suffered,   330
tell me these things from your memory. And tell me the whole truth.'
    Then deeply angered fair-haired Menelaos said to him:
'Oh, for shame, it was in the bed of a bold and strong man
they wished to lie, they themselves being all unwarlike.
As when a doe has brought her fawns to the lair of a lion   335
and put them there to sleep, they are newborn and still suckling,
then wanders out into the foothills and the grassy corners,
grazing there, but now the lion comes back to his own lair
and visits a shameful destruction on both mother and children;
so Odysseus will visit shameful destruction on these men.   340
O father Zeus and Athene and Apollo, I wish that
as he was when upon a time in strong-founded Lesbos
he stood up and wrestled Philomeleides from a challenge
and threw him strongly, so delighting ail the Achaians,
I wish that such an Odysseus would come now among the suitors.   345
They all would find death was quick and marriage a painful matter.
But for what you entreat me for and ask me about, I will not
turn away from the tale and speak idly, nor will I deceive you,
but of what the ever-truthful Old Man of the Sea told me
I will tell all without concealment, and hold back nothing,   350
    'The gods held me still in Egypt when I was eager to come back
here, for I had not rendered complete hecatombs to them.
The gods have always desired that their orders should be listened to.
There is an island there in the heavy wash of the open
sea, In front of Egypt, and they call it Pharos, as far out   355
as the distance a hollow ship can make in a whole day's sailing
when a sharp and following wind is blowing it onward.

And there is a harbor there with good anchorage, whence they put forth
their balanced ships to sea, after they have drawn dark water.
There the gods held me twenty days, nor did the sea winds   360
ever appear and blow across the salt water, such winds
as act to send ships sailing over the sea's wide ridges.
And now the food would all have been gone, and the men's strength with it,
if one of the gods had not been sorry for me, and shown mercy,
Eidothea, daughter to mighty Proteus, the Old Man   365
of the Sea, for it was her heart that I moved mostly
when she met me wandering by myself without my companions.
For always ranging about the island they would go fishing
with crooked fishhooks, and always the hunger oppressed their bellies.
She came and stood close beside me and spoke a word and addressed me: 370
"Are you so simple then, O stranger, and flimsy-minded,
or are you willingly giving up, and enjoying your hardships?
See, you are held so long on the island, and can find no way
out of it, while the heart in your companions diminishes."
So she spoke, and I in turn spoke up and made answer: 375
"So I will tell, whoever you may be of the goddesses,
that I am not detained of my own free will, but it must be
I have offended the immortals who hold wide heaven.
But do you then tell me, for the gods know everything, which one
of the immortals hampers me here and keeps me from my journey   380
and tell me how to make my way home on the sea where the fish swarm."
So I spoke, and she, shining among the goddesses, answered:
"See, I will accurately answer all that you ask me.
The ever truthful Old Man of the Sea ranges in these parts,
This is the Egyptian, immortal Proteus, and he knows   385
all the depths of the sea. He is Poseidon's underthegn.
And they say also he is my father, that he begot me.
If somehow you could lie in ambush and catch hold of him,
he could tell you the way to go, the stages of your journey,
and tell you how to make your way home on the sea where the fish swarm.   390
And he could tell you too, illustrious one, if you wish it,
what evil and what good has been done in your palace
while you have been gone away on your long and arduous voyage."
So she spoke, but then I answered her and said to her:
"Show me the way to lie in wait for this divine ancient,   395
for fear he may somehow see me first and be warned and avoid me.
A god is difficult for a mortal man to master."
So I spoke, and she, shining among goddesses, answered:

"See, I will accurately answer all that you ask me.
At the time when the sun has gone up to bestride the middle of heaven,   400
then the ever-truthful Old Man of the Sea will come out of the water
under the blast of the West Wind, circled in a shudder of darkening
water, and when he comes out he will sleep, under hollow caverns,
and around him seals, those darlings of the sea's lovely lady,
sleep in a huddle, after they have emerged from the gray sea,   405
giving off the sour smell that comes from the deep salt water.
There I will take you myself when dawn shows and arrange you
orderly in your ambush; you must choose from your companions
those three who are your best beside your strong-benched vessels.
Now I will tell you all the devious ways of this old man.   410
First of all he will go among his seals and count them,
but after he has reviewed them all and noted their number,
he will lie down in their midst, like a herdsman among his sheepflocks.
Next, as soon as you see that he is asleep, that will be
the time for all of you to use your strength and your vigor,   415
and hold him there while he strives and struggles hard to escape you.
And he will try you by taking the form of all creatures that come forth
and move on the earth, he will be water and magical fire.
You must hold stiffly on to him and squeeze him the harder.
But when at last he himself, speaking in words, questions you,   420
being now in the same form he was in when you saw him sleeping,
then, hero, you must give over your force and let the old man
go free, and ask him which one of the gods is angry with you,
and ask him how to make your way home on the sea where the fish swarm."
So she spoke, and dived back into the surf of the water.   425
Then I went back again to our ships where they were stationed
along the sand, but my heart was a storm in me as I went. Now
when I had come back to where my ship lay by the seaside,
we made ready our dinner, and the immortal night came over,
and then we lay down to sleep along the break of the sea beach.   430
But when the young Dawn showed again with her rosy fingers,
then I made my way along the beach of the wide-wayed
sea, praying much to the gods, and I took along with me
those three companions I trusted most for any adventure.

  'Meanwhile she had dived down into the sea's great cavern   435
and brought back the skins of four seals out of the water.
All were newly skinned. She was planning a trick on her father.
And hollowing out four beds in the sand of the sea, she sat there
waiting for us, and we came close up to her. Thereupon

she bedded us down in order, and spread a skin over each man.   440
That was a most awful ambush, for the pernicious
smell of those seals, bred in the salt water, oppressed us terribly.
Who would want to lie down to sleep by a sea-bred monster?
But she herself came to our rescue and devised a great help.
She brought ambrosia, and put it under the nose of each man,   445
and it smelled very sweet, and did away with the stench of the monster.
All that morning we waited there, with enduring spirit,
and the seals came crowding out of the sea, and when they came out
they lay down to sleep in order along the break of the sea beach.
At noon the Old Man came out of the sea and found his well-fed   450
seals, and went about to them all, and counted their number,
and we were among the first he counted; he had no idea
of any treachery. Then he too lay down among us.
We with a cry sprang up and rushed upon him, locking him
in our arms, but the Old Man did not forget the subtlety   455
of his arts. First he turned into a great bearded lion,
and then to a serpent, then to a leopard, then to a great boar,
and he turned into fluid water, to a tree with towering branches,
but we held stiffly on to him with enduring spirit
But when the Old Man versed in devious ways grew weary   460
of all this, he spoke to me in words and questioned me:
"Which of the gods now, son of Atreus, has been advising you
to capture me from ambush against my will What do you want?"
So he spoke, and I in turn spoke up and made answer:
"YOU know, Old Man. Why try to put me off with your answer?   465
See, I am held so long on the island, and can find no way
out of it, while the inward heart in me diminishes.
Do you then tell me, for the gods know everything, which one
of the immortals hampers me here and keeps me from my journey,
and tell me how to make my way home on the sea where the fish swarm."   470
So I spoke, and he in turn spoke up and made answer:
"But you should have made grand sacrifices to Zeus and the other
immortal gods, and so gone on board, so most quickly
to reach your own country, sailing over the wine-blue water.
It is not your destiny now to see your own people and come back   475
to your strong-founded house and to the land of your fathers,
until you have gone back once again to the water of Egypt,
the sky-fallen river, and there have accomplished holy hecatombs
in honor of all the immortal gods who hold wide heaven.
Then the gods will grant you that journey that you so long for."   480

So he spoke, and the inward heart in me was broken
because he ordered me to go back on the misty surface
of the water to Egypt again, a long way and a hard one,
but even so I answered him in words and said to him:
"All these things I will do, Old Man, in the way you tell me. 485
But come now, tell me this and give me an accurate answer.
Did all those Achaians Nestor and I left behind when we went
sailing from Troy come back in their ships, without injury,
or did any of them die by a dismal death on shipboard
or in the arms of his friends after he had wound up the fighting?" 490
So I spoke, and he in turn spoke up and made answer:
"Son of Atreus, why did you ask me that? You should not
learn it, nor know what my mind knows, and I think you will not be
free of tears for long, once you have heard the whole story.
There were many of these men who were lost, and many left over, 495
but two alone who were leaders of the bronze-armored Achaians
died on the way home. You yourself were there at the fighting.
And there is one who is being held alive on the wide sea
somewhere. Aias was lost, and his long-oared vessels with him.
First of all Poseidon drove him against the great rocks 500
of Gyrai, and yet he saved him out of the water,
and Aias would have escaped his doom, though Athene hated him,
had he not gone wildly mad and tossed out a word of defiance;
for he said that in despite of the gods he escaped the great gulf
of the sea, and Poseidon heard him, loudly vaunting, 505
and at once with his ponderous hands catching up the trident
he drove it against the Gyrean rock, and split a piece off it,
and part of it stayed where it was, but a splinter crashed in the water,
and this was where Aias had been perched when he raved so madly.
It carried him down to the depths of the endless and tossing main sea. 510
So Aias died, when he had swallowed down the salt water.
Your brother somehow got away and escaped the death spirits
with his hollow ships. It was the lady Hera who saved him.
But now as he had come close to the point of making the sheer peak
Maleia, then the stormwinds caught him away and carried him, 515
groaning heavily, out on the open sea where the fish swarm. 516
But since even from out there an easy homecoming was manifest 519
for him, the gods twisted the wind back, and they made the homeland 520
at the uttermost edge of his estate, where before now Thyestes 517
had made his home, but now Aigisthos son of Thyestes 518
lived. Agamemnon stepped rejoicing on the soil of his country 521

and stroked the ground with his hand and kissed it, and his thronging
hot tears streamed down, so dear to him was the sight of his country.
But a watchman saw him from his lookout, a man whom Aigisthos
had treacherously taken and stationed there, and promised him   525
two talents of gold as pay. For a year he had been watching
so Agamemnon would not go by unnoticed and mindful
of his furious valor. The man ran to the house of the war lord
with his news, and at once Aigisthos devised a treacherous stratagem.
Choosing out the twenty best fighting men in the district,   530
he set an ambush, and beside it had them arrange a festival,
and went down to welcome Agamemnon, shepherd of the people,
with horses and chariots, and with shameful thoughts in his mind, then
led him in all unsuspicious of death, and feasted him
and killed him feasting, as one strikes down an ox at his manger.   535
Not one of Agamemnon's men who followed him was left
alive, nor one of Aigisthos' men. All were killed in the palace."
So he spoke, and the inward heart in me was broken,
and I sat down on the sand and cried, nor did the heart in me
wish to go on living any longer nor to look on the sunlight.   540
But when I had glutted myself with rolling on the sand and weeping,
then the ever-truthful Old Man of the Sea said to me:
"No longer now, son of Atreus, spend your time on these wasting
tears, for I know no good that will come of it. Rather with all speed
endeavor to make good your way back to the land of your fathers.   545
You might find Aigisthos still alive, or perhaps Orestes
has beaten you to the kill, but you might be there for the burying."
So he spoke, and the heart within me and the proud spirit
of the breast were softened, even though I was so sorrowful,
and now I spoke aloud to him and addressed him in winged words: 550
"These then I know. But do you tell me the name of the third man,
whoever it is who is being held alive on the wide sea,
or else he has died, but for all my sorrow, I would hear this."
So I spoke, and he in turn spoke up and made answer:
"That was Odysseus son of Laertes, who makes his home in   555
Ithaka, whom I saw on an island, weeping big tears
in the palace of the nymph Kalypso, and she detains him
by constraint, and he cannot make his way to his country,
 for he has not any ships by him, nor any companions
who can convey him back across the sea's wide ridges.   560
But for you, Menelaos, O fostered of Zeus, it is not the gods' will
that you shall die and go to your end in horse-pasturing Argos,

but the immortals will convoy you to the Elysian
Field, and the limits of the earth, where fair-haired Rhadamanthys
is, and where there is made the easiest life for mortals,   565
for there is no snow, nor much winter there, nor is there ever
rain, but always the stream of the Ocean sends up breezes
of the West Wind blowing briskly for the refreshment of mortals.
This, because Helen is yours and you are son-in-law therefore
to Zeus." He spoke, and dived back into the tossing deep water.   570
But I went back again to my ships, and my godlike companions
went with me, but my heart was a storm in me as I went. Now
when we. had come back to where our ship lay by the seaside,
we made ready our dinner, and the immortal night came over,
and then we lay down to sleep along the break of the sea beach.   575
But when the young Dawn showed again with her rosy fingers,
first of all we dragged the ship down into the bright water,
and in the balanced ships set the masts in place, and set sails,
and we ourselves also went aboard and sat to the oarlocks,
and sitting well in order we dashed the oars in the gray sea,   580
back to where Egypt is, the sky-fallen river, and there
I stranded my ships, and there I rendered complete hecatombs.
But when I had ended the anger of the gods, who are everlasting,
I piled a mound for Agamemnon, so that his memory
might never die. I did this, and set sail, and the immortals   585
gave me a wind, so brought me back to my own dear country
with all speed. Come, now, stay here with me in my palace
until it is the eleventh day and even the twelfth day,
and then I will send you well on your way, and give you glorious
gifts, three horses and a well-finished chariot; also   590
I will give you a fine goblet so that you can pour libations
to the immortals; and think of me, all your days, when you do so,'
Then the thoughtful Telemachos said to him in answer:
'Son of Atreus, do not keep me with you here for a long time,
since I could well be satisfied to sit here beside you   595
for a year's time, without any longing for home or parents,
such strange pleasure do I take listening to your stories
and sayings, but by now my companions in sacred Pylos
are growing restless, yet for some time you would keep me with you.
And let the gift you give me be something that can be stored up.   600
I will not take the horses to Ithaka, but will leave them
here, for your own delight, since you are lord of a spreading
plain, there is plenty of clover here, there is galingale,

and there is wheat and millet here and white barley, wide grown.
There are no wide courses in Ithaka, there is no meadow;   605
a place to feed goats; but lovelier than a place to feed horses;
for there is no one of the islands that has meadows for driving horses;
they are all sea slopes; and Ithaka more than all the others.'
    He spoke, and Menelaos of the great war cry smiled on him,
and stroked him with his hand and called him by name and spoke to him: 610
'You are of true blood, dear child, in the way you reason.
So I shall change all this for you, since I am able to,
and of all those gifts that lie stored away in my house I will give you
the one which is most splendid and esteemed at the highest value.
I will give you a fashioned mixing bowl. It is of silver   615
all but the edges, and these are finished in gold. This is
the work of Hephaistos. The hero Phaidimos, the Sidonians'
king, gave it to me, when his house took me in and sheltered me
there on my way home. I would give it to you for a present.'
    So these two remained conversing this way together   620
and the banqueters came now into the divine king's palace,
and they drove sheep and carried heartening wine, and with them
their wives, in handsome hoods, brought food along. In this way
they about the palace were busy preparing dinner
but meanwhile before the palace of Odysseus the suitors   625
amused themselves with discs and with light spears for throwing
on a leveled floor, unruly men as they always had been,
but Antinoös and Eurymachos the godlike were seated
as lords of the suitors, out and away the best men among them,
and to them now came Phronios' son Noëmon, approaching   630
Antinoös, and spoke to him and asked him a question:
'Antinoös, do we have an idea in our minds or do we
not, when Telemachos will come back from sandy Pylos?
He has gone, and taken my ship, and now I find that I need her
for crossing over to spacious Elis, where I have a dozen   635
horses, mares, and suckling from them hard-working unbroken
males; I would like to break one in, taking it from the others.'
    So he spoke, and they were amazed at heart; they had not thought
he had gone to Pylos, the city of Neleus, but that he was somewhere
near, on his lands, among the flocks, or else with the swineherd.   640
It was Antinoös the son of Eupeithes that answered:
'Tell me the truth now, when did he go, and which of the young men
went with him? The choice men of Ithaka, or were they his own
following, henchmen and servants? Even he could accomplish so much.

And tell me this and tell me truly, so I can be certain, 645
did he take your black ship from you by force, when you were unwilling,
or did you willingly give it him, when he spoke to you for it?'
    Then the son of Noëmon, Phronios, gave him an answer:
'I gave it to him of my free will What else could one do
when a man like this, with so many cares to trouble his spirit, 650
asked for it? It would be hard to deny him the giving.
And the young men who are going along with him are the noblest
in our neighborhood. Also, I saw going aboard as leader
Mentor, or it was a god, but he was in every way like him,
and yet I wonder, for yesterday early I saw the splendid 655
Mentor here; before, he was boarding a ship for Pylos.'
    So he spoke, and went away to the house of his father,
and the proud heart in both these suitors was filled with amazement.
They had the suitors sit down in a group and stopped their contests.
It was Antinoös the son of Eupeithes who spoke to them, 660
raging, the heart within filled black to the brim with anger
from beneath, but his two eyes showed like fire in their blazing:
'Here now is a monstrous thing, this voyage made by Telemachos,
and insolently put through. We thought he would never achieve it.
A young boy, in despite of so many of us, has hauled down 665
his ship, and gone away, choosing out the best men in the country.
The evil will begin to go further. May Zeus grant destruction
of the life in him, before he comes to full measure of manhood.
But come now, give me a fast ship and twenty companions,
so that I can watch his return and lie in wait for him 670
in the narrow strait between Ithaka and towering Samos,
and make him sorry for this sea-going in search of his father.'
    So he spoke, and they all approved what he said and urged it,
and at once they stood up and went inside the house of Odysseus.
    Nor did Penelope go for a long time without knowing 675
of the counsels which the suitors had been secretly planning,
for Medon the herald told her, having overheard their counsels.
He had been standing outside the court while they plotted inside it,
and he went on his way with the message into the house of Penelope.
Penelope spoke to him as he stepped over the threshold: 680
'Herald, on what errand have the proud suitors sent you?
Is it to tell the serving maids of godlike Odysseus
to stop their work, so as to prepare the suitors a dinner?
Could this not be the last and the latest time of their dining
here, whether coming to court me or meeting for some other reason? 685

You, who keep gathering here, and consuming away much livelihood,
the property of wise Telemachos, nor have you listened
to what you heard from your fathers before you, when you were children,
what kind of man Odysseus was among your own parents,
how he did no act and spoke no word in his own country   690
that was unfair; and that is a way divine kings have, one
will be hateful to a certain man, and favor another,
but Odysseus was never outrageous at all to any man.
But in you the spirit is plain to see, and your unjust action
how you have no gratitude thereafter for good things done you.'   695
    Medon in turn, a man of thoughtful mind, said to her:
'If only, my queen, that could be the worst of the evil.
But the suitors now are devising another thing that is much worse
and harder to bear. May the son of Kronos not see it accomplished.
Now they are minded to kill Telemachos with the sharp bronze   700
on his way home. He went in quest of news of his father
to Pylos the sacrosanct and to glorious Lakedaimon.'
    So he spoke, and her knees gave way and the heart in her.
She stayed a long time without a word, speechless, and her eyes
filled with tears, the springing voice was held still within her.   705
At long last she found words to speak to him and answer:
'Herald, why is my child gone from me? There was no reason
for him to board fast-running ships, which serve as horses
for men on the salt sea, and they cross the expanses of water.
Must it be so that even his name shall be gone from men's minds?'   710
    Medon then, a thoughtful man, spoke to her in answer:
'I do not know whether some god moved him, or whether his own mind
had the impulse to go to Pylos, in order to find out
about his father's homecoming, or what fate he had met with.'
    So speaking he went away back into the house of Odysseus,   715
and a cloud of heart-wasting sorrow was on her, she had no strength left
to sit down in a chair, though there were many there in the palace,
but sat down on the floor of her own well-wrought bedchamber
weeping pitifully, and about her her maids were wailing
all, who were here in the house with her, both young and old ones,   720
To them, weeping constantly Penelope spoke now:
'Hear me, dear friends. The Olympian has given me sorrows
beyond all others who were born and brought up together
with me, for first I lost a husband with the heart of a lion
and who among the Danaans surpassed in all virtues,   725
and great, whose fame goes wide through Hellas and midmost Argos;

and now again the stormwinds have caught away my beloved
son, without trace, from the halls, and I never heard when he left me.
Hard-hearted, not one out of all of you then remembered
to wake me out of my bed, though your minds knew all clearly,   730
when he went out and away to board the hollow black ship.
For if I had heard that he was considering this journey,
then he would have had to stay, though hastening to his voyage,
or he would have had to leave me dead in the halls. So now
let someone make her way quickly and summon the old man Dolios,   735
my own servant, whom my father gave me to have as I came here,
and he keeps an orchard full of trees for me, so that he may
go with speed to Laertes and sit beside him and tell him
all, and perhaps he, weaving out the design in his heart,
may go outside and complain to the people of those who are striving   740
to waste away his own seed and that of godlike Odysseus.'
    Then in turn Eurykleia her dear nurse said to her:
'Kill me then, dear girl, with the pitiless bronze, or else
let me be in the halls. I will not hide the story from you.
I did know all these things, and I gave him all that he asked for,   745
both bread and sweet wine, but he took a great oath from me
never to tell you of it until it came to the twelfth day,
or until you might miss him yourself or hear he was absent,
so that you might not ruin your lovely skin with weeping.
But go, wash with water and put clean clothing upon your body,   750
and going on to the upper story with your attendant
women, pray to Athene daughter of Zeus of the aegis,
for she would then be able to save him, even from dying.
But do not embitter the bitterness of the old man. I think
the seed of Arkeisios is not altogether hated   755
by the blessed gods, but there will still be one left to inherit
the high-roofed house and the rich fields that lie at a distance.'
    So she spoke, and stilled her grieving and stopped the weeping
of her eyes, and she washed and put clean clothing upon her body;
and went to the upper story with her attendant women,   760
and laid the barley grains in the basket and prayed to Athene:
'Hear me, Atrytone, child of Zeus of the aegis,
If ever here in his own palace resourceful Odysseus
burned the rich thigh pieces of an ox or sheep in your honor,
remember it now for my sake and save for me my beloved   765
son, and fend off the suitors who are evilly overbearing.'
    She spoke, and raised the outcry, and the goddess listened to her praying.

But the suitors all through the shadowy halls were raising a tumult
and thus would go the word of one of the arrogant young men:
'Surely our much sought-after queen is consenting to marriage   770
with one of us, not knowing how the murder of her son is appointed.'
   Thus one of them would speak, not knowing what was appointed.
But it was Antinoös who now stood forth and addressed them:
'You are all mad. Keep clear of all this kind of disorderly
talk, for fear somebody may go inside and report us.   775
But come let us silently rise up now and put into action
that counsel which has been resolved in the hearts of all of us.'
   So he spoke, and chose out the twenty best men among them
and they went along to the fast ship and the sand of the seashore,
and first of all they dragged the ship out to the deepening water,   780
and in the black hull set the mast in place, and set sails,
and made the oars fast in the leather slings of the oarlocks
all in good order, and hoisted the white sails and set them,
and their high-hearted henchmen carried their gear on for them.
They anchored her deep enough in the channel, and then disembarking   785
themselves, prepared their dinner and waited for the coming of evening.
   But she in the upper chamber, circumspect Penelope,
lay there fasting, she had tasted no food nor drink, only
pondering whether her stately son would escape from dying
or have to go down under the hands of the insolent suitors;   790
and as much as a lion caught in a crowd of men turns about
in fear, when they have made a treacherous circle about him,
so she was pondering, when the painless sleep came upon her
and all her joints were relaxed so that she slept there reclining.
   Then the gray-eyed goddess Athene thought what to do next.   795
She made an image, and likened it to Penelope's sister
Iphthime, the daughter of great-hearted Ikarios,
whose husband was Eumelos, and he lived in his home at Pherai.
She sent her now into the house of godlike Odysseus
in order to stop Penelope, who was grieving, lamenting,   800
from her crying and tearful lamentation. The dream figure
went into the bedchamber passing beside the thong of the door bar,
and came and stood above her head and spoke a word to her:
'Penelope, are you sleeping so sorrowful in the inward
heart? But the gods who live at their ease do not suffer you   805
to weep and to be troubled, since your son will have his homecoming
even yet, since he has done no wrong in the gods' sight.'
   Circumspect Penelope said to her in answer,

sleeping very sweetly now in the dreams' gateway:
'Why have you come here, sister, now, when you were not used to   810
come before, since the home where you live is far away from us,
and now you tell me to give over from the grieving and sorrows
that are many upon me and trouble me in my heart and spirit,
since first I lost a husband with the heart of a lion,
and who among the Danaans surpassed in all virtues,   815
a great man, whose fame goes wide through Hellas and midmost Argos;
and now again a beloved son is gone on a hollow
ship, an innocent all unversed in fighting and speaking,
and it is for him I grieve even more than for that other one,
and tremble for him and fear, lest something should happen to him   820
either in the country where he has gone, or on the wide sea,
for he has many who hate him and are contriving against him
and striving to kill him before he comes back into his own country.'
Then in turn the dark dream image spoke to her in answer:
"Take courage, let not your heart be too altogether frightened,   825
such an escort goes along with him, and one that other
men would have prayed to have standing beside them, for she has power,
Pallas Athene, and she has pity on you in your grieving,
and it is she who has sent me to you to tell you of these things.'
Circumspect Penelope said to her in answer: 830
'If then you are a god, and have heard the voice of the goddess,
come then, tell me of that other unfortunate, tell me
whether he still lives and looks upon the sun's shining,
or whether he has died and is now in the house of Hades.'

    Then in turn the dark dream image spoke to her in answer: 835
'As for that other one, I will not tell you the whole story
whether he lives or has died. It is bad to babble emptily.'
So she spoke, and drifted away by the bolt and the door post
and out and into the blowing winds. Ikarios' daughter
started up from her sleep, soothed in the inward heart, because   840
this clear dream in the dim of the night had come to visit her.

    But the suitors went aboard and sailed out into the flowing
ways, in their hearts devising sudden death for Teiemachos.
There is a rocky, island there in the middle channel
halfway between Ithaka and towering Samos,   845
called Asteris, not large, but it has a double anchorage
where ships can be hidden. There the Achaians waited in ambush.

ALCMAN

Translated by M.L. West

… Among the dead, Lykaithos concerns me not,   1
nor Enarsphoros and fleet-foot Sebros
and the mighty … and the warrior … ,
Euteiches, lord Areitos, and …
outstanding among the heroes of old …
great Eurytos … the nobles;
all these we shall pass by:
Measure and Means are senior of the gods,
and help from Zeus comes prompt, nor waits
to do up shoes. Let no man seek to fly
to heaven, possess in love
fair Aphrodite, or the queen of gods,
or some delicious nymph;
but the sweet-eyed Graces of music may go in
to the hall of Zeus.

         • • •

One was slain with an arrow, one laid low
with a bright millstone … Hades …
So they paid dearly for their wickedness.
There's such a thing
as God's requital. Fortunate is he
who in good heart plaits up his day sans tears.
Now my song's of the radiance
of Agido: she to my eyes
shines like the sun she calls to be our witness.
But I must not speak good or ill of her
when the dancers' famous principal herself
stands out like a racehorse set among the sheep,
a thundering winner, the sort you see in dreams

as you doze in a cavern's shade.
Ah, look—the mount's a Venetian;
that combed-out hair
of cousin Hagesichora has a sheen
like purest gold,
and that silver face—why say it in words?
There's Hagesichora;
while Agido's nearest challenger for looks
will be a Scythian nag to an Ibenian.
The Pleiades that go up before daybreak
fight it out with us as we bear
the plough, our Sirius, through the ambrosial
     night.

Our purple finery is not
the treasure that defends us,
no coiled snake-bangle of solid gold,
nor Lydian headband splendid upon girls
with big dark eyes,
nor Nanno's hair, no, nor nymphlike Areta,
nor Thulakis, nor Klesithera; nor
will you go to Ainesimbrota's and say
'Oh please make Astaphis mine'
or 'Make Philylla look my way',
Damareta, or sweet Vianthemis.
No, it's Hagesichora—
she is my heartache.

For her beauty of ankles is not here in the dance:
she bides by Agido, commends
our ceremonial. Gods, receive their prayers—
in the gods' hands lies fulfilment.
Dance-leader, I may say that in myself
I'm just a maid that vainly hoots
like the owl in the roof: Aotis is the one
I chiefly hope to please,
who gives us relief from toil; but Hagesichora
brings girls into sweet concord.

For the team must turn with the trace-horse,
and the helmsman rules the ship.

The Sirens' tone indeed
is music more than ours;
they are divine, and not eleven girls
but ten sing in this choir. Yet it gives voice
like the swan on the waters of Xanthos,
and she with her darling flaxen hair,
Hagesichora …

There, in highest respect from gods and men,   2
they dwell … in a chamber divinely built,
masters of swift colts—Castor—
skilled horsemen—and glorious Polydeuces.

Muses of Olympus, my heart is rapt   3
with desire of hearing a new song
and the unison of girls in lovely melody
… will dispel
the sweetness of sleepy eyelids.
… draws me along to the piazza,
there where I'll be tossing my flaxen hair
… a dance for tender feet …
                    •   •   •
and with crippling longing. Her glance
more melting than sleep or death;
hers is a potent sweetness.

But Astymeloisa gives me no response,
just flits with her garland
like a falling star through the splendour of the night,
a golden shoot, a tuft of down—
gone in a few strides of her long legs.
All Cinyras' glistening charm
sits on our damsel hair,

But as to milady Astymeloisa,
out in the crowd, she wins the public's heart.
                    •   •   •
If she would just come up, take my young hand,
I'd soon be begging her favour.
But as things are, in angry mood …
     … the girl …

Hey Muse, euphonious Muse, full of melodies,   14(*a*)
ever the singer,
make start of a new song for the girls to sing!

He was no yokel,   16
no fool even among experts;
not of Thessalian stock,
no shepherd from Nether Wallop,
but from the centre of Sardis.

And sometime I'll lend you a full-bellied cauldron   17
in which you can put all your oddments together.
It's never yet been on the fire, but soon it'll
stand full of soup, the sort Alcman the trencherman
dotes on, all hot in the depths of midwinter.
For really, he doesn't eat anything fancy,
but looks for the ordinary, just like the people.

Seven couches, and to each a table   19
bedecked with poppy-seed rolls,
linseed and sesame, and bowls
of … stuck with golden honey.

Of seasons he created three,   20
summer, winter, and autumn to boot;
and for a fourth, the spring, when things
are growing, but a man can't eat his fill.

My legs can support me no longer, young ladies   26
with voices of honey and song divine!
Ah, would that I could be a kingfisher, flying
sea-blue, fearless, amid you halcyons
down to rest on the foaming brine!
Hey Muse, daughter of Zeus, Calliope,   27
make me a start of delightful poetry:
give my song charm, and beautiful dancing.

And all the young girls among us   38
speak highly of the man that plays the lyre.

These verses and melody Alcman   39, 40
found by harking to the voice
of chattering partridges …
I know the tunes of all the birds.

May our chorus be pleasing to all Zeus' house   45
and to thee, lord Apollo.

Often enough, in the heights of the mountains   56
when festival torches pleasure the gods,
you've taken a golden bowl, a big one
like shepherds have; filled it with milk of a lioness,
then made a big firm cheese for Hermes slayer of
        Argus.

It's not the goddess of love,   58
just wild Cupid playing his boyish games,
alighting on the petals—please don't touch!—
of my galingale garland,

Cupid once more by the goddess's grace   59*a*
trickles down in his sweetness, warming my heart.

Such is the offering of pleasant Muses   59*b*
made manifest by Megalostrata
the flaxen-haired, a girl for girls to envy.

'And I pray to you, bringing this garland   60
of helichryse and lovely galingale.'

And the girls all say,   81
'Father Zeus, I wish he could be *my* husband!'

They sleep, the mountain peaks,   89
the clefts, ridges, and gullies,
and all the creatures that the dark earth feeds,
the animals of the glen, the tribe of bees,
the monsters of the salt purple deeps.
They sleep, the tribes
of winging birds …

Soon he'll be serving bean-pottage,   96
white groats, and the fruit of the honeycomb.

At feasts and at men's mess unions   98
with banqueters gathered it's fitting to start on the
          paean.

P. Oxy. 2443 fr. 1 +3213
… as I went up from Trygeai
to the White Goddesses' beautiful precinct
with two sweet pomegranates.
The girls, having prayed to the fair-flowing river
for lovely fulfilment of marriage
and the supreme experience
that men and women know, the bridal bed,

                    • • •

TYRTAEUS

Translated by M.L. West

… let us obey [the kings, who are] 2
nearer the line [of the gods].
For fair-crowned Hera's husband, Kronos' son
    himself,
    Zeus, gave the sons of Heracles this state.
Under their lead we left windswept Erineos
    and came to Pelops' broad sea-circled land.

This was the oracle from Phoebus that, they heard 4
    at Delphi, and brought back the god's decree:
First in debate shall heaven's favourites, the kings,
    the guardians of fair Sparta's polity,
speak, and the elders. After them the commoners
    shall to direct proposals make response
with conscientious speech and all just
       consequence,
    making no twisted plans against our realm;
and commoners' majority shall win the day.
    Phoebus brought forth this guidance for the state.

… our sovereign Theopompus, whom the gods 5
      did love,
    through whom we took Messene's broad
      dance-grounds,
Messene good to plough and good to plant for
      fruit.
    To conquer her they fought full nineteen years
steadfastly ever, with endurance in their hearts,
    those spearmen of our fathers' fathers' time,

and in the twentieth the foe took flight, and left
their fertile farms among Ithome's heights.

(*The enslaved Messenians were*)   6
   like donkeys suffering under heavy loads,
by painful force compelled to bring their masters
    half
     of all the produce that the soil brought forth.
… making a wailing funeral chorus, they and   7
    their wives,
    when one of their masters met his destiny.

For it is fine to die in the front line,   10
   a brave man fighting for his fatherland,
and the most painful fate's to leave one's town
   and fertile farmlands for a beggar's life,
roaming with mother dear and aged father,
   with little children and with wedded wife.
He'll not be welcome anywhere he goes,
   bowing to need and horrid poverty,
his line disgraced, his handsome face belied;
   every humiliation dogs his steps.
This is the truth: the vagrant is ignored
   and slighted, and his children after him.
So let us fight with spirit for our land,
   die for our sons, and spare our lives no more.
You young men, keep together, hold the line,
   do not start panic or disgraceful rout.
Keep grand and valiant spirits in your hearts,
   be not in love with life—the fight's with men!
Do not desert your elders, men with legs
   no longer nimble, by recourse to flight:
it is disgraceful when an older man
   falls in the front line while the young hold back,
with head already white, and grizzled beard,
   gasping his valiant breath out in the dust
and clutching at his bloodied genitals,
   his nakedness exposed: a shameful sight
and scandalous. But for the young man, still
   in glorious prime, it is all beautiful:
alive, he draws men's eyes and women's hearts;

felled in the front line, he is lovely yet.
Let every man then, feet set firm apart,
    bite on his lip and stand against the foe.

But Heracles unvanquished sowed your stock: 11
    take heart! Zeus bows not yet beneath the yoke.
Fear not the throng of men, turn not to flight,
    but straight toward the front line bear your
       shields,
despising life and welcoming the dark
    contingencies of death like shafts of sun.
You know what wreck the woeful War-god makes,
    and are well to the grim fight's temper tuned.
You have been with pursuers and pursued,
    you young men, and had bellyful of both.
You know that those who bravely hold the line
    and press toward' engagement at the front
die in less numbers, with the ranks behind
    protected; those who run, lose all esteem.
The list is endless of the ills that hurt
    the man who learns to think the coward's
       thoughts:
for it's a bad place, as he flees the fray,
    to have his wound, between the shoulder-blades,
and it's a shameful sight to see him lie
    dead in the dust, the spear-point in his back.
Let every man, then, feet set firm apart,
    bite on his lip and stand against the foe,
his thighs and shins, his shoulders and his chest
    all hidden by the broad bulge of his shield.
Let his right hand brandish the savage lance,
    the plume nod fearsomely above—his head.
By fierce deeds let him teach himself to fight,
    and not stand out of fire—he has a shield—
but get in close, engage, and stab with lance
    or sword, and strike his adversary down.
Plant foot by foeman's foot, press shield on shield,
    thrust helm at helm, and tangle plume with
       plume,
opposing breast to breast that's how to fight,
    with the long lance or sword-grip in your hand.

You light-armed men, wherever you can aim
    from the shield-cover, pelt them with great rocks
and hurl at them your smooth-shaved javelins,
    helping the armoured troops with close support.

I would not rate a man worth mention or account   12
    either for speed of foot or wrestling skill,
not even if he had a Cyclops' size and strength
    or could outrun the fierce north wind of Thrace;
I would not care if he surpassed Tithonus' looks,
    or Cinyras' or Midas' famous wealth,
or were more royal than Pelops son of Tantalus,
    or had Adrastus' smooth persuasive tongue,
or fame for everything save only valour: no,
    no man's of high regard in time of war
unless he can endure the sight of blood and death,
    and stand close to the enemy, and fight.
This is the highest worth, the finest human prize
    and fairest for a bold young man to win.
It benefits the whole community and state,
    when with a firm stance in the foremost rank
a man bides steadfast, with no thought of shameful
        flight,
    laying his life and stout heart on the line,
and standing by the next man speaks
        encouragement.
    This is the man of worth in time of war.
Soon he turns back the foemen's sharp-edged
        battle lines
    and strenuously stems the tide of arms;
his own dear life he loses, in the front line felled,
    his breast, his bossed shield pierced by many a
        wound,
and of his corselet all the front, but he has brought
    glory upon his father, army, town.
His death is mourned alike by young and old; the
        whole
community feels the keen loss its own.
People point out his tomb, his children in the
        street,
    his children's children and posterity.

His name and glorious reputation never die;
    he is immortal even in his grave,
that man the furious War-god kills as he defends
    his soil and children with heroic stand.
Or if in winning his proud spear-vaunt he escapes
    the doom of death and griefs long shadow-cast,
then all men do him honour, young and old alike;
    much joy is his before he goes below.
He grows old in celebrity, and no one thinks
    to cheat him of his due respect and rights,
but all men at the public seats make room for him,
    the young, the old, and those of his own age.
This is the excellence whose heights one now must seek
    to scale, by not relenting in the fight.

... a tawny lion's spirit in your breast.   13

... until it ends   14
    in highest heroism, or in death.

... throwers of stones, and archers,   19
    ... like hordes of wasps ...
... the man-destroying War-god ...

         • • •

... protected by your convex shields,
Pamphyloi, Hylleis, and Dymanes, each distinct,
    your murderous lances levelled in your hands.
... (not?) leave it all to the immortal gods

         • • •

but with concerted charge at once we'll crush their
    front,
    meeting the enemy spearmen face to face.
A fearsome clangour will be heard, as the two sides
    dash shields against round shields ...
               ... falling upon each other,
and corselets on men's breasts will fend away
destruction, yet be dented by the points of spears.
    The brazen helmets will resound beneath the battering of rocks ...

But as they fight, Athena, pale-eyed daughter   23*a*
of Zeus who holds the Aegis/ checks the wild

spears' flight.
    A multitude will throw with javelins
sharp-pointed …
    in light arms running forward …
Arcadians … the Argives' … along the wall …
    … from pale-eyed Athena … ditch …
They will kill every Spartan that they catch
    fleeing the battle …

THE LANDMARK HERODOTUS

Edited by Robert B. Strassler

THE SPARTAN STATE IN WAR AND PEACE

Herodotus as Ethnographer of the Spartans

§1. Herodotus the "father of history" (Cicero's *pater historiae*) is also the father of comparative ethnography. He is a generally fair-minded and balanced ethnographer not only of non-Greek "others" but of the Greeks, too. He explicitly describes the ethnicity, customs, and beliefs of many "barbarian" peoples in elaborate, if not always entirely accurate, detail. By contrast, his discourse on Greek ethnicity, customs, and beliefs is for the most part implicit, with one huge exception: his treatment of the Spartans. In Book 6, between his descriptions of the Ionian Revolt (499–494) and the battle of Marathon (490), Herodotus provides a long excursus on the prerogatives of the odd dual kingship of the Spartans (6.51–60). This is followed not long after by a story of the birth of a Spartan king, Demaratos, who was to play a key role in Herodotus' version of Xerxes' invasion of Greece (6.63–69). Part of that story (6.69) is told, moreover, from the point of view of a woman—Demaratos' mother.

§2. These two extended passages in Book 6 convey two important messages, as forcefully as narrative skill can. First, that the Spartans, though they are of course Hellenes, are also, in some vital respects, "other"—in their political arrangements and their social customs they depart significantly from Greek norms. Second, that not the least important way in which they differ from other Greeks is in the role they allocated to, or that was assumed by, Spartan women, at any rate royal women. There is a growing consensus among scholars that Herodotus was a master of the art of historiography as embedded narrative. Herodotus' account—or rather multiple accounts—of Sparta and Spartans are an excellent illustration of his narrative mastery.

Lykourgos

§3. The chronological starting point of the *Histories* in our terms would be somewhere about the year 550, roughly three generations before Herodotus' birth. At that time, the two most powerful mainland Greek cities were Sparta and Athens. Herodotus is quite conventional in ascribing most of Sparta's basic political and military institutions to the reforms of the famed lawgiver Lykourgos (1.65). He writes of Lykourgos as a human being, though he records a Delphic oracle which suggests that he was to be paid divine, not heroic, cult honors after his death. He does not date Lykourgos precisely; later writers dated him variously within a huge span of several centuries. That was only one of many such disagreements as to the details of Lykourgos' life and achievement; other sources differed on, for example, whether or not he played a role in the origins of the ephorate. So great indeed was the disagreement surrounding him that Plutarch (c. C.E. 100) begins his "biography" of Lykourgos by saying that there is nothing that is asserted of him by one writer that has not been contradicted by another. It is very noticeable that Herodotus does not mention Lykourgos again, not even when he comes to describe in detail what is supposed to have been Lykourgos' arrangement for the prerogatives of the two joint kings (6.56–60).

The Names for Sparta, the Spartans and Their Territory

§4. Herodotus comments sharply on the Spartans' own local tradition about their original settlement of their territory, saying that in one respect they contradicted "all the poets" (6.52.1). From this we would have been likely to infer not only that Herodotus was very learned but also that he had gained direct access to local Spartan genealogical and mythical history. That inference is explicitly confirmed elsewhere (§15 below). Here I concentrate on one reflection of his local knowledge, namely his use of the Spartans' own terminology for themselves, their city, and their city-state territory. Unfortunately, Herodotus was not always rigorously consistent in applying his undoubted firsthand knowledge.

§5. The strict technical term for Spartan citizens of full status was Spartiatai (which Herodotus spells in the Ionic way, with an ēta instead of a long alpha in the third syllable, Spartiētai, 9.85.2). Lakōn (7.161.1; feminine Lakaina, 3.134.5) was an alternative form; it is from the adjectival form of *lakōn*, *lakōnikos*, that we get our word "laconic" (see also 3.46 for a classic anecdote illustrating this quintessentially Spartan mode of speech). But Herodotus, like other authors, more usually calls them Lakedaimonioi, meaning either inhabitants of or citizens of Lakedaimōn. For Lakedaimōn could mean either the entire territory of the Spartan state, for which Lakonikē (sc.*gē*, "land," 1.69, 6.58, 7.235) or "*gē* of the Lakedaimonioi" (7.158.2) were alternative usages, or just specifically the city—or town, more correctly—of Sparta (which might also be called Spartē).

§6. The entire civic territory of Sparta consisted of pretty much the southern portion of the Peloponnese, some 8,000 square kilometers (3,000 square miles) in all, easily the largest city-state territory in the entire Greek world. It may be divided into two roughly equal halves separated by the Taygetos mountain range (rising to more than 2,400 meters or 8,000 feet). On the west lay Messenia, the ancient term. This was territory that the Spartans had acquired by conquest beginning in the late eighth century, not without fierce resistance from the Messenians. Spartan control was firmly established by 550, but Messenian recalcitrance (alluded to at 5.49.8) remained high; and in the 460s a major revolt broke out (§9 below), mentioned at 9.64.2

(Stenykleros is in the main river valley of the Pamisos). On the east, where the town of Sparta lies toward the head of the valley of the River Eurotas, is what we call anachronistically Laconia (which is in fact the late Roman, not a classical Greek, name).

Other Inhabitants of *Lakedaimōn: Perioikoi* and Helots

§7. The problem with the term Lakedaimonioi, for us rather than for them, is that it could also encompass inhabitants of Lakedaimōn who were not full citizens of Sparta, namely the *perioikoi* or "outdwellers." There were perhaps as many as eighty communities of *perioikoi*, situated on the periphery of the two great riverine valleys of Laconia and Messenia and all around the very long and indented coastline. Within these communities there was clear class differentiation: the wealthier *perioikoi* served the Spartans either as hoplites or as cavalrymen, and some even rose to hold positions of command in the fleet. It was when *perioikoi* served in Spartan or larger allied armies together with Spartan citizens that they were most naturally called Lakedaimonioi.

§8. Apart from the status and behavior of women (§25 below), the other great social oddity of Sparta was the helots. These were local Greek natives of Laconia and Messenia whom the Spartans reduced to a serflike status and exploited mainly for performing agricultural functions but also several other tasks, for instance on campaign as body-servants (7.229) and even as lightly armed fighters (9.29). The helots who died at Thermopylae (8.25.1) may have been both.

§9. Herodotus does justice to them in a number of ways. Apart from a variety of individual helots featured, such as the one who was set to guard King Kleomenes and was persuaded with fatal consequences to hand the king his knife (6.75.2), Herodotus also mentions the Messenian helots collectively, not least in the context of his tale of Teisamenos the seer and his five "contests" (9.33–36). Teisamenos was originally from Elis, but he and his brother were made a unique grant of Spartan citizenship, for the sake of their indispensable gift of prophecy. Teisamenos had said that, if the Spartans accepted him and his brother as citizens, he would help them to be successful in five "contests," as predicted by a Delphic oracle (9.33, 9.35). The fourth of the "contests" won by the Spartans with his aid was against the Messenian helots, when they revolted en masse in the 460s, taking advantage of the Great Earthquake of c. 464. The development of Sparta as a peculiarly military society (a mere armed camp to critics like Isokrates) was necessitated as much as anything by the helot enemy within.

Political System.

§10. As a military society, Sparta predictably ordered its political arrangements from the top down. At the very pinnacle of the hierarchy were the two kings, each from a different aristocratic house and claiming divine descent ultimately from Zeus via Herakles and his descendants Agis and Eurypon. Herodotus quite rightly appreciated the uniqueness of the Spartan dyarchy and devoted several pages to setting out his understanding of the two kings' special privileges and prerogatives (*gerea:* 6.51–60). These included lavish funeral rituals that were the very opposite of the austerely restrained burial practices prescribed for nonroyal Spartans, and indeed they recalled "barbarian" (Egyptian, Scythian) rather than normal Greek funerary customs. The importance and oddity of the Spartan kingship are further brought out by Herodotus' dwelling on succession crises (e.g., 5.39–40) and dynastic marriage practices (e.g., 6.63–69) more redolent of an oriental court than of a Greek citizen-state.

§11. Not all the details of the kings' powers are absolutely clear. For example, Thucydides (1.20.3) perhaps unfairly accused Herodotus (without mentioning him by name) of foolishly believing that kings had two votes each in the thirty-member senate called the Gerousia (§12), whereas in fact they had only one. It is anomalous, moreover, that the kings allegedly appointed diplomatic representatives (*proxenoi*) of other Greek cities from among the citizens of Sparta: normally, that was the prerogative of the partner city itself. Thus Athens would appoint its own *proxenos* or multiple *proxenoi* from among the Spartan citizens, and so forth. And although Herodotus says (6.56) it was the kings' prerogative to declare and wage war on whom they wished, it is clear that the Spartan Assembly would have to vote affirmatively for war for it to become official (§14).

§12. The Gerousia (1.65, 5.40.1, 6.57.5) was a tiny permanent body of thirty senior citizens who—except for the two kings, who were members ex officio and by birthright—were elected for life by the Spartan citizenry as a whole. Candidates had to be over sixty, that is, beyond active-service military age, and probably also aristocrats, members of families that, like those of the two kings, called themselves collectively "descendants of Herakles" (Herakleidai). The election was carried out by votes delivered in the same manner as for other decisions, by the members of the Assembly shouting out loud. Aristotle considered this procedure "childish." The Gerousia acted as a probouleutic (pre-deliberative) body for the Assembly and also functioned as Sparta's supreme court. Even Spartan kings might be tried before the Gerousia, on which occasions it would probably be joined by the members of the Board of Ephors (§13). At 6.82 Herodotus gives his untechnical account of the trial of Kleomenes in about 494. Voting in such cases was open, each member having one vote, but trials took place in camera. There were no truly popular courts at Sparta, as there were in Athens.

§13. The Board of Five Ephors ("overseers," "supervisors") was elected annually by the Assembly (§14). All Spartan citizens were eligible for election, which was conducted according to the same "childish" procedure as elections for the Gerousia. Even quite poor Spartans might stand and be elected. Re-election was banned, so ephors might be very powerful for a year but unheard of before or after. The board constituted the effective day-to-day government of Sparta. Among their many powers, the ephors supervised a king's behavior, even in the most intimate matter of dynastic marriage (5.39.1–2, 5.42.1), and it was their responsibility when need arose to decide, by majority, whether or not a king should be required to stand trial. Besides supervising the kings, ephors were also responsible for military mobilization and in peacetime for the conduct of the Agōgē ("upbringing"), the unique state education system through whose carefully defined stages all Spartan boys, except the two heirs apparent, were required to pass between the ages of seven and eighteen. The military character and purposes of this education (*paideia*) were explicit.

§14. The Assembly (Ekklesia) consisted of all Spartan citizens in good standing—that is, males aged twenty or over who had passed successfully through the compulsory educational system and been duly elected members of a dining society, or "mess." The Assembly met statutorily once a month on the feast day of Apollo but could be summoned to extraordinary sessions if need be (as at 7.134.2, where the Assembly is given the generic name *haliē*, or "gathering"). Meetings were presided over by the senior member of the Board of Ephors, who would invite ephors, members of the Gerousia, and perhaps other senior office-holders to speak to the issue at hand. The matter would then be put to the popular vote of the Assembly, which would be registered by shouting in the usual Spartan way (*Thucydides* 1.87.2). The outcome would depend on the presiding ephor's judgment as to which shout—for or against the motion—had been the louder. Scope for manipulation seems manifest. The Assembly decided mainly matters of peace and war. Occasionally, that involved legislation. At 5.75.2 Herodotus cites the "law" introduced in about 505 decreeing that only one of the two kings might at any one time be in command of a particular Spartan or Spartan-led combined force. The passage of that law would have been the outcome of a complicated legislative procedure, the details of which are again hugely disputed among scholars (Herodotus himself, in his usual way, simply takes the process for granted). According to what I consider the most probable reconstruction, any new legislation would have to originate within the elite Gerousia. Presumably, except in the cases where it acted as a supreme court, it would operate by consensus rather than by formally registering votes. If a proposal commanded majority support in the Gerousia, a motion would then be put before a meeting of the Assembly for its final decision.

Army Organization

§15. Herodotus states that he personally visited Sparta. Indeed, he names Archias, a leading Spartan, as one of his informants there (3.55), and this is one of only three cases in the entire *Histories* where he cites an individual informant by name. Moreover, he also names the village from which Archias came, namely Pitana, one of the four that together constituted the town of Sparta. Thereby hangs an intriguing historiographical tale. In his account of the battle of Plataea, Herodotus mentions a "Pitanate *lokhos*" (9.53.2), or "Pitanate brigade," a detail about which he was presumably informed by Archias. Yet Thucydides, in one of his opening methodological chapters (1.20.3), pours scorn on a benighted predecessor who was naïve enough to believe there had once been a Pitanate *lokhos* when in fact no such unit had ever existed. The unnamed predecessor he had in his sights was of course Herodotus. Presumably the reason Thucydides was so sure Herodotus was wrong was that in his own day such a regiment did not exist, and he seems to have been one of those who held the view—widespread but false (see §14, on 5.75.2)—that all Spartan political and military institutions were of timeless antiquity.

§16. It is far more plausible to infer that a major military reform was enacted sometime between the battle of Plataea (479) and Thucydides' Atheno-Peloponnesian War (431–404), in which the Spartan army of the early fifth century, described by Herodotus and based on regiments called *lokhoi*, was replaced by one based on regiments called "divisions" (*morai*), as described by Xenophon, who fought with a Spartan army in the early fourth century. Regimental commanders in both cases were known as polemarchs (7.173.2), which may further account for Thucydides' confusion. The chief reason for such a major organizational reform is not hard to find: namely, the growing shortage or shrinkage of adult Spartan military manpower (what Aristotle was to call *oliganthrōpia*).

§17. In 480 there were reportedly some 8,000 Spartan citizens of military age and capacity (7.234.2), but by 371 there were only about 1,000. Between 480 and 371 there had been a major loss of life among young as well as mature Spartans caused by a massive earthquake in about 464 whose epicenter was near Sparta itself. The Atheno-Peloponnesian War had also taken its toll, but to these natural and military causes must be added certain social factors, including the increasing concentration of privately owned land in ever fewer and ever richer hands. Spartiate citizen-soldiers were required to feed themselves from foodstuffs produced by helots on land they themselves owned. Thus the concentration of land ownership directly reduced the number of men able to contribute food to the common messes that were at the basis of the political and military systems. One vital purpose of the postulated army reform (which I would date to the later 440s, during a brief interlude of peace with Athens) was therefore to compensate for the decrease in the number of frontline citizen-status hoplites by incorporating selected *perioikoi* into the new mixed "divisions." There is no sign that the inclusion of *perioikoi* hoplites in what had formerly been exclusively Spartiate regiments had any deleterious effect on Sparta's military capacity or efficiency. Rather the opposite, as the battle of Mantiniea in 418 proved.

§18. *Perioikoi* had been regarded as a necessary complement to Spartan citizen troops since at least the Plataea campaign of 479, when an equal number (5,000) of *perioikoi* hoplites was sent out alongside the Spartiate contingent (9.11.3). They presumably fought separately in the line of battle, and when it came to burying their dead, the Spartans interred them in three separate mounds. However, Herodotus fails to mention the *perioikoi* dead at all, though he does mention the mound given exclusively to the helot corpses.

Religion

§19 Herodotus' treatment of the Spartans' religious beliefs and practices is evenhand-ed. He makes it quite clear that the Spartans were perceived to be exceptionally pious. On several major occasions—not least the battles of Marathon and Thermopylae—he reports without comment that the Spartans felt unable to act immediately or in full force because they had prior religious obligations to perform. For the Spartans, as he twice puts it (5.63.2, 9.7), "considered the things of the gods more weighty than the things of men." More skeptical modern historians have inferred that the Spartans were merely using religion as a self-serving pretext. But if the manuscript reading at 9.85.2 is correct, the Spartans erected a special mound at Plataea for those dead Spartiates who were priests. Likewise Herodotus is careful to point out that Spartan kings were themselves priests and maintained close connections with the holiest of all Greek shrines, that of Apollo at Delphi (6.56–57). The perceived importance to Sparta both of Delphi and of military divination is apparent not least from the special grant of citizenship to the seer Teisamenos of Elis (§9). The conduct of Regent Pausanias at Plataea, refusing to order the Greek advance until the sacrificial omens were right (9.61–62), is another telling illustration. The Spartans earned from Xenophon the title of "craftsmen of war" precisely because of the minute attention they paid to the conduct of pre-battle sacrifices and other divinatory signs.

The Peloponnesian League and King Kleomenes I

§20. The Spartan history that Herodotus wanted to discuss with Archias undoubt-edly included the expansion of Sparta into the eastern Mediterranean about 525. He believed that the Spartans already had brought most of the Peloponnese under their control as early as 550 (1.68). This, as we can see with hindsight, was part of the process that many of us refer to now as the establishment of the Peloponnesian League (a modern term). The league in fact extended outside the Peloponnese, although it never included all Peloponnesian cities—most notably not Argos.* This alliance de-vised and led by Sparta was a privileged system of separate offensive and defensive military treaties between Sparta and several other states. It mainly benefited Sparta, which was protected by it against hostile invasion and whose relatively few hoplites were transformed by it into an army of formidable proportions. One propaganda claim that Sparta seems regularly to have used in order to legitimate its alliance was an alleged principled opposition to tyrannies—one-man dictatorships (5.92.⊠C.2). But Sparta's foreign relations took a new and more expansive turn in the reign of King Kleomenes I (c. 520–490).

§21. Herodotus' description of Kleomenes and his reign is one of the most puzzling, even contradictory, accounts in the whole *Histories*. On the one hand Kleomenes was a great and powerful king who—at any rate in the late 490s—had the best interests of Hellas at heart (6.61.1). On the other hand, Kleomenes was at

least a bit of a madman (5.39.1), who died horribly by self-mutilation (6.75) in divinely just retribution, according to Herodotus, for an act of gross sacrilege (6.84;

here once again Herodotus explicitly contradicts the official local Spartan explanation). He certainly was instrumental in ending the tyranny of the Peisistratid family led by Hippias at Athens in 510 (5.64–65), but Herodotus was probably right that in the long run the major impact of his clumsy interventions here (again in the years 508 and 506; 5.70, 5.72–76) was to prompt Athens to implement the reforms of Kleisthenes and become a democracy (6.131; see also 5.78). A direct consequence of the failure of the 506 expedition was the calling of the first Peloponnesian League congress in about 504 (5.91–93). Sparta proposed to reinstate Hippias as tyrant of Athens, but Sparta's allies had now secured a collective right of veto on the decisions of the alliance's leader, and in this first case, led by Corinth, they rejected Sparta's proposal.

Other Great Spartan Men—and Women

§22. When it came to choosing between Athens and Sparta as to which of those two states contributed most to saving mainland Greece from total Persian conquest in 480–479, Herodotus delivers what he knows will be to many an objectionable judgment, but the one that he considers to be true: namely, that it was the Athenians who—above all by their conduct at the battle of Salamis—were the principal saviors of Greece (7.139.1, 7139.5). Yet that does not mean that he (unlike some modern historians, perhaps) in any way downplays the almost equally critical and decisive contribution of the Spartans to the Persians' eventual defeat in the battle of Plataea in 479.

§23. The Spartan who led the Greeks to victory in that battle was Regent Pausanias, another hugely controversial character like Kleomenes, both in Sparta and outside, and both in his own lifetime and after his death. Like Kleomenes he came to a bad end (near murder by the Spartan authorities for his alleged treason). But unlike Kleomenes, Pausanias predominantly earns plaudits from Herodotus. After victory has been won at Plataea, "the most splendid of all those we know" (9.64.1), Herodotus relates two telling episodes in which Pausanias is featured as an exemplar of the best Spartan—and Greek—values. A hotheaded Greek from Aegina urges Pausanias to mutilate the corpse of Mardonios in revenge for the mutilation of the corpse of Leonidas by Mardonios and Xerxes at Thermopylae the previous year. Pausanias sharply rebukes the man and tells him that such barbarity is not the Greek way (9.78–79). Then, when Pausanias is shown the rampant luxuriousness of Mardonios' tent and the vast amounts of lavish food prepared for the Persian commander, Pausanias quietly orders his helot attendants to prepare a Spartan—indeed, as we say, a "spartan," meaning frugal—meal in order to demonstrate the superior virtue of Greek self-restraint (9.82).

§24. Leonidas, a half brother of Kleomenes, was also Kleomenes' son-in-law, since his wife Gorgo was Kleomenes' only daughter. Unusually, Gorgo is named by Herodotus—whereas the mother of Demaratos remains anonymous (§1). And whenever Gorgo gets a mention by Herodotus, she cuts a fine figure. She warns her father not to be taken in by a plausible Greek suitor from Samos (5.50–51), and it is she alone who can figure out how to read the vital message concealed beneath an apparently blank wax tablet (7.239).

§25. These two Spartan women are, admittedly, not ordinary, everyday Spartan women and wives. Indeed, the anonymous mother of Demaratos was not just a queen but had had what can only be called a magical experience: as an unprepossessing infant she had been graced by the presence of the legendary Helen in her shrine at Therapne and thereafter grew up to be a great beauty herself (6.61). Yet behind these two exceptional figures we sense the perception widespread in the rest of Greece that Spartan women were not as other Greek women were. They had something to say and were not afraid to say it, even in public in front of other, unrelated men. Many centuries later, Plutarch was to collect a number of these "apophthegmata" in his *Sayings of Spartan Women*. Their formidable presence was based ultimately on legal entitlement: unlike almost all other Greek women, they were allowed to own landed property in their own right, and as such were quite properly referred to by Herodotus as "heiresses" (*patroukhoi*: 6.57.4).

§26. It is doubtful therefore that Persian Great King Darius I's wife Atossa (daughter of Cyrus the Great) would have found the Spartan maids she professed to desire (3.134.5) to be altogether amenable and docile. But whether their relatively enhanced social status amounts to the existence of a certain feminism in Sparta is another matter. At any rate, the treatment of the anonymous mother of Demaratos as a political pawn in a game of dynastic matchmaking suggests otherwise. Her testimony in a key royal succession dispute was not deemed worthy of delivery or public record.

Paul Cartledge
Professor of Greek History
University of Cambridge
Cambridge, UK

6.52
SPARTA
The Spartan version of
how the early Spartans
determined which
of the royal twins was the
firstborn.

For according to the Lacedaemonians—though no poet agrees with them in this—it was not the sons of Aristodemos, but Aristodemos himself the son of Aristomachos son of Kleodaios who was the son of Hyllos, who had, during his reign, led them to the land they now possess. [2] And not much time had passed before the wife of Aristodemos, whose name was Argeia, gave birth. They say that she was the daughter of Autesion son of Teisamenos the son of Thersandros, who was the son of Polynices, and that she gave birth to twins, and that Aristodemos lived to see his infant sons, but then died of an illness. [3] So the Lacedaemonians of that time followed their custom and resolved to make the elder son king. But they did not know which to choose, because the boys were so much alike and they were in fact, identical. Since they were incapable of distinguishing between them, they asked the boys' mother (or perhaps had done so even before this). [4] But she said that not even she could tell them apart. Now she was actually well able to distinguish between them but denied that she could because she wanted both of them to be kings if possible. So the Lacedaemonians, now at a complete loss, sent to Delphi asking what they should do about this problem. [5] The Pythia ordered them to regard both children as kings, but to award the senior brother greater honor. This response by the Pythia left the Lacedaemonians no less bewildered than they had been before, because they had no way to determine which of the boys was the elder. Finally a Messenian man by the name of Panites suggested [6] that the Lacedaemonians watch the mother carefully to see which of the boys she would bathe and feed first. And if she clearly and consistently followed the same sequence, they would obtain the object of their search and find out what they were seeking to discover. But if she alternated between the two, then it would be obvious that she knew no more than they did, in which case they would have to try another method of investigation. [7] The Spartans followed the Messenian's advice, and as they watched the mother of the sons of Aristodemos (who did not know why she was being watched), they indeed saw her consistently picking up and honoring one of the boys by bathing and feeding him before the other. So they took the child that they had found to be more highly honored by its mother, on the grounds that it must be the firstborn, and raised it at public expense. The name given to this boy was Eurysthenes; that given to the other was Prokles. [8] And they say that even though they were brothers, after they grew up they disagreed with each other throughout their entire lives, just as their descendants continue to do.

Of the Hellenes, the Lacedaemonians are the only ones who tell that version of the story. Now I shall put in writing what other Hellenes report. They correctly list the Dorian kings as far back as Perseus son of Danae, omitting the god and showing that these kings were Hellenes, and that even in those early days they were classified as Hellenes. [2] I said "as far back as Perseus" since I cannot trace the lineage back any further than that because no one is named as the mortal father of Perseus—as Amphitryon, for example, is named the father of Herakles. Therefore I was correct to say "as far back as Perseus." But if someone were to recount the ancestors of Danae daughter of Akrisios and trace them all the way back in a continuous sequence, it would become obvious that the leaders of the Dorians are actually genuine Egyptians by direct descent.

6.53
SPARTA
The Greek version of this story, with proofs of its correctness.

That, then, is the genealogy of the Spartan kings according to the Hellenes. The account of the Persians is that Perseus was an Assyrian who became a Hellene, and that his ancestors did not. The forefathers of Akrisios, they say, were not related to Perseus at all but were, as the Hellenes also say, Egyptians.

6.54
Persians say Perseus was originally Assyrian.

Let that be the extent of what is said on this topic. For others have told of the deeds they performed to obtain their positions as kings over the Dorians, even though they were Egyptians, so I shall leave that subject alone. I shall, however, record what the accounts of others have not already covered.

6.55
Herodotus finishes with this subject.

The Spartans have granted the following privileges to their kings: two priesthoods, one of Zeus Lacedaemon, the other of Zeus of Heaven; the prerogative to wage war against any land they wish, and no Spartan can hinder them from doing so; if anyone tries, he is subject to a curse; and when they wage war, the kings go out first and return last. On their expeditions, the kings have 100 picked men to serve as their guards, and as they depart for war, they may sacrifice as many flocks as they wish and take all the hides and backs of the victims for themselves.

6.56
SPARTA
Privileges of the Spartan kings in war.

6.56
SPARTA
Privileges of the
Spartan kings in peace.

Those are their privileges in war. Their privileges in peace are as follows: whenever someone performs a sacrifice at public expense, the kings are the first to sit down and the first to be served at the feast, and they are given a portion twice as large as any other person dining there. They also begin the libations and receive the hides of the sacrificial victims. [2] At every new moon, as well as on the seventh day of every month, they are provided from the public treasury with a full-grown sacrificial victim for the sanctuary of Apollo, a medimnos of barley meal, and a Laconian fourth of wine. They receive special seats up front at all the contests. The kings also have the prerogative of appointing whomever of the citizens they want as *proxenoi*, and they are empowered to choose two *Pythioi* as well. The *Pythioi* are sacred delegates who are sent to Delphi, and who eat their meals with the kings at public expense. [3] If the kings do not come to dinner, they receive two choinikes of barley meal and a kotyle of wine to their homes. And when the kings do attend dinner, they receive double portions of everything. If they are invited to dine with private citizens, they receive the same honors from them. [4] The kings are in charge of keeping the oracles received that pertain to the state, and the *Pythioi* share their knowledge of the contents of these oracles. The kings act as sole judges only in the following cases: they decide who will marry a girl possessing an inheritance if her deceased father has not arranged a marriage for her; and they also judge cases concerning public roads. [5] In addition anyone who wants to adopt a child must do so in the presence of the kings. The kings sit with the Council of Elders, who number twenty-eight, during their meetings, and if the kings do not attend, the Elders most closely related to the kings assume their prerogatives and cast two votes for the kings and a third for themselves.

6.58
SPARTA
Spartan customs and
ceremonies when the
king dies.

Those are the privileges granted by the Spartan community to the kings while they live; after their death they receive the following honors. Horsemen carry the news of the king's death throughout all of Laconia, and in every city, women walk about beating on cauldrons; and whenever this occurs, two free people from each household, a man and a woman, must defile themselves, otherwise they incur large fines. [2] One custom observed by the Lacedaemonians at the death of their kings is the same as that practiced by a majority of the barbarians in Asia when their kings die: whenever a king of the

Lacedaemonians dies, a fixed number of the *perioikoi* from all of Lacedaemon, in addition to the Spartans, must attend the funeral to grieve. [3] And when many thousands of people have gathered there—*perioikoi,* helots and Spartans—men mingling together with women, all beating their heads vigorously, they wail continuously and loudly, proclaiming that this king who has just died had proved himself to be the best. If one of the kings should die in war, they make an image of him and carry it out on a bier with sumptuous coverings. After the king is buried, all business in the agora as well as meetings to elect officials are suspended for ten days, during which they mourn.

The customs they follow when a king dies also resemble those of the Persians. Whenever a Spartan king dies and a new king is installed, the new king forgives the debt of every Spartan who owes anything to the king or the state; in the same way, among the Persians, a new king releases all the cities from their obligation to pay back-tribute.

6.59
SPARTA
Debts to the king or state are forgiven when the king dies.

Lacedaemonian practices also conform to the following customs of the Egyptians. Their heralds, flute players, and cooks inherit their professions from their father, so that a flute player is the son of a flute player, a cook the son of a cook, a herald the son of a herald; and others do not apply themselves to these skills. One cannot become a herald on the strength of one's voice and thus try to take the place of hereditary heralds; instead, these occupations are performed only by those who have inherited them from their ancestors. Those, then, are their customs.

6.60
SPARTA
Like the Egyptians, Spartans inherit their crafts from their fathers.

So while Kleomenes was in Aegina trying to work for the common good of Hellas, Demaratos was maligning him, not because he cared much about the Aeginetans, but from jealousy and malice. After Kleomenes returned home from Aegina, he considered how to depose Demaratos from the kingship, and when the following circumstances provided him with an opportunity he moved against him.

6.61
SPARTA
The story of how King Ariston's third wife went from being very ugly to becoming the most beautiful woman in Sparta.

While Ariston had reigned in Sparta, he had married twice, but neither of his wives had borne him any children. [2] And because he knew that he was not the cause of this problem, he married a third wife, and this is how that marriage came about. There was a Spartan man who was a close friend of Ariston's; in fact, of all citizens, Ariston was attached to him the most. This man happened to have a wife who was by far the most beautiful woman in Sparta, and who in fact had become the most beautiful only after having been the ugliest. [3] For her appearance was once quite homely. Her nurse, however, realizing that the unattractive girl was the daughter of wealthy people who regarded her appearance as a disaster, developed the following plan. Every day she took the girl to the sanctuary of Helen, which is located in the district called Therapne above the sanctuary of Phoibos. Whenever the nurse brought her here she would stand her at the statue and pray that the goddess would deliver the child from her ugliness. [4] And it is said that once, while the nurse was leaving the sanctuary, a woman appeared before her and asked what she was carrying in her arms, to which the nurse replied that she was carrying a child. The woman then requested that the nurse show her the child, which the nurse refused to do, since the parents had forbidden her to show the child to anyone. But the woman ordered her to reveal it anyway [5] And because the woman kept trying to see the child and was making a huge fuss about viewing it, the nurse finally showed it to her. The woman then touched the child's head, and said that she would be the most beautiful of all the women in Sparta. From that day on her appearance changed, and when she reached marriageable age, Agetos son of Alkeides, the man who was the friend of Ariston, married her.

6.62
SPARTA
How King Ariston outwitted his friend so that he could marry this woman.

But it turned out that Ariston began to be disturbed by passion for this woman, and so he devised the following strategy. He promised Agetos, his good friend and the husband of this woman, that he would give to him any object from his possessions that he would select, and he asked his friend to grant the same favor to himself Agetos had no fear for his wife since he could see that Ariston already had a wife, and so he consented to the terms of this agreement, and they confirmed it by exchanging strong and binding oaths. [2] Then Ariston gave Agetos what he chose to take from his store of treasures, and when the time came for Ariston himself to seek a gift of equal value, he attempted to take away his friend's wife. Agetos argued that he had agreed to give anything except for this; but because he was compelled by his oath, after his friend had thoroughly misled and deceived him he allowed Ariston to take his wife away.

So that is how Ariston came to divorce his second wife and married a third. But in less than a ten-month interval, this wife gave birth to Demaratos. [2] Ariston was sitting in council with the ephors when one of his household servants announced that a son had been born to him. And he after remembering when he had married the woman and counting out the months on his fingers, swore an oath: "He could not be my own son!" The ephors heard this, but for the moment, thought nothing of it. As the child grew, Ariston repented these words, for he indeed came to regard Demaratos as his very own son. [3] He named him Demaratos because before he was born, the entire population of Sparta had said a prayer that a son would be born to Ariston, since of all the kings of Sparta, he was held in the highest esteem. So that is how Demaratos received his name.

In the course of time, Ariston died, and Demaratos succeeded him as king. But it seems that what had happened was destined to become known and would bring the reign of Demaratos to an end. This occurred as a consequence of the hostility between the two kings. Demaratos and Kleomenes had been antagonistic toward each other before, when Demaratos had led the army out of Eleusis, and the hostility between them grew more intense now, when Kleomenes crossed over to Aegina to oppose the Aeginetans who were medizing.

Kleomenes now ardently sought revenge, and entered into a pact with Leotychidas son of Menares son of Agis, who belonged to the same branch of the royal family as Demaratos. The terms of the agreement were that if Kleomenes were to make Leotychidas king in place of Demaratos, then Leotychidas would join him against the medizing Aeginetans. [2] Leotychidas was already a personal enemy of Demaratos, particularly because when Leotychidas had arranged to marry Perkalos, the daughter of Chiton son of Demarmenos, Demaratos had conspired to rob Leotychidas of his marriage by seizing Perkalos and making her his own wife. [3] That is how Leotychidas' hatred of Demaratos had begun, and now, following the desire of Kleomenes, Leotychidas swore an oath accusing Demaratos of not rightfully ruling as king of the Spartans, since he was not the son of Ariston. And after swearing this oath, he prosecuted Demaratos in court and resurrected what Ariston had said when the household servant had announced the birth of a son to him, and he had counted the months and

6.63
SPARTA
Demaratos is born a bit too soon after the marriage of his mother with King Ariston, creating doubt that he is Ariston's son.

6.64
495-491?
SPARTA
Demaratos became king, but Kleomenes questions the legitimacy of his royal birth.

6.65
SPARTA
Kleomenes joins with Leotychidas—who hates Demaratos for having robbed him of his betrothed—and now declares that Demaratos is not Ariston's son and therefore cannot be king.

had declared the child was not his own. [4] Resting his case on this statement, Leotychidas tried to demonstrate over and over again that Demaratos was not the son of Ariston and therefore did not rightfully reign as king of Sparta, and he provided as witnesses the ephors who had happened to be sitting in council with Ariston at the time and who had heard what he said.

The controversy continued until finally the Spartans decided to ask the oracle at Delphi whether Demaratos was or was not the son of Ariston. [2] It was Kleomenes who had come up with the idea to refer this question to the Pythia, and he next gained the support of Kobon son of Aristophantos, who wielded the. greatest influence at Delphi and who then persuaded Periallos the Pythia to proclaim what Kleomenes wanted her to say. [3] And thus, when the sacred delegates presented their question, the Pythia asserted that Demaratos was not the son of Ariston. Later, however, these intrigues became known, and as a result, Kobon was exiled from Delphi, while Periallos the Pythia was ousted from her position of honor.

So that is how Demaratos was deposed from his kingship. He subsequently fled from Sparta to the Medes because of the following affront. After his kingship had come to an end, Demaratos was elected to a certain magistracy. [2] Now Demaratos was in the audience watching the events at the Gymnopaidiai when Leotychidas, now king in his place, sent a servant to ridicule and insult Demaratos by asking him how it felt to be a magistrate after having been king. [3] Grievously offended by this question, Demaratos answered by saying that while he himself was now experienced in both, Leotychidas was not, adding that the asking of this question would be the beginning of either a multitude of evils or a multitude of blessings for the Lacedaemonians. After saying this, Demaratos covered his head, left the theater, and returned home, where he immediately prepared and performed the sacrifice of an ox to Zeus. Then he summoned his mother.

When his mother came to him, he placed some of the entrails in her hands and entreated her, saying, "Mother, I appeal to the other gods and especially to Zeus Protector of Our Household right here, and I beseech you to tell me the truth: who is my real father? [2] For Leotychidas said during our disputes that you were pregnant from your former husband when you came to Ariston while others tell an even more insulting

6.66
DELPHI
The Delphic priestess is secretly persuaded to rule against Demaratos and declare that he is not the son of Ariston.

6.67
SPARTA
Leotychidas, who takes Demaratos' place as king, insults Demaratos in public.

6.68
SPARTA
Demaratos asks his mother for the truth about his paternity.

story, that one of the stableboys visited you and that I am his son. [3] Now I implore you by the gods: tell me the truth! Even if you have done anything like what is rumored, you are not alone; many women have done such things. And besides, there is much talk in Sparta about how Ariston lacked the seed to produce offspring; otherwise, they say, his earlier wives would have given him children."

After he had appealed to her in this way, she replied, "My son, you have implored me with prayers to tell you the truth, and that is what I will tell you, and in detail. On the third night after the night on which Ariston had brought me to his home, an apparition in the likeness of Ariston came to me, and after lying with me, put the garlands it had been wearing on me. [2] The apparition left, and then Ariston came; when he saw me wearing the garlands, he asked who had given them to me. I told him it was he himself, but he refused to admit it. Then I swore an oath and said that it was not right for him to deny it, since only a short time before, he had come in and given me the garlands after lying with me. [3] Seeing that I had sworn to it on oath, Ariston realized that this had been the act of a divinity. For the garlands had evidently come from the shrine of the hero called Astrabakos which is set up at the doors of the courtyard, and the prophets had proclaimed this very Astrabakos to be a hero. [4] So now I have told you the whole story, my son, all that you wanted to know: either your father is the hero Astrabakos, or else your father is Ariston. For that was the night I conceived you. As to your enemies' exploiting the story that Ariston denied that you could have been his son when your birth was announced because ten months had not yet passed, it was his ignorance regarding these matters that led him to blurt out such a comment. [5] For some women give birth at nine months, or even seven; not all of them carry a full ten months of pregnancy, and I, my son, gave birth to you in the seventh month. Not long afterward, Ariston himself recognized that he had uttered these words out of stupidity. So do not believe other stories about your birth, for you have now heard the whole truth, and may it be Leotychidas and those who say such things whose wives will bear the children of stableboys."

6.70
491
SPARTA-PERSIA
Demaratos escapes from
the Spartans and goes into
exile in Persia, where King
Darius treats him well.

Those were the words of his mother, and now that Demaratos had found out what he wanted to know, he took provisions for a journey and made his way to Elis, after giving as a pretext that he was going to Delphi to consult the oracle. But the Lacedaemonians suspected that Demaratos was trying to run away, and they pursued him. [2] Demaratos somehow managed to cross over from Elis to the island of Zacynthus before they caught up with him. But then the Lacedaemonians crossed over in pursuit, took away his servants, and tried to apprehend him. The Zacynthians, however, refused to give Mm up, so he was then able to cross over to Asia and travel to the court of King Darius.

The King gave him a lavish welcome and furnished him with both land and cities. [3] Such was the fortune of Demaratos, and that is the story of how he came to Asia. He was famous among the Lacedaemonians for his brilliant deeds and good judgment on many occasions, and in particular for having conferred on them an Olympic victory when he won in the four-horse chariot race; he was the only one of all the kings in Sparta who had ever done this.

After Demaratos had been deposed, Leotychidas son of Menares succeeded to his kingship. Now Leotychidas had a son named Zeuxidemos, who was called Kyniskos by some of the Spartans. But this Zeuxidemos did not become a king of Sparta, because he died before Leotychidas did, leaving behind a son of his own, Archidamos. [2] After Leotychidas had lost Zeuxidemos, he married a second wife, Eurydame, the sister of Menios and daughter of Diactoridas. She bore him no sons, but she did bear a daughter named Lampito, who was given in marriage by Leotychidas to Archidamos son of Zeuxidemos.

6.72
SPARTA
Much later, Leotychidas
is banished for having
accepted a bribe.

Leotychidas did not grow old in Sparta but paid the penalty for what he had done to Demaratos in the following way. He had led the army of the Lacedaemonians into Thessaly, and although it would have been possible for him to subjugate all of that land, he accepted a large bribe instead [2] and was caught in the act, sitting in camp on a glove full of money. For this, Leotychidas was put on trial, with the result that he was exiled from Sparta and his house was demolished. He then fled to Tegea, where he died.

But all that happened much later. Now, after Kleomenes' plot against Demaratos had succeded, he at once took Leotychidas with him and advanced on the Aeginetans, against whom he bore a a bitter grudge for their having treated him so contemptuously before. [2] Now that both kings had come against them, the Aeginetans decided not to offer any further resistance, so the Spartan kings selected ten Aeginetans of the highest value in terms of wealth and lineage and took them away. Among them were the most powerful Aeginetans, Krios son of Polykritos and Kasambos son of Aristokrates. The kings brought these men to Attica and deposited them as hostages with the Athenians, who were the most hostile enemies of the Aeginetans.

After that, Kleomenes' evil plot against Demaratos became known and so, in fear of the Spartans, he slipped away secretly to Thessaly. From there, he went to Arcadia and tried to instigate a revolt by uniting the Arcadians against Sparta and having them swear oaths that they would follow wherever he would lead them. In particular, he was eager to bring the leading men of Arcadia to the city of Nonakris and make them swear that oath by the waters of the River Styx, [2] for the Arcadians say that the waters of the Styx lie in this city and that a small stream of water emerges from a rock and drips into a hollow surrounded by a circular enclosure of stones. This spring happens to be located in Nonakris, a city of Arcadia near Pheneos.

When the Lacedaemonians learned what Kleomenes was up to, they became afraid and brought him back to Sparta, where he resumed ruling on the same terms as he had before. But as soon as he had returned, he was stricken by madness (although he had been somewhat deranged even before this). For now, whenever he encountered a Spartan, he would thrust his staff into his face. [2] Because he was doing this and not in his right mind, his relatives confined him in a wooden pillory, and while he was thus confined, he noticed that one of the guards had been left alone with him, and he asked the guard to give him a knife. The guard refused him at first, but when Kleomenes threatened what he would do to him when he was released, the frightened guard, who was a helot, gave him a knife. [3] Kleomenes then took the weapon and started to mutilate himself, beginning from his shins. Cutting his flesh lengthwise, he proceeded to his thighs, and from his thighs, his

6.73
491
AEGINA
Kleomenes and the new king, Leotychidas, now punish the Aeginetans, sending ten of the most prominent of them as hostages to Athens.

6.74
491
ARCADIA
Later Kleomenes' plot against Demaratos becomes known, and he flees to the Arcadians, whom he attempts to unite against Sparta.

6.75
491
SPARTA
The Spartans bring Kleomenes home, but he goes mad, abuses others, and kills himself. The Athenians and Argives each have their explanations for his downfall.

hips, and then his sides, until he reached his abdomen, which he thoroughly shredded and then died. Many of the Hellenes say this happened because he had bribed the Pythia to give those responses concerning Demaratos; but according to the Athenians, it was because when he had invaded Eleusis, he had ravaged the precinct of the goddesses. The Argives, however, say it was because he had brought the fugitives out of the sanctuary of Argos and executed them, and had no regard for the grove itself, but had burned it down.

6.76
494
ARGOLID
Kleomenes withdraws from the Erasinos when the omens are unfavorable, and approaches Argos by sea via Nauplia and Tiryns.

For Kleomenes had once received an oracle at Delphi, predicting that he would capture Argos. On his way to Argos, he came to the Erasinos River, which is said to flow out of the Stymphalian Lake and to disappear into an invisible chasm, only to reappear in Argos, where the river is called the Erasinos by the Argives. Upon his arrival at these waters, he performed a sacrifice, [2] but the omens were not favorable for his crossing of the river. Kleomenes then commented that while he admired the Erasinos for not betraying its local citizens, the Argives would not escape unharmed.

Then he retreated and led his army down to Thyrea, where, after sacrificing a bull to the sea, he took his army on boats to the territory of Tiryns and Nauplia.

When the Argives learned of this, they rushed to the coast to oppose him, and, drawing near to Tiryns, at the place called Sepeia, they deployed against the Lacedaemonians, leaving very little space between the two armies. Now the Argives were not afraid of open battle, but rather of being conquered by guile, [2] for that was what the Pythia had indicated in the double oracle that she had given to the Argives and the Milesians. It said to the Argives:

6.77
494
SEPEIA
The Argives approach the Spartans and prepare for battle, but, made wary by an oracle, they decide to avoid being tricked by carrying out all instructions given by the Spartan herald.

When the female conquers and drives out the male,
And among the Argives is exalted in glory,
Many women of Argos will tear at their cheeks,
And thus someday in the future a mortal will say:
"A terrible snake, triple in coils, was subdued and destroyed by the spear."

[3] The concurrence of all the omens frightened the Argives, so they resolved to protect themselves by making use of the enemies' herald: whatever the Lacedaemonian herald announced

to the Lacedaemonians, they, the Argives, would carry out the same instructions.

When Kleomenes realized that the Argives were doing whatever his herald ordered, he commanded that when the herald announced that his troops were to eat breakfast, they should instead pick up their weapons and advance against the Argives. [2] The Lacedaemonians successfully carried out this scheme, for their attack caught the Argives while they were eating their breakfast in accordance with the herald's order, and they were able to slaughter many of them. Many more Argives, however, fled for refuge to the grove of Argos, where the Lacedaemonians surrounded them and stood on guard.

6.78
494
SEPEIA
Kleomenes sees the Argives perform his herald's instructions and uses this to rout them in a surprise attack.

Next Kleomenes questioned some deserters he had with him and then sent a herald to summon by name those Argives who were confined within the sanctuary and to announce to them that their ransom money had been paid. (Among the Peloponnesians, two minas is fixed as the payment of ransom for a prisoner of war.) In this way, Kleomenes managed to induce about fifty of the Argives whose names had been called to come out, and as they did so he killed every one of them. [2] The rest of those in the precinct remained unaware of what was happening outside, since the foliage of the grove was thick and they could not see what was happening to the men outside it until finally one of them climbed a tree and, looking down, discovered what was happening. After that, the Argives no longer went out when they were summoned.

6.79
494
SEPEIA
Speaking falsely, Kleomenes lures out and kills many of the Argives who have taken refuge in a shrine in a grove, until his ruse is discovered.

At that point, Kleomenes ordered the helots with the army to pile up wood around the grove, and after they had obeyed this command, he set the entire grove on fire. As it burned, he asked one of the deserters which of the gods this grove belonged to and was told that it was the grove of Argos. When he heard this, Kleomenes heaved a great sigh and said, "Apollo god of prophecy, you certainly deceived me when you told me that I would capture Argos; I assume your prophecy has now been fulfilled."

6.80
494
SEPEIA
Kleomenes burns down the grove and discovers that this fulfills his own prophecy.

Kleomenes then sent the greater part of the army back to Sparta, but he himself took 1,000 of his best men to the sanctuary of Hera, where he wanted to perform a sacrifice at the altar. The priest, however, forbade him from doing so, saying that it was a sacrilege for an outsider to sacrifice there. Kleomenes ordered the helots to lead the priest away from the altar and to

6.81
494
ARGOS-SPARTA
After worshiping at the sanctuary of Hera, Kleomenes returns to Sparta.

whip him, and then performed the sacrifice by himself; then he, too, went back to Sparta.

After his return, his enemies brought him to trial before the ephors, claiming that he had accepted bribes to refrain from taking Argos when he could easily have captured it. In his reply to this charge—which I cannot judge if it was a lie or the truth—he said that when he had taken the sanctuary of Argos, he supposed that the god's oracle had been fulfilled, and thus he had not thought it right to make an attempt on the city until he had performed a sacrifice and learned whether the god would surrender Argos to him or stand in his way. [2] But while he was hoping to obtain favorable omens in the sanctuary of Hera, a flame of fire blazed from the chest of the statue of the goddess, which convinced him that he would not take Argos. For if it had been the head of the statue that had blazed, he would have taken over the city from top to bottom, but since the fire had blazed out of the chest, he knew that he had already done all that the god willed for him to do. What he said was both plausible and credible to the Spartans, and so his judges voted by a large margin to acquit him.

Argos was now so bereft of its male citizens that their slaves took control of affairs there, governing and managing the city until the sons of those who had perished reached maturity. When that happened, the sons regained control over Argos for themselves and threw out the slaves, who, being compelled to leave, took possession of Tiryns by force. [2] These two cities were on good terms with each other for some time, but then a prophet Kleandros, a man of Arcadian Phigaleia by origin, came to the slaves and persuaded them to attack their masters. This gave rise to a long war between them until finally the Argives prevailed, though with much difficulty.

According to the Argives, then, that is why Kleomenes went mad and died an evil death. The Spartans, however, say that Kleomenes became deranged not because of any divine force, but because he had become through his association with Scythians, a drinker of undiluted wine. [2] For the Scythian nomads, eager to punish Darius for having invaded their land, had sent an embassy to Sparta to form an alliance and to organize a plan whereby they themselves would attempt to invade Media from the Phasis River, and they wanted to arrange that the Spartans would march inland from Ephesus and meet them

6.82
494?
SPARTA
Kleomenes successfully defends himself against a suit brought by his enemies that he accepted bribes to spare Argos.

6.83
ARGOS
Argos is ruled by slaves until the sons of those slain grow up. The cast-out slaves capture Tiryns.

6.84
SPARTA
The Spartans say that Kleomenes went mad from an addiction to strong drink he had acquired by keeping company with the Scythians.

at the same place. [3] They say that when the Scythians had come to Sparta for this purpose, Kleomenes spent a great deal of time in their company, and in fact associated with them more than was appropriate; and it was from them that he learned to drink unmixed wine, which the Spartans believe was the cause of his madness. And they claim that ever since then, whenever they wish to drink stronger wine, they call for a "Scythian" drink. So that is what the Spartans tell about Kleomenes. For myself, I think that the best explanation is that Kleomenes was punished for his treatment of Demaratos.

When the Aeginetans found out that Kleomenes had died, they sent messengers to Sparta to denounce Leotychidas for the hostages being held in Athens. The Lacedaemonians organized a trial and decided that the Aeginetans had suffered an egregious insult at the hands of Leotychidas and sentenced him to be surrendered to the Aeginetans as compensation for the hostages held in Athens. [2] But just as the Aeginetans were about to lead Leotychidas away, Theasides son of Leoprepes, a man of some distinction in Sparta, spoke up: "What are you planning to do, Aeginetans? Will you really seize the king of the Spartans now being surrendered by his own citizens? Even if the Spartans have made this decision now out of anger, you, if you do this, will have to worry that they will later invade and utterly destroy your land." [3] Upon hearing this warning, the Aeginetans halted their abduction of Leotychidas and instead negotiated an agreement whereby he would accompany them to Athens, where he would make sure that their hostages were returned to them.

When Leotychidas came to Athens, he asked for the return of the hostages that he had deposited with them, but the Athenians were unwilling to give them back. They spun out excuses, claiming that since two kings had deposited them, it would not be right if the Athenians should now return the hostages to just one king without the other.

6.85
490
SPARTA
At the instigation of the Aeginetans after the death of Kleomenes, a Spartan court condemns Leotychidas, but the Aeginetans refrain from punishing him and agree that he will accompany them to Athens to ask for the Aeginetan hostages.

6.86
490
ATHENS
The Athenians at first refuse to give back the Aeginetan hostages.

6.86.α*
490
ATHENS
Leotychidas speaks to the
Athenians, telling them
the tale of the Spartan
Glaukos, known
everywhere for justice,
who accepted money
for safekeeping from a
Milesian stranger.

Leotychidas replied to their refusal, "Athenians, you may do whatever you wish; either return them, which would be the pious thing to do, or not, which would be the opposite. I would like to tell you, however, about a certain deposit that once was made in Sparta. [2] We Spartans tell the story of Glaukos son of Epikydas, who lived in Lacedaemon in about the third generation before my own. We tell how this man was preeminent in all respects, and especially in his reputation for justice; he was the best among all who dwelled in Lacedaemon at this time. [3] And we tell what happened to him in the fullness of time, how a certain Milesian who wanted to talk to him once came to Sparta and presented him with the following proposition: 'I am a Milesian, but I have come to your land, Glaukos, because I would like to benefit from your justice, [4] which is much talked of throughout all Hellas, and especially in Ionia. I have been thinking about how Ionia is always in danger, while the Peloponnese is secure, established, and stable; in my land, it is impossible for one to see wealth remaining in the hands of the same people continuously. [5] After I had considered all this and thought it through, I decided to convert half of all my property into silver and to deposit the money with you, because I am absolutely certain that what I deposit with you will be safe and secure. So accept my money and take also these tokens to keep safe with it; restore the silver to whoever comes to you with the same tokens and asks you for it.'

6.86.β
ATHENS
When asked for the return
of the money by the
stranger's sons, Glaukos
procrastinates.

"When the visitor from Miletus had said just that and no more than that, Glaukos accepted the deposit and the stated conditions. And after a great deal of time had passed, the sons of the man who had made the deposit came to Sparta, arranged to talk to Glaukos, and, showing him the tokens, asked for the return of the money. [2] But Glaukos tried to put them off, saying: 'I really do not remember this matter, and I can't think of anything that would help me recall what you are talking about. Of course, if I do come to remember something of it, I would do only what is just; if I did take the money, I shall do the right thing and return it, but if I never took it in the first place, I shall abide by the customs of the Hellenes in my dealings with you. I shall postpone my decision until the fourth month from this one.'

"The Milesians thought themselves most unfortunate and departed under the impression that they had been robbed of their money. Glaukos then journeyed to Delphi to consult the oracle. He inquired whether he could seize the money for himself by swearing a solemn oath, and the Pythia attacked him with these verses:

[2] Glaukos son of Epikydas, right now you will gain the
    greater advantage
To plunder and win the money by oath.
Then swear, since even the trustworthy man meets death in
    the end.
But the child of oath is a nameless force, with no hands
And no feet, yet swiftly pursues and destroys with its grasp
All his kin, his whole house will afterward perish,
While the line of the trustworthy man will fare better.

"After hearing this response, Glaukos begged the god to grant him forgiveness for what he had said. But the Pythia replied that the testing of the god and the commission of the crime were one and the same thing.

"Glaukos then sent for the Milesian visitors and returned the money to them. But I tell this story to you, Athenians, because no descendant of Glaukos exists today, and not a single hearth is acknowledged to belong to his family; his line has been wiped out root and branch from Sparta. Therefore, when it comes to a deposit, it is best to think only of returning it to those who ask for its return." That was what Leotychidas said, but the Athenians still did not heed his words, so he left them.

Now the Aeginetans had not yet paid the penalty for the crimes which they committed earlier against the Athenians in order to please the Thebans. Nevertheless, they now prepared to punish the Athenians, claiming that it was they themselves who had suffered injustice and that the Athenians were to blame. At that time the Athenians were celebrating their quadrennial festivalb off Cape Sounion, so the Aeginetans set up an ambush and seized the ship carrying the sacred officials, with many of the leading men of Athens on board. After capturing these men, they bound them in chains.

Having suffered this insult at the hands of the Aeginetans, the Athenians no longer postponed developing every conceivable scheme against them. Now there lived on Aegina a distinguished man called Nikodromos son of Knoithos, who resented the Aeginetans for having exiled him from the island earlier and who now, when he learned that the Athenians were preparing to harm the Aeginetans, arranged to betray Aegina to the Athenians, designating a certain day on which he would make his attempt and when they should come to his assistance. To fulfill his part of this arrangement, Nikodromos seized what is called the Old City, but the Athenians did not appear at the appointed time.

It so happened that they did not then have enough battle-worthy ships to engage the Aeginetan fleet, so they asked the Corinthians to lend them ships, but by the time they obtained them, the project was ruined. The Corinthians and the Athenians were the best of friends at this time, so the Corinthians did give twenty ships in response to the Athenian request, but they had to charge five drachmas each for them, since the law did not permit them to give the ships as a gift. Adding these ships to their own, the Athenians manned a total of seventy ships when they left for Aegina, but they sailed one day after the agreed-upon date.

When the Athenians did not show up on time, Nikodromos went on board a boat and fled from Aegina, accompanied by other Aeginetans; the Athenians permitted them to settle at Cape Sounion, from where they raided and plundered the Aeginetans on the island.

That, however, is what happened afterward. But at this time, Nikodromos led the common people in an attempted revolt, which was put down by the affluent Aeginetans. The victors led out the captive rebels in order to execute them, and because of what happened next, they came under a curse that they were unable to counter through sacrifice, since they were driven off the island before they could appease the goddess. [2] They had taken 700 of the people alive, and while they were leading them out to be executed, one of the captives broke out of his bonds and fled to the porch of Demeter Thesmophoros. There he grasped the door handles and clung to them so tightly that, although they tried to drag him away, they were unable to loosen his grip on the doors, so they cut off his hands and took him like that, with his hands still clinging fast to the door handles.

So that is what the Aeginetans had done to their own people. And when the Athenians arrived with the fleet of seventy ships, the Aeginetans fought a sea battle against them but were defeated. The Aeginetans then called for assistance from the Argives,a the same people to whom they had appealed before, but this time the Argives did not rush to their aid, since they were angry that the Aeginetan ships that Kleomenes had seized by force had put in to shore on Argive territory and that the ships' crews had disembarked with the Lacedaemonians and invaded their territory; in addition, the men from Sicyonianc ships had also participated in this invasion. [2] So the Argives imposed a fine of 1,000 talents, 500 to be paid by each of the two peoples. But while the Sicyonians admitted that they had done wrong and agreed to be freed from further expense by paying 100 talents now, the Aeginetans would not admit their guilt and in fact were rather perversely stubborn and remorseless about the whole thing. As a result, when they now requested the Argive state to help them, not a single Argive was officially sent to assist them, although about 1,000 of them did volunteer to go. The general leading these volunteers was a man by the name of Eurybates, who had trained for the pentathlon. [3] The majority of these volunteers never returned home again but were killed by the Athenians on Aegina. The general himself, Eurybates, showed his skill in single combat by killing three men, but he then died at the hands of the fourth, one Sophanes of Dekeleia.

Sometime later, when the Aeginetans spotted the Athenian ships floundering in disorder, they attacked and this time won the battle, taking four Athenian ships with all their crews.

So the Athenians waged war against the Aeginetans. Meanwhile, the Persian was attending to his own concerns, as he was constantly being reminded by his servant to remember the Athenians, and the Peisistratids were at his side maligning the Athenians; moreover, Darius himself wanted to seize this pretext to subjugate all those Hellenes who had refused to give him earth and water. [2] Since Mardonios had failed on his expedition, Darius relieved him of his command and appointed other generals: Datis, a Mede by race, and Artaphrenes son of his brother Artaphrenes. Darius sent these generals off,

6.91
490
AEGINA-ARGOS
The Athenians defeat the Aeginetans in a sea fight. Argos refuses to help Aegina as before, but 1,000 volunteers come anyway, most of whom are killed by the Athenians on Aegina.

6.93
490
AEGINA-ARGOS
The Aeginetans defeat the Athenians at sea.

6.94
491
SUSA-SARDIS?
While Athens and Aegina fought, Darius appointed new generals to lead an expedition against Athens and Eretria.

instructing them to enslave Athens and Eretria and to bring back the captive slaves into his presence.

So the newly appointed generals left the King and set out on their journey. They went first to the plain of Aleion in Cilicia, bringing along a huge and well-equipped land army. As they camped there, all the ships that had been levied from the various districts arrived to join their forces, as well as the horse-transport ships, which Darius had ordered his tribute-paying peoples to prepare the year before. [2] After putting the horses on board these ships, the land army embarked, and the expedition sailed to Ionia with a fleet of 600 triremes. From there, instead of keeping their ships close to the mainland and sailing toward the Hellespont and Thrace, they set out from Samos, went past Ikaros, and made their voyage through the islands. I suppose they took this route because they were afraid to sail around Mount Athos, since the year before they had suffered catastrophic losses on this route. Moreover, the fact that Naxos had not yet been conquered provided another compelling reason for them to go this way.

The Persians left the Ikarian Sea, and since they intended to attack Naxos first, they approached the island and put in to shore there. The Naxians, remembering their previous experience, did not await them but fled for the hills. The Persians caught and enslaved some of them and set fire to their sanctuaries and the city. After that, they set sail for the other islands.

Meanwhile, the Delians left their own island and fled to Tenos. As the Persian forces approached Delos, Datis sailed ahead of them and did not allow the ships to anchor off Delos, but had them put in across from it at the island of Rheneia instead. Upon learning where the Delians were now he sent a herald to them with the following message: [2] "Holy men, why have you gone in flight and condemned me without good reason? For I myself have enough good sense to know, and besides the King has instructed me, not to harm the site on which the two gods were born, nor the rest of the island or its inhabitants. Therefore return to your homes and inhabit your own island again." After Datis had proclaimed this message through the herald, he piled up 300 talents of frankincense upon the altar and burned it as a sacrifice.

6.95
490
IONIA-AEGEAN SEA
The Persian expedition crosses the Aegean westward from island to island to avoid the passage around Mount Athos.

6.96
490
NAXOS
The Persians conquer Naxos, enslaving all those they catch.

6.97
490
DELOS
The Delians flee before the Persian approach, but Datis, the Persian general, promises good treatment and honor to the holy place and bids them to return.

When the sacrifice had been completed, Datis next sailed with his forces to Eretria, taking Ionians and Aeolians with him. And according to the Delians, it was at this point, just after he had put out to sea, that Delos was shaken by an earthquake—the first and last one up until my own day. This was, I suppose, a portent by which the god revealed to mortals the evils that were going to befall them. [2] For in three successive generations, during the reigns of Darius son of Hystaspes, Xerxes son of Darius, and Artaxerxes son of Xerxes, more evils befell Hellas than in all the other generations prior to that of Darius. Some of these evils were caused by the Persians, but others by the leading states of Hellas waging war for political domination among themselves. [3] So it was not at all odd that Delos should be shaken now, although it had never been before. In fact an oracle predicting this had been written down:

I shall shake even Delos, though it was unshaken before.

In Greek the names of the kings mean the following: Darius means "Achiever," Xerxes "Warlike," and Artaxerxes "Extremely Warlike." These are the names the Hellenes would correctly use to refer to these Kings in their own language.

After the barbarians sailed from Delos, they put in at the islands, where they enlisted men to join their forces and took sons of the islanders as hostages. [2] But when, as they made their rounds of the islands, they put in at Karystos, the inhabitants there refused to give them hostages or to march against their neighbors, by whom they meant the Eretrians and Athenians. So the Persians besieged the city and ravaged the land until the Karystians adopted the Persian way of thinking and came over to their side.

When the Eretrians learned that Persian forces were sailing against them, they appealed to the Athenians to come to their assistance, and the Athenians, not wishing to refuse them military aid, offered them as allies their 4,000 klerouchs who had taken over the land of the Chalcidian horse-breeders. The planning of the Eretrians, however, was not at all sound, for although they had sent for Athenian assistance, they were divided among themselves over what they should do. [2] Some of them considered leaving the place and heading for the rough

6.98
490
DELOS
After Datis leaves, Delos suffers an earthquake, its first according to Herodotus, who thinks it a portent from the gods of all the evils the Hellenes were to suffer in the ensuing years.

6.99
490
KARYSTOS
The Persians recruit soldiers from the islands. Karystos at first refuses them, but then gives in.

6.100
490
ERETRIA
When the Eretrians ask Athens for help, she sends 4,000 klerouchs from Chalcis, but finding divisions among the Eretrians, these go away.

headlands of Euboea, while others, expecting to win personal gains from the Persians, were preparing to betray their city. [3] When Aischines son of Nothon, the leading man of Eretria, became aware of this situation, he informed those Athenians who had arrived about the present state of affairs and begged them to depart for their own land so that they would not perish along with the Eretrians. The Athenians followed his advice, [6.101] and by crossing over to Oropos, they saved themselves. Now the Persians put in their ships at Tamynai, Choereai, and Aigilia in Eretrian territory, and as soon as they landed, they disembarked the horses and prepared to attack their enemies. [2] The Eretrians had no intention of marching out to meet them in battle, so now their prevailing plan was to stay in the city, and their main concern was to defend its walls if they possibly could. The assault on the walls was fierce and lasted for six days, and many fell on both sides. On the seventh day, two prominent citizens, Euphorbos son of Alkimachos and Philagros son of Kyneas, betrayed their city and surrendered it to the Persians. [3] After entering the city, the Persians plundered and set fire to the sanctuaries, exacting vengeance for the sanctuaries burned down in Sardis, and as Darius had instructed, they enslaved the people.

After their conquest of Eretria, the Persians lingered for a few days and then sailed for Attica, thus applying pressure on the Athenians and fully expecting that they would do to the Athenians what they had done to the Eretrians.

Since Marathon was the region of Attica most suitable for cavalry as well as the one closest to Eretria, that is where Hippias son of Peisistratos led them.

As soon as they heard about this, the Athenians rushed to Marathon to defend it themselves, led by the ten generals of whom Miltiades was the tenth. His father, Kimon son of Stesagoras, had been driven into exile from Athens by Peisistratos son of Hippocrates. [2] And during his exile he won a race with his four-horse team at Olympia, achieving the same victory that had been won by Miltiades, his half brother by the same mother. At the next Olympiad, Kimon won again with the same mares, but this time gave up his victory so that it could be proclaimed in the name of Peisistratos. By relinquishing his victory, he was able to return from exile to his own land. [3] But when he had won with the same mares yet again,

6.101
490
ERETRIA
After resisting Persian assaults for six days, the Eretrians are betrayed by two of their own citizens, the city is taken, and they are enslaved.

6.102
490
MARATHON
Hippias then leads the Persians to Marathon.

6.103
490
MARATHON
The Athenians march to Marathon, led by ten generals—among them Miltiades, whose father, Kimon, had won the four-horse chariot race at Olympia three times in a row, and who was murdered by the sons of Peisistratos.

it was his fate to die at the hands of the sons of Peisistratos after Peisistratos was no longer alive. They killed him by placing men at the Prytaneion at night to ambush him; he now lies buried at the entrance to the city, across the road called "Through the Hollow," and the horses that won his three Olympic victories are buried opposite him. [4] The horses of Euagoras of Laconia accomplished this same feat, but no others have ever done so. Kimon's elder son Stesagoras was at the time being raised in the Chersonese with his uncle Miltiades, while the younger son was with Kimon himself in Athens. He was named Miltiades after the Miltiades who had settled the Chersonese.

This was the Miltiades who had escaped death twice and who had left the Chersonese and was now a general of the Athenians. For the Phoenicians, judging his capture and delivery to the King to be of great importance, had pursued him as far as Imbros. [2] But he escaped them and returned to his own land, thinking he was now safe. There, however, his enemies caught up with him and prosecuted him in court for having behaved like a tyrant in the Chersonese. But he was acquitted and escaped them, too, and thus came to be a general of the Athenians, elected by the people.

6.104
493
IMBROS-ATHENS
Miltiades escapes from the Phoenicians only to be sued for tyranny in Athens, but he is acquitted and elected general instead.

The first thing the generals did, while still in the city, was to send a message sage to Sparta by dispatching a herald named Philippides, who was an Athenian long-distance runner and a professional in this work. Now Philippides himself reported to the Athenians afterward that when he was running in the vicinity of Mount Parthenion overlooking Tegea, the god Pan fell in with him [2] and, shouting out his name, "Philippides," ordered him to ask the Athenians why they were paying no attention to him, although he was well disposed toward them, had already and often been of service to them, and would serve them further in the future. [3] The Athenians believed this report was true, and once their affairs were settled and stable again, they set up a shrine to Pan below the Acropolis, and in response to his message to them, they propitiate Pan with sacrifices and a torch race every year.

6.105
490
TEGEA
Philippides, sent by Athens to summon help from Sparta, meets the god Pan near Tegea. The god asks him why the Athenians ignore him. Later a shrine to Pan is established under the Acropolis.

So after Philippides had been sent off by the generals and, as he claimed, Pan had appeared to him, he arrived in Sparta on the day after he had left Athens. There he said to the magistrates, [2] "Lacedaemonians, the Athenians beg you to rush to their defense and not look on passively as the most ancient city in Hellas falls into slavery imposed by barbarians. For in fact Eretria has already been enslaved, and thus Hellas has become weaker by one important city." [3] When he had announced this as he had been instructed the Spartans resolved to help the Athenians, but it was impossible for them to do so at that moment, since they did not wish to break their law. For that day was the ninth of the month, and on the ninth, they said, they could not march out to war, but must instead wait until the moon was full.

So they waited for the full moon while Hippias son of Peisistratos was leading the barbarians to Marathon. During the previous night Hippias dreamt that he was sleeping with his own mother. [2] He interpreted this vision to mean that he would return to Athens, recover his rule, and die as an old man there in his native land; at least that was his interpretation of his dream at the time. After Hippias led the captive slaves from Eretria to the island of the Styrians, which is called Aigilia, and had them disembark there, he directed the ships to put in at Marathon. When the barbarians had come ashore, he set about assigning them to their various positions. [3] In the midst of this work, however, he was seized by an unusually severe fit of sneezing and coughing, and since he was getting on in age, most of his teeth were loose, and one of them fell out with the force of his coughing and landed on the sand. Hippias tried very hard to find it, [4] but the tooth was nowhere to be seen. He then groaned to those standing nearby, "This land is not ours, and we shall not make it subject to us, either, for my tooth now holds all that was to be my share."

In this way, then, Hippias concluded that his vision had been fulfilled.

Now just when the Athenians had taken up their positions in the precinct of Herakles, the Plataeans arrived in full force to assist them. They had earlier placed themselves under the protection of the Athenians, who had then exerted much effort on their behalf. [2] This had happened in the following way. Once, when the Plataeans were being hard pressed by the Thebans, they had offered themselves to Kleomenes son of Anaxandridas and the Lacedaemonians, since the Lacedaemonians happened to be present in their region at the time. But the Lacedaemonians refused to accept them, saying, "We live too far away, and any assistance we could offer you would be cold and remote. You could be enslaved many times over before we ever heard anything about it. [3] So we advise you to give yourselves to the Athenians for protection instead; they not only are your close neighbors, but also are no sluggards when it comes to lending military assistance." The Lacedaemonians gave this advice not so much out of goodwill toward the Plataeans as out of their wish to create trouble for the Athenians by provoking them into active hostilities against the Boeotians. [4] The Plataeans did not reject their advice, so while the Athenians were conducting their sacrifices to the twelve gods, the Plataeans sat down at the altar and offered themselves to the Athenians. As soon as the Thebans learned of this, they marched against the Plataeans, and the Athenians rushed to their assistance. [5] Battle was about to be joined when the Corinthians who happened to be present, would not allow them to fight, and were entrusted by both sides with the task of arbitration. The Corinthians reconciled the parties by defining the boundaries of their respective territories on the condition that the Thebans should leave anyone alone who did not wish to be classified as members of the Boeotian League. After rendering this decision, the Corinthians departed, but as the Athenians, too, were marching away, the Boeotians attacked them, and in the ensuing battle were defeated. [6] The Athenians then extended the boundaries of the Plataeans beyond those set by the Corinthians, making the River Asopos itself the border that divided the territory of Thebes from that of Plataea and Hysiai. That, then, is how the Plataeans had offered themselves to the Athenians and thus gained their protection. And now they had arrived to help the Athenians at Marathon.

6.108
PLATAEA
The Plataeans arrive at Marathon to fight alongside the Athenians. Herodotus tells how thirty years earlier, following Spartan advice, they allied themselves with Athens for protection against Thebes.

6.109
490
MARATHON
The Athenian generals
are equally divided
between attacking and
remaining on the
defensive. Miltiades
tries to persuade the
polemarch Kallimachos
to cast the tie-breaking
vote in favor of
attacking the Persians.

The Athenian generals were divided in their opinions: some were against joining battle, thinking their own numbers were too few to engage the forces of the Medes, while others, including Miltiades, urged that they fight. [2] So they disagreed, and the worst of the two proposals seemed to be prevailing when Miltiades went up to the polemarch at that time, one Kallimachos of Apfaidna, who had been selected by lot for his office as polemarch of the Athenians. It was he who had the eleventh vote, for in the old days the Athenians used to grant the polemarch an equal vote with their generals. [3] Miltiades said to Kallimachos, "It is now up to you, Kallimachos, whether you will reduce Athens to slavery or ensure its freedom and thus leave to all posterity a memorial for yourself which will exceed even that of Harmodios and Aristogeiton. For from the time Athenians first came into existence up until the present, this is the greatest danger they have ever confronted. If they bow down before the Medes, it is clear from our past experience what they will suffer when handed over to Hippias; but if this city prevails, it can become the first among all Greek cities. [4] I shall explain to you how matters really stand and how the authority to decide this matter has come to rest with you. We ten generals are evenly divided in our opinions, some urging that we join battle, others that we do not. [5] If we fail to fight now, I expect that intense factional strife will fall upon the Athenians and shake their resolve so violently that they will medize. But if we join battle before any rot can infect some of the Athenians, then, as long as the gods grant both sides equal treatment, we can prevail in this engagement. [6] All this is now in your hands and depends on you. If you add your vote for my proposal, your ancestral land can be free and your city the first of Greek cities. But if you choose the side of those eager to prevent a battle, you will have the opposite of all the good things I have described."

6.110
490
MARATHON
Kallimachos votes to
attack, and leadership of
the army is granted by all
to Miltiades.

Miltiades' arguments persuaded Kallimachos, and when the polemarch's vote was added to the tally, the decision was made to join battle. And afterward, the generals in favor of the battle each in their turn ceded their day of command to Miltiades when the day came around for each to be in charge. But while Miltiades accepted this, he would not make the attack until it was his day to preside.

When his turn came, he deployed the Athenians for battle with the polemarch Kallimachos leading the right wing, for at that time the Athenians observed a custom that the polemarch was always to command the right wing. Once Kallimachos had taken his position there as their leader, the tribes were posted next to one another in succession according to their numerical order, and the Plataeans were posted at the end of the line, holding the extreme left wing. [2] In fact, as a consequence of this battle, whenever the Athenians perform sacrifices at their quadrennial festivals, the Athenian herald prays that both the Athenians and the Plataeans together will be blessed with good fortune. [3] The result of the Athenians' deployment at Marathon was that the line of the Athenian army was equal in length to that of the Medes, but the center of the Athenian line was only a few rows deep and thus the army was at its weakest there; each wing, however, was strong in numbers.

6.111
490
MARATHON
Miltiades arrays the army in line, with more strength in the wings than in the center.

After the troops were in position and the sacrifices had proven favorable, when the Athenians were let loose and allowed to advance, they charged at a run toward the barbarians. The space between the two armies was about a mile, [2] and the Persians, who saw the Athenians advancing toward them on the double, prepared to meet their attack; they assumed that the Athenians were seized by some utterly self-destructive madness, as they observed how few the Athenians were in number and how they were charging toward them with neither cavalry nor archers in support. [3] So the barbarians suspected that the Athenians had gone mad, but when the Athenians closed with them in combat, they fought remarkably well For they were the first of all Hellenes we know of to use the running charge against their enemies, as well as the first to endure the sight of the Medes' clothing and the men wearing it. In fact, until then, even to hear the name "Medes" spoken would strike terror into Hellenes.

6.112
490
MARATHON
After the sacrifices prove favorable, the Athenians charge at the run, the first Hellenes to do so and not fear the sight of the Medes.

They fought in the battle at Marathon for a long time. The barbarians prevailed in the center of the line, where the Persians themselves and the Sakai were deployed, and as the barbarians were winning here, they broke through the line of the Hellenes and chased them inland; but at the same time, the Athenians and Plataeans were prevailing on the wings. [2] In their victory there, they allowed the barbarian troops that they had routed to flee and then, drawing both of their wings together, they

6.113
490
MARATHON
The Athenian wings prevail and then unite to defeat the initially victorious Persian center, driving the enemy to their ships.

fought those enemy troops who had broken through the center; in this encounter, too, the Athenians were victorious, and as the Persians fled, the Athenians pursued them and cut them down until they reached the sea, where they called for fire and started to seize the ships.

It was in this struggle that the polemarch Kallimachos perished, having proven himself a noble and courageous warrior; Stesilaos son of Thrasylaos, one of the generals, also died. In addition, Kynegeiros son of Euphorion fell, for while seizing the sternpost of a ship, his hand was chopped off by an axe. Many other famous Athenians died in this conflict as well.

In their attempts, the Athenians gained possession of seven ships. The barbarians pushed off from shore with their fleet and, after picking up the captive slaves from Eretria whom they had left on the island, sailed around Sounion, hoping to arrive at the city of Athens before the Athenians could march there. At Athens, the Alkmeonids were later blamed for having contrived a scheme whereby a shield would be displayed to send a signal to the Persians aboard their ships.

Now while the Persians were sailing around Sounion, the Athenians were marching back as fast as they could to defend their city, and they managed to arrive there in advance of the barbarian fleet. Coming from the sanctuary of Herakles in Marathon, they arrived and set up their camp in another sanctuary of Herakles, the one in Kynosarges. The barbarians anchored their ships off Phaleron (for that was the harbor of the Athenians at the time), held their ships there for a while, and then sailed back to Asia.

In the battle of Marathon, about 6,400 of the barbarians died, and of the Athenians, 192. Those were the casualties from both sides. [2] It happened that an amazing occurrence took place there, when Epizelus son of Cuphagoras, an Athenian who was fighting in the battle and proving himself to be a noble and courageous warrior, was stricken with blindness, though he had not been struck or hit on any part of his body. But from this time on and for the rest of his life, he continued to be blind. [3] I have heard that the story he told about it went something like this: he thought he saw a huge hoplite whose beard overshadowed his entire shield and who was standing opposite him; but this phantom passed by Epizelus and killed

6.114
490
MARATHON
Some of the famous Athenians who fell in the fighting.

6.115
490
MARATHON
The Persians sail off and head for Athens, hoping to find the city undefended.

6.116
490
ATHENS
The Athenians march home in time to confront the enemy fleet when it arrives.

6.117
490
MARATHON
Herodotus notes the very unequal number of casualties suffered by each side in the battle. The tale of Epizelus.

the man standing next to him. At least that is what I have heard that Epizelus said.

Datis was well on his way to Asia with his forces when he came to Mykonos, where he had a vision in his sleep. What he saw is not reported, but as soon as the light of day arrived, he made a search of his ships and found in a Phoenician vessel a gilded statue of Apollo. Upon inquiring about the site from which it had been looted, he learned the name of the sanctuary from which it had come and sailed to Delos in his own ship. [2] Datis deposited the statue in the sanctuary there and instructed the Delians, who had by now returned to their island, to take the statue to Delion in Thebes, which lies on the coast opposite Chakis. [3] After giving these orders, Datis sailed away. The Delians, however, did not deliver the image; but twenty years later, the Thebans brought it to Delion because of a prophecy.

Datis and Artaphrenes sailed to Asia and brought the captive Eretrian slaves to Susa. Darius the King had been nursing a bitter grudge against the Eretrians before they were brought to him as slaves, because they had struck first and been the aggressors. [2] But when he saw them delivered up to him as his subjects, he did them no further harm but instead settled them at his royal station in the land of the Kissians called Arderikka, about twenty-three miles from Susa, and almost four and a half miles from the well which supplies three types of products. For bitumen, salt, and oil are drawn from this well in the following way. [3] A shadoof is used, to which is fastened half a wineskin to serve as a bucket. They dip this into the well and draw up the liquid and pour it into a container, from which it is then poured into another, where it is diverted into three separate channels. The bitumen and salt immediately congeal, while the oil [...] The Persians call this oil *rhadinake*. It is black and has a heavy acrid odor. [4] So the Eretrians were settled in this place by King Darius, and they continue to inhabit this land up to my own time, still speaking their original language.

That, then, is what happened to the Eretrians. After the full moon 2,000 Lacedaemonians marched to Athens in such great haste that they arrived in Attica on the third day out of Sparta. They were too late to engage in battle, but nevertheless wished to see the Medes, which they did when they reached Marathon. Then they praised the Athenians for their achievement and went home.

6.118
DELOS
The story of Datis' dream and the image of Apollo he left at Delos.

6.119
490-?
ERETRIA-KISSIA
Darius settles the Eretrians near a well that produces asphalt, salt, and oil.

6.120
490
MARATHON
The Spartans arrive, go to Marathon to view the dead Persians.

I am astonished by that story about the Alkmeonids. I do not believe that they could ever have displayed a shield to the Persians pursuant to an agreement that was motivated by any desire on their part to subject the Athenians to Hippias and the barbarians. For the Alkmeonids are obviously more vehement tyrant haters than even Kallias son of Phainippos and father of Hipponikos. [2] Kallias was the only one of all the Athenians, after Peisistratos had been exiled, who dared to buy the tyrant's property when it was put up for sale by the public auctioneer, and he devised every other land of hostile act against him as well.

BOOK 7.101 – 7.105

After sailing through them, he disembarked from the ship and sent for Demaratos son of Ariston, who had joined him in the expedition against Hellas and when he had answered the summons, Xerxes said, Demaracos, it is now my pleasure to ask you something that I wish to know. You are a Hellene, and according to what I have heard from you as well as from the other Hellenes who have spoken with me, you come from a city that is neither one of the smallest nor one of the weakest. [2] So tell me, will the Hellenes stand their ground and use force to resist me? For I think that even if all the Hellenes were assembled together, and even if they joined the peoples who dwell west of them, they still could not match me in battle, and therefore they will not stand their ground when I attack them—unless, that is, they should unite. [3] However, I would like to hear your opinion; do tell me anything you can say about them." That was what Xerxes asked, and Demaratos replied, "Sire, shall I tell you the truth or shall I say what will please you?" Xerxes ordered him to tell the truth, saying that by doing so, Demaratos would please him just as much as he had before.

Upon hearing this, Demaratos said, "Sire, since you insist that I speak the truth and say nothing for which you could later accuse me of falsehood here it is: in Hellas, poverty is always and forever a native resident, while excellence is something acquired through intelligence and the force of strict law. It is through the exercise of this excellence that Hellas wards off both poverty and despotism. [2] Now while I commend all the Hellenes who live in the Dorian lands, what I shall next tell you applies not to all of them, but only to the Lacedaemonians. First of all, there is no way that they will accept your stated intention to enslave Hellas; next, even if all the other Hellenes come to see things your way, the Spartans will certainly oppose you in battle. [3] And you need not ask as to their number in order to consider how they could possibly do this, for if there are 1,000 of them marching out, they will fight you, and if they number more or less than that—it makes no difference—they will fight you all the same."

When Xerxes heard this, he laughed and said, "Demaratos, how can you make such a statement—that 1,000 men will fight my troops! Tell me, you claim that you were a king of these men, so would you then be willing to fight against ten men on the spot? Yet if your citizens are at all as you describe them, it would be fitting that you as their king should be ready to stand up to twice as many antagonists as they would, in accordance with your own laws and customs. [2] So if each one of them is worth ten of my troops, then I would expect you to be the equal of twenty. That, at least, would square with what you have told me. But if these men are like you and about the same size as you and similar to the other men who have come from Hellas to visit and speak with me, then you Hellenes may go ahead and boast, but see to it that your story is not just empty bragging. [3] Now please allow me to look at this in an entirely rational manner. How could 1,000 or even 10,000 or 50,000 men, all of them alike being free and lacking one man to rule over them, stand up to an army as great as mine? Even if there are 5,000 of them, we will outnumber them by more than 1,000 to one. [4] Now if they were under the rule of one man, as is our way, they would fear that man and be better able, in spite of their natural inclinations, to go out and confront larger forces, despite their being outnumbered, because they would then be compelled by the lash. But they would never dare to do such a thing if they were allowed their freedom! I myself think that even if the Hellenes were equal in numbers to us, they would have difficulty fighting just us, the Persians, alone. [5] I must admit that among our men, the kind of courage you described is rare rather than common, but I do have Persian spearmen who would gladly fight three Hellenes at once, So you are simply talking nonsense and are clearly ignorant concerning these matters."

7.103
480
DORISKOS
Xerxes thinks Demaratos makes idle boasts; that the Hellenes might oppose his great army if compelled by a single ruler, but being free, they will certainly not do so.

7.104
480
DORISKOS
Demaratos replies that he
only speaks what he
believes to be the truth:
that the Spartans are the
best warriors on earth,
that they fear their law
more than the Persians
fear Xerxes and will
obey it and fight bravely.

To that, Demaratos replied, "Sire, from the beginning of this conversation I knew that if I told you the truth you would not like it. But since you compelled me to speak the absolute truth, I have told you how things stand with the Spartans. [2] You yourself, however, are well aware of how I happen to love them right now, given my circumstances: they have deprived me of my office and ancestral privileges and have rendered me an exile belonging to no city. It was your father who took me in, supported me, and gave me a home. Now surely it would be unreasonable for a prudent man to turn away goodwill when it appears to him. On the contrary, he should welcome it with open arms. [3] I do not claim to have the ability myself to fight ten men at once, nor even two, and I would not fight even one in a duel if I had the choice. But if I were compelled or urged on by some great challenge, I would indeed take the utmost pleasure in fighting one of those men who says that he by himself is equal to three Hellenes. [4] The Lacedaemonians are in fact no worse than any other men when they fight individually, but when they unite and fight together, they are the best warriors of all. For though they are free, they are not free in all respects, for they are actually ruled by a lord and master: law is their master, and it is the law that they inwardly fear—much more so than your men fear you. [5] They do whatever it commands, which is always the same: it forbids them to flee from battle, and no matter how many men they are fighting, it orders them to remain in their rank and either prevail or perish. Now if I appear to you to be talking nonsense when I say this, I am quite willing to hold my tongue from now on; I said all this because you compelled me to do so. Nevertheless, sire, I hope that everything turns out in accord with your wishes."

That was the reply of Demaratos. Xerxes expressed no anger at all; in fact he made a joke of it and sent him away gently. After concluding his talk with Demaratos, Xerxes appointed a new governor for Doriskos, Maskames son of Megadostes, ousting the man that had been appointed by Darius. Then he proceeded on his way toward Hellas, leading the army through Thrace.

Those Hellenes who gave earth and water were the Thessalians, Dolopians, Ainianes, Perraibians, Locrians, Magnesians, Malians, Achaeans of Phthiotis, Thebans, and all the Boeotians except for the Thespians and the Plataeans. [2] Concerning these peoples, the Hellenes who were undertaking war against the barbarians swore a solemn oath, vowing that all the Hellenes who had surrendered themselves to the Persian without being forced to do so would have to pay the tithe to the god at Delphi once they had succeeded and their affairs were settled. That, then, was the oath sworn by the Hellenes.

Xerxes did not send heralds to Athens and Sparta to ask for earth and water, because when Darius had sent heralds to these cities some years before, the Athenians had cast these heralds, when they made their request, down into a pit, and the Spartans had thrown theirs into a well; and the heralds were told to take their earth and water to the King from there! [2] So that is why Xerxes did not send anyone to Athens or Sparta to make the request. Now I cannot say whether it was because the Athenians had dealt with the heralds in this way that they later suffered the disaster of having their land and city laid waste, but in my opinion it was not on account of what they had done to the heralds.

In any case, the wrath of Talthybios, the herald of Agamemnon, struck the Lacedaemonians. There is a sanctuary of Talthybios in Sparta where his descendants, who are called Talthybiads, are granted the office and honor of serving on all embassies sent out by Sparta. [2] Now after the incident of the heralds, the Spartans were unable to obtain good omens when they sacrificed, and as they found this to be the case for a long time, the Lacedaemonians became troubled and vexed that this kept happening; and so they held frequent assemblies and made a proclamation asking whether any Lacedaemonian was willing to die on behalf of Sparta. The men who volunteered to undertake the punishment imposed by Xerxes for the loss of Darius' heralds were Sperthias son of Aneristos and Boulis son of Nikolaos, Spartans of noble birth who had also attained the first rank in wealth. [3] And so the Spartans sent them off to the Medes to die.

7.132
480
PIERIA
A list of those Hellenes who gave earth and water to Xerxes' heralds and thus submitted.

7.133
491
ATHENS-SPARTA
Athens and Sparta were guilty of having sacrilegiously killed heralds sent by Darius.

7.134
480
SPARTA
To atone for the murder of Darius' heralds, the Spartans sent two volunteers to Persia to face death or any punishment imposed by Xerxes.

7.135
480
ASIA
Herodotus tells the
anecdote of these men's
sharp reply to Hydarnes
the Persian, who talked
of the advantages of
the King's friendship.

The courage of these men is certainly worthy of awe, as are also the words they spoke. For along their journey to Susa, they came to Hydarnes, a Persian by race, who was general of the peoples along the coast of Asia. He entertained them by serving them a feast during which he asked them, [2] "Lacedaemonians, why are you trying to avoid becoming the King's friends? You can see that the King knows how to honor good men when you look at me and the state of my affairs. This could be the same for you if only you would surrender yourselves to the King, since he would surely think you to be good men and allow each of you Greek territory to rule over." [3] To this they replied, "Hydarnes, you offer us this advice only because you do not have a fair and proper perspective. For you counsel us based on your experience of only one way of life, but you have had no experience of the other: you know well how to be a slave but have not yet experienced freedom, nor have you felt whether it is sweet or not. But if you could try freedom, you would advise us to fight for it, and not only with spears, but with axes!"

7.136
480
SUSA
The Spartans nobly tell
Xerxes their mission, but
he refuses to execute
them and thus imitate
the Spartan blasphemy.

After giving that answer to Hydarnes, they traveled inland to Susa and gained an audience with the King. At first the King's bodyguards ordered them and actually tried to force them to prostrate themselves before the King; but they refused to do so, saying that they would never do that, even if the bodyguards should try to push them down to the ground headfirst, since it was not their custom to prostrate themselves before any human being, and besides, that was not the reason for which they had come. So they succeeded in fighting off this command, and next made a speech with words to this effect: [2] "King of the Medes, the Lacedaemonians have sent us here to make up for the heralds you lost in Sparta, so that we may bear the punishment for what happened to them." Xerxes responded to their speech with proud magnanimity. He said he would not act like the Lacedaemonians, who had violated laws observed by all humanity when they killed the heralds; no, he himself would not do the kind of thing for which he was reproaching them: he would not kill these two men to release the Lacedaemonians from their guilt.

So Sperthias and Boulis returned home, but the Spartans had nevertheless managed for the time being to stop the wrath of Talthybios. Much later, however, as the Lacedaemonians say, this wrath was reawakened during the war between the Peloponnesians and the Athenians. And it is apparent to me that this phenomenon was especially divine, [2] for this wrath of Talthybios struck messengers in particular, and did not stop until it had been vented completely, which implies the idea of justice. Moreover, it fell upon the very sons of those men who had gone to the King to placate it earlier—Nikolas son of Boulis and Aneristos son of Sperthios. Aneristos was the man who took Halieis, an offshoot of Tiryns, after sailing there in a merchant ship full of men. In any case, it is quite clear to me that what occurred was divine and a result of this wrath. [3] For when these men were sent by the Lacedaemonians as messengers to Asia, they were betrayed by Sitalkes son of Teras, the king of the Thracians, and by Nymphodoros of Abdera, the son of Pytheas; after they were captured in Bisanthe on the Hellespont, they were carried off to Attica, where the Athenians executed both of them along with Aristeas of Corinth, son of Adeimantos.

7.137
430
ATHENS
The two Spartans return home safe, but their sons, while on their way to Persia as envoys from Sparta, are captured by Thracians friendly to Athens and sent to Athens, where they are executed. Herodotus considers this divine retribution for the killing of the envoys of Darius.

But that happened many years after the King's expedition, and so I shall now return to my earlier account.

The proclaimed goal of the King's expedition was to attack Athens, but his real objective was all of Hellas. The Hellenes had known this for a long time, but they did not all react to it in the same way now. [2] Those who had given earth and water to the Persian felt confident that they would come to no harm at the hands of the barbarian, but others, who had refused to give earth and water, were now absolutely terrified that there were not enough battleworthy ships in Hellas to face the invader, and that most of the men were unwilling to engage in the war actively, but were instead eager to medize.

7.138
480
THRACE
The King's intent to conquer all of Hellas is clear. Many Hellenes are afraid and unwilling to go to war.

7.139
480
ATHENS
Herodotus declares that
Athens saved Hellas,
although this might be a
displeasing statement
to many Hellenes, for if
Athens had submitted,
the Persians would have
been supreme at sea, and
no land defense by
the Peloponnesians
could have succeeded.

I have now reached a point at which I am compelled to declare an opinion that will cause offense to many people, but which nevertheless appears to me to be true, so I shall not restrain myself. [2] If the Athenians had evacuated their land in terror of the danger approaching them, or if they had not left their land but remained and surrendered themselves to Xerxes, no one at all would have tried to oppose the King at sea. And if no one had then opposed Xerxes at sea, this is what would have happened on land. [3] The Peloponnesians, even if they had covered over their isthmus with walls, would have been abandoned by their allies, who, seeing their cities conquered one by one by the barbarian fleet, would have been forced to submit against their will. Finally those thus deserted, now all alone, would have performed great feats and died honorably. [4] Of course that might not be their fate if they had earlier seen how the rest of the Hellenes were medizing and would have come to an agreement of their own with Xerxes. Thus, either way, Hellas would have been conquered by the Persians. For I cannot discern what advantage could have been derived from walls extended across the isthmus if the King had control of the sea. [5] So anyone who said that the Athenians proved to be the saviors of Hellas would not have strayed from the truth. For whichever course they chose to follow was certain to tip the scales of war. They chose that Hellas should survive in freedom; and after rousing to that cause all the other Hellenes who had not medized, they repelled the King with the help of the gods. [6] Indeed, not even the frightening oracles they received from Delphi threw them into a panic or persuaded them to abandon Hellas. Instead, they stood fast and had the courage to confront the invader of their land.

7.140
480
DELPHI
Herodotus recounts an
oracle predicting disaster
and ruin for the
Athenians at the hands
of the Persians.

For the Athenians had prepared to consult the oracle by sending sacred delegates to Delphi, who, after performing the usual preliminaries at the sanctuary, entered the inner shrine and took their seats. The Pythia, whose name was Aristonike, gave them the following oracular response: [2]

Why sit so idle, you poor wretched men? To the ends of the
  land you should flee.
Leave your homes, leave the heights of your circular fortress,
For neither the head nor the body remains in its place,
Nor the feet underneath, nor the hands nor the middle

Is left as it was, but now all is obscure. For casting it down
Is fire and Ares so sharp on the heels of a Syrian chariot
[3] And he will destroy many cities with towers, and not
yours alone;
And into the devouring fire he will give the temples of
eternal gods
Which now drip with sweat and shake in their fear
As blood gushes darkly from the tops of their roofs,
Foreseeing the force of compelling disaster.
Now step out of this shrine, and shroud over your heart
with the evils to come.

When the sacred delegates of the Athenians heard this, they felt that they had met with the greatest disaster; and as they were giving themselves up for lost over the evils predicted by the oracle, Timon son of Androboulos, a man of Delphi and a prominent citizen equal to their best, advised them to take olive branches and to consult the oracle a second time, this time as suppliants. [2] Following his advice, the Athenians went again and said to the god, "Lord, deliver to us a better oracle concerning our fatherland out of respect for these branches which we carry, coming, here as suppliants, or else we shall not leave your shrine but shall remain here until we die." After they said this, the prophetess gave them a second oracle, as follows:

7.141
480
DELPHI
The Athenians return to Delphi as suppliants for a better answer. The priestess now says that wooden walls may save them and mentions Salamis.

[3] Unable is Pallas to appease Zeus Olympian
With copious prayers, with counsel quite cunning.
Now to you once again my word I shall speak, making it
    adamantine:
The rest will be taken, all lying within the boundary of
    Kekrops
And that of the hollow of sacred Cithaeron.
But a wall made of wood does farsighted Zeus to Tritogenes
    grant
Alone and unravaged, to help you and your children.
[4] Do not await peacefully the horse and the foot,
The army gigantic that comes from the mainland;
Withdraw, turn your backs, though someday you still will
    meet
face to face. O Salamis Divine, the children of women you
    will yet destroy

While Demeter is scattered or while she is gathered.

7.142
480
ATHENS
The Athenians could not agree whether the oracle's "wooden walls"were the ancient walls of the Acropolis or Athens' new fleet of triremes.

Since this oracle seemed, and really was, less harsh to them than the earlier one, they copied it down and departed for Athens. When they arrived the sacred delegates proclaimed the oracle to the assembly of the people, and many sought to interpret what it meant, but the following two interpretations were particularly contradictory. Some of the elders said that in their opinion, the god was prophesying that the Acropolis would be preserved; for in ancient times the Acropolis of the Athenians had been enclosed by a thorn hedge, [2] so they concluded that this oracle's "wall made of wood" corresponded to the enclosing fence. Others in turn said that the god was referring to their ships, and they urged them to abandon everything else and to make their ships ready. But those who said that the wooden wall referred to ships were perplexed by the last two lines spoken by the Pythia:

O Salamis Divine, the children of women you will yet destroy
While Demeter is scattered or while she is gathered.

[3] These verses thwarted the proposal of those who interpreted the oracle's wooden wall to represent ships, for the oracle interpreters took these lines to mean that once they had made preparations for a sea battle, they were destined to be defeated around Salamis.

7.143
480
ATHENS
Themistokles persuades the Athenians that the wooden walls means their navy and that they should prepare to fight at sea.

But among the Athenians was a certain man who had just recently come into the highest prominence; his name was Themistokles, and he was called the son of Neoldes. Now this man asserted that the explanation of the oracle interpreters was not entirely correct. He said that if the real import of these verses to the Athenians was that the inhabitants were to end their lives around Salamis, then he did not think it would have used such mild language, but would have said something like "O Salamis Cruel" rather than "O Salamis Divine." [2] But if, in fact, one understood the oracle properly this part of it was directed by the god not to the Athenians but to their enemies. And so the god had advised them to prepare for a sea battle, and their fleet was what he meant by the wooden wall. [3] When Themistokles proclaimed this opinion, the Athenians decided that his interpretation was preferable to that of the oracle experts, who would not have allowed them to prepare for a sea battle and who said, in a word, that they should abandon Attica and settle in some other land.

There was an earlier occasion on which Themistokles proposed a measure that proved to be optimal for the predicament of that moment. At the time when, the Athenians were receiving large revenues into their public treasury from the silver mines at Laureion, and they were intending to apportion it so that each one of them would individually receive ten drachmas, Themistoldes stopped this plan to divide the money by persuading the Athenians to use it instead to build 200 ships for the war, by which he meant the war against the Aeginetans. [2] It was actually the onset of this war that saved Hellas by forcing the Athenians to take to the sea. For although the ships were not after all used for the purpose for which they had been constructed, they were there for the benefit of all of Hellas when they were needed. These ships, then, had been built in advance and were therefore ready for the Athenians to use, although they now had to build others in addition. [3] After their deliberations concerning the oracle, they resolved to confront the barbarian's invasion of Hellas with all their people and their ships in obedience to the god, together with those of Hellenes who wished to join them.

So those were the oracles that had been delivered to the Athenians. And now those Hellenes who wanted what was best for Hellas gathered together, engaged in discussions, and exchanged pledges. As they deliberated, the first of the matters they decided was that all existing hostilities and wars between one another were to be brought to an end. For wars had been stirred up between some Hellenes and others—the most serious of them being that between the Athenians and the Aeginetans. [2] Then, after learning that Xerxes and his army were in Sardis, they agreed to send men as spies to Asia to determine the extent of the King's power. They also resolved to send some messengers to Argos to attempt to establish a military alliance with the Argives against the Persian, and they decided to dispatch other envoys to Gelon son of Deinomenes in Sicily, to Corcyra, and to Crete to urge them all to come to the aid of Hellas. They did this in the hope that if they put their heads together and worked toward a common goal,

7.144
483
ATHENS
Themistokles had earlier persuaded the Athenians to use a sudden increase in the production of the Laureion silver mines for the construction of a fleet of 200 triremes.

7.145
481? 480?
ISTHMUS OF CORINTH
The Hellenes who oppose Persia meet to resolve their current quarrels, to send spies to Asia, and to send envoys to other Hellenes inviting them to join in the common defense.

Hellas could then somehow unite into a single state, since the invasion threatened all Hellenes alike. Gelon's power was said to be great, and of all the other Greek states, none had power greater than his.

BOOK 7.199 – 7.239

7.199
480
TRACHIS
Herodotus describes the geography of the Trachis region.

The city of Trachis lies about a half a mile away from the Black River. It was built on land which has the widest expanse of the entire region from the mountains to the sea, for the plain here covers some 5,500 acres. To the north of Trachis, cutting through the foothills of the mountain enclosing Trachinian territory, is a ravine in which the Asopos River flows.

7.200
480
THERMOPYLAE
Herodotus describes the geography of the Thermopylae region.

There is another river to the south of the Asopos—the Phoinix—which is not very big; it flows out of the mountains and empties into the Asopos. Right here at the Phoinix is the narrowest part of the region, where a path has been built up just wide enough for a single wagon. From the Phoinix River it is a little less than one and three-quarter miles to Thermopylae, [2] and between the Phoinix River and Thermopylae lies a village by the name of Anthela. The Asopos flows beside this village and from there continues on until it empties into the sea. The plain around Anthela is broader, and on it stands the sanctuary of Demeter Amphiktyonis. Here are the seats of the Amphiktyones and the sanctuary of Amphiktyon himself.

7.201
480
THERMOPYLAE
The situation of the two armies encamped near Thermopylae.

Now King Xerxes made his base in the Trachinian part of Malls, while the Hellenes were camped at the pass. Most of the Hellenes call this place Thermopylae, but the inhabitants dwelling here called it Pylae. So that is where each army made its camp, one controlling everything toward the north down to Trachis, the other in control of the regions toward the south on that side of the Greek mainland.

7.202
480
THERMOPYLAE
The origins and numbers of the Hellenes waiting at Thermopylae.

The Hellenes who were waiting for the Persian in this region were 300 Spartan hoplites, 1,000 men from Tegea and Mantineia (each providing 500), 120 from Orchomenos in Arcadia, and 1,000 from the rest of Arcadia. These were all the troops that came from Arcadia. From Corinth there were 400 hoplites, from Phleious 200; and there were also 80 Mycenaeans. Those, then, were the troops that had come from the Peloponnese. From Boeotia there were 700 Thespians and 400 Thebans.

In addition to these, both the Opuntian Locrians, who had come in full force, and 1,000 Phocians had responded to the Greek call for assistance. For the Hellenes had sent messengers to summon their help, saying to them that those who had come to Thermopylae were merely an advance guard of the rest of the allies who were expected to arrive any day now; more-over, they said, the sea was being guarded by the Athenians, Aeginetans,and those others who had been assigned to the fleet, so that they had nothing to fear; [2] for it was not a god but a human being who was invading Hellas, and no mortal existed now, nor would ever exist, who did not have a mixture of adversity in his life from the moment of his birth; indeed the greatest men encountered the greatest adversities. Therefore it was bound to happen that the one who was marching against them, since he was mortal, would fail in his glorious expectations. When they heard this the Locrians and Phocians hurried to Trachis to help.

Each contingent of these troops was under the command of generals assigned by their individual cities, but the most ad-mired and the leader of the whole army was a Lacedaemonian: Leonidas son of Anaxandridas the son of Leon son of Eurykratides, the son of Anaxandros son of Eurykrates, the son of Polydoros son of Alkamenes, the son of Teleklos son of Archelaos, the son of Hrgesilaos son of Doryssos, the son of Leobotas son of Echestratos, the son of Agis son of Eurysthenes, the son of Aristodemosson of Aristomachos, the son of Kleodaios son of Hyllos, who was the son of Herakles. Leonidas had become a king of Sparta unexpectedly.

For since he had two older brothers, Kleomenes and Dorieus, he had long before cleared his mind of any thoughts that he might become king. But then Kleomenes died without a male heir, and Dorieus, who had met his end in Sicily, was no longer in the picture either. Since Leonidas was older than Kleombrotos, the youngest son of Anaxandridas, and, more-over, because he had married the daughter of Kleomenes, the kingship came to devolve upon him. [2] So Leonidas arrived at Thermopylae with his assigned force of 300 men, whom he had selected from those who had sons living at the time. He took with him also the Thebans I mentioned when I listed the number of Greek troops; they were under the command of Leontiades son of Eurymachos. [3] Leonidas had made a special

7.203
480
THERMOPYLAE
The Opuntian Locrians and the Phocians also send troops to Trachis to join the Hellenic forces.

7.204
480
THERMOPYLAE
The most admired leader of the Hellenes was the Spartan king Leonidas, who became king unexpectedly.

7.205
480
THERMOPYLAE
Leonidas became king after his two older brothers died. He now leads his picked force of 300 Spartans to Thermopylae. He also brought the Thebans with him because they were accused of medizing.

effort to bring the Thebans from among all of the Hellenes, because they had been strongly accused of medizing. So he had summoned them to come to war with him, wanting to find out whether they would send men to go with him or whether they would publicly refuse to endorse the alliance of the Hellenes. And though their hearts were not in it, they did send men.

7.206
480
THERMOPYLAE
Leonidas was sent out to show other Hellenes that Sparta would be there, although their main force was delayed by the Karneia.

The Spartans sent Leonidas with his men first so that their allies would see them and join in the war, since if they learned that the Spartans were delaying, they too might medize. The rest of the Spartans were held back to celebrate the festival of the Karneia, but they intended to go as soon as they had concluded it. They planned to leave some men behind to guard Sparta, but for the rest of them to march out immediately afterward with all speed and in full force. [2] The rest of the allies had similar intentions for themselves, since the Olympic festival also coincided with these events. And as they did not expect that the battle at Thermopylae would be decided so swiftly, they sent only their advance guards.

7.207
480
THERMOPYLAE
As the Persians approach Thermopylae, the Hellenes deliberate about whether to retire.

That, then, was what the allies intended, but the Hellenes at Thermopylae became terrified when the Persian drew near the pass, and began to discuss whether or not they should leave. The rest of the Peloponnesians thought it best to return to the Peloponnese to protect the isthmus, but this proposal infuriated the Phocians and Locrians, and Leonidas voted to remain where they were and to dispatch messengers to the cities asking them to send help because their numbers were too few to repel the army of the Medes by themselves.

7.208
480
THERMOPYLAE
When Xerxes learns of the Greek forces at Thermopylae, he sends a scout to spy on them.

As they deliberated, Xerxes sent a mounted scout to see how many of them there were and what they were doing. While still in Thessaly, the King had heard that a small army was gathered here, and that its leaders were the Lacedaemonians and Leonidas, who traced his lineage to Herakles. [2] When the scout rode up to the camp, he looked around and watched, but could not see the whole army, since some men were posted within the wall that they had rebuilt and were now guarding it, so that it was impossible for the spy to see them. But he did see those outside, whose arms were lying in front of the wall, and it just so happened that at the moment, the Lacedaemonians were the ones posted outside. [2] The scout saw some of these men exercising and others combing their hair, which astonished him. After he had ascertained their number and every other detail, he rode back undisturbed, for no one pursued him; in fact he was practically ignored. When he returned, he reported all that he had seen to Xerxes.

Xerxes listened but could not understand: that the Lacedaemonians were really preparing to kill or be killed, to fight as much as was in their power, seemed to him to be the height of folly, the action of fools. So he sent for Demaratos son of Ariston, who was in the camp, and [2] when Demaratos arrived, Xerxes questioned him about everything he had been told, trying to understand the meaning behind what the Lacedaemonians were doing. Demaratos answered, "You heard what I said about these men before, when we were just setting out against Hellas, and you made me a laughingstock when you heard my view of how these matters would turn out. But it is my greatest goal to tell the truth in your presence, [3] so hear me now once again. These men have come to fight us for control of the road, and that is really what they are preparing to do. For it is their tradition that they groom their hair whenever they are about to put their lives in danger. [4] Now know this: if you subjugate these men and those who have remained behind in Sparta, there is no other race of human beings that will be left to raise their hands against you. For you are now attacking the most noble kingdom of all the Hellenes, and the best of men." [5] What Demaratos said seemed quite incredible to Xerxes, and he asked for the second time how they could possibly intend to fight his whole army, since there were so few of them. Demaratos replied, "Sire, if things do not turn out just as I claim they will, treat me like a liar." But even by saying this he did not convince Xerxes.

Xerxes let four whole days elapse, all the while expecting that the Hellenes would run away. But when, on the fifth day, they had still not gone away but were instead holding their positions in what seemed to him a display of reckless impudence, he lost his temper and ordered the Medes and the Kissians out against them, with instructions to bring them back alive and to conduct them into his presence. [2] The Medes charged headlong into the Hellenes and great numbers of them fell. Although others rushed forth to replace them, even they could not drive the Hellenes away, though they, too, suffered great losses in the attempt. Indeed, the Hellenes made it clear to everyone, and especially to the King himself, that although there were many

7.211
480
THERMOPYLAE
After the Medes fail,
Xerxes orders the Persians
to attack, but they, too,
fail to exploit their
superior number and fare
no better. The Spartans
show themselves to be
superior in training, s
kill, and arms.

in his army, there were few real men. The fighting went on all day.

Since the Medes were suffering extremely rough treatment, they now withdrew, and the Persians under the command of Hydarnes, whom the King called the Immortals, came forth to take their place. There was every expectation that they, at least, would easily prevail, [2] but when they joined battle with the Hellenes, they fared no better than the Medes, and indeed they suffered the very same setbacks. The fighting continued to take place in a confined space, with the Persians using shorter spears than those of the Hellenes and unable to derive any advantage from their superior numbers. [3] The Lacedaemonians fought remarkably well, proving that they were experts in battle who were fighting among men who were not, especially whenever they would turn their backs and feign flight all together, and the barbarians, seeing this, would pursue them with much clatter and shouting; the Lacedaemonians would allow the barbarians to catch up with them and then suddenly turn around to face them, at which point they would slay countless numbers of them. Of the Spartans themselves, however, only a few fell there. Finally the Persians retreated, since despite all their efforts to attack by regiments or by any other means, they could not gain any ground in the pass.

7.212
480
THERMOPYLAE
The Persians continue
the assault the next day
but withdraw after failing
to move the Hellenes.

It is said that during these assaults, the King, who was watching, leapt up from his throne three times in fear for his army. Thus ended the contest that day, and on the next, the barbarians did no better. They attacked with the expectation that such a small number of Hellenes would be covered with wounds and unable to lift a hand against them. [2] But the Hellenes had formed ranks in their national contingents, and each group fought in its turn except for the Phocians, who had been posted to guard the path on the mountain. When the Persians found that nothing had changed from what they had seen the day before, they retreated again.

The King was at a loss about how to deal with this impasse, but just then Ephialtes of Malis, son of Eurydemos, came to speak with him, expecting to win some great reward for telling the King of the path that led through the mountain to Thermopylae. By so doing, he caused the destruction of the Hellenes stationed there. [2] This man later fled to Thessaly in fear of the Lacedaemonians, and during his exile a price was set on his head by the Pylagoroi during a meeting of the Amphiktyones at Pylaia. After a while he went back to Antikyra, where he died at the hands of Athenades, a man of Trachis. [3] This Athenades killed Ephialtes for another reason, which I shall explain in a later section of my story, but Athenades was honored nonetheless by the Lacedaemonians. That is how Ephialtes was later killed.

7.213
480
THERMOPYLAE
Xerxes is baffled until a Hellene named Ephialtes reveals a path over the mountain by which the Persians can outflank the Hellenes. How Ephialtes was later killed.

Another version of these events is that Onetes of Karystos, son of Phanagoras, and Korydallos of Antikyra were the ones who gave this information to the King and who guided the Persians around the mountain, but I find this version to be completely inconceivable. [2] For on balance, the weight of consideration should be given to the fact that the Hellenes, that is the Pylagoroi, set a price of silver on the head of Ephialtes of Trachis, not on Onetes and Korydallos, and they would certainly have done so only after finding out exactly what had happened. Moreover, we know that it was for this reason that Ephialtes went into exile. [3] Now Onetes could indeed have known about this path, even though he was not a Malian, since he may have been familiar with this area anyway, but in fact it was Ephialtes who guided the Persians around the mountain along the path, and so I am recording in writing that he is the guilty one.

7.214
480
THERMOPYLAE
Herodotus describes an alternate story of the betrayal but denies it, asserting that Ephialtes was the true villain.

Xerxes was pleased and exhilarated by what Ephialtes promised to accomplish, and he at once sent off Hydarnes and those under his command, who set out from camp at the time the lamps were being lit. This path had been discovered by the local Malians, who had led the Thessalians along it against the Phocians at the time when the Phocians had barricaded the main pass with a wall to protect themselves from invasion. So long ago the Malians had found that this path could be put to ill use.

7.215
480
THERMOPYLAE
Xerxes orders the Persians to take the path over the mountain that evening.

The path begins from the Asopos River where it flows through the ravine; both the path and the mountain it crosses have the same name: Anopaia. This Anopaia Path extends along the ridge of the mountain and ends both at Alpenos (the first Locrian city one arrives at when coming from Malian territory) and at the rock called Melampygos and the seats of the Kerkopes; this is the narrowest part of the path.

So this was the path that the Persians took after crossing the Asopos; they marched all night long, keeping the mountains of Oeta on their right and those of Trachis on their left, and arrived at the summit of the mountain just as dawn was breaking. [2] As I mentioned earlier, there were 1,000 Phocian hoplites guarding this part of the mountain to protect their own country as well as to defend the path here. For while the pass below was being guarded by those I listed before, the Phocians had volunteered to guard this mountain path, holding themselves responsible to Leonidas for this task.

This is how the Phocians became aware that the Persians had reached the summit. They had not noticed them ascending the mountain because it was entirely covered with oak trees. But then, as no wind was blowing, they heard the loud sound of leaves being trampled under many feet, and at that point, the Phocians jumped up and began to arm themselves, but then, all of a sudden, the barbarians were right there in front of them.

[2] The barbarians were amazed to see men arming themselves, since they had not expected to encounter any opposition at all, but now they found themselves in the presence of an army. Hydarnes feared that these troops were Lacedaemonians. He asked exactly what country this army was from, and when he learned that they were Phocians, he formed up the Persians for battle. [3] The Phocians were at once hit with a dense hail of arrows and, thinking that the Persians had originally set out to attack them, they fled to the peak of the mountain and prepared to die. That was what they thought, but the Persians with Ephialtes and Hydarnes were now paying no attention to the Phocians; they were descending the mountain as fast as they could go.

As for the Hellenes at Thermopylae, the first news of the enemy's approach came from the prophet Megistias; he had inspected the sacrificial victims and now predicted that they would face death at dawn. After that, deserters came while it was still dark and reported that the Persians were making their way around the mountain toward them. And finally, as day dawned, their lookouts ran down from the heights and told them the same news. [2] At that point the Hellenes discussed what to do and found that they were divided in their opinions: some advised against deserting their post, while others argued the opposite course. After these deliberations they split up: some departed and scattered to their several cities, while the rest prepared to remain there with Leonidas.

7.219
480
THERMOPYLAE
The Hellenes at Thermopylae learn that they have been out flanked and will soon be surrounded.

It is also said, however, that Leonidas himself sent most of them away as he was worried that all of them might otherwise be killed. But he felt that for himself and the Spartans with him, it would not be decent to leave the post that they had originally come to guard. [2] I myself am most inclined to this opinion and think that when Leonidas perceived the allies' lack of zeal and their reluctance to share with him in the danger ahead, he ordered them to leave. He perceived that it would be ignoble for him to leave the pass, and that if he were to remain, he would secure lasting glory and assure that the prosperity of Sparta would not be obliterated. [3] For the Spartans had consulted the oracle about the war at its very outset, and the Pythia had told them that either Lacedaemon would be depopulated by the barbarians or their king would die. She answered them in these hexameter verses:

7.220
480
THERMOPYLAE
Leonidas tells his allies to depart, but he decides to remain with his Spartans, spurred by the prospect of fame and by an oracle predicting that Sparta would be saved if a Spartan king were to die.

> [4] As for you who dwell in the vast land of Sparta,
> Either your city of glory will perish, sacked by the
>   Perseids,
> Or else the boundaries of Lacedaemon will grieve for
>   the death of a king born of Herakles,
> Since neither bulls nor lions have enough might
> to oppose him, for the power of Zeus is his possession.
> And he, I declare, will not be restrained until one or the
>   other is torn apart.

Bearing in mind this oracle, and wanting to gain future glory for the Spartans alone, Leonidas sent the allies away, rather than have them leave. That is why they left, rather than because of a difference of opinion.

One of the most significant proofs that I can assert in order to support this claim has to do with Megistias of Acarnania, who is said to have been descended from Melampous. He was the prophet accompanying this army and had predicted what was going to happen from his inspection of the sacrificial victims. It is clear that Leonidas tried to send him away to prevent him from being killed with those who remained. But though Megistias was dismissed, he refused to leave, and instead sent away his son, who was serving in the army and was his only child.

Now those allies who had been dismissed left in obedience to Leonidas, and only the Thespians and the Thebans stayed behind with the Lacedaemonians. The Thebans did not want to be there, but Leonidas held them back, treating them as hostages and keeping them there against their will. The Thespians, however, were quite willing to stay; they refused to go away and to abandon Leonidas and his men; instead, they remained there to die with them. Their commander was Demophilos son of Diadromes.

At sunrise, Xerxes poured libations and then waited until about the time of peak market hour to make his attack. That is what Ephialtes had told him to do, since the way down the mountain was quicker and the ground theyhad to cover much shorter than the climb up and around the mountain. [2] Xerxes' men advanced, but so did the Hellenes with Leonidas, and since the latter were marching to their death, they now ventured much farther than they had at first onto the wider part of the strip of land, for on the preceding days they had been guarding the defensive wall and had kept back tofight at the narrower part. [3] Now, however, they joined battle beyond that sector. Many of the barbarians fell, for the leaders of the regiments were behind them with whips, flogging each and every man and urging them ever forward. Many fell into the sea and died, but even more were trampled alive by one another. There was no counting the number of the dead. [4] The Hellenes knew they were about to face death at the hands of the men who had come around the mountain, and so they exerted their utmost strength against the barbarians, with reckless desperation and no regard for their own lives.

7.221
480
THERMOPYLAE
Leonidas sends away the seer Megistias, but he will not leave.

7.222
480
THERMOPYLAE
Leonidas keeps the Thebans there as hostages. The Thespians remain gladly.

7.223
480
THERMOPYLAE
Battle is joined again at midmorning. The Hellenes fight recklessly and desperately, knowing they are to die, and inflict high casualties on the enemy.

By this time most of their spears had broken, so they were slaying the Persians with their swords. And it was during this struggle that Leonidas fell, the man who had proved himself the most valiant of all, and with him those other famous Spartans whose names I have learned because I think they also proved themselves to be worthy men; indeed, I have learned the names of all 300 of them. [2] Many Persians fell there, too, including some famous ones; in particular, two sons of Darius, Abrokomes and Hyperanthes, who had been born to Darius by Phratagoune daughter of Artanes. This Artanes was the brother of King Darius and the son of Hystaspes son of Arsames. After giving his daughter in marriage to Darius, he had given him also his whole estate, since she was his only child.

Two brothers of Xerxes also fell there, while they were fighting in the melée over the body of Leonidas, for the Persians and Lacedaemonians engaged in a violent struggle over the corpse until the Hellenes, after routing their opponents four times, managed with great valor to drag it out and away from the crowd. The fighting continued until the forces with Ephialtes arrived. [2] When the Hellenes learned that they had come, the contest took a different turn, as they retreated back to the narrow part of the road, and after passing the wall, all of them except for the Thebans stationed themselves together upon the hill that is located at the place on the road where the stone lion in honor of Leonidas now stands. [3] On this spot they tried to defend themselves with their daggers if they still had them, or if not, with their hands and their teeth. The barbarians pelted them with missiles, some running up to face the Hellenes directly and demolishing the defensive wall, and others coming to surround them on all sides.

Though the Lacedaemonians and the Thespians alike proved themselves to be brave in this battle, it is said that the Spartan Dienekes proved himself to be the most valiant man of all. It is reported that before the Hellenes engaged the Medes in battle, one of the Trachinians said that there were so many barbarians that whenever they shot their arrows, the sun was blocked by their number. [2] Dienekes was not alarmed to hear this but rather, in total disregard for the vast numbers of Medes, said that what his Trachinian friend had reported was in fact good news, since it meant that while the Medes were blocking the sun, they would fight them in the shade. This saying

7.224
480
THERMOPYLAE
Finally Leonidas and many famous Spartans fall there (Herodotus has learned all their names), and many eminent Persians.

7.225
480
THERMOPYLAE
The Hellenes rout the Persians four times and retire to the narrow pass for a last stand when the men with Ephialtes arrive.

7.226
480
THERMOPYLAE
The anecdote of Dienekes, who, hearing that the huge number of enemy missiles would darken the sun, said that he pould prefer to fight in he shade.

and others like it have been left as memorials of Dienekes the Lacedaemonian.

After Dienekes, the most outstanding men in this battle are said to be two Lacedaemonian brothers, Alpheos and Maron, sons of Orsiphantos. Of the Thespians, the man who earned the highest distinction was named Dithyrambos son of Harmatides.

They were buried just where they had fallen, and for these men as well as for those who had met their end before Leonidas could send them away, an inscription was erected which says:

Three million foes were once fought right here
By four thousand men from the Peloponnese.

[2] That inscription applied to them all, but the Spartans have one of their own:

Tell this, passerby, to the Lacedaemonians:
It is here that we lie, their commands we obey.

[3] That inscription is for the Lacedaemonians, and this one, for the prophet:

This is the monument of the famous Megistias,
Slain by the Medes when they crossed the Sperchias.
A prophet knowing for certain that Doom was approaching,
Yet he could not endure to forsake Sparta's leaders.

[4] The first two of these inscriptions and pillars were set up in honor of these men by the Amphiktyones. Simonides son of Leoprepes had the monument to the prophet Megistias inscribed for the sake of friendship.

It is said that two of the 300 men, Eurytos and Aristodemos, had the opportunity to return safely to Sparta if only they had come to an agreement since they had been released from the camp by Leonidas and were laid up in Alpenos with the most serious cases of eye disease. Or, if they had not wanted to return home, they could die together with the others. Though it was possible for both of them to take either of these courses of action they made different decisions about what to do. When Eurytos learned of the Persian advance around the mountain,

7.227
480
THERMOPYLAE
Other Hellenes who gained renown.

7.228
480
THERMOPYLAE
Herodotus recounts some epitaphs that were later inscribed at Thermopylae over the graves of Hellenes who fell there to memorialize them and the battle.

7.229
480
THERMOPYLAE
Two Spartans who were suffering from ophthalmia were ordered to leave. One, Eurytos, refused and died fighting blindly. The other, Aristodemos, went home and was received angrily by the Spartans.

he asked for his arms,put them on and ordered his helot to lead him to those who were fighting.After leading him to the fighting, the helot fled and disappeared from sight while Eurytos charged into the raging battle and was killed. But Aristodemos was left behind, faint and feeble. [2] Now if it had been only Aristodemos who became ill and returned to Sparta, or if both of them alike had taken the journey home together, I do not think the Spartans would have been provoked to any wrath at all against them. When, however, one of them was slain and the other had the same excuse but was unwilling to die, it became inevitable that the Spartans would be stirred to great wrath against Aristodemos.

While some say that Aristodemos returned safely to Sparta and report the illness as his excuse, others say that he had been sent from the camp as a messenger and that although he could have come back in time for the battle, he was unwilling to do so and instead lagged behind on his journey and thus survived while his fellow messenger came back for the battle and died in it.

7.230
480
THERMOPYLAE
Another version of the story of the two Spartans.

So after returning to Lacedaemon, Aristodemos met with disgrace and dishonor. The dishonor he suffered was that not a single Spartan would give him fire or speak to him, and his disgrace was that he was called "Aristodemos the Trembler." But at the battle of Plataea he acquitted himself of all blame that had been cast upon him.

7.231
480
SPARTA
How Aristodemos was punished, and how he redeemed himself.

It is also said that another of these 300 men was sent away as a messenger to Thessaly and that he survived as well; his name was Pantites, and when he returned to Sparta, he suffered such dishonor that he hanged himself.

7.232
480
SPARTA
Another Spartan who survived dishonored.

Now the Thebans, whose commander was Leontiades, fought alongside the Hellenes against the army of the King for a while, since they were being compelled to do so. But when they saw the Persian side prevailing and the Hellenes with Leonidas hurrying to the hill, the Thebans broke away and approached the barbarians with their hands outstretched, saying most truthfully that they had medized and had been among the first to give earth and water to the King, but had been compelled to come to Thermopylae, and were guiltless of inflicting any damages on the King. [2] By saying all this they survived, since they had the Thessalians as witnesses to their claims; they were not entirely fortunate, however. Some of them were seized

7.233
480
THERMOPYLAE
The Thebans surrendered when they could, saying they had been forced to fight against the Persians. Somewere killed, and many of the rest were branded by the Persians.

and killed by the barbarians as they approached, and Xerxes ordered that a majority of the rest be branded with the royal marks, beginning with the commander Leontiades. The son of this Leontiades, Eurymachos, was murdered long after this by the Plataeans after he had taken the city of Plataea with 400 Thebans under his command.

7.234
480
THERMOPYLAE
Xerxes questions Demaratos, admitting that what he had said had proved true, asking him for advice on how to overcome the Spartans at least cost to the Persians.

That, then, is how the Hellenes fought at Thermopylae. Now Xerxes summoned Demaratos and questioned him, beginning, "Demaratos, you are a good man. My evidence for this is your past truthfulness, for everything has turned out just as you said it would. But now tell me how many Lacedaemonians are left, and how many of them are warriors like these men were, or are they all like this?" [2] Demaratos replied, "Sire, the total numberof Lacedaemonians is quite large, and they have many cities. But I will tell you now what you really want to know. In Lacedaemon there is a citycalled Sparta, with about 8,000 men living in it, and these men are all the equals of those who fought here, while the other Lacedaemonians are not, though they are good men." [3] Xerxes responded, asking, "Demaratos, what would be the easiest way for us to conquer these men? Come now, give me your expert advice, for you know the details of how they plan their strategies, since you were once their king."

7.235
480
THERMOPYLAE
Demaratos advises Xerxes to send a naval force to occupy Cythera and to carry the war from there directly against Sparta to embroil the Spartans at home. He predicts that if the Persians do not do this, they will face harder and more costly battles than Thermopylae at the Isthmus of Corinth.

Demaratos replied, "Sire, if you really are seeking my advice in earnest, it is only right that I should give you the best counsel that I can. Suppose you were to send 300 ships from your fleet to Laconian territory. [2] Well, lying off the coast of that land is an island by the name of Cythera. And Chilon, the wisest man among our people, once said that the Spartans could profit more if this island would sink into the sea than they could if it continued to remain above water. He said this because he always expected that something like what I am now advising you to do would happen someday. He, of course, had no advance knowledge of your expedition, but he feared any and all such expeditions conducted by men. [3] My advice is that you should use this island as your base to frighten the Lacedaemonians. If theyhave a war of their own at home, you will then be able to conquer the restof Hellas with your land army and not have to fear that they will come to the assistance of the other Hellenes. Then, when the rest of Hellas has been enslaved, Laconia will be the only land left to oppose you, and it will be a weakened one at that.

[4] "If you do not follow this advice, however, this is what you should expect. There is, at the entrance to the Peloponnese, a narrow isthmus where all the Peloponnesians who will form a solemn league against you will join forces. There you may expect to face more difficult battles than those that have been fought so far. But if you do as I say, this isthmus and the cities will surrender to you without a fight."

After these words of Demaratos, Achaimenes, a brother of Xerxes and a commander of the fleet, spoke up. He had happened to be present and was afraid that Xerxes would be persuaded to take Demaratos' advice. "Sire," he said, "I can see that you approve of the words of this man who envies your success or perhaps is even acting treacherously against you and your interests. For these are exactly the sorts of things that Hellenes delight in doing. They envy prosperity and hate whoever is better and stronger than themselves. [2] Now in our present situation, having lost 400 ships wrecked in the storm, if you were to send 300 more ships from our fleet to sail around the Peloponnese, your adversary's fleet will certainly be a match for you in battle. But if our fleet stays concentrated, it will be very difficult for them to deal with it, and they will be no match for you at all. By keeping your entire fleet together, it can then assist your army, and the army can travel with the support of your fleet. But if you divide your fleet, you will not be able to help the separated forces, nor will they be able to help you. [3] So decide on a course that well serves your own interests instead of concerning yourself with your enemies: where they will take a stand to fight you, or what they will do, or how many of them there are. For they are quite capable of thinking for themselves, just as we are for ourselves. And even if the Lacedaemonians do advance against the Persians for battle, they will in no way be able to heal the injuries they have now suffered."

7.236
480
THERMOPYLAE
Achaimenes advises Xerxes not to follow Demaratos' advice. He asserts that all Hellenes hate power and are jealous of success. He advises that the Persians keep their forces concentrated as they advance, and predicts that Sparta will not recover from recent losses.

Xerxes replied, "Achaimenes, I think that you have given good advice, and I shall certainly follow it. Although Demaratos advised me to do what he thinks would be the best plan for me, his judgment has proved inferior to yours. [2] But I do not accept at all your assertion that he is antagonistic to my interests when I weigh what he said before, as well as the fact that a citizen normally envies another citizen who is successful and shows his hostility by his silence; he refuses to give good advice when consulted by someone from his own community

7.237
480
THERMOPYLAE
Xerxes decides to follow Achaimenes' advice, butpraises Demaratos as a friend and trustworthy adviser.

unless he has attained a high degree of virtue—but men like this are rare. [3] And a guest-friend is the most benevolent of all toward his guest-friend when the latter succeeds, and will give him the best advice when consulted; so since Demaratos is my guest-friend, I forbid anyone to utter any slander against him ever again."

After having said this, Xerxes made his way among the corpses, including that of Leonidas. Having heard that Leonidas was a king and the commander of the Lacedaemonians, he ordered that his head be cut off and impaled on a stake. [2] For me this is the clearest of many proofs that King Xerxes felt greater animosity for Leonidas while he was still alive than he felt for any other man. Otherwise he would not have treated the corpse so outrageously, since of all the peoples I know of, the Persians especially honor men who are good at waging war. So now, those to whom he had given these orders duly carried them out.

I shall now go back to a detail of my account that I left unexplained before. The Lacedaemonians had been the first to learn that the King would lead an expedition against Hellas, and so had sent to consult the oracle at Delphi, to which they received the response I quoted a little earlier. But the way in which they received this news is quite extraordinary. [2] When Demaratos son of Ariston was in exile among the Medes, I do not believe—and here reason is my ally—that he had good-will toward the Lacedaemonians, though one may conjecture whether he acted out of benevolence or out of spiteful satisfaction. For when Xerxes resolved to lead an expedition against Hellas, Demaratos was in Susa, and upon learning Xerxes' plans, immediately wanted to communicate this information to the Lacedaemonians. [3] There was a risk that he would be caught, so there was no other way he could inform them except by the following scheme. Taking a double writing tablet, he scraped off the wax and inscribed the plan of the King onto the wood of the tablet. After doing this, he melted some wax back over what he had written, so that the tablet would be apparently blank and thus cause no trouble from the guards as it was conveyed to its destination. [4] When it arrived at Lacedaemon, the Lacedaemonians could not understand what it meant until, according to what I have heard, Gorgo the daughter of Kleomenes and wife of Leonidas deduced the

7.238
480
THERMOPYLAE
Xerxes orders that the head of Leonidas should be cutoff and impaled.

7.239
485?
SUSA
How Demaratos used a clever trick to send a message of warning to the Spartans of the aggressive plans of the Persians, and how Gorgo, Kleomenes' daughter, discovered the message.

answer herself. She ordered them to scrape off the wax and said that they would then discover a message written on the wood. When they followed her advice, they did discover the message and, after reading it, dispatched the news to the rest of the Hellenes. That, then, is how this is said to have happened.

BOOK 9.25 – 9.85

The Hellenes gained much courage from the fact that they had stood up to the attack of the cavalry and had repelled it. The first thing they did was to place the corpse on a wagon and have it drawn past the army's various units in their assigned positions. They displayed it this way because the body of Masistios was worth seeing for its size and its beauty, and the men left their ranks in order to see it. [2] Next, the Hellenes decided to advance down into Plataea, for they could see that the Plataean land was much more suitable for their camp than that of Erythrai; among other advantages, it had a better supply of water. So they decided to advance to the Spring of Gargaphia located there, and to establish their camps in that location after deploying into their various separate units. [3] And so, taking up their arms, they advanced through the foothills of Cithaeron, past Hysiai and into Plataean territory. There they deployed in their national contingents near the Spring of Gargaphia and the precinct of the hero Androkrates. Their forces extended across the low hills and the level land there.

9.25
479
ERYTHRAI
The Hellenes are encour aged by their victory over the enemy cavalry, and decide to move their positions from Erythrai down to Plataea, where water is more plentiful.

But while they were drawing up in their ranks, fierce wrangling arose between the Tegeans and the Athenians; for both thought it only right that they should occupy the other wing of the army, and both of them justified their claims by citing both recent and ancient deeds. The Tegeans said [2] "Of all the allies, we have always been worthy of this position in every previous joint expedition of the Peloponnesians—both long ago and recently—ever since the Heraklids tried to return to the Peloponnese after the death of Eurystheus. [3] We gained this position because of what happened at that time. We had gone to help in the fight at the isthmus together with the Achaeans and the Ionians who then lived in the Peloponnese, and we took up our positions against the returning exiles. But then the story goes, Hyllos proclaimed that it was unnecessary for the armies to risk an engagement, but instead, the Peloponnesians

9.26
479
ERYTHRAI
There is a dispute between the Tegeans and the Athenians as to who should hold the left wing in the battle order. The Tegeans give their argu ment why they should have that honorific position.

should select the best man in their camp, and he would then fight Hyllos in single combat on agreed-upon terms. [4] The Peloponnesians decided that they had to carry out his proposal, and they swore a solemn oath with Hyllos on these conditions: if Hyllos won the victory over the leader of the Peloponnesians, the Heraklids should return to the land of their father, but if he lost, then the opposite would happen; the Heraklids would depart and Hyllos would lead their army away, and they would not seek to return to the Peloponnese for 100 years. [5] Out of all the allies, our general and king, Echemos son of Aeropos, the son of Phegeus, volunteered and was chosen. He fought Hyllos in single combat and killed him. And because of that feat we obtained several important privileges from the Peloponnesians, and we continue to hold them today. In particular, we always lead one of the two wings on a joint expedition. [6] We do not oppose you, men of Lacedaemon; we offer you the choice of whichever wing you want, and we yield the command of it to you. But we claim the other wing, which belongs under our command, just as it has in times past. And apart from the achievement just described, we are more worthy to win a victory in this position than the Athenians, for we have been successful in many battles fought against you as well as against many others. And so it is only right and just that we, rather than the Athenians, should hold the other wing, for they have not accomplished such feats as we have, neither in recent nor ancient times."

9.27
479
ERYTHRAI
The Athenians give their arguments about why they deserve to hold the left wing, but state that they will take any position chosen for them by the Spartans and endeavor to acquit themselves valiantly there.

That was the speech of the Tegeans, and the Athenians responded to it as follows: "We know that this meeting has been convened to prepare for battle against the barbarians and not for speeches, but since this man from Tegea has put before you accounts of valiant deeds that each of us has accomplished in both ancient and recent times, we are forced to demonstrate to you that the most prominent positions belong to us as our ancestral right rather than to the Arcadians, because we are truly valiant. [2] Now the Heraklids, whose leader they claim to have killed at the isthmus, had earlier fled enslavement by the Mycenaeans, and were driven away by all the Hellenes wherever they sought refuge, until we alone received them and subdued the arrogance of Eurystheus; and with them we won the victory in battle over those who held the Peloponnese at that time. [3] Secondly, when the Argives who marched against

Thebes with Polyneikes met their end, they lay unburied until we fought the Kadmeians, and it is our claim to fame that we picked up their bodies and buried them in our own territory of Eleusis. [4] We also did well against the Amazons who at one time invaded from the Thermodon River into Attica; and in the struggles at Troy we were inferior to none. But there is no profit in recalling all this, for the same men who were valiant back then could now be inferior, and those who are inferior now could have been superior then. [5] So let that be enough talk about deeds performed long ago. And even if there were nothing else for us to show as our achievement—as if any of the other Hellenes had as many successes as we have had—our accomplishment at Marathon certainly makes us worthy to hold this privilege and others besides: there we alone of the Hellenes fought the Persian all by ourselves and not only survived such are markable endeavor, but won a victory over forty-six nations. [6] Well,then, should we not justly be entitled to hold this post because of this one feat alone? But since it is not really appropriate to engage in such disputes at a time like this, we are ready and willing to obey you, Lacedaemonians, and we shall take our position in the line wherever, and opposite whomever, you decide is most suitable. We shall try to be valiant in any post we occupy."

That was how the Athenians replied, and the whole camp of Lacedaemonians shouted out that the Athenians were more worthy than the Arcadians to win the glory of victory holding this wing. And thus the Athenians prevailed over the Tegeans and obtained the post. [2] After this, the Hellenes, both those who had come there first and those who were joining the army now, took up their positions in the following order. Ten thousand Lacedaemonians held the right wing, and of these there were 5,000 Spartans with 35,000 light-armed troops of helots guarding them, seven posted around each man. [3] The Spartans chose the Tegeans to stand next to them in line to show them honor and because of their valor. There were 1,500 Tegeans who served as hoplites. After them stood 5,000 Corinthians, and Pausanias gave them the 300 Poteidaians from Pallene who were there to join them in their ranks. [4] Next to them stood 600 Arcadians of Orchomenos, followed by 3,000 men of Sicyon. After these were 800 Epidaurians, and next to them were posted 1,000 Troizenians, then 200 men of Lepreon,

9.28
479
PLATAEA
The whole army awards the wing position to the Athenians by acclamation. Herodotus describes the Greek order of battle from the Spartans on the right to the Athenians on the left, citing their numbers by city as well as by their position.

followed by 400 men of Mycenae and Tiryns; then 1,000 Phleiasians, next to whom stood 3,000 troops from Hermione. [5] After the Hermionians 600 Eretrians and Styrians, were posted, and they were followed by 400 Chalcidians, and next to them, 500 Ambraciots. Next came 800 Leucadians and Anactorians, then 200 Palees from Cephallania. [6] Posted after them were 500 Aeginetans, and next to them stood 3,000 Megarians, followed by 600 Plataeans. Finally, leading the ranks were the Athenians, 8,000 of them holding the left wing, and their commander was Aristeides son of Lysimachos.

9.29
479
PLATAEA
Herodotus lists the total number of hoplites and lightly armed men in the Greek army.

All these (except for the seven helots posted with each Spartan) were hoplites, and added together their number was 38,700. That is the numberof hoplites that had gathered to oppose the barbarians. The numbers of lightly armed troops were as follows: posted with the Spartans were 35,000, seven for each hoplite, and every one of these was equipped for war. [2] The lightly armed troops of the other Lacedaemonians and Hellenes were assigned one to each hoplite, and they numbered 34,500, bringing the total number of lightly armed troops to 69,500.

9.30
479
PLATAEA
The Greek forces number 110,000.

So the sum of the entire Greek force assembled at Plataea, including both the hoplites and the lightly armed troops, was 1,800 less than110,000, but when the Thespians who had survived and were now in the camp, although not wearing armor, are added to the total, their number comes to a full 110,000.

Deployed in these positions, they camped beside the Asopos River.

9.31
479
PLATAEA
Herodotus lists by nationality Mardonios' order of battle of the Persian forces as they advance against the Greek position at Plataea.

After the barbarians under the command of Mardonios had finished their mourning for Masistios, they learned that the Hellenes were at Plataea, so they also advanced to where the Asopos flowed nearby. When they arrived there, Mardonios arranged them opposite the Hellenes in the following manner. He placed the Persians so that they faced the Lacedaemonians; [2] but since the Persians actually far outnumbered the Lacedaemonians they faced the Tegeans also, and they were deployed in more ranks than usual. That was the position of the Persians. As the Thebans had informed and instructed him, Mardonios chose the most powerful part of his forces to stand opposite the Lacedaemonians and deployed the weaker units against the Tegeans. [3] Next to the Persians he posted the Medes to stand opposite the Corinthians, Poteidaians, Orchomenians, and Sicyonians. And next to the Medes he marshaled the Baktrians, who faced the Epidaurians, Troizenians, Lepreans, Mycenaeans, and Phleiasians. [4] After the Baktrians he posted the Indians to stand opposite the Hermionians, Eretrians, Styrians, and Chalcidians. Next to the Indians he had the Sakai stand to face the Ambraciots, Anaktorians, Leucadians, Palees, and Aeginetans.[5] Opposite the Athenians, Plataeans, and Megarians, he deployed the Boeotians, Locrians, Malians, Thessalians, and the 1,000 troops from Phocis; Not all of the Phocians were medizing; some of them were supporting the Greek cause by taking refuge around Parnassus and using this as their base from which to plunder and rob the army of Mardonios and the Hellenes who were with him. Mardonios also positioned the Macedonians and the inhabitants of the region, surrounding Thessaly so that they faced the Athenians.

These ethnic contingents just listed were the greatest of those deployed by Mardonios, in that they were the most noteworthy and most important. But there were men of other nations mingled among them: Phrygians, Thracians, Mysians, Paionians, and the rest, including Ethiopians and Egyptians—namely, the Ermotybians and those called the Kalasiries, who bear knives and are the only Egyptians classed as warriors. [2] These Egyptians were really marines, but Mardonios had ordered them to disembark at Phaleron, for they had not been originally assigned to the army that went with Xerxes to Athens. So as I mentioned earlier, there were 300,000 barbarians. There is no number reported for the Hellenes allied with Mardonios, but if I may venture a guess, I would estimate that up to 50,000 of them had assembled there and were drawn up as infantry; the cavalry was stationed apart from them.

9.32
479
PLATAEA
Herodotus lists other ethnic units fighting with the Persians, including their Greek allies. He says the barbarians number 300,000, and estimates the number of Greek allies as 50,000.

On the day after they had all been marshaled into their ethnic contingents and units, both sides conducted sacrifices. The man who performed the sacrifice for the Hellenes was Teisamenos son of Antiochos, who had accompanied this army as its seer. He was an Elean of the Iamid clan, but the Lacedaemonians had made him one of their own people. [2] It seems that once, when Teisamenos had consulted the oracle at Delphi about offspring, the Pythia had replied that he would win the greatest contests—five of them, in fact. Missing the point of the oracular response, he turned his attention to athletics, thinking that he would win gymnastic contests. He practiced the

9.33
479
PLATAEA
How Teisamenos, the army diviner, almost wins the pentathlon at Olympia, gains the freedom of Sparta, and asks for citizenship for himself and his brother.

pentathlon and missed an Olympic victory in wrestling by just one fall in a competition against Hieronymos of Andros. [3] The Lacedaemonians, however, realized that the prophecy to Teisamenos referred not to athletic but to military contests, and they tried to bribe him to lead them in war together with the Heraklids who were their kings. [4] Now, Teisamenos could see that the Spartans thought it very important to win him over as their friend, and because he realized this, he began to demand a higher price, stipulating that if they made him a Spartan citizen and granted him his share of all their privileges, he would do as they requested, but for any other or lesser compensation he would refuse them. [5] Upon hearing this, the Spartans became outraged and withdrew their request entirely; but in the end, when they grew very frightened due to the impending Persian campaign, they pursued him again and consented to his demands. Perceiving the change in their attitude, he said that he was now not satisfied with just these conditions, but that his brother Hegias should also be made a Spartan on the same terms as himself.

9.34
ARGOS
How Melampous earlier extorted kingship from the Argives for himself and his brother as the price for curing the Argive women.

By making this demand, he was imitating Melampous, if a demand for kingship can be compared with one for citizenship. For when the women of Argos had gone mad, the Argives tried to pay Melampous to come from Pylos and bring an end to the illness of their women, and he proposed that they give him half the kingship as his reward. [2] This the Argives could not endure, and they went away. But after many more of their women had gone mad, they accepted his demand, and went to him and offered what he had proposed. But then, seeing their change in attitude, he asked for more, claiming that unless they gave to his brother Bias a third part of the kingship, he would not do what they wanted. The Argives were in dire straits, so they consented to this demand also.

9.35
479
SPARTA
The Spartans give Teisamenos everything he wants, and he helps them to win five victories.

And so the Spartans, since they were in desparate need of Teisamenos' help, agreed to all his demands. And after they had consented to both his requests, Teisamenos of Elis, now a Spartan, helped them to win their five greatest contests by serving as their seer. These two were the only people we know of who ever were made Spartan citizens. [2] The five contests were, first, the one at Plataea; next, one at Tegea against the Tegeans and Argives; after that, at Dipaia against all the Arcadians except for the Mantineians; then against the Messenians near Ithome;

and finally, in Tanagra against the Athenians and Argives, and the last one completed the series of five contests.

This was the Teisamenos whom the Spartans led to Plataea to be a seer for the Hellenes. The sacrificial omens for the Hellenes were favorable if they fought to defend themselves, but not if they crossed the Asopos and initiated battle.

The sacrifices conducted for Mardonios also turned out to be adverse if he were eager to initiate battle, but favorable if he fought in self-defense. He too obtained sacrificial omens in the Greek way; his seer was Hegesistratos of Elis, the most noteworthy of the Telliads. Earlier, the Spartans had arrested, imprisoned, and condemned Hegesistratos to death for the many and terrible damages they had suffered because of him. [2] Caught in this dire situation, Hegesistratos, recognizing that he was in a race against death, resolved to suffer severe pain rather than to die, and he then performed a feat that beggars description. Although he was confined in wooden stocks rimmed with iron, he gained possession of an iron implement that had somehow been brought there. As soon as he obtained it, he devised the bravest of all deeds that we know of: he first measured how much of his foot could be freed from the stocks, and then proceeded to cut it off between the toes and the heel. [3] After he had done this, he still had to evade his guards, so he tunneled through the wall and fled to Tegea, traveling during the nights and hiding in the woods to rest during the days until, on the third night, he arrived in Tegea. Meanwhile, the Lacedaemonians, who were struck with amazement when they saw half of his foot lying in the stocks, were out searching for him in full force, but they could not find him. [4] Thus he escaped the Lacedaemonians on that occasion and took refuge in Tegea, which was not on friendly terms with the Lacedaemonians at that time. When he had recovered his health and had a wooden foot made for himself, he became openly hostile to the Lacedaemonians. In the end, however, his enmity toward them brought him no good, for while he was serving as a seer on Zacynthus, they captured and killed him.

9.36
479
PLATAEA
Teisamenos is the diviner at Plataea.

9.37
479
PLATAEA
Mardonios' sacrifices predict a bad outcome if he should attack first. The story of his diviner, Hegesistratos of Elis, and how he escapes from the Spartans and is their enemy until they capture and kill him.

9.38
479
PLATAEA
The omens remain
unfavorable as the
Greek army grows more
numerous. A man from
Thebes advises Mardonios
to guard the passover
Mount Cithaeron.

But of course the death of Hegesistratos occurred after the events at Plataea. At this time he was serving by the Asopos, receiving no small payment from Mardonios for performing sacrifice, which he carried out enthusiastically both because of his hatred for the Lacedaemonians and because of the profit he was making. [2] Now the omens concerning battle were unfavorable not only for the Persians themselves but also for the Hellenes who were allied with them (since they had a seer of their own, Hippomachos of Leucas).

But as time passed, and the Greek army grew larger as more and more Hellenes streamed in to join it, a Theban named Timagenides son of Herpys advised Mardonios to occupy the pass at Cithaeron, telling him that the Hellenes were pouring through it every day and that great numbers of them could be intercepted there.

9.39
479
MOUNT
CITHAERON
Mardonios sends his
cavalry on a successful
raid against supply trains
coming over the
Cithaeron pass.

Eight days had already passed since the two sides had been camping opposite each other when Timagenides counseled Mardonios to do this. Realizing that this was good advice, Mardonios waited until night fell and then sent his cavalry to the pass of Cithaeron, which opens toward Plataea and is called Three Heads by the Boeotians and Oaks Heads by the Athenians. [2] And these horsemen did not go there in vain, for as they raided the plain, they captured 500 beasts of burden carrying food from the Peloponnese toward the Greek camp, and the people tending the wagons as well. After they had taken this quarry, the Persians proceeded to slaughter everything without mercy, sparing neither man nor beast. When they had their fill of killing, they surrounded what was left and drove them back to Mardonios and his camp.

9.40
479
PLATAEA
Neither side will begin
the battle, but
Mardonios'cavalry, aided
by the Thebans,harass
the Hellenes.

Two more days elapsed after they had done this deed, as neither side wanted to initiate battle. The barbarians tested the Hellenes by going as far as the Asopos, but neither side crossed the river. Mardonios' cavalry, however, continually harassed the Hellenes and pressed them hard. For the Thebans, who were staunch medizers and eager participants in the war, always led the way until the actual battle, at which point the Persians and the Medes took over and were the ones who performed feats of great valor.

But for the first ten days nothing happened other than what I have related. Then, with the arrival of the eleventh day after the armies had camped opposite each other at Plataea, by which time the Greeks had indeed greatly increased their numbers, Mardonios son of Gobryas grew exasperated at the continued standoff; at that point he held a conference with Artabazos son of Pharnakes, one of the few Persian men highly esteemed by Xerxes. [2] During their discussion, Artabazos expressed the opinion that they should have the whole army pack up as quickly as possible and retreat behind the walls of Thebes, where much food for them and fodder for the pack animals had been taken, and where they could accomplish their goals at their leisure; [3] for they had there a great store of gold, both coined and uncoined, and much silver and many drinking vessels as well. They should spare none of this, he said, but send it off to be distributed among the Hellenes, especially among those who were prominent in their cities; if they did this, the Hellenes would quickly surrender their freedom and the Persians would not have to be exposed to the risks of battle. [4] This proposal of Artabazos was really the same advice as that which the Thebans had given, as he also had more foresight than the Persian commander. Indeed, Mardonios' attitude was the more forceful and competitiveof the two, and in no way submissive, for he believed that his army was much stronger than that of the Hellenes, and that it should engage in battle as quickly as possible rather than allow the Hellenes to marshal still more men than they had already assembled. As for the pre-battle sacrifices of Hegesistratos, he said they should forget about them rather than try to force them to become favorable. Instead, he thought that they should join battle in the Persian tradition.

That is what Mardonios thought was the right course of action, and since no one opposed him, his opinion prevailed. For it was he, and not Artabazos, who had received control over the army from the King. He sent for the subordinate commanders of the regiments and the generals of the Hellenes serving with them and asked them if they knew of any prophecy predicting that the Persians would be destroyed in Hellas. [2] These specially summoned men responded with silence, some of them because they did not know the oracles, others knowing them but thinking that it was unsafe to speak about them. So

9.41
479
PLATAEA
After many days of skirmishing, Artabazos and the Thebans counsel Mardonios to withdraw inside the walls of Thebes and attempt to break the unity of he Hellenes by bribing the chief men of the various cities, Mardonios, however, wants to bring about a battle immediately, before the Greek army grows stronger.

9.42
479
PLATAEA
Mardonios is the com mander, so his view prevails. Steps are ordered to prepare the army for battle the next day.

Mardonios himself said, "Well, then, since you either know nothing or do not dare to speak up, I shall tell you, because I am quite knowledgeable about this matter. [3] There is an oracle that the Persians are destined to come to Hellas and that they will all die, but only after they plunder the sanctuary at Delphi. So since we know this, we shall not go to this sanctuary or try to plunder it, and for that reason we shall not die. [4] All of you who happen to be well disposed toward the Persians may take pleasure in this, since it means that we shall prevail over the Hellenes." After saying this, he gave the signal for the second time to make all the preparations and put everything in good order for the battle to be joined on the following day.

As to the oracle that Mardonios said applied to the Persians, I know that it was not composed about the Persians but actually about the Illyrians and the army of the Encheles. But there is another one composed by Bakis which does refer to this battle:

> [2] Beside the River Thermodon and grassy banks of Asopos,
> Greek armies will assemble; barbarian tongues will shriek;
> Medes who wield bows will fall here in great numbers,
> Before their time allotted, when this day of death arrives.

I also know other prophecies referring to the Persians similar to this one, by Mousaios. The Thermodon River flows between Tanagra and Glisas.

After this inquiry about the oracles and the exhortation offered by Mardonios, night fell, and men were stationed at the guard posts. The night was well advanced; all was quiet throughout the camp, and most of the men were fast asleep when Alexandros son of Amyntas rode up on horseback to a guard post of the Athenians, seeking to speak to their generals. [2] While most of the guards remained at their posts, some ran to their generals, and when they found them they told them that someone on horseback had arrived from the camp of the Medes, and that he would say nothing more than that he wished to speak to some of their generals, whom he named.

9.43
479
PLATAEA
Herodotus says that the oracle quoted by Mardonios really refers to the Illyrians, and not the Persians.

9.44
479
PLATAEA
Late in the night, Alexandros of Macedon rides to the Athenian lines and asks to speak to the generals.

As soon as they heard this, the generals followed the guards back to their post, and when they arrived there, Alexandros said to them, "Men of Athens, I entrust you with what I am about to say, charging you to keep it an absolute secret and to tell no one but Pausanias, lest you utterly destroy me. You must know that I would not be speaking to you if I did not care greatly about all of Hellas, [2] for I myself am a Hellene of ancient lineage and would not wish to see Hellas exchange its freedom for slavery. And so I am here to tell you that Mardonios and his army are unable to obtain from their sacrifices the omens they desire. Otherwise you would have fought a long time ago. Now, however, Mardonios has resolved to dismiss the oracles and to engage in battle beginning at the break of day; my guess is that he is very worried that more men will come here to join you. So you should prepare yourselves for this. If it turns out that Mardonios delays the encounter and does nothing, you should remain and persevere, for they have enough food left for only a few days. [3] And if this war ends in your favor, then you must remember me and my own quest for liberation, for it is on my own initiative that I have performed this dangerous feat as a service to the Hellenes; I wish to reveal the intent of Mardonios to you so that the barbarians will not be able to fall upon you suddenly and unexpectedly. I am Alexandros of Macedon." After saying this he rode away, back to his camp and his own post.

The Athenian generals went to the right wing and told Pausanias exactly what they had heard from Alexandros. With the report of this news, Pausanias grew frightened at the very thought of the Persians and said, [2] "Well, then, since the battle will begin at dawn, it would be best for you, the Athenians, to oppose the Persians, and for us to face the Boeotians and the Hellenes now posted opposite you. After all, you are familiar with the Medes and how they fight, since you fought them at Marathon, while not a single one of us, the men of Sparta, has any experience or knowledge of the Medes in battle, although we are quite familiar with the Boeotians and Thessalians. [3] Therefore you should take up your arms and come over to this wing, and we shall go to the left." To this the Athenians replied, "Actually, for a long time now, indeed from the very beginning when we saw you deployed opposite the Persians, we ourselves have been thinking about suggesting just what

9.45
479
PLATAEA
Alexandros warns the Hellenes that although Mardonios has not received favorable omens, he plans to attack at dawn, having only enough food to hold his position for a few days more. He asks that the Hellenes, if success ful, remember to liberate Macedon, too, from Persian rule.

9.46
479
PLATAEA
When Pausanias is told of the Persian plans, he suggests that the Athenians and Spartans exchange positions in the Greek line, so each will oppose a familiar foe—the Athenians against the Persians, the Spartans against the Boeotians.

you have now proposed, but we feared that our advice would displease you. Now that you have suggested it, we are pleased with your proposal and are most ready and willing to carry it out.

Since this plan satisfied both parties, they exchanged positions as dawn was breaking. But when the Boeotians found out what was happening and reported it to Mardonios, he immediately tried to shift positions, too, so as to again place the Persians opposite the Lacedaemonians. Then, when Pausanias learned what was going on and realized that his maneuver had been detected and countered, he brought the Spartans back to the right wing, and Mardonios, in the same way, brought the Persians back to the left.

When everyone had settled back into their original positions, Mardonios sent a herald to the Spartans with this message: "Lacedaemonians, you are *said* to be the best and bravest of men by the people of these parts; they are overcome with awe for you because, so they say, you neither flee from battle nor desert your posts, but stand fast and either destroy your foes or are destroyed yourselves. [2] But it turns out that none of this is true. For even before we have joined battle and come to close combat, we have seen you flee and abandon your assigned positions to make the Athenians test us first, while you deploy yourselves opposite our slaves. [3] These are certainly not the deeds of noble and courageous men! We have been altogether deceived about you, for we expected that you, given your glorious reputation, would send a herald to challenge us, and that you would want to fight only the Persians; and we were ready to act accordingly. Now we find that you are making no such proposal but are cringing before us instead. Well, then, since you have not initiated the challenge, we shall do so ourselves. [4] Why don't you fight for the Hellenes, since you are reputed to be the most valiant of them, and we shall fight for the barbarians, with equal numbers on each side. If you think the others should fight, too, fine: let them fight afterward. Or if not, and if you should think we alone are enough, we shall fight it out to the end, and whichever of us wins will then claim the victory over the entire army of the other."

9.47
479
PLATAEA
The Persians counter the Greek maneuver, which leads Pausanias to return the Spartans to the right wing.

9.48
479
PLATAEA
Mardonios sends a message to the Spartans, mocking them for attempting to avoid battle with the Persians and challenging them to a decisive encounter of equal numbers.

The herald paused after saying this, and when no one replied here turned to Mardonios and informed him of what had happened. Mardonios, overjoyed and exalted by this phantom victory, sent out his cavalry against the Hellenes. [2] The horsemen rode out and attacked, inflicting injuries on the entire Greek army with their javelins and arrows, for they were mounted archers and it was impossible for the Hellenes to close with them. They also blocked and destroyed the Spring of Gargaphia, which had been the source of water for the whole Greek army. [3] The Lacedaemonians were the only ones posted at the spring, and the rest of the Helleneswere farther away from it, according to the position in which each of their units was stationed. Though the Asopos was nearby, they had been blocked off from it and had to go back and forth to the spring, since the cavalry and archers prevented them from transporting water from the river.

So that was their situation; and with the army now deprived of water and suffering under the harassment of the cavalry, the generals of the Hellenes gathered together and went to Pausanias on the right wing to discuss these and other matters. There were in fact other problems that distressed them even more than these: they no longer had any food, since the auxiliaries they had sent to the Peloponnese to bring back provisions had been completely blocked by the enemy's cavalry and were unable to reach their camp.

Taking counsel together, the generals resolved that if the Persians delayed and did not give battle that day, they would retreat to the island which was situated in front of the city of Plataea, a little more than a mile from the Asopos and the Spring of Gargaphia, where they were camping at the time. [2] It could be thought of as an island on the mainland, in that there is a river which divides upstream and flows down from Cithaeron to the plain, so that its two streams are separated from each other by approximately 2,000 yards before joining again into one stream. The river's name is Oëroë; according to the local inhabitants, Oëroë is the daughter of Asopos. [3] So it was to this place they planned to move, in order to have an unlimited supply of water and so that the cavalry could not inflict harm on them from positions directly opposite them, as it was doing now. They decided to make the move that night during the second watch, so that the Persians would not see

9.49
479
PLATAEA
The Spartans do not respond to Mardonios' challenge, so he sends his cavalry to spoil the spring from which the Greek army draws water, as the Persian horsemen already barred them from the Asopos River.

9.50
479
PLATAEA
The loss of the spring and the lack of food due to the cutting of their supply line worry the Hellenes.

9.51
479
PLATAEA
The Hellenes in council decide to move the army during the night to the "island," where there would be plentiful water, and tore open their supply line over Mount Cithaeron.

them set out and their horsemen would not be able to harass them in pursuit. [4] They also decided that during the same night, upon their arrival at the island around which Oëroë daughter of Asopos flows from Cithaeron, they would dispatch half the army to Cithaeron to rescue the auxiliaries who were supposed to be transporting their provisions, since they were stranded there on Cithaeron.

After they had discussed and planned this move, they suffered throughout the whole day from attacks by the Persian cavalry; and it was not until the day was drawing to a close that the horsemen finally ceased their assaults. After night fell and the hour they had arranged to leave arrived, most of them departed, though they had no intention of going to the destination upon which they had previously agreed. For once they were in motion, they were so happy to flee from the cavalry that they continued their flight toward the city of Plataea until they arrived at the sanctuary of Hera, which lies in front of the city and is a little more than two miles from the Spring of Gargaphia. Upon their arrival there they set down their arms in front of the sanctuary.

Thus they made their camp around the sanctuary of Hera. Now when Pausanias saw them departing from their previous camp, he gave orders to the Lacedaemonians to take up their arms and follow the others who had gone before them and who he assumed were on their way to the place upon which they had previously agreed. [2] The other subordinate commanders were all ready to obey Pausanias, but Amompharetos son of Poliades, the commander of the Pitana brigade, would not move, saying that he was unwilling to flee from the outsiders and bring disgrace upon Sparta; he was amazed by what was happening, because he had not been present at the earlier conference. [3] Pausanias and Euryanax were infuriated at his disobedience, but they were even more upset by the fact that they would have to leave the Pitana brigade behind if he persisted in his refusal. They feared that by carrying out the agreement they had made with the other Hellenes, they would have to desert Amompharetos and his men, who, being left behind there, would surely be destroyed. [4] As they were reasoning this through, they kept the Laconian army from moving off, and tried to persuade Amompharetos that he was wrong to act this way.

9.52
479
PLATAEA
The Hellenes suffer attacks all day from the Persian cavalry, so that when they depart for their assigned places, most of them go instead to Plataea.

9.53
479
PLATAEA
Pausanias gives orders to the Spartans to move to their assigned position, but one captain, Amompharetos, refuses. Rather than abandon his unit, the Spartans remain there while Pausanias and others try to persuade Amompharetos to go with the rest.

And while they were thus urging Amompharetos, who was the only one of the Lacedaemonians and Tegeans who was about to be left behind, the Athenians also refused to move, but stayed where they had been originally posted, firmly believing that the Lacedaemonians' disposition was to say one thing while intending to do another. [2] So when the army had started to move, they had sent one of their horsemen to see whether the Spartans were making an attempt to leave or whether they actually did not intend to depart at all, and also to ask Pausanias what they themselves should do.

When the herald reached the Lacedaemonians, he saw that they were deployed in their original positions and that their most prominent men were involved in a quarrel. For Euryanax and Pausanias had no success at all in persuading Amompharetos not to risk leaving himself and his men isolated as the only Lacedaemonians to remain there, and their discussion had finally developed into an open quarrel, just as the Athenian herald arrived and stood next to them. [2] During this argument Amompharetos picked up a rock with both hands and, placing it before the feet of Pausanias, said that with this voting pebble he was casting his vote not to flee from the outsiders. Pausanias then called him a madman and said he was out of his mind. The Athenians' herald inquired as he had been instructed, and in reply, Pausanias ordered him to tell the Athenians about his current situation, and to request that they come now to join his troops; as for what to do about retreating, he said they should follow the lead of the Lacedaemonians.

The herald then returned to the Athenians. When dawn came, the Spartans were still bickering. Pausanias had not moved all this time, but now, thinking that Amompharetos would not really stay behind if the rest of the Lacedaemonians marched away (which is just what happened), he gave the signal and led off all the rest of the troops through the hills, while the Tegeans followed. [2] The Athenians marched in the opposite direction, as they had been assigned, for while the Lacedaemonians kept close to the ridges and the foothills of Cithaeron in fear of the cavalry, the Athenians turned down toward the plain.

9.54
479
PLATAEA
The Athenians ask Pausanias whether the Spartans are marching and what the Athenians should do.

9.55
479
PLATAEA
The Athenian messenger arrives during the argument with Amompharetos, and Pausanias asks the Athenians to join the Spartans and to follow their lead.

9.56
479
PLATAEA
The Spartans march off, keeping to the hills to avoid Persian cavalry. The Athenians march down into the plain.

9.57
479
PLATAEA
After the rest of the
Spartans marched off,
Amompharetos follows,
and finds them waiting
for him not far away.
Then they are attacked
by the Persian cavalry.

At first Amompharetos had expected that Pausanias would not dare to leave him and his men behind, and he remained determined to stay and not to abandon his post. But then, as Pausanias and his troops continued to march away, he concluded that they were quite clearly abandoning him. At this point he had his brigade take up their arms, and he led them forth at a walking pace toward the main body of troops. [2] The latter had gone ahead a little less than half a mile, but then had stopped to wait for the brigade of Amompharetos around the River Moloeis at the place called Argiopion, where there is a sanctuary of Eleusinian Demeter. Pausanias and his men waited there so that if Amompharetos and his company remained at their formerly appointed post, they would be able to hurry back to help them. [3] Now, just as Amompharetos and his men reached Pausanias and his troops, the entire cavalry of the barbarians pressed hard upon them. For the horsemen were acting as they usually did: when they saw empty space where the Hellenes had been in position on the previous days, they rode forward and, as soon as they caught up with the Hellenes, they attacked them.

9.58
479
PLATAEA
Mardonios, seeing the
Spartans had retreated
during the night, mocks
them as cowards who
are afraid to face the
braver Persians. He
orders an immediate
pursuit.

When Mardonios learned that the Hellenes had gone away during the night and he saw that the place where they had been was deserted, he summoned Thorax of Larissa and his brothers Eurypylos and Thrasydaios and said to them, [2] "So, sons of Aleuas, will you still talk as you did, now that you see this place is deserted? For you who are neighbors of the Lacedaemonians used to say that they do not flee from battle. You claimed that they are the best of all warriors, but earlier you saw them leave their battle positions, and now we can all see that during the night just past, they have scattered and fled, just when they would have had to contend in battle against people who are indisputably the best. Thus they have made it plain that they are people of no account, trying to distinguish themselves among Hellenes, who are also people of no account. [3] Now I at least shall certainly pardon you, since you had no experience of the Persians before and were praising those about whom you had some knowledge. But I am rather amazed at how Artabazos was utterly terrified of the Lacedaemonians, and how because of his fear he declared that most cowardly proposal, namely, that we should break up our camp and retreat to the city of Thebes, where we would have been besieged. The King will hear about this from me, [4] but the accounting for all that will take place elsewhere. As for now, the Hellenes must not be permitted to get away from us; they must be pursued until they are overtaken and made to pay the penalty for all that they have inflicted on the Persians."

After saying this, he led the Persians at a run across the Asopos and along what he assumed was the path of the fleeing Hellenes. He was actually directing his troops toward the Lacedaemonians and Tegeans alone, for because of the ridges, he had not perceived the Athenians turning toward the plain. [2] When the rest of the barbarian regiments saw the Persians setting out to pursue the Hellenes, their commanders immediately raised the signal and joined in the chase as fast as they could, without marshaling the troops into any order or assigned positions. They rushed against the Hellenes in a mass, shouting the battle cry and determined to take them bystorm.

9.59
479
PLATAEA
Thinking the Hellenes are fleeing, the Persians charge the Spartans at top speed and without order.

As the enemy cavalry approached, Pausanias sent a horseman to the Athenians with this message: "Men of Athens, as our greatest contest, one which will determine the freedom or enslavement of Hellas, lies before us, we Lacedaemonians and you Athenians have been betrayed during the past night by our allies, who have run away. [2] So now it is obvious what we must do from this point on: we must defend and protect each other to the best of our abilities. If the enemy cavalry had rushed out against you first, then we along with the Tegeans, who have refused to betray Hellas, would have been obliged to come to your aid. But as it is, their whole cavalry has advanced against us, and so it is only right and just that you come to defend the division that is being pressed the hardest. [3] But if some circumstance makes it impossible for you to come to our aid, you will gain our gratitude by sending us your archers. We know, because you have shown such great zeal throughout this war, that you will certainly comply with this request."

9.60
479
PLATAEA
Pausanias sends a message to the Athenians asking them to assist the Spartans, who bear the full brunt of the Persian attack. Should they be unable to march to his aid, he asks them to at least send their archers.

9.61
479
PLATAEA
The Athenians are attacked by the enemy Hellenes, and cannot send assistance to the Spartans. The Spartans stand their ground and suffer many casualties from Persian archers shooting from behind a shield wall. Spartan sacrifices do not prove favorable.

When the Athenians heard this, they set out to assist the Lacedaemonians and to support them as best they could; but along the way they were attacked by Greek allies of the King who were posted opposite them, and this attack caused them such distress that they were no longer able to go to their aid. [2] Thus the Lacedaemonians and Tegeans were left to stand, alone; the number of the Lacedaemonians, including the lightly armed troops, came to 50,000, and of the Tegeans (who had never left the Lacedaemonians), 3,000. Since they were about to engage in combat with Mardonios and his army before them, they performed pre-battle sacrifices, [3] but the omens turned out to be unfavorable for them. And during all this time, many of them fell to their deaths and many more by far were wounded. The Persians had set up a barricade of their wicker shields and were relendessly shooting volleys of arrows at them, so that, as the Spartans were being pressed hard and the sacrifices continued to prove unfavorable, Pausanias turned to gaze toward the Plataeans' sanctuary of Hera and called upon the goddess, entreating her that they would not be cheated of their hope for victory

9.62
479
PLATAEA
As the Tegeans suddenly charge, the sacrifices prove favorable, and the Spartans charge also. Now the Persian lack of armor and skill in close-quarters fighting proves decisive.

While he was still invoking the aid of the goddess with this prayer, the Tegeans took up a position against the barbarians in the front line ahead of the others and began to advance toward them. And just then, as Pausanias concluded his prayer, the Lacedaemonians' sacrifices yielded favorable omens. Now that this had finally happened, the Lacedaemonians also advanced against the Persians, who threw down their bows as they confronted them. [2] They fought their first battle around the wicker shields,and when these had fallen over, they waged a fierce struggle beside the sanctuary of Demeter itself, which went on for a long time, until they reached the point of close-quarters pushing and shoving, for the barbarians seized the Hellenes' spears and broke them. [3] The Persians were not inferior in courage or strength, but they did not have hoplite arms, and besides, they were untrained and no match for their opponents in tactical skill. They were dashing out beyond the front lines individually or in groups often, joining together in larger or smaller bands, and charging right into the Spartan ranks, where they perished.

The place where the Lacedaemonians pressed their opponents the hardest was at the spot where Mardonios was fighting. He was mounted on a white horse and surrounded by 1,000 picked men, the best of the Persians and for as long as he survived, the Persians maintained their resistance; and as they defended themselves, they struck down many of the Lacedaemonians. [2] But when Mardonios was killed and the troops posted around him who made up the most formidable division of the army, had also fallen, the others turned to flee and gave way to the Lacedaemonians. They were hurt the most by how they were equipped, namely by their lack of armor, for they were fighting as unarmed soldiers in a contest against well-equipped hoplites.

9.63
479
PLATAEA
The Persians hold their ground, although fighting without armor against armored Hellenes, until Mardonios and his guards fall.

Thus, in accordance with the oracle, Mardonios paid a just and full retribution to the Spartans for the murder of Leonidas, and Pausanias son of Kleombrotos, the son of Anaxandridas, achieved the finest victory of all those known to us. [2] The names of his earlier ancestors have been listed with reference to Leonidas, since they happen to be the same for both. Mardonios died at the hands of a notable Spartan named Arimnestos, who later, after the wars of the Medes, led a troop of 300 men against the entire army of the Messenians in the war at Stenykleros, where he himself and all his men were killed.

9.64
479
PLATAEA
Herodotus praises the victory over Mardonios as the finest "of all those known to us."

But at Plataea, when the Persians were routed by the Lacedaemonians, they fled in disorder to their camp and the wooden wall they had built in Theban territory. What really amazes me is that, though they were fighting beside the grove of Demeter, not one of the Persians was seen entering the precinct or dying there; for the majority of the Persians who fell that day died on the unconsecrated ground immediately surrounding the sanctuary, I assume, if it is necessary to assume anything about matters of the divine, that the goddess herself refused to admit them because they had set fire to her inner hall at Eleusis.

9.65
479
PLATAEA
The Persians flee in disorder to their camp.

That was what happened in the battle. Now, Artabazos son of Pharnakes had from the very beginning disapproved of the King's having placed Mardonios in charge; and after that he had repeatedly tried to dissuade Mardonios from joining battle, but had accomplished nothing. So it was his displeasure with Mardonios' direction of their affairs that motivated what he did now. [2] Artabazos was the commander of no small

9.66
479
PLATAEA
Artabazos, whose advice not to engage had been ignored by Mardonios, leads his forces away from the battle to Phocis and toward the Hellespont.

force, having up to 40,000 men with him. When the battle was joined, he knew very well what the outcome of the fight would be, and as he led his men out, he deployed them in close formation and commanded them all to stay together and go wherever he led them at the same pace as his own. [3] After giving this order, he led his force as though to take it into battle, but as he advanced farther along the road and saw the Persians already in flight he no longer kept his men in the same good order as before, but took off at a run by the quickest route—not to the wooden wall of their camp or to the city walls of Thebes, but directly toward Phocis—because he wanted to reach the Hellespont as soon as possible.

So they turned in that direction, and meanwhile, most of the Greek allies of the King were behaving like cowards, but not the Boeotians, who fought the Athenians a long time, for those Thebans who had medized were so keen to fight and not play the coward that 300 of the best and most prominent of them fell there at the hands of the Athenians. But finally, when they too had been routed, they fled to Thebes, though not along the path taken in flight by the Persians and the whole throng of the other allies, who had neither fought to the end with anyone nor accomplished any remarkable feats.

It is clear to me that the barbarians depended entirely for their success on the Persians, since it was because they saw that the other Persians were fleeing that Artabazos and his troops fled from the enemy, though they had not yet even joined in the battle. Thus they were all in flight except for the cavalry, particularly the Boeotian division, which provided vital assistance to the fleeing troops by riding up close to the Hellenes and blocking them from the fleeing allies; the Hellenes, now that they had won the victory, were intent on pursuing and slaughtering the troops of Xerxes.

Now while this rout was well under way, the other Hellenes who had stationed themselves around the sanctuary of Hera and who had not taken part in the fight received the news that the battle was over and that Pausanias and his men had won. Upon hearing this, they set off without bothering to organize themselves into any battle order or assigned positions; the Corinthians and those with them took the route leading through the foothills and knolls, straight up to the sanctuary of Demeter, while the Megarians, thePhleiasians, and those with them advanced through the plain along the most level of the roads in this region. [2] When the Megarians and Phleiasians drew near their enemies, the Theban horsemen caught sight of them rushing ahead in disorder, and charged them on horseback, under the command of Asopodoros son of Timandros. Falling upon them, they cut down 600 of them and drove the rest back all the way to Cithaeron.

These troops perished without accomplishing anything-noteworthy at all. Meanwhile, the Persians and the crowd of allies that were with them had taken refuge within the wooden wall and climbed the towers before the Lacedaemonians could get there, and ascending the wall, they strengthened it as well as they could. When the Lacedaemonians arrived and began their assault, the battle at the wall grew increasingly fierce, [2] for as long as the Athenians were absent, the Persian troops defended themselves effectively and had the advantage over the Lacedaemonians, since the latter had little experience of siege warfare. But when the Athenians arrived and joined the attack, the assaults intensified and went on for quite some time. Finally, by their valor and perseverance, the Athenians mounted the wall and tore it down, and the Hellenes streamed in. [3] The Tegeans, who were the first to enter inside the wall, were the ones who plundered the tent of Mardonios; among the various items they took from it was a feeding trough for horses made entirely of bronze, which is certainly worth seeing. Later, the Tegeans dedicated this feeding trough of Mardonios at the temple of Athena Alea, but everything else they had taken they contributed to the common stockpile of spoils collected by all the Hellenes. [4] Once the wall had been torn down, the barbarians no longer formed up in military order. Not one of them any longer thought of resistance; they had fallen into a state of panic, as tens of thousands of people were trapped there in a confined space. [5] The Hellenes were thus provided with such a great opportunity for slaughter that out of an army numbering 300,000, not counting the 40,000 troops with whom Artabazos had fled, not even 3,000 survived. Of the Lacedaemonians from Sparta, in all ninety-one died in this encounter; of the Tegeans, sixteen; and of the Athenians, fifty-two.

9.70
479
PLATAEA
The Persians defend their walled camp successfully against the Spartans, but the Athenians, after a long struggle, finally breach the wall. The Hellenes enter and plunder the camp, slaughtering all but 3,000 Persians. Herodotus lists Greek losses from the battle.

9.71
479
PLATAEA
Herodotus describes the
post-battle discussion
of who was the bravest
and deserves the most
praise. Among themselves,
the Spartans select
Poseidonios over
Aristodemos, because
the latter clearly wished
to die.

The barbarians who proved the best and bravest were the Persian infantry and the cavalry of the Sacae, while Mardonios is said to have been the best and bravest of individual men. Of the Hellenes, the Tegeans andAthenians proved noble and courageous, but the Lacedaemonians surpassed them in valor. [2] I can present no proof of this judgment, since they all shared in the victory against their opponents, except that the Lacedaemonians attacked the strongest division and conquered it. And in my opinion, the man who proved the best and bravest by far was Aristodemos, the only one of the 300 to have survived Thermopylae, for which he had met with disgrace and dishonor. After him, the best were the Spartans Poseidonois, Philokyon, and Amompharetos. [3] When the question of which man had proven himself the best came up for discussion, however, the surviving Spartans recognized that Aristodemos had wanted to die in front of everyone because of the charge against him, and so had left his post in a rage and displayed great feats, while Poseidonios did not want to die, but proved himself a noble and courageous man all the same, and was therefore much the better man for it. [4] But perhaps it was jealousy that motivated them to render this judgment. Of those who died in this battle, all the men I have listed except for Aristodemos were awarded official honors, while Aristodemos was not because he had wanted to die for the reason I have just mentioned.

9.72
479
PLATAEA
Herodotus describes the
sad fate of Kallikrates,
who was killed by an
arrow before he could
strike a blow for Hellas.

Those were the men who won the greatest fame at Plataea. For Kallikrates died away from the battle; he had come to the camp as the most handsome man of the Hellenes at that time, not only among the Lacedaemonians, but among all the other Hellenes, too. What happened was that while Pausanias was conducting the pre-battle sacrifices, Kallikrates was sitting at his assigned post when he was wounded in his side by an arrow. [2] So as the others fought, he had been carried out of the ranks, and while he struggled against death he said to Arimnestos, a Plataean, that he did not mind dying for Hellas, but regretted that he had not struck a blow or performed any feats to show his worth, though he had been eager to do so.

It is said that of the Athenians, Sophanes son of Eutychides, from the deme of Dekeleia, distinguished himself in the battle. According to the Athenians, the Dekeleians had once performed a deed whose worth endures forever. [2] A long time ago, the sons of Tyndareos invaded Attica with a large army to recover Helen, and ravaged the demes, since they did notknow where Helen, for her own safety, had been hidden. Some say that it was the Dekeleians, others say that it was Dekelos himself, who, annoyed by the arrogance of Theseus and fearing for all of the Athenian territory, guided the sons of Tyndareos in this matter and led them to Aphidna, which Titakos, who was born of this land, then betrayed by handing it over to them. [3] Because of this deed, when the Dekeleians are in Sparta, theyare exempt from payments and are provided front-row seats, and these privileges still continue without interruption to this day, so that even in the war many years later between the Athenians and Lacedaemonians, the Lacedaemonians spoiled the rest of Attica but stayed away from Dekeleia.

9.73
479
PLATAEA
The Athenian Sophanes of Dekeleia wins renown. Herodotus tells the tale of how the Dekeleians helped the Spartan Tyndaridae to locate Helen at Aphidna.

Sophanes had come from this deme, and it was he who proved to be the best and bravest of the Athenians at that time. Two different stories are told about him: one, that from the belt of his breastplate he carried an iron anchor slung from a bronze chain, which he would throw whenever he drew near his enemies so that when they broke out of their position in the ranks to assault him, they would be unable to budge him; then, when his opponents were in flight, his tactic was to pick up the anchor and chase them with it. [2] That is one of the stories; according to the other, which conflicts with the first, he did not actually wear an anchor attached to his breastplate but instead had an anchor as an emblem on his shield, which never ceased moving and was always in swift motion.

9.74
479
PLATAEA
Herodotus recounts two tales about Sophanes' bravery and his "anchor" in the battle.

And there is another illustrious deed that Sophanes performed: when the Athenians were blockading Aegina, on a challenge he fought and killed Eurybates of Argos, a victor in the pentathlon. Much later, it happened that Sophanes, while proving himself noble and courageous as general of the Athenians in joint command with Leagros son of Glaukon, died at the hands of the Edonians as he was fighting for the gold mines at Baton.

9.75
479
PLATAEA
Herodotus describes another glorious deed by Sophanes, and how he met his death.

A woman of Cos deserts the Persians and, as a suppliant, begs Pausanias to protect her. He proves to be a friend of her father's and promises to treat her well.

The Mantineians and the Eleans arrive after the battle is over, and are so upset to have missed it that they banish their leaders.

After the Hellenes had overwhelmed the barbarians at Plataea, a woman came to them of her own accord; she had been a concubine of a Persian named Pharandates son of Teaspis, and when she realized that the Persians had been destroyed and the Hellenes victorious, she adorned herself lavishly with gold and dressed herself and her servants in the finest clothes they had with them; then she stepped down from her carriage and went to the Lacedaemonians, who were still in the midst of the slaughter. She was already quite familiar with the name of Pausanias and his homeland, since she had often heard them mentioned, and when she saw that Pausanias was in charge of everything, she knew who he was. Clasping his knees, she said to him, [2] "King of Sparta, save me, your suppliant, from captive slavery. For you have helped me even before this by destroying these men who respect neither divinities nor gods. I am from Cos by birth, the daughter of Hegetorides son of Antagoras, and the Persian took me by force from Cos and kept me against my will." Pausanias answered her, [3] "Woman, you are a suppliant, and if indeed you are telling the truth and really are the daughter of Hegetorides of Cos, then have no fear. Hegetorides happens to be my closest guest-friend of all the people who live in that region." After saying this, he entrusted her to the ephors who were with him and later sent her to Aegina in accord with her own wishes.

Immediately following the appearance of this woman, the Mantineians arrived, but the battle was now over. When they found out that they had come too late for the engagement, they thought it a terrible calamity and said that they deserved to be punished. [2] And then, when they heard that the Medes with Artabazos were fleeing, they were about to set out to pursue and drive them as far as Thessaly, but the Lacedaemonians would not allow them to chase down the fleeing enemy. So they went back to their own land, where they drove their military leader out of their country. [3] After the Mantineians, the Eleans arrived, and they likewise thought it a terrible calamity to have missed the battle and departed, and when they returned home, they also drove out their leaders. So much for the Mantineians and the Eleans.

Back at Plataea there was in the camp of the Aeginetans one Lampon son of Pytheas, one of the most prominent men of Aegina, who now rushed to Pausanias and, speaking with great zeal, made this most ungodly proposal: [2] "Son of Kleombrotos, you have accomplished a feat that is extraordinary in both its magnitude and its nobility; god granted that you should be the one to protect Hellas and gain the greatest glory of all Hellenes known to us. But now you should carry out what still remains to be done so that you will have an even greater reputation and so that in the future, every barbarian will beware of initiating reckless acts against the Hellenes. [3] For after Leonidas died at Thermopylae, Mardonios and Xerxes cut off his head and suspended it from a stake; and if you now pay back Mardonios by treating him in the same fashion, you will win praise first from all the Spartans, and then from the rest of the Hellenes, since by impaling Mardonios, you will have vengeance for what happened to your uncle Leonidas." Though he thought he would please Pausanias by saying this, Pausanias replied as follows:

"My friend from Aegina, I commend and appreciate that you mean well and are trying to look out for my future interests, but this idea of yours falls short of good judgment. After you have raised me up on high, together with exalting my homeland and my achievement, you cast me down to nothing by encouraging me to abuse a corpse, claiming that if I did so, I would have a better reputation. But this is a deed more appropriate to barbarians than to Hellenes, though we resent them for it all the same. [2] In any case, because of this, I could hardly please the Aeginetans or anyone else who approves of such deeds as this. It is quite enough for me to please the Spartans by committing no sacrilege and by speaking with respect for what is lawful and sacred. As for Leonidas, whom you urge me to avenge, I tell you that he and the others who met their ends at Thermopylae have already achieved great vengeance by the countless souls of those who lie here dead. As for you, do not ever again approach me with such a suggestion or try to advise me, and be thankful to leave here without suffering harm."

9.78
479
PLATAEA
Lamport of Aegina advises Pausanias to take revenge for the Persians' ill-treatment of the body of Leonidas at Thermopylae by impaling the corpse of Mardonios.

9.79
479
PLATAEA
Pausanias rejects the advice of Lampon as unworthy of a Greek and a Spartan, and sends him away, warning him not to return with such counsel.

<table>
<tr><td>

9.80
479
PLATAEA
At Pausanias' order, the
helots gather the spoils,
but they sell some of
the gold secretly to the
Aeginetans as though it
were bronze, thereby
making many Aeginetan
fortunes.

</td><td>

After hearing this reply, Lampon departed. Pausanias now
issued a proclamation that no one should touch the spoils, and
he ordered the helots to gather all the goods together in one
place. They scattered throughout the camp and found tents
adorned with gold and silver, couches gilded with gold and
silver, golden mixing bowls, libation bowls, and other drinking
vessels. [2] On the wagons they discovered sacks in which they
saw cauldrons of gold and silver. And they stripped the bodies
lying there of their bracelets, necklaces, and golden daggers,
but they paid no attention at all to the embroidered clothing.
[3] The helots presented and accounted for much of these
spoils—as much as they were unable to hide—but they stole
quite a bit and sold it to the Aeginetans. And so it was from this
time on that theAeginetans became very wealthy, as they were
buying gold from the helots as though it were bronze.

</td></tr>
<tr><td>

9.81
479
PLATAEA
After one-tenth of the
loot is dedicated to each
of three gods, Apollo,
Zeus, and Poseidon,
the rest—gold, silver,
women, horses, camels,
and other goods—is
distributed to the soldiers,
with ten of each category
set apart for Pausanias.

</td><td>

After bringing all the goods together, the Hellenes took out
a tenth for the god at Delphi, and from this they dedicated
a golden tripod set upon a three-headed serpent of bronze,
which stands next to the altar. They removed another tenth for
the god at Olympia, and from it dedicated a bronze statue of
Zeus fifteen feet tall, and another for the god at the isthmus,
from which was made a bronze Poseidon seven feet tall. After
taking out these tithes, they divided the rest, and each took
what he deserved of the Persians' concubines, gold, silver, other
goods, and the pack animals.[2] There are no reports about
everything that was taken and distributed to those who proved
the best at Plataea, but I for my part suppose that of what
remained, ten of every type of spoil were separated out and
given to Pausanias—women, horses, talents, camels, as well as
the other types of goods in the same proportion.

</td></tr>
<tr><td>

9.82
479
PLATAEA
Herodotus tells the
anecdote of
Pausanias'comparison
of the sumptuous
Persian dinner to that
of the Spartans.

</td><td>

It is also reported that Xerxes had left his tent to Mardonios
when he fled from Hellas, and that when Pausanias saw these
quarters of Mardonios and how they were furnished with
embroidered draperies, he ordered the breadbakers and the
cooks to prepare a meal for him like those they had made for
Mardonios. [2] When they had carried out their orders and
Pausanias saw the golden and silver couches with sumptuous
coverings and the tables, also of gold and silver, all set out with
a magnificent feast, he was struck with wonder at the good
things lying before him, and then, as a joke, ordered his servants
to prepare a Laconian meal. [3] When the banquet was ready,

</td></tr>
</table>

the difference between the two was great indeed, and Pausanias laughed, and then sent for the generals of the Hellenes. When they had all come to him, Pausanias, as he pointed to each of the meals that had been served, said, "Men of Hellas, I have brought you here together, because I wanted to show you what an idiot the leader of the Medes was. This was his lifestyle, but he came to us, who have this miserable way of life, in order to deprive us of it." That is what Pausanias is reported to have said to the generals of the Hellenes.

But later, well after these events, the Plataeans found chests made of gold and silver as well as other goods. And still later, something else appeared among the corpses, now bare of their flesh (for the Plataeans had collected all the bones in one place): a skull was found which had not a single suture, but was apparently all of bone. And the jaw on its upper part apparently has teeth all joined in one piece, also as a single bone, both the front teeth and the molars. The skeleton of this man measured seven and a half feet long.

The corpse of Mardonios had disappeared by the day after the battle, and I cannot say for certain who might have been responsible for its disappearance, but I have heard of many people from various places who allegedly buried Mardonios, and I know that many by now have received large rewards from Artontes, the son of Mardonios, in return for this deed. Although I am unable to tell for certain who secretly took the corpse of Mardonios and buried it, there is a rumor about that the one who did it was Dionysophanes, a man from Ephesus.

In any case, it seems that Mardonios was buried in some way or other. When the Hellenes at Plataea had finished dividing up the spoils, each group buried their own dead separately. The Lacedaemonians made three different tombs: [2] in one they buried the priests, who included Poseidonios, Amompharetos, Philokyon, and Kallikrates. So the priests were buried in one grave, and in another were the rest of the Spartiates, and in the third were the helots. That is how the Lacedaemonians buried their men. The Tegeans buried all their men together in a separate place, the Athenians had graves of their own, and the Megarians and Phleiasians also separately buried their men who had been killed by the cavalry. [3] The graves of all these were full of bodies, but according to what I have heard about all the other graves that are seen at Plataea, each of the peoples who felt disgraced by their absence from the battle piled up empty mounds for the sake of posterity, and even the so-called grave of the Aeginetans there, so I have been told, was heaped up ten years later at the request of the Aeginetans by Kleades son of Autodikos, a Plataean and their *proxenos*.

THE LANDMARK
THUCYDIDES

Edited by Robert B. Strassler

SPARTAN INSTITUTIONS AT THUCYDIDES

Social Structure

§1. Sparta was different, "other," almost un-Greek—or so it could be made to seem from the Athenian side of the fifth-century B.C. "Great Powers," divide (1.77.5; 5.105.3–4). Only a few favored non-Spartans knew Sparta well from the inside. Conversely, unwelcome foreign visitors might find themselves summarily expelled (2.39.1). But the experience of Thucydides was probably more typical. He complains in exasperation of "the secrecy of their government" (5.68.2), and his Athenian speakers emphasize the polar opposition between themselves and their principal foes in character as in institutions (1.69.4–71; 2.39; 8.96.5). These fundamental differences can almost all be traced to two Spartan peculiarities: their educational system and their relationship with the Helots of Laconia and Messenia.

§2. Unlike all other Greek city-states, Sparta had a comprehensively, minutely, and centrally organized system of education that was prescribed as a condition of attaining full Spartan, adult, citizen status. Its main emphasis was military. Boys were separated early from their mothers—indeed, from all females—and educated roughly in rigidly controlled packs divided and subdivided by age. Fighting, stealing, and finally even murdering (see §4) were enjoined as integral parts of the educative process. Basic literacy was apparently taught, so some Spartans at least could presumably read the few official documents their city chose to record and display (5.18.23). Music (5.70) and dancing (5.16) were also part of the prescribed curriculum, since they were crucial to performing the major religious festivals devoted to Apollo, such as the Carneia (5.54; 5.76.1), but they were also learned in significant measure for their military benefits. Hence, too, the conscious development of a clipped, military-style form of utterance (4.17.2; 4.84.2), which is still called by us "laconic" (after the Greek adjective meaning "Spartan"), just as we still speak of a "spartan"—that is, a spare, austere, self-denying—mode of existence. Between the ages of seven and thirty Spartan males spent almost their entire lives in communal dormitories, messes, or barracks; even married men were required to make their conjugal visits furtively, briefly, and under cover of darkness.

§3 The Helots, especially the more numerous portion living in Messenia to the west of Sparta on the far side of the eight-thousand-foot Taygetus mountain range, were the Spartans' enemy within, not least because they always and appreciably outnumbered their masters. Most were farmers producing the food, drink, and other basics (especially barley, pork, wine, and olive oil) that enabled all Spartans to live a barrack-style military life in Sparta instead of working for a living. But the Helots, though native Greeks, farmed the Spartans' land under a harsh yoke of servitude, so that many of them vehemently opposed the Spartan regime, yearned to regain the liberty and autonomy they imagined they had lost through earlier defeats (their name probably means "captives"), and were prepared to stake all on revolt (1.101.2; 2.27.2; 4.56.2). Spartan policy, therefore, as Thucydides starkly and accurately asserts, was "at all times … governed by the necessity of taking precautions against them" (4.80.2; cf. 1.132.4–5; 5.23.3—"the slave population").

§4 Precautions might exceptionally be intensified, as in 425–24, when, in response to the Athenians' exploitation of Helot disaffection following the vital loss of Pylos and Cythera (4.3.3; 4.55.1; 5.35.7), some two thousand selected troublemakers were secretly liquidated (4.80.5). But Spartans were routinely brought up, within the normal framework of their educational curriculum, to put Helots to death in peacetime. This occurred under cover of a general proclamation, repeated every autumn by each new board of ephors (see below), declaring war on the Helots collectively and thereby exonerating their Spartan killers in advance from the ritual pollution of homicide. There could not be a more perfect illustration of the Spartans' intense religiosity bordering on superstition that was perhaps another by-product of their military style of life.

Government Institutions

§5 The five ephors, chosen by a curious form of election from any Spartans who wished to stand, were Sparta's chief executive officials. They possessed very extensive powers in both the formulation and the execution of foreign and domestic policy (1.85.3; 1.86; 1.131.1; 2.2.1; 6.88.10). Collegiality and the majority principle did impose some constraints, but the annual oath they exchanged with the two Spartan hereditary kings indicates where the balance of authority rested: the ephors swore on behalf of the Spartan collectively to uphold the kingship so long as the kings themselves observed the laws (which the ephors interpreted and applied).

§6 Ephors, though, were annual officials, and the office could apparently be held only once. The two kings, on the other hand, and the other members of the thirty-strong Gerousia (Sparta's senate, also curiously elected, but only from men aged sixty or over who probably also had to belong to certain aristocratic families), held office for life and partly for that reason enjoyed exceptional prestige and authority. However, not even the kings' supposed direct descent from Heracles, "the demigod son of Zeus"

(5.16.2), nor their hereditary right to the overall command of any Spartan army or Spartan-led allied force, prevented them from being disciplined (5.63.2–4), and sometimes deposed and exiled (5.16). An adroit king such as Archidamus might seek to exploit his aura of prestige and abundant opportunities for patronage to exercise a decisive and sometimes lasting influence on policy. But in 432 not even Archidamus (1.80–85) and his supporters in the Gerousia could persuade the assembly of citizen warriors, which had the final say in matters of peace and war, from voting against immediate war with Athens—in this one known instance by a formal division rather than by its usual crude procedure of shouting (1.87).

Military Organization

§7. In his account of the great battle of Mantinea in 418, Thucydides provides a privileged glimpse of Sparta's unique and complex military organization in decisive and successful action (esp. 5.66, 5.69.2–7; cf. 4.34.1; 5.9). The goal of the Spartan educational system was to produce exceptionally disciplined and efficient hoplite infantrymen (see Appendix F, §7); the navy was very much an inferior Spartan service (1.142.2). For almost two centuries, indeed, the Spartans suffered no major reverses of any sort. Yet partly because of the constant internal Helot threat, the Spartans did not lightly undertake aggressive foreign wars (1.118.2; cf. 5.107), and they very rarely fought without large-scale allied support.

§8. Moreover, the Spartans experienced a growing and increasingly critical shortage of citizen military manpower, caused basically by internal socioeconomic deficiencies. Each Spartan citizen had to contribute a minimum of natural produce from the land worked for him by Helots toward the upkeep of the communal "mess" in which he lived and ate, and through which he exercised his military and other civic responsibilities. But in the period after the Persian Wars the number of Spartan citizens who could contribute the required minimum declined, through a process not entirely understood today, but which probably was the result of an increasing concentration of land in fewer hands. This socioeconomic manpower shortage was aggravated by the catastrophic earthquake of the 460s (1.101.2; 1.128.1; 2.27.2; 4.56.2) and by important losses in the Peloponnesian War.

§9 The Spartans therefore drew ever more heavily on non-Spartan troops to make up their frontline infantry force. In the first place, they had regular and increasing recourse to the hoplites of the perioikoi (literally, "dwellers around") whom they even brigaded in the same regiments as themselves. These perioikoi were free Greeks who lived in their own semiautonomous communities, mainly along the coasts of both Laconia (e.g., Epidaurus Limera and Thyrea [4.56.2]) and Messenia (e.g., Methone [2.25.1]), but also along the vulnerable northern border with Arcadia and Argos (e.g., the Sciritae [5.67.2; 5.68.3; 5.71.2–3; 5.73.1–2; cf. 5.33.1]). The perioikoi spoke the same dialect as the Spartans and resembled them in other cultural ways, but they enjoyed no political rights at Sparta and so had no say in Sparta's foreign affairs (3.92.5;

4.8.1; 4.53.2; 5.54.1; 5.67.1; 8.6.4; 8.22.1). Secondly, and paradoxically, the Spartans also had regular and increasing military recourse to Helots and various categories of liberated Helots, of which the most privileged but still awkwardly unassimilated were the neodamodeis (4.21; 5.67; 7.19.3; 7.58.3). All the same, the Peloponnesian War was decided not on land but at sea and above all by Persian money, rather than by traditional Spartan military prowess.

Paul Cartledge
Clare College
Cambridge University
Cambridge, England

But at last a time came when the tyrants of Athens and the far older tyrannies of the rest of Hellas were, with the exception of those in Sicily, once and for all put down by Sparta; for this city, though after the settlement of the Dorians, its present inhabitants, it suffered from factions for an unparalleled length of time, still at a very early period obtained good laws, and enjoyed a freedom from tyrants which was unbroken; it has possessed the same form of government for more than four hundred years, reckoning to the end of the late war, and has thus been in a position to arrange the affairs of the other states. Not many years after the deposition of the tyrants, the battle of Marathon was fought between the Medes and the Athenians. [2] Ten years afterwards the barbarian returned with the armada for the subjugation of Hellas. In the face of this great danger the command of the confederate Hellenes was assumed by the Spartans in virtue of their superior power; and the Athenians having made up their minds to abandon their city, broke up their homes, threw themselves into their ships, and became a naval people. This coalition, after repulsing the barbarian, soon afterwards split into two sections, which included the Hellenes who had revolted from the King, as well as those who had shared in the war. At the head of the one stood Athens, at the head of the other Sparta, one the first naval, the other the first military power in Hellas. [3] For a short time the league held together, till the Spartans and Athenians quarreled, and made war upon each other with their allies, a duel into which all the Hellenes sooner or later were drawn, though some might at first remain neutral. So that the whole period from the Median war to this, with some peaceful intervals, was spent by each power in war, either with its rival, or with its own revolted allies, and consequently afforded them constant practice in military matters, and that experience which is learnt in the school of danger.

1.18
HELLAS
Sparta put down Hellenic tyrants and led Greek resistance to Persia. After the Persians' defeat Athens and Sparta quarreled.

The policy of Sparta was not to exact tribute from her allies, but merely to secure their subservience to her interests by establishing oligarchies among them; Athens, on the contrary, had by degrees deprived hers of their ships, and imposed instead contributions in money on all except Chios and Lesbos. Both found their resources for this war separately to exceed the sum of their strength when the alliance flourished intact.

1.19
HELLAS
Thucydides describes the different policies of the Spartan and Athenian alliances.

1.20
ATHENS
Thucydides notes that
people accept traditions
that are clearly in error,
for example, the tale
about Harmodius and
Aristogiton.

Having now given the result of my inquiries into early times, I grant that there will be a difficulty in believing every particular detail. The way that most men deal with traditions, even traditions of their own country, is to receive them all alike as they are delivered, without applying any critical test whatever. [2] The Athenian public generally believe that Hipparchus was tyrant when he fell by the hands of Harmodius and Aristogiton. They do not know that Hippias, the eldest of the sons of Pisistratus, was really supreme; that Hipparchus and Thessalus were his brothers; and that Harmodius and Aristogiton, suspecting on the very day—indeed at the very moment fixed for the deed—that information had been conveyed to Hippias by their accomplices, concluded that he had been warned. They did not attack Hippias but, not liking to risk their lives and be apprehended for nothing, they fell upon Hipparchus near the temple of the daughters of Leos and slew him as he was arranging the Panathenaic procession. [3] There are many other unfounded ideas current among the rest of the Hellenes, even on matters of contemporary history which have not been obscured by time. For instance, there is the notion that the Spartan kings have two votes each, the fact being that they have only one; and that there is a military company of Pitane, there being simply no such thing. So little pains do the vulgar take in the investigation of truth, accepting readily the first story that comes to hand.

1.21
HELLAS
Thucydides believes his
conclusions to be reliable,
and notes that this war
was much greater than
earlier ones.

On the whole, however, the conclusions I have drawn from the proofs quoted may, I believe, safely be relied upon. Assuredly they will not be disturbed either by the verses of a poet displaying the exaggeration of his craft, or by the compositions of the chroniclers that are attractive at truth's expense; the subjects they treat of being out of the reach of evidence, and time having robbed most of them of historical value by enthroning them in the region of legend. Turning from these, we can rest satisfied with having proceeded upon the clearest data, and having arrived at conclusions as exact as can be expected in matters of such antiquity. [2] To come to this war; despite the known disposition of the actors in a struggle to overrate its importance, and when it is over to return to their admiration of earlier events, yet an examination of the facts will show that it was much greater than the wars which preceded it.

With reference to the speeches in this history, some were delivered before the war began, others while it was going on; some I heard myself, others I got from various quarters; it was in all cases difficult to carry them word for word in one's memory, so my habit has been to make the speakers say what was in my opinion demanded of them by the various occasions, of course adhering as closely as possible to the general sense of what they really said. [2] And with reference to the narrative of events, far from permitting myself to derive it from the first source that came to hand, I did not even trust my own impressions, but it rests partly on what I saw myself, partly on what others saw for me, the accuracy of the report being always tried by the most severe and detailed tests possible. [3] My conclusions have cost me some labor from the want of coincidence between accounts of the same occurrences by different eyewitnesses, arising sometimes from imperfect memory, sometimes from undue partiality for one side or the other. [4] The absence of romance in my history will, I fear, detract somewhat from its interest; but if it be judged useful by those inquirers who desire an exact knowledge of the past as an aid to the understanding of the future, which in the course of human things must resemble if it does not reflect it, I shall be content. In fine, I have written my work, not as an essay which is to win the applause of the moment, but as a possession for all time.

1.22
HELLAS
Thucydides discusses the speeches in his text. He says it lacks romance because he intends it to be "a possession for all time."

The Median war, the greatest achievement of past times, yet found a speedy decision in two actions by sea and two by land. The Peloponnesian War went on for a very long time and there occurred during it disasters of a kind and number that no other similar period of time could match. [2] Never had so many cities been taken and laid desolate, here by the barbarians, here by the parties contending (the old inhabitants being sometimes removed to make room for others); never was there so much banishing and bloodshedding, now on the field of battle, now in political strife. [3] Old stories of occurrences handed down by tradition, but scantily confirmed by experience, suddenly ceased to be incredible; there were earthquakes of unparalleled extent and violence; eclipses of the sun occurred with a frequency unrecorded in previous history; there were great droughts in sundry places and consequent famines, and that most calamitous and awfully fatal visitation, the plague. All this came upon them with the late war, [4] which was begun by

1.23
HELLAS
Thucydides compares the Persian war and the much longer Peloponnesian War, and states that the latter's true cause was Spartan fear of the growth of Athenian power.

the Athenians and Peloponnesians with the dissolution of the Thirty Years' Peace made after the conquest of Euboea. [5] To the question why they broke the treaty, I answer by placing first an account of their grounds of complaint and points of difference, that no one may ever have to ask the immediate cause which plunged the Hellenes into a war of such magnitude. [6] The real cause, however, I consider to be the one which was formally most kept out of sight. The growth of the power of Athens, and the alarm which this inspired in Sparta, made war inevitable. Still it is well to give the grounds alleged by either side, which led to the dissolution of the treaty and the breaking out of the war.

BOOK 1.66 – 1.146

1.66
432
HELLAS
Athens and Corinth complain much about Potidaea, yet there is still peace.

The Athenians and Peloponnesians had these antecedent grounds of complaint against each other: the complaint of Corinth was that her colony of Potidaea, and Corinthian and Peloponnesian citizens within it, was being besieged; that of Athens against the Peloponnesians that they had incited one of the cities in their alliance and liable for tribute, to revolt, and that they had come and were openly fighting against her on the side of the Potidaeans. For all this, war had not yet broken out: there was still truce for a while; for this was a private enterprise on the part of Corinth.

1.67
432
SPARTA
Many cities denounce Athens to the allies assembled at Sparta. The Corinthians speak last.

But the siege of Potidaea put an end to her inaction; she had men inside it: besides, she feared for the place. Immediately summoning the allies to Sparta, she came and loudly accused Athens of breach of the treaty and aggression on the rights of the Peloponnesus. [2] With her, the Aeginetans, formally unrepresented from fear of Athens, in secret proved not the least urgent of the advocates for war, asserting that they had not the independence guaranteed to them by the treaty. [3] After extending the summons to any of their allies and others who might have complaints to make of Athenian aggression, the Spartans held their ordinary assembly, and invited them to speak. [4] There were many who came forward and made their several accusations; among them the Megarians, in a long list of grievances, called special attention to the fact of their exclusion from the ports of the Athenian empire and the market of Athens, in defiance of the treaty. [5] Last of all the Corinthians came forward, and having let those who preceded them inflame the Spartans, now followed with a speech to this effect:

"Spartans! the confidence which you feel in your constitution and social order inclines you to receive any reflections of ours on other powers with a certain skepticism. Hence springs your moderation, but hence also the rather limited knowledge which you betray in dealing with foreign politics. [2] Time after time was our voice raised to warn you of the blows about to be dealt us by Athens, and time after time, instead of taking the trouble to ascertain the worth of our warnings, you contented yourselves with suspecting the speakers of being inspired by private interest. And so, instead of calling these allies together before the blow fell, you have delayed to do so till we are smarting under it; and of the allies it is not unfitting that we make this speech for we have very great complaints of highhanded treatment by the Athenians and of neglect by you. [3] Now if these assaults on the rights of Hellas had been made in the dark you might be unacquainted with the facts, and it would be our duty to enlighten you. As it is, long speeches are not needed where you see servitude accomplished for some of us, meditated for others—in particular for our allies—and prolonged preparations by the aggressor for the hour of war. [4] Or what, pray, is the meaning of their reception of Corcyra by fraud, and their holding it against us by force? What of the siege of Potidaea?—places one of which lies most conveniently for any action against the Thracian cities; while the other would have contributed a very large navy to the Peloponnesians?"

1.68
432
SPARTA
The Corinthians complain of Athenian aggression against them at Corcyra and Potidaea, and also of Spartan inaction, which both injures Sparta's allies and strengthens Sparta's rival.

The Corinthians assert that Spartan inaction has permitted Athens to grow at the expense of the Hellenes, and that Athens' perception of Sparta's acquiescence encourages her to commit further aggression. Once the Spartans could have stopped her easily, but Athens has now become such a formidable adversary that Hellenic confidence in Sparta is shaken.

"For all this you are responsible. You it was who first allowed them to fortify their city after the Persian war, and afterwards to erect the long walls—you who, then and now, are always depriving of freedom not only those whom they have enslaved, but also those who have as yet been your allies. For the true author of the subjugation of a people is not so much the immediate agent, as the power which permits it having the means to prevent it; particularly if that power aspires to the glory of being the liberator of Hellas. We are at last assembled. [2] It has not been easy to assemble, nor even now are our objects defined. We ought not to be still inquiring into the facts of our wrongs, but into the means for our defense. For the aggressors with matured plans to oppose to our indecision have cast threats aside and betaken themselves to action. [3] And we know what are the paths by which Athenian aggression travels, and how insidious is its progress. A degree of confidence she may feel from the idea that your bluntness of perception prevents your noticing her; but it is nothing to the impulse which her advance will receive from the knowledge that you see, but do not care to interfere. [4] You, Spartans, of all the Hellenes are alone inactive, and defend yourselves not by doing anything but by looking as if you would do something; you alone wait till the power of an enemy is becoming twice its original size, instead of crushing it in its infancy. [5] And yet the world used to say that you were to be depended upon; but in your case, we fear, it said more than the truth. The Mede, we ourselves know, had time to come from the ends of the earth to the Peloponnesus, without any force of yours worthy of the name advancing to meet him. But this was a distant enemy. Well, Athens at all events is a near neighbor, and yet Athens you utterly disregard; against Athens you prefer to act on the defensive instead of on the offensive, and to make it an affair of chances by deferring the struggle till she has grown far stronger than at first. And yet you know that on the whole the rock on which the barbarian was wrecked was himself, and that if our present enemy Athens has not again and again annihilated us, we owe it more to her blunders than to your protection. [6] Indeed, expectations from you have before now been the ruin of some, whose faith induced them to omit preparation."

"We hope that none of you will consider these words of remonstrance to be rather words of hostility; men remonstrate with friends who are in error, accusations they reserve for enemies who have wronged them."

"Besides, we consider that we have as good a right as anyone to point out a neighbor's faults, particularly when we contemplate the great contrast between the two national characters; a contrast of which, as far as we can see, you have little perception, having never yet considered what sort of antagonists you will encounter in the Athenians, how widely, how absolutely different from yourselves. [2] The Athenians are addicted to innovation, and their designs are characterized by swiftness alike in conception and execution; you have a genius for keeping what you have got, accompanied by a total want of invention, and when forced to act you never go far enough. [3] Again, they are adventurous beyond their power, and daring beyond their judgment, and in danger they are sanguine; your wont is to attempt less than is justified by your power, to mistrust even what is sanctioned by your judgment, and to fancy that from danger there is no release. [4] Further, there is promptitude on their side against procrastination on yours; they are never at home, you are most disinclined to leave it, for they hope by their absence to extend their acquisitions, you fear by your advance to endanger what you have left behind. [5] They are swift to follow up a success, and slow to recoil from a reverse. [6] Their bodies they spend ungrudgingly in their country's cause; their intellect they jealously husband to be employed in her service. [7] A scheme unexecuted is with them a positive loss, a successful enterprise a comparative failure. The deficiency created by the miscarriage of an undertaking is soon filled up by fresh hopes; for they alone are enabled to call a thing hoped for a thing got, by the speed with which they act upon their resolutions. [8] Thus they toil on

1.70
432
SPARTA
The Corinthians characterize the Athenians and the Spartans as opposites: where the Athenians are active, innovative, daring, quick, enterprising, acquisitive, and opportunistic, the Spartans are passive, cautious, conservative, timid, and slow. The Athenians take no rest and allow none to others.

in trouble and danger all the days of their life, with little opportunity for enjoying, being ever engaged in getting: their only idea of a holiday is to do what the occasion demands, and to them laborious occupation is less of a misfortune than the peace of a quiet life. [9] To describe their character in a word, one might truly say that they were born into the world to take no rest themselves and to give none to others."

"Such is Athens, your antagonist. And yet, Spartans, you still delay, and fail to see that peace stays longest with those who are not more careful to use their power justly than to show their determination not to submit to injustice. On the contrary, your ideal of fair dealing is based on the principle that if you do not injure others, you need not risk your own fortunes in preventing others from injuring you. [2] Now you could scarcely have succeeded in such a policy even with a neighbor like yourselves; but in the present instance, as we have just shown, your habits are old-fashioned as compared with theirs. [3] It is the law, as in the arts so in politics, that improvements ever prevail; and though fixed usages may be best for undisturbed communities, constant necessities of action must be accompanied by the constant improvement of methods. Thus it happens that the vast experience of Athens has carried her further than you on the path of innovation."

[4] "Here, at least, let your procrastination end. For the present, assist your allies and Potidaea in particular, as you promised, by a speedy invasion of Attica, and do not sacrifice friends and kindred to their bitterest enemies, and drive the rest of us in despair to some other alliance. [5] Such a step would not be condemned either by the gods who received our oaths, or by the men who witnessed them. The blame for a breach of a treaty cannot be laid on the people whom desertion compels to seek new relations, but on the power that fails to assist its confederate. [6] But if only you will act, we will stand by you; it would be unnatural for us to change, and never should we meet with such a congenial ally. [7] For these reasons choose the right course, and endeavor not to let the Peloponnesus under

1.71
432
SPARTA
The Corinthians conclude by blaming Sparta's old-fashioned ways for her failure to perceive the effectiveness of Athenian innovation. They beg Sparta "to assist Potidaea now as she had promised." They threaten to seek another alliance if the Spartans continue to fail them.

your supremacy degenerate from the prestige that it enjoyed under that of your ancestors."

Such were the words of the Corinthians. There happened to be Athenian envoys present at Sparta on other business. On hearing the speeches they thought themselves called upon to come before the Spartans. Their intention was not to offer a defense on any of the charges which the cities brought against them, but to show on a comprehensive view that it was not a matter to be hastily decided on, but one that demanded further consideration. There was also a wish to call attention to the great power of Athens, and to refresh the memory of the old and enlighten the ignorance of the young, from a notion that their words might have the effect of inducing them to prefer tranquillity to war. [2] So they came to the Spartans and said that they too, if there was no objection, wished to speak to their assembly. They replied by inviting them to come forward. The Athenians advanced, and spoke as follows:

1.72
432
SPARTA
Some Athenian envoys at Sparta ask for permission to address the assembly; it is granted.

"The object of our mission here was not to argue with your allies, but to attend to the matters on which our state despatched us. However, the vehemence of the outcry that we hear against us has prevailed on us to come forward. It is not to combat the accusations of the cities (indeed you are not the judges before whom either we or they can plead), but to prevent your taking the wrong course on matters of great importance by yielding too readily to the persuasions of your allies. We also wish to show on a review of the whole indictment that we have a fair title to our possessions, and that our country has claims to consideration. [2] We need not refer to remote antiquity; there we could appeal to the voice of tradition, but not to the experience of our audience. But to the Persian wars and contemporary history we must refer, although we are rather tired of continually bringing this subject forward. In our action during that war we ran great risk to obtain certain advantages: you had your share in the solid results, do not try to rob us of all share in the good that the glory may do us. [3] However, the story shall be told not so much to seek to be spared hostility as to testify against

1.73
432
SPARTA
The Athenians hope to show that their country merits consideration for its achievements, particularly in the Persian wars in which all Hellenes benefited from extraordinary and courageous Athenian efforts.

it, and to show, if you are so ill-advised as to enter into a struggle with Athens, what sort of an antagonist she is likely to prove. [4] We assert that at Marathon we were in the forefront of danger and faced the barbarian by ourselves. That when he came the second time, unable to cope with him by land we went on board our ships with all our people, and joined in the action at Salamis. This prevented his taking the Peloponnesians city by city, and ravaging them with his fleet; when the multitude of his vessels would have made any combination for self-defense impossible. [5] The best proof of this was furnished by the invader himself. Defeated at sea, he considered his power to be no longer what it had been, and retired as speedily as possible with the greater part of his army."

1.74
432
SPARTA

The Athenians claim to have provided the most powerful and essential contributions to the Hellenic success at Salamis, which proved to be the decisive blow to the Persian advance. They remind the Spartans that they courageously abandoned their homes and fought on even before the Peloponnesians arrived to help.

"Such, then, was the result of the matter, and it was clearly proved that it was on the fleet of Hellas that her cause depended. Well, to this result we contributed three very useful elements, namely, the largest number of ships, the ablest commander, and the most unhesitating patriotism. Our contingent of ships was little less than two-thirds of the whole four hundred; the commander was Themistocles, through whom chiefly it was that the battle took place in the straits, the acknowledged salvation of our cause. Indeed, this was the reason for your receiving him with honors such as had never been accorded to any foreign visitor. [2] While for daring patriotism we had no competitors. Receiving no reinforcements from behind, seeing everything in front of us already subjugated, we had the spirit, after abandoning our city, after sacrificing our property (instead of deserting the remainder of the league or depriving them of our services by dispersing), to throw ourselves into our ships and meet the danger, without a thought of resenting your having neglected to assist us. [3] We assert, therefore, that we conferred on you quite as much as we received. For you had a stake to fight for; the cities which you had left were still filled with your homes, and you had the prospect of enjoying them again; and your coming was prompted quite as much by fear for yourselves as for us; at all events, you never appeared till we had nothing left to lose. But we left behind us a city that was a city no longer, and staked our lives for a city that had an existence only in desperate hope, and so bore our full share in your deliverance and in ours. [4] But if we had copied others, and allowed fears for our territory to make us go over to the Mede before you came, or if we had allowed our ruin to break our spirit and prevent us embarking in our ships, your naval inferiority would have made a sea fight unnecessary, and his objects would have been peaceably attained."

"Surely, Spartans, neither by the patriotism that we displayed at that crisis, nor by the wisdom of our counsels, do we merit our extreme unpopularity with the Hellenes, not at least unpopularity for our empire. [2] That empire we acquired not by violence, but because you were unwilling to prosecute to its conclusion the war against the barbarian, and because the allies attached themselves to us and spontaneously asked us to assume the command. [3] And the nature of the case first compelled us to advance our empire to its present height; fear being our principal motive, though honor and interest afterwards came in. [4] And at last, when almost all hated us, when some had already revolted and had been subdued, when you had ceased to be the friends that you once were, and had become objects of suspicion and dislike, it appeared no longer safe to give up our empire; especially as all who left us would fall to you. [5] And no one can quarrel with a people for making, in matters of tremendous risk, the best provision that it can for its interest."

"You, at all events, Spartans, have used your supremacy to settle the states in the Peloponnesus as is agreeable to you. And if at the period of which we were speaking you had persevered to the end of the matter, and had incurred hatred in your command, we are sure that you would have made yourselves just as galling to the allies, and would have been forced to choose between a strong government and danger to yourselves. [2] It follows that it was not a very remarkable action, or contrary to the common practice of mankind, if we

1.74
The Athenians claim to have provided the most powerful and essential contributions to the Hellenic success at Salamis, which proved to be the decisive blow to the Persian advance. They remind the Spartans that they courageously abandoned their homes and fought on even before the Peloponnesians arrived to help.

1.76
432
SPARTA
The Athenians argue that Athens acted normally within the common practices of mankind to maintain her empire; fear, honor, and interest motivate her as they would any others in her place.

did accept an empire that was offered to us, and refused to give it up under the pressure of three of the strongest motives, fear, honor, and interest. And it was not we who set the example, for it has always been the law that the weaker should be subject to the stronger. Besides, we believed ourselves to be worthy of our position, and so you thought us till now, when calculations of interest have made you take up the cry of justice—a consideration which no one ever yet brought forward to hinder his ambition when he had a chance of gaining anything by might. [3] And praise is due to all who, if not so superior to human nature as to refuse dominion, yet respect justice more than their position compels them to do."

[4] "We imagine that our moderation would be best demonstrated by the conduct of who should be placed in our position; but even our equity has very unreasonably subjected us to condemnation instead of approval."

1.77
432
SPARTA
The Athenians speculate that Sparta would be equally hated were she to take Athens' place, and perhaps more so, because her peculiar institutions render her people unfit to rule other Hellenes.

"Our abatement of our rights in the contract trials with our allies, and our causing them to be decided by impartial laws at Athens, have gained us the character of being litigious. [2] And none care to inquire why this reproach is not brought against other imperial powers, who treat their subjects with less moderation than we do; the secret being that where force can be used, law is not needed. [3] But our subjects are so habituated to associate with us as equals, that any defeat whatever that clashes with their notions of justice, whether it proceeds from a legal judgment or from the power which our empire gives us, makes them forget to be grateful for being allowed to retain most of their possessions, and more vexed at a part being taken, than if we had from the first cast law aside and openly gratified our covetousness. If we had done so, they would not have disputed that the weaker must give way to the stronger. [4] Men's indignation, it seems, is more excited by legal wrong than by violent wrong; the first looks like being cheated by an equal, the second like being compelled by a superior. [5] At all events they contrived to put up with much worse treatment than this from the Persians, yet they think our rule severe, and this is to be expected, for the present always weighs heavy on the conquered. This at least is certain. [6] If you were to succeed in overthrowing us and in taking our place, you would speedily lose the popularity with which fear of us has invested you, if your policy now were to be at all like the sample you gave during the brief period of your command against the Mede. Not only is your life at home regulated by rules and institutions incompatible with those of others, but your citizens abroad act neither on these rules nor on those which are recognized by the rest of Hellas."

"Take time then in forming your resolution, as the matter is of great importance; and do not be persuaded by the opinions and complaints of others and so bring trouble on yourselves, but consider the vast influence of accident in war, before you are engaged in it. [2] As it continues, it generally becomes an affair of chances, chances from which neither of us is exempt, and whose event we must risk in the dark. [3] It is a common mistake in going to war to begin at the wrong end, to act first, and wait for disaster to discuss the matter. [4] But we are not yet by any means so misguided, nor, so far as we can see, are you; accordingly, while it is still open to us both to choose aright, we bid you not to dissolve the treaty, or to break your oaths, but to have our differences settled by arbitration according to our agreement. Or else we take the gods who heard the oaths to witness, and if you begin hostilities, whatever line of action you choose, we will endeavor to defend ourselves against you."

1.78
432
SPARTA
In conclusion, the Athenians advise the Spartans to decide carefully, reminding them of the chances of war and noting that the treaty calls for disputes to be submitted to arbitration.

Such were the words of the Athenians. After the Spartans had heard the complaints of the allies against the Athenians, and the observations of the latter, they made all withdraw, and consulted by themselves on the question before them. [2] The opinions of the majority all led to the same conclusion; the Athenians were open aggressors, and war must be declared at once. But Archidamus, the Spartan king, who had the reputation of being at once a wise and a moderate man, came forward and made the following speech:

1.79
432
SPARTA
The Spartans declare the Athenians to be aggressors.

1.80
432
SPARTA
The Spartan king,
Archidamus, warns the
Spartans that Athens is a
powerful adversary with
many advantages in war.
He advises them to prepare
carefully for such a struggle
and not to act rashly.

"I have not lived so long, Spartans, without having had the experience of many wars, and I see those among you of the same age as myself, who will not fall into the common misfortune of longing for war from inexperience or from a belief in its advantage and its safety. [2] This, the war on which you are now debating, would be one of the greatest magnitude, on a sober consideration of the matter. [3] In a struggle with Peloponnesians and neighbors our strength is of the same character, and it is possible to move swiftly on the different points. But a struggle with a people who live in a distant land, who have also an extraordinary familiarity with the sea, and who are in the highest state of preparation in every other department; with wealth private and public, with ships, and horses, and hoplites, and a population such as no one other Hellenic place can equal, and lastly a large number of tributary allies—what can justify us in rashly beginning such a struggle? Wherein is our trust that we should rush on it unprepared? [4] Is it in our ships? There we are inferior; while if we are to practice and become a match for them, time must intervene. Is it in our money? There we have a far greater deficiency. We neither have it in our treasury, nor are we ready to contribute it from our private funds."

1.81
432
SPARTA
Archidamus points out
that Sparta can only
devastate Attica, which will
not harm Athens materially.
He warns that the war will
not be short, and wonders
aloud how Sparta can win.

"Confidence might possibly be felt in our superiority in hoplites and population, which will enable us to invade and devastate their lands. [2] But the Athenians have plenty of other land in their empire, and can import what they want by sea. [3] Again, if we are to attempt an insurrection of their allies, these will have to be supported with a fleet, most of them being islanders. [4] What then is to be our war? For unless we can either beat them at sea, or deprive them of the revenues which feed their navy, we shall meet with little but disaster. [5] Meanwhile our honor will be pledged to keeping on, particularly if it be the opinion that we began the quarrel. [6] For let us never be elated by the fatal hope of the war being quickly ended by the devastation of their lands. I fear rather that we may leave it as a legacy to our children; so improbable is it that the Athenian spirit will be the slave of their land, or Athenian experience be cowed by war."

"Not that I would bid you be so unfeeling as to suffer them to injure your allies, and to refrain from unmasking their intrigues; but I do bid you not to take up arms at once, but to send and remonstrate with them in a tone not too suggestive of war, nor again too suggestive of submission, and to employ the interval in perfecting our own preparations. The means will be, first, the acquisition of allies, Hellenic or barbarian it matters not, so long as they are an accession to our strength naval or financial—I say Hellenic or barbarian, because the odium of such an accession to all who like us are the objects of the designs of the Athenians is taken away by the law of self-preservation—and secondly the development of our home resources. [2] If they listen to our embassy, so much the better; but if not, after the lapse of two or three years our position will have become materially strengthened, and we can then attack them if we think proper. [3] Perhaps by that time the sight of our preparations, backed by language equally significant, will have disposed them to submission, while their land is still untouched, and while their counsels may be directed to the retention of advantages as yet undestroyed. [4] For the only light in which you can view their land is that of a hostage in your hands, a hostage the more valuable the better it is cultivated. This you ought to spare as long as possible, and not make them desperate, and so increase the difficulty of dealing with them. [5] For if while still unprepared, hurried on by the complaints of our allies, we are induced to lay it waste, have a care that we do not bring deep disgrace and deep perplexity upon the Peloponnesus. [6] Complaints, whether of communities or individuals, it is possible to adjust; but war undertaken by a coalition for sectional interests, whose progress there is no means of foreseeing, may not be easily or creditably settled."

1.83
432
SPARTA
Archidamus asserts that
Sparta must accumulate
money for a war with
Athens.

1.84
432
SPARTA
Archidamus tells Sparta to
ignore her allies' impatient
calls for action and to move
slowly and moderately. He
praises Spartan character,
a product of practical,
limited education, and adds
that Sparta traditionally
assumes that her adversaries
will plan wisely and not
blunder.

"And none need think it cowardice for a large number of confederates to pause before they attack a single city. [2] The Athenians have allies as numerous as our own, and allies that pay tribute, and war is a matter not so much of arms as of money, which makes arms of use. And this is more than ever true in a struggle between a continental and a maritime power. [3] First, then, let us provide money, and not allow ourselves to be carried away by the talk of our allies before we have done so: as we shall have the largest share of responsibility for the consequences be they good or bad, we have also a right to a tranquil inquiry respecting them."

"And the slowness and procrastination, the parts of our character that are most assailed by their criticism, need not make you blush. If we undertake the war without preparation, we should by hastening its commencement only delay its conclusion: further, a free and a famous city has through all time been ours. [2] The quality which they condemn is really nothing but a wise moderation; thanks to its possession, we alone do not become insolent in success and give way less than others in misfortune; we are not carried away by the pleasure of hearing ourselves cheered on to risks which our judgment condemns; nor, if annoyed, are we any the more convinced by attempts to exasperate us by accusation. [3] We are both warlike and wise, and it is our sense of order that makes us so. We are warlike, because self-control contains honor as a chief constituent, and honor bravery. And we are wise, because we are educated with too little learning to despise the laws, and with too severe a self-control to disobey them, and are brought up not to be too knowing in useless matters—such as the knowledge which can give a specious criticism of an enemy's plans in theory, but fails to assail them with equal success in practice—but are taught to consider that the schemes of our enemies are not dissimilar to our own, and that the freaks of chance are not determinable by calculation. [4] In practice we always base our preparations against an enemy on the assumption that his plans are good; indeed, it is right to rest our hopes not on a belief in his blunders, but on the soundness of our provisions. Nor ought we to believe that there is much difference between man and man, but to think that the superiority lies with him who is reared in the severest school."

"These practices, then, which our ancestors have delivered to us, and by whose maintenance we have always profited, must not be given up. And we must not be hurried into deciding in a day's brief space a question which concerns many lives and fortunes and many cities, and in which honor is deeply involved—but we must decide calmly. This our strength peculiarly enables us to do. [2] As for the Athenians, send to them on the matter of Potidaea, send on the matter of the alleged wrongs of the allies, particularly as they are prepared to submit matters to arbitration, for one should not proceed against a party who offers arbitration as one would against a wrongdoer. Meanwhile do not omit preparation for war. This decision will be the best for yourselves and the most terrible to your opponents."

1.85
432
SPARTA
Archidamus concludes that the Spartans must decide calmly. He reminds them that Athens offers arbitration, but asks them to continue to prepare for war.

[3] Such were the words of Archidamus. Last came forward Sthenelaidas, one of the *ephors* for that year, and spoke to the Spartans as follows:

"The long speech of the Athenians I do not pretend to understand. They said a good deal in praise of themselves, but nowhere denied that they are injuring our allies and the Peloponnesus. And yet if they behaved well against the Persians in the past, but ill toward us now, they deserve double punishment for having ceased to be good and for having become bad. [2] We meanwhile are the same then and now, and shall not, if we are wise, disregard the wrongs of our allies, or put off till tomorrow the duty of assisting those who must suffer today. [3] Others have much money and ships and horses, but we have good allies whom we must not give up to the Athenians, nor by lawsuits and words decide the matter, as it is anything but in word that we are harmed, but render instant and powerful help. [4] And let us not be told that it is fitting for us to deliberate under injustice; long deliberation is rather fitting

1.86
432
SPARTA
The Spartan ephor Sthenelaidas demands a declaration of war against Athens.

for those who have injustice in contemplation. [5] Vote therefore, Spartans, for war, as the honor of Sparta demands, and neither allow the further aggrandizement of Athens, nor betray our allies to ruin, but with the gods let us advance against the aggressors."

1.87
432
SPARTA
The Spartans vote by acclamation to declare war and to convene a decisive meeting of all their allies.

With these words he, as ephor, himself put the question to the assembly of the Spartans. [2] He said that he could not determine which was the loudest acclamation (their mode of decision is by acclamation, not by voting); the fact being that he wished to make them declare their opinion openly and thus to increase their ardor for war. Accordingly he said, "All Spartans who are of opinion that the treaty has been broken, and that Athens is guilty, leave your seats and go there," pointing out a certain place; "all who are of the opposite opinion, there." [3] They accordingly stood up and divided; and those who held that the treaty had been broken were in a decided majority. [4] Summoning the allies, they told them that their opinion was that Athens had been guilty of injustice, but that they wished to convoke all the allies and put it to the vote; in order that they might make war, if they decided to do so, on a common resolution. [5] Having thus gained their point, the delegates returned home at once; the Athenian envoys a little later, when they had dispatched the objects of their mission. [6] This decision of the assembly judging that the treaty had been broken, was made in the fourteenth year of the Thirty Years' Peace, which was entered into after the affair of Euboea.

1.88
431
SPARTA
Fearing Athen's growing power, Sparta votes for war.

The Spartans voted that the treaty had been broken, and that war must be declared, not so much because they were persuaded by the arguments of the allies, as because they feared the growth of the power of the Athenians, seeing most of Hellas already subject to them.

1.89
479/8
PENTECONTAETIA
HELLESPONT
Thucydides tells how Athens grew powerful after Persia's defeat.

The way in which Athens came to be placed in the circumstances under which her power grew was this. [2] After the Persians had returned from Europe, defeated by sea and land by the Hellenes, and after those of them who had fled with their ships to Mycale had been destroyed, Leotychides, king of the Spartans, the commander of the Hellenes at Mycale, departed home with the allies from the Peloponnesus. But the Athenians and the allies from Ionia and Hellespont, who had now revolted from the King, remained and laid siege to Sestos, which was still held by the Persians. After wintering before it, they became masters of the place on its evacuation by the barbarians; and after this they sailed away from Hellespont to their respective cities. [3] Meanwhile the Athenian people, after the departure of the barbarian from their country, at once proceeded to bring over their children and wives, and such property as they had left, from the places where they had deposited them, and prepared to rebuild their city and their walls. For only isolated portions of the circumference had been left standing, and most of the houses were in ruins; though a few remained, in which the Persian grandees had taken up their quarters.

Perceiving what they were going to do, the Spartans sent an embassy to Athens. They would have themselves preferred to see neither her nor any other city in possession of a wall; though here they acted principally at the instigation of their allies, who were alarmed at the strength of her newly acquired navy, and the valor which she had displayed in the war with the Persians. [2] They begged her not only to abstain from building walls for herself, but also to join them in throwing down the remaining walls of the cities outside the Peloponnesus. They did not express openly the suspicious intention with regard to the Athenians that lay behind this proposal but urged that by these means the barbarians, in the case of a third invasion, would not have any strong place, such as in this invasion he had in Thebes, for his base of operation; and that the Peloponnesus would suffice for all as a base both for retreat and offense. [3] After the Spartans had thus spoken, they were, on the advice of Themistocles, immediately dismissed by the Athenians, with the answer that ambassadors should be sent to Sparta to discuss the question. Themistocles told the Athenians to send him off with all speed to Lacedaemon, but not to despatch his colleagues as soon as they had selected them, but to wait until they had raised their wall to the height from which defense was possible. Meanwhile the whole population in the city was to labor at the wall, the Athenians, their wives, and their children, sparing no edifice, private or public, which might be of any use to the work, but throwing all down. [4] After giving these instructions, and adding that he would be responsible for all other matters there, he departed. [5] Arrived at Sparta he did not seek an audience with the magistrates, but tried to gain time and made excuses. When any of the authorities asked

1.90
479/8
ATHENS
Sparta asks Athens not to rebuild its city wall. Themistocles goes to Sparta to discuss the matter and to delay a Spartan response while the Athenians hastily build a new city wall.

him why he did not appear in the assembly, he would say that he was waiting for his colleagues, who had been detained in Athens by some engagement; however, that he expected their speedy arrival, and wondered that they were yet there.

1.91
479/8
SPARTA
Themistocles' stratagem succeeds. After the wall is completed, Themistocles tells Sparta that Athens will look after her own interests.

At first the Spartans trusted the words of Themistocles, through their friendship for him; but when others arrived, all distinctly declaring that the work was going on and already attaining some elevation, they could not fail to believe them. [2] Aware of this, he told them that rumors are deceptive, and should not be trusted; they should send some reputable persons from Sparta to inspect, whose report might be trusted. [3] They despatched them accordingly. Concerning these Themistocles secretly sent word to the Athenians to detain them as far as possible without putting them under open constraint, and not to let them go until they had themselves returned. For his colleagues had now joined him, Abronichus son of Lysicles, and Aristides son of Lysimachus, with the news that the wall was sufficiently advanced; and he feared that when the Spartans heard the facts, they might refuse to let them go. [4] So the Athenians detained the envoys according to his message, and Themistocles had an audience with the Spartans and at last openly told them that Athens was now fortified sufficiently to protect its inhabitants; that any embassy which the Spartans or their allies might wish to send to them should in future proceed on the assumption that the people to whom they were going was able to distinguish both its own and the general interests; [5] that when the Athenians thought fit to abandon their city and to embark in their ships, they ventured on that perilous step without consulting them, and that on the other hand, wherever they had deliberated with the Spartans, they had proved themselves to be in judgment second to none; [6] and that they now thought it fit that their city should have a wall, and that this would be more for the advantage of both the citizens of Athens and the Hellenic confederacy, [7] for without equal military strength it was impossible to contribute equal or fair counsel to the common interest. It followed, he observed, either that all the members of the confederacy should be without walls, or that the present step should be considered a right one.

The Spartans did not betray any open signs of anger against the Athenians at what they heard. The embassy, it seems, was prompted not by a desire to obstruct, but to guide the counsels of their government: besides, Spartan feeling was at that time very friendly toward Athens on account of the patriotism which she had displayed in the struggle with the Mede. Still the defeat of their wishes could not but cause them secret annoyance. The envoys of each state departed home without complaint.

In this way the Athenians walled their city in a short space of time. [2] To this day the building shows signs of the haste of its execution; the foundations are laid of stones of all kinds, and in some places not wrought or fitted, but placed just in the order in which they were brought by the different hands; and many columns, too, from tombs and sculptured stones were put in with the rest. For the bounds of the city were extended at every point of the circumference; and so they laid hands on everything without exception in their haste. [3] Themistocles also persuaded them to finish the walls of the Piraeus, which had been begun before, in his year of office as archon; being influenced alike by the fineness of a locality that has three natural harbors, and by the great start which the Athenians would gain in the acquisition of power by becoming a naval people. [4] For the first ventured to tell them to stick to the sea and forthwith began to lay the foundations of the empire. [5] It was by his advice, too, that they built the walls of that thickness which can still be discerned round the Piraeus, the stones being brought up by two wagons meeting each other. Between the walls thus formed there was neither rubble nor mortar, but great stones hewn square and fitted together, cramped to each other on the outside with iron and lead. About half the height that he intended was finished. [6] His idea was by their size and thickness to keep off the attacks of an enemy; he thought that they might be adequately defended by a small garrison of invalids, and the rest be freed for service in the fleet. [7] For the fleet claimed most of his attention. He saw, as I think, that the approach by sea was easier for the King's army than that by land: he also thought the Piraeus more valuable than the upper city; indeed, he was always advising the Athenians, if a day should come when they were hard pressed by land, to go down into the Piraeus, and defy the world with their fleet. In this way, therefore, the Athenians completed their wall, and

1.92
478
SPARTA
Sparta accepts the Athenian wall with outward grace but secret annoyance.

1.93
478
ATHENS
Themistocles fortifies the Piraeus, foreseeing that Athens would grow great through naval power.

commenced their other buildings immediately after the retreat of the Persians.

Meanwhile Pausanias son of Cleombrotus was sent out from Sparta as commander-in-chief of the Hellenes, with twenty ships from the Peloponnesus. With him sailed the Athenians with thirty ships, and a number of the other allies. [2] They made an expedition against Cypras and subdued most of the island, and afterwards against Byzantium, which was in the hands of the Persians, and compelled it to surrender. This event took place while the Spartans were still supreme. [1.95.1] But the violence of Pausanias had already begun to be disagreeable to the Hellenes, particularly to the Ionians and the newly liberated populations. These resorted to the Athenians and requested them as their kinsmen to become their leaders, and to stop any attempt at violence on the part of Pausanias. [2] The Athenians accepted their overtures, and determined to put down any attempt of the kind and to settle everything else as their interests might seem to demand. [3] In the meantime the Spartans recalled Pausanias for an investigation of the reports which had reached them. Manifold and grave accusations had been brought against him by Hellenes arriving in Sparta; and, to all appearance, his conduct seemed more like that of a despot than of a general. [4] As it happened, his recall came just at the time when the hatred which he had inspired had induced the allies to desert him, the soldiers from the Peloponnesus excepted, and to range themselves by the side of the Athenians. [5] On his arrival at Lacedaemon, he was censured for his private acts of oppression, but was acquitted on the heaviest counts and pronounced not guilty; it must be known that the charge of Medism formed one of the principal, and to all appearance one of the best-founded, articles against him. [6] The Spartans did not, however, restore him to his command, but sent out Dorkis and certain others with a small force; who found the allies no longer inclined to concede to them the command. [7] Perceiving this they departed, and the Spartans did not send out any to succeed them. They feared for those who went out a deterioration similar to that observable in Pausanias; besides, they desired to be rid of the war against the Persians, and were satisfied of the competency of the Athenians for the position, and of their friendship at the time toward themselves.

1.94
478
HELLESPONT
Pausanias leads a fleet against Cyprus and Byzantium.

1.95
478
HELLESPONT
Pausanias grows arrogant and unpopular. Spartan leadership at sea is rejected by the allies in favor of Athens. Sparta accepts this decision.

The Athenians having thus succeeded to the supremacy by the voluntary act of the allies through their hatred of Pausanias, determined which cities were to contribute money against the barbarian, and which ships; their professed object being to retaliate for their sufferings by ravaging the King's country. [2] Now was the time that the office of "Treasurers for Hellas" was first instituted by the Athenians. These officers received the tribute, as the money contributed was called. The tribute was first fixed at four hundred and sixty talents. The common treasury was at Delos, and the congresses were held in the temple.

Initially, the Athenians commanded autonomous allies and made their decisions in general congresses. Their supremacy grew during the interval between the present war and the Persian wars, through their military and political actions recounted below against the barbarians, against their own allies in revolt, and against the Peloponnesians whom they encountered on various occasions. [2] My reason for relating these events, and for venturing on this digression, is that this passage of history has been omitted by all my predecessors, who have confined themselves either to Hellenic history before the Persian wars, or to the Persian wars itself. Hellanicus, it is true, did touch on these events in his Athenian history; but he is somewhat concise and not accurate in his dates. Besides, the history of these events contains an explanation of the growth of the Athenian empire.

First, under the command of Cimon son of Miltiades, the Athenians besieged and captured Eion on the Strymon from the Persians, and made slaves of the inhabitants. [2] Next they enslaved Scyros the island in the Aegean, containing a Dolopian population, and colonized it themselves. [3] This was followed by a war against Carystus, in which the rest of Euboea remained neutral, and which was ended by surrender on conditions. [4] After this Naxos left the confederacy, and a war ensued, and she had to return after a siege; this was the first instance of the confederation being forced to subjugate an allied city, a precedent which was followed by that of the rest in the order which circumstances prescribed.

1.96
478
DELOS
Athens forms a new anti-Persian alliance.

1.97
477–31
HELLAS
Thucydides describes the growth of Athenian power, noting that no other historian has covered this topic adequately.

1.98
476–67
AEGEAN AREA
Athens' new alliance attacks Eion, Scyros, and Carystus, and defeats a revolt by Naxos.

1.99
AEGEAN AREA
Athens grows less popular as it strictly requires military and monetary contributions to the alliance.

Of all the causes of defection, that connected with arrears of tribute and vessels, and with failure of service, was the chief; for the Athenians were very severe and exacting, and made themselves offensive by applying the screw of necessity to men who were not used to and in fact not disposed for any continuous labor. [2] In some other respects the Athenians were not the old popular rulers they had been at first; and if they had more than their fair share of service, it was correspondingly easy for them to reduce any that tried to leave the confederacy. [3] For this the allies had themselves to blame; the wish to get off service making most of them arrange to pay their share of the expense in money instead of in ships, and so to avoid having to leave their homes. Thus while Athens was increasing her navy with the funds which they contributed, a revolt always found them without resources or experience for war.

1.100
467?
ASIA
The Persians are defeated on the Eurymedon River.
465?
THRACE
Thasos revolts.
The Athenians are defeated at Amphipolis.

Next we come to the actions by land and by sea at the river Eurymedon, between the Athenians with their allies, and the Persians, when the Athenians won both battles on the same day under the leadership of Cimon son of Miltiades, and captured and destroyed the whole Phoenician fleet, consisting of two hundred vessels. [2] Some time afterwards occurred the defection of the Thasians, caused by disagreements about the markets on the opposite coast of Thrace, and about the mine in their possession. Sailing with a fleet to Thasos, the Athenians defeated them at sea and effected a landing on the island. [3] About the same time they sent ten thousand settlers of their own citizens and the allies to settle the place then called Ennea Hodoi (or Nine Ways), now Amphipolis. They succeeded in gaining possession of Ennea Hodoi from the Edonians, but on advancing into the interior of Thrace were cut off in Brabescus, a city of the Edonians, by the assembled Thracians, who regarded the settlement of the place Ennea Hodoi as an act of hostility.

1.101
466–62?
SPARTA
Promised Spartan aid to Thasos is prevented by earthquake and Helot revolt. Thasos surrenders on terms.

Meanwhile the Thasians being defeated in the field and suffering siege, appealed to Sparta, and desired her to assist them by an invasion of Attica. [2] Unknown to the Athenians, she promised and intended to do so, but was prevented by the occurrence of the earthquake, accompanied by the secession of the Helots and the Thuriats and Aethaeans of the perioikoi to Ithome. Most of the Helots were the descendants of the old Messenians that were enslaved in the famous war; and so all of them came to be called Messenians. [3] The Spartans thus being engaged in a war with the rebels in Ithome, the Thasians in the third year of the siege obtained terms from the Athenians by razing their walls, delivering up their ships, and arranging to pay the moneys demanded at once, and tribute in future; giving up their possessions on the mainland together with the mine.

The Spartans meanwhile finding the war against the rebels in Ithome was likely to be a long one, invoked the aid of their allies, and especially of the Athenians, who came in some force under the command of Cimon. [2] The reason for this pressing summons lay in their reputed skill in siege operations; a long siege had taught the Spartans their own deficiency in this art, else they would have taken the place by assault. [3] The first open quarrel between the Spartans and Athenians arose out of this expedition. The Spartans, when an assault failed to take the place, apprehensive of the enterprising and revolutionary character of the Athenians, and further looking upon them as of alien extraction, began to fear that if they remained, they might be persuaded by the besieged in Ithome to attempt some political changes. They accordingly dismissed them alone of the allies, without declaring their suspicions, but merely saying that they had now no need of them. [4] But the Athenians, aware that their dismissal did not proceed from the more honorable reason of the two, but from suspicions which had been conceived, went away deeply offended, and conscious of having done nothing to merit such treatment from the Spartans; and the instant that they returned home they broke off the alliance which had been made against the Mede, and allied themselves with Sparta's enemy Argos; each of the contracting parties taking the same oaths and making the same alliance with the Thessalians.

Meanwhile the rebels in Ithome, unable to prolong further a ten years' resistance, surrendered to Sparta; the conditions being that they should depart from the Peloponnesus under safe conduct, and should never set foot in it again: [2] anyone who might hereafter be found there was to be the slave of his captor. It must be known that the Spartans had an old oracle from Delphi, to the effect that they should let go the suppliant of Zeus at Ithome. [3] So they went forth with their children and their wives, and being received by Athens because of the hatred

1.102
462–61?
MESSENE
Athens sends troops to help the Spartans fight the Helots. When they are rudely dismissed, Athens renounces her alliance with Sparta.

1.103
457–56
MESSENE
Given permission to leave Laconia, the Helots surrender and are settled in Naupactus by the Athenians.
MEGARA
A dispute with Corinth leads Megara to ally herself with Athens.

that she now felt for the Spartans, were located at Naupactus, which she had lately taken from the Ozolian Locrians. [4] The Athenians received another addition to their confederacy in the Megarians; who left the Spartan alliance, annoyed by a war about boundaries forced on them by Corinth. The Athenians occupied Megara and Pegae, and built for the Megarians their long walls from the city to Nisaea, in which they placed an Athenian garrison. This was the principal cause of the Corinthians conceiving such a deadly hatred against Athens.

1.104
460?
EGYPT
An Athenian fleet sails to Egypt to assist a revolt there against the Persians.

Meanwhile Inaros son of Psammetichus, a Libyan king of the Libyans on the Egyptian border, having his headquarters at Marea, the city above Pharos, caused a revolt of almost the whole of Egypt from King Artaxerxes, and placing himself at its head, invited the Athenians to his assistance. [2] Abandoning a Cyprian expedition upon which they happened to be engaged with two hundred ships of their own and their allies, the Athenians arrived in Egypt and sailed from the sea into the Nile, made themselves masters of the river and two-thirds of Memphis, and addressed themselves to the attack of the remaining third, which is called White Castle. Within it were Persians and Medes who had taken refuge there, and Egyptians who had not joined the rebellion.

1.105
459?
TROEZEN
An Athenian attack on Halieis is repelled, but the Peloponnesian fleet is defeated off Cecryphalia.
458?
AEGINA
Athens defeats the Aeginetans at sea and besieges their city.
MEGARID
A Corinthian attack on Megara is stopped by a reserve Athenian army.

At this time, other Athenians, making a descent from their fleet upon Halieis, were engaged by a force of Corinthians and Epidaurians; and the Corinthians were victorious. Afterwards the Athenians engaged the Peloponnesian fleet off Cecryphalia; and the Athenians were victorious. [2] Subsequently, war broke out between Aegina and Athens, and there was a great battle at sea off Aegina between the Athenians and Aeginetans, each being aided by their allies; in which victory remained with the Athenians, who took seventy of the enemy's ships, and landed in the country and commenced a siege under the command of Leocrates son of Stroebus. [3] Upon this the Peloponnesians, desirous of aiding the Aeginetans, threw into Aegina a force of three hundred hoplites, who had before been serving with the Corinthians and Epidaurians. Meanwhile the Corinthians and their allies occupied the heights of Geraneia, and marched down into the Megarid, in the belief that with a large force absent in Aegina and Egypt, Athens would be unable to help the Megarians without raising the siege of Aegina. [4] But the Athenians, instead of moving the army at Aegina, raised a force of the old and young men that had been left in the city, and marched into the Megarid under the command of Myronides. [5] After a drawn battle with the Corinthians, the rival hosts parted, each with the impression that they had gained the victory. [6] The Athenians, however, if anything, had rather the advantage, and on the departure of the Corinthians set up a trophy. Urged by the taunts of the elders in their city, the Corinthians made their preparations, and about twelve days afterwards came and set up their trophy as victors. Sallying out from Megara, the Athenians destroyed the party that was employed in erecting the trophy, and engaged and defeated the rest.

In the retreat of the vanquished army, a considerable division, pressed by the pursuers and mistaking the road, dashed into a field on some private property, with a deep trench all round it and no way out. [2] Being acquainted with the place, the Athenians hemmed their front with hoplites, and placing the light troops round in a circle, stoned all who had gone in. Corinth here suffered a severe blow. The bulk of her army continued its retreat home.

About this time the Athenians began to build the long walls to the sea, that toward Phaleram and that toward the Piraeus. [2] Meanwhile the Phocians made an expedition against Doris, the old home of the Spartans, containing the cities of Boeum, Cytinium, and Erineum. They had taken one of these cities, when the Spartans under Nicomedes son of Cleombrotus, commanding for King Pleistoanax son of Pausanias, who was still a minor, came to the aid of the Dorians with fifteen hundred hoplites of their own, and ten thousand of their allies. After compelling the Phocians to restore the city on conditions, they began their retreat. [8] The route by sea across the Crisaean gulf exposed them to the risk of being stopped by the Athenian fleet; that by land across Geraneia seemed scarcely safe with the Athenians holding Megara and Pegae, for the pass was a difficult one, and was always guarded by the Athenians; and in the present instance, the Spartans had information that they meant to dispute their passage. [4] So they resolved to remain in Boeotia, and to consider which would be the safest line of march. They had also another reason for this resolve. Secret encouragement had been given them by a party in Athens, who hoped to put an end to the reign of democracy and the building

1.106
458?
MEGARID
A division of Corinthians is destroyed.

1.107
457
ATHENS
Athens begins work on the Long Walls.
PHOCIS
A Spartan army rescues Doris from Phocis but retires to Boeotia when the routes home are blocked.
BOEOTIA
The Athenian army advances to engage the Peloponnesians; Thessalian cavalry joins them but defects during the battle.

of the long walls. [5] Meanwhile the Athenians marched against them with their whole levy and a thousand Argives and the respective contingents of the rest of their allies. Altogether they were fourteen thousand strong. [6] The march was prompted by the notion that the Spartans were at a loss how to effect their passage, and also by suspicions of an attempt to overthrow the democracy. [7] Some cavalry also joined the Athenians from their Thessalian allies; but these went over to the Spartans during the battle.

The battle was fought at Tanagra in Boeotia. After heavy loss on both sides victory declared for the Spartans and their allies. [2] After entering the Megarid and cutting down the fruit trees, the Spartans returned home across Geraneia and the isthmus. Sixty-two days after the battle the Athenians marched into Boeotia under the command of Myronides, [3] defeated the Boeotians in battle at Oenophyta, and became masters of Boeotia and Phocis. They dismantled the walls of the Tanagraeans, took a hundred of the richest men of the Opuntian Locrians as hostages, and finished their own long walls. [4] This was followed by the surrender of the Aeginetans to Athens on conditions; they pulled down their walls, gave up their ships, and agreed to pay tribute in future. [5] The Athenians sailed round the Peloponnesus under Tolmides son of Tolmaeus, burnt the arsenal of Sparta, took Chalcis, a city of the Corinthians, and in a descent upon Sicyon defeated the Sicyonians in battle.

Meanwhile the Athenians in Egypt and their allies stayed on and encountered all the vicissitudes of war. [2] First the Athenians were masters of Egypt, and the King sent Megabazus, a Persian, to Sparta with money to bribe the Peloponnesians to invade Attica and so draw off the Athenians from Egypt. [3] Finding that the matter made no progress, and that the money was only being wasted, he recalled Megabazus with the remainder of the money, and sent Megabyzus son of Zopyrus, a Persian, with a large army to Egypt. [4] Arriving by land he defeated the Egyptians and their allies in a battle, and drove the Hellenes out of Memphis, and at length shut them up in the island of Prosopitis, where he besieged them for a year and six months. At last, draining the canal of its waters, which he diverted into another channel, he left their ships high and dry and joined most of the island to the mainland, and then marched over on foot and captured it.

Thus the enterprise of the Hellenes came to ruin after six years of war. Of all that large host a few traveling through Libya reached Cyrene in safety, but most of them perished. [2] And thus Egypt returned to its subjection to the King, except Amyrtaeus, the king in the marshes whom they were unable to capture from the extent of the marsh; the marshmen being also the most warlike of the Egyptians. [3] Inaros, the Libyan king, the sole author of the Egyptian revolt, was betrayed, taken, and crucified. [4] Meanwhile a relieving squadron of fifty triremes had sailed from Athens and the rest of the confederacy for Egypt. They put in to shore at the Mendesian mouth of the Nile, in total ignorance of what had occurred. Attacked on the land side by the troops, and from the sea by the Phoenician navy, most of the ships were destroyed; the few remaining being saved by retreat. Such was the end of the great expedition of the Athenians and their allies to Egypt.

Meanwhile Orestes son of the Thessalian king Echecratides, being an exile from Thessaly, persuaded the Athenians to restore him. Taking with them the Boeotians and the Phocians their allies, the Athenians marched to Pharsalus in Thessaly. They became masters of the country, though only in the immediate vicinity of the camp; beyond which they could not go for fear of the Thessalian cavalry. But they failed to take the city or to attain any of the other objects of their expedition, and returned home with Orestes without having effected anything. [2] Not long after this a thousand of the Athenians embarked in the vessels that were at Pegae (Pegae, it must be remembered, was now theirs), and sailed along the coast to Sicyon under the command of Pericles son of Xanthippus. Landing in Sicyon and defeating the Sicyonians who engaged them, [3] they immediately took with them the Achaeans and sailing across, marched against and laid siege to Oeniadae in Acarnania. Failing however to take it, they returned home.

1.110
454?
EGYPT
Most of Athens' fleet in Egypt is lost. An Athenian relief fleet, unaware of the defeat, is surprised and destroyed.

1.111
454?
THESSALY
Athens attempts to restore Orestes in Thessaly but fails.
SICYON
Pericles' fleet defeats the Sicyonians but fails to take Oeniadae.

Three years afterwards a truce was made between the Peloponnesians and Athenians for five years. [2] Released from Hellenic war, the Athenians made an expedition to Cyprus with two hundred vessels of their own and their allies, under the command of Cimon. [3] Sixty of these were detached to Egypt at the request of Amyrtaeus, the king in the marshes; the rest laid siege to Citium, from which, however, [4] they were compelled to retire by the death of Cimon and by scarcity of provisions. Sailing off Salamis in Cyprus, they fought with the Phoenicians, Cyprians, and Cilicians by land and sea, and being victorious on both elements departed home, and with them the squadron that had returned from Egypt. [5] After this the Spartans marched out on a sacred war, and becoming masters of the temple at Delphi, placed it in the hands of the Belphians. Immediately after their retreat, the Athenians marched out, became masters of the temple, and placed it in the hands of the Phocians.

Some time after this, a thousand Athenians with allied contingents under the command of Toimides son of Tolmaeus, marched against Orchomenus, Chaeronea, and some other places in Boeotia that were in the hands of the Boeotian exiles. They took Chaeronea, made slaves of the inhabitants, and leaving a garrison, commenced their return. [2] On their way they were attacked at Coronea by the Boeotian exiles from Orchomenus, with some Locrians and Euboean exiles, and others who were of the same way of thinking. The Athenians were defeated in battle and some were killed, others taken captive. [3] The Athenians evacuated all Boeotia by a treaty providing for the recovery of the men; [4] and the exiled Boeotians returned, and with all the rest regained their independence.

This was soon afterwards followed by the revolt of Euboea from Athens. Pericles had already crossed over with an army of Athenians to the island, when news was brought to him that Megara had revolted, that the Peloponnesians were on the point of invading Attica, and that the Athenian garrison had been cut off by the Megarians, with the exception of a few who had taken refuge in Nisaea. The Megarians had introduced the Corinthians, Sicyonians, and Epidaurians into the city before they revolted. Meanwhile Pericles brought his army back in all haste from Euboea. [2] After this the Peloponnesians, under the command of King Pleistoanax son of Pausanias, marched into Attica as far as Eleusis and Thria, ravaging the country and without advancing further returned home. [3] The Athenians then crossed over again to Euboea under the command of Pericles, and subdued the whole of the island. While they settled all the rest of the island by means of agreed terms, they expelled the people of Histiaea and occupied their territory themselves.

Not long after their return from Euboea, they made a peace treaty with the Spartans and their allies for thirty years, giving up the posts which they occupied in the Peloponnesus, Nisaea, Pegae, Troezen, and Achaea. [2] In the sixth year of the truce, war broke out between the Samians and Milesians about Priene. Worsted in the war, the Milesians came to Athens with loud complaints against the Samians. In this they were joined by certain private persons from Samos itself, who wished to change the constitution by revolution. [3] Accordingly the Athenians sailed to Samos with forty ships and set up a democracy; took hostages from the Samians, fifty boys and as many men, lodged them in Lemnos, and after leaving a garrison in the island returned home. [4] Some of the Samians, however, had not remained in the island, but had fled to the continent. Making an agreement with the most powerful of those in the city, and an alliance with Pissuthnes son of Hystaspes, who at that time controlled Sardis for the Persians, they got together a force of seven hundred mercenaries, and under cover of night crossed over to Samos. [5] Their first step was to rise against The People, most of whom they secured, their next to steal their hostages from Lemnos; after which they revolted, gave up the Athenian garrison left with them and its commanders to Pissuthnes, and instantly prepared for an expedition against Miletus. The Byzantians also revolted with them.

As soon as the Athenians heard the news, they sailed with sixty ships against Samos. Sixteen of these went to Caria to look out for the Phoenician fleet, and to Chios and Lesbos carrying round orders for reinforcements, and so never engaged; but forty-four ships under the command of Pericles and nine colleagues gave battle off the island of Tragia to seventy Samian vessels—of which twenty were transports—as they were sailing from Miletus. Victory remained with the Athenians. [2] Reinforced afterwards by forty ships from Athens, and twenty-five Chian and Lesbian vessels, the Athenians landed, and

1.115
446
PELOPONNESUS
Athens gives up bases in the Megarid and Peloponnesus to secure the Thirty Years' Peace.
441/0
SAMOS
Samos and Byzantium revolt; Persian troops assist Samos.

1.116
441/0
SAMOS
The Athenians win a battle off Samos and prepare to engage the Phoenician fleet.

having the superiority by land besieged the city with three walls and also blockaded it from the sea. [3] Meanwhile Pericles took sixty ships from the blockading squadron and departed in haste for Caunus and Caria, intelligence having been brought in of the approach of the Phoenician fleet to the aid of the Sarnians; indeed Stesagoras and others had left the island with five ships to bring them. [1.117.1] But in the meantime the Samians made a sudden sally, and fell on the camp, which they found unfortified. Destroying the lookout vessels, and engaging and defeating such as were being launched to meet them, they remained masters of their own seas for fourteen days, and carried in and carried out what they pleased. [2] But on the arrival of Pericles, they were once more shut up. Fresh reinforcements afterwards arrived—forty ships from Athens with Thucydides, Hagnon, and Phormio; twenty with Tlepolemus and Anticles, and thirty vessels from Chios and Lesbos. [3] After a brief attempt at fighting, the Samians unable to hold out after a nine-month siege, were forced to surrender on terms; they razed their walls, gave hostages, delivered up their ships, and arranged to pay the expenses of the war by installments. The Byzantians also agreed to be subject as before.

1.117
440
SAMOS
Samos resists for nine months but finally surrenders to Athens.

After this, though not many years later, we at length come to what has been already related, the affairs of Corcyra and Potidaea and the events that served as a pretext for the present war. [2] All these actions of the Hellenes against each other and the barbarian occurred in the fifty years' interval between the retreat of Xerxes and the beginning of the present war. During this interval the Athenians succeeded in placing their empire on a firmer basis, and themselves advanced their own power to a very great height. The Spartans, though fully aware of it, opposed it only for a little while, but remained inactive during most of the period, being of old slow to go to war except under the pressure of necessity, and in the present instance being hampered by wars at home. Finally, the growth of the Athenian power could no longer be ignored as their own confederacy became the object of its encroachments. They then felt that they could endure it no longer, but that the time had come for them to throw themselves heart and soul upon the hostile power, and break it, if they could, by commencing the present war. [3] And though the Spartans had made up their own minds on the fact of the breach of the treaty and the guilt

1.118
432
HELLAS
Thus in the fifty years after the defeat of Persia, the power of Athens grew until Sparta felt compelled to oppose it. This chapter concludes the Pentecontaetia.

of the Athenians, yet they sent to Delphi and inquired of the god whether it would be well with them if they went to war and, as it is reported, received from him the answer that if they put their whole strength into the war, victory would be theirs, and the promise that he himself would be with them, whether invoked or uninvoked.

Still they wished to summon their allies again, and to take their vote on the propriety of making war. After the ambassadors from the confederates had arrived and a congress had been convened, they all spoke their minds, most of them denouncing the Athenians and demanding that the war should begin, especially the Corinthians. They had before on their own account canvassed the cities separately to induce them to vote for the war, in the fear that it might come too late to save Potidaea; they were present also on this occasion, and came forward the last, and made the following speech:

1.119
432/1
SPARTA
The Corinthians speak at a meeting of the Spartans and their allies.

"Fellow allies, we can no longer accuse the Spartans of having failed in their duty: they have not only voted for war themselves, but have assembled us here for that purpose. We say their duty, for supremacy has its duties. Besides equitably administering private interests, leaders are required to show a special care for the common welfare in return for the special honors accorded to them by all in other ways. [2] All of us who have already had dealings with the Athenians require no warning to be on their guard against them. The states more inland and away from the main routes should understand that if they omit to support the coast powers, the result will be to injure the transit of their produce for exportation and the reception in exchange of their imports from the sea; and they must not be careless judges of what is now said, as if it had nothing to do with them, but must expect that the sacrifice of the powers on the coast will one day be followed by the extension of the danger to the interior, and must recognize that their own interests are deeply involved in this discussion. [3] For these reasons they should not hesitate to exchange peace for war. If wise men remain quiet while they are not injured, brave men abandon peace for war when they are injured, returning to an

1.120
432/1
SPARTA
Corinth applauds Sparta's vote for war and urges all states in the Peloponnesian League to recognize their common interests and potential for injury, and to vote for war.

understanding on a favorable opportunity. In fact, they are neither intoxicated by their success in war nor disposed to take an injury for the sake of the delightful tranquillity of peace. [4] Indeed, to falter for the sake of such delights is, if you remain inactive, the quickest way of losing the sweets of repose to which you cling; while to conceive extravagant pretensions from success in war is to forget how hollow is the confidence by which you are elated. [5] For if many ill-conceived plans have succeeded through the still greater lack of judgment of an opponent, many more, apparently well laid, have on the contrary ended in disgrace. The confidence with which we form our schemes is never completely justified in their execution; speculation is carried on in safety, but, when it comes to action, fear causes failure."

"To apply these rules to ourselves, if we are now kindling war it is under the pressure of injury, and with adequate grounds of complaint; and after we have chastised the Athenians we will in season desist. [2] We have many reasons to expect success—first, superiority in numbers and in military experience, and secondly our general and unvarying obedience in the execution of orders. [3] The naval strength which they possess shall be raised by us from our respective present resources, and from the moneys at Olympia and Delphi. A loan from these enables us to seduce their foreign sailors by the offer of higher pay. For the power of Athens is more mercenary than national; while ours will not be exposed to the same risk, as its strength lies more in men than in money. [4] A single defeat at sea is in all likelihood their ruin: should they hold out, in that case there will be the more time for us to exercise ourselves in naval matters; and as soon as we have arrived at an equality in science, we need scarcely ask whether we shall be their superiors in courage. For the advantages that we have by nature they cannot acquire by education; while their superiority in science must be removed by our practice. [5] The money required for these objects shall be provided by our contributions: nothing indeed could be more monstrous than the suggestion that,

1.121
432/1
SPARTA
The Corinthians optimistically assert that the Peloponnesians can raise enough money by contributions and by loans from Delphi and Olympia to finance a fleet and to subvert that of Athens; they say that, the Peloponnesians with practice will soon equal the Athenians at sea.

while their allies never tire of contributing for their own servitude, we should refuse to spend for vengeance and self-preservation the treasure which by such refusal we shall forfeit to Athenian rapacity, and see employed for our own ruin."

"We have also other ways of carrying on the war, such as revolt of their allies, the surest method of depriving them of their revenues, which are the source of their strength, and establishment of fortified positions in their country, and various operations which cannot be foreseen at present. For war of all things proceeds least upon definite rules, but draws principally upon itself for contrivances to meet an emergency; and in such cases the party who faces the struggle and keeps his temper best meets with most security, and he who loses his temper about it with correspondent disaster. [2] Let us also reflect that if it was merely a number of disputes of territory between rival neighbors, it might be borne; but here we have in Athens an enemy that is a match for our whole coalition, and more than a match for any of its members; so that unless as a body and as individual nationalities and individual cities we make a unanimous stand against her, she will easily conquer us divided and city by city. That conquest, terrible as it may sound, would, it must be known, have no other end than slavery pure and simple; [3] a word which the Peloponnesus cannot even hear whispered without disgrace, or without disgrace see so many states abused by one. Meanwhile the opinion would be either that we were justly so used, or that we put up with it from cowardice, and were proving degenerate sons in not even securing for ourselves the freedom which our fathers gave to Hellas; and in allowing the establishment in Hellas of a tyrant state, though in individual states we think it our duty to put down sole rulers. [4] And we do not know how this conduct can be held free from three of the gravest failings, want of sense, of courage, or of vigilance. For we do not suppose that you have taken refuge in that contempt of an enemy which has proved so fatal in so many instances—a feeling which

1.122 432/1
SPARTA
The Corinthians add that the Peloponnesians can suborn Athenian allies and establish fortified posts in Attica. They call for unity in the face of Athenian aggression since the alternative is slavery. They assert that the Peloponnesians must prevent Athens from ruling all Hellas as a tyrant state just as they have put down tyrants in individual states.

1.123
432/1
SPARTA
The Corinthians claim that
the god of Delphi sanctions
war, which proves that the
treaty has already been
violated by Athens.

1.124
432/1
SPARTA
The Corinthians conclude
with an appeal to their allies
to vote for war in order
to deny Athens her goal of
universal empire.

from the numbers that it has ruined has come to be
thought not to express contempt but to deserve it."

"There is, however, no advantage in reflections on
the past further than may be of service to the present.
For the future we must provide by maintaining what
the present gives us and redoubling our efforts; it is
hereditary to us to win virtue as the fruit of labor,
and you must not change the habit, even though you
should have a slight advantage in wealth and resources;
for it is not right that what was won in want should
be lost in plenty. No, we must boldly advance to the
war for many reasons; the god has commanded it and
promised to be with us, and the rest of Hellas will all
join in the struggle, part from fear, part from interest.
[2] You will not be the first to break a treaty which the
god, in advising us to go to war, judges to be violated
already, but rather to support a treaty that has been
outraged: indeed, treaties are broken not by resistance
but by aggression."

"Your position, therefore, from whatever quarter
you may view it, will amply justify you in going to
war; and this step we recommend in the interests of all,
bearing in mind that identity of interests is the surest of
bonds whether between states or individuals. Delay not,
therefore, to assist Potidaea, a Dorian city besieged by
Ionians, which is quite a reversal of the order of things;
nor to assert the freedom of the rest. [2] It is impossible
for us to wait any longer when waiting can only mean
immediate disaster for some of us and, if it comes to be
known that we have conferred but do not venture to
protect ourselves, likely disaster in the near future for
the rest. Delay not, fellow allies, but convinced of the
necessity of the crisis and the wisdom of this counsel,
vote for the war, undeterred by its immediate terrors,
but looking beyond to the lasting peace by which it will
be succeeded. Out of war peace gains fresh stability,
but to refuse to abandon repose for war is not so sure
a method of avoiding danger. [3] We must believe that
the tyrant city that has been established in Hellas has
been established against all alike, with a program of
universal empire, part fulfilled, part in contemplation;

let us then attack and reduce it, and win future ⟨...⟩ for ourselves and freedom for the Hellenes ⟨...⟩ now enslaved."

Such were the words of the Corinthians. [1⟨...⟩ Spartans having now heard all give their opinion, ⟨...⟩ of all the allied states present in order, great an⟨...⟩ and the majority voted for war. [2] This decide⟨...⟩ impossible for them to commence at once, from ⟨...⟩ preparation; but it was resolved that the means ⟨...⟩ to be procured by the different states, and that t⟨...⟩ no delay. And indeed, in spite of the time occupied with the necessary arrangements, less than a year elapsed before Attica was invaded, and the war openly begun.

This interval was spent in sending embassies to Athens charged with complaints, in order to obtain as good a pretext for war as possible, in the event of her paying no attention to them. [2] The first Spartan embassy was to order the Athenians to drive out the curse of the goddess; the history of which is as follows. [8] In former generations there was an Athenian of the name of Cylon, a victor at the Olympic games, of good birth and powerful position, who had married a daughter of Theagenes, a Megarian, at that time tyrant of Megara. [4] Now this Cylon was inquiring at Delphi when he was told by the god to seize the Acropolis of Athens on the grand festival of Zeus. [5] Accordingly, procuring a force from Theagenes and persuading his friends to join him, he seized the Acropolis when the Olympic festival in the Peloponnesus began with the intention of making himself tyrant, thinking that this was the grand festival of Zeus, and also an occasion appropriate for a victor at the Olympic games. [6] Whether the grand festival that was meant was in Attica or elsewhere was a question which he never thought of, and which the oracle did not offer to solve. For the Athenians also have a festival which is called the grand festival of Zeus Meilichios or Gracious, namely, the Diasia. It is celebrated outside the city, and the whole people sacrifice not real victims but a number of bloodless offerings peculiar to the country. However, fancying he had chosen the right time, he made the attempt. [7] As soon as the Athenians perceived it, they flocked in, one and all, from the country, and sat down, and laid siege to the citadel. [8] But as time went on, weary

1.126
432/1
ATHENS
As a pretext for war, Sparta tells Athens to drive out the curse of the goddess. Thucydides describes Cylon's attempted coup, from which the curse derived.

of the labor of blockade, most of them departed; the responsibility of keeping guard being left to the nine archons, with plenary powers to arrange everything according to their good judgment. It must be known that at that time most political functions were discharged by the nine archons. [9] Meanwhile Cylon and his besieged companions were distressed for want of food and water. [10] Accordingly Cylon and his brother made their escape; but the rest being hard pressed, and some even dying of famine, seated themselves as suppliants at the altar in the Acropolis. [11] The Athenians who were charged with the duty of keeping guard, when they saw them at the point of death in the temple, raised them up on the understanding that no harm should be done to them, led them out, and slew them. Some who as they passed by took refuge at the altars of the awful goddesses were dispatched on the spot. From this deed the men who killed them were called accursed and guilty against the goddess, they and their descendants. [12] Accordingly these cursed ones were driven out by the Athenians, and driven out again by Cleomenes of Sparta and an Athenian faction; the living were driven out, and the bones of the dead were taken up; thus they were cast out. For all that, they came back afterwards, and their descendants are still in the city.

This, then, was the curse that the Spartans ordered them to drive out. They were actuated primarily, as they pretended, by care for the honor of the gods; but they also knew that Pericles son of Xanthippus was connected with the curse on his mother's side, and they thought that his banishment would materially advance their designs on Athens. [2] Not that they really hoped to succeed in procuring this; they rather thought to create a prejudice against him in the eyes of his countrymen from the feeling that the war would be partly caused by his misfortune. [3] For being the most powerful man of his time, and the leading Athenian statesman, he opposed the Spartans in everything, and would have no concessions, but ever urged the Athenians on to war.

1.126
432/1
ATHENS
As a pretext for war, Sparta tells Athens to drive out the curse of the goddess. Thucydides describes Cylon's attempted coup, from which the curse derived.

The Athenians retorted by ordering the Spartans to drive out the curse of Taenarus. The Spartans had once raised up some Helot suppliants from the temple of Poseidon at Taenaras, led them away, and slain them; for which they believe the great earthquake at Sparta to have been a retribution. [2] The Athenians also ordered them to drive out the curse of the goddess of the Bronze House; the history of which is as follows. [3] After Pausanias the Spartan had been recalled by the Spartans from his command in the Hellespont (this is his first recall), and had been tried by them and acquitted, not being again sent out in a public capacity, he took a trireme of Hermione on his own responsibility, without the authority of the Spartans, and arrived as a private person in the Hellespont. He came ostensibly for the Hellenic war, but really to carry on his intrigues with the King, which he had begun before his recall, being ambitious of reigning over Hellas. [4] The circumstance which first enabled him to lay the King under an obligation, and to make a beginning of the whole design was this. [5] Some connections and kinsmen of the King had been taken in Byzantium on its capture from the Persians, when he was first there after the return from Cyprus. These captives he sent off to the King without the knowledge of the rest of the allies, the account being that they had escaped from him. [6] He managed this with the help of Gongylus, an Eretrian, whom he had placed in charge of Byzantium and the prisoners. He also gave Gongylus a letter for the King, the contents of which were as follows, as was afterwards discovered: [7] "Pausanias, the general of Sparta, anxious to do you a favor, sends you these his prisoners of war. I propose also, with your approval, to marry your daughter, and to make Sparta and the rest of Hellas subject to you. I may say that I think I am able to do this, with your cooperation. Accordingly if any of this please you, send a safe man to the sea through whom we may in future conduct our correspondence."

This was all that was revealed in the writing, and Xerxes was pleased with the letter. He sent off Artabazus son of Pharnaces to the sea with orders to supersede Megabates, the previous governor in the province of Dascylium, and to send over as quickly as possible to Pausanias at Byzantium a letter which he entrusted to him; to show him the royal signet, and to execute any commission which he might receive from Pausanias on the

1.128
432/1
SPARTA
Athens in turn tells Sparta to drive out the curse of Taenarus and the curse of the goddess of the Bronze House, the latter involving Pausanias' attempt to betray the Greeks to Xerxes.

1.129
HELLESPONT
The account of the curse of the goddess of the Bronze House begins with Xerxes' favorable response to Pausanias' letter.

King's business, with all care and fidelity. [2] Artabazus on his arrival carried the King's orders into effect, and sent over the letter, [3] which contained the following answer: "Thus saith King Xerxes to Pausanias. For the men whom you have saved for me from Byzantium across sea, an obligation is laid up to you in our house, recorded forever; and with your proposals I am well pleased. Let neither night nor day stop you from diligently performing any of your promises to me, neither for cost of gold nor of silver let them be hindered, nor yet for number of troops, wherever it may be that their presence is needed; but with Artabazus, an honorable man whom I send you, boldly advance my objects and yours, as may be most for the honor and interest of us both."

1.130
HELLESPONT
Pausanias adopts Persian ways and antagonizes the Greeks.

Previously held in high honor by the Hellenes as the hero of Plataea, Pausanias, after the receipt of this letter, became prouder than ever, and could no longer live in the usual style, but went out of Byzantium in a Median dress, was attended on his march through Thrace by a bodyguard of Medes and Egyptians, kept a Persian table, and was quite unable to contain his intentions, but he betrayed by his conduct in trifles what his ambition looked one day to enact on a grander scale. [2] He also made himself difficult of access, and displayed so violent a temper to everyone without exception that no one could come near him. Indeed, this was the principal reason why the confederacy went over to the Athenians.

1.131
SPARTA
Suspecting treachery, the ephors recall Pausanias.

The above-mentioned conduct, coming to the ears of the Spartans, occasioned his first recall. And after his second voyage out in the ship of Hermione, without their orders, he gave proofs of similar behavior. Besieged and expelled from Byzantium by the Athenians, he did not return to Sparta; but news came that he had settled at Colonae in the Troad, and was intriguing with the barbarians, and that his stay there was for no good purpose; and the ephors, now no longer hesitating, sent him a herald and a scytale with orders to accompany the herald or be declared a public enemy. [2] Anxious above everything to avoid suspicion, and confident that he could quash the charge by means of money, he returned a second time to Sparta. At first thrown into prison by the ephors (whose powers enable them to do this to the king), he soon compromised the matter and came out again, and offered himself for trial to any who wished to institute an inquiry concerning him.

Now the Spartans had no tangible proof against him—neither his enemies nor the city as a whole—of that indubitable kind required for the punishment of a member of the royal family, and at that moment in high office; he being regent for his first cousin King Pleistarchus, Leonidas' son, who was still a minor. But by his contempt of the laws and imitation of the barbarians, [2] he gave grounds for much suspicion of his being discontented with things established; all the occasions on which he had in any way departed from the regular customs were passed in review, and it was remembered that he had taken upon himself to have inscribed on the tripod at Delphi, which was dedicated by the Hellenes, as the first-fruits of the spoil of the Medes, the following couplet:

The Mede defeated, great Pausanias raised
This monument, that Phoebus might be praised.

[3] At the time Spartans had at once erased the couplet, and inscribed the name of the cities that had aided in the overthrow of the barbarian and dedicated the offering. Yet it was considered that Pausanias had here been guilty of a grave offense, which, interpreted by the light of the attitude which he had since assumed, gained a new significance, and I seemed to be quite in keeping with his present schemes. [4] Besides, they were informed that he was even intriguing with the Helots; and such indeed was the fact, for he was promising them freedom and citizenship if they would join him in insurrection, and would help him to carry out his plans to the end. [5] Even now, mistrusting the evidence even of the Helots themselves, the ephors would not consent to take any decided step against him; in accordance with their regular custom toward themselves, namely, to be slow in taking any irrevocable resolve in the matter of a Spartan citizen, without indisputable proof. At last, it is said, the person who was going to carry to Artabazus the last letter for the King, a man of Argilus, once the favorite and most trusty servant of Pausanias, turned informer. Alarmed by the reflection that none of the previous messengers had ever returned, having counterfeited the seal, in order that, if he found himself mistaken in his surmises, or if Pausanias should ask to make some correction, he might not be discovered, he

1.132
SPARTA
The ephors suspect Pausanias but they lack proof, until one of his servants betrays him.

THE LANDMARK THUCYDIDES · 181

undid the letter, and found the postscript that he had suspected, namely, an order to put him to death.

On being shown the letter the ephors now felt more certain. Still, they wished with their own ears to hear Pausanias commit himself. Accordingly the man went by appointment to Taenaras as a suppliant, and there found shelter for himself in a hut divided into two by a partition; within which he concealed some of the ephors and let them hear the whole matter plainly. For Pausanias came to him and asked him the reason of his suppliant position; and the man reproached him with the order that he had written concerning him, and one by one declared all the rest of the circumstances, how he who had never yet brought him into any danger, while employed as agent between him and the King, was yet just like the mass of his servants, to be rewarded with death. Admitting all this, and telling him not to be angry about the matter, Pausanias gave him guarantee of safety in getting him to leave the temple, and begged him to set off as quickly as possible, and not to hinder the business in hand.

The ephors listened carefully, and then departed, taking no action for the moment, but, having at last reached certainty, were preparing to arrest him in the city. It is reported that, as he was about to be arrested in the street, he saw from the face of one of the ephors what he was coming for; another, too, made him a secret signal, and betrayed it to him from kindness. Setting off at a run for the temple of the goddess of the Bronze House, the enclosure of which was near at hand, he succeeded in taking sanctuary before they took him, and entering into a small chamber, which formed part of the temple, to avoid being exposed to the weather, he remained there. [2] The ephors, for the moment distanced in the pursuit, afterwards took off the roof of the chamber, and having made sure that he was inside, shut him in, barricaded the doors, and staying before the place, reduced him by starvation. [3] When they found that he was on the point of expiring, just as he was, in the chamber, they brought him out of the temple, while the breath was still in him, and as soon as he was brought out he died. [4] They were going to throw him into the Kaiadas, where they cast criminals, but finally decided to inter him somewhere near. But the god at Delphi afterwards ordered the Spartans to remove the tomb to the place of his death—where he now lies in the consecrated

1.133
471?
SPARTA
Posing as a suppliant at Taenaras, the servant tricks Pausanias into disclosing his crimes to the ephors in hiding.

1.134
471 ?
SPARTA
Pausanias takes sanctuary in the temple of the goddess of the Bronze House. The ephors shut him in there and he starves to death, causing the curse.

ground, as an inscription on a monument declares—and, as what had been done was a curse to them, to give back two bodies instead of one to the goddess of the Bronze House. So they had two bronze statues made, and dedicated them as a substitute for Pausanias. [1.135.1] Accordingly the Athenians retorted by telling the Spartans to drive out what the god himself had pronounced to be a curse.

[2] To return to the Medism of Pausanias, matter was found in the course of the inquiry to implicate Themistocles; and the Spartans accordingly sent envoys to the Athenians and required them to punish him as they had punished Pausanias. The Athenians consented to do so. [3] He had, as it happened, been ostracized and, from a residence at Argos, was in the habit of visiting other parts of the Peloponnesus. So they sent with the Spartans, who were ready to join in the pursuit, persons with instructions to take him wherever they found him.

1.135
471?
ATHENS
The investigation of Pausanias implicates Themistocles, who had been ostracized from Athens.

Themistocles became aware of their intentions, however, and fled from the Peloponnesus to Corcyra, which was under obligations toward him. But the Corcyraeans alleged that they could not venture to shelter him at the cost of offending Athens and Sparta, and they conveyed him over to the continent opposite. [2] Pursued by the officers who hung on the report of his movements, and at a loss where to turn, he was compelled to stop at the house of Admetus, the Molossian king, though they were not on friendly terms. [3] Admetus happened not to be indoors, but his wife, to whom he made himself a suppliant, instructed him to take their child in his arms and sit down by the hearth. [4] Soon afterwards Admetus came in, and Themistocles told him who he was, and begged him not to take revenge on Themistocles in exile for any opposition which his requests might have experienced from Themistocles at Athens. Indeed, he was now far too low for such revenge; retaliation was only honorable between equals. Besides, his opposition to the king had only affected the success of a request, not the safety of his person; if the king were to give him up to the pursuers that he mentioned, and the fate which they intended for him, he would just be consigning him to certain death.

1.136
470?
MOLOSSIA
Unable to remain at Corcyra, Themistocles flees to Molossia, to whose king, Admetus, a former adversary, he now becomes a suppliant.

The king listened to him and raised him up with his son, as he was sitting with him in his arms after the most effectual method of supplication, and on the arrival of the Spartans not long afterwards, refused to give him up for anything they could say, but sent him off by land to the other sea to Pydna in Alexander's dominions, as he wished to go to the Persian King. [2] There he met with a merchant ship on the point of starting for Ionia. Going on board, he was carried by a storm to the Athenian squadron which was blockading Naxos. In his alarm—he was luckily unknown to the people in the vessel—he told the master who he was and what he was flying for, and said that, if he refused to save him, he would declare that the captain had been bribed into taking him. Meanwhile their safety consisted in letting no one leave the ship until a favorable time for sailing should arise. If he complied with his wishes, Themistocles promised him a proper recompense. The master acted as he desired, and, after lying at anchor for a day and a night out of the reach of the squadron, at length arrived at Ephesus.

[3] After having rewarded him with a present of money, as soon as he received some from his friends at Athens and from his secret hoards at Argos, Themistocles started inland with a Persian from the coast, and sent a letter to King Artaxerxes, Xerxes' son, who had just come to the throne. Its contents were as follows: [4] "I, Themistocles, am come to you, who did your house more harm than any of the Hellenes, when I was compelled to defend myself against your father's invasion—harm, however, far surpassed by the good that I did him during his retreat, which brought no danger for me but much for him. For the past, you owe me a good turn"—here he alluded to the warning sent to Xerxes from Salamis to retreat, as well as his finding the bridges unbroken, which, as he falsely pretended, was due to him—"for the present, able to do you great service, I am here, pursued by the Hellenes for my friendship for you. However, I desire a year's grace, when I shall be able to declare in person the objects of my coming."

It is said that the King approved his intention, and told him to do as he said. He employed the interval in making what progress he could in the study of the Persian tongue, and of the customs of the country. [2] Arrived at court at the end of the year, he attained to very high consideration there, such as no Hellene has ever possessed before or since; partly from his splendid reputation, partly from the hopes which he held out of effecting the subjugation of Hellas, but principally by the proof which experience daily gave of his intelligence. [3] For Themistocles was a man who exhibited the most indubitable signs of genius; indeed, in this particular he has a claim on our admiration quite extraordinary and unparalleled. By his own native capacity, which was neither shaped by education nor developed by later training, he was at once the best judge in those sudden crises which admit of little or of no deliberation, and the best prophet of the future, even to its most distant possibilities. An able theoretical expositor of all that came within the sphere of his practice, he was not without the power of passing an adequate judgment in matters in which he had no experience. He could also excellently divine the good and evil which lay hidden in the unseen future. To sum up, whether we consider the extent of his natural powers, or the slightness of his application, this extraordinary man must be allowed to have surpassed all others in the faculty of intuitively meeting an emergency. [4] Disease was the real cause of his death; though there is a story of his having ended his life by poison, on finding himself unable to fulfill his promises to the King. [5] However this may be, there is a monument to him in the agora of Asiatic Magnesia. He was governor of the district, the King having given him Magnesia, which brought in fifty talents a year for bread, Lampsacus, which was considered to be the richest wine country, for wine, and Myos for other provisions. [6] His bones, it is said, were conveyed home by his relatives in accordance with his wishes, and interred in Attic ground. This was done without the knowledge of the Athenians; as it is against the law to bury in Attica an outlaw for treason. So ends the history of Pausanias and Themistocles, the Spartan and the Athenian, the most famous men of their time in Hellas.

1.138
461?
PERSIAN ASIA
Themistocles is well received by Xerxes, Thucydides applauds Themistocles' extraordinary ability to foresee events and make decisions. Xerxes appoints him a governor.

1.139
432/1
ATHENS
Sparta also demands
that Athens raise the siege
of Potidaea, restore
independence to Aegina,
and rescind the Megarian
Decree. A final ultimatum
orders Athens to let the
Hellenes be independent.
As the Athenians debate
these demands, Pericles
rises to speak.

To return to the Spartans. The history of their first embassy, the injunctions which it conveyed and the rejoinder which it provoked concerning the expulsion of the accursed persons, have been related already. It was followed by a second, which ordered Athens to raise the siege of Potidaea, and to respect the independence of Aegina. Above all, it made very clear to the Athenians that war might be prevented if they revoked the Megara Decree, excluding the Megarians from the use of Athenian harbors and of the market of Athens. [2] But Athens was not inclined either to revoke the decree, or to entertain their other proposals; she accused the Megarians of pushing their cultivation into the consecrated ground and the unenclosed land on the border, and of harboring her runaway slaves. [3] At last an embassy arrived with the Spartan ultimatum. The ambassadors were Ramphias, Melesippus, and Agesander. Not a word was said on any of the old subjects; there was simply this: "Sparta wishes the peace to continue, and there is no reason why it should not, if you would let the Hellenes be independent." Upon this the Athenians held an assembly, and laid the matter before their consideration. It was resolved to deliberate once and for all on all their demands, and to give them an answer. [4] There were many speakers who came forward and gave their support to one side or the other, urging the necessity of war, or the revocation of the decree and the folly of allowing it to stand in the way of peace. Among them came forward Pericles son of Xanthippus, the first man of his time at Athens, ablest alike in counsel and in action, and gave the following advice:

1.140
432/1
ATHENS
Pericles demands no
concession to Sparta
because she has not offered
or accepted arbitration,
as called for in the treaty,
and her demands have
grown more dictatorial
and threatening. He says
the Megarian Decree is
not a trifle, but a symbol of
Athenian response to
Spartan pressure.

"There is one principle, Athenians, which I hold to through everything, and that is the principle of no concession to the Peloponnesians. I know that the spirit which inspires men while they are being persuaded to make war is not always retained in action, that as circumstances change, resolutions change. Yet I see that now as before the same, almost literally the same, counsel is demanded of me; and I put it to those of you who are allowing yourselves to be persuaded, to support the decisions of the assembly even in the case of reverses, or to forfeit all credit for their wisdom in the event of success. For sometimes the course of things is as arbitrary as the plans of man; indeed this is why we usually blame chance for whatever does not happen as we expected. [2] Now it was clear before that Sparta entertained designs against us; it is still more clear now. The treaty provides that we shall mutually submit our differences to arbitration, and that we shall meanwhile each keep what we have. Yet the Spartans never yet made us any such offer, never yet would accept from us any such offer; on the contrary, they wish complaints to be settled by war instead of by negotiation; and in the end we find them here dropping the tone of protest and adopting that of command. [3] They order us to raise the siege of Potidaea, to let Aegina be independent, to revoke the Megara decree; and they conclude with an ultimatum warning us to leave the Hellenes independent.

[4] I hope that you will none of you think that we shall be going to war for a trifle if we refuse to revoke the Megara decree, which appears in front of their complaints, and the revocation of which is to save us from war, or let any feeling of self-reproach linger in your minds, as if you went to war for slight cause. [5] Why, this trifle contains the whole seal and trial of your resolution. If you give way, you will instantly have to meet some greater demand, as having been frightened into obedience in the first instance; while a firm refusal will make them clearly understand that they must treat you as equals."

"Make your decision therefore at once, either to submit before you are harmed, or if we are to go to war, as I for one think we ought, to do so without caring whether the ostensible cause be great or small, resolved against making concessions or consenting to a precarious tenure of our possessions. For all claims from an equal, urged upon a neighbor as commands, before any attempt at arbitration, be they great or be they small, have only one meaning, and that is slavery."

[2] "As to the war and the resources of either party, a detailed comparison will not show you the inferiority of Athens. [3] Personally engaged in the cultivation of their land, without funds either private or public, the Peloponnesians are also without experience in long wars

1.141
432/1
ATHENS
Pericles says that to heed Sparta's demands can lead only to slavery. He points out that the Peloponnesians lack funds to sustain conflicts and, being farmers, they will not be able to mobilize for long campaigns; that they cannot threaten Athens at sea; and, as a league of states with divergent interests, they will find it hard to act quickly or decisively.

across sea, from the strict limit which poverty imposes on their attacks upon each other. [4] Powers of this description are quite incapable of often manning a fleet or often sending out an army: they cannot afford the absence from their homes, the expenditure from their own funds; and besides, they have not command of the sea. [5] Capital, it must be remembered, maintains a war more than forced contributions. Farmers are a class of men that are always more ready to serve in person than in purse. Confident that the former will survive the dangers, they are by no means so sure that the latter will not be prematurely exhausted, especially if the war last longer than they expect, which it very likely will. [6] In a single battle the Peloponnesians and their allies may be able to defy all Hellas, but they are incapacitated from carrying on a war against a power different in character from their own, by the want of the single council chamber requisite to prompt and vigorous action, and the substitution of a congress composed of various peoples, in which every state possesses an equal vote, and each presses its own ends—a condition of things which generally results in no action at all. [7] The great wish of some is to avenge themselves on some particular enemy, the great wish of others to save their own pocket. Slow in assembling, they devote a very small fraction of the time to the consideration of any matter of common concern, most of it to the prosecution of their own affairs. Meanwhile each fancies that no harm will come of his neglect, that it is the business of somebody else to look after this or that for him; and so, by the same notion' being entertained by all separately, the common cause imperceptibly decays."

"But the principal point is the hindrance that they will experience from want of money. The slowness with which it comes in will cause delay; but the opportunities of war wait for no man. [2] Again, we need not be alarmed either at the possibility of their raising fortifications in Attica, or at their navy. [3] It would be difficult for any system of fortifications to establish a rival city, even in time of peace, much more, surely, in an enemy's country, with Athens just as much fortified against it, as it against Athens; [4] while a mere post might be able to do some harm to the country by incursions and by the facilities which it would afford for desertion, it can never prevent our sailing into their country and raising fortifications there, and making reprisals with our powerful fleet. [5] For our naval skill is of more use to us for service on land, than their military skill for service at sea. [6] Familiarity with the sea they will not find an easy acquisition. [7] If you who have been practicing at it ever since the Persian invasion have not yet brought it to perfection, is there any chance of anything considerable being effected by an agricultural, unseafaring population, who will besides be prevented from practicing by the constant presence of strong squadrons of observation from Athens? [8] With a small squadron they might hazard an engagement, encouraging their ignorance by numbers; but the restraint of a strong force will prevent their moving, and through want of practice they will grow more clumsy, and consequently more timid. [9] It must be kept in mind that seamanship, just like anything else, is a matter requiring skill, and will not admit of being taken up occasionally as an occupation for times of leisure; on the contrary, it is so exacting as to leave leisure for nothing else."

1.142
432/1
ATHENS
Pericles argues that the enemy's principal handicap will be lack of money; that Athenian sea power will be more effective against them on land than their land power against Athens at sea; and that they will not easily acquire the skill to challenge Athens at sea, especially if Athenian fleets limit their opportunities to practice.

1.143
432/1
ATHENS

Pericles asserts that Sparta, even if she obtains funds, will never match Athens at sea, for Athens has enough citizen-sailors to match all of Hellas. Athens has lands across the sea that Sparta cannot harm. "Thus we must forgo our properties in Attica and, viewing ourselves as islanders, value most our sea power and its ability to provide, us resources from our empire."

"Even if they were to touch the moneys at Olympia or Delphi, and try to seduce our foreign sailors by the temptation of higher pay, that would only be a serious danger if we could not still be a match for them, by embarking our own citizens and the resident aliens. But in fact by this means we are always a match for them; and, best of all, we have a larger and higher class of native coxswains and sailors among our own citizens than all the rest of Hellas. [2] And to say nothing of the danger of such a step, none of our foreign sailors would consent to become an outlaw from his country, and to take service with them and their hopes, for the sake of a few days' high pay."

[3] "This, I think, is a tolerably fair account of the position of the Peloponnesians; that of Athens is free from the defects that I have criticized in them, and has other advantages of its own, which they can show nothing to equal. [4] If they march against our country we will sail against theirs, and it will then be found that the desolation of the whole of Attica is not the same as that of even a fraction of the Peloponnesus; for they will not be able to supply the deficiency except by a battle, while we have plenty of land both on the islands and the continent. [5] The rule of the sea is indeed a great matter. Consider for a moment. Suppose that we were islanders: can you conceive a more impregnable position? Well, this in future should, as far as possible, be our conception of our position. Dismissing all thought of our land and houses, we must vigilantly guard the sea and the city. No irritation that we may feel for the former must provoke us to a battle with the numerical superiority of the Peloponnesians. A victory would only be succeeded by another battle against the same superiority: a reverse involves the loss of our allies, the source of our strength, who will not remain quiet a day after we become unable to march against them. We must cry not over the loss of houses and land but of men's lives; since houses and land do not gain men, but men them. And if I had thought that I could persuade you, I would have bid you go out and lay them waste

with your own hands, and show the Peloponnesians that this at any rate will not make you submit."

"I have many other reasons to hope for a favorable outcome, if you can consent not to combine schemes of fresh conquest with the conduct of the war, and will abstain from willfully involving yourselves in other dangers; indeed, I am more afraid of our own blunders than of the enemy's devices. [2] But these matters shall be explained in another speech, as events require; for the present dismiss these men with the answer that we will allow Megara the use of our market and harbors when the Spartans suspend their alien acts against us and our allies, there being nothing in the treaty to prevent either one or the other; that we will leave the cities independent if independent we found them when we made the treaty, and when the Spartans grant to their cities an independence not involving subservience to Spartan interest, but such as each severally may desire; that we are willing to give the legal satisfaction which our agreements specify; and that we shall not commence hostilities, but shall resist those who do commence them. This is an answer agreeable at once to the rights and the dignity of Athens. [3] It must be thoroughly understood that war is a necessity, and that the more readily we accept it, the less will be the ardor of our opponents, and that out of the greatest dangers communities and individuals acquire the greatest glory. Did not our fathers resist the Persians not only with resources far different from ours, but even when those resources had been abandoned; and more by wisdom than by fortune, more by daring than by strength, did not they beat off the barbarian and advance their affairs to their present height? We must not fall behind them, but must resist our enemies in any way and in every way, and attempt to hand down our power to our posterity unimpaired."

1.144
432/1
ATHENS
Pericles concludes his speech by advising the Athenians to accept this war as inevitable, and to avoid any new conquests or unnecessary risks until the war is over. He suggests that they let the Peloponnesians commence hostilities and reminds the Athenians of their glorious past.

1.145
432/1
ATHENS
The Athenians vote as
Pericles advises and the
Spartan envoys return
home.

Such were the words of Pericles. The Athenians, persuaded of the wisdom of his advice, voted as he desired, and answered the Spartans as he recommended, both on the separate points and in general: they would not respond to commands, but were ready to have the complaints settled in a fair and impartial manner by arbitration, which the terms of the truce prescribe. So the envoys departed home, and did not return again.

These were the charges and differences existing between the rival powers before the war, arising immediately from the affair at Epidamnus and Corcyra. Still intercourse continued in spite of them, and mutual communication. It was carried on without heralds, but not without suspicion, as events were occurring which were equivalent to a breach of the treaty and matter for war.

BOOK 3.52 – 3.68

About the same time in this summer, the Plataeans being now without provisions, and unable to support the siege, surrendered to the Peloponnesians in the following manner. [2] An assault had been made upon the wall, which the Plataeans were unable to repel. The Spartan commander, perceiving their weakness, wished to avoid taking the place by storm; his instructions from Sparta having been so conceived, in order that if at any future time peace should be made with Athens, and they should agree each to restore the places that they had taken in the war, Plataea might be held to have come over voluntarily, and not be included in the list. He accordingly sent a herald to them to ask if they were willing voluntarily to surrender the city to the Spartans, and accept them as their judges, upon the understanding that the guilty should be punished, but no one without form of law. [3] The Plataeans were now in the last state of weakness, and the herald had no sooner delivered his message than they surrendered the city. The Peloponnesians fed them for some days until the judges from Sparta, who were five in number, arrived. [4] Upon their arrival no charge was preferred; they simply called up the Plataeans, and asked them whether they had done the Spartans and allies any service in the war then raging. The Plataeans asked leave to speak at greater length, and deputed two of their number to represent them, Astymachus son of Asopolaus, and Lacon son of Aeimnestus, *proxenus* of the Spartans, who came forward and spoke as follows:

"Spartans, when we surrendered our city we trusted in you, and looked forward to a trial more agreeable to the forms of law than the present, to which we had no idea of being subjected; the judges also in whose hands we consented to place ourselves were you, and you only (from whom we thought we were most likely to obtain justice), and not other persons, as is now the case. [2] As matters stand, we are afraid that we have been doubly deceived. We have good reason to suspect, not only that the issue to be tried is the most terrible of all, but that you will not prove impartial; if we may argue from the fact that no accusation was first brought forward for us to answer, but we had ourselves to ask leave to speak, and from the question being put so shortly, that a true answer to it tells against us, while a false one can be contradicted.

[3] In this dilemma, our safest, and indeed our only course, seems to be to say something at all risks: placed as we are, we could scarcely be silent without being tormented by the damning thought that speaking might have saved us. [4] Another difficulty that we have to encounter is the difficulty of convincing you. Were we unknown to each other we might profit by bringing forward new matter with which you were unacquainted: as it is, we can tell you nothing that you do not know already, and we fear, not that you have condemned us in your own minds of having failed in our duty toward you, and make this our crime, but that to please a third party we have to submit to a trial the result of which is already decided."

"Nevertheless, we will place before you what we can justly urge, not only on the question of the quarrel which the Thebans have against us, but also as addressing you and the rest of the Hellenes; and we will remind you of our good services, and endeavor to prevail with you, [2] To your short question, whether we have done the Spartans and allies any service in this war, we say, if you ask us as enemies, that to refrain from serving you was not to do you injury; if as friends, that you are more in fault for having marched against us. [3] During the peace, and against the Mede, we acted well: we have not now been the first to break the peace, and we were the only Boeotians who then joined in defending the liberty of Hellas against the Persian. [4] Although an inland people, we were present at the action at Artemisium; in the battle that took place in our territory we fought by the side of yourselves and Pausanias; and in all the other Hellenic exploits of the time we took a part quite out of proportion to our strength. [5] Besides, you, as Spartans, ought not to forget that at the time of the great panic at Sparta, after the earthquake, caused by the secession of the Helots to Ithome, we sent the third part of our citizens to assist you."

"On these great occasions in the past such was the part that we chose, although afterwards we became your enemies. For this you were to blame. When we asked for your alliance against our Theban oppressors, you rejected our petition, and told us to go to the Athenians who were our neighbors, as you lived too far off. [2] In the war we never have done to you, and never would have done to you, anything unreasonable. [3] If we refused to desert the Athenians when you asked us, we did no wrong; they had helped us against the Thebans when you drew back, and we could no longer give them, up with honor; especially as we had obtained their alliance and had been admitted to their citizenship at our own request, and after receiving benefits at their hands; but it was plainly our duty loyally to obey their orders. [4] Besides, the faults that either of you may commit in your supremacy must be laid, not upon the followers, but on the chiefs that lead them astray."

"With regard to the Thebans, they have wronged us repeatedly, and their last aggression, which has been the means of bringing us into our present position, is within your own knowledge. [2] In seizing our city in time of peace, and what is more at a holy time in the month, they justly encountered our vengeance,

3.55
427
5th Year/Summer
PLATAEA
The Plataeans argue that since Sparta sent Plataea to Athens for alliance, Sparta must now accept Plataean loyalty to Athens.

3.56
427
5th Year/Summer
PLATAEA
The Plataeans call on Sparta to deny Theban wrath and to reward past Plataean help.

in accordance with the universal law which sanctions resistance to an invader; and it cannot now be right that we should suffer on their account. [3] By taking your own immediate interest and their animosity as the test of justice, you will prove yourselves to be servants of expediency rather than judges of right; [4] although if they seem useful to you now, we and the rest of the Hellenes gave you much more valuable help at a time of greater need. Now you are the assailants, and others fear you; but at the crisis to which we allude, when the barbarian threatened all with slavery, the Thebans were on his side. [5] It is just, therefore, to put our patriotism then against our error now, if error there has been; and you will find the merit outweighing the fault, and displayed at a juncture when there were few Hellenes who would set their valor against the strength of Xerxes, and when greater praise was theirs who preferred the dangerous path of honor to the safe course of consulting their own interest with respect to the invasion. [6] To these few we belonged, and highly were we honored for it; and yet we now fear to perish by having again acted on the same principles, and chosen to act well with Athens sooner than wisely with Sparta. [7] Yet in justice the same cases should be decided in the same way, and policy should not mean anything else than lasting gratitude for the service of a good ally combined with a proper attention to one's own immediate interest."

"Consider also that at present the Hellenes generally regard you as a model of worth and honor; and if you pass an unjust sentence upon us in this which is no obscure cause—but one in which you, the judges, are as illustrious as we, the prisoners, are blameless—take care that displeasure be not felt at an unworthy decision in the matter of honorable men made by men yet more honorable than they, and at the consecration in the national temples of spoils taken from the Plataeans, the benefactors of Hellas. [2] Shocking indeed will it seem for Spartans to destroy Plataea, and for the city whose name your fathers inscribed upon the tripod at Delphi for its good service, to be by you blotted out

3.57
427
5th Year/Summer
PLATAEA
The Plataeans say that Sparta's reputation will suffer if she permits Thebes to destroy Plataea.

from the map of Hellas to please the Thebans. [3] To such a depth of misfortune have we fallen, that while the Medes' success had been our ruin, Thebans now supplant us in your once fond regards; and we have been subjected to two dangers, the greatest of any—that of dying of starvation then, if we had not surrendered our city, and now of being tried for our lives. [4] So that we Plataeans, after exertions beyond our power in the cause of the Hellenes, are rejected by all, forsaken and unassisted; helped by none of our allies, and reduced to doubt the stability of our only hope, yourselves."

"Still, in the name of the gods who once presided over our confederacy, and of our own good service in the Hellenic cause, we appeal to you to relent; to rescind the decision which we fear that the Thebans may have obtained from you; to ask back the gift that you have given them, that they disgrace not you by slaying us; to gain a pure instead of a guilty gratitude, and not to gratify others to be yourselves rewarded with shame. [2] Our lives may be quickly taken, but it will be a heavy task to wipe away the infamy of the deed; as we are no enemies whom you might justly punish, but friends forced into taking arms against you. [3] To grant us our lives would be, therefore, a righteous judgment; if you consider also that we are prisoners who surrendered of their own accord, stretching out our hands for quarter, whose slaughter Hellenic law forbids, and who besides were always your benefactors. [4] Look at the tombs of your fathers, slain by the Persians and buried in our country, whom year by year we honored with garments and all other dues, and the first fruits of all that our land produced in their season, as friends from a friendly country and allies to our old companions in arms! Should you not decide aright, your conduct would be the very opposite to ours. Consider only: [5] Pausanias buried them thinking that he was laying them in friendly ground and among men as friendly; but you, if you kill us and make the Plataean territory Theban, will leave your fathers and kinsmen in a hostile soil and among their murderers, deprived of the honors which they now enjoy. What is

3.58
427
5th Year/Summer
PLATAEA
The Plataeans contrast themselves, who care for the graves of Spartans who fell beside them fighting the Persians, with the Thebans, who fought against the Spartans with the Persians.

more, you will enslave the land in which the freedom of the Hellenes was won, make desolate the temples of the gods to whom they prayed before they overcame the Persians, and take away your ancestral, sacrifices from those who founded and instituted them."

"It were not to your glory, Spartans, either to offend in this way against the common-law of the Hellenes and against your own ancestors, or to kill us, your benefactors, to gratify another's hatred without having been wronged yourselves: it would be more to your glory to spare us and to yield to the impressions of a reasonable compassion; reflecting not merely on the awful fate in store for us, but also on the character of the sufferers, and on the impossibility of predicting how soon misfortune may fall even upon those who deserve it not. [2] We, as we have a right to do and as our need impels us, entreat you, calling aloud upon the gods at whose common altar all the Hellenes worship, to hear our request, to be not unmindful of the oaths which your fathers swore, and which we now plead. We supplicate you by the tombs of your fathers and appeal to those that are gone to save us from falling into the hands of the Thebans and prevent the dearest friends of the Hellenes from being given up to their most detested foes. We also remind you of that day on which we did the most glorious deeds by your fathers' sides, we who now on this day are likely to suffer the most dreadful fate. [3] Finally, to do what is necessary and yet most difficult for men in our situation—that is, to make an end of speaking, since with that ending the peril of our lives draws near—[4] we say in conclusion that we did not surrender our city to the Thebans (to that we would have preferred inglorious starvation), but trusted in and capitulated to you; and it would be just, if we fail to persuade you, to put us back in the same position and let us take the chance that falls to us: And at the same time we Plataeans, foremost among the Hellenic patriots, and suppliants to you, beseech you not to give us up out of your hands and faith to our most hated enemies, the Thebans, but to be our saviors.

3.59
427
5th Year/Summer
PLATAEA
The Plataeans conclude that they surrendered their city to Sparta, not to Thebes.

Do not, while you free the rest of the Hellenes, bring us to destruction."

Such were the words of the Plataeans. The Thebans, afraid that the Spartans might be moved by what they had heard, came forward and said that they too desired to address them, since the Plataeans had, against their wish, been allowed to speak at length instead of being confined to a simple answer to the question. Leave being granted, the Thebans spoke as follows:

"We should never have asked to make this speech if the Plataeans on their side had contented themselves with briefly answering the question, and had not turned round and made charges against us, coupled with a long defense of themselves upon matters outside the present inquiry and not even the subject of accusation, and with praise of what no one finds fault with. However, since they have done so, we must answer their charges and refute their self-praise, in order that neither our bad name nor their good may help them, but that you may hear the real truth on both points, and so decide. [2] The origin of our quarrel was this. We settled Plataea some time after the rest of Boeotia, together with other places out of which we had driven the mixed population. The Plataeans not choosing to recognize our supremacy, as had been first arranged, but separating themselves from the rest of the Boeotians, and proving traitors to their nationality, we used compulsion; upon which they went over to the Athenians, and with them did us much harm, for which we retaliated."

"Next, when the barbarian invaded Hellas, they say that they were the only Boeotians who did not Medize; and this is where they most glorify themselves and abuse us. We say that if they did not Medize, it was because the Athenians did not do so either; just as afterwards when the Athenians attacked the Hellenes they, the Plataeans, were again the only Boeotians who Atticized. [2] And yet consider the forms of our respective governments when we so acted. Our city at that juncture had neither an oligarchic constitution in which all the nobles enjoyed equal rights nor a democracy, but that which is most opposed to law and good government and nearest a tyranny—the rule of a close cabal. [3] These, hoping to strengthen their individual power by the success of the Persians, kept the people down by force, and brought them into the city. The city as a whole was not its own mistress when it so acted, and ought not to be reproached for the errors that it committed while deprived of its constitution. [4] Examine only how we acted after the departure of the Persians and the recovery of the constitution; when the Athenians attacked the rest of Hellas and endeavored to subjugate our country, of the greater part of which faction had already made them masters. Did we not fight and conquer at Coronea and liberate Boeotia, and do we not now actively contribute to the liberation of the rest, providing horses to the cause and a force unequaled by that of any other state in the confederacy?"

3.62
427
5th Year/Summer
PLATAEA
The Thebans say their government was a tyranny when it Medized, acting against the desires of the people. Now that they have recovered their constitution, Thebes is foremost in the fight against Athenian hegemony.

"Let this suffice to excuse us for our Medism. We will now endeavor to show that you have injured the Hellenes more than we, and are more deserving of condign punishment. [2] It was in defense against us, say you, that you became allies and citizens of Athens. If so, you ought only to have called in the Athenians against us, instead of joining them, in attacking others: it was open to you to do this if you ever felt that they were leading you where you did not wish to follow, as Sparta was already your ally against the Mede, as you so much insist; and this was surely sufficient to keep us off, and above all to allow you to deliberate in security. Nevertheless, of your own choice and without

3.63
427
5th Year/Summer
PLATAEA
The Thebans criticize the Plataeans for helping the Athenians to subjugate other Hellenes.

3.64
427
5th Year/Summer
PLATAEA
The Thebans emphasize
the willingness of the
Plataeans to serve Athens,
pointing out that they
rejected an offer to remain
neutral in the current
struggle.

compulsion you chose to throw your lot in with Athens. [3] And you say that it had been base for you to betray your benefactors; but it was surely far baser and more iniquitous to sacrifice the whole body of the Hellenes, your fellow confederates, who were liberating Hellas, than the Athenians only, who were enslaving it. [4] The return that you made them was therefore neither equal nor honorable, since you called them in, as you say, because you were being oppressed yourselves, and then became their accomplices in oppressing others; one should indeed return like for like, but it is base to do so when such repayment unjustly harms others."

"Meanwhile, after thus plainly showing that it was not for the sake of the Hellenes that you alone then did not Medize, but because the Athenians did not do so either, and you wished to side with them and to be against the rest; [2] you now claim the benefit of good deeds done to please your neighbors. This cannot be admitted: you chose the Athenians, and with them you must stand or fall. Nor can you plead the league then made and claim that it should now protect you. [3] You abandoned that league, and offended against it by helping instead of hindering the subjugation of the Aeginetans and others of its members, and that not under compulsion, but while in enjoyment of the same institutions that you enjoy to the present hour, and no one forcing you as in our case. Lastly, an invitation was addressed to you before you were besieged to be neutral and join neither party: this you did not accept. [4] Who then merit the detestation of the Hellenes more justly than you, you who sought their ruin under the mask of honor? The former virtues that you allege you now show not to be proper to your character; the real bent of your nature has been at length damningly proved: when the Athenians took the path of injustice you followed them."

[5] "Of our unwilling Medism and your willful Atticizing this, then, is our explanation."

"The last wrong of which you complain consists in our having, as you say, lawlessly invaded your city in time of peace and festival. Here again we cannot think that we were more in fault than yourselves. [2] If of our own proper motion we made an armed attack upon your city and ravaged your territory, we are guilty; but if the first men among you in estate and family, wishing to put an end to the foreign connection and to restore you to the common Boeotian country, of their own free will invited us, wherein is our crime? Where wrong is done, those who lead, as you say, are more to blame than those who follow. [3] Not that, in our judgment, wrong was done either by them or by us. Citizens like yourselves, and with more at stake than you, they opened their own walls and introduced us into their own city, not as foes but as friends, to prevent the bad among you from becoming worse; to give honest men their due; to reform principles without attacking persons, since you were not to be banished from your city, but brought home to your kindred, nor to be made enemies to any, but friends alike to all."

"That our intention was not hostile is proved by our behavior. We did no harm to anyone, but publicly invited those who wished to live under a national, Boeotian government to come over to us; [2] which at first you gladly did, and made an agreement with us and remained tranquil, until you became aware of the smallness of our numbers. Now it is possible that there may have been something not quite fair in our entering without the consent of your People. At any rate you did not repay us in kind. Instead of refraining, as we had done, from violence, and inducing us to retire by negotiation, you fell upon us in violation of your agreement, and slew some of us in fight, of which we do not so much complain, for in that there was a certain justice; but others who held out their hands and received quarter, and whose lives you subsequently promised us, you lawlessly butchered. If this was not abominable, what is? [3] And after these three crimes committed one after the other—the violation of your agreement, the murder of the men afterwards, and the lying breach

3.65
427
5th Year/Summer
PLATAEA
Though Theban Medizing was unwilling, Plataean Atticizing was willful. Some Plataean citizens acted honorably to help Thebes in the attack on their city to save it from its worst elements.

3.66
427
5th Year/Summer
PLATAEA
The Thebans say their intentions were not hostile, but that the Plataeans criminally violated their own agreement when they slew their prisoners.

of your promise not to kill them, if we refrained from injuring your property in the country—you still affirm that we are the criminals and yourselves pretend to escape justice. Not so, if these your judges decide aright, but you will be punished for all together."

"Such, Spartans, are the facts. We have gone into them at some length both on your account and on our own, that you may feel that you will justly condemn the prisoners, and we, that we have given an additional sanction to our vengeance. [2] We would also prevent you from being melted by hearing of their past virtues, if any such they had: these may be fairly appealed to by the victims of injustice, but only aggravate the guilt of criminals, since they offend against their better nature. Nor let them gain anything by crying and wailing, by calling upon your fathers' tombs and their own desolate condition. [3] Against this we point to the far more dreadful fate of our youth, butchered at their hands; the fathers of whom either fell at Coronea, bringing Boeotia over to you, or seated, forlorn old men by desolate hearths, who with far more reason implore your justice upon the prisoners. [4] The pity which they appeal to is due rather to men who suffer unworthily; those who suffer justly, as they do, are on the contrary subjects for triumph. [5] For their present desolate condition they have themselves to blame, since they willfully rejected the better alliance. Their lawless act was not provoked by any action of ours; hate, not justice, inspired their decision; and even now the satisfaction which they afford us is not adequate; they will suffer by a legal sentence not, as they pretend, as suppliants asking for quarter in battle, but as prisoners who have surrendered upon agreement to take their trial. [6] Vindicate, therefore, the Hellenic law which they have broken, Spartans, and grant to us, the victims of its violation, the reward merited by our zeal. Nor let us be supplanted in your favor by their harangues, but offer an example to the Hellenes that the contests to which you invite them are of deeds, not words: good deeds can be shortly stated, but where wrong is done a wealth of language is needed to veil its deformity. [7]

3.67
427
5th Year/Summer
PLATAEA
The Thebans conclude that the Plataeans are unworthy of pity, for they bear full responsibility for their plight after rejecting the Hellenes.

However, if leading powers were to do what you are now doing, and putting one short question to all alike, were to decide accordingly, men would be less tempted to seek fine phrases to cover bad actions."

Such were the words of the Thebans. The Spartan judges decided that the question, whether they had received any service from the Plataeans in the war, was a fair one for them to put; as they had always invited them to be neutral, agreeably to the original covenant of Pausanias after the defeat of the Persians, and had again definitely offered them the same conditions before the blockade. This offer having been refused, they were now, they conceived, by the loyalty of their intention released from their covenant; and having, as they considered, suffered evil at the hands of the Plataeans, they brought them in again one by one and asked each of them the same question, that is to say, whether they had done the Spartans and allies any service in the war; and upon their saying that they had not, took them out and slew them all without exception. [2] The number of Plataeans thus massacred was not less than two hundred, with twenty-five Athenians who had shared in the siege. The women were taken as slaves. [3] The city the Thebans gave for about a year to some political emigrants from Megara, and to the surviving Plataeans of their own party to inhabit, and afterwards razed it to the ground from the very foundations, and built on to the precinct of Hera an inn two hundred feet square, with rooms all round above and below, making use for this purpose of the roofs and doors of the Plataeans : of the rest of the materials in the wall, the brass and the iron, they made couches which they dedicated to Hera, for whom they also built a stone chapel of a hundred feet square. The land they confiscated and let out on a ten-years' lease to Theban occupiers. [4] The adverse attitude of the Spartans in the whole Plataean affair was mainly adopted to please the Thebans, who were thought to be useful in the war at that moment raging. Such was the end of Plataea in the ninety-third year after she became the ally of Athens.

3.68
427
5th Year/Summer
PLATAEA.
The Plataeans are executed and their city razed.

4.1
425
7th Year/Summer
SICILY
Messana invites
occupation by Syracuse
and Locris, and revolts
from Athens.

Next summer, about the time of the grain's coming into ear, ten Syracusan and as many Locrian vessels sailed to Messana, in Sicily, and occupied the city upon the invitation of the inhabitants; and Messana revolted from the Athenians. [2] The Syracusans contrived this chiefly because they saw that the place afforded an approach to Sicily, and feared that the Athenians might hereafter use it as a base for attacking them with a larger force; the Locrians because they wished to carry on hostilities from both sides of the Strait and to reduce their enemies, the people of Rhegium. [3] Meanwhile, the Locrians had invaded the Rhegian territory with all their forces, to prevent their assisting Messana, and also at the request of some exiles from Rhegium who were with them. Moreover, the long-standing factions by which that city had been torn rendered it for the moment incapable of resistance, and thus furnished an additional temptation to the invaders, [4] After devastating the country the Locrian land forces retired, their ships remaining to guard Messana, while others, were being manned for the same destination to carry on the war from there.

4.2
425
7th Year/Summer
PELOPONNESUS
The Peloponnesians
invade Attica again. An
Athenian fleet leaves the
Piraeus for Sicily.

About the same time in the spring, before the corn was ripe, the Peloponnesians and their allies invaded Attica under Agis son of Archidamus, king of the Spartans, and established themselves there and laid waste the country. [2] Meanwhile the Athenians sent off to Sicily the forty ships which they had been preparing, with the remaining generals Eurymedon and Sophocles; [3] their colleague Pythodorus having already preceded them there. These had also instructions as they sailed by to assist the Corcyraeans in the city, who were being plundered by the exiles in the mountain. To support these exiles sixty Peloponnesian vessels had recently sailed, it being thought that the famine raging in the city would make it easy for them to reduce it. [4] Demosthenes also, who had remained without employment since his return from Acarnania, applied for and obtained permission to use the fleet, if he wished, upon the coast of the Peloponnesus.

Off Laconia they heard that the Peloponnesian ships were already at Corcyra, upon which Eurymedon and Sophocles wished to hasten to the island, but Demosthenes required them first to touch at Pylos and do what was wanted there, before continuing their voyage. While they were making objections, a squall chanced to come on and carried the fleet into Pylos. [2] Demosthenes at once urged them to fortify the place, as this was the reason why he had come on the voyage. He made them observe that there was plenty of stone and timber on the spot and that the place was strong by nature, and together with much of the country round unoccupied; Pylos, or Coryphasium, as the Spartans call it, lies about forty-five miles distant from Sparta in the former country of the Messenians. [3] The commanders told him that there was no lack of desert headlands in the Peloponnesus if he wished to put the city to expense by occupying them. He, however, thought that this place was distinguished from others of the kind by having a harbor close by; while the Messenians, the old natives of the country, speaking the same dialect as the Spartans, could do them the greatest harm by their incursions from it, and would at the same time be a trusty garrison.

After speaking to the captains of companies on the subject, and failing to persuade either the generals or the soldiers, he remained inactive with the rest from stress of weather; until the soldiers themselves wanting occupation were seized with, a sudden impulse to go round and fortify the place. [2] Accordingly they set to work in earnest, and having no iron tools, picked up stones, and put them together as they happened to fit, and where mortar was needed, carried it on their backs for want of hods, stooping down to make it stay on, and clasping their hands together behind to prevent it falling off; [3] sparing no effort to complete the most vulnerable points before the arrival of the Spartans, most of the place being sufficiently strong by nature without further fortification.

Meanwhile the Spartans were celebrating a festival, and also at first made light of the news, thinking that whenever they chose to take the field the place would be immediately evacuated by the enemy or easily taken by force. The absence of their army before Athens also had something to do with, their delay. [2] The Athenians fortified the place on the land side and where it most required it in six days, and leaving Demosthenes

4.3
425
7th year/Summer
PYLOS
A storm forces the Athenian fleet to put into Pylos. Demosthenes wants to fortify the place but the generals refuse.

4.4
425
7th year/Summer
PYLOS
The bored Athenian soldiers suddenly and impulsively decide to build a fort.

4.5
425
7th year/Summer
SPARTA
The Spartans make light of the news about Pylos and permit the Athenians to complete their fort.

with five ships to garrison it, hastened with the main body of the fleet on their voyage to Corcyra and Sicily.

4.6
425
7th year/Summer
ATTICA
But when Agis learns of the fort, he marches his army back to Sparta.

As soon as the Peloponnesians in Attica heard of the occupation of Pylos, they hurried back home, the Spartans and their king Agis thinking that the matter touched them nearly. Besides having made their invasion early in the season while the grain was still green, most of their troops were short of provisions: the weather also was unusually bad for the time of year, and greatly distressed their army. [2] Many reasons thus combined to hasten their departure and to make this invasion a very short one; indeed they stayed only fifteen days in Attica.

4.7
425
7th year/Summer
THRACE
The Athenians take but then fail to hold Mendaean Eion.

About the same time the Athenian general Simonides getting together a few Athenians from the garrisons, and a number of the allies in those parts, took by treachery the Mendaean colony of Eion in Thrace, which was hostile to Athens, but he had no sooner done so than the Chalcidians and Bottiaeans came up and beat him out of it, with the loss of many of his soldiers.

4.8
425
7th year/Summer
PYLOS
The Spartans concentrate land and sea forces to attack Pylos. Demosthenes sends for help from the Athenian fleet at Zacynthus. The Spartans plan to blockade Pylos and take it by siege. They occupy the island of Sphacteria.

On the return of the Peloponnesians from Attica the Spartans themselves and the nearest of the *perioikoi* at once set for Pylos, the other Spartans following more slowly as they had just come in from another campaign. [2] Word was also sent round the Peloponnesus to come as quickly as possible to Pylos; while the sixty Peloponnesian ships were sent for from Corcyra, and being dragged by their crews across the isthmus of Leucas, passed unperceived by the Athenian squadron at Zacynthus, and reached Pylos, where the land forces had arrived before them. [3] Before the Peloponnesian fleet sailed in, Demosthenes found time to send out unobserved two ships to inform Eurymedon and the Athenians on board the fleet at Zacynthus of the danger to Pylos and to summon them to his assistance. [4] While the ships hastened on their voyage in obedience to the orders of Demosthenes, the Spartans prepared to assault the fort by land and sea, hoping to capture with ease a work constructed in haste, and held by a feeble garrison. [5] Meanwhile, as they expected the Athenian ships to arrive from Zacynthus, they intended, if they failed to take the place before, to block the entrances of the harbor to prevent their being able to anchor inside it. [6] For the island of Sphacteria stretches along in a line close in front of the harbor and at once makes it safe and narrows its entrances, leaving a passage for two ships on the side nearest Pylos and the Athenian fortifications, and for eight or nine skips on that next the mainland on the other side: for the rest, the island was entirely covered with wood, and without paths through not being inhabited, and about fifteen *stades* in length. [7] The Spartans meant to close the entrances with a line of ships placed close together with their prows turned toward the sea and, meanwhile, fearing that the enemy might make use of the island to operate against them, carried over some *hoplites* to it, stationing others along the coast. [8] By this means both the island and the continent would be hostile the shore of Pylos itself outside the inlet toward the open sea had no harbor, there would be no point that the Athenians could use as a base from which to relieve their countrymen. Thus the Spartans would in all probability become master of the place without a sea fight or risk, as there had been little preparation for the occupation and there was no food there. [9]

This being decided, they carried the hoplites over to the island, drafting them by lot from all the companies. Some others had crossed over before in relief parties, but these last who were left there were four hundred and twenty in number, with their *Helot* attendants, and were commanded by Epitadas son of Molobrus.

Meanwhile Demosthenes, seeing that the Spartans were about to attack him by sea and land simultaneously, was himself not idle. He drew up under the fortification the *triremes* remaining to him of those which had been left him and enclosed them in a stockade, arming the sailors taken out of them with poor shields, most of them made of osier, it being impossible to procure arms in such a desert place. Indeed, even these were obtained from a thirty-oared Messenian privateer and a boat belonging to some Messenians who happened to have come to them. Among these Messenians were forty hoplites, whom he made use of with the rest. [2] Posting most of his men, unarmed and armed, upon the best fortified and strong points of the place facing the interior, with orders to repel any attack of the land forces, he picked sixty hoplites and a few archers from his whole force, and with these went outside the wall down to the sea, where he thought that the enemy would most likely attempt to land. Although the ground was difficult and rocky, looking toward the open sea, the fact that this was the

4.9
425
7th year/Summer
PYLOS
Demosthenes, joined bysome Messenians, prepares to defend Pylos and personally leads the defense against an anticipated Spartan amphibious attack.

weakest part of the wall would, he thought, encourage their ardor, [3] as the Athenians, confident in their naval superiority, had here paid little attention to their defenses, and the enemy, if he could force a landing, might feel sure of taking the place. [4] At this point, accordingly, going down to the water's edge, he posted his hoplites to prevent, if possible, a landing, and encouraged them in the following terms:

4.10
425
7th year/Summer
PYLOS
Demosthenes addresses his troops, advising them to offer firm resistance at the water's edge to repulse the enemy's amphibious assault.

"Soldiers and comrades in this adventure, I hope that none of you in our present strait will think to show his wit by exactly calculating all the perils that encompass us, but that you will rather hasten to close with the enemy, without staying to weigh the odds, seeing in this your best chance of safety. In emergencies like ours calculation is out of place; the sooner the danger is faced the better. [2] To my mind also most of the chances are for us, if we will only stand fast and not throw away our advantages, overawed by the numbers of the enemy. [3] One of the points in our favor is the awkwardness of the landing. This, however, only helps us if we stand our ground. If we give way it will, without a defender, prove practicable enough, in spite of its natural difficulty, without a defender; and the enemy will instantly become more formidable from the difficulty he will have in retreating, supposing that we succeed in repulsing him. Surely we shall find it easier to repel him while he is on board his ships, than after he has landed and meets us on equal terms. [4] As to his numbers, these need not too much alarm you. Large as they may be he can only engage in small detachments, from the difficulty of landing. Besides, the numerical superiority that we have to meet is not that of an army on land with everything else equal, but of troops on board ship, upon an element where many favorable accidents are required to act effectively. [5] I therefore consider that his difficulties may be fairly set against our numerical deficiencies, and at the same time I charge you as Athenians who know by experience what landing from ships on a hostile territory means, and how impossible it is to drive back an enemy determined enough to stand his ground and not to be frightened away by the surf and the terrors of the ships sailing in, to stand fast in the present emergency, beat back the enemy at the water's edge, and save yourselves and the place."

Thus encouraged by Demosthenes, the Athenians felt more confident, and went down to meet the enemy, posting themselves along the edge of the sea. [2] The Spartans now put themselves in motion and simultaneously assaulted the fortification with their land forces and with their ships, forty-three in number, under their admiral, Thrasymelidas son of Cratesicles, a *Spartiate*, who made his attack just where Demosthenes expected. [3] The Athenians had thus to defend themselves on both sides, from the land and from the sea; the enemy rowing up in small detachments, the one relieving the other—it being impossible for many to engage at once—and showing great ardor and cheering each other on, in the endeavor to force a landing and to take the fortification. [4] He who most distinguished himself was Brasidas, captain of a trireme, Seeing that the captains and steersmen, impressed by the difficulty of the position, hung back even where a landing might have seemed possible, for fear of wrecking their vessels, he shouted out to them that they must never allow the enemy to fortify himself in their country for the sake of saving timber, but must shiver their vessels and force a landing. He bade the allies, instead of hesitating in such a moment, to sacrifice their ships for Sparta in return for her many benefits, to run them boldly aground, land in one way or another, and make themselves masters of the place and its garrison.

4.11
425
7th year/Summer
PYLOS
The Spartans attack both by land and sea. Brasidas displays unusual zeal and bravery.

Not content with this exhortation, he forced his own steersman to run his ship ashore, and stepping onto the gangway, was endeavoring to land when he was beaten back by the Athenians and after receiving many wounds fainted away. Falling into the bow, his shield slipped off his arm into the sea, and being thrown ashore was picked up by the Athenians and afterwards used for the trophy which they set up for this attack. [2] The rest also did their best, but were not able to land, owing to the difficulty of the ground and the unflinching tenacity of the Athenians. [3] It was a strange reversal of the order of things for Athenians to be fighting from the land and from Laconian land too, against Spartans coming from the sea; while Spartans

4.12
425
7th year/Summer
PYLOS
Brasidas is wounded and faints. The Athenians recover his shield and use it for their victory trophy. Thucydides notes the irony of Athenians defending Spartan land against Spartans attacking from the sea.

were trying to land from shipboard in their own country, now become hostile, to attack Athenians, although the former were chiefly famous at the time as an inland people and superior by land, the latter as a maritime people with a navy that had no equal.

After continuing their attacks during that day and most of the next, the Peloponnesians desisted, and the day after sent some of their ships to Asine for timber to make siege engines with which they hoped to take, in spite of its height, the wall opposite the harbor where the landing was easiest. [2] At this moment the Athenian fleet from Zacynthus arrived, now numbering fifty sail, having been reinforced by some of the ships on guard at Naupactus and by four Chian vessels. [3] Seeing both the coast and the island crowded with hoplites, and the hostile ships in the harbor showing no signs of sailing out, and at a loss where to anchor, they sailed for the moment to the desert island of Prote, not far off, where they passed the night. The next day they got under weigh in readiness to engage in the open sea if the enemy chose to put out to meet them, being determined in the event of his not doing so to sail in and attack him. [4] The Spartans did not put out to sea, and having omitted to close the entrances as they had intended, remained quiet on shore, engaged in manning their ships and getting ready, in the case of any one sailing in, to fight in the harbor, which is a fairly large one.

Perceiving this, the Athenians advanced against them through both entrances and falling on the enemy's fleet, most of which was by this time afloat and in line, they at once put it to flight, and giving chase as far as the short distance allowed, disabled a good many vessels and took five, one with its crew on board. Then, dashing in at the rest that had taken refuge on shore, they rammed some that were still being manned before they could put out, and lashed on to their own ships and towed off empty others whose crews had fled. [2] At this sight the Spartans, maddened by a disaster which cut off their men on the island, rushed to the rescue, and going into the sea with their heavy armor, laid hold of the ships and tried to drag them back, each man thinking that success depended on his individual exertions. [3] Great was the melee, and quite in contradiction to the naval tactics usual to the two. combatants; the Spartans in their excitement and dismay being actually

4.13
425
7th year/Summer
The Spartans attack Pylos for two days without success. The Athenian fleet from Zacynthus arrives and, unable to land at Pylos, camps for the night at Prote. The next morning it attacks the Spartans, who are taken by surprise.

4.14
425
7th year/Summer
PYLOS
The Peloponnesian fleet is routed, but Spartan troops prevent the Athenians from dragging off their beached triremes. The Athenians cruise around Sphacteria to cut off the island's garrison.

engaged in a sea fight on land, while the victorious Athenians, in their eagerness to push their success as far as possible, were carrying on a land fight from their ships. [4] After great exertions and numerous wounds on both sides they separated, the Spartans saving their empty ships, except those first taken; [5] and both parties returning to their camp, the Athenians set up a trophy, gave back the dead, secured the wrecks, and at once began to cruise round and carefully watch the island, with its intercepted garrison, while the Peloponnesians on the mainland, whose contingents had now all come up, stayed where they were before Pylos.

When the news of what had happened at Pylos reached Sparta, the disaster was thought so serious that the Spartans resolved that the authorities should go down to the camp and decide on the spot what was best to be done. [2] There, seeing that it was impossible to help their men and not wishing to risk their being reduced by hunger or overpowered by numbers, they determined, with the consent of the Athenian generals, to conclude an armistice at Pylos, to send envoys to Athens to obtain a convention, and to endeavor to get back their men as quickly as possible.

4.15
425
7th year/Summer
PYLOS
Worried Spartan authorities arrive at Pylos and quickly conclude an armistice.

The generals accepting their offers, an armistice was concluded upon the following terms:

That the Spartans should bring to Pylos and deliver to the Athenians the ships that had fought in the late engagement, and all in Laconia that were vessels of war, and should make no attack on the fortification either by land or by sea. That the Athenians should allow the Spartans on the mainland to send to the men in the island a certain fixed quantity of already kneaded grain, that is to say, two quarts of barley meal, one pint of wine, and a piece of meat for each man, and half the same quantity for a servant. That this allowance should be sent in under the eyes of the Athenians, and that no boat should sail to the island except openly. That the Athenians should continue to guard the island the same as before, without however landing upon it, and should refrain from attacking the Peloponnesian troops either by land or by sea. [2] That if either party should infringe any of these terms in the slightest particular, the armistice should be at once void. That the armistice should hold good until the return of the Spartan envoys from Athens—the Athenians sending them thither in a trireme and bringing them

4.16
425
7th year/Summer
PYLOS
Thucydides lists the terms of the armistice.

back again—and upon the arrival of the envoys should be at an end, and the ships be restored by the Athenians in the same state as they received them. [3] Such were the terms of the armistice, and the ships were delivered over to the number of sixty, and the envoys sent off accordingly. When they arrived at Athens they spoke as follows:

4.17
425
7th year/Summer
ATHENS
Addressing the Athenian Assembly, Spartan envoys convey their wish to settle the war in a manner consistent with Athenian interests and Spartan dignity in its time of misfortune.

"Athenians, the Spartans sent us to try to find some way of settling the affair of our men on the island, that shall be at once satisfactory to your interests, and as consistent with our dignity in our misfortune as circumstances permit. [2] We can venture to speak at some length without any departure from the habit of our country. Men of few words where many are not wanted, we can be less brief when there is a matter of importance to be discussed and an end to be served by its illustration. [3] Meanwhile we beg you to take what we may say, not in a hostile spirit, nor as if we thought you ignorant and wished to lecture you, but rather as a suggestion on the best course to be taken, addressed to intelligent judges. [4] You can now, if you choose, employ your present success to advantage, so as to keep what you have got and gain honor and reputation besides, and you can avoid the mistake of those who meet with an extraordinary piece of good fortune, and are led on by hope to grasp continually at something further, through having already succeeded without expecting it. [5] While those who have known most vicissitudes of good and bad, have also and rightly, least confidence in their prosperity; and experience has not been wanting to teach your city and ours this lesson."

4.18
425
7th year/Summer
ATHENS
The Spartan envoys blame Sparta's current troubles on errors of judgment, not loss of power, and urge the Athenians to use their success wisely and moderately.

"To be convinced of this you have only to look at our present misfortune. What power in Hellas stood higher than we did? And yet we have come to you, although we formerly thought ourselves more able to grant what we are now here to ask. [2] Nevertheless, we have not been brought to this by any decay in. our power, or through having our heads turned by aggrandizement; no, our resources are what they have always been, and our error has been an error of judgment, to which all are equally liable. [3] Accordingly the prosperity which your city now enjoys, and the accessions that it has lately received, must not make you suppose that fortune will be always with you. [4] Indeed sensible men are prudent enough to treat their gains as precarious, just as they would also keep a clear head in adversity, and think that war, so far from staying within the limit to which a combatant may wish to confine it, will run the course that its chances prescribe; and thus, not being puffed up by confidence in military success, they are less likely to come to grief and most ready to make peace, if they can, while their fortune lasts. [5] This, Athenians, you have a good opportunity to do now with us, and thus to escape the possible disasters which may follow upon your refusal, and the consequent imputation of having owed to accident even your present advantages when you might have left behind you a reputation for power and wisdom which nothing could endanger."

"The Spartans accordingly invite you to make a treaty and to end the war, and offer peace and alliance and the most friendly and intimate relations in every way and on every occasion between us; and in return ask for the men on the island, thinking it better for both parties not to hold out to the end, hoping that some favorable accident will enable the men to force their way out, or of their being compelled to succumb under the pressure of blockade. [2] Indeed if great enmities are ever to be really settled, we think it will be, not by the system of revenge and military success, and by forcing an opponent to swear to a treaty to his disadvantage; but when the more fortunate combatant waives his privileges and, guided by gentler feelings, conquers his rival in generosity and accords peace on more moderate conditions than expected. [3] From that moment, instead of the debt of revenge which violence must entail, his adversary owes a debt of generosity to be paid in kind, and is inclined by honor to stand by his agreement. [4] And men more often act in this manner toward their greatest enemies than where the quarrel is of less importance; they are also by nature as glad to give way to those who first yield to them,

4.19
425
7th year/Summer
ATHENS
The Spartan envoys offer Athens a treaty of peace and alliance, pointing out that real peace must arise through generosity, not through military success that spawns a desire for revenge.

as they are apt to be provoked by arrogance to risks condemned by their own judgment."

"To apply this to ourselves: if peace was ever desirable for both parties, it is surely so at the present moment, before anything irremediable befall us and force us to hate you eternally, personally as well as politically, and you to miss the advantages that we now offer you. [2] While the issue is still in doubt, and you have reputation and our friendship in prospect, and we the compromise of our misfortune before anything fatal occur, let us be reconciled, and for ourselves choose peace instead of war, and grant to the rest of the Hellenes a remission from their sufferings, for which be sure they will think they have chiefly you to thank."

"They know not who began this war, but their gratitude for concluding it, as it depends on your decision, will surely be laid at your door. [3] By such a decision you can become firm friends with the Spartans at their own invitation, which you do not force from them, but oblige them by accepting. [4] And from this friendship consider the advantages that are likely to follow: when Attica and Sparta are in concord, the rest of Hellas, you may be sure, will remain in respectful inferiority before its heads."

Such were the words of the Spartans, their idea being that the Athenians, already desirous of a truce and only kept back by their opposition, would joyfully accept a peace freely offered, and give back the men. [2] The Athenians, however, having the men on the island, thought that the treaty would be ready for them whenever they chose to make it, and grasped at something further. [8] Foremost to encourage them in this policy was Cleon son of Cleaenetus, a popular leader of the time and very powerful with the multitude, who persuaded them to answer as follows: First, the men in the island must surrender themselves and their arms and be brought to Athens. Next, the Spartans must restore Nisaea, Pegae, Troezen, and Achaea, all places acquired not by arms, but by the previous convention, under which they had been ceded by Athens herself at a moment of disaster, when a truce was more necessary

4.20
425.
7th year/Summer
ATHENS
The Spartan envoys conclude by saying that Athens will receive credit for the ensuing peace, which will endure, since no one in Hellas could challenge the combined hegemony of Athens and Sparta.

4.21
425
7th year/Summer
ATHENS
The Athenians, swayed by the demagogic Cleon, refuse Sparta's offer of peace and alliance, and instead "grasp for something more."

to her than at present. This done they might take back their men, and make a truce for as long as both parties might agree.

To this answer the envoys made no reply, but asked that commissioners might be chosen with whom they might confer on each point, and quietly talk the matter over and try to come to some agreement. [2] Hereupon Cleon violently assailed them, saying that he knew from the first that they had no right intentions, and that it was clear enough now by their refusing to speak before the people, and wanting to confer in secret with a committee of two or three. No! if they meant anything honest let them say it out before all. [3] The Spartans, however, seeing that whatever concessions they might be prepared to make in their misfortune, it was impossible to express them before the multitude and lose credit with their allies for a negotiation which might after all miscarry, and on the other hand, that the Athenians would never grant what they asked upon moderate terms, returned from Athens without having effected anything.

Their arrival at once put an end to the armistic at Pylos, and the Spartans asked for the return of their ships according to the truce. The Athenians, however, alleged an attack on the fort in violation of the truce, and other grievances seemingly not worth mentioning, and refused to give them back, insisting upon the clause by which the slightest infringement made the armistice void. The Spartans, after denying the violation and protesting against their bad faith in the matter of the ships, went away and earnestly addressed themselves to the war. [2] Hostilities were now carried on at Pylos by both sides with vigor. The Athenians cruised round the island all day with two ships going different ways; and by night, except on the seaward side in windy weather, anchored round it with their whole fleet, which having been reinforced by twenty ships from Athens come to aid in the blockade, now numbered seventy sail; while the Peloponnesians remained encamped on the mainland, making attacks on the fort, and on the lookout for any opportunity which might offer itself for the deliverance of their men.

4.22
425
7th year/Summer
ATHENS
When Cleon attacks a Spartan proposal to confer in private with Athenian commissioners, the Spartan envoys recognize that Athens will not negotiate moderately, and return to Sparta.

4.23
425
7th year/Summer
PYLOS
War resumes at Pylos; the Athenians refuse to return the Peloponnesian ships, and they reinforce the blockade of Sphacteria.

4.24
425
7th Year/Summer
SICILY
The Syracusans reinforce
their fleet at Messana
and prepare to attack the
Athenians at Rhegium
to take control of the
strait between the two
cities.

Meanwhile the Syracusans and their allies in Sicily had brought up to the squadron guarding Messana the reinforcement which they had been preparing, and carried on the war from there, [2] incited chiefly by the Locrians from their hatred of the Rhegians, whose territory they had invaded with all their forces. [3] The Syracusans also wished to try their fortune at sea, seeing that the Athenians had only a few ships actually at Rhegium, and hearing that the main fleet destined to join them was engaged in blockading the island. [4] A naval victory, they thought, would enable them to blockade Rhegium by sea and land, and to reduce it easily; a success which would at once place their affairs upon a solid basis, as the promontory of Rhegium in Italy and Messana in Sicily are so near each other that it would be impossible for the Athenians to cruise against them and command the strait. [5] The strait in question consists of the sea between Rhegium and Messana, at the point where Sicily approaches nearest to the continent, and is the Charybdis through which the story makes Odysseus sail; and the narrowness of the passage, and the strength, of the current that pours in from the vast Tyrrhenian and Sicilian mains, have rightly given it a bad reputation.

4.25
425
7th Year/Summer
SICILY
Fighting on land and
sea Seen Athenians,
Namns, Rhegians,
Sicels, and Leontines,
on one side, and
Syracusans, Locrians
and Messanians, on the
other, is inconclusive.

In this strait the Syracusans and their allies were compelled to engage, late in the day, about a merchant ship sailing through, putting out with rather more than thirty ships against sixteen Athenian and eight Rhegian vessels. [2] Defeated by the Athenians they hastily set off, each for himself, to their own stations at Messana and Rhegium, with the loss of one ship; night coming on before the battle was finished. [3] After this the Locrians retired from the Rhegian territory, and the ships of the Syracusans and their allies united and came to anchor at Cape Peloras, in the territory of Messana, where their land forces joined them. [4] Here the Athenians and Rhegians sailed up, and seeing the ships unmanned made an attack, in which they in their turn lost one vessel, which was caught by a grappling iron, the crew saving themselves by swimming. [5] After this the Syracusans got on board their ships, and while they were being towed along shore to Messana, were again attacked by the Athenians, but suddenly headed out to sea and became the assailants, and caused the Athenians to lose another vessel [6] After thus holding their own in the voyage along shore and in the engagement as above described, the Syracusans sailed on into the harbor of Messana.

[7] Meanwhile the Athenians, having received warning that Camarina was about to be betrayed to the Syracusans by Archias and his party, sailed to that place; and the Messanians took this opportunity to attack their Chalcidian neighbor, Naxos by sea and land with all their forces. [8] The first day they forced the Naxians to stay within their walls, and laid waste their country; the next they sailed round with their ships, and laid waste their land on the river Akesines, while their land forces menaced the city. [9] Meanwhile the Sicels came down from the high country in great numbers to aid against the Messanians; and the Naxians, elated at the sight, and animated by a belief that the Leontines and their other Hellenic allies were coming to their support, suddenly sallied out from the city, and attacked and routed the Messanians killing more than a thousand of them; while the remainder suffered severely in their retreat home, being attacked by the barbarians on the road, and most of them cut down. [10] The ships put in to Messana, and afterwards dispersed to their different homes. The Leontines and their allies, with the Athenians, upon this at once turned their arms against the now weakened Messana, and attacked, the Athenians with their ships on the side of the harbor, and the land forces on that of the city. [11] The Messanians, however, sallying out with Demoteles and some Locrians who had been left to garrison the city after the disaster, suddenly attacked and routed most of the Leontine army, killing a great number; upon seeing which the Athenians landed from their ships, and failing on the disordered Messanians, chased them back into the city, and setting up a trophy retired to Rhegium. [12] After this the Hellenes in Sicily continued to make war on each other by land, without the Athenians.

Meanwhile the Athenians at Pylos were still besieging the Spartans in the island, the Peloponnesian forces on the continent remaining where they were. [2] The blockade was very laborious for the Athenians from want of food and water; there was no spring except one in the citadel of Pylos itself, and that not a large one, and most of them were obliged to scrape away the gravel on the sea beach and drink such water as they could find. [3] They also suffered from want of room, being encamped in a narrow space; and as there was no anchorage for the ships,

4.26
425
7th year/Summer
PYLOS
The hardships of the blockading Athenians are described. Spartan Helots risk their lives to bring food to the Sphacteria garrison, and thus win their freedom.

some took their meals on shore in their turn, while the others were anchored out at sea. [4] But their greatest discouragement arose from the unexpectedly long time which it took to reduce a body of men shut up in a desert island, with only brackish water to drink, a matter which they had imagined would take them only a few days. [5] The fact was, that the Spartans had made advertisement for volunteers to carry into the island flour, wine, cheese, and any other food useful in a siege; high prices being offered, and freedom promised to any of the Helots who should succeed in doing so. [6] The Helots accordingly were most forward to engage in this risky traffic, putting off from this or that part of the Peloponnesus, and running in by night on the seaward side of the island. [7] They were best pleased, however, when they could catch a wind to carry them in. It was more easy to elude the triremes on guard, when it blew from the seaward, as it then became impossible for them to anchor round the island; while the Helots had their boats valued at their worth in money, and ran them ashore without caring how they landed, being sure to find the soldiers waiting for them at the landing places. But all who risked it in fair weather were taken. [8] Divers also swam in under water from the harbor, dragging by a cord in skins poppyseed mixed with honey, and bruised linseed; these at first escaped notice, but afterwards a lookout was kept for them. [9] In short, both sides tried every possible contrivance, the one to throw in provisions, and the other to prevent their introduction.

4.27
425
7th Year/Summer
ATHENS
The Athenians begin to regret not making peace with the Spartans and blame Cleon, who in turn blames the general Nicias for not attacking and capturing the Spartans on Sphacteria.

At Athens, meanwhile, the news that the army was in great distress and that grain found its way in to the men in the island caused no small perplexity; and the Athenians began to fear that winter might come on and find them still engaged in the blockade. They saw that the convoying of provisions round the Peloponnesus would be then impossible. The country offered no resources in itself, and even in summer they could not send round enough. The blockade of a place without harbors could then no longer be kept up; and the men would either escape by the siege being abandoned, or would watch for bad weather and sail out in the boats that brought in their grain. [2] What caused still more alarm was the attitude of the Spartans, who must, it was thought by the Athenians, feel themselves on strong ground not to send them any more envoys; and they began to repent having rejected the treaty. [3] Cleon, perceiving the disfavor with which he was regarded for having stood in the way of the convention, now said that their informants did not speak the truth; and upon the messengers recommending that, if they did not believe them, they send some commissioners to see, Cleon himself and Theagenes were chosen by the Athenians as commissioners. [4] Aware that he would now be obliged either to say what had been already said by the men whom he was slandering, or be proved a liar if he said the contrary, he told the Athenians, whom he saw to be not altogether disinclined for a fresh expedition, that instead of sending commissioners and wasting their time and opportunities, if they believed what was told them, they ought to sail against the men. [5] And pointing at Nicias son of Niceratus, then general, whom he hated, he tauntingly said that it would be easy, if they had men for generals, to sail with a force and take those in the island, and that if he had himself been in command, he would have done it.

Nicias, seeing the Athenians murmuring against Cleon for not sailing now if it seemed to him so easy, and further seeing himself the object of attack, told him that for all that the generals cared, he might take what force he chose and make the attempt. [2] At first Cleon fancied that this resignation was merely a figure of speech, and was ready to go, but finding that it was seriously meant, he drew back, and said that Nicias, not he, was general, being now frightened, and having never supposed that Nicias would go so far as to retire in his favor. [3] Nicias, however, repeated his offer and resigned the command against Pylos, calling upon the Athenians to witness that he did so. And as the multitude is wont to do, the more Cleon shrank from the expedition and tried to back out of what he had said, the more they encouraged Nicias to hand over his command, and clamored at Cleon to go. [4] At last, not knowing how to get out of his words, he undertook the expedition, and came forward and said that he was not afraid of the Spartans, but would sail without taking anyone from the city with him except the Lemnians and Imbrians that were at Athens, with some *peltasts* that had come up from Aenus, and four hundred archers from elsewhere. With these and the soldiers at Pylos, he would within twenty days either bring the Spartans alive, or kill them on the spot. [5] The Athenians could not help laughing at his empty words, while sensible men comforted themselves

4.28
425
7th Year/Summer
ATHENS
Nicias withdraws from the command. The Athenian People now insist that Cleon take it and he does so, asking only for peltasts and archers, and promising to return victorious in twenty days.

with the reflection that they must gain in either circumstance; either they would be rid of Cleon, which they rather hoped, or if disappointed in this expectation, would reduce the Spartans.

After he had settled everything in the assembly, and the Athenians had voted him the command of the expedition, he chose as his colleague Demosthenes, one of the generals at Pylos, and pushed forward the preparations for his voyage. [2] His choice fell upon Demosthenes because he heard that he was contemplating a descent on the island and because the soldiers, distressed by the difficulties of the position and feeling more like besieged than besiegers, were eager to fight it out. Moreover, the firing of the island had increased the confidence of the general. [3] At first he had been afraid that the uninhabited island's pathless woods would favor the enemy, as he might land a large force and yet suffer losses from an attack from an unseen position. He thought the woods would in great measure conceal from him the mistakes and forces of the enemy, while the blunders of his own troops would be quickly detected by the enemy who, retaining always the ability to attack, would fall upon his troops unexpectedly wherever they pleased. [4] If, on the other hand, he should force them to engage in the thicket, the smaller number who knew the country would, he thought, have the advantage over the larger who were ignorant of it, and thus his own army might be imperceptibly destroyed in spite of its numbers, as his men would not be able to see where to support each other.

The Aetolian disaster, which had been mainly caused by the wood, had not a little to do with these reflections. [2] Meanwhile, one of the soldiers who were compelled by want of room to land on the extremities of the island and take their dinners, with outposts fixed to prevent a surprise, set fire to a little of the wood without meaning to do so; and as it came on to blow soon afterwards, almost the whole was consumed before they were aware of it. [3] Demosthenes was now able for the first time to see how numerous the Spartans really were, having up to this moment been under the impression that they took in provisions for a smaller number; he also saw that the Athenians thought success important and were anxious about it, and that it was now easier to land on the island, and accordingly got ready for the attempt, sending for troops from the allies in the neighborhood, and pushing forward his other preparations. [4] At this moment Cleon arrived at Pylos with the troops which he had asked for, having sent on word to say that he was coming. The first step taken by the two generals after their meeting was to send a herald to the camp on the mainland, to ask if they were disposed to avoid all risk and to order the men on the island to surrender themselves and their arms, to be kept in gentle custody until some general settlement should be concluded.

On the rejection of this proposition the generals let one day pass, and the next embarking all their hoplites on board a few ships, put out by night, and a little before dawn landed on both sides of the island from the open sea and from the harbor, being about eight hundred strong, and advanced with a run against the first post in the island. [2] The enemy had distributed his force as follows: In this first post there were about thirty hoplites; the center and most level part, where the water was, was held by the main body, and by Epitadas their commander; while a small party guarded the very end of the island, toward Pylos, which was precipitous on the sea side and very difficult to attack from the land, and where there was also a sort of old fort of stones rudely put together, which they thought might be useful to them, in case they should be forced to retreat. Such was their disposition.

The advanced post thus attacked by the Athenians was at once put to the sword, the men being scarcely out of bed and still arming, the landing having taken them by surprise, as they fancied the ships were only sailing as usual to their stations for the night. [2] As soon as day broke, the rest of the army landed, that is to say, all the crews of rather more than seventy ships, except the lowest rank of oars, with the arms they carried, eight hundred archers, and as many peltasts, the Messenian reinforcements, and all the other troops on duty round Pylos, except the garrison in the fort. [3] The tactics of Demosthenes had divided them into companies of two hundred, more or less, and made them occupy the highest points in order to paralyze the enemy by surrounding him on every side. By refusing to engage closely, the Athenians would leave him without any tangible adversary and expose him to the cross-fire of their host; plied by those in his rear if he attacked in front, and by those on one flank if he moved against those on the other. [4] In short, wherever he went he would have assailants behind him, and

4.31
425
7th Year/Summer
PYLOS
The Athenians embark at night and land on Sphacteria just before dawn. Spartan troops are divided into three unequal forces.

4.32
425
7th Year/Summer
PYLOS
The Spartan advance post is taken by surprise, and the rest of the Athenians land. Demosthenes' plan to refuse close combat and to attack the Spartans from all sides with missiles is described.

these light-armed attackers would prove the most difficult to deal with; their arrows, darts, stones, and slings making them formidable at a distance, and there being no means of getting at them at close quarters, as they could flee if pursued, and the moment their pursuer turned they would be upon him. Such was the idea that Demosthenes had in the first place when he was planning the landing and so he arranged its execution.

4.33
425
7th Year/Summer
PYLOS
The main Spartan force advances but is thwarted by Demosthenes' tactics.

Meanwhile the main body of the troops in the island (that under Epitadas), seeing their outpost cut off and an army advancing against them, serried their ranks and pressed forward to close with the Athenian hoplites in front of them, the light troops being upon their flanks and rear. [2] However, they were not able to engage or to profit by their superior skill, the light troops keeping them in check on either side with their missiles, and the hoplites remaining stationary instead of advancing to meet them; and although they routed the light troops wherever they ran up and approached too closely, yet they retreated fighting, being lightly equipped, and easily getting away in their flight, from the difficult and rugged nature of the ground, in an island hitherto uninhabited, over which the Spartans could not pursue them in their heavy armor.

4.34
425
7th Year/Summer
PYLOS
As the Spartans tire, the Athenians grow more confident. Blinded by dust and deafened by the noise of battle, the Spartans find it impossible either to attack or to defend themselves effectively.

After this skirmishing had lasted some little while, the Spartans became unable to dash out with the same rapidity as before upon the points attacked, and the light troops, finding that they now fought with less vigor, became more confident. They could see with their own eyes that they were many times more numerous than the enemy; they were now more familiar with his aspect and found him less terrible, the event not having justified the apprehensions which they had suffered when they first landed in slavish dismay at the idea of attacking Spartans; and accordingly their fear changing to disdain, they now rushed upon them all together with loud shouts, and pelted them with stones, darts, and arrows, whichever came first to hand. [2] The shouting accompanying their onset confounded the Spartans, unaccustomed to this mode of fighting; dust rose from the newly burnt wood, and it was impossible to see in front of one with the arrows and stones flying through clouds of dust from the hands of numerous assailants. [3] The Spartans had now to sustain a difficult conflict; their caps would not keep out the arrows, and darts had broken off in the bodies of the wounded. They themselves were unable to retaliate, being prevented from using their eyes to see what was before them, and unable to hear the words of command for the hubbub raised by the enemy; danger encompassed them on every side, and there was no hope of any means of defense or safety.

At last, after many had been already wounded in the confined space in which they were fighting, they formed in close order and retired to the fort at the end of the island, which was not far off, and to their friends who held it.

[2] The moment they gave way, the light troops became bolder and pressed upon them, shouting louder than ever, and lolled as many as they caught up with in their retreat, but most of the Spartans made good their escape to the fort, and with the garrison in it ranged themselves all along its whole extent to repulse the enemy wherever it was assailable. [3] The Athenians pursuing, unable to surround and hem them in, owing to the strength of the ground, attacked them in front and tried to storm the position. [4] For a long time, indeed for most of the day, both sides held out against all the torments of the battle, thirst, and sun, the one endeavoring to drive the enemy from the high ground, the other to maintain himself upon it, it being now more easy for the Spartans to defend themselves than before, as they could not be surrounded upon the flanks.

The struggle began to seem endless, when the commander of the Messenians came to Cleon and Demosthenes, and told them that they were wasting their efforts but that if they would give him some archers and light troops to go round on the enemy's rear by a way he would undertake to find, he thought he could force the approach. [2] Upon receiving what he asked for, he started from a point out of sight in order not to be seen by the enemy, and creeping on wherever the precipices of the island permitted, and where the Spartans, trusting to the strength of the ground, kept no guard, succeeded after the greatest difficulty in getting round without their seeing him, and suddenly appeared on the high ground in their rear, to the dismay of the surprised enemy and the still greater joy of his expectant friends. [3] The Spartans thus placed between two fires, and in the same dilemma, to compare small things with great, as at Thermopylae, where the defenders were cut off through the Persians getting round by the path, being now attacked in front and behind, began to give way, and overcome

4.35
425
7th Year/Summer
PYLOS
After many Spartans are wounded, they retire to an old fort at the end of the island, and the Athenians pursue them. There the ground favors defense and prevents encirclement. Both sides endure the torments of sun and thirst.

4.36
425
7th Year/Summer
PYLOS
The Messenian commander leads a force by a hidden route to a position above and behind the Spartans, surprising them and forcing them to give way.

4.37
425
7th Year/Summer
PYLOS
Demosthenes and Cleon
halt the advance and ask
the Spartans if they will
now surrender.

4.38
425
7th Year/Summer
PYLOS
The Spartans surrender
after consulting their
forces on the mainland.
The Spartans have lost
about 130 men.
Athenian losses are small,
as there was no fighting
at close-quarters.

by the odds against them and exhausted from want of food, retreated.

The Athenians were already masters of the approaches [4.37.1] when Cleon and Demosthenes, perceiving that the enemy, should he give way a single step farther, would be destroyed by their soldiery, put a stop to the battle and held their men back. They wished to take the Spartans alive to Athens and hoped that their stubbornness might relax on hearing the offer of terms, and that they might surrender and yield to the present overwhelming danger. [2] Proclamation was accordingly made, to determine whether they would surrender themselves and their arms to the Athenians to be dealt with at their discretion.

When the Spartans heard this offer, most of them lowered their shields and waved their hands to show that they accepted it. Hostilities now ceased, and a parley was held between Cleon and Demosthenes, and Styphon son of Pharax, for the other side; since Epitadas, the first of the previous commanders, had been killed, and Hippagretas, the next in command, left for dead among the slain, though still alive; and thus the command had devolved upon Styphon according to the law in case of anything happening to his superiors. [2]

Styphon and his companions said they wished to send a herald to the Spartans on the mainland, to know what they were to do. [3] The Athenians would not let any of them go, but themselves called for heralds from the mainland, and after questions had been carried backwards and forwards two or three times, the last man that passed over from the Spartans on the continent brought this message: "The Spartans bid you to decide for yourselves so long as you do nothing dishonorable"; upon which after consulting together they surrendered themselves and their arms. [4] The Athenians, after guarding them that day and night, the next morning set up a trophy in the island, and got ready to sail, giving their prisoners in batches to be guarded by the captains of the triremes; and the Spartans sent a herald and took up their dead. [5] The number of the killed and prisoners taken in the island was as follows: of the four hundred and twenty hoplites who had passed over originally, two hundred and ninety-two were taken alive to Athens; the rest were killed. About a hundred and twenty of the prisoners were Spartiates. The Athenian loss was small, the battle not having been fought at close quarters.

The blockade lasted seventy-two days in all, counting from the naval fight to the battle on the island. [2] For twenty of these, during the absence of the envoys sent to negotiate for peace, the men had provisions given them; for the rest they were fed by the smugglers. Grain and other victuals were found in the island, the commander Epitadas having kept the men upon half rations. [3] The Athenians and Peloponnesians now each withdrew their forces from Pylos, and went home, and mad as Cleon's promise was, he fulfilled it, by bringing the men to Athens within the twenty days as he had pledged himself to do.

Nothing that happened in the war surprised the Hellenes so much as this. It was the general opinion that no force or famine could make the Spartans give up their arms, but that they would fight on as they could, and die with them in their hands: [2] indeed people could scarcely believe that those who had surrendered were of the same stuff as the fallen; and an Athenian ally, who some time after insultingly asked one of the prisoners from the island if those that had fallen were noble and good men, received for answer that the *atraktos*—that is, the arrow—would be worth a great deal if it could, pick out noble and good men from the rest; in allusion to the fact that the lolled were those whom the stones and the arrow happened to hit.

Upon the arrival of the men the Athenians determined to keep them in prison until the peace, and if the Peloponnesians invaded their country in the interval, to bring them out and put them to death. [2] Meanwhile the defense of Pylos was not forgotten; the Messenians from Naupactus sent to their old country, to which Pylos formerly belonged, some of the most suitable of their number, and began a series of incursions into Laconia, which their common dialect rendered most destructive. [3] The Spartans, hitherto with experience of incursions or a warfare of the kind, finding the Helots deserting, and fearing the march of revolution in their country, began to be seriously, and in spite of their unwillingness to betray this to the Athenians began to send envoys to Athens, and tried to recover Plyos and the prisoners. [4] The Athenians, however, kept grasping at

4.39
425
7th Year/Summer
PYLOS
The blockade lasted seventy-two days. Cleon returns to Athens with the prisoners, his promise fulfilled.

4.40
425
7th Year/Summer
PYLOS
All Greece is amazed that the Spartans at Sphacteria surrendered. Thucydides' recounts the anecdote of the clever arrows.

4.41
425
7th Year/Summer
PYLOS-ATHENS
The captured Spartans are imprisoned at Athens. The Messenians launch effective raids on Laconia. The Spartans send envoys to Athens to negotiate a peace, but the Athenians reject their proposals, "always grasping for more."

more, and dismissed envoy after envoy without their having effected anything. Such was the history of the affair of Pylos.

BOOK 5.1 – 5.20

The next summer the truce for a year ended, after lasting until the Pythian games. During the armistice the Athenians expelled the Delians from Delos, concluding that they must have been polluted by some old offense at the time of their consecration, and that this had been the omission in the previous purification of the island which, as I have related, had been thought to have been duly accomplished by the removal of the graves of the dead. The Delians had Atramyttium in Asia given them by Phamaces, and settled there when they left Delos.

Meanwhile Cleon prevailed on the Athenians to let him set sail at the expiration of the armistice for the cities in the Thracian district with twelve hundred *hoplites* and three hundred horse from Athens, a larger force of the allies, and thirty ships. [2] First touching at the still-besieged Scione, and taking some hoplites from the army there, he next sailed into Cophosa harbor in the territory of Torone, which is not far from the city. [3] From thence, having learnt from deserters that Brasidas was not in Torone, and that its garrison was not strong enough to give him battle, he advanced with his army against the city, sending ten ships to sail round into the harbor. [4] He came first to the fortification recently built in front of the city by Brasidas in order to take in the suburb, to do which he had pulled down part of the original wall and made it one city [5.3.1] Pasitelidas, the Spartan commander, with such garrison as there was in the place, hurried to this point to repel the Athenian assault; but finding himself hard pressed, and seeing the ships that had been sent round sailing into the harbor, Pasitelidas began to be afraid that they might get up to the city before its defenders were there, and the fortification being also carried, he might be taken prisoner, and so abandoned the outer fortification and ran into the city. [2] But the Athenians from the ships had already taken Torone, and their land forces following at his heels burst in with him with a rush over the part of the old wall that had been pulled down, killing some of the Peloponnesians and Toronaeans in the mêlée, and making prisoners of the rest, and Pasitelidas their commander amongst them. [3] Brasidas meanwhile had advanced to relieve Torone, and had only about four miles more to go when he heard of its fall on the road and turned back again. [4] Cleon and the Athenians set up two trophies, one by the harbor, the other by the fortification, and making slaves of the wives and children of the Toronaeans, sent the men with the Peloponnesians and any Chalcidians that were there, to the number of seven hundred, to Athens; from which, however, they all came home afterwards, the Peloponnesians on the conclusion of peace, and the rest by being exchanged against other prisoners with the Olynthians [5] About the same time Panactum, a fortress on the Athenian border, was taken by treachery by the Boeotians. [6] Meanwhile Cleon, after placing a garrison in Torone, weighed anchor and sailed round Athos6a on his way to Amphipolis.

About the same time Phaeax son of Erasistratus set sail with two colleagues as ambassador from Athens to Italy and Sicily. [2] The Leontines, upon the departure of the Athenians from Sicily after the peace agreement, had enrolled many new citizens and The People planned to redistribute the land; but those in power, aware of their intention, called in the Syracusans and expelled The People. [3] These last were scattered in various directions; but the upper classes came to an agreement with the Syracusans, abandoned and laid waste their city, and went to live at Syracuse, where they were made citizens. [4] Afterwards some of them were dissatisfied, and leaving Syracuse occupied Phocaeae, a quarter of the city of Leontini, and Bricinniae, a fortified place in the Leontine country, and being there joined by most of the exiled People carried on war from the fortifications. [5] The Athenians hearing this, sent Phaeax to see if they could not by some means so convince their allies there and the rest of the Sicilians of the ambitious designs of Syracuse, as to induce them to form a general coalition against her, and thus save The People of Leontini. [6] Arrived in Sicily, Phaeax succeeded at Camarina and Agrigentum, but meeting with a repulse at Gela did not go on to the rest, as he saw that he should not succeed with them, but returned through the country of the Sicels to Catana, and after visiting Bricinniae as he passed, and encouraging its inhabitants, sailed back to Athens.

5.4
422
10th Year/Summer
SICILY
The Athenians send Phaeax to Sicily to form a coalition against Syracuse and to rescue the exiled Leontines. Phaeax returns to Athens unsuccessful.

5.5
422
10th Year/Summer
ITALY
Phaeax tries to secure
the friendship of some
Italian cities for Athens.
Epizephyrian Locri, at
war with its neighbors,
makes peace with
Athens.

During his voyage along the coast to and from Sicily, he talked with some cities in Italy on the subject of friendship with Athens, and also encountered some Locrian settlers exiled from Messana, who had been sent there when the Locrians were called in by one of the factions that divided Messana after the pacification of Sicily,10 and Messana came for a time into the hands of the Locrians. [2] These being met by Phaeax on their return home received no injury at his hands, as the Locrians had agreed with him for a treaty with Athens. [3] They were the only people of the allies of Syracuse who, when the reconciliation between the Sicilians took place, had not made peace with Athens; nor indeed would they have done so now, if they had not been pressed by a war with the Hipponians and Medmaeans who lived on their border, and were colonists of theirs. Phaeax meanwhile proceeded on his voyage, and at length arrived at Athens.

5.6
422
10th Year/Summer
THBACE.
Cleon makes Eion his
base and calls upon local
allies for additional
troops. Brasidas
establishes a base at
Amphipolis.

Cleon, having sailed round from Torone to Amphipolis, made Eion his base, and after an unsuccessful assault upon the Andrian colony of Stagiras, took Galepsus, a colony of Thasos, by storm. [2] He now sent envoys to Perdiccas to command his attendance with an army, as provided by the alliance; and others to Thrace, to Polles, king of the Odomantians, who was to bring as many Thracian mercenaries as possible; and himself remained inactive in Eion, awaiting their arrival. [3] Informed of this, Brasidas on his part took up a position of observation upon Cerdylium, a place situated in the Argilian country on high ground across the river, not far from Amphipolis, and commanding a view on all sides, and thus made it impossible for Cleon's army to move without his seeing it; for he fully expected that Cleon, contemptuous of the scanty numbers of his opponent, would march against Amphipolis with the force that he had with him. [4] At the same time Brasidas made his preparations, calling to his standard fifteen hundred Thracian mercenaries, and all the Edonians, horse and peltasts. he also had a thousand Myrcinian and Chalcidian peltasts, besides those in Amphipolis, [5] and a force of hoplites numbering altogether about two thousand, and three hundred Hellenic horse. Fifteen hundred of these he had with him upon Cerdylium; the rest were stationed with Clearidas in Amphipolis.

After remaining quiet for some time, Cleon was at length obliged to do as Brasidas expected, [2] His soldiers, tired of their inactivity, began seriously to reflect on the weakness and incompetence of their commander and the skill and valor that would be opposed to him, and on their own original unwillingness to accompany him. These murmurs coming to the ears of Cleon, he resolved not to disgust the army by keeping it in the same place, and broke up his camp and advanced. [3] The temper of the general was what it had been at Pylos, his success on that occasion having given him confidence in his capacity. He never dreamed of anyone coming out to fight him, but said that he was rather going up to view the place; and if he waited for his reinforcements it was not in order to make victory secure in case he should be compelled to engage, but to be enabled to surround and storm the city. [4] He accordingly came and posted his army upon a strong hill in front of Amphipolis, and proceeded to examine the lake formed by the Strymon, and how the city lay on the side of Thrace. [5] He thought to retire when he chose without fighting, as there was no one to be seen upon the wall or coming out of the gates, all of which were shut. Indeed, it seemed a mistake not to have brought down siege engines with him; he could then have taken the city, there being no one to defend it.

5.7
422
10th Year/Summer
AMPHIPOLIS
In order to satisfy his men, Cleon makes a reconnaissance in force to Amphipoiis. He does not expect to fight or to be attacked.

As soon as Brasidas saw the Athenians in motion he descended himself from Cerdylium and entered Amphipolis. [2] He did not venture to go out in regular order against the Athenians: he mistrusted his strength, and thought it inadequate to the attempt; not in numbers—these were not so unequal—but in quality, the flower of the Athenian army being in the field, with the best of the Lemnians and Imbrians. He therefore prepared to assail them by stratagem. [3] For if he let the enemy see both the numbers of his men and the makeshift nature of their armament, he thought he was less likely to win than if the enemy did not have a view of them in advance and thus come rightly to despise them. [4] He accordingly picked out a hundred and fifty hoplites, and putting the rest under Clearidas, determined to attack suddenly before the Athenians retired; thinking that he should not again have such a chance of catching them alone if their reinforcements were once allowed to come up; and so calling all his soldiers together in order to encourage them and explain his intention, spoke as follows:

5.8
422
10th Year/Summer
AMPHIPOLIS
Recognizing Cleon s ineptitude, Brasidas decides that this is an opportune moment to attack, and explains his plan to his troops.

5.9
422
10th Year/Summer
AMPHIPOLIS
Brasidas says that the
Athenians are careless and
their advance to
Amphipolis is a blunder.
He divides his force and
plans to launch a double
surprise attack in order to
panic the enemy. He
promises to set an example
by his own courage.

"Peloponnesians, the character of the country from which we have come, one which has always owed its freedom to valor, and the fact that you are Dorians and the enemy you are about to fight Ionians whom you are accustomed to beat, are things that do not need further comment. [2] But as for the plan of attack that I propose to pursue, this it is well to explain, in order that the fact of our adventuring with a part instead of with the whole of our forces may not damp your courage by the apparent disadvantage at which it places you. [3] I imagine it is the poor opinion that he has of us, and the fact that he has no idea of anyone coming out to engage him, that has made the enemy march up to the place and carelessly look about him as he is doing, without noticing us. [4] But the most successful soldier will always be the man who most happily detects a blunder like this, and who carefully consulting his own means makes his attack not so much by open and regular approaches, as by seizing the opportunity of the moment; [5] and these stratagems, which do the greatest service to our friends by most completely deceiving our enemies, have the most brilliant name in war. [6] Therefore, while their careless confidence continues, and they are still thinking, as in my judgment they are now doing, more of retreat than of maintaining their position, while their spirit is slack and not high-strung with expectation, I with the men under my command will, if possible, take them by surprise and fall with a run upon their center; [7] and do you, Clearidas, afterwards, when you see me already upon them, and, as is likely, dealing terror among them, take with you the Amphipolitans, and the rest of the allies, and suddenly open the gates and dash at them, and hasten to engage as quickly as you can. [8] That is our best chance of establishing a panic among them, as a fresh assailant has always more terrors for an enemy than the one he is immediately engaged with. [9] Show yourself a brave man, as a *Spartiate* should; and do you, allies, follow him like men, and remember that zeal, honor, and obedience mark the good soldier, and that this day will make you either free men and allies of Sparta, or slaves of Athens; even if you escape without personal loss of liberty or life, your bondage will be on harsher terms than before, and you will also hinder the liberation of the rest of the Hellenes. [10] Make no show of cowardice then on your part, seeing the greatness of the issues at stake, and I will show that what I preach to others I can practice myself."

After this brief speech Brasidas himself prepared for the sally, and placed the rest with Clearidas at the Thracian gates to support him as had been agreed. [2] Meanwhile he had been seen coming down from Cerdylium and then in the city (which is overlooked from the outside), sacrificing near the temple of Athena; in short, all his movements had been observed, and word was brought to Cleon, who had at the moment gone on to look about him, that the whole of the enemy's force could be seen in the city, and that the feet of horses and men in great numbers were visible under the gates, as if a sally were intended. [3] Upon hearing this he went up to look, and having done so, being unwilling to venture upon the decisive step of a battle before his reinforcements came up, and thinking that he would have time to retire, bid the-retreat be sounded and sent orders to the men to execute it by moving on the left wing in the direction of Eion, which was indeed the only way practicable. [4] This however not being quick enough for him, he joined the retreat in person and made the right wing wheel round, thus turning its unarmed side to the enemy. [5] It was then that Brasidas seeing the Athenian force in motion and his opportunity come, said to the men with him and the rest, "Those fellows will never stand before us, one can see that by the way their spears and heads are going.

Troops which do as they do seldom stand a charge. Quick, someone, open the gates I spoke of, and let us be out and at them with no fears for the result." [6] Accordingly moving out by the palisade gate and by the first gate in the long wall then existing, he ran at top speed along the straight; road, where the trophy now stands as you go by the steepest part of the hill, and fell upon and routed the center of the Athenians, panic-stricken by their own disorder and astounded at his audacity. [7] At the same moment Clearidas in execution of his orders issued out from the Thracian gates to support him, and also attacked the

5.10
422
10th Year/Summer
AMPHIPOLIS
When Brasidas' preparations are observed by the Athenians, Cleon orders his army to return to Eion. Brasidas' sudden attack overwhelms the Athenians. Cleon is killed in the rout. Brasidas, however, is mortally wounded.

enemy. [8] The result was that the Athenians, suddenly and unexpectedly attacked on both sides, fell into confusion; and their left toward Eion, which had already got on some distance, at once broke and fled. Just as it was in fall retreat and Brasidas was passing on to attack the right, he received a wound; but his fall was not perceived by the Athenians, as he was taken up by those near him and carried off the field. [9] The Athenian right made a better stand, and though Cleon, who from the first had no thought of fighting, at once fled and was overtaken and skin by a Myrcinian peltast, his infantry forming in close order upon the hill twice or thrice repulsed the attacks of Clearidas, and did not finally give way until they were surrounded and routed by the missiles of the Myrcinian and Chakidian horse and the peltasts. [10] Thus all the Athenian army was now in flight; and those who escaped being killed in the battle by the Chalcidian horse and the peltasts dispersed among the hills, and with difficulty made their way to Eion. [11] The men who had taken up and rescued Brasidas, brought him into the city with the breath still in him: he lived to hear of the victory of his troops, and not long after expired. [12] The rest of the army returning with Clearidas from the pursuit stripped the dead and set up a trophy.

5.11
422
10th Year/Summer
AMPHIPOLIS
The Amphipolitans bury Brasidas and honor him as if he were their city's founder. The Athenian casualties are very heavy.

After this all the allies attended in arms and buried Brasidas at the public expense in the city, in front of what is now the marketplace, and the Amphipolitans having enclosed his tomb, ever afterwards sacrifice to him as a hero and have given to him the honor of games and annual offerings. They constituted him the founder of their colony, and pulled down the Hagnonic erections and obliterated everything that could be interpreted as a memorial of his [Hagnon] having founded the place; for they considered that Brasidas had been their preserver and courting as they did the alliance of Sparta for fear of Athens, in their present hostile relations with the latter they could no longer with the same advantage or satisfaction pay Hagnon his honors. [2] They also gave the Athenians back their dead. About six hundred of the latter had fallen and only seven of the enemy, owing to there having been no regular engagement, but the affair of accident and panic that I have described. [3] After taking up their dead the Athenians sailed off home, while Clearidas and his troops remained to arrange matters at Amphipolis.

About the same time three Spartans—Ramphias, Autocharidas, and Epicydidas—led a reinforcement of nine hundred hoplites to the cities in the Thracian region, and arriving at Heraclea in Trachis made changes and reforms there as they thought best. [2] While they delayed there, this battle took place and so the summer ended.

With the beginning of winter Ramphias and his companions penetrated as far as Pierium in Thessaly; but as the Thessalians opposed their farther advance, and Brasidas whom they came to reinforce was dead, they turned back home, thinking that the moment had gone by, the Athenians being defeated and gone, and themselves not equal to the execution of Brasidas' designs. [2] The main cause however of their return was because they knew that when they set out, Spartan opinion was really in favor of peace.

Indeed it so happened that directly after the battle of Amphipolis and the retreat of Ramphias from Thessaly, both sides ceased to prosecute the war and turned their attention to peace. Athens had suffered severely at Delium, and again shortly afterwards at Amphipolis, and had no longer that confidence in her strength which had made her before refuse to accept the offer of peace, in the belief of ultimate victory which her success at the moment had inspired; [2] besides, she was afraid of her allies being tempted by her reverses to rebel more generally, and repented having let go the splendid opportunity for peace which the affair of Pylos had offered. [3] Sparta, on the other hand, found the actuality of the war falsify her notion that devastating their land for a few years would suffice for the overthrow of the power of the Athenians. She had suffered on the island a disaster hitherto unknown at Sparta; she saw her country plundered from Pylos and Cythera; the *Helots* were deserting, and she was in constant apprehension that those who remained in the Peloponnesus would rely upon those outside and take advantage of the situation to renew their old attempts at revolution. [4] Besides this, as chance would have it, her thirty years' truce with the Argives was upon the point of expiring; and they refused to renew it unless Cynuria were restored to them; so that it seemed impossible to fight Argos and Athens at once. She also suspected some of the cities in the Peloponnesus of intending to go over to the enemy, as was indeed the case.

5.12
422
10th Year/Summer
HERACLEA
Spartan reinforcements for Thrace delay at Heraclea.

5.13
422/1
10th Year/Winter
THESSALY
The Spartan reinforcements halt because of Thessalian opposition and Spartan desire for peace.

5.14
422/1
10th Year/Winter
ATHENS-SPARTA
Both sides now desire peace, and Thucydides explains why this is so.

5.15
422/1
10th Year/Winter
ATHENS-SPARTA
The Spartans are eager
for peace in order to
liberate the prisoners
taken at Pylos, some of
whom belonged to the
first families of Sparta.

5.16
422/1
10th Year/Winter
ATHENS-SPARTA
With Brasidas and Cleon
dead, new leaders (King
Pleistoanax in Sparta and
Nicias in Athens) come
to prominence. They are
eager for peace. The
campaign behind
Pleistoanax's return from
exile is described.

These considerations made both sides disposed for an accommodation; the Spartans being probably the most eager, as they ardently desired to recover the men taken on the island, the Spartiates among whom belonged to the first families and were accordingly related to leading men in Sparta. [2] Negotiations had been begun directly after their capture, but the Athenians in their hour of triumph would not consent to any reasonable terms; though after their defeat at Delium Sparta, knowing that they would now be more inclined to listen, at once concluded the truce for a year, during which they were to confer together and see if a longer period could not be agreed upon.

Now, however, after the Athenian defeat at Amphipolis, and the death of Cleon and Brasidas, who had been the two principal opponents of peace on either side—the latter from the success and honor which war gave him, the former because he thought that, if tranquility were restored, his crimes would be more open to detection and his slanders less credited—the foremost candidates for power in either city, Pleistoanax son of Pausanias, king of Sparta, and Nicias son of Niceratus, the most fortunate general of his time, each desired peace more ardently than ever. Nicias, while still happy and honored, wished to secure his good fortune, to obtain a present release from trouble for himself and his countrymen, and hand down to posterity a name as an ever-successful statesman, and thought the way to do this was to keep out of danger and commit himself as little as possible to fortune, and that peace alone made this keeping out of danger possible, Pleistoanax, on the other hand, was assailed by his enemies for his restoration, and regularly criticized by them in front of his countrymen for every reverse that befell them, as though his unjust restoration were the cause. [2] They accused him and his brother Aristocles of having bribed the prophetess of Delphi to tell the Spartan deputations which successively arrived at the temple to bring home the seed of the demigod son of Zeus from abroad, else they would have to plough with a silver share. [3] They insisted that in time, he had in this way induced the Spartans to restore him with the same dances and sacrifices with which they had instituted their kings upon the first settlement of Sparta. This they did in the nineteenth year of his exile to Lycaeum where he had gone when banished on suspicion of having accepted a bribe to retreat from Attica, and where he had built half his house within the consecrated precinct of Zeus for fear of the Spartans.

The sting of this accusation, and the reflection that in peace no disaster could occur, and that when Sparta had recovered her men there would be nothing for his enemies to seize upon (whereas, while war lasted the highest station must always bear the scandal of everything that went wrong), made him ardently desire a settlement. [2] Accordingly this winter was employed in conferences; and as spring rapidly approached, the Spartans sent round orders to the cities to prepare for a fortified occupation of Attica, and held this as a sword over the heads of the Athenians to induce them to listen to their overtures; and at last, after many claims had been urged on either side at the conferences, a peace was agreed to upon the following basis: each party was to restore its conquests, but Athens was to keep Nisaea; her demand for Plataea being countered by the Thebans asserting that they had acquired the place not by force or treachery, but by the voluntary adhesion upon agreement of its citizens; and the same, according to the Athenian account, being the history of her acquisition of Nisaea. This arranged, the Spartans summoned their allies, and all voting for peace except the Boeotians, Corinthians, Eleans, and Megarians, who did not approve of these proceedings, they concluded the treaty and made peace, each of the contracting parties swearing to the following articles:

5.17
422/1
10th Year/Winter
ATHENS-SPARTA
As peace negotiations drag on, Sparta threatens to fortify a post in Attica. The final treaty involves compromises and is not approved by certain members of the Peloponnesian League.

The Athenians and Spartans and their allies made a treaty, and swear to it, city by city, as follows:

5.18
422/1
10th Year/Winter
ATHENS-SPARTA
Thucydides lists the articles of the treaty.

- [2] Regarding the national temples, there shall be a free passage by land and by sea to all who wish it, to sacrifice, travel, consult, and attend the oracle or games, according to the customs of their countries.
- The temple and shrine of Apollo at Delphi and the Delphians shall be governed by their own laws, taxed by their own state, and judged by their own judges, the land and the people, according to the customs of their country.
- [3] The treaty shall be binding for fifty years upon the Athenians and the allies of the Athenians, and upon the Spartans and the allies of the Spartans, without fraud or harm by land or by sea.
- [4] It shall not be lawful to take up arms, with intent to do injury either for the Spartans and their allies against

the Athenians and their allies, or for the Athenians and their allies against the Spartans and their allies, in any way or means whatsoever. But should any difference arise between them they are to have recourse to law and oaths, according as may be agreed between the parties.

- [5] The Spartans and their allies shall give back Amphipolis to the Athenians. Nevertheless, in the case of cities given up by the Spartans to the Athenians, the inhabitants shall be allowed to go where they please and to take their property with them; and the cities shall be independent, paying only the tribute of Aristides.

And it shall not be lawful for the Athenians or their allies to carry on war against them after the treaty has been, concluded, so long as the tribute is paid. The cities referred to are Argilus, Stagirus, Acanthus, Scolus, Olynthus, and Spartolus, These cities shall be neutral, allies neither of the Spartans nor of the Athenians; but if the cities consent, it shall be lawful for the Athenians to make them their allies, provided always that the cities wish it. [6] The Mecybernaeans, Sanaeans, and Singaeans shall inhabit their own cities, as also the Olynthians and Acanthians; [7] but the Spartans and their allies shall give back Panactum to the Athenians.

- The Athenians shall give back Coryphasium, Cythera, Methana, Pteleum, and Atalanta to the Spartans, and also all Spartans that are in the prison at Athens or elsewhere in the Athenian dominions, and shall let go the Peloponnesians besieged in Scione and all others in Scione that are allies of the Spartans, and all whom Brasidas sent in there, and any others of the allies of the Spartans that may be in the prison at Athens or elsewhere in the Athenian dominions.
- The Spartans and their allies shall in like manner give back any of the Athenians or their allies that they may have in their hands.
- [8] In the case of Scione, Torone, and Sermylium and any other cities that the Athenians may have, the Athenians may adopt such measures as they please.
- [9] The Athenians shall take an oath to the Spartans and their allies, city by city. Every man shall swear by the most binding oath of his country, seventeen from each city. The

oath shall be as follows:—"I will abide by this agreement and treaty honestly and without deceit." In the same way an oath shall be taken by the Spartans and their allies to the Athenians;

- [10] and the oath shall be renewed annually by both parties. Pillars shall be erected at Olympia, Pythia, the Isthmus, at Athens in the Acropolis, and at Sparta in the temple at Amyclae.

- [11] If anything be forgotten, whatever it be, and on whatever point, it shall be consistent with their oath for both parties the Athenians and Spartans to alter it, according to their discretion.

The treaty begins from the ephorate of Pleistolas in Sparta, on the 27th day of the month of Artemisium, and from the archonship of Alcaeus at Athens, on the 25th day of the month of Elaphebolion. [2] Those who took the oath and poured the libations for the Spartans were Pleistoanax, Agis, Pleistolas, Damagetus, Chionis, Metagenes, Acanthus, Daithus, Ischagoras, Philocharidas, Zeuxidas, Antippus, Tellis, Alcinadas, Empedias, Menas, and Laphilus; for the Athenians, Lampon, Isthmionicus, Nicias, Laches, Euthydemus, Procles, Pythodorus, Hagnon, Myrtilus, Thrasycles, Theagenes, Aristocrates, Iolcius, Timocrates, Leon, Lamachus, and Demosthenes.

5.19
422/1
10th Year/Winter
ATHENS-SPARTA
Thucydides gives the date of the treaty and names of the oath-takers who acted as the representatives for Sparta and Athens.

This treaty was made in the spring, just at the end of winter, directly after the city festival of Dionysus, just ten years, with the difference of a few days, from the first invasion of Attica and the commencement of this war. [2] This must be calculated by the seasons rather than by trusting to the enumeration of the names of the various magistrates or offices of honor that are used to mark past events. Accuracy is impossible where an event may have occurred in the beginning, or middle, or at any period in their tenure of office. [3] But by computing by summers and winters, the method adopted in this history, it will be found that, each of these amounting to half a year, there were ten summers and as many winters contained in this first war.

5.20
422/1
10th Year/Winter
HELLAS
Thucydides explains his method of dating by annual summer and winter seasons rather than by referring to magistrates' names.

BOOK 5.34 – 5.35

5.34
421
11th Year/Summer
SPARTA
Helots among Spartan troops returning from Thrace are freed and allowed to live where they like. The disgraced Spartans captured at Sphacteria are at first restricted, but later restored to their full rights.

The same summer the soldiers from Thrace who had gone out with Brasidas came back, having been brought from thence after the treaty by Clearidas; and the Spartans decreed that the Helots who had fought with Brasidas should be free and allowed to live where they Eked, and not long afterwards settled them with the Neodamodeis at Lepreum, which is situated on the Laconian and Elean border; Sparta being at this time at enmity with Elis. [2] Those, however, of the Spartans who had been taken prisoner on the island and had surrendered their arms might, it was feared, suppose that they were to be subjected to some degradation in con-, sequence of their misfortune, and so make some attempt at revolution, if left in possession of their full rights. These were therefore at once deprived of some of their rights, although some of them were in office at the time, and thus they were barred from taking office, or buying and selling anything. After some time, however, their rights were restored to them.

5.35
421
11th Year/Summer
THRACE
The Dians take Thyssus.
ATHENS-SPARTA
Athens and Sparta are still at peace, but Sparta's failure to fulfill her treaty obligations arouses Athenian suspicions. Athens holds onto Pylos and the other places she had agreed to give up, but does withdraw the Messenians and the Laconian deserters from Pylos.

The same summer the Dians took Thyssus, a city on Acte near Athosld and in alliance with Athens. [2] During the whole of this summer, intercourse between the Athenians and Peloponnesians continued, although each party began to suspect the other immediately after the treaty, because of the places specified in it not being restored. [3] Sparta, to whose lot it had fallen to begin by restoring Amphipolis and the other cities, had not done so. She had equally failed to get the treaty accepted by her Thracian allies, or by the Boeotians or the Corinthians; although she was continually promising to unite with Athens in compelling their compliance, if it were longer refused. She also kept fixing a time at which those who still refused to come in were to be declared enemies to both parties, but took care not to bind herself by any written agreement. [4] Meanwhile the Athenians, seeing none of these promises actually fulfilled, began to suspect the honesty of her intentions, and consequently not only refused to comply with her demands for Pylos, but also repented having given up the prisoners from the island, and kept tight hold of the other places, until Sparta's part of the treaty should be fulfilled. [5] Sparta, on the other hand, said she had done what she could, having given up the Athenian prisoners of war in her possession, evacuated Thrace, and performed everything else in her power. Amphipolis, she said, it was out of her ability to restore; but she would endeavor to bring the Boeotians and Corinthians in to the treaty, to recover Panactum, and send home all the Athenian prisoners of war in Boeotia. [6] Meanwhile she insisted that Pylos should be restored, or at least that the Messenians and Helots should be withdrawn (as her troops had been from Thrace), and the place garrisoned, if necessary, by the Athenians themselves. [7] After a number of different conferences held during the summer she succeeded in persuading Athens to withdraw the Messenians from Pylos and the rest of the Helots and deserters from Laco-nia, who were accordingly settled by her at Cranae in Cephallenia. [8] Thus during this summer there was peace and intercourse between the two peoples.

BOOK 6.88 – 6.93

Such were the words of Euphemus. What the Camarinaeans felt was this. They sympathized with the Athenians, except insofar as they might be afraid of their subjugating Sicily, and they had always been at enmity with their neighbor Syracuse. From the very fact, however, that they were their neighbors, they feared the Syracusans most of the two, and being apprehensive that the Syracusans might win even without their help, both sent them in the first instance the few horsemen mentioned and for the future determined to support them most in fact, although as sparingly as possible; but for the moment in order not to seem to slight the Athenians, especially as they had been successful in the engagement, to answer both alike. [2] In accordance with this resolution they answered that as both the contending parties happened to be allies of theirs, they thought it most consistent with their oaths, at present, to side with neither; with which answer the ambassadors of each party departed.

[3] In the meantime, while Syracuse pursued her preparations for war, the Athenians were encamped at Naxos, and tried by negotiation to gain as many of the Sicels as possible. [4] Those more in the lowlands, and subjects of Syracuse, mostly held aloof; but the peoples of the interior who had never been otherwise than independent, with few exceptions, at once joined the Athenians, and brought down grain to the army, and in some cases even money. [5] The Athenians marched against

6.88
415/4
17th Year/Winter
CAMARINA
Camarina decides to remain neutral, but to give limited aid to Syracuse in fear that she is nearby and will win.
CATANA
The Athenians obtain support and some new allies among the Sicels. They transfer their winter base to Catana.
PELOPONNESUS
The Syracusans send for help to the Italians, the Corinthians, and the Spartans. Corinth responds enthusiastically but Sparta refuses aid. Alcibiades, having just arrived, speaks to the Spartans to urge them to act.

those who refused to join, and forced some of them to do so; in the case of others they were stopped by the Syracusans sending garrisons and reinforcements.

Meanwhile the Athenians moved their winter quarters from Naxos to Catana, and reconstructed the camp burnt by the Syracusans, and stayed there the rest of the winter. [6] They also sent a trireme to Carthage, with offers of friendship, on the chance of obtaining assistance, and another to Tyrrhenia; some of the cities there having spontaneously offered to join them in the war. They also sent round to the Sicels and to Egesta, desiring them to send them as many horses as possible, and meanwhile prepared bricks, iron, and all other things necessary for the work of circumvallation, intending by the spring to begin hostilities.

[7] In the meantime the Syracusan envoys that had been dispatched to Corinth and Sparta tried as they passed along the coast to persuade the Italians to interfere with the proceedings of the Athenians which, they argued, threatened Italy quite as much as Syracuse, and having arrived at Corinth made a speech calling on the Corinthians to assist them on the ground of their common origin. [8] The Corinthians voted at once to aid them unstintingly themselves, and then sent on envoys with them to Sparta, to help them to persuade her also to prosecute the war with the Athenians more openly at home and to send assistance to Sicily. [9] The envoys from Corinth having reached Sparta found Alcibiades there with his fellow refugees, who had without delay crossed over in a trading vessel from Thurii, first to Cyllene in Elis, and afterwards from there to Sparta; upon the Spartans' own invitation, after first obtaining a safe conduct, as he feared them for the part he had taken in the affair of Mantinea. [10] The result was that the Corinthians, Syracusans, and Alcibiades, all pressing the same request in the assembly of the Spartans, succeeded in persuading them; but as the ephors and the authorities, although resolved to send envoys to Syracuse to prevent them surrendering to the Athenians, showed no inclination to send them any assistance, Alcibiades now came forward and inflamed and stirred the Spartans by speaking as follows:

"I am forced first to speak to you of the prejudice with which I am regarded, in order that suspicion may not make you disinclined to listen to me upon public matters. [2] The connection with you as your *proxeni* which the ancestors of our family by reason of some discontent renounced, I personally tried to renew by my good offices toward you, in particular upon the occasion of the disaster at Pylos. But although I maintained this friendly attitude, you yet chose to negotiate the peace with the Athenians through my enemies, and thus to strengthen them and to discredit me. [3] You had therefore no right to complain if I turned to the Mantineans and Argives, and seized other occasions of thwarting and injuring you; and the time has now come when those among you, who in the bitterness of the moment may have been then unfairly angry with me, should look at the matter in its true light, and take a different view. Those again who judged me unfavorably, because I leaned rather to the side of The People must not think that their dislike is any better founded. [4] We have always been hostile to tyrants, and all who oppose arbitrary power are called The People; hence we continued to act as leaders of the multitude; besides which, as democracy was the government of the city, it was necessary in most things to conform to established conditions. [5] However, we endeavored to be more moderate than the licentious temper of the times; and while there were others, formerly as now, who tried to lead the multitude astray (the same who banished me), [6] our party was that of the whole people, our creed being to do our part in preserving the form of government under which the city enjoyed the utmost greatness and freedom, and which we had found existing. As for democracy, the men of sense among us knew what it was, and I perhaps as well as any, as I have more cause to complain of it; but there is nothing new to be said of a patent absurdity—meanwhile we did not think it safe to alter it under the pressure of your hostility."

6.89
415/4
17th Year/Winter
SPARTA
Alcibiades addresses his Spartan critics and justifies his past actions against Sparta. He explains his role in Athenian politics. He agrees that democracy is absurd, but that it was successful at Athens, that he had inherited it there, and that it could not be altered in the face of Spartan pressure.

6.90
415/4
17th Year/Winter
SPARTA
Alcibiades says that Athens'
true purpose in Sicily
is the conquest of all the
Hellenes. She intends to
use the resources gained by
the conquest of Sicily and
Italy, and from alliances
with others, to return to
the Peloponnesus in
overwhelming force to
reduce it city by city.

6.91
415/4
17th Year/Winter
SPARTA
Alcibiades reiterates that
Sparta should act for
Peloponnesian interests by
preventing the fall of
Syracuse. He urges the
Spartans to fortify Decelea
in Attica and to send troops
and a general to Syracuse to
lead a professional defense.

"So much then for the prejudices with which I am regarded: I now can call your attention to the questions you must consider, and upon which superior knowledge perhaps permits me to speak. [2] We sailed to Sicily first to conquer, if possible, the Sicilians, and after them the Italians also, and finally to assail the empire and city of Carthage. [3] In the event of all or most of these schemes succeeding, we were then to attack the Peloponnesus, bringing with us the entire force of the Hellenes lately acquired in those parts, and taking a number of barbarians into our pay, such as the Iberians and others in those countries, recognized as the most warlike known, and building numerous triremes in addition to those which we had already (timber being plentiful in Italy); and with this fleet blockading the Peloponnesus from the sea and assailing it with our armies by land, taking some of the cities by storm, and besieging others, we hoped without difficulty to defeat them completely and after this, to rule the whole of the Hellenic world. [4] Money and grain for the better execution of these plans were to be supplied in sufficient quantities by the newly acquired places in those countries, independently of our revenues here at home."

"You have thus heard the history of the present expedition from the man who most exactly knows what our intentions were; and the remaining generals will, if they can, carry these out just the same. But that the states in Sicily must succumb if you do not help them, I will now show. [2] Although the Sicilians, with all their inexperience, might even now be saved if their forces were united, the Syracusans alone, beaten already in one battle with all their people and blockaded from the sea, will be unable to withstand the Athenian armament that is now there. [3] But if Syracuse falls, all Sicily falls also, and Italy immediately afterwards; and the danger which I just now spoke of from that quarter will before long be upon you. [4] None need therefore imagine that only Sicily is in question; the Peloponnesus will be so also, unless you speedily do as I tell you, and send on board ship to Syracuse troops that shall be able to row their ships themselves, and serve as hoplites the moment that they land; and what I consider even more important than the troops, a *Spartiate* as commanding officer to discipline the forces already on foot and to compel shirkers to serve. The friends that you have already will thus become more confident, and the waverers will be encouraged to join you. [5]

Meanwhile you must carry on the war here more openly, so that the Syracusans, seeing that you do not forget them, may put heart into their resistance, and that the Athenians may be less able to reinforce their armament. [6] You must fortify Decelea in Attica, the blow of which the Athenians are always most afraid and the only one that they think they have not experienced in the present war; the surest method of harming an enemy being to find out what he most fears, and to choose this means of attacking him, since everyone naturally knows best his own weak points and fears accordingly. [7] The fortification in question, while it benefits you, will create difficulties for your adversaries, of which I shall pass over many, and shall only mention the chief. Whatever property there is in the country will most of it become yours, either by capture or surrender; and the Athenians will at once be deprived of their revenues from the silver mines at Laurium, of their present gains from their land and from the law courts, and above all of the revenue from their allies, which will be paid less regularly, as they lose their awe of Athens and see you addressing yourselves with vigor to this war. [6.92.1] The zeal and speed with which all this shall be done depends, Spartans, upon yourselves; as to its possibility, I am quite confident, and I have little fear of being mistaken."

Alcibiades addresses his Spartan critics and justifies his past actions against Sparta. He explains his role in Athenian politics. He agrees that democracy is absurd, but that it was successful at Athens, that he had inherited it there, and that it could not be altered in the face of Spartan pressure.

Alcibiades argues that he is not a traitor because he cannot betray a country from which he was wrongfully driven and which is no longer his. Moreover, he adds, a true patriot will go to any length, even to aid his country's enemies, in order to recover it. He concludes by asking the Spartans to use his knowledge of Athens and Athenian plans to their best advantage.

[2] " Meanwhile I hope that none of you will think any the worse of me if after having hitherto passed as a lover of my country, I now actively join its worst enemies in attacking it, or will suspect what I say as the fruit of an outlaw's enthusiasm. [3] I am an outlaw from the iniquity of those who drove me forth, not, if you will be guided by me, from your service: my worst enemies are not you who only harmed your foes, but they who forced their friends to become enemies; [4] and love of country is what I do not feel when I am wronged, but what I felt when secure in my rights as a citizen. Indeed I do not consider that I am now attacking a country that is still mine; I am rather trying to recover one that is mine no longer; and the true lover of his country is not he who consents to lose it unjustly rather than attack it, but he who longs for it so much that he will go to all lengths to recover it. [5] For myself, therefore, Spartans, I beg you to use me without scruple for danger and trouble of every kind, and to remember the argument in everyone's mouth, that if 1 did you great harm as an enemy, I could likewise do you good service as a friend, inasmuch as I know the plans of the Athenians, while I only guessed yours. For yourselves I entreat you to believe that your most vital interests are now under consideration; and I urge you to send without hesitation the expeditions to Sicily and Attica; by the presence of a small part of your forces you will save important cities in that island, and you will destroy the power of Athens both present and prospective; after this you will dwell in security and enjoy the supremacy over all Hellas, resting not on force but upon consent and affection."

Such were the words of Alcibiades. The Spartans, who had previously intended to march against Athens themselves, but were still waiting and looking about them, at once became much more serious when they received this particular information from Alcibiades, and considered that they had heard it from the man who best knew the truth of the matter. [2] Accordingly they now turned their attention, to fortifying Decelea and sending immediate aid to the Sicilians; and naming Gylippus son of Cleandridas to the command of the Syracusans, instructed him to consult with that people and with the Corinthians and arrange for help to reach the island in the best and speediest way possible under the circumstances. [3] Gylippus requested the Corinthians to send him at once two ships to Asine, and to prepare the rest that they intended to send, and to have them ready to sail at the proper time. Having-settled this, the, envoys departed, from Sparta.

6.93
415/4
17th Year/Winter
SPARTA
Moved by Alcibiades, the Spartans vote to aid the Sicilians and send Gylippus to take command there. They prepare to fortify Decelea in Attica.
ATHENS
Athens votes to send funds and reinforcements to their forces in Sicily.

THE LIFE OF LYSANDER

From Plutarch, *The Parallel Lives*

1

The treasury of the Acanthians at Delphi bears this inscription: "Brasidas and the Acanthians, with spoil from the Athenians."[1] For this reason many think that the marble figure standing within the edifice, by the door, is a statue of Brasidas. But it really represents Lysander, with his hair very long, after the ancient custom, and growing a generous beard. For it is not true, as some state, that because the Argives, after their great defeat, shaved their heads for sorrow, the Spartans, in contrary fashion, let their hair grow long in exultation over their victory;[2] nor was it because the Bacchiadae,[3] when they fled from Corinth to Lacedaemon, looked mean and unsightly from having shaved their heads, that the Spartans, on their part, became eager to wear their hair long; but this custom also goes back to Lycurgus. And he is reported to have said that a fine head of hair makes the handsome more comely to look upon, and the ugly more terrible.[4]

2

The father of Lysander, Aristocleitus, is said to have been of the lineage of the Heracleidae, though not of the royal family. But Lysander was reared in poverty, and showed himself as much as any man conformable to the customs of his people; of a manly spirit, too, and superior to every pleasure, excepting only that which their good deeds bring to those who are successful and honoured. To this pleasure it is no disgrace for the youth in Sparta to succumb. Indeed, from the very first they wish their boys to be sensitive towards public opinion, distressed by censure, and exalted

---

1 In B.C. 424, Brasidas won Acanthus, a town on the Chalcidic peninsula, away from its alliance with Athens (Thuc.IV.84 88).

2 Herodotus, I.82

3 An oligarchical family, deposed from rule in Corinth by Cypselus, about 650 B.C. (Herod. V.92).

4 *Cf. Lycurgus*, xxii.1.

by praise; and he who is insensible and stolid in these matters, is looked down upon as without ambition for excellence, and a cumberer of the ground. Ambition, then, and the spirit of emulation, were firmly implanted in him by his Laconian training, and no great fault should be found with his natural disposition on this account. But he seems to have been naturally subservient to men of power and influence, beyond what was usual in a Spartan, and content to endure an arrogant authority for the sake of gaining his ends, a trait which some hold to be no small part of political ability. And Aristotle, when he sets forth that great natures, like those of Socrates and Plato and Heracles, have a tendency to melancholy, writes also[5] that Lysander, not immediately, but when well on in years, was a prey to melancholy.

But what is most peculiar in him is that, though he bore poverty well, and though he was never mastered nor even corrupted by money, yet he filled his country full of wealth and the love of wealth, and made her cease to be admired for not admiring wealth, importing as he did an abundance of gold and silver after the war with Athens, although he kept not a single drachma for himself. And when Dionysius the tyrant sent his daughters some costly tunics of Sicilian make, he would not receive them, saying he was afraid they would make his daughters look more ugly. But a little later, when he was sent as ambassador to the same tyrant from the same city, and was presented by him with two robes, and ordered to choose which of them he would, and carry it to his daughter, he said that she could choose better herself, and went off with both of them.

3

The Peloponnesian war had now been carried on for a long time, and after their disaster in Sicily[6] it was expected that the Athenians would straightway lose their control of the sea, and presently give up the struggle altogether. But Alcibiades, returning from exile and taking the command, wrought a great change, and made his countrymen again a match for their enemies by sea.[7] The Lacedaemonians, accordingly, were frightened again, and summoning up fresh zeal for the war, which required, as they thought, an able leader and a more powerful armament, sent out Lysander to take command upon the sea.[8] When he came to Ephesus, he found the city well disposed to him and very zealous in the Spartan cause, although it was then in a low state of prosperity and in danger of becoming utterly barbarized by the admixture of Persian customs, since it was enveloped by Lydia, and the King's generals made it their headquarters. He therefore pitched his camp there, and ordered the merchant

---

5 *Problems*, xxx.1.

6 413 B.C. *Cf.* Thuc. VIII.2.

7 *Cf. Alcibiades*, xxxii.4.

8 In the autumn of 408 B.C.

vessels from every quarter to land their cargoes there, and made preparations for the building of triremes. Thus he revived the traffic of their harbours, and the business of their market, and filled their houses and workshops with profits, so that from that time on, and through his efforts, the city had hopes of achieving the stateliness and grandeur which it now enjoys.

4

When he learned that Cyrus, the King's son, was come to Sardis,[9] he went up to confer with him and to accuse Tissaphernes, who, though he was commissioned to aid the Lacedaemonians and drive the Athenians from the sea, was thought to be remiss in his duty, through the efforts of Alcibiades,[10] showing lack of zeal, and destroying the efficiency of the fleet by the meagre subsidies which he gave. Now Cyrus was well pleased that Tissaphernes, who was a base man and privately at feud with him, should be accused and maligned. By this means, then, as well as by his behaviour in general, Lysander made himself agreeable, and by the submissive deference of his conversation, above all else, he won the heart of the young prince, and roused him to prosecute the war with vigour. At a banquet which Cyrus gave him as he was about to depart, the prince begged him not to reject the tokens of his friendliness, but to ask plainly for whatever he desired, since nothing whatsoever would be refused him. "Since, then," said Lysander in reply, "thou art so very kind, I beg and entreat thee, Cyrus, to add an obol to the pay of my sailors, that they may get four obols instead of three."[11] Cyrus, accordingly, delighted with his public spirit, gave him ten thousand darics, out of which he added the obol to the pay of his seamen, and, by the renown thus won, soon emptied the ships of his enemies. For most of their seamen came over to those who offered higher pay, and those who remained were listless and mutinous, and gave daily trouble to their officers. However, although he had thus injured and weakened his enemies, Lysander shrank from a naval battle, through fear of Alcibiades, who was energetic, had a greater number of ships, and in all his battles by land and sea up to that time had come off victorious.

5

But after this, Alcibiades sailed away from Samos to Phocaea, leaving Antiochus, his pilot, in command of the fleet; and Antiochus, as if in bold mockery of Lysander, put in to the harbour of Ephesus with two triremes, and rowed ostentatiously past his ships, as they lay drawn up on shore, with noise and laughter. Lysander was incensed,

---

9   He succeeded Tissaphernes as satrap of Lydia.

10   *Cf. Alcibiades*, xxv.1 2.

11   *Cf.* Xen. *Hell.* I.5.6 f.

and launching at first only a few of his triremes, pursued him; then seeing that the Athenians were coming to the rescue, he manned others, and at last the action became general. Lysander was victorious, too, captured fifteen triremes, and set up a trophy. Thereupon the people of Athens, flying into a passion, deposed Alcibiades from his command and finding himself slighted and abused by the soldiers at Samos, he left the camp and sailed off to the Chersonese. This battle, then, although actually not a great one, was made memorable by its bearing on the fortunes of Alcibiades.[12]

Lysander now summoned from their various cities to Ephesus men whom he saw to be most eminent for confidence and daring, and sowed in their minds the seeds of the revolutionary decadarchies[13] afterwards instituted by him, urging and inciting them to form political clubs in their several cities, and apply themselves to public affairs, assuring them that as soon as the Athenian empire was destroyed, they could rid themselves of their democracies and become themselves supreme in power. Moreover, by actual benefits he gave them all a confidence in this future, promoting those who were already his friends and allies to large enterprises and honours and commands, and taking a share himself in their injustice and wickedness in order to gratify their rapacity. Therefore all attached themselves to him, expecting to attain all their highest ambitions if only he remained in power. Therefore, too, they neither looked kindly upon Callicratidas at the first, when he came to succeed Lysander in the admiralty,[14] nor afterwards, when he had shown by manifest proofs that he was the justest and noblest of men, were they pleased with the manner of his leadership, which had a certain Doric simplicity and sincerity. They did, indeed, admire his virtue, as they would the beauty of a hero's statue; but they yearned for the zealous support of Lysander, and missed the interest which he took in the welfare of his partisans, so that when he sailed away they were dejected and shed tears.

6

Lysander made these men yet more disaffected towards Callicratidas. He also sent back to Sardis what remained of the money which Cyrus had given him for the navy, bidding Callicratidas ask for it himself, if he wished, and see to the maintenance of his soldiers. And finally, as he sailed away, he called Callicratides to witness that the fleet which he handed over to him was in command of the sea. But he, wishing to prove the emptiness and vanity of this ambitious boast, said: "In that case, keep Samos on the left, sail to Miletus, and there hand the triremes over to me; surely we

---

12   *Cf. Alcibiades*, xxxv xxxvi.

13   Governing bodies of ten men.

14   Late in the year 407 B.C. It was Spartan policy to change their admiral yearly.

need not fear to sail past the enemy at Samos if we are masters of the sea." To this Lysander answered that Callicratidas, and not he, was in command of the ships, and sailed off to Peloponnesus, leaving Callicratidas in great perplexity.[15] For neither had he brought money from home with him, nor could he bear to lay the cities under forced contribution when they were already in an evil plight. The only course left, therefore, was to go to the doors of the King's generals, as Lysander had done, and ask for money. For this he was of all men least fitted by nature, being of a free and lofty spirit, and one who thought any and every defeat of Greeks at the hands of Greeks more becoming to them than visits of flattery to the houses of Barbarians, who had much gold, but nothing else worthwhile.

Constrained, however, by his necessities, he went up into Lydia, proceeded at once to the house of Cyrus, and ordered word to be sent in that Callicratidas the admiral was come and wished to confer with him. And when one of the door-keepers said to him: "But Cyrus is not at leisure now, Stranger, for he is at his wine"; Callicratidas replied with the utmost simplicity: "No matter, I will stand here and wait till he has had his wine." This time, then, he merely withdrew, after being taken for a rustic fellow and laughed at by the Barbarians. But when he was come a second time to the door and was refused admittance, he was indignant, and set off for Ephesus, invoking many evils upon those who first submitted to the mockery of the Barbarians and taught them to be insolent because of their wealth, and swearing roundly to the bystanders that as soon as he got back to Sparta, he would do all he could to reconcile the Greeks with one another, in order that they might themselves strike fear into the Barbarians, and cease soliciting their power against each other.

7

But Callicratidas, after cherishing purposes worthy of Lacedaemon, and showing himself worthy to compete with the most eminent of the Greeks by reason of his righteousness, magnanimity, and valour, not long afterwards lost the sea-fight at Arginusae, and vanished from among men.[16] Then, their cause declining, the allies sent an embassy to Sparta and asked that Lysander be made admiral, declaring that they would grapple much more vigorously with the situation if he were their commander. Cyrus also sent to make the same request. Now the Lacedaemonians had a law forbidding that the same man should be admiral twice, and yet they wished to gratify their allies; they therefore invested a certain Aracus with the title of admiral, and sent out Lysander as vice-admiral,[17] nominally, but really with supreme power. So he came out, as most of those who had political power and influence in the cities

---

15 *Cf.* Xen. *Hell.* I.6.2 f.

16 In the late summer of 406 B.C. (Xen. *Hell.* I.6.33).

17 In the spring of 405 B.C. (Xen. *Hell.* II.1.7).

had long desired, for they expected to become still stronger by his aid when the popular governments had been utterly overthrown; but to those who loved simplicity and nobility in the character of their leaders, Lysander, compared with Callicratidas, seemed to be unscrupulous and subtle, a man who tricked out most of what he did in war with the varied hues of deceit, extolling justice if it was at the same time profitable, but if not, adopting the advantageous as the honourable course, and not considering truth as inherently better than falsehood, but bounding his estimate of either by the needs of the hour. Those who demanded that the descendants of Heracles should not wage war by deceit he held up to ridicule, saying that "where the lions' skin will not reach, it must be patched out with the fox's."

8

Of such a sort were his dealings with Miletus, according to the record. For when his friends and allies, whom he had promised to aid in overthrowing the democracy and expelling their opponents, changed their minds and became reconciled to their foes, openly he pretended to be pleased and to join in the reconciliation; but in secret he reviled and abused them, and incited them to fresh attacks upon the multitude. And when he perceived that the uprising was begun, he quickly came up and entered the city, where he angrily rebuked the first conspirators whom he met, and set upon them roughly, as though he were going to punish them, but ordered the rest of the people to be of good cheer and to fear no further evil now that he was with them. But in this he was playing a shifty part, wishing the leading men of the popular party not to fly, but to remain in the city and be slain. And this was what actually happened; for all who put their trust in him were slaughtered.

Furthermore, there is a saying of Lysander's, recorded by Androcleides, which makes him guilty of the greatest recklessness in the matter of oaths. It was his policy, according to this authority, "to cheat boys with knuckle-bones, but men with oaths," thus imitating Polycrates of Samos; not a proper attitude in a general towards a tyrant, nor yet a Laconian trait to treat the gods as one's enemies are treated, nay, more outrageously still; since he who overreaches his enemy by means of an oath, confesses that he fears that enemy, but despises God.

9

Well, then, Cyrus summoned Lysander to Sardis, and gave him this, and promised him that, ardently protesting, to gratify him, that he would actually squander his own fortune, if his father gave him nothing for the Spartans; and if all else failed, he said he would cut up the throne on which he sat when giving audience, a throne covered with gold and silver. And finally, as he was going up into Media to wait upon his father, he assigned to Lysander the tribute of the cities, and entrusted his own government to him; and embracing him in farewell, and begging him not to fight the Athenians at sea until he was come back, and promising to come back with many ships from Phoenicia and Cilicia, he set out to go up to the King.[18]

Then Lysander, who could neither fight a naval battle on equal terms, nor remain idle with the large fleet at his disposal, put out to sea and reduced some of the islands, and touching at Aegina and Salamis, overran them. Then he landed in Attica and saluted Agis, who came down in person from Deceleia[19] to meet him, and displayed to the land forces there the strength of his fleet, with the mien of one who sailed where he pleased and was master of the sea. But on learning that the Athenians were pursuing him, he fled by another route through the islands to Asia.

Finding the Hellespont unguarded, he himself attacked Lampsacus from the sea with his ships, while Thorax, co-operating with the land forces, assaulted the walls. He took the city by storm, and gave it up to his soldiers to plunder.[20]Meanwhile the Athenian fleet of a hundred and eighty triremes had just arrived at Elaeus in the Chersonese, and learning that Lampsacus had fallen, they straightway put in at Sestos. There they took in provisions, and then sailed along to Aegospotami, over against their enemies, who were still in station at Lampsacus. The Athenians were under the command of several generals, among whom was Philocles, the man who had recently persuaded the people to pass a decree that their prisoners of war should have the right thumb cut off, that they might not be able to wield a spear, though they might ply an oar.[21]

10

For the time being, then, all rested, expecting that on the morrow the fleets would engage. But Lysander was planning otherwise, and ordered his seamen and pilots, as though there would be a struggle at daybreak, to go on board their triremes in the early morning, and take their seats in order and in silence, awaiting the word of command, and that the land forces also, in the same manner, remain quietly in their ranks by the sea. When the sun rose, however, and the Athenians sailed up with all their ships in line and challenged to battle, although he had his ships drawn up in line to meet them and fully manned before it was light, he did not put out from his position, but sending despatch-boats to the foremost of his ships, ordered them to keep quiet and remain in line, not getting into confusion nor sailing out to meet the enemy. And

---

18   Cf. Xen. *Hell.* II.1.13 f.

19   In the spring of 413 B.C. the Spartans had fortified Deceleia, a few miles N.W. of Athens, and stationed there a permanent garrison under Agis the king. Lysander's ravaging of Aegina and Salamis was just before his siege of Athens, according to Xenophon (*Hell.* II.2.9).

20   *Cf.* Xen. *Hell.* II.1.18 f.

21   *Cf.* Xen. *Hell.* II.1.20 26; Plutarch, *Alcibiades,* xxxvi.4 xxxvii.1.

so about midday when the Athenians sailed back, he did not allow his men to leave their ships until two or three triremes, which he sent to reconnoitre, came back, after seeing that the enemy had disembarked. On the following day this was done again, and on the third, and at last on the fourth, so that the Athenians became very bold and contemptuous, believing that their enemies were huddling together in fear.

At this juncture, Alcibiades, who was living in his own fortress on the Chersonese, rode up to the Athenian army and censured the generals, first for having pitched their camp in a bad and even dangerous place on an open beach where there was no roadstead; and second, for the mistake of getting their provisions from distant Sestos, when they ought to sail round the coast a little way to the harbour and city of Sestos, where they would be at a longer remove from their enemies, who lay watching them with an army commanded by a single man, the fear of whom led it to obey his every order promptly. These were the lessons he gave them, but they would not receive them, and Tydeus actually gave him an insolent answer, saying that he was not general now, but others.[22]

11

Alcibiades, accordingly, suspecting that some treachery was afoot among them, went away. But on the fifth day, when the Athenians had sailed over to the enemy and back again, as was now their wont, very carelessly and contemptuously, Lysander, as he sent out his reconnoitring ships, ordered their commanders, as soon as they saw that the Athenians had disembarked, to put about and row back with all speed, and when they were half way across, to hoist a brazen shield at the prow, as a signal for the onset. And he himself sailed round and earnestly exhorted the pilots and trierarchs to keep all their crews at their post, sailors and soldiers alike, and as soon as the signal was given, to row with ardour and vigour against the enemy. When, therefore, the shield was hoisted on the lookout ships, and the trumpet on the admiral's ship signalled the attack, the ships sailed forth, and the land forces ran their fastest along the shore to seize the promontory. The distance between the two continents at this point is fifteen furlongs, and such was the zealous ardour of the rowers that it was quickly consumed. Conon, the Athenian general, who was the first to see from the land the onset of the fleet, suddenly shouted orders to embark, and deeply stirred by the threatening disaster, called upon some, besought others, and forced others to man the triremes. But his eager efforts were of no avail, since the men were scattered. For just as soon as they had disembarked, since they expected no trouble, some went to market, some walked about the country, some lay down to sleep in their tents, and some began to get their suppers ready, being as far as possible removed from any thought of what was to happen, through the inexperience of their commanders. The shouts and splashing

---

22   One of the sacred state-galleys. It now carried the news of the disaster to Athens (Xen. *Hell.* II.1.28).

oars of the oncoming enemy were already heard, when Conon, with eight ships, sailed stealthily away, and making his escape, proceeded to Cyprus, to Evagoras; but the Peloponnesians fell upon the rest of the ships, some of which they took entirely empty, and others they disabled while their crews were still getting aboard. And the men, coming up unarmed and in straggling fashion, perished at their ships, or if they fled by land, their enemies, who had disembarked, slew them. Lysander took three thousand men prisoners, together with their generals, and captured the whole fleet, excepting the Paralus[23] and the ships that had made their escape with Conon. So after plundering his enemy's camp and taking their ships in tow, he sailed back to Lampsacus, to the sound of pipes and hymns of victory. He had wrought a work of the greatest magnitude with the least toil and effort, and had brought to a close in a single hour a war which, in length, and the incredible variety of its incidents and fortunes, surpassed all its predecessors. Its struggles and issues had assumed ten thousand changing shapes, and it had cost Hellas more generals than all her previous wars together, and yet it was brought to a close by the prudence and ability of one man. Therefore some actually thought the result due to divine intervention.

12

There were some who declared that the Dioscuri[24] appeared as twin stars on either side of Lysander's ship just as he was sailing out of the harbour against the enemy, and shone out over the rudder-sweeps. And some say also that the falling of the stone was a portent of this disaster; for according to the common belief, a stone of vast size had fallen from heaven at Aegospotami,[25] and it is shown to this day by the dwellers in the Chersonese, who hold it in reverence. Anaxagoras is said to have predicted that if the heavenly bodies should be loosened by some slip or shake, one of them might be torn away, and might plunge and fall down to earth; and he said that none of the stars was in its original position; for being of stone, and heavy, their shining light is caused by friction with the revolving aether, and they are forced along in fixed orbits by the whirling impulse which gave them their circular motion, and this was what prevented them from falling to our earth in the first place, when cold and heavy bodies were separated from universal matter.

But there is a more plausible opinion than this, and its advocates hold that shooting stars are not a flow or emanation of aetherial fire, which the lower air quenches at the very moment of its kindling, nor are they an ignition and blazing up of a quantity

---

23   Castor and Pollux.

24   In 468–7 B.C., according to the Parian marble (*ep.* 57) and Pliny, *N. H.* II.149 f.

25   See chapter ix.5. According to Xenophon (*Hell.* II.1.31 f.), however, the Athenians had passed a decree that, if victorious in the sea-fight, they would cut off the right hand of every prisoner; and the crime of Philocles was that he had ordered the crews of two captured triremes to be thrown over a precipice.

of lower air which has made its escape into the upper regions; but they are plunging and falling heavenly bodies, carried out of their course by some relaxation in the tension of their circular most, and falling, not upon the inhabited region of the earth, but for the most part outside of it and into the great sea; and this is the reason why they are not noticed.

But Daïmachus, in his treatise "On Religion," supports the view of Anaxagoras. He says that before the stone fell, seventy-five days continually, there was seen in the heavens a fiery body of vast size, as if it had been a flaming cloud, not resting in one place, but moving along with intricate and irregular motions, so that fiery fragments, broken from it by its plunging and erratic course, were carried in all directions and flashed fire, just as shooting stars do. But when it had fallen in that part of the earth, and the inhabitants, after recovering from their fear and amazement, were assembled about it, no action of fire was seen, nor even so much as a trace thereof, but a stone lying there, of large size, it is true, but one which bore almost no proportion at all to the fiery mass seen in the heavens. Well, then, that Daïmachus must needs have indulgent readers, is clear; but if his story is true, he refutes utterly those who affirm that a rock, which winds and tempests had torn from some mountain top, was caught up and borne along like a spinning top, and that at the point where the whirling impetus given to it first relaxed and ceased, there it plunged and fell. Unless, indeed, what was seen in the heavens for many days was really fire, the quenching and extinction of which produced a change in the air resulting in unusually violent winds and agitations, and these brought about the plunge of the stone. However, the minute discussion of this subject belongs to another kind of writing.

13

Lysander, after the three thousand Athenians whom he had taken prisoners had been condemned to death by the special council of allies, calling Philocles, their general, asked him what punishment should be visited upon him for having given his fellow-citizens such counsel regarding Greeks.[26] But he, not one whit softened by his misfortunes, bade him not play the prosecutor in a case where there was no judge, but to inflict, as victor, the punishment he would have suffered if vanquished. Then, after bathing and putting on a rich robe, he went first to the slaughter and showed his countrymen the way, as Theophrastus writes. After this, Lysander sailed to the various cities, and ordered all the Athenians whom he met to go back to Athens, for he would spare none, he said, but would slaughter any whom he caught outside the city. He took this course, and drove them all into the city together, because he wished

---

26 The specific name for the governor whom the Lacedaemonians sent out to the islands and cities of Greece during their supremacy.

that scarcity of food and a mighty famine should speedily afflict the city, in order that they might not hinder him by holding out against his siege with plenty of provisions. He also suppressed the democratic, and the other forms of government, and left one Lacedaemonian harmost[27] in each city, and ten rulers chosen from the political clubs which he had organized throughout the cities. This he did alike in the cities which had been hostile, and in those which had become his allies, and sailed along in leisurely fashion, in a manner establishing for himself the supremacy over Hellas. For in his appointments of the rulers he had regard neither to birth nor wealth, but put control of affairs into the hands of his comrades and partisans, and made them masters of rewards and punishments. He also took part himself in many massacres, and assisted in driving out the enemies of his friends. Thus he gave the Greeks no worthy specimen of Lacedaemonian rule, nay, even the comic poet Theopompus was thought absurd in likening the Lacedaemonians to tavern-women, because they gave the Greeks a very pleasant sip of freedom, and then dashed the wine with vinegar; for from the very first the taste was harsh and bitter, since Lysander not only would not suffer the people to be masters of their affairs, but actually put the cities into the hands of the boldest and most contentious of the oligarchs.

14

After he had spent some little time in this business, and had sent messengers to Lacedaemon to report that he was sailing up with two hundred ships, he made a junction in Attica with the forces of Agis and Pausanias, the kings, believing that he would speedily capture the city.[28] But since the Athenians held out against them, he took his ships and crossed again to Asia. Here he suppressed the governments of all the remaining cities in like manner, and set up decadarchies, many citizens being slain in each city, and many banished; he also drove out all the Samians, and handed their cities over to the men whom they had banished.[29] Moreover, when he had taken Sestos out of the hands of the Athenians, he would not permit the Sestians to dwell there, but gave the city and its territory to be divided among men who had been pilots and boatswains under him. And this was the first step of his which was resisted by the Lacedaemonians, who restored Sestians again to their country. But there were other measures of Lysander upon which all the Greeks looked with pleasure, when, for instance, the Aeginetans, after a long time,[30] received back their own city, and

---

27 *Cf.* Xen. *Hell.* II.2.5 9.

28 This was after the fall of Athens (Xen. Hell. II.3.6 f.).

29 They had been expelled by the Athenians in 431 B.C.

30 The island and city of Melos were captured and depopulated by the Athenians in the winter of 416–415 B.C.

when the Melians[31] and Scionaeans[32] were restored to their homes by him, after the Athenians had been driven out and had delivered back the cities.

And now, when he learned that the people of Athens were in a wretched plight from famine, he sailed into the Piraeus, and reduced the city, which was compelled to make terms on the basis of his commands. It is true that one hears it said by Lacedaemonians that Lysander wrote to the ephors thus: "Athens is taken"; and that the ephors wrote back to Lysander: "'Taken' were enough"; but this actual story was invented for its neatness' sake.[33] The actual decree of the ephors ran thus: "This is what the Lacedaemonian authorities have decided: tear down the Piraeus and the long walls; quit all the cities and keep to your own land; if you do these things, and restore your causes, you shall have peace, if you want it. As regards the number of your ships, whatsoever shall be decided there, this do."[34] This edict was accepted by the Athenians, on the advice of Theramenes the son of Hagnon, who, they say, being asked at this time by Cleomenes, one of the young orators, if he dared to act and speak the contrary to Themistocles, by surrendering those walls to the Lacedaemonians which that statesman had erected in defiance of the Lacedaemonians, replied: "But I am doing nothing, young man, that is contrary to Themistocles; for the same walls which he erected for the safety of the citizens, we shall tear down for their safety. And if walls made cities prosperous, then Sparta must be in the worst plight of all, since she has none."

15

Lysander, accordingly, when he had taken possession of all the ships of the Athenians except twelve, and of their walls, on the sixteenth of the month Munychion, the same on which they conquered the Barbarian in the sea-fight at Salamis, took measures at once to change their form of government. And when the Athenians opposed him bitterly in this, he sent word to the people that he had caught the city violating the terms of its surrender; for its walls were still standing, although the days were past within which they should have been pulled down; he should therefore present their case anew for the decision of the authorities, since they had broken their agreements. And some say that in very truth a proposition to sell the Athenians into slavery was actually made in the assembly of the allies, and that at this time Erianthus the Theban also made a motion that the city be razed to the ground, and the country about it left for sheep to graze. Afterwards, however, when the leaders were gathered at a banquet,

---

31   The city of Scionè, on the Chalcidic peninsula, was captured and depopulated by the Athenians in 421 B.C.

32   To illustrate the Spartan passion for brevity of speech.

33   *Cf.* Xen. *Hell.* II.2.20.

34   Verses 167 f. (Kirchhoff).

and a certain Phocian sang the first chorus in the "Electra" of Euripides,[35] which begins with

> "O thou daughter of Agamemnon,
> I am come, Electra, to thy rustic court,"

all were moved to compassion, and felt it to be a cruel deed to abolish and destroy a city which was so famous, and produced such poets.

So then, after the Athenians had yielded in all points, Lysander sent for many flute-girls from the city, and assembled all those who were already in the camp, and then tore down the walls, and burned up the triremes, to the sound of the flute, while the allies crowned themselves with garlands and made merry together, counting that day as the beginning of their freedom. Then, without delay, he also made changes in the form of government, establishing thirty rulers in the city and ten in Piraeus. Further, he put a garrison into the acropolis, and made Callibius, a Spartan, its harmost. He it was who once lifted his staff to smite Autolycus, the athlete, whom Xenophon makes the chief character in his "Symposium";[36] and when Autolycus seized him by the legs and threw him down, Lysander did not side with Callibius in his vexation, but actually joined in censuring him, saying that he did not understand how to govern freemen. But the Thirty, to gratify Callibius, soon afterwards put Autolycus to death.

16

Lysander, after settling these matters, sailed for Thrace himself, but what remained of the public moneys, together with all the gifts and crowns which he had himself received,—many people, as was natural, offering presents to a man who had the greatest power, and who was, in a manner, master of Hellas,—he sent off to Lacedaemon by Gylippus, who had held command in Sicily.[37] But Gylippus, as it is said, ripped open the sacks at the bottom, and after taking a large amount of silver from each, sewed them up again, not knowing that there was a writing in each indicating the sum it held. And when he came to Sparta, he hid what he had stolen under the tiles of his house, but delivered the sacks to the ephors, and showed the seals upon them. When, however, the ephors opened the sacks and counted the money, its amount did not agree with the written lists, and the thing perplexed them, until a servant of Gylippus made the truth known to them by his riddle of many owls sleeping under the tiling.

---

35   *Cf.* Xen. *Hell.* II.2.23.

36   The scene of the ""Symposium"" is laid at the house of Callias, to which Autolycus and his father have been invited, together with Socrates and some of his friends.

37   As Spartan general sent out to aid the Syracusans, he had turned the success of the besieging Athenians into disaster. See the *Nicias,* chapters xviii–ff.

For most of the coinage of the time, as it seems, bore the forgery of an owl, owing to the supremacy of Athens.

17

Gylippus, then, after adding a deed so disgraceful and ignoble as this to his previous great and brilliant achievements, removed himself from Lacedaemon. And the wisest of the Spartans, being led by this instance in particular to fear the power of money, which they said was corrupting influential as well as ordinary citizens, reproached Lysander, and fervently besought the ephors to purify the city of all the silver and the gold, as imported curses. The ephors deliberated on the matter. And it was Sciraphidas, according to Theopompus, or Phlogidas, according to Ephorus, who declared that they ought not to receive gold and silver coinage into the city, but to use that of the country. Now this was of iron, and was dipped in vinegar as soon as it came from the fire, that it might not be worked over, but be made brittle and intractable by the dipping.[38] Besides, it was very heavy and troublesome to carry, and a great quantity and weight of it had but little value. Probably, too, all the ancient money was of this sort, some peoples using iron spits for coins, and some bronze; whence it comes that even to this day many small pieces of money retain the name of "oboli," or *spits*, and six "oboli" make a "drachma," or *handful*, since that was as many as the hand could grasp.

But since Lysander's friends opposed this measure, and insisted that the money remain in the city, it was resolved that money of this sort could be introduced for public use, but that if any private person should be found in possession of it, he should be punished with death; just as though Lycurgus had feared the coin, and not the covetousness which the coin produced. And this vice was not removed by allowing no private person to possess money, so much as it was encouraged by allowing the city to possess money, its use thereby acquiring dignity and honour.

Surely it was not possible for those who saw money publicly honoured, to despise it privately as of no service; or to consider as worthless for the individual's private use that which was publicly held in such repute and esteem. Moreover, it takes far less time for public practices to affect the customs of private life, than it does for individual lapses and failings to corrupt entire cities. For it is natural that the parts should rather be perverted along with the whole, when that deteriorates; but the diseases which flow from a part into the whole find many correctives and aids in the parts which remain sound. And so these magistrates merely set the fear of the law to guard the houses of the citizens, that money might have no entrance there, but did not keep their spirits undaunted by the power of money and insensible to it; they rather inspired them

---

38   *Cf. Lycurgus,* ix.2.

all with an emulous desire for wealth as a great and noble object of pursuit. On this point, however, we have censured the Lacedaemonians in another treatise.[39]

18

Out of the spoils, Lysander set up at Delphi bronze statues of himself and each of his admirals, as well as golden stars of the Dioscuri, which disappeared before the battle of Leuctra.[40] And in the treasury of Brasidas and the Acanthians[41] there was stored a trireme two cubits long, made of gold and ivory, which Cyrus sent Lysander as a prize for his victory. Moreover, Anaxandrides the Delphian writes that a deposit of Lysander's was also stored there, consisting of a talent of silver, and fifty-two minas, and eleven staters besides; a statement that is inconsistent with the generally accepted accounts of his poverty. At any rate, Lysander was at this time more powerful than any Greek before him had been, and was thought to cherish a pretentious pride that was greater even than his power. For he was the first Greek, as Duris writes, to whom the cities erected altars and made sacrifices as to a god, the first also to whom songs of triumph were sung. One of these is handed down, and begins as follows:—

> "The general of sacred Hellas
> who came from wide-space Sparta
> will we sing O! io! Paean."

The Samians, too, voted that their festival of Hera should be called Lysandreia. And the poet Choerilus was always kept in his retinue, to adorn his achievements with verse; while with Antilochus, who composed some verses in his honour, he was so pleased that he filled his cap with silver and gave it to him. And when Antimachus of Colophon and a certain Niceratus of Heracleia competed one another at the Lysandreia in poems celebrating his achievements, he awarded the crown to Niceratus, and Antimachus, in vexation, suppressed his poem. But Plato, who was then a young man, and admired Antimachus for his poetry, tried to cheer and console him in his chagrin at this defeat, telling him that it is the ignorant who suffer from their ignorance, just as the blind do from their blindness. However, when Aristonoüs the harper, who had been six times victor at the Pythian games, told Lysander in a patronizing way that if he should be victorious again, he would have himself proclaimed under Lysander's name, "That is," Lysander replied, "as my slave?"

---

39 *Inst. Lacon.* 42 (*Morals*, p239 f.).

40 An omen of the defeat of the Spartans in that battle (371 B.C.).

41 *Cf.* chapter i.1.

19

Now to the leading men, and to his equals, the ambition of Lysander was annoying merely. But since, owing to the court that was paid to him, great haughtiness and severity crept into his character along with his ambition, there was no such moderation as would become a popular leader either in his rewards or punishments, but the prizes he awarded to his friends and allies were irresponsible lordships over cities, and absolute sovereignties, while the sole punishment that could satisfy his wrath was the death of his enemy; not even exile was allowed. Nay, at a later time, fearing lest the active popular leaders of Miletus should go into exile, and desiring to bring from their retreats those also who were in hiding, he made oath that he would do them no harm; but when the first put faith in him and the second came forth, he delivered them all over to the oligarchs for slaughter, being no less than eight hundred of both classes. In the other cities also untold numbers of the popular party were slain, since he killed not only for his own private reasons, but also gratified by his murders the hatred and cupidity of his many friends everywhere, and shared the bloody work with them. Wherefore Eteocles the Lacedaemonian won great approval when he said that Hellas could not have borne two Lysanders. Now this same utterance was made by Archestratus concerning Alcibiades also,[42] as Theophrastus tells us. But in his case it was insolence, and wanton self-will, that gave most offence; whereas Lysander's power was made dreadful and oppressive by the cruelty of his disposition.

The Lacedaemonians paid little heed to the rest of his accusers, but when Pharnabazus, who was outraged by Lysander's pillaging and wasting his territory, sent men to Sparta to denounce him, the ephors were incensed, and when they found Thorax, one of Lysander's friends and fellow-generals, with money in his private possession, they put him to death, and sent a dispatch-scroll to Lysander, ordering him home.

The dispatch-scroll is of the following character. When the ephors send out an admiral or a general, they make two round pieces of wood exactly alike in length and thickness, so that each corresponds to the other in its dimensions, and keep one themselves, while they give the other to their envoy. These pieces of wood they call "scytalae." Whenever, then, they wish to send some secret and important message, they make a scroll of parchment long and narrow, like a leathern strap, and wind it round their "scytale," leaving no vacant space thereon, but covering its surface all round with the parchment. After doing this, they write what they wish on the parchment, just as it lies wrapped about the "scytale"; and when they have written their message, they take the parchment off, and send it, without the piece of wood, to the commander. He, when he has received it, cannot other get any meaning of it,—since the letters have no connection, but are disarranged,—unless he takes his own "scytale" and winds the strip of parchment about it, so that, when its spiral course is restored

---

42   *Cf. Alcibiades,* xvi.5.

perfectly, and that which follows is joined to that which precedes, he reads around the staff, and so discovers the continuity of the message. And the parchment, like the staff, is called "scytale," as the thing measured bears the name of the measure.

20

But Lysander, when the dispatch-scroll reached him at the Hellespont, was much disturbed, and since he feared the denunciations of Pharnabazus above all others, he hastened to hold a conference with him, hoping to compose their quarrel. At this conference he begged Pharnabazus to write another letter about him to the magistrates, stating that he had not been wronged at all, and had no complaints to make. 2 But in thus ""playing the Cretan against a Cretan,"" as the saying is, he misjudged his opponent. For Pharnabazus, after promising to do all that he desired, openly wrote such a letter as Lysander demanded, but secretly kept another by him ready written. And when it came to putting on the seals, he exchanged the documents, which looked exactly alike, and gave him the letter which had been secretly written. 3 Accordingly, when Lysander arrived at Sparta and went, as the custom is, into the senate-house, he gave the ephors the letter of Pharnabazus, convinced that the greatest of the complaints against him was thus removed; for Pharnabazus was in high favour with the Lacedaemonians, because he had been, of all the King"s generals, most ready to help them in the war. 4 But when the ephors, after reading the letter, showed it to him, and he understood that

"Odysseus, then, is not the only man of guile,"[43]

for the time being he was mightily confounded and went away. But a few days afterwards, on meeting the magistrates, he said that he was obliged to go up to the temple of Ammon[44] and sacrifice to the god the sacrifice which he had vowed before his battles. 5 Now some say that when he was besieging the city of Aphytae in Thrace, Ammon really stood by him in his sleep; wherefore he raised the siege, declaring that the god had commanded it, and ordered the Aphytaeans to sacrifice to Ammon, and was eager to make a journey into Libya and propitiate the god. But the majority believed that he made the god a pretext, and really feared the ephors, and was impatient of the yoke at home, and unable to endure being under authority, and therefore longed to wander and travel about somewhat, like a horse which comes back from unrestricted pasture in the meadows to his stall, and is put once more to his accustomed work. Ephorus,

---

43   An iambic trimeter of some unknown poet.

44   In an oasis of the great desert of Libya. *Cf. Cimon*, xviii.6 f.

it is true, assigns another reason for this absence abroad, which I shall mention by and by.[45]

21

After he had with great difficulty procured his release by the ephors, he set sail. But the kings, when he had gone abroad, became aware that by means of the societies which he had formed, he had the cities entirely in his power and was master of Hellas; they therefore took measures for deposing his friends everywhere and restoring the management of affairs to the people. However, fresh disturbances broke out in connection with these changes, and first of all the Athenians from Phyle attacked the Thirty and overpowered them. Lysander therefore came home in haste, and persuaded the Lacedaemonians to aid the oligarchies and chastise the democracies. Accordingly, they sent to the Thirty, first of all, a hundred talents for the war, and Lysander himself as general. But the kings were jealous of him, and feared to let him capture Athens a second time; they therefore determined that one of them should go out with the army. And Pausanias did go out, ostensibly in behalf of the tyrants[46] against the people, but really to put a stop to the war, in order that Lysander might not again become master of Athens through the efforts of his friends. This object, then, he easily accomplished, and by reconciling the Athenians and putting a stop to their discord, he robbed Lysander of his ambitious hopes. A short time afterwards, however, when the Athenians revolted again, he himself was censured for taking the curb of the oligarchy out of the mouth of the people, and letting them grow bold and insolent again; while Lysander won fresh repute as a man who exercised his command in downright fashion, not for the gratification of others, nor yet to win applause, but for the good of Sparta.

22

He was harsh of speech also, and terrifying to his opponents. For instance, when the Argives were disputing about boundaries, and thought they made a juster plea than the Lacedaemonians, he pointed to his sword, and said to them: "He who is master of this discourses best about boundaries." And when a Megarian, in some conference with him, grew bold in speech, he said: "Thy words, Stranger, lack a city." And when the Boeotians tried to play a double game with him, he asked them whether he should march through their territory with spears upright, or levelled. And once when the Corinthians had revolted, a hare was seen leaping across the moat; whereupon he said: "Are ye not ashamed to fear enemies who are so lazy that hares sleep on their walls?"

---

45 Chapter xxv.3.

46 That is, the Thirty in Athens.

When Agis the king died,[47]leaving a brother, Agesilaüs, and a reputed son, Leotychides, Lysander, who had been a lover of Agesilaüs, persuaded him to lay claim to the kingdom, on the ground that he was a genuine descendant of Heracles. For Leotychides was accused of being a son of Alcibiades, who had secret commerce with Timaea, the wife of Agis, while he was living in exile at export. Now Agis, as they tell us, being convinced by a computation of time that his wife had not conceived by him, ignored Leotychides, and manifestly repudiated him up to the last. But when he was carried sick to Heraea and was about to die, he yielded to the entreaties of the young man himself and of his friends, and declared in the hearing of many that Leotychides was his own son, and after begging those who were present to bear witness of this to the Lacedaemonians, died. Accordingly, they did so bear witness in favour of Leotychides. Moreover, Agesilaüs, who was otherwise illustrious, and had Lysander as a champion, was injured in his claim by Diopeithes, a man in high repute for his interpretation of oracles, who published the following prophecy with reference to the lameness of Agesilaüs:—[48]

> "Bethink thee now, O Sparta, although thou art very proud,
> Lest from thee, sound of foot, there spring a maimed royalty;
> For long will unexpected toils oppress thee,
> And onward rolling billows of man-destroying war."

Many, therefore, out of deference to the oracle, inclined to Leotychides, but Lysander declared that Diopeithes did not interpret the prophecy correctly; for it did not mean that the god would be displeased if one who was lame should rule the Lacedaemonians, but the kingdom would be maimed if bastards and ill-born men should be kings in a line with the posterity of Heracles. By such arguments, and because he had very great influence, he prevailed, and Agesilaüs became king.[49]

23

At once, then, Lysander tried to rouse and incite him to make an expedition into Asia, suggesting hopes that he would put down the Persians and become a very great man. He also wrote letters to his friends in Asia, bidding them ask Agesilaüs of the Lacedaemonians as general for their war against the Barbarians.[50]They obeyed, and sent ambassadors to Lacedaemon with the request, and thus an honour not inferior to that of being made king was obtained for Agesilaüs through the efforts of Lysander.

---

47 In 398 B.C., after returning home from a victorious campaign (Xen. *Hell.* III.3.1).
48 *Cf.* Plutarch's *Agesilaüs*, ii.2.
49 *Cf.* Plutarch's *Agesilaüs*, iii.3 5; Xen. *Hell.* III.3.2 f.
50 *Cf.* Plutarch's *Agesilaüs*, vi.1 f.

But with ambitious natures, which are otherwise not ill qualified for command, jealousy of their equals in reputation is no slight obstacle to the performance of noble deeds; for they make those their rivals in the path of virtue, whom they might have as helpers. Agesilaüs did indeed take Lysander with him among his thirty counsellors, intending to treat him with special favour as his chief friend; but when they were come into Asia, the people there, who were not acquainted with him, conferred with him but rarely and briefly, whereas Lysander, in consequence of their large intercourse with him in former times, had them always at his door and in his train, those who were his friends coming out of deference, and those whom he suspected, out of fear. And just as in tragedies it naturally happens that an actor who takes the part of some messenger or servant is in high repute and plays leading rôles, while the one who bears the crown and sceptre is not even listened to when he speaks, so in this case the whole honour of the government was associated with the counsellor, and there was left for the king only the empty name of power. It is true, perhaps, that there should have been some gentle handling of this excessive ambition, and that Lysander should have been reduced to the second place; but entirely to cast off and insult, for fame's sake, a benefactor and a friend, was not worthy of the character of Agesilaüs.

In the first place, then, he did not give him opportunities for achievement, nor even assign him to a command; and secondly, those in whose behalf he perceived that Lysander was earnestly exerting himself, these he always sent away with less reward than an ordinary suitor, or wholly unsuccessful, thus quietly undoing and chilling his influence. So when Lysander missed all his aims, and saw that his interested efforts for his friends were an obstacle to their success, he not only ceased to give them his own aid, but begged them not to wait upon him nor pay him their court, but to confer with the king, and with such as had more power to benefit those who showed them honour than was his at present. Most of those who heard this refrained from troubling him about their affairs, but did not cease paying him their court, nay rather, by waiting upon him in the public walks and places of exercise, they gave Agesilaüs even more annoyance than before, because he envied him the honour. Therefore, though he offered most of the Spartans[51] commands in the field and governments of cities, he appointed Lysander his carver of meats. And presently, as if by way of insult to the Ionians, he said: "Let them be off, and pay their court now to my carver of meats." Accordingly, Lysander determined to have a conference with him, at which a brief and laconic dialogue passed between them. "Verily, though knowest well, Agesilaüs, how to abase friends." To which Agesilaüs: "Yes, if they would be greater than I; but those who increase my power should also share in it." "Well, perhaps thy words, Agesilaüs, are fairer than my deeds; but I beg thee, even because of the strangers who have their

---

51   Agis took thirty Spartans with him as counsellors and captains (Plutarch's *Agesilaüs*, vi.3; Xenophon's *Agesilaüs*, i.7).

eyes upon us, to give me a post under thy command where thou believest that I shall be least annoying to thyself, and more serviceable than now."[52]

24

Upon this, he was sent as ambassador to the Hellespont; and though he was angry with Agesilaüs, he did not neglect to do his duty, but induced Spithridates the Persian, a high-minded man with forces at his command, to revolt from Pharnabazus, with whom he was at odds, and brought him to Agesilaüs.[53] The king made no further use of Lysander, however, in the war, and when his time had expired, he sailed back to Sparta without honour, not only enraged at Agesilaüs, but hating the whole form of government more than ever, and resolved to put into execution at once, and without delay, the plans for a revolutionary change which he is thought to have devised and concocted some time before.

They were as follows. Of the Heracleidae who united with the Dorians and came down into Peloponnesus, there was a numerous and glorious stock flourishing in Sparta; however, not every family belonging to it participated in the royal succession, but the kings were chosen from two houses only, and were called Eurypontidae and Agiadae. The rest had no special privileges in the government because of their high birth, but the honours which result from superior excellence lay open to all who had power and ability. Now Lysander belonged to one of these families, and when he had risen to great fame for his deeds, and had acquired many friends and great power, he was vexed to see the city increased in power by his efforts, but ruled by others who were of no better birth than himself. He therefore planned to take the government away from the two houses, and restore it to all the Heracleidae in common, or, as some say, not to the Heracleidae, but to the Spartans in general,[54] in order that its high prerogatives might not belong to those only who were descended from Heracles, but to those who, like Heracles, were selected for superior excellence, since it was this which raised him to divine honours. And he hoped that when the kingdom was awarded on this principle, no Spartan would be chosen before himself.

25

In the first place, then, he undertook and made preparations to persuade the citizens by his own efforts, and committed to memory a speech written by Cleon, the Halicarnassian, for the purpose. In the second place, seeing that the novelty and magnitude of his innovation demanded a more audacious support, he brought stage

---

52   *Cf.* Plutarch's *Agesilaüs*, vii viii.1 2; Xen. *Hell.* III.4.7 9.

53   *Cf.* Plutarch's *Agesilaüs*, viii.3; Xen. *Hell.* III.4.10.

54   *Cf.* Plutarch's *Agesilaüs*, viii.3.

machinery to bear upon the citizens,[55] as it were, by collecting and arranging responses and oracles of Apollo; convinced that Cleon's clever rhetoric would not help him at all unless he should first terrify and subdue his countrymen by vague religious fear and superstitious terror, and then bring them under the influence of his argument. Well, then, Ephorus tells us that after an attempt to corrupt the Pythian priestess, and after a second failure to persuade the priestesses of Dodona by means of Pherecles, he went up to the temple of Ammon and had a conference with the god's interpreters there, at which he offered them much money, but that they took this ill, and sent certain messengers to Sparta to denounce him; and further, that when Lysander was acquitted of their charges, the Libyans said, as they went away, "But we will pass better judgments than yours, O Spartans, when ye come to dwell with us in Libya"; for they knew that there was a certain ancient oracle bidding the Lacedaemonians to settle in Libya. But since the whole plot and concoction was no insignificant one, nor yet carelessly undertaken, but made many important assumptions, like a mathematical demonstration, and proceeded to its conclusion through premises which were difficult and hard to obtain, we shall follow, in our description of it, the account of one who was both a historian and a philosopher.[56]

26

There was a woman in Pontus who declared that she was with child by Apollo. Many disbelieved her, as was natural, but many also lent an ear to her, so that when she gave birth to a male child, many notable persons took an interest in its care and rearing. For some reason or other, the name given to the boy was Silenus. Lysander took these circumstances for his foundation, and supplied the rest of his cunning fabric himself, making use of not a few, nor yet insignificant, champions of the tale, who brought the story of the boy's birth into credit without exciting suspicion. They also brought back another response from Delphi, and caused it to be circulated in Sparta, which declared that sundry very ancient oracles were kept in secret writings by the priests there, and that it was not possible to get these, nor even lawful to read them, unless someone born of Apollo should come after a long lapse of time, give the keepers an intelligible token of his birth, and obtain the tablets containing the oracles. The way thus being prepared, Silenus was to come and demand the oracles as Apollo's son, and the priests who were in the secret were to insist on precise answers to all their questions about his birth, and finally, persuaded, forsooth, that he was the son of Apollo, were to show him the writing. Then Silenus, in the presence of many witnesses, was to read aloud the prophecies, especially the one relating to the kingdom, for the sake of

---

55 In the Greek theatre, gods were swung into view, above the plane of the action, by means of a huge crane. Cf. *Themistocles*, x.1.

56 Probably Ephorus.

which the whole scheme had been invented, and which declared that it was more for the honour and interest of the Spartans to choose their kings from the best citizens.

But when at last Silenus was grown to be a youth, and was ready for the business, Lysander's play was ruined for him by the cowardice of one of his actors, or co-workers, who, just as he came to the point, lost his courage and drew back. However, all this was actually found out, not while Lysander was alive, but after his death.

27

And he died before Agesilaüs returned from Asia, after he had plunged, or rather had plunged Hellas, into the Boeotian war.[57] For it is stated in both ways; and some hold him responsible for the war, others the Thebans, and others both together. It is charged against the Thebans that they cast away the sacrifices at Aulis,[58] and that, because Androcleides and Amphitheus[59] had been bribed with the King's money to stir up a war in Greece against the Lacedaemonians, they set upon the Phocians and ravaged their country. It is said, on the other hand, that Lysander was angry with the Thebans because they alone laid claim to a tenth part of the spoils of the war, while the rest of the allies held their peace; and because they were indignant about the money which he sent to Sparta; but above all, because they first put the Athenians in the way of freeing themselves from the thirty tyrants whom he had set up, whose terrorizing power the Lacedaemonians had increased by decreeing that fugitives from Athenians might be brought back from every place of refuge, and that all who impeded their return should be declared enemies of Sparta. In reply to this the Thebans issued counter decrees, akin in spirit to the beneficent deeds of Heracles and Dionysus, to the effect that every house and city in Boeotia should be open to such Athenians as needed succour; and that whosoever did not help a fugitive under arrest, should be fined a talent; and that if any one should carry arms through Boeotia against the tyrants in Athens, no Theban would either see him or hear about it. And they did not merely vote such Hellenic and humane decrees, without at the same time making their deeds correspond to their edicts; but Thrasybulus and those who with him occupied Phyle, set out from Thebes to do so,[60] and the Thebans not only provided them with arms and money, but also with secrecy and a base of operations. Such, then, were the grounds of complaint which Lysander had against the Thebans.

---

57 In 395 B.C., the aggressions of Sparta led to an alliance between Thebes and Athens against her. In the following year Corinth and Argos joined the alliance, and the whole war, which dragged along until 387 B.C., is usually known as the "Corinthian war."

58 In the spring of 396, when Agesilaüs vainly tried to sacrifice there, in imitation of Agamemnon (Plutarch's *Agesilaüs*, vi.4 6; Xen. *Hell.* III.4.3 f., and 5.5).

59 *Cf.* Xen. *Hell.* III.5.1 and 4.

60 *Cf.* Xen. *Hell.* II.4.1 f.

28

And since he was now of an altogether harsh disposition, owing to the melancholy which persisted into his old age, he stirred up the ephors, and persuaded them to fit out an expedition against the Thebans; and assuming the command, he set out on the campaign.[61] Afterwards the ephors sent out Pausanias the king also with an army. Now it was the plan that Pausanias should make a circuit by the way of Mount Cithaeron, and then invade Boeotia, while Lysander marched through Phocis to meet him, with a large force. He took the city of Orchomenus, which came over to him of its own accord, and assaulted and plundered Lebadeia. Then he sent a letter to Pausanias, bidding him move from Plataea and join forces with him at Haliartus, and promising that he himself would be before the walls of Haliartus at break of day. This letter was brought to Thebes by some scouts, into whose hands its bearer fell. The Thebans therefore entrusted their city to a force of Athenians which had come to their aid, while they themselves set out early in the night, and succeeded in reaching Haliartus a little before Lysander, and a considerable part of them entered the city. Lysander at first decided to post his army on a hill and wait for Pausanias; then, as the day advanced, being unable to remain inactive, he took his arms, encouraged his allies, and led them along the road in column towards the wall of the city. But those of the Thebans who had remained outside, taking the city on their left, advanced upon the rear of their enemy, at the spring called Cissusa. Here, as the story goes, his nurses bathed the infant Dionysus after his birth; for the water has the colour and sparkle of wine, is clear, and very pleasant to the taste. And not far away the Cretan storax-shrub grows in profusion, which the Haliartans regard as a proof that Rhadamanthus once dwelt there; and they show his tomb, which they call Alea. And near by is also the memorial of Alcmene; for she was buried there, as they say, having lived with Rhadamanthus after the death of Amphitryon.

But the Thebans inside the city, drawn up in battle array with the Haliartans, kept quiet for some time; when, however, they saw Lysander with his foremost troops approaching the wall, they suddenly threw open the gate and fell upon them, and killed Lysander himself with his soothsayer, and a few of the rest; for the greater part of them fled swiftly back to the main body.

And when the Thebans made no halt, but pressed hard upon them, the whole force turned to the hills in flight, and a thousand of them were slain. Three hundred of the Thebans also lost their lives by pursuing their enemies into rough and dangerous places. These had been accused of favouring the Spartan cause, and in their eagerness to clear themselves of this charge in the eyes of their fellow-citizens, they exposed themselves needlessly in the pursuit, and so threw away their lives.[62]

---

61   Lysander was commissioned to raise a force of allies in Phocis and the neighbouring country, with which Pausanias was to unite his troops (Xen. *Hell.* III.5.6). Plutarch's language is obscure.

62   *Cf.* Xen. *Hell.* III.5.17 20.

29

Tidings of the disaster were brought to Pausanias while he was on the march from Plataea to Thespiae, and putting his army in battle array, he came to Haliartus. Thrasybulus also came from Thebes, leading his Athenians. But when Pausanias was minded to ask for the bodies of the dead under a truce, the elders of the Spartans could not brook it, and were angry among themselves, and coming to the king, they protested that the body of Lysander must not be taken up under cover of a truce, but by force of arms, in open battle for it; and that if they conquered, then they would give him burial, but if they were vanquished, it would be a glorious thing to lie dead with their general. Such were the words of the elders; but Pausanias saw that it would be a difficult matter to conquer the Thebans, flushed as they were with victory, and that the body of Lysander lay near the walls, so that its recovery would be difficult without a truce, even if they were victorious; he therefore sent a herald, and after making a truce, led his forces back. And as soon as they had come beyond the boundary of Boeotia with Lysander's body, they buried it in the friendly soil of their allies, the Panopeans, where his monument now stands, by the road leading from Delphi to Chaeroneia.

Here the army bivouacked; and it is said that a certain Phocian, recounting the action to another who was not in it, said that the enemy fell upon them just after Lysander had crossed the Hoplites. Then a Spartan, who was a friend of Lysander, asked in amazement what he meant by Hoplites, for he did not know the name. "Indeed it was there," said the Phocian, "that the enemy slew the foremost of us; for the stream that flows past the city is called Hoplites." On hearing this, the Spartan burst into tears, and said that man could not escape his destiny. For Lysander, as it appears, had received an oracle running thus:—

"Be on thy guard, I bid thee, against a sounding Hoplites,
And an earth born dragon craftily coming behind thee."

Some, however, say that the Hoplites does not flow before Haliartus, but is a winter torrent near Coroneia, which joins the Philarus and then flows past that city; in former times it was called Hoplias, but now Isomantus. Moreover, the man of Haliartus who killed Lysander, Neochorus by name, had a dragon as emblem on his shield, and to this, it was supposed, the oracle referred. And it is said that the Thebans also, during the Peloponnesian war, received an oracle at the sanctuary of Ismenus which indicated beforehand not only the battle at Delium,[63] but also this battle at Haliartus, thirty years later. It ran as follows:—

"When thou huntest the wolf with the spear, watch closely the border,
Orchalides, too, the hill which foxes never abandon."

---

63   424 B.C.

Now by "border," the god meant the region about Delium, where Boeotia is conterminous with Attica; and by Orchalides, the hill which is now called Alopecus, or Fox-hill, in the parts of Haliartus which stretch towards Mount Helicon.

30

Now that Lysander had met with such an end, at the outset the Spartans were so indignant about it that they summoned the king to trial for his life; but he evaded it, and fled to Tegea, where he spent the end of his days as a suppliant in the sanctuary of Athena. For the poverty of Lysander, which was discovered at his death, made his excellence more apparent to all, since from the vast wealth and power in his hands, and from the great homage paid him by cities and the Great King, he had not, even in the slightest degree, sought to amass money for the aggrandizement of his family. This is the testimony of Theopompus, who is more to be trusted when he praises than when he blames; for he takes more pleasure in blaming than in praising. But after some time had passed, according to Ephorus, some dispute arose at Sparta with her allies, and it became necessary to inspect the writings which Lysander had kept by him; for which purpose Agesilaüs went to his house. And when he found the book containing the speech on the constitution,[64] which argued that the kingship ought to be taken from the Eurypontidae and Agiadae and made accessible to all Spartans alike, and that the choice should be made from the best of these, he was eager to produce the speech before his countrymen, and show them what the real character of Lysander's citizenship had been. But Lacratidas, a prudent man, and at that time the principal ephor, held Agesilaüs back, saying that they ought not to dig Lysander up again, but rather to bury the speech along with him, since it was composed with such a subtle persuasiveness.

However, they paid him many honours at his death. In particular, they imposed a fine upon the men who had engaged to marry his daughters, and then, after Lysander's death, had renounced the engagement. The reason given for the fine was that the men had paid court to Lysander while they thought him rich, but when his poverty showed them that he was just a good man, they forsook him. For there was, as it appears, a penalty at Sparta not only for not marrying at all, and for a late marriage, but also a bad marriage; and to this last they subjected those especially who sought alliance with the rich, instead of with the good and with their own associates. Such, then, are the accounts we have found given of Lysander.

---

64 *Cf.* chapter xxv.1.

THE REPUBLIC OF PLATO
Book II

Translated by Paul Shorey

When I had said this I supposed that I was done with the subject, but it all turned out to be only a prelude. For Glaucon, who is always an intrepid, enterprising spirit in everything, would not on this occasion acquiesce in Thrasymachus' abandonment of his case, but said, Socrates, is it your desire to seem to have persuaded us or really to persuade us that it is without exception better to be just than unjust?

Really, I said, if the choice rested with me.

Well, then, you are not doing what you wish. For tell me, do you agree that there is a kind of good which we would choose to possess, not from desire for its aftereffects, but welcoming it for its own sake? As, for example, joy and such pleasures as are harmless and nothing results from them afterward save to have and to hold the enjoyment.

I recognize that kind, said I.

And again a kind that we love both for its own sake and for its consequences, such as understanding, sight, and health? For these I presume we welcome for both reasons.

Yes, I said.

And can you discern a third form of good under which fall exercise and being healed when sick and the art of healing and the making of money generally? For of them we would say that they are laborious and painful yet beneficial, and for their own sake we would not accept them, but only for the rewards and other benefits that accrue from them.

Why yes, I said, I must admit this third class also. But what of it?

In which of these classes do you place justice? he said.

In my opinion, I said, it belongs in the fairest class, that which a man who is to be happy must love both for its own sake and for the results.

Yet the multitude, he said, do not think so, but that it belongs to the toilsome class of things that must be practiced for the sake of rewards and repute due to opinion but that in itself is to be shunned as an affliction.

I am aware, said I, that that is the general opinion and Thrasymachus has for some time been disparaging it as such and praising injustice. But I, it seems, am somewhat slow to learn.

Come now, he said, hear what I too have to say and see if you agree with me. For Thrasymachus seems to me to have given up to you too soon, as if he were a serpent that you had charmed, but I am not yet satisfied with the proof that has been offered about justice and injustice. For what I desire is to hear what each of them is and what potency and effect each has in and of itself dwelling in the soul, but to dismiss their rewards and consequences. This, then, is what I propose to do, with your concurrence. I will renew the argument of Thrasymachus and will first state what men say is the nature and origin of justice, secondly, that all who practice it do so reluctantly, regarding it as something necessary and not as a good, and thirdly, that they have plausible grounds for thus acting, since forsooth the life of the unjust man is far better than that of the just man—as they say, though I, Socrates, don't believe it. Yet I am disconcerted when my ears are dinned by the arguments of Thrasymachus and innumerable others. But the case for justice, to prove that it is better than injustice, I have never yet heard stated by any as I desire to hear it. What I desire is to hear an encomium on justice in and by itself. And I think I am most likely to get that from you. For which reason I will lay myself out in praise of the life of injustice, and in so speaking will give you an example of the manner in which I desire to hear from you in turn the dispraise of injustice and the praise of justice. Consider whether my proposal pleases you.

Nothing could please me more, said I, for on what subject would a man of sense rather delight to hold and hear discourse again and again?

That is excellent, he said, and now listen to what I said would be the first topic—the nature and origin of justice.

By nature, they say, to commit injustice is a good and to suffer it is an evil, but that the excess of evil in being wronged is greater than the excess of good in doing wrong, so that when men do wrong and are wronged by one another and taste of both, those who lack the power to avoid the one and take the other determine that it is for their profit to make a compact with one another neither to commit nor to suffer injustice, and that this is the beginning of legislation and of covenants between men, and that they name the commandment of the law the lawful and the just, and that this is the genesis and essential nature of justice—a compromise between the best, which is to do wrong with impunity, and the worst, which is to be wronged and be impotent
to get one's revenge. Justice, they tell us, being midway between the two, is accepted and approved, not as a real good, but as a thing honored in the lack of vigor to do injustice, since anyone who had the power to do it and was in reality 'a man' would never make a compact with anybody neither to wrong nor to be wronged, for he would be mad. The nature, then, of justice is this and such as this, Socrates, and such are the conditions in which it originates, according to the theory.

But as for the second point, that those who practice it do so unwillingly and from want of power to commit injustice, we shall be most likely to apprehend that if we entertain some such supposition as this in thought—if we grant to both the just and the unjust license and power to do whatever they please, and then accompany them in imagination and see whither desire will conduct them. We should then catch the just man in the very act of resorting to the same conduct as the unjust man because of the self-advantage which every creature by its nature pursues as a good, while by the convention of law it is forcibly diverted, to paying honor to 'equality.' The license that I mean would be most nearly such as would result from supposing them to have the power which men say once came to the ancestor of Gyges the Lydian. They relate that he was a shepherd in the service of the ruler at that time of Lydian, and that after a great deluge of rain and an earthquake the ground opened and a chasm appeared in the place where he was pasturing, and they say that he saw and wondered and went down into the chasm. And the story goes that he beheld other marvels there and a hollow bronze horse with little doors, and that he peeped in and saw a corpse within, as it seemed, of more than mortal stature, and that there was nothing else but a gold ring on its hand, which he took off, and so went forth. And when the shepherds held their customary assembly to make their monthly report to the king about the flocks, he also attended, wearing the ring. So as he sat there it chanced that he turned the collet of the ring toward himself, toward the inner part of his hand, and when this took place they say that he became invisible to those who sat by him and they spoke of him as absent, and that he was amazed, and again fumbling with the ring turned the collet outward and so became visible. On noting this he experimented with the ring to see if it possessed this virtue, and he found the result to be that when he turned the collet inward he became invisible, and when outward visible, and becoming aware of this, he immediately managed things so that he became one of the messengers who went up to the king, and on coming there he seduced the king's wife and with her aid set upon the king and slew him and possessed his kingdom.

If now there should be two such rings, and the just man should put on one and the unjust the other, no one could be found, it would seem, of such adamantine temper as to persevere in justice and endure to refrain his hands from the possessions of others and not touch them, though he might with impunity take what he wished even rom the market place, and enter into houses and lie with whom he pleased, and slay and loose from bonds whomsoever he would, and in all other things conduct himself among mankind as the equal of a god. And in so acting he would do no differently from the other man, but both would pursue the same course. And yet this is a great proofs, one might argue, that no one is just of his own will but only from constraint, in the belief that justice is not his personal good, inasmuch as every man, when he supposes himself to have the power to do wrong, does wrong. For that there is far more profit for him personally
in injustice than in justice is what every man believes, and believes truly, as the proponent of this theory will maintain. For if anyone who had got such a license within his grasp should refuse to do any wrong or lay his hands on others' possessions, he would be regarded as most pitiable and a great fool by all who took note of it, though they

would praise him before one another's faces, deceiving one another because of their fear of suffering injustice. So much for this point.

But to come now to the decision between our two kinds of life, if we separate the most completely just and the most completely unjust man, we shall be able to decide rightly, but if not, not. How, then, is this separation to be made? Thus. We must subtract nothing of his injustice from the unjust man or of his justice from the just, but assume the perfection of each in his own mode of conduct. In the first place, the unjust man must act as clever craftsmen do. A first-rate pilot or physician, for example, feels the difference between impossibilities and possibilities in his art and attempts the one and lets the others go, and then, too, if he does happen to trip, he is equal to correcting his error. Similarly, the unjust man who attempts injustice rightly must be supposed to escape detection if he is to be altogether unjust, and we must regard the man who is caught as a bungler. For the height of injustice is to seem just without being so. To the perfectly unjust man, then, we must assign perfect injustice and withhold nothing of it, but we must allow him, while committing the greatest wrongs, to have secured for himself the greatest reputation for justice, and if he does happen to trip, we must concede to him the power to correct his mistakes by his ability to speak persuasively if any of his misdeeds come to light, and when force is needed, to employ force by reason of his manly spirit and vigor and his provision of friends and money. And when we have set up an unjust man of this character, our theory must set the just man at his side—a simple and noble man, who, in the phrase of Aeschylus, does not wish to seem but to be good. Then we must deprive him of the seeming. For if he is going to be thought just he will have honors and gifts because of that esteem. We cannot be sure in that case whether he is just for justice' sake or for the sake of the gifts and the honors. So we must strip him bare of everything but justice and make his state the opposite of his imagined counterpart. Though doing no wrong he must have the repute of the greatest injustice, so that he may be put to the test as regards justice through not softening because of ill repute and the consequences thereof. But let him hold on his course unchangeable even unto death, seeming all his life to be unjust though being just, so that, both men attaining to the limit, the one of injustice, the other of justice, we may pass judgment which of the two is the happier.

Bless me, my dear Glaucon, said I. How strenuously you polish off each of your two men for the competition for the prize as if it were a statue!

To the best of my ability, he replied, and if such is the nature of the two, it becomes an easy matter, I fancy, to unfold the tale of the sort of life that awaits each. We must tell it, then, and even if my language is somewhat rude and brutal, you must not suppose, Socrates, that it is I who speak thus, but those who commend injustice above justice. What they will say is this, that such being his disposition the just man will have to endure the lash, the rack, chains, the branding iron in his eyes, and finally, after every extremity of suffering, he will be crucified, and so will learn his lesson that not to be but to seem just is what we ought to desire. And the saying of Aeschylus was, it seems, far more correctly applicable to the unjust man. For it is literally true, they will say, that the unjust man, as pursuing what clings closely to reality, to truth, and not regulating his life by opinion, desires not to seem but to be unjust,

> Exploiting the deep furrows of his wit
> From which there grows the fruit of counsels shrewd,[1]

first office and rule in the state because of his reputation for justice, then a wife from any family he chooses, and the giving of his children in marriage to whomsoever he pleases, dealings and partnerships with whom he will, and in all these transactions advantage and profit for himself because he has no squeamishness about committing injustice. And so they say that if he enters into lawsuits, public or private, he wins and gets the better of his opponents, and, getting the better, is rich and benefits his friends and harms his enemies, and he performs sacrifices and dedicates votive offerings to the gods adequately and magnificently, and he serves and pays court to men whom he favors and to the gods far better than the just man, so that he may reasonably expect the favor of heaven also to fall rather to him than to the just. So much better they say, Socrates, is the life that is prepared for the unjust man from gods and men than that which awaits the just.

When Glaucon had thus spoken, I had a mind to make some reply thereto, but his brother Adimantus said, You surely don't suppose, Socrates, that the statement of the case is complete?

Why, what else? I said.

The very most essential point, said he, has not been mentioned.

Then, said I, the proverb has it, 'Let a brother help a man—and so, if Glaucon omits any word or deed, do you come to his aid. Though for my part what he has already said is quite enough to overthrow me and incapacitate me for coming to the rescue of justice.

Nonsense, he said, but listen to this further point. We must set forth the reasoning and the language of the opposite party, of those who commend justice and dispraise injustice, if what I conceive to be Glaucon's meaning is to be made more clear. Fathers, when they address exhortations to their sons, and all those who have others in their charge, urge the necessity of being just, not by praising justice itself, but the good repute with mankind that accrues from it, the object that they hold before us being that by seeming to be just the man may get from the reputation office and alliances and all the good things that Glaucon just now enumerated as coming to the unjust man from his good name. But those people draw out still further this topic of reputation. For, throwing in good standing with the gods, they have no lack of blessings to describe,

---

1 Septem 592 sq.

which they affirm the gods give to pious men, even as the worthy Hesiod and Homer declare—the one that the gods make the oaks bear for the just

Acorns on topmost branches and swarms of bees on their mid-trunks,

and he tells how the

Flocks of the fleece-bearing sheep are laden and weighted with soft wool,[2]

and of many other blessings akin to these, and similarly the other poet,

Even as when a good king, who rules in the fear of the high gods,
Upholds justice and right, and the black earth yields him her foison,
Barley and wheat, and his trees are laden and weighted with fair fruits,
Increase comes to his flocks and the ocean is teeming with fishes.[3]

And Musaeus and his son have a more excellent song than these of the blessings that the gods bestow on the righteous. For they conduct them to the house of Hades in their tale and arrange a symposium of the saints, where, reclined on couches and crowned with wreaths, they entertain the time henceforth with wine, as if the fairest meed of virtue were an everlasting drunk. And others extend still further the rewards of virtue from the gods. For they say that the children's children of the pious and oath-keeping man and his race thereafter never fail. Such and suchlike are their praises of justice. But the impious and the unjust they bury in mud in the house of Hades and compel them to fetch water in a sieve, and, while they still live, they bring them into evil repute, and all the sufferings that Glaucon enumerated as befalling just men who are thought to be unjust, these they recite about the unjust, but they have nothing else to say. Such is the praise and the censure of the just and of the unjust.

Consider further, Socrates, another kind of language about justice and injustice employed by both laymen and poets. All with one accord reiterate that soberness and righteousness are fair and honorable, to be sure, but unpleasant and laborious, while licentiousness and injustice are pleasant and easy to win and are only in opinion and by convention disgraceful. They say that injustice pays better than justice, for the most part, and they do not scruple to felicitate bad men who are rich or have other kinds of power and to do them honor public and private, and to dishonor and disregard those who are in any way weak or poor, even while admitting that they are better men than the others. But the strangest of all these speeches are the things they say about the gods and virtue—how it is that the gods themselves assign to many good men misfortunes

2   Works and Days 232 sq.
3   Odyssey 19.109 sq.

and an evil life, but to their opposites a contrary lot, and begging priests and soothsayers go to rich men's doors and make them believe that they by means of sacrifices and incantations have accumulated a treasure of power from the gods that can expiate and cure with pleasurable festivals any misdeed of a man or his ancestors, and that if a man wishes to harm an enemy, at slight cost he will be enabled to injure just and unjust alike, since they are masters of spells and enchantments that constrain the gods to serve their end. And for all these sayings they cite the poets as witnesses, with regard to the ease and plentifulness of vice, quoting,

> Evildoing in plenty a man shall find for the seeking.
> Smooth is the way, and it lies near at hand and is easy to enter,
> But on the pathway of virtue the gods put sweat from the first step,[4]

and a certain long and uphill road. And others cite Homer as a witness to the beguiling of gods by men, since he too said,

> The gods themselves are moved by prayers,
> And men by sacrifice and soothing vows,
> And incense and libation turn their wills
> Praying, whene'er they have sinned and made transgression.[5]

And they produce a bushel of books of Musaeus and Orpheus, the offspring of the Moon and of the Muses, as they affirm, and these books they use in their ritual, and make not only ordinary men but states believe that there really are remissions of sins and purifications for deeds of injustice, by means of sacrifice and pleasant sport for the living, and that there are also special rites for the defunct, which they call functions, that deliver us from evils in that other world, while terrible things await those who have neglected to sacrifice.

What, Socrates, do we suppose is the effect of all such sayings about the esteem in which men and gods hold virtue and vice upon the souls that hear them, the souls of young men who are quick-witted and capable of flitting, as it were, from one expression of opinion to another and inferring from them all the character and the path whereby a man would lead the best life? Such a youth would most likely put to himself the question Pindar asks, 'Is it by justice or by crooked deceit that I the higher tower shall scale and so live my life out in fenced and guarded security?' The consequences of my being just are, unless I likewise seem so, not assets, they say, but liabilities, labor, and total loss, but if I am unjust and have procured myself a reputation for justice, a godlike life is promised. Then since it is 'the seeming,' as the wise men show me, that 'masters

---

4   Hesiod, Works and Days 287 sq.
5   Iliad 9.497 sq.

the reality' and is lord of happiness, to this I must devote myself without reserve. For a front and a show I must draw about myself a shadow outline of virtue, but trail behind me the fox of the most sage Archilochus, shifty and bent on gain. Nay, 'tis objected, it is not easy for a wrongdoer always to lie hid. Neither is any other big thing facile, we shall reply. But all the same if we expect to be happy, we must pursue the path to which the footprints of our arguments point. For with a view to lying hid we will organize societies and political clubs, and there are teachers of cajolery who impart the arts of the popular assembly and the courtroom, so that, partly by persuasion, partly by force, we shall contrive to overreach with impunity. But against the gods, it may be said, neither secrecy nor force can avail. Well, if there are no gods, or they do not concern themselves with the doings of men, neither need we concern ourselves with eluding their observation. If they do exist and pay heed, we know and hear of them only from such discourses and from the poets who have described their pedigrees. But these same authorities tell us that the gods are capable of being persuaded and swerved from their course by 'sacrifice and soothing vows' and dedications. We must believe them in both or neither. And if we are to believe them, the thing to do is to commit injustice and offer sacrifice from the fruits of our wrongdoing. For if we are just, we shall, it is true, be unscathed by the gods, but we shall be putting away from us the profits of injustice, but if we are unjust, we shall win those profits, and, by the importunity of our prayers, when we transgress and sin we shall persuade them and escape scot free. Yes, it will be objected, but we shall be brought to judgment in the world below for our unjust deeds here, we or our children's children. Nay, my dear sir, our calculating friend will say, here again the rites for the dead have much efficacy, and the absolving divinities, as the greatest cities declare, and the sons of gods, who became the poets and prophets of the gods, and who reveal that this is the truth.

On what further ground, then, could we prefer justice to supreme injustice? If we combine this with a counterfeit decorum, we shall prosper to our heart's desire, with gods and men, in life and death, as the words of the multitude and of men of the highest authority declare. In consequence, then, of all that has been said, what possibility is there, Socrates, that any man who has the power of any resources of mind, money, body, or family should consent to honor justice and not rather laugh when he hears her praised? In sooth, if anyone is able to show the falsity of these arguments, and has come to know with sufficient assurance that justice is best, he feels much indulgence for the unjust, and is not angry with them, but is aware that except a man by inborn divinity of his nature disdains injustice, or, having won to knowledge, refrains from it, no one else is willingly just, but that it is from lack of manly spirit or from old age or some other weakness that men dispraise injustice, lacking the power to practice it. The fact is patent. For no sooner does such a one come into the power than he works injustice to the extent of his ability.

And the sole cause of all this is the fact that was the starting point of this entire plea of my friend here and of myself to you, Socrates, pointing out how strange it is that of all you self-styled advocates of justice, from the heroes of old whose discourses survive to the men of the present day, not one has ever censured injustice or commended justice otherwise than in respect of the repute, the honors, and the gifts that accrue from each. But what each one of them is in itself, by its own inherent force, when it is within the soul of the possessor and escapes the eyes of both gods and men, no one has ever adequately set forth in poetry or prose—the proof that the one is the greatest of all evils that the soul contains within itself, while justice is the greatest good. For if you had all spoken in this way from the beginning and from our youth up had sought to convince us, we should not now be guarding against one another's injustice, but each would be his own best guardian, for fear lest by working injustice he should dwell in communion with the greatest of evils.

This, Socrates, and perhaps even more than this, Thrasymachus and haply another might say in pleas for and against justice and injustice, inverting their true potencies, as I believe, grossly. But I—for I have no reason to hide anything from you—am laying myself out to the utmost on the theory, because I wish to hear its refutation from you. Do not merely show us by argument that justice is superior to injustice, but make clear to us what each in and of itself does to its possessor, whereby the one is evil and the other good. But do away with the repute of both, as Glaucon urged. For, unless you take away from either the true repute and attach to each the false, we shall say that it is not justice that you are praising but the semblance, nor injustice that you censure, but the seeming, and that you really are exhorting us to be unjust but conceal it, and that you are at one with Thrasymachus in the opinion that justice is the other man's good, the advantage of the stronger, and that injustice is advantageous and profitable to oneself but disadvantageous to the inferior. Since, then, you have admitted that justice belongs to the class of those highest goods which are desirable both for their consequences and still more for their own sake, as sight, hearing, intelligence, yes and health too, and all other goods that are productive by their very nature and not by opinion, this is what I would have you praise about justice—the benefit which it and the harm which injustice inherently works upon its possessor. But the rewards and the honors that depend on opinion, leave to others to praise. For while I would listen to others who thus commended justice and disparaged injustice, bestowing their praise and their blame on the reputation and the rewards of either, I could not accept that sort of thing from you unless you say I must, because you have passed your entire life in the consideration of this very matter. Do not, then, I repeat, merely prove to us in argument the superiority of justice to injustice, but show us what it is that each inherently does to its possessor—whether he does or does not escape the eyes of gods and men—whereby the one is good and the other evil.

While I had always admired the genius of Glaucon and Adimantus, I was especially pleased by their words on this occasion, and said, It was excellently spoken of you, sons of the man we know, in the beginning of the elegy which the admirer of Glaucon wrote when you distinguished yourselves in the battle of Megara—'Sons of Ariston, whose race from a glorious sire is godlike.' This, my friends, I think, was well said. For there must indeed be a touch of the godlike in your disposition if you are not convinced that injustice is preferable to justice though you can plead its case in such fashion. And I believe that you are really not convinced. I infer this from your general character, since from your words alone I should have distrusted you. But the more I trust you the more I am at a loss what to make of the matter. I do not know how I can come to the rescue. For I doubt my ability for the reason that you have not accepted the arguments whereby I thought I proved against Thrasymachus that justice is better than injustice. Nor yet again do I know how I can refuse to come to the rescue. For I fear lest it be actually impious to stand idly by when justice is reviled and be fainthearted and not defend her so long as one has breath and can utter his voice. The best thing, then, is to aid her as best I can.

Glaucon, then, and the rest besought me by all means to come to the rescue and not to drop the argument but to pursue to the end the investigation as to the nature of each and the truth about their respective advantages. I said then as I thought, The inquiry we are undertaking is no easy one but calls for keen vision, as it seems to me. So, since we are not clever persons, I think we should employ the method of search that we should use if we, with not very keen vision, were bidden to read small letters from a distance, and then someone had observed that these same letters exist elsewhere larger and on a larger surface. We should have accounted it a godsend, I fancy, to be allowed to read those letters first, and then examine the smaller, if they are the same.

Quite so, said Adimantus, but what analogy to this do you detect in the inquiry about justice?

I will tell you, I said. There is a justice of one man, we say, and, I suppose, also of an entire city?

Assuredly, said he.

Is not the city larger than the man?

It is larger, he said.

Then, perhaps, there would be more justice in the larger object, and more easy to apprehend. If it please you, then, let us first look for its quality in states, and then only examine it also in the individual, looking for the likeness of the greater in the form of the less.

I think that is a good suggestion, he said.

If, then, said I, our argument should observe the origin of a state, we should see also the origin of justice and injustice in it?

It may be, said he.

And if this is done, we may expect to find more easily what we are seeking?

Much more.

Shall we try it, then, and go through with it? I fancy it is no slight task. Reflect, then.

We have reflected, said Adimantus. Proceed and don't refuse.

The origin of the city, then, said I, in my opinion, is to be found in the fact that we do not severally suffice for our own needs, but each of us lacks many things. Do you think any other principle establishes the state?

No other, said he.

As a result of this, then, one man calling in another for one service and another for another, we, being in need of many things, gather many into one place of abode as associates and helpers, and to this dwelling together we give the name city or state, do we not?

By all means.

And between one man and another there is an interchange of giving, if it so happens, and taking, because each supposes this to be better for himself.

Certainly.

Come, then let us create a city from the beginning in our theory. Its real creator, as it appears, will be our needs.

Obviously.

Now the first and chief of our needs is the provision of food for existence and life.

Assuredly.

The second is housing and the third is raiment and that sort of thing.

That is so.

Tell me, then, said I, how our city will suffice for the provision of all these things. Will there not be a farmer for one, and a builder, and then again a weaver? And shall we add thereto a cobbler and some other purveyor for the needs of the body?

Certainly.

The indispensable minimum of a city, then, would consist of four or five men.

Apparently.

What of this, then? Shall each of these contribute his work for the common use of all? I mean, shall the farmer, who is one, provide food for four and spend fourfold time and toil on the production of food and share it with the others, or shall he take no thought for them and provide a fourth portion of the food for himself alone in a quarter of the time and employ the other three-quarters, the one in the provision of a house, the other of a garment, the other of shoes, and not have the bother of associating with other people, but, himself for himself, mind his own affairs?

And Adimantus said, But, perhaps, Socrates, the former way is easier.

It would not, by Zeus, be at all strange, said I, for now that you have mentioned it, it occurs to me myself that, to begin with, our several natures are not all alike but different. One man is naturally fitted for one task, and another for another. Don't you think so?

I do.

Again, would one man do better working at many tasks or one at one?

One at one, he said.

And, furthermore, this, I fancy, is obvious—that if one lets slip the right season, the favorable moment in any task, the work is spoiled.

Obvious.

That, I take it, is because the business will not wait upon the leisure of the workman, but the workman must attend to it as his main affair, and not as a bywork.

He must indeed.

The result, then, is that more things are produced, and better and more easily when one man performs one task according to his nature, at the right moment, and at leisure from other occupations.

By all means.

Then, Adimantus, we need more than four citizens for the provision of the things we have mentioned. For the farmer, it appears, will not make his own plow if it is to be a good one, nor his hoe, nor his other agricultural implements, nor will the builder, who also needs many, and similarly the weaver and cobbler.

True.

Carpenters, then, and smiths and many similar craftsmen, associating themselves with our hamlet, will enlarge it considerably.

Certainly.

Yet it still wouldn't be very large even if we should add to them neatherds and shepherds and other herders, so that the farmers might have cattle for plowing, and the builders oxen to use with the farmers for transportation, and the weavers and cobblers hides and fleeces for their use.

It wouldn't be a small city, either, if it had all these.

But further, said I, it is practically impossible to establish the city in a region where it will not need imports.

It is.

There will be a further need, then, of those who will bring in from some other city what it requires.

There will.

And again, if our servitor goes forth empty-handed, not taking with him any of the things needed by those from whom they procure what they themselves require, he will come back with empty hands, will he not?

I think so.

Then their home production must not merely suffice for themselves but in quality and quantity meet the needs of those of whom they have need.

It must.

So our city will require more farmers and other craftsmen.

Yes, more.

And also of other ministrants who are to export and import the merchandise. These are traders, are they not?

Yes.

We shall also need traders, then.

Assuredly.

And if the trading is carried on by sea, we shall need quite a number of others who are expert in maritime business.

Quite a number.

But again, within the city itself how will they share with one another the products of their labor? This was the very purpose of our association and establishment of a state.

Obviously, he said, by buying and selling.

A market place, then, and money as a token for the purpose of exchange will be the result of this.

By all means.

If, then, the farmer or any other craftsman taking his products to the market place does not arrive at the same time with those who desire to exchange with him, is he to sit idle in the market place and lose time from his own work?

By no means, he said, but there are men who see this need and appoint themselves for this service—in well-conducted cities they are generally those who are weakest in body and those who are useless for any other task. They must wait there in the agora and exchange money for goods with those who wish to sell, and goods for money with as many as desire to buy.

This need, then, said I, creates the class of shopkeepers in our city. Or is not 'shopkeepers' the name we give to those who, planted in the agora, serve us in buying and selling, while we call those who roam from city to city merchants?

Certainly.

And there are, furthermore, I believe, other servitors who in the things of the mind are not altogether worthy of our fellowship, but whose strength of body is sufficient for toil; so they, selling the use of this strength and calling the price wages, are designated, I believe, 'wage earners,' are they not?

Certainly.

Wage earners, then, it seems, are the complement that helps to fill up the state.

I think so.

Has our city, then, Adimantus, reached its full growth, and is it complete?

Perhaps.

Where, then, can justice and injustice be found in it? And along with which of the constituents that we have considered do they come into the state?

I cannot conceive, Socrates, he said, unless it be in some need 372 that those very constituents have of one another.

Perhaps that is a good suggestion, said I. We must examine it and not hold back.

First of all, then, let us consider what will be the manner of life of men thus provided. Will they not make bread and wine and garments and shoes? And they will build themselves houses and carry on their work in summer for the most part unclad and unshod and in winter clothed and shod sufficiently. And for their nourishment they will provide meal from their barley and flour from their wheat, and kneading and cooking these they will serve noble cakes and loaves on some arrangement of reeds or clean leaves. And, reclined on rustic beds strewed with bryony and myrtle, they will feast with their children, drinking of their wine thereto, garlanded and singing hymns to the gods in pleasant fellowship, not begetting offspring beyond their means lest they fall into poverty or war.

Here Glaucon broke in, No relishes apparently, he said, for the men you describe as feasting.

True, said I, I forgot that they will also have relishes—salt, of course, and olives and cheese, and onions and greens, the sort of things they boil in the country, they will boil up together. But for dessert we will serve them figs and chick-peas and beans, and they will toast myrtle berries and acorns before the fire, washing them down with moderate potations. And so, living in peace and health, they will probably die in old age and hand on a like life to their offspring.

And he said, If you were founding a city of pigs, Socrates, what other fodder than this would you provide?

Why, what would you have, Glaucon? said I.

What is customary, he replied. They must recline on couches, I presume, if they are not to be uncomfortable, and dine from tables and have dishes and sweetmeats such as are now in use.

Good, said I. I understand. It is not merely the origin of a city, it seems, that we are considering but the origin of a luxurious city. Perhaps that isn't such a bad suggestion, either. For by observation of such a city it may be we could discern the origin of justice and injustice in states. The true state I believe to be the one we have described—the healthy state, as it were. But if it is your pleasure that we contemplate also a fevered state, there is nothing to hinder. For there are some, it appears, who will not be contented with this sort of fare or with this way of life, but couches will have to be added thereto and tables and other furniture, yes, and relishes and myrrh and incense and girls and cakes—all sorts of all of them. And the requirements we first mentioned, houses and garments and shoes, will no longer be confined to necessities, but we must set painting to work and embroidery, and procure gold and ivory and similar adornments, must we not?

Yes, he said.

Then shall we not have to enlarge the city again? For that healthy state is no longer sufficient, but we must proceed to swell out its bulk and fill it up with a multitude of things that exceed the requirements of necessity in states, as, for example, the entire class of huntsmen, and the imitators, many of them occupied with figures and colors and many with music—the poets and their assistants, rhapsodists, actors, chorus dancers, contractors—and the manufacturers of all kinds of articles, especially those that have to do with women's adornment. And so we shall also want more servitors. Don't you think that we shall need tutors, nurses wet and dry, beauty-shop ladies, barbers, and yet again cooks and chefs? And we shall have need, further of swineherds; there were none of these creatures in our former city, for we had no need of them, but in this city there will be this further need. And we shall also require other cattle in great numbers if they are to be eaten, shall we not?

Yes.

Doctors, too, are something whose services we shall be much more likely to require if we live thus than as before?

Much.

And the territory, I presume, that was then sufficient to feed the then population, from being adequate will become too small. Is that so or not?

It is.

Then we shall have to cut out a cantle of our neighbor's land if we are to have enough for pasture and plowing, and they in turn of ours if they too abandon themselves to the unlimited acquisition of wealth, disregarding the limit set by our necessary wants.

Inevitably, Socrates.

We shall go to war as the next step, Glaucon—or what will happen?

What you say, he said.

And we are not yet to speak, said I, of any evil or good effect of war, but only to affirm that we have further discovered the origin of war, namely, from those things from which the greatest disasters, public and private, come to states when they come.

Certainly.

Then, my friend, we must still further enlarge our city by no small increment, but by a whole army, that will march forth and fight it out with assailants in defense of all our wealth and the luxuries we have just described.

How so? he said. Are the citizens themselves not sufficient for that?

Not if you, said I, and we all were right in the admission we made when we were molding our city. We surely agreed, if you remember, that it is impossible for one man to do the work of many arts well.

True, he said.

Well, then, said I, don't you think that the business of fighting is an art and a profession?

It is indeed, he said.

Should our concern be greater, then, for the cobbler's art than for the art of war?

By no means.

Can we suppose, then, that while we were at pains to prevent the cobbler from attempting to be at the same time a farmer, a weaver, or a builder instead of just a cobbler, to the end that we might have the cobbler's business well done, and similarly assigned to each and every one man one occupation, for which he was fit and naturally adapted and at which he was to work all his days, at leisure from other pursuits and not letting slip the right moments for doing the work well, and that yet we are in doubt whether the right accomplishment of the business of war is not of supreme moment? Is it so easy

that a man who is cultivating the soil will be at the same time a soldier and one who is practicing cobbling or any other trade, though no man in the world could make himself a competent expert at draughts or the dice who did not practice that and nothing else from childhood but treated it as an occasional business? And are we to believe that a man who takes in hand a shield or any other instrument of war springs up on that very day a competent combatant in heavy armor or in any other form of warfare—though no other tool will make a man be an artist or an athlete by his taking it in hand, nor will it be of any service to those who have neither acquired the science of it nor sufficiently practiced themselves in its use?

Great indeed, he said, would be the value of tools in that case!

Then, said I, in the same degree that the task of our guardians is the greatest of all, it would require more leisure than any other business and the greatest science and training.

I think so, said he.

Does it not also require a nature adapted to that very pursuit?

Of course.

It becomes our task, then, it seems, if we are able, to select which and what kind of natures are suited for the guardianship of a state.

Yes, ours.

Upon my word, said I, it is no light task that we have taken upon ourselves. But we must not faint so far as our strength allows.

No, we mustn't.

Do you think, said I, that there is any difference between the nature of a well-bred hound for this watchdog's work and that of a wellborn lad?

What point have you in mind?

I mean that each of them must be keen of perception, quick in pursuit of what it has apprehended, and strong too if it has to fight it out with its captive.

Why, yes, said he, there is need of all these qualities.

And it must, further, be brave if it is to fight well.

Of course.

And will a creature be ready to be brave that is not high-spirited, whether horse or dog or anything else? Have you never observed what an irresistible and invincible thing is spirit, the presence of which makes every soul in the face of everything fearless and unconquerable?

I have.

The physical qualities of the guardian, then, are obvious.

Yes.

And also those of his soul, namely that he must be of high spirit.

Yes, this too.

How then, Glaucon, said I, will they escape being savage to one another and to the other citizens if this is to be their nature?

Not easily, by Zeus, said he.

That is so.

That, then, is what I meant by saying that we must take up music before gymnastics.

You were right, he said.

Do you not know, then, that the beginning in every task is the chief thing, especially for any creature that is young and tender? For it is then that it is best molded and takes the impression that one wishes to stamp upon it.

Quite so.

Shall we, then, thus lightly suffer our children to listen to any chance stories fashioned by any chance teachers and so to take into their minds opinions for the most part contrary to those that we shall think it desirable for them to hold when they are grown up?

By no manner of means will we allow it.

We must begin, then, it seems, by a censorship over our storymakers, and what they do well we must pass and what not, reject. And the stories on the accepted list we will induce nurses and mothers to tell to the children and so shape their souls by these stories far rather than their bodies by their hands. But most of the stories they now tell we must reject.

What sort of stories? he said.

The example of the greater stories, I said, will show us the lesser also. For surely the pattern must be the same, and the greater and the less must have a like tendency. Don't you think so?

I do, he said, but I don't apprehend which you mean by the greater, either.

Those, I said, that Hesiod and Homer and the other poets related to us. These, methinks, composed false stories which they told and still tell to mankind.

Of what sort? he said. And with what in them do you find fault?

With that, I said, which one ought first and chiefly to blame, especially if the lie is not a pretty one.

What is that?

When anyone images badly in his speech the true nature of gods and heroes, like a painter whose portraits bear no resemblance to his models.

It is certainly right to condemn things like that, he said, but just what do we mean and what particular things?

There is, first of all, I said, the greatest lie about the things of greatest concernment, which was no pretty invention of him who told how Uranus did what Hesiod says he did to Cronus, and how Cronus in turn took his revenge, and then there are the doings and sufferings of Cronus at the hands of his son. Even if they were true I should not think that they ought to be thus lightly told to thoughtless young persons. But the best way would be to bury them in silence, and if there were some necessity for relating them, only a very small audience should be admitted under pledge of secrecy and after sacrificing, not a pig, but some huge and unprocurable victim, to the end that as few as possible should have heard these tales.

Why, yes, said he, such stories are hard sayings.

Yes, and they are not to be told, Adimantus, in our city, nor is it to be said in the hearing of a young man that in doing the utmost wrong he would do nothing to surprise anybody, nor again in punishing his father's wrongdoings to the limit, but would only be following the example of the first and greatest of the gods.

No, by heaven, said he, I do not myself think that they are fit to be told.

Neither must we admit at all, said I, that gods war with gods and plot against one another and contend—for it is not true either—if we wish our future guardians to deem nothing more shameful than lightly to fall out with one another. Still less must we make battles of gods and giants the subject for them of stories and embroideries, and other enmities many and manifold of gods and heroes toward their kith and kin. But if there is any likelihood of our persuading them that no citizen ever quarreled with his fellow citizen and that the very idea of it is an impiety, that is the sort of thing that ought rather to be said by their elders, men and women, to children from the beginning and as they grow older, and we must compel the poets to keep close to this in their compositions. But Hera's fetterings by her son and the hurling out of heaven of Hephaestus by his father when he was trying to save his mother from a beating, and the battles of the gods in Homer's verse are things that we must not admit into our city either wrought in allegory or without allegory. For the young are not able to distinguish what is and what is not allegory, but whatever opinions are taken into the mind at that age are wont to prove indelible and unalterable. For which reason, maybe, we should do our utmost that the first stories that they hear should be so composed as to bring the fairest lessons of virtue to their ears.

Yes, that is reasonable, he said, but if again someone should ask us to be specific and say what these compositions may be and what are the tales, what could we name?

And I replied, Adimantus, we are not poets, you and I at present, but founders of a state. And to founders it pertains to know the patterns on which poets must compose their fables and from which their poems must not be allowed to deviate, but the founders are not required themselves to compose fables.

Right, he said, but this very thing—the patterns or norms of right speech about the gods—what would they be?

Something like this, I said. The true quality of God we must always surely attribute to him whether we compose in epic, melic, or tragic verse.

We must.

And is not God of course good in reality and always to be spoken of as such?

Certainly.

But further, no good thing is harmful, is it?

I think not.

Can what is not harmful harm?

By no means.

Can that which does not harm do any evil?

Not that either.

But that which does no evil would not be cause of any evil either?

How could it?

Once more, is the good beneficent?

Yes.

It is the cause, then, of welfare?

Yes.

Then the good is not the cause of all things, but of things that are well it is the cause—of things that are ill it is blameless.

Entirely so, he said.

Neither, then, could God, said I, since he is good, be, as the multitude say, the cause of all things, but for mankind he is the cause of few things, but of many things not the cause. For good things are far fewer with us than evil, and for the good we must assume no other cause than God, but the cause of evil we must look for in other things And not in God.

What you say seems to me most true, he replied.

Then, said I, we must not accept from Homer or any other poet the folly of such error as this about the gods, when he says,

Two urns stand on the floor of the palace of Zeus and are filled with Dooms he allots, one of blessings, the other of gifts that are evil.[6]

And to whomsoever Zeus gives of both commingled

Now upon evil he chances and now again good is his portion.
But the man for whom he does not blend the lots, but to whom he gives unmixed evil—

Hunger devouring drives him, a wanderer over the wide world.

Nor will we tolerate the saying that

Zeus is dispenser alike of good and of evil to mortals.

But as to the violation of the oaths and the truce by Pandarus, if anyone affirms it to have been brought about by the action of Athena and Zeus, we will not approve,

---

6   Iliad 24.527 sq.

nor that the strife and contention of the gods were the doing of Themis and Zeus, nor again must we permit our youth to hear what Aeschylus says.

> A god implants the guilty cause in men
> When he would utterly destroy a house.

But if any poets compose a 'Sorrows of Niobe,' the poem that contains these iambics, or a tale of the Pelopidae or of Troy, or anything else of the kind, we must either forbid them to say that these woes are the work of God, or they must devise some such interpretation as we, now require, and must declare that what God did was righteous and good, and they were benefited by their chastisement. But that they were miserable who paid the penalty, and that the doer of this was God, is a thing that the poet must not be suffered to say. If on the other hand he should say that for needing chastisement the wicked were miserable and that in paying the penalty they were benefited by God, that we must allow. But as to saying that God, who is good, becomes the cause of evil to anyone, we must contend in every way that neither should anyone assert this in his own city if it is to be well governed, nor anyone hear it, neither younger nor older, neither telling a story in meter or without meter, for neither would the saying of such things, if they are said, be holy, nor would they be profitable to us or concordant with themselves.

I cast my vote with yours for this law, he said, and am well pleased with it.

This, then, said I, will be one of the laws and patterns concerning the gods to which speakers and poets will be required to conform, that God is not the cause of all things, but only of the good.

And an entirely satisfactory one, he said.

And what of this, the second? Do you think that God is a wizard and capable of manifesting himself by design, now in one aspect, now in another, at one time himself changing and altering his shape in many transformations and at another deceiving us and causing us to believe such things about him, or that he is simple and less likely than anything else to depart from his own form?

I cannot say offhand, he replied.

But what of this? If anything went out from its own form, would it not be displaced and changed, either by itself or by something else?

Necessarily.

Is it not true that to be altered and moved by something else happens least to things that are in the best condition, as, for example, a body by food and drink and toil, and plants by the heat of the sun and winds and similar influences—is it not true that the healthiest and strongest is least altered?

Certainly.

And is it not the soul that is bravest and most intelligent that would be least disturbed and altered by any external affection?

Yes.

And, again, it is surely true of all composite implements, edifices, and habiliments, by parity of reasoning, that those which are well made and in good condition are least liable to be changed by time and other influences.

That is so.

It is universally true, then, that that which is in the best state by nature or art or both admits least alteration by something else.

So it seems.

But God, surely, and everything that belongs to God, is in every way in the best possible state.

Of course.

From this point of view, then, it would be least of all likely that there would be many forms in God.

Least indeed.

But would he transform and alter himself?

Obviously, he said, if he is altered.

Then does he change himself for the better and to something fairer, or for the worse and to something uglier than himself?

It must necessarily, said he, be for the worse if he is changed. For we surely will not say that God is deficient in either beauty or excellence.

Most rightly spoken, said I. And if that were his condition, do you think, Adimantus, that any one god or man would of his own will worsen himself in any way?

Impossible, he replied.

It is impossible then, said I, even for a god to wish to alter himself, but, as it appears, each of them, being the fairest and best possible, abides forever simply in his own form. An absolutely necessary conclusion to my thinking.

No poet then, I said, my good friend, must be allowed to tell us that 'The gods, in the likeness of strangers, many disguises assume as they visit the cities of mortals.'[7] Nor must anyone tell falsehoods about Proteus and Thetis, nor in any tragedy or in other poems bring in Hera disguised as a priestess collecting alms 'for the life-giving sons of Inachus, the Argive stream.'[8] And many similar falsehoods they must not tell. Nor again must mothers under the influence of such poets terrify their children with harmful tales, how there are certain gods whose apparitions haunt the night in the likeness of many strangers from all manner of lands, lest while they speak evil of the gods they at the same time make cowards of the children.

They must not, he said.

But, said I, may we suppose that while the gods themselves are

---

7   Odyssey 17.485 sq.

8   Aeschylus, Xanthians, fr. 159.

incapable of change they cause us to fancy that they appear in many shapes deceiving and practicing magic upon us?

Perhaps, said he.

Consider said I. Would a god wish to deceive, or lie, by presenting in either word or action what is only appearance?

I don't know, said he.

Don't you know, said I, that the veritable lie, if the expression is permissible, is a thing that all gods and men abhor?

What do you mean? he said.

This, said I, that falsehood in the most vital part of themselves, and about their most vital concerns, is something that no one willingly accepts, but it is there above all that everyone fears it.

I don't understand yet either.

That is because you suspect me of some grand meaning, I said, but what I mean is, that deception in the soul about realities, to have been deceived and to be blindly ignorant and to have and hold the falsehood there, is what all men would least of all accept, and it is in that case that they loathe it most of all.

Quite so, he said.

But surely it would be most wholly right, as I was just now saying, to describe this as in very truth falsehood—ignorance namely in the soul of the man deceived. For the falsehood in words is a copy of the affection in the soul, an afterrising image of it and not an altogether unmixed falsehood. Is not that so?

By all means.

Essential falsehood, then, is hated not only by gods but by men.

I agree.

But what of the falsehood in words—when and for whom is it serviceable so as not to merit abhorrence? Will it not be against enemies? And when any of those whom we call friends owing to madness or folly attempts to do some wrong, does it not then become useful to avert the evil—as a medicine? And also in the fables of which we were just now speaking, owing to our ignorance of the truth about antiquity, we liken the false to the true as far as we may and so make it edifying.

We most certainly do, he said.

Tell me, then, on which of these grounds falsehood would be serviceable to God. Would he because of his ignorance of antiquity make false likenesses of it?

An absurd supposition, that, he said.

Then there is no lying poet in God.

I think not.

Well then, would it be through fear of his enemies that he would lie?

Far from it.

Would it be because of the folly or madness of his friends?

Nay, no fool or madman is a friend of God.

Then there is no motive for God to deceive.

None.

So from every point of view the divine and the divinity are free from falsehood.

By all means.

Then God is altogether simple and true in deed and word, and neither changes himself nor deceives others by visions or words or the sending of signs in waking or in dreams.

I myself think so, he said, when I hear you say it.

You concur then, I said, in this as our second norm or canon for speech and poetry about the gods—that neither are they wizards in shape shifting nor do they mislead us by falsehoods in words or deed?

I concur.

Then, though there are many other things that we praise in Homer, this we will not applaud, the sending of the dream by Zeus to Agamemnon, nor shall we approve of Aeschylus when his Thetis avers that Apollo, singing at her wedding, 'foretold the happy fortunes of her issue,'

Their days prolonged, from pain and sickness free,
And rounding out the tale of heaven's blessings,
Raised the proud paean, making glad my heart.
And I believed that Phoebus' mouth divine,
Filled with the breath of prophecy, could not lie.
But he himself, the singer, himself who sat
At meat with us, himself who promised all,
Is now himself the slayer of my son.

When anyone says that sort of thing about the gods, we shall be wroth with him, we will refuse him a chorus. Neither will we allow teachers to use him for the education of the young if our guardians are to be god-fearing men and godlike in so far as that is possible for humanity.

By all means, he said, I accept these norms and would use them as canons and laws.

THE REPUBLIC OF PLATO
Book III

Translated by Paul Shorey

Concerning the gods then, said I, this is the sort of thing that we must allow or not allow them to hear from childhood up, if they are to honor the gods and their fathers and mothers, and not to hold their friendship with one another in light esteem.

That was our view and I believe it right.

What then of this? If they are to be brave, must we not extend our prescription to include also the sayings that will make them least likely to fear death? Or do you suppose that anyone could ever become brave who had that dread in his heart?

No indeed, I do not, he replied.

And again, if he believes in the reality of the underworld and its terrors, do you think that any man will be fearless of death and in battle will prefer death to defeat and slavery?

By no means.

Then it seems we must exercise supervision also, in the matter of such tales as these, over those who undertake to supply them and request them not to dispraise in this undiscriminating fashion the life in Hades but rather praise it, since what they now tell us is neither true nor edifying to men who are destined to be warriors.

Yes, we must, he said.

Then, said I, beginning with this verse we will expunge everything of the same kind,

Liefer were I in the fields up above to be serf to another
Tiller of some poor plot which yields him a scanty subsistence,
Than to be ruler and king over all the dead who have perished,[1]

and this,

Lest unto men and immortals the homes of the dead be uncovered

---

1 Odyssey 11.489 sq.

Horrible, noisome, dank, that the gods too hold in abhorrence,[2]

and,

Ah me! So it is true that e'en in the dwellings of Hades
Spirit there is and wraith, but within there is no understanding,[3]

and this [of Tiresias],

Sole to have wisdom and wit, but the others are shadowy phantoms,[4]

and,

Forth from his limbs unwilling his spirit flitted to Hades,
Wailing its doom and its lustihood lost and the May of its manhood,[5]

and,

Under the earth like a vapor vanished the gibbering soul,[6] and,
Even as bats in the hollow of some mysterious grotto
Fly with a flittermouse shriek when one of them falls from the cluster,
Whereby they hold to the rock and are clinging the one to the other,
Flitted their gibbering ghosts.[7]

We will beg Homer and the other poets not to be angry if we cancel those and all similar passages, not that they are not poetic and pleasing to most hearers, but because the more poetic they are the less are they suited to the ears of boys and men who are destined to be free and to be more afraid of slavery than of death.

By all means.

Then we must further taboo in these matters the entire vocabulary of terror and fear, Cocytus named of lamentation loud, abhorred Styx, the flood of deadly hate, the people of the infernal pit and of the charnel house, and all other terms of this type, whose very names send a shudder through all the hearers every year. And they may be

---

2 Iliad 20.64.

3 Iliad 23.103.

4 Odyssey 10.495.

5 Iliad 16.856.

6 Iliad 23.100.

7 Odyssey 24.6 sq.

excellent for other purposes, but we are in fear for our guardians lest the habit of such thrills make them more sensitive and soft than we would have them.

And we are right in so fearing.

We must remove those things then?

Yes.

And the opposite type to them is what we must require in speech and in verse?

Obviously.

And shall we also do away with the wailings and lamentations of men of repute?

That necessarily follows, he said, from the other.

Consider, said I, whether we shall be right in thus getting rid of them or not. What we affirm is that a good man will not think that for a good man, whose friend he also is, death is a terrible thing.

Yes, we say that.

Then it would not be for his friend's sake as if he had suffered something dreadful that he would make lament.

Certainly not.

But we also say this, that such a one is most of all men sufficient unto himself for a good life and is distinguished from other men in having least need of anybody else.

True, he replied.

Least of all then to him is it a terrible thing to lose son or brother or his wealth or anything of the sort.

Least of all.

Then he makes the least lament and bears it most moderately when any such misfortune overtakes him.

Certainly.

Then we should be right in doing away with the lamentations of men of note and in attributing them to women, and not to the most worthy of them either, and to inferior men, in order that those whom we say we are breeding for the guardianship of the land may disdain to act like these.

We should be right, said he.

Again then we shall request Homer and the other poets not to portray Achilles, the son of a goddess, as, 'lying now on his side, and then again on his back, and again on his face,'[8] and then rising up and 'drifting distraught on the shore of the waste unharvested ocean,'[9] nor as clutching with both hands the sooty dust and strewing it over his head, nor as weeping and lamenting in the measure and manner attributed to him by the poet, nor yet Priam, near kinsman of the gods, making supplication and rolling in the dung, 'calling aloud unto each, by name to each man appealing.'[10] And

---

8 Iliad 24.10 sq.

9 Iliad 24.12 sq.

10 Iliad 22.414 sq.

yet more than this shall we beg of them at least not to describe the gods as lamenting and crying, 'Ah, woe is me, woeful mother who bore to my sorrow the bravest,'[11] and if they will so picture the gods, at least not to have the effrontery to present so unlikely a likeness of the supreme god as to make him say,

> Out on it, dear to my heart is the man whose pursuit around Troy town
> I must behold with my eyes while my spirit is grieving within me,[12]

and,

> Ah, woe is me! Of all men to me is Sarpedon the dearest,
> Fated to fall by the hands of Patroclus, Menoetius' offspring.[13]

For if, dear Adimantus, our young men should seriously incline to listen to such tales and not laugh at them as unworthy utterances, still less likely would any man be to think such conduct unworthy of himself and to rebuke himself if it occurred to him to do or say anything of that kind, but without shame or restraint full many a dirge for trifles would he chant and many a lament.

You say most truly, he replied.

But that must not be, as our reasoning but now showed us, in which we must put our trust until someone convinces us with a better reason.

No, it must not be.

Again, they must not be prone to laughter. For ordinarily when one abandons himself to violent laughter his condition provokes a violent reaction.

I think so, he said.

Then if anyone represents men of worth as overpowered by laughter we must not accept it, much less if gods.

Much indeed, he replied.

Then we must not accept from Homer such sayings as these either about the gods.

> Quenchless then was the laughter that rose from the blessed immortals
> When they beheld Hephaestus officiously puffing and panting.[14]

We must not accept them on your view.

If it pleases you to call it mine, he said. At any rate we must not accept them.

But further we must surely prize truth most highly. For if we were

---

11   Iliad 18.54.

12   Iliad 22.168.

13   Iliad 16.433 sq.

14   Iliad 1.599.

right in what we were just saying and falsehood is in very deed useless to gods, but to men useful as a remedy or form of medicine, it is obvious that such a thing must be assigned to physicians, and laymen should have nothing to do with it.

Obviously, he replied.

The rulers then of the city may, if anybody, fitly lie on account of enemies or citizens for the benefit of the state; no others may have anything to do with it. But for a layman to lie to rulers of that kind we shall affirm to be as great a sin, nay a greater, than it is for a patient not to tell his physician or an athlete his trainer the truth about his bodily condition, or for a man to deceive the pilot about the ship and the sailors as to the real condition of himself or a fellow sailor, and how they fare.

Most true, he replied.

If then the ruler catches anybody else in the city lying, any of the craftsmen, 'whether a prophet or healer of sickness or joiner of timbers,'[15] he will chastise him for introducing a practice as subversive and destructive of a state as it is of a ship.

He will, he said, if deed follows upon word.

Again, will our lads not need the virtue of self-control?

Of course.

And for the multitude are not the main points of self-control these—to be obedient to their rulers and themselves to be rulers over the bodily appetites and pleasures of food, drink, and the rest?

I think so.

Then, I take it, we will think well said such sayings as that of Homer's Diomedes,

Friend, sit down and be silent and hark to the word of my bidding,[16] and what follows,

Breathing high spirit the Greeks marched silently fearing their captains,[17]

and all similar passages.

Yes, well said.

But what of this sort of thing,

Heavy with wine, with the eyes of a dog and the heart of a fleet deer,[18]

and the lines that follow? Are these well—and other impertinences in prose or verse of private citizens to their rulers?

They are not well.

---

15 Odyssey 17.383 sq.

16 Iliad 4.412.

17 Iliad 3.8 and 4.431.

18 Iliad 1.225.

They certainly are not suitable for youth to hear for the inculcation of self-control. But if from another point of view they yield some pleasure we must not be surprised, or what is your view of it?

This, he said.

Again, to represent the wisest man as saying that this seems to him the fairest thing in the world,

When the bounteous tables are standing Laden with bread and with meat and the cupbearer ladles the sweet wine
Out of the mixer and bears it and empties it into the beakers,[19]

do you think the hearing of that sort of thing will conduce to a young man's temperance or self-control? Or this?

Hunger is the most piteous death that a mortal may suffer.[20]

Or to hear how Zeus lightly forgot all the designs which he devised, awake while the other gods men slept, because of the excitement of his passions, and was so overcome by the sight of Hera that he is not even willing to go to their chamber, but wants to lie with her there on the ground and says that he is possessed by a fiercer desire than when they first consorted with one another, 'deceiving their dear parents'?[21] Nor will it profit them to hear of Hephaestus' fettering of Ares and Aphrodite for a like motive.

No, by Zeus, he said, I don't think it will.

But any words or deeds of endurance in the face of all odds attributed to famous men are suitable for our youth to see represented and to hear, such as,

He smote his breast and chided thus his heart,
Endure, my heart, for worse hast thou endured.[22]

By all means, he said.
It is certain that we cannot allow our men to be accepters of
bribes or greedy for gain.

By no means.

Then they must not chant, 'Gifts move the gods and gifts persuade dread kings.' Nor should we approve Achilles' attendant Phoenix as speaking fairly when he counseled him if he received gifts for it to defend the Achaeans, but without gifts not to lay aside

---

19   Odyssey 9.8 sq.
20   Odyssey 12.342.
21   Iliad 14-2-94 sq.
22   Odyssey 20.17 sq.

his wrath. Nor shall we think it proper nor admit that Achilles himself was so greedy as to accept gifts from Agamemnon and again to give up a dead body after receiving payment but otherwise to refuse.

It is not right, he said, to commend such conduct.

But, for Homer's sake, said I, I hesitate to say that it is positively impious to affirm such things of Achilles and to believe them when told by others, or again to believe that he said to Apollo,

> Me them hast balked, far-darter, the most pernicious of all gods,
> Mightily would I requite thee if only my hands had the power,[23]

and how he was disobedient to the river, who was a god, and was ready to fight with him, and again that he said of the locks of his hair, consecrated to the other river, Spercheus,

> This let me give to take with him my hair to the hero, Patroclus,[24]

who was a dead body. And that he did so we must not believe. And again the trailings of Hector's body round the grave of Patroclus and the slaughter of the living captives upon his pyre, all these we will affirm to be lies, nor will we suffer our youth to believe that Achilles, the son of a goddess and of Peleus, the most chaste of men, grandson of Zeus, and himself bred under the care of the most sage Chiron, was of so perturbed a spirit as to be affected with two contradictory maladies, the greed that becomes no free man and at the same time overweening arrogance toward gods and men.

You are right, he said.

Neither, then, said I, must we believe this, or suffer it to be said, that Theseus, the son of Poseidon, and Pirithous, the son of Zeus, attempted such dreadful rapes, nor that any other child of a god or hero would have brought himself to accomplish the terrible and impious deeds that they now falsely relate of them. But we must constrain the poets either to deny that these are their deeds or that they are the children of gods, but not to make both statements or attempt to persuade our youth that the gods are the begetters of evil, and that heroes are no better than men. For, as we were saying, such utterances are both impious and false. For we proved, I take it, that for evil to arise from gods is an impossibility.

Certainly.

And they are furthermore harmful to those that hear them. For every man will be very lenient with his own misdeeds if he is convinced that such are and were the actions of

---

23 Iliad 22.15
24 Iliad 23.151

The near-sown seed of gods,
Close kin to Zeus, for whom on Ida's top
Ancestral altars flame to highest heaven,
Nor in their lifeblood fails the fire divine.[25]

For which cause we must put down such fables, lest they breed in our youth great laxity in turpitude.

Most assuredly.

What type of discourse remains for our definition of our prescriptions and proscriptions? We have declared the right way of speaking about gods and daemons and heroes and that other world?

We have.

Speech, then, about men would be the remainder.

Obviously.

It is impossible for us, my friend, to place this here.

Why?

Because I presume we are going to say that so it is that both poets and writers of prose speak wrongly about men in matters of greatest moment, saying that there are many examples of men who, though unjust, are happy, and of just men who are wretched, and that there is profit in injustice if it be concealed, and that justice is the other man's good and your own loss, and I presume that we shall forbid them to say this sort of thing and command them to sing and fable the opposite. Don't you think so?

Nay, I well know it, he said.

Then, if you admit that I am right, I will say that you have conceded the original point of our inquiry?

Rightly apprehended, he said.

Then, as regards men, that speech must be of this kind, that is a point that we will agree upon when we have discovered the nature of justice and the proof that it is profitable to its possessor whether he does or does not appear to be just.

Most true, he replied.

So this concludes the topic of tales. That of diction, I take it, is to be considered next. So we shall have completely examined both the matter and the manner of speech.

And Adimantus said, I don't understand what you mean by this.

Well, said I, we must have you understand. Perhaps you will be more likely to apprehend it thus. Is not everything that is said by fabulists or poets a narration of past, present, or future things?

What else could it be? he said.

---

25 Aeschlyus, Niobe, fr. 146

Do not they proceed either by pure narration or by a narrative that is effected through imitation, or by both?

This too, he said, I still need to have made plainer.

I seem to be a ridiculous and obscure teacher, I said. So, like men who are unable to express themselves I won't try to speak in wholes and universals but will separate off a particular part and by the example of that try to show you my meaning. Tell me, do you know the first lines of Iliad in which the poet says that Chryses implored Agamemnon to release his daughter, and that the king was angry and that Chryses, failing of his request, imprecated curses on the Achaeans in his prayers to the god?

You know then that as far as these verses,

And prayed unto all the Achaeans,
Chiefly to Atreus's sons, twin leaders who marshaled the people,[26]

the poet himself is the speaker and does not even attempt to suggest to us that anyone but himself is speaking. But what follows he delivers as if he were himself Chryses and tries as far as may be to make us feel that not Homer is the speaker, but the priest, an old man. And in this manner he has carried on nearly all the rest of his narration about affairs Ilium, all that happened in Ithaca, and the entire Odyssey.

Quite so, he said.

Now, it is narration, is it not, both when he presents the several speeches and the matter between the speeches?

Of course.

But when he delivers a speech as if he were someone else, shall we not say that he then assimilates thereby his own diction as far as possible to that of the person whom he announces as about to speak?

We shall, obviously.

And is not likening oneself to another in speech or bodily bearing an imitation of him to whom one likens oneself?

Surely.

In such case then, it appears, he and the other poets effect their narration through imitation.

Certainly.

But if the poet should conceal himself nowhere, then his entire poetizing and narration would have been accomplished without imitation. And lest you may say again that you don't understand, I will explain to you how this would be done. If Homer, after telling us that Chryses came with the ransom of his daughter and as a suppliant of the Achaeans but chiefly of the kings, had gone on speaking not as if made or being Chryses but still as Homer, you are aware that it would not be imitation but narration,

---

26 Iliad 1.15 sq.

pure and simple. It would have been somewhat in this wise. I will state it without meter for I am not a poet. The priest came and prayed that to them the gods should grant to take Troy and come safely home, but that they should accept the ransom and release his daughter, out of reverence for the god, and when he had thus spoken the others were of reverent mind and approved, but Agamemnon was angry and bade him depart and not come again lest the scepter and the fillets of the god should not avail him. And ere his daughter should be released, he said, she would grow old in Argos with himself, and he ordered him to be off and not vex him if he wished to get home safe. And the old man on hearing this was frightened and departed in silence, and having gone apart from the camp he prayed at length to Apollo, invoking the appellations of the god, and reminding him of and asking requital for any of his gifts that had found favor whether in the building of temples or the sacrifice of victims. In return for these things he prayed that the Achaeans should suffer for his tears by the god's shafts.

It is in this way, my dear fellow, I said, that without imitation simple narration results.

I understand, he said.

Understand then, said I, that the opposite of this arises when one removes the words of the poet between and leaves the alternation of speeches.

This too I understand, he said. It is what happens in tragedy.

You have conceived me most rightly, I said, and now I think I can make plain to you what I was unable to before, that there is one kind of poetry and taletelling which works wholly through imitation, as you remarked, tragedy and comedy, and another which employs the recital of the poet himself, best exemplified, I presume, in the dithyramb, and there is again that which employs both, in epic poetry and in many other places, if you apprehend me.

I understand now, he said, what you then meant.

Recall then also the preceding statement that we were done with the 'what' of speech and still had to consider the 'how.'

I remember.

What I meant then was just this, that we must reach a decision whether we are to suffer our poets to narrate as imitators or in part as imitators and in part not, and what sort of things in each case, or not allow them to imitate at all.

I divine, he said, that you are considering whether we shall admit tragedy and comedy into our city or not.

Perhaps, said I, and perhaps even more than that. For I certainly do not yet know myself, but whithersoever the wind, as it were, of the argument blows, there lies our course.

Well said, he replied.

This then, Adimantus, is the point we must keep in view. Do we wish our guardians to be good mimics or not? Or is this also a consequence of what we said before, that each one could practice well only one pursuit and not many, but if he attempted the latter, dabbling in many things, he would fail of distinction in all?

Of course it is.

And does not the same rule hold for imitation, that the same man is not able to imitate many things well as he can one?

No, he is not.

Still less, then, will he be able to combine the practice of any worthy pursuit with the imitation of many things and the quality of a mimic, since, unless I mistake, the same men cannot practice well at once even the two forms of imitation that appear most nearly akin, as the writing of tragedy and comedy. Did you not just now call these two imitations?

I did, and you are right in saying that the same men are not able to succeed in both.

Nor yet to be at once good rhapsodists and actors?

True.

But neither can the same men be actors for tragedies and comedies—and all these are imitations, are they not?

Yes, imitations.

And to still smaller coinage than this, in my opinion, Adimantus, proceeds the fractioning of human faculty, so as to be incapable of imitating many things or of doing the things themselves of which the imitations are likenesses.

Most true, he replied.

If, then, we are to maintain our original principle, that our guardians, released from all other crafts, are to be expert craftsmen of civic liberty, and pursue nothing else that does not conduce to this, it would not be fitting for these to do nor yet to imitate anything else. But if they imitate they should from childhood up imitate what is appropriate to them—men, that is, who are brave, sober, pious, free, and all things of that kind—but things unbecoming the free man the should neither do nor be clever at imitating, nor yet any other shameful thing, lest from the imitation they imbibe the reality. Or have you not observed that imitations, if continued from youth far into life, settle down into habits and second nature in the body, the speech, and the thought?

Yes, indeed, said he.

We will not then allow our charges, whom we expect to prove good men, being men, to play the parts of women and imitate a woman young or old wrangling with her husband, defying heaven, loudly boasting, fortunate in her own conceit, or involved in misfortune and possessed by grief and lamentation—still less a woman that is sick, in love, or in labor.

Most certainly not, he replied.

Nor may they imitate slaves, female and male, doing the offices of slaves.

No, not that either.

Nor yet, as it seems, bad men who are cowards and who do the opposite of the things we just now spoke of, reviling and lampooning one another, speaking foul words in their cups or when sober and in other ways sinning against themselves and others in word and deed after the fashion of such men. And I take it they must not form the habit of likening themselves to madmen either in words nor yet in deeds. For while knowledge they must have both of mad and bad men and women, they must do and imitate nothing of this kind.

Most true, he said.

What of this? I said. Are they to imitate smiths and other craftsmen or the rowers of triremes and those who call the time to them or other things connected therewith?

How could they, he said, since it will be forbidden them even to pay any attention to such things?

Well, then, neighing horses and lowing bulls, and the noise of rivers and the roar of the sea and the thunder and everything of that kind—will they imitate these?

Nay, they have been forbidden, he said, to be mad or liken themselves to madmen.

If, then, I understand your meaning, said I, there is a form of diction and narrative in which the really good and true man would narrate anything that he had to say, and another form unlike this to which the man of the opposite birth and breeding would cleave and in which he would tell his story.

What are these forms? he said.

A man of the right sort, I think, when he comes in the course of his narrative to some word or act of a good man will be willing to impersonate the other in reporting it, and will feel no shame at that kind of mimicry, by preference imitating the good man when he acts steadfastly and sensibly, and less and more reluctantly when he is upset by sickness or love or drunkenness or any other mishap. But when he comes to someone unworthy of himself, he will not-wish to liken himself in earnest to one who is inferior, except in the few cases where he is doing something good, but will be embarrassed both because he is unpracticed in the mimicry of such characters, and also because he shrinks in distaste from molding and fitting himself to the types of baser things. His mind disdains them, unless it be for jest.

Naturally, he said.

Then the narrative that he will employ will be of the kind that we just now illustrated by the verses of Homer, and his diction will be one that partakes of both, of imitation and simple narration, but there will be a small portion of imitation in a long discourse—or is there nothing in what I say?

Yes, indeed, he said, that is the type and pattern of such a speaker.

Then, said I, the other kind of speaker, the more debased he is the less will he shrink from imitating anything and everything. He will think nothing unworthy of himself, so that he will attempt, seriously and in the presence of many, to imitate all things, including those we just now mentioned—claps of thunder, and the noise of wind and hail and axles and pulleys, and the notes of trumpets and flutes and

Panpipes, and the sounds of all instruments, and the cries of dogs, sheep, and birds—and so his style will depend wholly on imitation in voice and gesture, or will contain but a little of pure narration.

That too follows of necessity, he said.

These, then, said I, were the two types of diction of which I was speaking.

There are those two, he replied.

Now does not one of the two involve slight variations, and if we assign a suitable pitch and rhythm to the diction, is not the result that the right speaker speaks almost on the same note and in one cadence—for the changes are slight—and similarly in a rhythm of nearly the same kind?

Quite so.

But what of the other type? Does it not require the opposite, every kind of pitch and all rhythms, if it too is to have appropriate expression, since it involves manifold forms of variation?

Emphatically so.

And do all poets and speakers hit upon one type or the other of diction or some blend which they combine of both?

They must, he said.

What, then, said I, are we to do? Shall we admit all of these into the city, or one of the unmixed types, or the mixed type?

If my vote prevails, he said, the unmixed imitator of the good.

Nay, but the mixed type also is pleasing, Adimantus, and far most pleasing to boys and their tutors and the great mob is the opposite of your choice.

Most pleasing it is.

But perhaps, said I, you would affirm it to be ill suited to our polity, because there is no twofold or manifold man among us, since every man does one thing.

It is not suited.

And is this not the reason why such a city is the only one in which we shall find the cobbler a cobbler and not a pilot in addition to his cobbling, and the farmer a farmer and not a judge added to his farming, and the soldier a soldier and not a money-maker in addition to his soldiery, and so of all the rest?

True, he said.

If a man, then, it seems, who was capable by his cunning of assuming every kind of shape and imitating all things should arrive in our city, bringing with himself the poems which he wished to exhibit, we should fall down and worship him as a holy and wondrous and delightful creature, but should say to him that there is no man of that kind among us in our city, nor is it lawful for such a man to arise among us, and we should send him away to another city, after pouring myrrh down over his head and crowning him with fillets of wool, but we ourselves, for our souls' good, should continue to employ the more austere and less delightful poet and taleteller, who would imitate the diction of the good man and would tell his tale in the patterns which we prescribed in the beginning, when we set out to educate our soldiers.

We certainly should do that if it rested with us.

And now, my friend, said I, we may say that we have completely finished the part of music that concerns speeches and tales. For we have set forth what is to be said and how it is to be said.

I think so too, he replied.

After this, then, said I, comes the manner of song and tunes?

Obviously.

And having gone thus far, could not everybody discover what we must say of their character in order to conform to what has already been said?

I am afraid that 'everybody' does not include me, laughed Glaucon. I cannot sufficiently divine offhand what we ought to say, though I have a suspicion.

You certainly, I presume, said I, have a sufficient understanding of this—that the song is composed of three things, the words, the tune, and the rhythm?

Yes, said he, that much.

And so far as it is words, it surely in no manner differs from words not sung in the requirement of conformity to the patterns and manner that we have prescribed?

True, he said.

And again, the music and the rhythm must follow the speech.

Of course.

But we said we did not require dirges and lamentations in words.

We do not.

What, then, are the dirgelike modes of music? Tell me, for you are a musician.

The mixed Lydian, he said, and the tense or higher Lydian, and similar modes.

These, then, said I, we must do away with. For they are useless even to women who are to make the best of themselves, let alone to men.

Assuredly.

But again, drunkenness is a thing most unbefitting guardians, and so is softness and sloth.

Yes.

What, then, are the soft and convivial modes?

There are certain Ionian and also Lydian modes that are called lax.

Will you make any use of them for warriors?

None at all, be said, but it would seem that you have left the Dorian and the Phrygian.

I don't know the musical modes, I said, but leave us that mode that would fittingly imitate the utterances and the accents of a brave man who is engaged in warfare or in any enforced business, and who, when he has failed, either meeting wounds or death or having fallen into some other mishap, in all these conditions confronts fortune with steadfast endurance and repels her strokes. And another for such a man engaged in works of peace, not enforced but voluntary, either trying to persuade somebody of something and imploring him—whether it be a god, through prayer, or a man, by teaching and admonition—or contrariwise yielding himself to another who is petitioning or teaching him or trying to change his opinions, and in consequence faring according to his wish, and not bearing himself arrogantly, but in all this acting modestly and moderately and acquiescing in the outcome. Leave us these two modes—the enforced and the voluntary—that will best imitate the utterances of men failing or succeeding, the temperate, the brave—leave us these.

Well, said he, you are asking me to leave none other than those I just spoke of.

Then, said I, we shall not need in our songs and airs instruments of many strings or whose compass includes all the harmonies.

Not in my opinion, said he.

Then we shall not maintain makers of triangles and harps and all other many-stringed and polyharmonic instruments.

Apparently not.

Well, will you admit to the city flute makers and flute players? Or is not the flute the most 'many-stringed' of instruments and do not the panharmonics themselves imitate it?

Clearly, he said.

You have left, said I, the lyre and the cithara. These are useful in the city, and in the fields the shepherds would have a little piccolo to pipe on.

So our argument indicates, he said.

We are not innovating, my friend, in preferring Apollo and the instruments of Apollo to Marsyas and his instruments.

No, by heaven I he said. I think not.

And by the dog, said I, we have all unawares purged the city which a little while ago we said was luxurious.

In that we show our good sense, he said.

Come then, let us complete the purification. For upon harmonies would follow the consideration of rhythms; we must not pursue complexity nor greats variety in the basic movements, but must observe what are the rhythms of a life that is orderly and brave, and after observing them require the foot and the air to conform to that kind of man's speech and not the speech to the foot and the tune. What those rhythms would be, it is for you to tell us as you did the musical modes.

Nay, in faith, he said, I cannot tell. For that there are some three forms from which the feet are combined, just as there are four in the notes of the voice whence come all harmonies, is a thing that I have observed and could tell. But which are imitations of which sort of life, I am unable to say.

Well, said I, on this point we will take counsel with Damon, too, as to which are the feet appropriate to illiberality, and insolence or madness or other evils, and what rhythms we must leave for their opposites. And I believe I have heard him obscurely speaking of a foot that he called the enoplios, a composite foot, and a dactyl and a heroic foot, which he arranged, I know not how, to be equal up and down in the interchange of long and short, and unless I am mistaken he used the term iambic, and there was another foot that he called the trochaic, and he added the quantities long and short. And in some of these, I believe, he censured and commended the tempo of the foot no less than the rhythm itself, or else some combination of the two, I can't say. But, as I said, let this matter be postponed for Damon's consideration. For to determine the truth of these would require no little discourse. Do you think otherwise?

No, by heaven, I do not.

But this you are able to determine—that seemliness and unseemliness are attendant upon the good rhythm and the bad.

Of course.

And, further, that good rhythm and bad rhythm accompany, the one fair diction, assimilating itself thereto, and the other the opposite, and so of the apt and the unapt, if, as we were just now saying, the rhythm and harmony follow the words and not the words these.

They certainly must follow the speech, he said.

And what of the manner of the diction, and the speech? said I. Do they not follow and conform to the disposition of the soul?

Of course.

And all the rest to the diction?

Yes.

Good speech, then, good accord, and good grace, and good rhythm wait upon a good disposition, not that weakness of head which we euphemistically style goodness of heart, but the truly good and fair disposition of the character and the mind.

By all means, he said.

And must not our youth pursue these everywhere if they are to do what it is truly theirs to do?

They must indeed.

And there is surely much of these qualities in painting and in all similar crafts-manship—weaving is full of them and embroidery and architecture and likewise the manufacture of household furnishings and thereto the natural bodies of animals and plants as well. For in all these there is grace or gracelessness. And gracelessness and evil rhythm and disharmony are akin to evil speaking and the evil temper, but the opposites are the symbols and the kin of the opposites, the sober and good disposition.

Entirely so, he said.

Is it, then, only the poets that we must supervise and compel to embody in their poems the semblance of the good character or else not write poetry among us, or must we keep watch over the other crafts-men, and forbid them to represent the evil disposition, the licentious, the illiberal, the graceless, either in the likeness of living creatures or in buildings or in any other product of their art, on penalty, if unable to obey, of being forbidden to practice their art among us, that our guardians may not be bred among symbols of evil, as it were in a pasturage of poisonous herbs, lest grazing freely and cropping from many such day by day they little by little and all unawares accumulate and build up a huge mass of evil in their own souls. But we must look for those craftsmen who by the happy gift of nature are capable of following the trail of true beauty and grace, that our young men, dwelling as it were in a salubrious region, may receive benefit from all things about them, whence the influence that emanates from works of beauty may waft itself to eye or ear like a breeze that brings from wholesome places health, and so from earliest childhood insensibly guide them to likeness, to friendship, to harmony with beautiful reason.

Yes, he said, that would be far the best education for them.

And is it not for this reason, Glaucon, said I, that education in music is most sovereign, because more than anything else rhythm and harmony find their way to the inmost soul and take strongest hold upon it, bringing with them and imparting grace, if one is rightly trained, and otherwise the contrary? And further, because omissions and the failure of beauty in things badly made or grown would be most quickly perceived by one who was properly educated in music, and so, feeling distaste rightly, he would praise beautiful things and take delight in them and receive them into his soul to foster its growth and become himself beautiful and good. The ugly he would rightly disapprove of and hate while still young and yet unable to apprehend the reason, but when reason came the man thus nurtured would be the first to give her welcome, for by this affinity he would know her.

I certainly think, he said, that such is the cause of education in music.

It is, then, said I, as it was when we learned our letters and felt that we knew them sufficiently only when the separate letters did not elude us, appearing as few elements in all the combinations that convey them, and when we did not disregard them in small things or great and think it unnecessary to recognize them, but were eager to distinguish them everywhere, in the belief that we should never be literate and letter-perfect till we could do this.

True.

And is it not also true that if there are any likenesses of letters reflected in water or mirrors, we shall never know them until we know the originals, but such knowledge belongs to the same art and discipline?

By all means.

Then, by heaven, am I not right in saying that by the same token we shall never be true musicians, either—neither we nor the guardians that we have undertaken to educate—until we are able to recognize the forms of soberness, courage, liberality, and high-mindedness, and all their kindred and their opposites, too, in all the combinations that contain and convey them, and to apprehend them and their images wherever found, disregarding them neither in trifles nor in great things, but believing the knowledge of them to belong to the same art and discipline?

The conclusion is inevitable, he said.

Then, said I, when there is a coincidence of a beautiful disposition in the soul and corresponding and harmonious beauties of the same type in the bodily form—is not this the fairest spectacle for one who is capable of its contemplation?

Far the fairest.

And surely the fairest is the most lovable.

Of course.

The true musician, then, would love by preference persons of this sort, but if there were disharmony he would not love this.

No, he said, not if there was a defect in the soul, but if it were in the body he would bear with it and still be willing to bestow his love.

I understand, I said, that you have or have had favorites of this sort and I grant your distinction. But tell me this—can there be any communion between soberness and extravagant pleasure?

How could there be, he said, since such pleasure puts a man beside himself no less than pain?

Or between it and virtue generally?

By no means.

But is there between pleasure and insolence and license?

Most assuredly.

Do you know of greater or keener pleasure than that associated with Aphrodite?

I don't, he said, nor yet of any more insane.

But is not the right love a sober and harmonious love of the orderly and the beautiful?

It is indeed, said he.

Then nothing of madness, nothing akin to license, must be air lowed to come nigh the right love?

No.

Then this kind of pleasure may not come nigh, nor may lover and beloved who rightly love and are loved have anything to do with it?

No, by heaven, Socrates, he said, it must not come nigh them.

Thus, then, as it seems, you will lay down the law in the city that we are founding, that the lover may kiss and pass the time with and touch the beloved as a father would a son, for honorable ends, if he persuade him. But otherwise he must so associate with the objects of his care that there should never be any suspicion of anything further, on penalty of being stigmatized for want of taste and true musical culture.

Even so, he said.

Do you not agree, then, that our discourse on music has come to an end? It has certainly made a fitting end, for surely the end and consummation of culture is the love of the beautiful.

I concur, he said.

After music our youth are to be educated by gymnastics?

Certainly.

In this too they must be carefully trained from boyhood through life, and the way of it is this, I believe, but consider it yourself too. For I, for my part, do not believe that a sound body by its excellence makes the soul good, but on the contrary that a good soul by its virtue renders the body the best that is possible. What is your opinion?

I think so too.

Then if we should sufficiently train the mind and turn over to it the minutiae of the care of the body, and content ourselves with merely indicating the norms or patterns, not to make a long story of it, we should be acting rightly?

By all means.

From intoxication we said that they must abstain. For a guardian is surely the last person in the world to whom it is allowable to get drunk and not know where on earth he is.

Yes, he said, it would be absurd that a guardian should need a guard.

What next about their food? These men are athletes in the greatest of contests, are they not?

Yes.

Is, then, the bodily habit of the athletes we see about us suitable for such?

Perhaps.

Nay, said I, that is a drowsy habit and precarious for health. Don't you observe that they sleep away their lives, and that if they depart ever so little from their prescribed regimen these athletes are liable to great and violent diseases?

I do.

Then, said I, we need some more ingenious form of training for our athletes of war, since these must be as it were sleepless hounds, and have the keenest possible perceptions of sight and hearing, and in their campaigns undergo many changes in their drinking water, their food, and in exposure to the heat of the sun and to storms, without disturbance of their health.

I think so.

Would not, then, the best gymnastics be akin to the music that we were just now describing?

What do you mean?

It would be a simple and flexible gymnastic training, and especially so in the training for war.

In what way?

One could learn that, said I, even from Homer. For you are aware that in the banqueting of the heroes on campaign he does not feast them on fish, though they are at the seaside on the Hellespont, nor on boiled meat, but only on roast, which is what soldiers could most easily procure. For everywhere, one may say, it is of easier provision to use the bare fire than to convey pots and pans along.

Indeed it is.

Neither, as I believe, does Homer ever make mention of sweetmeats. Is not that something which all men in training understand—that if one is to keep his body in good condition he must abstain from such things altogether?

They are right, he said, in that they know it and do abstain.

Then, my friend, if you think this is the right way, you apparently do not approve of a Syracusan table and the Sicilian variety of dishes.

I think not.

You would frown, then, on a little Corinthian maid as the chère amie of men who were to keep themselves fit?

Most certainly.

And also on the seeming delights of Attic pastry?

Inevitably.

In general, I take it, if we likened that kind of food and regimen to music and song expressed in the panharmonic mode and in every variety of rhythm it would be a fair comparison.

Quite so.

And there variety engendered licentiousness, did it not, but here disease, while simplicity in music begets sobriety in the souls, and in gymnastic training it begets health in bodies?

Most true, he said.

And when licentiousness and disease multiply in a city, are not many courts of law and dispensaries opened? And the arts of chicane and medicine give themselves airs when even free men in great numbers take them very seriously.

How can they help it? he said.

Will you be able to find a surer proof of an evil and shameful state of education in a city than the necessity of first-rate physicians and judges, not only for the base and mechanical, but for those who claim to have been bred in the fashion of free men? Do you not think it disgraceful and a notable mark of bad breeding to have to make use of a justice imported from others, who thus become your masters and judges, from lack of such qualities in yourself?

The most shameful thing in the world.

Is it? said I. Or is this still more shameful—when a man not only wears out the better part of his days in the courts of law as defendant or accuser, but from the lack of all true sense of values is led to plume himself on this very thing, as being a smart fellow to 'put over' an unjust act and cunningly to try every dodge and practice, every evasion, and wriggle out of every hold in defeating justice, and that too for trifles and worthless things, because he does not know how much nobler and better it is to arrange his life so as to have no need of a nodding juryman?

That is, said he, still more shameful than the other.

And to require medicine, said I, not merely for wounds or the incidence of some seasonal maladies, but, because of sloth and such a regimen as we described, to fill one's body up with winds and humors like a marsh and compel the ingenious sons of Asclepius to invent for diseases such names as fluxes and flatulences—don't you think that disgraceful?

Those surely are, he said, newfangled and monstrous strange names of diseases.

There was nothing of the kind, I fancy, said I, in the days of Asclepius. I infer this from the fact that at Troy his sons did not find fault with the damsel who gave to the wounded Eurypylus to drink a posset of Pramnian wine plentifully sprinkled with barley and gratings of cheese, inflammatory ingredients of a surety, nor did they censure Patroclus, who was in charge of the case.

It was indeed, said he, a strange potion for a man in that condition.

Not so strange, said I, if you reflect that the former Asclepiads made no use of our modern coddling medication of diseases before the time of Herodicus. But Herodicus was a trainer and became a valetudinarian, and blended gymnastics and medicine, for the torment first and chiefly of himself and then of many successors.

How so? he said.

By lingering out his death, said I. For living in perpetual observance of his malady, which was incurable, he was not able to effect a cure, but lived through his days unfit for the business of life, suffering the tortures of the damned if he departed a whit from his fixed regimen. And struggling against death, by reason of his science he won the prize of a doting old age.

A noble prize indeed for his science, he said.

The appropriate one, said I, for a man who did not know that it was not from ignorance or inacquaintance with this type of medicine that Asclepius did not discover it to his descendants, but because he knew that for all well-governed peoples there is a work assigned to each man in the city which he must perform, and no one has leisure to be sick and doctor himself all his days. And this we absurdly enough perceive in the case of a craftsman, but don't see in the case of the rich and so-called fortunate.

How so? he said.

A carpenter, said I, when he is sick expects his physician to give him a drug which will operate as an emetic on the disease, or to get rid of it by purging or the use of cautery or the knife. But if anyone prescribes for him a long course of treatment with swathings about the head and their accompaniments, he hastily says that he has no leisure to be sick, and that such a life of preoccupation with his illness and neglect of the work that lies before him isn't worth living. And thereupon he bids farewell to that kind of physician, enters upon his customary way of life, regains his health, and lives attending to his affairs—or, if his body is not equal to the strain, he dies and is freed from all his troubles.

For such a man, he said, that appears to be the right use of medicine.

And is not the reason, I said, that he had a task and that life wasn't worth acceptance on condition of not doing his work?

Obviously, he said.

But the rich man, we say, has no such appointed task, the necessity of abstaining from which renders life intolerable.

I haven't heard of any.

Why, haven't you heard that saying of Phocylides, that after a man has 'made his pile' he ought to practice virtue?

Before, too, I fancy, he said.

Let us not quarrel with him on that point, I said, but inform ourselves whether this virtue is something for the rich man to practice, and life is intolerable if he does not, or whether we are to suppose that while valetudinarianism is a hindrance to single-minded attention to carpentry and the other arts, it is no obstacle to the fulfillment of Phocylides' exhortation.

Yes, indeed, he said, this excessive care for the body that goes beyond simple gymnastics is about the greatest of all obstacles.

For it is troublesome in household affairs and military service and sedentary offices in the city. And, chief of all, it puts difficulties in the way of any kind of instruction, thinking, or private meditation—forever imagining headaches and dizziness and attributing their origin to philosophy. So that wherever this kind of virtue is practiced and tested it is in every way a hindrance. For it makes the man always fancy himself sick and never cease from anguishing about his body.

Naturally, he said.

Then shall we not say that it was because Asclepius knew this, that for those who were by nature and course of life sound of body but had some localized disease, that for such, I say, and for this habit he revealed the art of medicine, and, driving out their disease by drugs and surgery, prescribed for them their customary regimen in order not to interfere with their civic duties, but that, when bodies were diseased inwardly and throughout, he did not attempt by diet and by gradual evacuations and infusions to prolong a wretched existence for the man and have him beget in all likelihood similar wretched offspring? But if a man was incapable of living in the established round and order of life, he did not think it worth while to treat him, since such a fellow is of no use either to himself or to the state.

A most politic Asclepius you're telling us of, he said.

Obviously, said I, that was his character. And his sons too, don't you see that at Troy they proved themselves good fighting men and practiced medicine as I described it? Don't you remember that in the case of Menelaus too, from the wound that Pandarus inflicted 'they sucked the blood, and soothing simples sprinkled'?[27] But what he was to eat or drink thereafter they no more prescribed than for Eurypylus, taking it for granted that the remedies sufficed to heal men who before their wounds were healthy and temperate in diet even if they did happen for the nonce to drink a posset. But they thought that the life of a man constitutionally sickly and intemperate was of no use to

---

27 Iliad 4.218.

himself or others, and that the art of medicine should not be for such nor should they be given treatment even if they were richer than Midas.

Very ingenious fellows, he said, you make out these sons of Asclepius to be.

'Tis fitting, said I, and yet in disregard of our principles the tragedians and Pindar affirm that Asclepius, though he was the son of Apollo, was bribed by gold to heal a man already at the point of death, and that for this cause he was struck by the lightning. But we in accordance with the aforesaid principles refuse to believe both statements. If he was the son of a god he was not avaricious, we will insist, and if he was greedy of gain he was not the son of a god.

That much, said he, is most certainly true. But what have you to say to this, Socrates? Must we not have good physicians in our city? And they would be the most likely to be good who had treated the greatest number of healthy and diseased men, and so good judges would be those who had associated with all sorts and conditions of men.

Most assuredly I want them good, I said, but do you know whom I regard as such? I'll know if you tell, he said.

Well, I will try, said I. You, however, have put unlike cases in one question.

How so? said he.

Physicians, it is true, I said, would prove most skilled if, from childhood up, in addition to learning the principles of the art they had familiarized themselves with the greatest possible number of the most sickly bodies, and if they themselves had suffered all diseases and were not of very healthy constitution. For you see they do not treat the body by the body. If they did, it would not be allowable for their bodies to be or to have been in evil condition. But they treat the body with the mind—and it is not competent for a mind that is or has been evil to treat anything well.

Right, he said.

But a judge, mark you, my friend, rules soul with soul and it is not allowable for a soul to have been bred from youth up among evil souls and to have grown familiar with them, and itself to have run the gauntlet of every kind of wrongdoing and injustice so as quickly to infer from itself the misdeeds of others as it might diseases in the body, but it must have been inexperienced in evil natures and uncontaminated by them while young, if it is to be truly fair and good and judge soundly of justice. For which cause the better sort seem to be simple-minded in youth and are easily deceived by the wicked, since they do not have within themselves patterns answering to the affections of the bad.

That is indeed their experience, he said.

Therefore it is, said I, that the good judge must not be a youth but an old man, a late learner of the nature of injustice, one who has not become aware of it as a property in his own soul, but one who has through the long years trained himself to understand it as an alien thing in alien souls, and to discern how great an evil it is by the instrument of mere knowledge and not by experience of his own.

That at any rate, he said, appears to be the noblest kind of judge.

And what is more, a good one, I said, which was the gist of your question. For he who has a good soul is good. But that cunning fellow quick to suspect evil, and who has himself done many unjust acts and who thinks himself a smart trickster, when he associates with his like does appear to be clever, being on his guard and fixing his eyes on the patterns within himself. But when the time comes for him to mingle with the good and his elders, then on the contrary he appears stupid. He is unseasonably distrustful and he cannot recognize a sound character because he has no such pattern in himself. But since he more often meets with the bad than the good, he seems to himself and to others to be rather wise than foolish.

That is quite true, he said.

Well then, said I, such a one must not be our ideal of the good and wise judge but the former. For while badness could never come to know both virtue and itself, native virtue through education will at last acquire the science of both itself and badness. This one, then, as I think, is the man who proves to be wise and not the bad man.

And I concur, he said.

Then will you not establish by law in your city such an art of medicine as we have described in conjunction with this kind of justice? And these arts will care for the bodies and souls of such of your citizens as are truly wellborn, but those who are not, such as are defective in body, they will suffer to die, and those who are evil-natured and incurable in soul they will themselves put to death.

This certainly, he said, has been shown to be the best thing for the sufferers themselves and for the state.

And so your youths, said I, employing that simple music which we said engendered sobriety will, it is clear, guard themselves against falling into the need of the justice of the courtroom.

Yes, he said.

And will not our musician, pursuing the same trail in his use of
gymnastics, if he please, get to have no need of medicine save when indispensable?

I think so.

And even the exercises and toils of gymnastics he will undertake with a view to the spirited part of his nature to arouse that rather than for mere strength, unlike ordinary athletes, who treat diet and exercise only as a means to muscle.

Nothing could be truer, he said.

Then may we not say, Glaucon, said I, that those who established an education in music and gymnastics had not the purpose in view that some attribute to them in so instituting, namely to treat the body by one and the soul by the other?

But what? he said.

It seems likely, I said, that they ordained both chiefly for the soul's sake.

How so?

Have you not observed, said I, the effect on the disposition of the mind itself of lifelong devotion to gymnastics with total neglect of music? Or the disposition of those of the opposite habit?

In what respect do you mean? he said.

In respect of savagery and hardness or, on the other hand, of softness and gentleness?

I have observed, he said, that the devotees of unmitigated gymnastics turn out more brutal than they should be and those of music softer than is good for them.

And surely, said I, this savagery is a quality derived from the high-spirited element in our nature, which, if rightly trained, becomes brave, but if overstrained, would naturally become hard and harsh.

I think so, he said.

And again, is not the gentleness a quality which the philosophical nature would yield? This if relaxed too far would be softer than is desirable but if rightly trained gentle and orderly?

That is so.

But our requirement, we say, is that the guardians should possess both natures.

It is.

And must they not be harmoniously adjusted to one another?

Of course.

And the soul of the man thus attuned is sober and brave?

Certainly.

And that of the ill-adjusted is cowardly and rude?

It surely is.

Now when a man abandons himself to music, to play upon him and pour into his soul as it were through the funnel of his ears those sweet, soft, and dirgelike airs of which we were just now speaking, and gives his entire time to the warblings and blandishments of song, the first result is that the principle of high spirit, if he had it, is softened like iron and is made useful instead of useless and brittle. But when he continues the practice without remission and is spellbound, the effect begins to be that he melts and liquefies till he completely dissolves away his spirit, cuts out as it were the very sinews of his soul and makes of himself a 'feeble warrior.'[28]

Assuredly, he said.

And if, said I, he has to begin with a spiritless nature he reaches this result quickly, but if a high-spirited, by weakening the spirit he makes it unstable, quickly irritated by slight stimuli, and as quickly quelled. The outcome is that such men are choleric and irascible instead of high-spirited, and are peevish and discontented.

Precisely so.

---

28 Iliad 17.588.

On the other hand, if a man toils hard at gymnastics and eats right lustily and holds no truck with music and philosophy, does he not at first get very fit and full of pride and high spirit and become more brave and bold than he was?

He does indeed.

But what if he does nothing but this and has no contact with the Muse in any way? Is not the result that even if there was some principle of the love of knowledge in his soul, since it tastes of no instruction nor of any inquiry and does not participate in any discussion or any other form of culture, it becomes feeble, deaf, and blind, because it is not aroused or fed nor are its perceptions purified and quickened?

That is so, he said.

And so such a man, I take it, becomes a misologist and a stranger to the Muses. He no longer makes any use of persuasion by speech but achieves all his ends like a beast by violence and savagery, and in his brute ignorance and ineptitude lives a life of disharmony and gracelessness.

That is entirely true, he said.

For these two, then, it seems there are two arts which I would say some god gave to mankind, music and gymnastics for the service of the high-spirited principle and the love of knowledge in them—not for the soul and the body except incidentally, but for the harmonious adjustment of these two principles by the proper degree of tension and relaxation of each.

Yes, so it appears, he said.

Then he who best blends gymnastics with music and applies them most suitably to the soul is the man whom we should most rightly pronounce to be the most perfect and harmonious musician, far rather than the one who brings the strings into unison with one another.

That seems likely, Socrates, he said.

And shall we not also need in our city, Glaucon, a permanent overseer of this kind if its constitution is to be preserved?

We most certainly shall.

Such would be the outlines of their education and breeding. For why should one recite the list of the dances of such citizens, their hunts and chases with hounds, their athletic contests and races? It is pretty plain that they must conform to these principles and there is no longer any difficulty in discovering them.

There is, it may be, no difficulty, he said.

Very well, said I. What, then, have we next to determine? Is it not which ones among them shall be the rulers and the ruled?

Certainly.

That the rulers must be the elder and the ruled the younger is obvious.

It is.

And that the rulers must be their best?

This too.

And do not the best of the farmers prove the best farmers?

Yes.

And in this case, since we want them to be the best of the guardians, must they not be the best guardians, the most regardful of the state?

Yes.

They must then to begin with be intelligent in such matters and capable, and furthermore careful of the interests of the state?

That is so.

But one would be most likely to be careful of that which he loved.

Necessarily.

And again, one would be most likely to love that whose interests he supposed to coincide with his own, and thought that when it prospered he too would prosper and if not, the contrary.

So it is, he said.

Then we must pick out from the other guardians such men as to our observation appear most inclined through the entire course of their lives to be zealous to do what they think for the interest of the e state, and who would be least likely to consent to do the opposite.

That would be a suitable choice, he said.

I think, then, we shall have to observe them at every period of life, to see if they are conservators and guardians of this conviction in their minds and never by sorcery nor by force can be brought to expel from their souls unawares this conviction that they must do what is best for the state.

What do you mean by the 'expelling'? he said.

I will tell you, said I. It seems to me that the exit of a belief from the mind is either voluntary or involuntary. Voluntary is the departure of the false belief from one who learns better, involuntary that of every true belief.

The voluntary, he said, I understand, but I need instruction about the involuntary.

How now, said I, don't you agree with me in thinking that men are unwillingly deprived of good things but willingly of evil? Or is it not an evil to be deceived in respect of the truth and a good to possess truth? And don't you think that to opine the things that are is to possess the truth?

Why, yes, said he, you are right, and I agree that men are unwillingly deprived of true opinions.

And doesn't this happen to them by theft, by the spells of sorcery, or by force?

I don't understand now either, he said.

I must be talking in high tragic style, I said. By those who have their opinions stolen from them I mean those who are overpersuaded and those who forget, because in the one case time, in the other argument strips them unawares of their beliefs. Now I presume you understand, do you not?

Yes.

Well then, by those who are constrained or forced I mean those whom some pain or suffering compels to change their minds.

That too I understand and you are right.

And the victims of sorcery I am sure you too would say are they who alter their opinions under the spell of pleasure or terrified by some fear.

Yes, he said, everything that deceives appears to cast a spell upon the mind.

Well then, as I was just saying, we must look for those who are the best guardians of the indwelling conviction that what they have to do is what they at any time believe to be best for the state. Then we must observe them from childhood up and propose for them tasks in which one would be most likely to forget this principle or be deceived, and he whose memory is sure and who cannot be beguiled we must accept and the other kind we must cross off from our list. Is not that so?

Yes.

And again we must subject them to toils and pains and competitions in which we have to watch for the same traits.

Right, he said.

Then, said I, must we not institute a third kind of competitive test with regard to sorcery and observe them in that? Just as men conduct colts to noises and uproar to see if they are liable to take fright, so we must bring these lads while young into fears and again pass them into pleasures, testing them much more carefully than men do gold in the fire, to see if the man remains immune to such witchcraft and preserves his composure throughout, a good guardian of himself and the culture which he has received, maintaining the true rhythm and harmony of his being in all those conditions, and the character that would make him most useful to himself and to the state. And he who as boy, lad, and man endures the test and issues from it unspoiled we must establish as ruler over our city and its guardian, and bestow rewards upon him in life, and in death the allotment of the supreme honors of burial rites and other memorials. But the man of the other type we must reject. Such, said I, appears to me, Glaucon, the general notion of our selection and appointment of rulers and guardians as sketched in outline, but not drawn out in detail.

I too, he said, think much the same.

Then would it not truly be most proper to designate these as guardians in the full sense of the word, watchers against foemen without and friends within, so that the latter shall not wish and the former shall not be able to work harm, but to name those youths whom we were calling guardians just now helpers and aids for the decrees of the rulers?

I think so, he replied.

How, then, said I, might we contrive one of those opportune falsehoods of which we were just now speaking, so as by one noble lie to persuade if possible the rulers themselves, but failing that the rest of the city?

What kind of a fiction do you mean? said he.

Nothing unprecedented, said I, but a sort of Phoenician tale, something that has happened ere now in many parts of the world, as the poets aver and have induced men to believe, but that has not happened and perhaps would not be likely to happen in our day and demanding no little persuasion to make it believable.

You act like one who shrinks from telling his thought, he said.

You will think that I have right good reason for shrinking when I have told, I said.

Say on, said he, and don't be afraid.

Very well, I will. And yet I hardly know how to find the audacity or the words to speak and undertake to persuade first the rulers themselves and the soldiers and then the rest of the city that in good sooth all our training and educating of them were things that they imagined and that happened to them as it were in a dream, but that in reality at that time they were down within the earth being molded and fostered themselves while their weapons and the rest of their equipment were being fashioned. And when they were quite finished the earth as being their mother delivered them, and now as if their land were their mother and their nurse they ought to take thought for her and defend her against any attack and regard the other citizens as their brothers and children of the selfsame earth.

It is not for nothing, he said, that you were so bashful about coming out with your lie.

It was quite natural that I should be, I said, but all the same hear the rest of the story. While all of you in the city are brothers, we will say in our tale, yet God in fashioning those of you who are fitted to hold rule mingled gold in their generation, for which reason they are the most precious—but in the helpers silver, and iron and brass in the farmers and other craftsmen. And as you are all akin, though for the most part you will breed after your kinds, it may sometimes happen that a golden father would beget a silver son and that a golden offspring would come from a silver sire and that the rest would in like manner be born of one another. So that the first and chief injunction that the god lays upon the rulers is that of nothing else are they to be such careful guardians and so intently observant as of the intermixture of these metals in the souls of their offspring, and if sons are born to them with an infusion of brass or iron they shall by no means give way to pity in their treatment of them, but shall assign to each the status due to his nature and thrust them out among the artisans or the farmers. And again, if from these there are born sons with unexpected gold or silver in their composition they shall honor such and bid them go up higher, some to the office of guardian, some to the assistantship, alleging that there is an oracle that the state shall then be overthrown when the man of iron or brass is its guardian. Do you see any way of getting them to believe this tale?

No, not these themselves, he said, but I do their sons and successors and the rest of mankind who come after.

Well, said I, even that would have a good effect in making them more inclined to care for the state and one another. For I think I apprehend your meaning. And this shall fall out as tradition guides. But let us arm these sons of earth and conduct them under the leadership of their rulers. And when they have arrived they must look out for the fairest site in the city for their encampment, a position from which they could best hold down rebellion against the laws from within and repel aggression from without as of a wolf against the fold. And after they have encamped and sacrificed to the proper gods they must make their lairs, must they not?

Yes, he said.

And these must be of a character to keep out the cold in winter and be sufficient in summer?

Of course. For I presume you are speaking of their houses.

Yes, said I, the houses of soldiers, not of money-makers.

What distinction do you intend by that? he said.

I will try to tell you, I said. It is surely the most monstrous and shameful thing in the world for shepherds to breed the dogs who are to help them with their flocks in such wise and of such a nature that from indiscipline or hunger or some other evil condition the dogs themselves shall attack the sheep and injure them and be likened to wolves instead of dogs.

A terrible thing, indeed, he said.

Must we not then guard by every means in our power against our

helpers' treating the citizens in any such way and, because they are the stronger, converting themselves from benign assistants into savage masters?

We must, he said.

And would they not have been provided with the chief safeguard if their education has really been a good one?

But it surely has, he said.

That, said I, dear Glaucon, we may not properly affirm, but what we were just now saying we may, that they must have the right education, whatever it is, if they are to have what will do most to make them gentle to one another and to their charges.

That is right, he said.

In addition, moreover, to such an education a thoughtful man would affirm that their houses and the possessions provided for them ought to be such as not to interfere with the best performance of their own work as guardians and not to incite them to wrong the other citizens.

He will rightly affirm that.

Consider then, said I, whether, if that is to be their character, their habitations and ways of life must not be something after this fashion. In the first place, none must possess any private property save the indispensable. Secondly, none must have any habitation or treasure house which is not open for all to enter at will. Their food, in such quantities as are needful for athletes of war sober and brave, they must receive as an agreed stipend from the other citizens as the wages of their guardianship, so measured that there shall be neither superfluity at the end of the year nor any lack. And resorting to a common mess like soldiers on campaign they will live together. Gold and silver, we will tell them, they have of the divine quality from the gods always in their souls, and they have no need of the metal of men nor does holiness suffer them to mingle and contaminate that heavenly possession with the acquisition of mortal gold, since many impious deeds have been done about the coin of the multitude, while that which dwells within them is unsullied. But for these only of all the dwellers in the city it is not lawful to handle gold and silver and to touch them nor yet to come under the same roof with them, nor to hang them as ornaments on their limbs nor to drink from silver and gold. So living they would save themselves and save their city. But whenever they shall acquire for themselves land of their own and houses and coin, they will be householders and farmers instead of guardians, and will be transformed from the helpers of their fellow citizens to their enemies and masters, and so in hating and being hated, plotting and being plotted against, they will pass their days fearing far more and rather the townsmen within than the foemen without—and then even then laying the course of near shipwreck for themselves and the state. For all these reasons, said I, let us declare that such must be the provision for our guardians in lodging and other respects and so legislate. Shall we not?

By all means, said Glaucon.

THE REPUBLIC OF PLATO
Book IV

Translated by Paul Shorey

And Adimantus broke in and said, What will be your defense, Socrates, if anyone objects that you are not making these men very happy, and that through their own fault? For the city really belongs to them and yet they get no enjoyment out of it as ordinary men do by owning lands and building fine big houses and providing them with suitable furniture and winning the favor of the gods by private sacrifices and entertaining guests and enjoying too those possessions which you just now spoke of, gold and silver and all that is customary for those who are expecting to be happy. But they seem, one might say, to be established in idleness in the city, exactly like hired mercenaries, with nothing to do but keep guard.

Yes, said I, and what is more, they serve for board wages and do not even receive pay in addition to their food as others do, so that they will not even be able to take a journey on their own account, if they

Tell me first, I said, whether, if they have to fight, they will not be fighting as athletes of war against men of wealth?

Yes, that is true, he said.

Answer me then, Adimantus. Do you not think that one boxer perfectly trained in the art could easily fight two fat rich men who knew nothing of it?

Not at the same time perhaps, said he.

Not even, said I, if he were allowed to retreat and then turn and strike the one who came up first, and if he repeated the procedure many times under a burning and stifling sun? Would not such a fighter down even a number of such opponents?

Doubtless, he said, it wouldn't be surprising if he did.

Well, don't you think that the rich have more of the skill and practice of boxing than of the art of war?

I do, he said.

It will be easy, then, for our athletes in all probability to fight with double and triple their number.

I shall have to concede the point, he said, for I believe you are right.

Plato, *Republic*. Trans. Paul Shorey. Free Press. Copyright © 1930. In the public domain.

Well then, if they send an embassy to the other city and say what is in fact true, 'We make no use of gold and silver nor is it lawful for us, but it is for you; do then join us in the war and keep the spoils of the enemy'—do you suppose any who heard such a proposal would choose to fight against hard and wiry hounds rather than with the aid of the hounds against fat and tender sheep?

I think not. Yet consider whether the accumulation of all the wealth of other cities in one does not involve danger for the state that has no wealth.

What happy innocence, said I, to suppose that you can properly use the name city of any other than the one we are constructing.

Why, what should we say? he said.

A greater predication, said I, must be applied to the others. For they are each one of them many cities, not a city, as it goes in the game. There are two at the least at enmity with one another, the city of the rich and the city of the poor, and in each of these there are many. If you deal with them as one you will altogether miss the mark, but if you treat them as a multiplicity by offering to the one faction the property, the power, the very persons of the other, you will continue always to have few enemies and many allies. And so long as your city is governed soberly in the order just laid down, it will be the greatest of cities. I do not mean greatest in repute, but in reality, even though it have only a thousand defenders. For a city of this size that is really one you will not easily discover either among Greeks or barbarians—but of those that seem so you will find many and many times the size of this. Or do you think otherwise?

No, indeed I don't, said he.

Would not this, then, be the best rule and measure for our governors of the proper size of the city and of the territory that they should mark off for a city of that size and seek no more?

What is the measure?

I think, said I, that they should let it grow so long as in its growth it consents to remain a unity, but no further.

Excellent, he said.

Then is not this still another injunction that we should lay upon our guardians, to keep guard in every way that the city shall not be too small, nor great only in seeming, but that it shall be a sufficient city and one?

That behest will perhaps be an easy one for them, he said.

And still easier, haply, I said, is this that we mentioned before when we said that if a degenerate offspring was born to the guardians he must be sent away to the other classes, and likewise if a superior to the others he must be enrolled among the guardians, and the purport of all this was that the other citizens too must be sent to the task for which their natures were fitted, one man to one work, in order that each of them fulfilling his own function may be not many men, but one, and so the entire city may come to be not a multiplicity but a unity.

Why yes, he said, this is even more trifling than that.

These are not, my good Adimantus, as one might suppose, numerous and difficult injunctions that we are imposing upon them, but they are all easy, provided they guard, as the saying is, the one great thing—or instead of great let us call it sufficient.

What is that? he said.

Their education and nurture, I replied. For if a right education makes of them reasonable men they will easily discover everything of this kind—and other principles that we now pass over, as that the possession of wives and marriage, and the procreation of children and all that sort of thing should be made as far as possible the proverbial goods of friends that are common.

Yes, that would be the best way, he said.

And, moreover, said I, the state, if it once starts well, proceeds as it were in a cycle of growth. I mean that a sound nurture and education if kept up create good natures in turn receiving an education of this sort develop into better man than their predecessors both for other purposes and for the production of offspring, as among animals also.

It is probable, he said.

To put it briefly, then, said I, it is to this that the overseers of our state must cleave and be watchful against its insensible corruption. They must throughout be watchful against innovations in music and gymnastics counter to the established order, and to the best of their power guard against them, fearing when anyone says that that song is most regarded among men 'which hovers newest on the singer's lips,'[1] lest haply it be supposed that the poet means not new songs but a new way of song and is commending this. But we must not praise that sort of thing nor conceive it to be the poet's meaning. For a change to a new type of music is something to beware of as a hazard of all our fortunes. For the modes of music are never disturbed without unsettling of the most fundamental political and social conventions, as Damon affirms and as I am convinced.

Set me too down in the number of the convinced, said Adimantus.

It is here, then, I said, in music, as it seems, that our guardians must build their guardhouse and post of watch.

It is certain, he said, that this is the kind of lawlessness that easily insinuates itself unobserved.

Yes, said I, because it is supposed to be only a form of play and to work no harm.

Nor does it work any, he said, except that by gradual infiltration it softly overflows upon the characters and pursuits of men and from these issues forth grown greater to attack their business dealings, and from these relations it proceeds against the laws and the constitution with wanton license, Socrates, till finally it overthrows all things public and private.

Well, said I, are these things so?

I think so, he said.

---

1   Odyssey 1.351.

Then, as we were saying in the beginning, our youth must join in a more law-abiding play, since, if play grows lawless and the children likewise, it is impossible that they should grow up to be men of serious temper and lawful spirit.

Of course, he said.

And so we may reason that when children in their earliest play are imbued with the spirit of law and order through their music, the opposite of the former supposition happens—this spirit waits upon them in all things and fosters their growth, and restores and sets up again whatever was overthrown in the other type of state.

True indeed, he said.

Then such men rediscover for themselves those seemingly trifling conventions which their predecessors abolished altogether.

Of what sort?

Such things as the becoming silence of the young in the presence of their elders, the giving place to them and rising up before them, and dutiful service of parents, and the cut of the hair and the garments and the fashion of the footgear, and in general the deportment of the body and everything of the kind. Don't you think so?

I do.

Yet to enact them into laws would, I think, be silly. For such laws are not obeyed nor would they last, being enacted only in words and on paper.

How could they?

At any rate, Adimantus, I said, the direction of the education from whence one starts is likely to determine the quality of what follows. Does not like ever summon like?

Surely.

And the final outcome, I presume, we would say is one complete and vigorous product of good or the reverse.

Of course, said he.

For my part, then, I said, for these reasons I would not go on to try to legislate on such matters.

With good reason, said he.

But what, in heaven's name, said I, about business matters, the deals that men make with one another in the agora—and, if you please, contracts with workmen and actions for foul language and assault, the filing of declarations, the impaneling of juries, the payment and exaction of any dues that may be needful in markets or harbors and in general market, police, or harbor regulations and the like—can we bring ourselves to legislate about these?

Nay, 'twould not be fitting, he said, to dictate to good and honorable men. For most of the enactments that are needed about these things they will easily, I presume, discover.

Yes, my friend, provided God grants them the preservation of the principles of law that we have already discussed.

Failing that, said he, they will pass their lives multiplying such petty laws and amending them in the expectation of attaining what is best.

You mean, said I, that the life of such citizens will resemble that of men who are sick, yet from intemperance are unwilling to abandon their unwholesome regimen.

By all means.

And truly, said I, these latter go on in a most charming fashion. For with all their doctoring they accomplish nothing except to complicate and augment their maladies. And they are always hoping that someone will recommend a panacea that will restore their health.

A perfect description, he said, of the state of such invalids.

And isn't this a charming trait in them, that they hate most in all the world him who tells them the truth, that until a man stops drinking and gorging and wenching and idling, neither drugs nor cautery nor the knife, no, nor spells nor periapts nor anything of that kind will fee of any avail?

Not altogether charming, he said, for there is no grace or charm being angry with him who speaks well.

You do not seem to be an admirer of such people, said I.

No, by heaven, I am not.

Neither then, if an entire city, as we were just now saying, acts in this way, will it have your approval, or don't you think that the way of such invalids is precisely that of those cities which being badly governed forewarn their citizens not to meddle with the general constitution of the state, denouncing death to whosoever attempts that—while whoever most agreeably serves them governed as they are and who curries favor with them by fawning upon them and anticipating their desires and by his cleverness in gratifying them, him they will account the good man, the man wise in worthwhile things, the man they will delight to honor?

Yes, he said, I think their conduct is identical, and I don't approve it in the very least.

And what again of those who are willing and eager to serve such states? Don't you admire their valiance and lighthearted irresponsibility?

I do, he said, except those who are actually deluded and suppose themselves to be in truth statesmen because they are praised by the many.

What do you mean? Can't you make allowances for the men? Do you think it possible for a man who does not know how to measure when a multitude of others equally ignorant assure him that he is four cubits tall not to suppose this to be the fact about himself?

Why no, he said, I don't think that.

Then don't be harsh with them. For surely such fellows are the most charming spectacle in the world when they enact and amend such laws as we just now described and are perpetually expecting to find a way of putting an end to frauds in business and in the other matters of which I was speaking because they can't see that they are in very truth trying to cut off a Hydra's head.

Indeed, he said, that is exactly what they are doing.

I, then, said I, should not have supposed that the true lawgiver ought to work out matters of that kind in the laws and the constitution of either an ill-governed or a well-governed state—in the one because they are useless and accomplish nothing, in the other because some of them anybody could discover and others will result spontaneously from the pursuits already described.

What part of legislation, then, he said, is still left for us?

And I replied, For us nothing, but for the Apollo of Delphi, the chief, the fairest, and the first of enactments.

What are they? he said.

The founding of temples, and sacrifices, and other forms of worship of gods, daemons, and heroes, and likewise the burial of the dead and the services we must render to the dwellers in the world beyond to keep them gracious. For of such matters we neither know anything nor in the founding of our city if we are wise shall we entrust them to any other or make use of any other interpreter than the god of our fathers. For this god surely is in such matters for all mankind the interpreter of the religion of their fathers who from his seat in the middle and at the very navel of the earth delivers his interpretation.

Excellently said, he replied, and that is what we must do.

At last, then, son of Ariston, said I, your city may be considered as established. The next thing is to procure a sufficient light somewhere and to look yourself, and call in the aid of your brother and of Polemarchus and the rest, if we may in any wise discover where justice and injustice should be in it, wherein they differ from one another, and which of the two he must have who is to be happy, alike whether his condition is known or not known to all gods and men.

Nonsense, said Glaucon, you promised that you would carry on the search yourself, admitting that it would be impious for you not to come to the aid of justice by every means in your power.

A true reminder, I said, and I must do so, but you also must lend a hand.

Well, he said, we will.

I expected then, said I, that we shall find it in this way. I think our city, if it has been rightly founded, is good in the full sense of the word.

Necessarily, he said.

Clearly, then, it will be wise, brave, sober, and just

Clearly.

Then if we find any of these qualities in it, the remainder will be that which we have not found?

Surely.

Take the case of any four other things. If we were looking for any one of them in anything and recognized the object of our search first, that would have been enough for us, but if we had recognized the other three first, that in itself would have made known to us the thing we were seeking. For plainly there was nothing left for it to be but the remainder.

Right, he said.

And so, since these are four, we must conduct the search in the same way.

Clearly.

And, moreover, the first thing that I think I clearly see therein is the wisdom, and there is something odd about that, it appears.

What? said he.

Wise in very deed I think the city that we have described is, for it is well counseled, is it not?

Yes.

And surely this very thing, good counsel, is a form of wisdom. For is not by ignorance but by knowledge that men counsel well.

Obviously.

But there are many and manifold knowledges or sciences in the city.

Of course.

Is it then owing to the science of her carpenters that a city is to be called wise and well advised?

By no means for that, but rather mistress of the arts of building. Then a city is not to be styled wise because of the deliberations of the science of wooden utensils for their best production?

No, I grant you.

Is it, then, because of that of brass implements or any other of that kind?

None whatsoever, he said.

Nor yet because of the science of the production of crops from the soil, but the name it takes from that is agricultural.

I think so.

Then, said I, is there any science in the city just founded by us residing in any of its citizens which does not take counsel about some particular thing in the city but about the city as a whole and the betterment of its relations with itself and other states?

Why, yes, there is.

What is it, said I, and in whom is it found?

It is the science of guardianship or government and it is to be found in those rulers to whom we just now gave the name of guardians in the full sense of the word.

And what term then do you apply to the city because of this knowledge?

Well-advised, he said, and truly wise.

Which class, then, said I, do you suppose will be the more numerous in our city, the smiths or these true guardians?

The smiths, by far, he said.

And would not these rulers be the smallest of all the groups of those who possess special knowledge and receive distinctive appellations?

By far.

Then it is by virtue of its smallest class and minutest part of itself, and the wisdom that resides therein, in the part which takes the lead and rules, that a city established on principles of nature would be wise as a whole. And as it appears these are by nature the fewest, the class to which it pertains to partake of the knowledge which alone of all forms of knowledge deserves the name of wisdom.

Most true, he said.

This one of our four, then, we have, I know not how, discovered, the thing itself and its place in the state.

I certainly think, said he, that it has been discovered sufficiently.

But again there is no difficulty in seeing bravery itself and the part of the city in which it resides for which the city is called brave.

How so?

Who, said I, in calling a city cowardly or brave would fix his eyes on any other part of it than that which defends it and wages war in its behalf?

No one at all, he said.

For the reason, I take it, said I, that the cowardice or the bravery of the other inhabitants does not determine for it the one quality or the other.

It does not.

Bravery too, then, belongs to a city by virtue of a part of itself owing to its possession in that part of a quality that under all conditions will preserve the conviction that things to be feared are precisely those which and such as the lawgiver inculcated in their education. Is not that what you call bravery?

I don't altogether understand what you said, he replied, but say it again.

A kind of conservation, I said, is what I mean by bravery.

What sort of a conservation?

The conservation of the conviction which the law has created by education about fearful things—what and what sort of things are to be feared. And by the phrase 'under all conditions' I mean that the brave man preserves it both in pain and pleasures and in desires and fears and does not expel it from his soul. And I may illustrate it by a similitude if you please.

I do.

You are aware that dyers when they wish to dye wool so as to hold the purple hue begin by selecting from the many colors there be the one nature of the white and then give it a careful preparatory treatment so that it will take the hue in the best way, and after the treatment, then and then only, dip it in the dye. And things that are dyed, by this process become fast-colored and washing, either with or without lyes cannot take away the sheen of their hues. But otherwise you know what happens to them, whether anyone dips other colors or even these without the preparatory treatment.

I know, he said, that they present a ridiculous and washed-out appearance.

By this analogy, then, said I, you must conceive what we too to the best of our ability were doing when we selected our soldiers and educated them in music and exercises of the body. The sole aim of our contrivance was that they should be convinced and receive our laws like a dye as it were, so that their belief and faith might be fast-colored about both the things that are to be feared and all other things because of the fitness of their nature and nurture, and that so their dyes might not be washed out by those lyes that have such dread power to scour our faiths away, pleasure more potent than any detergent or abstergent to accomplish this, and pain and fear, and desire more sure than any lye. This power in the soul, then, this unfailing conservation of right and lawful belief about things to be and not to be feared is what I call and would assume to be courage, unless you have something different to say.

No, nothing, said he, for I presume that you consider mere right opinion about the same matters not produced by education, that which may manifest itself in a beast or a slave, to have little or nothing to do with law and that you would call it by another name than courage.

That is most true, said I.

Well then, he said, I accept this as bravery.

Do so, said I, and you will be right, with the reservation that it is the courage of a citizen. Some other time, if it please you, we will discuss it more fully. At present we were not seeking this but justice, and for the purpose of that inquiry I believe we have done enough.

You are quite right, he said.

Two things still remain, said I, to make out in our city, soberness
and the object of the whole inquiry, justice.

Quite so.

If there were only some way to discover justice so that we need not further concern ourselves about soberness.

Well, I, for my part, he said, neither know of any such way nor would I wish justice to be discovered first if that means that we are not to go on to the consideration of soberness. But if you desire to please me, consider this before that.

It would certainly be very wrong of me not to desire it, said I.

Go on with the inquiry then, he said.

I must go on, I replied, and viewed from here it bears more likeness to a kind of concord and harmony than the other virtues did.

How so?

Soberness is a kind of beautiful order and a continence of certain pleasures and appetites, as they say, using the phrase 'master of himself' I know not how, and there are other similar expressions that as it were point us to the same trail. Is that not so?

Most certainly.

Now the phrase 'master of himself' is an absurdity, is it not? For he who is master of himself would also be subject to himself, and he who is subject to himself would be master. For the same person is spoken of in all these expressions.

Of course.

But, said I, the intended meaning of this way of speaking appears to me to be that the soul of a man within him has a better part and a worse part, and the expression self-mastery means the control of the worse by the naturally better part. It is, at any rate, a term of praise. But when, because of bad breeding or some association, the better part, which is the smaller, is dominated by the multitude of the worse,

I think that our speech censures this as a reproach, and calls the man in this plight unself-controlled and licentious.

That seems likely, he said.

Turn your eyes now upon our new city, said I, and you will find one of these conditions existent in it. For you will say that it is justly spoken of as master of itself if that in which the superior rules the inferior is to be called sober and self-mastered.

I do not turn my eyes upon it, he said, and it is as you say.

And again, the mob of motley appetites and pleasures and pains one would find chiefly in children and women and slaves and in the base rabble of those who are free men in name.

By all means.

But the simple and moderate appetites which with the aid of reason and right opinion are guided by consideration you will find in few and those the best born and best educated.

True, he said.

And do you not find this too in your city and a domination there of the desires in the multitude and the rabble by the desires and the wisdom that dwell in the minority of the better sort?

I do, he said.

If, then, there is any city that deserves to be described as master of its pleasures and desires and self-mastered, this one merits that designation.

Most assuredly, he said.

And is it not also to be called sober in all these respects?

Indeed it is, he said.

And yet again, if there is any city in which the rulers and the ruled are of one mind as to who ought to rule, that condition will be found in this. Don't you think so?

I most emphatically do, he said.

In which class of the citizens, then, will you say that the virtue of soberness has its seat when this is their condition? In the rulers or in the ruled?

In both, I suppose, he said.

Do you see then, said I, that our intuition was not a bad one just now that discerned a likeness between soberness and a kind of harmony?

Why so?

Because its operation is unlike that of courage and wisdom, which residing in separate parts respectively made the city, the one wise and the other brave. That is not the way of soberness, but it extends literally through the entire gamut throughout, bringing about the unison in the same chant of the strongest, the weakest, and the intermediate, whether in wisdom or, if you please, in strength, or for that matter in numbers, wealth, or any similar criterion. So that we should be quite right in affirming this unanimity to be soberness, the concord of the naturally superior and inferior as to which ought to rule in both the state and the individual.

I entirely concur, he said.

Very well, said I, we have made out these three forms in our city to the best of our present judgment. What can be the remaining form that would give the city still another virtue? For it is obvious that the remainder is justice.

Obvious.

Now then, Glaucon, is the time for us like huntsmen to surround the covert and keep close watch that justice may not slip through and get away from us and vanish from our sight. It plainly must be somewhere hereabout. Keep your eyes open then and do your best to descry it. You may see it before I do and point it out to me.

Would that I could, he said, but I think rather that if you find in me one who can follow you and discern what you point out to him you will be making a very fair use of me.

Pray for success then, said I, and follow along with me.

That I will do, only lead on, he said.

And truly, said I, it appears to be an inaccessible place, lying in deep shadows.

It certainly is a dark covert, not easy to beat up.

But all the same, on we must go.

Yes, on.

And I caught view and gave a halloo and said, Glaucon, I think we have found its trail and I don't believe it will get away from us.

I am glad to hear that, said he.

Truly, said I, we were slackers indeed.

How so?

Why, all the time, bless your heart, the thing apparently was tumbling about our feet from the start and yet we couldn't see it, but were most ludicrous, like people who sometimes hunt for what they holds in their hands. So we did not turn our eyes upon it, but looked off into the distance, which was perhaps the reason it escaped us.

What do you mean? he said.

This, I replied, that it seems to me that though we were speaking of it and hearing about it all the time we did not understand ourselves or realize that we were speaking of it in a sense.

That is a tedious prologue, he said, for an eager listener.

Listen then, said I, and learn if there is anything in what I say. For what we laid down in the beginning as a universal requirement when we were founding our city, this I think, or some form of this, is justice. And what we did lay down, and often said, if you recall, was that each one man must perform one social service in the state for which his nature was best adapted.

Yes, we said that.

And again, that to do one's own business and not to be a busybody is justice is a saying that we have heard from many and have very often repeated ourselves.

We have.

This, then, I said, my friend, if taken in a certain sense appears to be justice, this principle of doing one's own business. Do you know whence I infer this?

No, but tell me, he said.

I think that this is the remaining virtue in the state after our consideration of soberness, courage, and intelligence, a quality which made it possible for them all to grow up in the body politic and which when they have sprung up preserves them as long as it is present. And I hardly need to remind you that we said that justice would be the residue after we had found the other three.

That is an unavoidable conclusion, he said.

But moreover, said I, if we were required to decide what it is whose indwelling presence will contribute most to making our city good, it would be a difficult decision whether it was the unanimity of rulers and ruled or the conservation in the minds of the soldiers of the convictions produced by law as to what things are or are not to be feared, or the watchful intelligence that resides in the guardians, or whether this is the chief cause of its goodness, the principle embodied in child, woman, slave, free, artisan, ruler, and ruled, that each performed his one task as one man and was not a versatile busybody.

Hard to decide indeed, he said.

A thing, then, that in its contribution to the excellence of a state vies with and rivals its wisdom, its soberness, its bravery, is this principle of everyone in it doing his own task.

It is indeed, he said.

And is not justice the name you would have to give to the principle that rivals these as conducting to the virtue of a state?

By all means.

Consider it in this wise too, if so you will be convinced. Will you not assign the conduct of lawsuits in your state to the rulers?

Of course.

Will not this be the chief aim of their decisions, that no one shall have what belongs to others or be deprived of his own?

Nothing else but this.

On the assumption that this is just?

Yes.

From this point of view too, then, the having and doing of one's own and what belongs to oneself would admittedly be justice.

That is so.

Consider now whether you agree with me. A carpenter undertaking to do the work of a cobbler or a cobbler of a carpenter or their interchange of one another's tools or honors or even the attempt of the same man to do both—the confounding of all other functions would not, think you, greatly injure a state, would it?

Not much, he said.

But when, I fancy, one who is by nature an artisan or some kind of money-maker tempted and incited by wealth or command of votes or bodily strength or some similar advantage tries to enter into the class of the soldiers or one of the soldiers into the class of counselors and guardians, for which he is not fitted, and these interchange their tools and their honors or when the same man undertakes all these functions at once, then, I take it, you too believe that this kind of substitution and meddlesomeness is the ruin of a state.

By all means.

The interference with one another's business, then, of three existent classes, and the substitution of the one for the other, is the greatest injury to a state and would most rightly be designated as the thing which chiefly works it harm.

Precisely so.

And the thing that works the greatest harm to one's own state,

will you not pronounce to be injustice?

Of course.

This, then, is injustice. Again, let us put it in this way. The proper functioning of the money-makers, the helpers, and the guardians, each doing his own work in the state, being the reverse of that just described, would be justice and would render the city just.

I think the case is thus and no otherwise, said he.

Let us not yet affirm it quite fixedly, I said, but if this form, when applied to the individual man, is accepted there also as a definition of justice, we will then concede the point—for what else will there be to say? But if not, then we will look for something else. But now let us work out the inquiry in which we supposed that, if we found some larger thing that contained justice and viewed it there, we should more easily discover its nature in the individual man. And we agreed that this larger thing is the city, and so we constructed the best city in our power, well knowing that in the good city it would of course be found. What, then, we thought we saw there we must refer back to the individual and, if it is confirmed, all will be well. But if something different manifests itself in the individual, we will return again to the state and test it there and it may be that, by examining them side by side and rubbing them against one another, as it were from the fire sticks we may cause the spark of justice to flash forth, and when it is thus revealed confirm it in our own minds.

Well, he said, that seems a sound method and that is what we must do.

Then, said I, if you call a thing by the same name whether it is big or little, is it unlike in the way in which it is called the same or like?

Like, he said.

Then a just man too will not differ at all from a just city in respect of the very form of justice, but will be like it.

Yes, like.

But now the city was thought to be just because three natural kinds existing in it performed each its own function, and again it was sober, brave, and wise because of certain other affections and habits of these three kinds.

True, he said.

Then, my friend, we shall thus expect the individual also to have these same forms in his soul, and by reason of identical affections of these with those in the city to receive properly the same appellations.

Inevitable, he said.

Goodness gracious, said I, here is another trifling inquiry into which we have plunged, the question whether the soul really contains these three forms in itself or not.

It does not seem to me at all trifling, he said, for perhaps, Socrates, the saying is true that 'fine things are difficult.'

Apparently, said I, and let me tell you, Glaucon, that in my opinion we shall never apprehend this matter accurately from such methods as we are now employing in discussion. For there is another longer and harder way that conducts to this. Yet we may perhaps discuss it on the level of our previous statements and inquiries.

May we not acquiesce in that? he said. I for my part should be quite satisfied with that for the present.

And I surely should be more than satisfied, I replied.

Don't you weary then, he said, but go on with the inquiry.

Is it not, then, said I, impossible for us to avoid admitting this much, that the same forms and qualities are to be found in each one of us that are in the state? They could not get there from any other source. It would be absurd to suppose that the element of high spirit was not derived in states from the private citizens who are reputed to have this quality, as the populations of the Thracian and Scythian lands and generally of northern regions, or the quality of love of knowledge, which would chiefly be attributed to the region where we dwell, or the love of money which we might say is not least likely to be found in Phoenicians and the population of Egypt.

One certainly might, he replied.

This is the fact then, said I, and there is no difficulty in recognizing it.

Certainly not.

But the matter begins to be difficult when you ask whether we do all these things with the same thing or whether there are three things and we do one thing with one and one with another—learn with one part of ourselves, feel anger with another, and with yet a third desire the pleasures of nutrition and generation and their kind, or whether it is with the entire soul that we function in each case when we once begin. That is what is really hard to determine properly.

I think so too, he said.

Let us then attempt to define the boundary and decide whether they are identical with one another in this way.

How?

It is obvious that the same thing will never do or suffer opposites in the same respect in relation to the same thing and at the same time. So that if ever we find these contradictions in the functions of the mind we shall know that it was not the same thing functioning but a plurality.

Very well.

Consider, then, what I am saying.

Say on, he replied.

Is it possible for the same thing at the same time in the same respect to be at rest and in motion?

By no means.

Let us have our understanding still more precise, lest as we proceed we become involved in dispute. If anyone should say of a man standing still but moving his hands and head that the same man is at the same time at rest and in motion we should not, I take it, regard that as the right way of expressing it, but rather that a part of him is at rest and a part in motion. Is not that so?

It is.

Then if the disputant should carry the jest still further with the subtlety that tops at any rate stand still as a whole at the same time that they are in motion when with the peg fixed in one point they revolve, and that the same is true of any other case of circular motion about the same spot—we should reject the statement on the ground that the repose and the movement in such cases were not in relation to the same parts of the objects. But we would say that there was a straight line and a circumference in them and that in respect of the straight line they are standing still since they do not incline to either side, but in respect of the circumference they move in a circle, but that when as they revolve they incline the perpendicular to right or left or forward or back, then they are in no wise at rest.

And that would be right, he said.

No such remarks then will disconcert us or any whit the more make us believe that it is ever possible for the same thing at the same time in the same respect and the same relation to suffer, be,or do opposites.

They will not me, I am sure, said he.

All the same, said I, that we may not be forced to examine at tedious length the entire list of such contentions and convince ourselves that they are false, let us proceed on the hypothesis that this is so, with the understanding that, if it ever appear otherwise, everything that results from the assumption shall be invalidated.

That is what we must do, he said.

Will you not then, said I, set down as opposed to one another assent and dissent, and the endeavor after a thing to the rejection of it, and embracing to repelling—do not these and all things like these belong to the class of opposite actions or passions, it will make no difference which?

None, said he, but they are opposites.

What then, said I, of thirst and hunger and the appetites generally, and again consenting and willing—would you not put them all somewhere in the classes just described? Will you not say, for example, that the soul of one who desires either strives for that which he desires or draws toward its embrace what it wishes to accrue to it, or again, in so far as it wills that anything be presented to it, nods assent to itself thereon as if someone put the question, striving toward its attainment?

I would say so, he said.

But what of not-willing and not-consenting nor yet desiring? Shall we not put these under the soul's rejection and repulsion from itself and generally into the opposite class from all the former?

Of course.

This being so, shall we say that the desires constitute a class and that the most conspicuous members of that class are what we call thirst and hunger?

We shall, said he.

Is not the one desire of drink, the other of food?

Yes.

Then in so far as it is thirst, would it be of anything more than that of which we say it is a desire in the soul? I mean is thirst thirst for hot drink or cold or much or little or in a word for a draught of any particular quality, or is it the fact that if heat is attached to the thirst it would further render the desire—a desire of cold, and if cold of hot? But if owing to the presence of muchness the thirst is much it would render it a thirst for much and if little for little. But mere thirst will never be desire of anything else than that of which it is its nature to be, mere drink, and so hunger of food.

That is so, he said. Each desire in itself is of that thing only of which it is its nature to be. The epithets belong to the quality—such or such.

Let no one then, said I, disconcert us when off our guard with the objection that everybody desires not drink but good drink and not food but good food, because, the argument will run, all men desire good, and so, if thirst is desire, it would be of good drink or of good whatsoever it is, and so similarly of other desires.

Why, he said, there perhaps would seem to be something in that objection.

But I need hardly remind you, said I, that of relative terms those that are somehow qualified are related to a qualified correlate, those that are severally just themselves to a correlate that is just itself.

I don't understand, he said.

Don't you understand, said I, that the greater is such as to be greater than something?

Certainly.

Is it not than the less?

Yes.

But the much greater than the much less. Is that not so?

Yes.

And may we add the onetime greater than the onetime less and that which will be greater than that which will be less?

Surely.

And similarly of the more toward the fewer, and the double toward the half and of all like cases, and again of the heavier toward the lighter, the swifter toward the slower, and yet again of the hot toward the cold and all cases of that kind—does not the same hold?

By all means.

But what of the sciences? Is not the way of it the same? Science, which is just that, is of knowledge which is just that, or is of whatsoever we must assume the correlate of science to be. But a particular science of a particular kind is of some particular thing of a particular kind. I mean something like this. As there was a science of making a house it differed from other sciences so as to be named architecture.

Certainly.

Was not this by reason of its being of a certain kind such as no other of all the rest?

Yes.

And was it not because it was of something of a certain kind that it itself became a certain kind of science? And similarly of the other arts and sciences?

That is so.

This then, said I, if haply you now understand, is what you must say I then meant, by the statement that of all things that are such as to be of something, those that are just themselves only are of things just themselves only, but things of a certain kind are of things of a kind. And I don't at all mean that they are of the same kind as the things of which they are, so that we are to suppose that the science of health and disease is a healthy and diseased science and that of evil and good, evil and good. I only mean that as science became the science not of just the thing of which science is but of some particular kind of thing, namely, of health and disease, the result was that it itself became some kind of science and this caused it to be no longer called simply science but, with the addition of the particular kind, medical science.

I understand, he said, and agree that it is so.

To return to thirst, then, said I, will you not class it with the things that are of something and say that it is what it is in relation to something—and it is, I presume, thirst?

I will, said he, namely of drink.

Then if the drink is of a certain kind, so is the thirst, but thirst that is just thirst is neither of much nor little nor good nor bad, nor in a word of any kind, but just thirst is naturally of just drink only.

By all means.

The soul of the thirsty then, in so far as it thirsts, wishes nothing else than to drink, and yearns for this and its impulse is toward this.

Obviously.

Then if anything draws it back when thirsty it must be something different in it from that which thirsts and drives it like a beast to drink. For it cannot be, we say, that the same thing with the same part of itself at the same time acts in opposite ways about the same thing.

We must admit that it does not.

So I fancy it is not well said of the archer that his hands at the same time thrust away the bow and draw it nigh, but we should rather say that there is one hand that puts it away and another that draws it to.

By all means, he said.

Are we to say, then, that some men sometimes though thirsty refuse to drink?

We are indeed, he said, many and often.

What then, said I, should one affirm about them? Is it not that there is a something in the soul that bids them drink and a something that forbids, a different something that masters that which bids?

I think so.

And is it not the fact that that which inhibits such actions arises when it arises from the calculations of reason, but the impulses which draw and drag come through affections and diseases?

Apparently.

Not unreasonably, said I, shall we claim that they are two and different from one another, naming that in the soul whereby it reckons and reasons the rational, and that with which it loves, hungers, thirsts, and feels the flutter and titillation of other desires, the irrational and appetitive—companion of various repletions and pleasures.

It would not be unreasonable but quite natural, he said, for us to think this.

These two forms, then, let us assume to have been marked off as actually existing in the soul. But now the thumos, or principle of high spirit, that with which we feel anger, is it a third, or would it be identical in nature with one of these?

Perhaps, he said, with one of these, the appetitive.

But, I said, I once heard a story which I believe, that Leontius the son of Aglaion, on his way up from the Piraeus under the outer side of the northern wall, becoming aware of dead bodies that lay at the place of public execution at the same time felt a desire to see them and a repugnance and aversion, and that for a time he resisted and veiled his head, but overpowered in despite of all by his desire, with wide staring eyes he rushed up to the corpses and cried, There, ye wretches, take your fill of the fine spectacle !

I too, he said, have heard the story.

Yet, surely, this anecdote, I said, signifies that the principle of anger sometimes fights against desires as an alien thing against an alien.

Yes, it does, he said.

And do we not, said I, on many other occasions observe when his desires constrain a man contrary to his reason that he reviles himself and is angry with that within which masters him, and that as it were in a faction of two parties the high spirit of such a man becomes the ally of his reason? But its making common cause with the desires against the reason when reason whispers low, Thou must not—that, I think, is a kind of thing you would not affirm ever to have perceived in yourself, nor, I fancy, in anybody else either.

No, by heaven, he said.

Again, when a man thinks himself to be in the wrong, is it not true that the nobler he is the less is he capable of anger though suffering hunger and cold and whatsoever else at the hands of him whom he believes to be acting justly therein, and as I say his spirit refuses to be aroused against such a one?

True, he said.

But what when a man believes himself to be wronged? Does not his spirit in that case seethe and grow fierce—and also because of his suffering hunger, cold, and the like—and make itself the ally of what he judges just? And in noble souls it endures and wins the victory and will not let go until either it achieves its purpose, or death ends all, or, as a dog is called back by a shepherd, it is called back by the reason within and calmed.

Your similitude is perfect, he said, and it confirms our former statements that the helpers are as it were dogs subject to the rulers who are as it were the shepherds of the city.

You apprehend my meaning excellently, said I. But do you also take note of this?

Of what?

That what we now think about the spirited element is just the opposite of our recent surmise. For then we supposed it to be a part of the appetitive, but now, far from that, we say that, in the factions of the soul, it much rather marshals itself on the side of the reason.

By all means, he said.

Is it then distinct from this too, or is it a form of the rational, so that there are not three but two kinds in the soul, the rational and the appetitive? Or just as in the city there were three existing kinds that composed its structure, the money-makers, the helpers, the counselors, so also in the soul does there exist a third kind, this principle of high spirit, which is the helper of reason by nature unless it is corrupted by evil nurture?

We have to assume it as a third, he said.

Yes, said I, provided it shall have been shown to be something different from the rational, as it has been shown to be other than the appetitive.

That is not hard to be shown, he said, for that much one can see in children, that they are from their very birth chock-full of rage and high spirit, but as for reason, some of them, to my thinking, never participate in it, and the majority quite late.

Yes, by heaven, excellently said, I replied, and further, one could see in animals that what you say is true. And to these instances we may add the testimony of Homer quoted above, 'He smote his breast and chided thus his heart.'[2] For there Homer has clearly represented that in us which has reflected about the better and the worse as rebuking that which feels unreasoning anger as if it were a distinct and different thing.

You are entirely right, he said.

Through these waters, then, said I, we have with difficulty made our way and we are fairly agreed that the same kinds equal in number are to be found in the state and in the soul of each one of us.

That is so.

Then does not the necessity of our former postulate immediately follow, that as and whereby the state was wise, so and thereby is the individual wise?

Surely.

And so whereby and as the individual is brave, thereby and so is the state brave, and that both should have all the other constituents of virtue in the same way?

Necessarily.

Just too, then, Glaucon, I presume we shall say a man is in the same way in which a city was just.

That too is quite inevitable.

But we surely cannot have forgotten this, that the state was just by reason of each of the three classes found in it fulfilling its own function.

I don't think we have forgotten, he said.

We must remember, then, that each of us also in whom the several parts within him perform each their own task—he will be a just man and one who minds his own affair.

We must indeed remember, he said.

Does it not belong to the rational part to rule, being wise and exercising forethought in behalf of the entire soul, and to the principle of high spirit to be subject to this and its ally?

Assuredly.

Then is it not, as we said, the blending of music and gymnastics that will render them concordant, intensifying and fostering the one with fair words and teachings and relaxing and soothing and making gentle the other by harmony and rhythm?

Quite so, said he.

---

2 Odyssey 20.17.

And these two, thus reared and having learned and been educated to do their own work in the true sense of the phrase, will preside over the appetitive part which is the mass of the soul in each of us and the most insatiate by nature of wealth. They will keep watch upon it, lest, by being filled and infected with the so-called pleasures associated with the body and so waxing big and strong, it may not keep to its own work but may undertake to enslave and rule over the classes which it is not fitting that it should, and so overturn the entire life of all.

By all means, he said.

Would not these two, then, best keep guard against enemies from without also in behalf of the entire soul and body, the one taking counsel, the other giving battle, attending upon the ruler, and by its courage executing the ruler's designs?

That is so.

Brave, too, then, I take it, we call each individual by virtue of this part in him, when, namely, his high spirit preserves in the midst of pains and pleasures the rule handed down by the reason as to what is or is not to be feared.

Right, he said.

But wise by that small part that ruled in him and handed down these commands, by its possession in turn within it of the knowledge of what is beneficial for each and for the whole, the community composed of the three.

By all means.

And again, was he not sober by reason of the friendship and concord of these same parts, when, namely, the ruling principle and its two subjects are at one in the belief that the reason ought to rule, and do not raise faction against it?

The virtue of soberness certainly, said he, is nothing else than this, whether in a city or an individual.

But surely, now, a man is just by that which and in the way we have so often described.

That is altogether necessary.

Well then, said I, has our idea of justice in any way lost the edge of its contour so as to look like anything else than precisely what it showed itself to be in the state?

I think not, he said.

We might, I said, completely confirm your reply and our own conviction thus, if anything in our minds still disputes our definition—by applying commonplace and vulgar tests to it.

What are these?

For example, if an answer were demanded to the question concerning that city and the man whose birth and breeding was in harmony with it, whether we believe that such a man, entrusted with a deposit of gold or silver, would withhold it and embezzle it, who do you suppose would think that he would be more likely so to act than men of a different kind?

No one would, he said.

And would not he be far removed from sacrilege and theft and betrayal of comrades in private life or of the state in public?

He would.

And, moreover, he would not be in any way faithless either in the keeping of his oaths or in other agreements.

How could he?

Adultery, surely, and neglect of parents and of the due service of the gods would pertain to anyone rather than to such a man.

To anyone indeed, he said.

And is not the cause of this to be found in the fact that each of the principles within him does its own work in the matter of ruling and being ruled?

Yes, that and nothing else.

Do you still, then, look for justice to be anything else than this potency which provides men and cities of this sort?

No, by heaven, he said, I do not.

Finished, then, is our dream and perfected—the surmise we spoke of, that, by some providence, at the very beginning of our foundation of the state, we chanced to hit upon the original principle and a sort of type of justice.

Most assuredly.

It really was, it seems, Glaucon, which is why it helps, a sort of adumbration of justice, this principle that it is right for the cobbler by nature to cobble and occupy himself with nothing else, and the carpenter to practice carpentry, and similarly all others.

Clearly.

But the truth of the matter was, as it seems, that justice is indeed something of this kind, yet not in regard to the doing of one's own business externally, but with regard to that which is within and in the true sense concerns one's self, and the things of one's self. It means that a man must not suffer the principles in his soul to do each the work of some other and interfere and meddle with one another, but that he should dispose well of what in the true sense of the word is properly his own, and having first attained to self-mastery and beautiful order within himself, and having harmonized these three principles, the notes or intervals of three terms quite literally the lowest, the highest, and the mean, and all others there may be between them, and having linked and bound all three together and made of himself a unit, one man instead of many, self-controlled and in unison, he should then and then only turn to practice if he find aught to do either in the getting of wealth or the tendance of the body or it may be in political action or private business—in all such doings believing and naming the just and honorable action to be that which preserves and helps to produce this condition of soul, and wisdom the science that presides over such conduct, and believing and naming the unjust action to be that whichever tends to overthrow this spiritual constitution, and brutish ignorance to be the opinion that in turn presides over this.

What you say is entirely true, Socrates.

Well, said I, if we should affirm that we had found the just man and state and what justice really is in them, I think we should not be much mistaken.

No indeed, we should not, he said.

Shall we affirm it, then?

Let us so affirm.

So be it, then, said I. Next after this, I take it, we must consider injustice.

Obviously.

Must not this be a kind of civil war of these three principles, their meddlesomeness and interference with one another's functions, and the revolt of one part against the whole of the soul that it may hold therein a rule which does not belong to it, since its nature is such that it befits it to serve as a slave to the ruling principle? Something of this sort, I fancy, is what we shall say, and that the confusion of these principles and their straying from their proper course is injustice and licentiousness and cowardice and brutish ignorance and, in general, all turpitude.

Precisely this, he replied.

Then, said I, to act unjustly and be unjust and in turn to act justly—the meaning of all these terms becomes at once plain and clear, since injustice and justice are so.

How so?

Because, said I, these are in the soul what the healthful and the diseaseful are in the body; there is no difference.

In what respect? he said.

Healthful things surely engender health and diseaseful disease.

Yes.

Then does not doing just acts engender justice and unjust injustice?

Of necessity.

But to produce health is to establish the elements in a body in the natural relation of dominating and being dominated by one another, while to cause disease is to bring it about that one rules or is ruled by the other contrary to nature.

Yes, that is so.

And is it not likewise the production of justice in the soul to establish its principles in the natural relation of controlling and being controlled by one another, while injustice is to cause the one to rule or be ruled by the other contrary to nature?

Exactly so, he said.

Virtue, then, as it seems, would be a kind of health and beauty and good condition of the soul, and vice would be disease, ugliness, and weakness.

It is so.

Then is it not also true that beautiful and honorable pursuits tend to the winning of virtue and the ugly to vice?

Of necessity.

And now at last, it seems, it remains for us to consider whether it is profitable to do justice and practice honorable pursuits and be just, whether one is known to be such or not, or whether injustice profits, and to be unjust, if only a man escape punishment and is not bettered by chastisement.

Nay, Socrates, he said, I think that from this point on our inquiry becomes an absurdity—if, while life is admittedly intolerable with a ruined constitution of body even though accompanied by all the food and drink and wealth and power in the world, we are yet to be asked to suppose that, when the very nature and constitution of that whereby we live is disordered and corrupted, life is going to be worth living, if a man can only do as he pleases, and pleases to do anything save that which will rid him of evil and injustice and make him possessed of justice and virtue—now that the two have been shown to be as we have described them.

Yes, it is absurd, said I, but nevertheless, now that we have won to this height, we must not grow weary in endeavoring to discover with the utmost possible clearness that these things are so.

That is the last thing in the world we must do, he said.

Come up here then, said I, that you may see how many are the kinds of evil, I mean those that it is worth while to observe and distinguish.

I am with you, he said. Only do you say on.

And truly, said I, now that we have come to this height of argument I seem to see as from a point of outlook that there is one form of excellence, and that the forms of evil are infinite, yet that there are some four among them that it is worth while to take note of.

What do you mean? he said.

As many as are the varieties of political constitutions that constitute specific types, so many, it seems likely, are the characters of soul.

How many, pray?

There are five kinds of constitutions, said I, and five kinds of soul.

Tell me what they are, he said.

I tell you, said I, that one way of government would be the constitution that we have just expounded, but the names that might be applied to it are two. If one man of surpassing merit rose among the rulers, it would be denominated royalty; if more than one, aristocracy.

True, he said.

Well, then, I said, this is one of the forms I have in mind. For neither would a number of such men, nor one if he arose among them, alter to any extent worth mentioning the laws of our city—if he preserved the breeding and the education that we have described.

It is not likely, he said.

THE REPUBLIC OF PLATO
Book V

Translated by Paul Shorey

To such a city, then, or constitution I apply the terms good and right—and to the corresponding kind of man—but the others I describe as bad and mistaken, if this one is right, in respect both to the administration of states and to the formation of the character of the individual soul, they falling under four forms of badness.

What are these? he said.

And I was going on to enumerate them in what seemed to me the order of their evolution from one another, when Polemarchus—he sat at some little distance from Adimantus—stretched forth his hand, and, taking hold of his garment from above by the shoulder, drew the other toward him and, leaning forward himself, spoke a few words in his ear, of which we overheard nothing else save only this. Shall we let him off, then, he said, or what shall we do?

By no means, said Adimantus, now raising his voice.

What, pray, said I, is it that you are not letting off?

You, said he.

And for what special reason, pray? said I.

We think you are a slacker, he said, and are trying to cheat us out of a whole division, and that not the least, of the argument to avoid the trouble of expounding it, and expect to 'get away with it' by observing thus lightly that, of course, in respect to women and children it is obvious to everybody that the possessions of friends will be in common.

Well, isn't that right, Adimantus? I said.

Yes, said he, but this word 'right,' like other things, requires defining as to the way and manner of such a community. There might be many ways. Don't, then, pass over the one that you have in mind. For we have long been lying in wait for you, expecting that you would say something both of the procreation of children and their bringing-up, and would explain the whole matter of the community of women and children of which you speak. We think that the right or wrong management of this makes a great difference, all the difference in the world, in the constitution of a state; so now, since you are beginning on another constitution before sufficiently defining this, we are firmly resolved, as you overheard, not to let you go till you have expounded all this as fully as you did the rest.

Set me down, too, said Glaucon, as voting this ticket.

Surely, said Thrasymachus, you may consider it a joint resolution of us all, Socrates.

What a thing you have done, said I, in thus challenging me! What a huge debate you have started afresh, as it were, about this polity, in the supposed completion of which I was rejoicing, being only too glad to have it accepted as I then set it forth! You don't realize what a swarm of arguments you are stirring up by this demand, which I foresaw and evaded to save us no end of trouble.

Well, said Thrasymachus, do you suppose this company has come here to prospect for gold and not to listen to discussions?

Yes, I said, in measure.

Nay, Socrates, said Glaucon, the measure of listening to such discussions is the whole of life for reasonable men. So don't consider us, and do not you yourself grow weary in explaining to us what we ask for, your views as to how this communion of wives and children among our guardians will be managed, and also about the rearing of the children while still young in the interval between birth and formal schooling which is thought to be the most difficult part of education. Try, then, to tell us what must be the manner of it.

It is not an easy thing to expound, my dear fellow, said I, for even more than the provisions that precede it, it raises many doubts. For one might doubt whether what is proposed is possible and, even conceding the possibility, one might still be skeptical whether it is best. For which reason one, as it were, shrinks from touching on the matter lest the theory be regarded as nothing but a 'wish-thought,' my dear friend.

Do not shrink, he said, for your hearers will not be inconsiderate nor distrustful nor hostile.

And I said, My good fellow, is that remark intended to encourage me?

It is, he said.

Well then, said I, it has just the contrary effect. For, if I were confident that I was speaking with knowledge, it would be an excellent encouragement. For there are both safety and boldness in speaking the truth with knowledge about our greatest and dearest concerns to those who are both wise and dear. But to speak when one doubts himself and is seeking while he talks, as I am doing, is a fearful and slippery venture. The fear is not of being laughed at, for that is childish, but, lest, missing the truth, I fall down and drag my friends with me in matters where it most imports not to stumble. So I salute Nemesis, Glaucon, in what I am about to say. For, indeed, I believe that involuntary homicide is a lesser fault than to mislead opinion about the honorable, the good, and the just. This is a risk that it is better to run with enemies than with friends, so that your encouragement is none.

And Glaucon, with a laugh, said, Nay, Socrates, if any false note in the argument does us any harm, we release you as in a homicide case, and warrant you pure of hand and no deceiver of us. So speak on with confidence.

Well, said I, he who is released in that case is counted pure as the law bids, and, presumably, if there, here too.

Speak on, then, he said, for all this objection.

We must return then, said I, and say now what perhaps ought to have been said in due sequence there. But maybe this way is right, that after the completion of the male drama we should in turn go through with the female, especially since you are so urgent.

For men, then, born and bred as we described, there is in my opinion no other right possession and use of children and women than that which accords with the start we gave them. Our endeavor, I believe, was to establish these men in our discourse as the guardians of a flock?

Yes.

Let us preserve the analogy, then, and assign them a generation and breeding answering to it, and see if it suits us or not.

In what way? he said.

In this. Do we expect the females of watchdogs to join in guarding what the males guard and to hunt with them and share all their pursuits or do we expect the females to stay indoors as being incapacitated by the bearing and the breeding of the whelps while the males toil and have all the care of the flock?

They have all things in common, he replied, except that we treat the females as weaker and the males as stronger.

Is it possible, then, said I, to employ any creature for the same ends as another if you do not assign it the same nurture and education?

It is not possible.

If, then, we are to use the women for the same things as the men, we must also teach them the same things.

Yes.

Now music together with gymnastics was the training we gave the men.

Yes.

Then we must assign these two arts to the women also and the offices of war and employ them in the same way.

It would seem likely from what you say, he replied.

Perhaps, then, said I, the contrast with present custom would make much in our proposals look ridiculous if our words are to be realized in fact.

Yes, indeed, he said.

What then, said I, is the funniest thing you note in them? Is it not obviously the women exercising unclad in the palaestra together with the men, not only the young, but even the older, like old men in gymnasiums, when, though wrinkled and unpleasant to look at, they still persist in exercising?

Yes, on my word, he replied, it would seem ridiculous under present conditions.

Then, said I, since we have set out to speak our minds, we must not fear all the gibes with which the wits would greet so great a revolution, and the sort of things they would say about gymnastics and culture, and most of all about the bearing of arms and the bestriding of horses.

You're right, he said.

But since we have begun we must go forward to the rough part of our law, after begging these fellows not to mind their own business but to be serious, and reminding them that it is not long since the Greeks thought it disgraceful and ridiculous, as most of the barbarians do now, for men to be seen naked. And when the practice of athletics began, first with the Cretans and then with the Lacedaemonians, it was open to the wits of that time to make fun of these practices, don't you think so?

I do.

But when, I take it, experience showed that it is better to strip than to veil all things of this sort, then the laughter of the eyes faded away before that which reason revealed to be best, and this made it plain that he talks idly who deems anything else ridiculous but evil, and who tries to raise a laugh by looking to any other pattern of absurdity than that of folly and wrong or sets up any other standard of the beautiful as a mark for his seriousness than the good.

Most assuredly, said he.

Then is not the first thing that we have to agree upon with regard to these proposals whether they are possible or not? And we must throw open the debate to anyone who wishes either in jest or in earnest to raise the question whether female human nature is capable of sharing with the male all tasks or none at all, or some but not others, and under which of these heads this business of war falls. Would not this be that best beginning which would naturally and proverbially lead to the best end?

Far the best, he said.

Shall we then conduct the debate with ourselves in behalf of those others so that the case of the other side may not be taken defenseless and go by default?

Nothing hinders, he said.

Shall we say then in their behalf, There is no need, Socrates and Glaucon, of others disputing against you, for you yourselves at the beginning of the foundation of your city agreed that each one ought to mind as his own business the one thing for which he was fitted by nature? We did so agree, I think, certainly! Can it be denied then that there is by nature a great difference between men and women?

Surely there is. Is it not fitting, then, that a different function should be appointed for each corresponding to this difference of nature? Certainly. How, then, can you deny that you are mistaken and in contradiction with yourselves when you turn around and affirm that the men and the women ought to do the same thing, though their natures are so far apart? Can you surprise me with an answer to that question?

Not easily on this sudden challenge, he replied, but I will and do beg you to lend your voice to the plea in our behalf, whatever it may be.

These and many similar difficulties, Glaucon, said I, I foresaw and feared, and so shrank from touching on the law concerning the getting and breeding of women and children.

It does not seem an easy thing, by heaven, he said, no, by heaven.

No, it is not, said I, but the fact is that whether one tumbles into a little diving pool or plump into the great sea he swims all the same.

By all means.

Then we, too, must swim and try to escape out of the sea of argument in the hope that either some dolphin will take us on its back or some other desperate rescue,

So it seems, he said.

Come then, consider, said I, if we can find a way out. We did agree that different natures should have differing pursuits and that the natures of men and women differ. And yet now we affirm that these differing natures should have the same pursuits. That is the indictment?

It is.

What a grand thing, Glaucon, said I, is the power of the art of contradiction!

Why so?

Because, said I, many appear to me to fall into it even against their wills, and to suppose that they are not wrangling but arguing, owing to their inability to apply the proper divisions and distinctions to the subject under consideration. They pursue purely verbal oppositions, practicing eristic, not dialectic on one another.

Yes, this does happen to many, he said, but does this observation apply to us too at present?

Absolutely, said I. At any rate I am afraid that we are unawares slipping into contentiousness.

In what way?

The principle that natures not the same ought not to share in the same pursuits we are following up most manfully and eristically in the literal and verbal sense, but we did not delay to consider at all what particular kind of diversity and identity of nature we had in mind and with reference to what we were trying to define it when we assigned different pursuits to different natures and the same to the same.

No, we didn't consider that, he said.

Wherefore, by the same token, I said, we might ask ourselves whether the natures of bald and long-haired men are the same and not, rather, the contrary. And, after agreeing that they were opposed, we might, if the bald cobbled, forbid the long-haired to do so, or vice versa.

That would be ridiculous, he said.

Would it be so, said I, for any other reason than that we did not then posit likeness and difference of nature in any and every sense, but were paying heed solely to the kind of diversity and homogeneity that was pertinent to the pursuits themselves? We meant, for example, that a man and a woman who have a physician's mind have the same nature. Don't you think so?

I do.

But that a man physician and a man carpenter have different natures?

Certainly, I suppose.

Similarly, then, said I, if it appears that the male and the female sex have distinct qualification for any arts or pursuits, we shall affirm that they ought to be assigned respectively to each. But if it appears that they differ only in just this respect that the female bears and the male begets, we shall say that no proof has yet been produced that the woman differs from the man for our purposes, but we shall continue to think that our guardians and their wives ought to follow the same pursuits.

And rightly, said he.

Then, is it not the next thing to bid our opponent tell us precisely

for what art or pursuit concerned with the conduct of a state the woman's nature differs from the man's?

That would be at any rate fair.

Perhaps, then, someone else, too, might say what you were saying a while ago, that it is not easy to find a satisfactory answer on a sudden, but that with time for reflection there is no difficulty.

He might say that.

Shall we, then, beg the raiser of such objections to follow us, if we may perhaps prove able to make it plain to him that there is no pursuit connected with the administration of a state that is peculiar to woman?

By all means.

Come then, we shall say to him, answer our question. Was this the basis of your distinction between the man naturally gifted for anything and the one not so gifted— that the one learned easily, the other with difficulty, that the one with slight instruction could discover much for himself in the matter studied, but the other, after much instruction and drill, could not even remember what he had learned, and that the bodily faculties of the one adequately served his mind, while, for the other, the body was a hindrance? Were there any other points than these by which you distinguish the well-endowed man in every subject and the poorly endowed?

No one, said he, will be able to name any others.

Do you know, then, of anything practiced by mankind in which the masculine sex does not surpass the female on all these points? Must we make a long story of it by alleging weaving and the watching of pancakes and the boiling pot, whereon the sex plumes itself and wherein its defeat will expose it to most laughter?

You are right, he said, that the one sex is far surpassed by the other in everything, one may say. Many women, it is true, are better than many men in many things, but broadly speaking, it is as you say.

Then there is no pursuit of the administrators of a state that belongs to a woman because she is a woman or to a man because he is a man. But the natural capacities are distributed alike among both creatures, and women naturally share in all pursuits and men in all—yet for all the woman is weaker than the man.

Assuredly.

Shall we, then, assign them all to men and nothing to women?

How could we?

We shall rather, I take it, say that one woman has the nature of a physician and another not, and one is by nature musical, and another unmusical?

Surely.

Can we, then, deny that one woman is naturally athletic and warlike and another unwarlike and averse to gymnastics?

I think not.

And again, one a lover, another a hater, of wisdom? And one high-spirited, and the other lacking spirit?

That also is true.

Then it is likewise true that one woman has the qualities of a guardian and another not. Were not these the natural qualities of the men also whom we selected for guardians?

They were.

The women and the men, then, have the same nature in respect to the guardianship of the state, save in so far as the one is weaker, the other stronger.

Apparently.

Women of this kind, then, must be selected to cohabit with men of this kind and to serve with them as guardians since they are capable of it and akin by nature.

By all means.

And to the same natures must we not assign the same pursuits?

The same.

We come round, then, to our previous statement, and agree that it does not run counter to nature to assign music and gymnastics to the wives of the guardians.

By all means.

Our legislation, then, was not impracticable or Utopian, since the law we proposed accorded with nature. Rather, the other way of doing things, prevalent today, proves, as it seems, unnatural.

Apparently.

The object of our inquiry was the possibility and the desirability of what we were proposing?

It was.

That it is possible has been admitted.

Yes.

The next point to be agreed upon is that it is the best way.

Obviously.

For the production of a female guardian, then, our education

will not be one thing for men and another for women, especially since the nature which we hand over to it is the same.

There will be no difference.

How are you minded, now, in this matter?

In what?

In the matter of supposing some men to be better and some worse, or do you think them all alike?

By no means.

In the city, then, that we are founding, which do you think will prove the better men, the guardians receiving the education which we have described or the cobblers educated by the art of cobbling?

An absurd question, he said,

I understand, said I, and are not these the best of all the citizens?

By far.

And will not these women be the best of all the women?

They, too, by far.

Is there anything better for a state than the generation in it of the best possible women and men?

There is not.

And this, music and gymnastics applied as we described will effect.

Surely.

Then the institution we proposed is not only possible but the best for the state.

That is so.

The women of the guardians, then, must strip, since they will be clothed with virtue as a garment, and must take their part with the men in war and the other duties of civic guardianship and have no other occupation. But in these very duties lighter tasks must be assigned to the women than to the men because of their weakness as a class. But the man who ridicules unclad women, exercising because it is best that they should, 'plucks the unripe fruit' of laughter and does not know, it appears, the end of his laughter nor what he would be at. For the fairest thing that is said or ever will be said is this, that the helpful is fair and the harmful foul.

Assuredly.

In this matter, then, of the regulation of women, we may say that we have surmounted one of the waves of our paradox and have not been quite swept away by it in ordaining that our guardians and female guardians must have all pursuits in common, but that in some sort the argument concurs with itself in the assurance that what it proposes is both possible and beneficial.

It is no slight wave that you are thus escaping.

You will not think it a great one, I said, when you have seen the one that follows.

Say on then and show me, said he.

This, said I, and all that precedes has for its sequel, in my opinion, the following law. What?

That these women shall all be common to all these men, and that none shall cohabit with any privately, and that the children shall be common, and that no parent shall know its own offspring nor any child its parent.

This is a far bigger paradox than the other, and provokes more distrust as to its possibility and its utility.

I presume, said I, that there would be no debate about its utility, no denial that the community of women and children would be the greatest good, supposing it possible. But I take it that its possibility or the contrary would be the chief topic of contention.

Both, he said, would be right sharply debated.

You mean, said I, that I have to meet a coalition of arguments. But I expected to escape from one of them, and that if you agreed that the thing was beneficial, it would remain for me to speak only of its feasibility.

You have not escaped detection, he said, in your attempted flight, but you must render an account of both.

I must pay the penalty, I said, yet do me this much grace. Permit me to take a holiday, just as men of lazy minds are wont to feast themselves on their own thoughts when they walk alone. Such persons, without waiting to discover how their desires may be realized, dismiss that topic to save themselves the labor of deliberating about possibilities and impossibilities, assume their wish fulfilled, and proceed to work out the details in imagination, and take pleasure in portraying what they will do when it is realized, thus making still more idle a mind that is idle without that. I too now succumb to this weakness and desire to postpone and examine later the question of feasibility, but will at present assume that, and will, with your permission, inquire how the rulers will work out the details in practice, and try to show that nothing could be more beneficial to the state and its guardians than the effective operation of our plan. This is what I would try to consider first together with you, and thereafter the other topic, if you allow it.

I do allow it, he said. Proceed with the inquiry.

I think, then, said I, that the rulers, if they are to deserve that name, and their helpers likewise, will, the one, be willing to accept orders, and the other, to give them, in some things obeying our laws, and imitating them in others which we leave to their discretion.

Presumably.

You, then, the lawgiver, I said, have picked these men and similarly will select to give over to them women as nearly as possible of the same nature. And they, having houses and meals in common, and no private possessions of that kind, will dwell together, and being commingled in gymnastics and in all their life and education, will be conducted by innate necessity to sexual union. Is not what I say a necessary consequence?

Not by the necessities of geometry, he said, but by those of love, which are perhaps keener and more potent than the other to persuade and constrain the multitude.

They are, indeed, I said. But next, Glaucon, disorder and promiscuity in these unions or in anything else they do would be an unhallowed thing in a happy state and the rulers will not suffer it.

It would not be right, he said.

Obviously, then, we must arrange marriages, sacramental so far as may be. And the most sacred marriages would be those that were most beneficial.

By all means.

How, then, would the greatest benefit result? Tell me this, Glaucon. I see that you have in your house hunting dogs and a number of pedigreed cocks. Have you ever considered something about their unions and procreations?

What? he said.

In the first place, I said, among these themselves, although they are a select breed, do not some prove better than the rest?

They do.

Do you then breed from all indiscriminately, or are you careful to breed from the best?

From the best.

And, again, do you breed from the youngest or the oldest, or, so far as may be, from those in their prime?

From those in their prime.

And if they are not thus bred, you expect, do you not, that your birds' breed and hounds will greatly degenerate?

I do, he said.

And what of horses and other animals? I said. Is it otherwise with them?

It would be strange if it were, said he.

Gracious, said I, dear friend, how imperative, then, is our need of the highest skill in our rulers, if the principle holds also for mankind.

Well, it does, he said, but what of it?

This, said I, that they will have to employ many of those drugs of which we were speaking. We thought that an inferior physician sufficed for bodies that do not need drugs but yield to diet and regimen. But when it is necessary to prescribe drugs we know that a more enterprising and venturesome physician is required.

True, but what is the pertinency?

This, said I. It seems likely that our rulers will have to make considerable use of falsehood and deception for the benefit of their subjects. We said, I believe, that the use of that sort of thing was in the category of medicine.

And that was right, he said.

In our marriages, then, and the procreation of children, it seems there will be no slight need of this kind of 'right.'

How so?

It follows from our former admissions, I said, that the best men must cohabit with the best women in as many cases as possible and the worst with the worst in the fewest, and that the offspring of the one must be reared and that of the other not, if the flock is to be as perfect as possible. And the way in which all this is brought to pass must be unknown to any but the rulers, if, again, the herd of guardians is to be as free as possible from dissension.

Most true, he said.

We shall, then, have to ordain certain festivals and sacrifices, in which we shall bring together the brides and the bridegrooms, and our poets must compose hymns suitable to the marriages that then take place. But the number of the marriages we will leave to the discretion of the rulers, that they may keep the number of the citizens as nearly as may be the same, taking into account wars and diseases and all such considerations, and that, so far as possible, our city may not grow too great or too small.

Right, he said.

Certain ingenious lots, then, I suppose, must be devised so that the inferior man at each conjugation may blame chance and not the rulers.

Yes, indeed, he said.

And on the young men, surely, who excel in war and other pursuits we must bestow honors and prizes, and, in particular, the opportunity of more frequent intercourse with the women, which will at the same time be a plausible pretext for having them beget as many of the children as possible.

Right.

And the children thus born will be taken over by the officials appointed for this, men or women or both, since, I take it, the official posts too are common to women and men.

Yes.

The offspring of the good, I suppose, they will take to the pen or crèche, to certain nurses who live apart in a quarter of the city, but the offspring of the inferior, and any of those of the other sort who are born defective, they will properly dispose of in secret, so that no one will know what has become of them.

That is the condition, he said, of preserving the purity of the guardians' breed.

They will also supervise the nursing of the children, conducting the mothers to the pen when their breasts are full, but employing every device to prevent anyone from recognizing her own infant. And they will provide others who have milk if the mothers are insufficient. But they will take care that the mothers themselves shall not suckle too long, and the trouble of wakeful nights and similar burdens they will devolve upon the nurses, wet and dry.

You are making maternity a soft job for the women of the guardians.

It ought to be, said I, but let us pursue our design. We said that the offspring should come from parents in their prime.

True.

Do you agree that the period of the prime may be fairly estimated at twenty years for a woman and thirty for a man?

How do you reckon it? he said.

The women, I said, beginning at the age of twenty, shall bear for the state to the age of forty, and the man shall beget for the state from the time he passes his prime in swiftness in running to the age of fifty-five.

That is, he said, the maturity and prime for both of body and mind.

Then, if anyone older or younger than the prescribed age meddles with procreation for the state, we shall say that his error is an impiety and an injustice, since he is begetting for the city a child whose birth, if it escapes discovery, will not be attended by the sacrifices and the prayers which the priests and priestesses and the entire city prefer at the ceremonial marriages, that ever better offspring may spring from good sires and from fathers helpful to the state sons more helpful still. But this child will be born in darkness and conceived in foul incontinence.

Right, he said.

And the same rule will apply, I said, if any of those still within the age of procreation goes in to a woman of that age with whom the ruler has not paired him. We shall say that he is imposing on the state a baseborn, uncertified, and unhallowed child.

Most rightly, he said.

But when, I take it, the men and the women have passed the age of lawful procreation, we shall leave the men free to form such relations with whomsoever they please, except daughter and mother and their direct descendants and ascendants, and likewise the women, save with son and father, and so on, first admonishing them preferably not even to bring to light anything whatever thus conceived, but if they are unable to prevent a birth to dispose of it on the understanding that we cannot rear such an offspring.

All that sounds reasonable, he said, but how are they to distinguish one another's fathers and daughters, and the other degrees of kin that you have just mentioned?

They won't, said I, except that a man will call all male offspring born in the tenth and in the seventh month after he became a bridegroom his sons, and all female, daughters, and they will call him father. And, similarly, he will call their offspring his grandchildren and they will call his group grandfathers and grandmothers. And all children born in the period in which their fathers and mothers were procreating will regard one another as brothers and sisters. This will suffice for the prohibitions of intercourse of which we just now spoke. But the law will allow brothers and sisters to cohabit if the lot so falls out and the Delphic oracle approves.

Quite right, said he.

This, then, Glaucon, is the manner of the community of wives and children among the guardians. That it is consistent with the rest of our polity and by far the best way is the next point that we must get confirmed by the argument. Is not that so?

It is, indeed, he said.

Is not the logical first step toward such an agreement to ask ourselves what we could name as the greatest good for the constitution of a state and the proper aim of a lawgiver in his legislation, and what would be the greatest evil, and then to consider whether the proposals we have just set forth fit into the footprints of the good and do not suit those of the evil?

By all means, he said.

Do we know of any greater evil for a state than the thing that distracts it and makes it many instead of one, or a greater good than that which bind it together an makes it one?

We do not.

Is not, then, the community of pleasure and pain the tie that binds, when, so far as may be, all the citizens rejoice and grieve alike at the same births and deaths?

By all means, he said.

But the individualization of these feelings is a dissolvent, when some grieve exceedingly and others rejoice at the same happenings to the city and its inhabitants?

Of course.

And the chief cause of this is when the citizens do not utter in unison such words as 'mine' and 'not mine,' and similarly with regard to the word 'alien'?

Precisely so.

That city, then, is best ordered in which the greatest number use the expression 'mine' and 'not mine' of the same things in the same way.

Much the best.

And the city whose state is most like that of an individual man. For example, if the finger of one of us is wounded, the entire community of bodily connections stretching to the soul for 'integration' with the dominant part is made aware, and all of it feels the pain as a whole, though it is a part that suffers, and that is how we come to say that the man has a pain in his finger. And for any other member of the man the same statement holds, alike for a part that labors in pain or is eased by pleasure.

The same, he said, and, to return to your question, the best-governed state most nearly resembles such an organism.

That is the kind of a state, then, I presume, that, when anyone of the citizens suffers aught of good or evil, will be most likely to speak of the part that suffers as its own and will share the pleasure or the pain as a whole.

Inevitably, he said, if it is well governed.

It is time, I said, to return to our city and observe whether it, rather than any other, embodies the qualities agreed upon in our argument.

We must, he said.

Well, then, there are to be found in other cities rulers and the people as in our city, are there not?

There are.

Will not all these address one another as fellow citizens?

Of course.

But in addition to citizens, what do the people in other states call their rulers?

In most cities, masters, in democratic cities, just this—rulers.

But what of the people in our city. In addition to citizens, what do they call their rulers ?

Saviors and helpers, he said.

And what term do these apply to the people?

Payers of their wage and supporters.

And how do the rulers in other states denominate the populace?

Slaves, he said.

And how do the rulers describe one another?

Corulers, he said.

And ours?

Coguardians.

Can you tell me whether any of the rulers in other states would speak of some of their corulers as 'belonging' and others as outsiders?

Yes, many would.

And such a one thinks and speaks of the one that 'belongs' as his own, doesn't he, and of the outsider as not his own?

That is so.

But what of your guardians? Could any of them think or speak of his coguardian as an outsider?

By no means, he said, for no matter whom he meets, he will feel that he is meeting a brother, a sister, a father, a mother, a son, a daughter, or the offspring or forebears of these.

Excellent, said I, but tell me this further. Will it be merely the names of this kinship that you have prescribed for them or must all their actions conform to the names in all customary observance toward fathers and in awe and care and obedience for parents, if they look for the favor of either gods or men, since any other behavior would be neither just nor pious? Shall these be the unanimous oracular voices that they hear from all the people, or shall some other kind of teaching beset the ears of your children from their birth, both concerning what is due to those who are pointed out as their fathers and to their other kin?

These, he said, for it would be absurd for them merely to pronounce with their lips the names of kinship without the deeds.

Then, in this city more than in any other, when one citizen fares well or ill, men will pronounce in unison the word of which we spoke, It is *mine* that does well, or, It is *mine* that does ill.

That is most true, he said.

And did we not say that this conviction and way of speech brings with it a community in pleasures and pains?

And rightly, too.

Then these citizens, above all others, will have one and the same thing in common which they will name mine, and by virtue of this communion they will have their pleasures and pains in common.

Quite so.

And is not the cause of this, besides the general constitution of the state, the community of wives and children among the guardians?

It will certainly be the chief cause, he said.

But we further agreed that this unity is the greatest blessing for a state, and we compared a well-governed state to the human body in its relation to the pleasure and pain of its parts.

And we were right in so agreeing.

Then it is the greatest blessing for a state of which the community of women and children among the helpers has been shown to be the cause.

Quite so, he said.

And this is consistent with what we said before. For we said, I believe, that these helpers must not possess houses of their own or land or any other property, but that they should receive from the other citizens for their support the wage of their guardianship and all spend it in common. That was the condition of their being true guardians.

Right, he said.

Is it not true, then, as I am trying to say, that those former and these present prescriptions tend to make them still more truly guardians and prevent them from distracting the city by referring mine not to the same but to different things, one man dragging off to his own house anything he is able to acquire apart from the rest, and another doing the same to his own separate house, and having women and children apart, thus introducing into the state the pleasures and pains of individuals? They should all rather, we said, share one conviction about their own, tend to one goal, and so far as practicable have one experience of pleasure and pain.

By all means, he said.

Then will not lawsuits and accusations against one another vanish, one may say, from among them, because they have nothing in private possession but their bodies, but all else in common? So that we can count on their being free from the dissensions that arise among men from the possession of property, children, and kin.

They will necessarily be quit of these, he said.

And again, there could not rightly arise among them any lawsuits for assault or bodily injury. For as between agefellows we shall say that self-defense is honorable and just, thereby compelling them to keep their bodies in condition.

Right, he said.

And there will be the further advantage in such a law that an angry man, satisfying his anger in such wise, would be less likely to carry the quarrel to further extremes.

Assuredly.

As for an older man, he will always have the charge of ruling and chastising the younger.

Obviously.

Again it is plain that the young man, except by command of the rulers, will probably not do violence to an elder or strike him, or, I take it, dishonor him in any other way. There being the two competent guardians to prevent that, fear and awe, awe restraining him from laying hands on one who may be his parent, and fear in that the others will rush to the aide of the sufferer, some as sons, some as brothers, some as fathers.

That is the way it works out he said.

Then in all cases the laws will leave these men to dwell in peace together.

Great peace.

And if these are free from dissensions among themselves, there is no fear that the rest of the city will ever start faction against them or with one another.

No, there is not.

But I hesitate, so unseemly are they, even to mention the pettiest troubles of which they would be rid, the flatterings of the rich, the embarrassments and pains of the poor in the bringing-up of their children and the procuring of money for the necessities of life for their households, the borrowings, the repudiations, all the devices with which they acquire what they deposit with wives and servitors to husband, and all the indignities that they endure in such matters, which are obvious and ignoble and not deserving of mention.

Even a blind man can see these, he said.

From all these, then, they will be finally free, and they will live a happier life than that men count most happy, the life of the victors at Olympia.

How so?

The things for which those are felicitated are a small part of what is secure for these. Their victory is fairer and their public support more complete. For the prize of victory that they win is the salvation of the entire state, the fillet that binds their brows is the public support of themselves and their children—they receive honor from the city while they live and when they die a worthy burial.

A fair guardian, indeed, he said.

Do you recall, said I, that in the preceding argument the objection of somebody or other rebuked use for not making our guardians happy, since, though it was in their power to have everything of the citizens, they had nothing, and we, I believe, replied that this was a consideration to which we would not return of occasion offered, but that at present we were making our guardians guardians and the city as a whole happy as possible, and that we were not modeling our ideal of happiness with reference to any one class?

I do remember, he said.

Well then, since now the life of our helpers has been shown to be far fairer and better than that of the victors at Olympia, need we compare it with the life of cobblers and other craftsmen and farmers?

I think not, he said.

But further, we may fairly repeat what I was saying then also, that if the guardian shall strive for a kind of happiness that will unmake him as a guardian and shall not be content with the way of life that is so moderate and secure and, as we affirm, the best, but if some senseless and childish opinion about happiness shall beset him and impel him to use his power to appropriate everything in the city for himself, then he will find out that Hesiod was indeed wise, who said that the half was in some sort more than the whole.

If he accept my counsel, he said, he will abide in this way of life.

You accept, then, as we have described it, this partnership of the women with our men in the matter of education and children and the guardianship of the other citizens, and you admit that both within the city and when they go forth to war they ought to keep guard together and hunt together as it were like hounds, and have all things in every way, so far as possible, in common, and that so doing they will do what is for the best and nothing that is contrary to female human nature in comparison with male or to their natural fellowship with one another.

I do admit it, he said.

Then, I said, is not the thing that it remains to determine this, whether, namely, it possible for such a community to be brought about among men as it is in the other animals, and in what way it is possible?

You have anticipated, he said, the point I was about to raise.

For as for their wars, I said, the manner in which they will conduct them is too obvious for discussion.

How so? said he.

It is obvious that they will march out together, and, what is more, will conduct their children to war when they are sturdy, in order that, like the children of other craftsmen, they may observe the processes of which they must be master in their maturity, and in addition to looking on they must assist and minister in all the business of war and serve their fathers and mothers. Or have you never noticed the practice in the arts, how for example the sons of potters look on as helpers a long time before they put their hands to the clay?

They do, indeed.

Should these then be more concerned than our guardians to train the children by observation and experience of what is to be their proper business?

That would be ridiculous, he said.

But, further, when it comes to fighting, every creature will do better in the presence of its offspring?

That is so, but the risk, Socrates, is not slight, in the event of disasters such as may happen in war, that, losing their children as well as themselves, they make it impossible for the remnant of the state to recover.

What you say is true, I replied, but, in the first place, is it your idea that the one thing for which we must provide is the avoidance of all danger?

By no means.

And, if they must incur danger, should it not be for something in which success will make them better?

Clearly.

Do you think it makes a slight difference and not worth some risk whether men who are to be warriors do or do not observe war as boys?

No, it makes a great difference for the purpose of which you speak.

Starting, then, from this assumption that we are to make the boys spectators of war, we must further contrive security for them and all will be well, will it not?

Yes.

To begin with, then, said I, will not the fathers be, humanly speaking, not ignorant of war and shrewd judges of which campaigns are hazardous and which not?

Presumably, he said.

They will take the boys with them to the one and avoid the others?

Rightly.

And for officers, I presume, said I, they will put in charge of them not those who are good for nothing else but men who by age and experience are qualified to serve at once as leaders and as caretakers of children.

Yes, that would be the proper way.

Still, we may object, it is the unexpected that happens to many in many cases.

Yes, indeed.

To provide against such chances, then, we must wing the children from the start so that if need arises they may fly away and escape.

What do you mean? he said.

We must mount them when very young, said I, and first have them taught to ride, and then conduct them to the scene of war, not on mettlesome war steeds, but on the swiftest and gentlest horses possible, for thus they will have the best view of their own future business and also, if need arises, will most securely escape to safety in the train of elder guides.

I think you are right, he said.

But now what of the conduct of war? What should be the attitude of the soldiers to one another and the enemy? Am I right in my notions or not?

Tell me what notions, he said.

Any one of them who deserts his post, or flings away his weapons, or is guilty of any similar act of cowardice, should be reduced, to the artisan or farmer class, should he not?

By all means.

And anyone who is taken alive by the enemy we will make a present of to his captors, shall we not, to deal with their catch as they please?

Quite so.

And don't you agree that the one who wins the prize of valor and distinguishes himself shall first be crowned by his fellows in the campaign, by the lads and boys each in turn?

I do.

And be greeted with the right hand?

That, too.

But I presume you wouldn't go as far as this?

What?

That he should kiss and be kissed by everyone?

By all means, he said, and I add to the law the provision that during that campaign none whom he wishes to kiss be allowed to refuse, so that if one is in love with anyone, male or female, he may be the more eager to win the prize.

Excellent, said I, and we have already said that the opportunity of marriage will be more readily provided for the good man, and that he will be more frequently selected than the others for participation in that sort of thing, in order that as many children as possible may be born from such stock.

We have, he replied.

But, furthermore, we may cite Homer too for the justice of honoring in such ways the valiant among our youth. For Homer says that Ajax, who had distinguished himself in the war, was honored with the long chine, assuming that the most fitting meed for a brave man in the prime of his youth is that from which both honor and strength will accrue to him.

Most rightly, he said.

We will then, said I, take Homer as our guide in this at least. We, too, at sacrifices and on other like occasions, will reward the good so far as they have proved themselves good with hymns and the other

privileges of which we have just spoken, and also with 'seats of honor and meat and full cups,'[1] so as to combine physical training with honor for the good, both men and women.

---

1 Iliad 8.162.

Nothing could be better, he said.

Very well, and of those who die on campaign, if anyone's death has been especially glorious, shall we not, to begin with, affirm that he belongs to the golden race?

By all means.

And shall we not believe Hesiod who tells us that when men of this race die, so it is that they become

Hallowed spirits dwelling on earth, averters of evil,
Guardians watchful and good of articulate-speaking mortals? [2]

We certainly shall believe him.

We will inquire of Apollo, then, how and with what distinction we are to bury men of more than human, of divine, qualities, and deal with them according to his response.

How can we do otherwise?

And ever after we will bestow on their graves the tendance and worship paid to spirits divine. And we will practice the same observance when any who have been adjudged exceptionally good in the ordinary course of life die of old age or otherwise?

That will surely be right, he said.

But again, how will our soldiers conduct themselves toward enemies?

In what respect?

First, in the matter of making slaves of the defeated, do you think it right for Greeks to reduce Greek cities to slavery, or rather that, so far as they are able, they should not suffer any other city to do so, but should accustom Greeks to spare Greeks, foreseeing the danger of enslavement by the barbarians?

Sparing them is wholly and altogether the better, said he.

They are not, then, themselves to own Greek slaves, either, and they should advise the other Greeks not to?

By all means, he said. At any rate in that way they would be more likely to turn against the barbarians and keep their hands from one another.

And how about stripping the dead after victory of anything except their weapons— is that well? Does it not furnish a pretext to cowards not to advance on the living foe, as if they were doing something needful when poking about the dead? Has not this snatching at the spoils ere now destroyed many an army?

Yes, indeed.

And don't you think it illiberal and greedy to plunder a corpse, and is it not the mark of a womanish and petty spirit to deem the body of the dead an enemy when the real foeman has flown away and left behind only the instrument with which he fought? Do you see any difference between such conduct and that of the dogs who snarl at the stones that hit them but don't touch the thrower?

Not the slightest.

---

2   Works and Days 121 sq.

We must abandon, then, the plundering of corpses and the refusal to permit their burial.

By heaven, we certainly must, he said.

And again, we will not take weapons to the temples for dedicatory offerings, especially the weapons of Greeks, if we are at all concerned to preserve friendly relations with the other Greeks. Rather we shall fear that there is pollution in bringing such offerings to the temples from our kind unless in a case where the god bids otherwise.

Most rightly, he said.

And in the matter of devastating the land of Greeks and burning their houses, how will your soldiers deal with their enemies? I would gladly hear your opinion of that.

In my view, said I, they ought to do neither, but confine themselves to taking away the annual harvest. Shall I tell you why?

Do.

In my opinion, just as we have the two terms, war and faction, so there are also two things, distinguished by two differentiae. The two things I mean are the friendly and kindred on the one hand and the alien and foreign on the other. Now the term employed for the hostility of the friendly is faction, and for that of the alien is war.

What you say is in nothing beside the mark, he replied.

Consider, then, if this goes to the mark. I affirm that the Hellenic race is friendly to itself and akin, and foreign and alien to the barbarian.

Rightly, he said.

We shall then say that Greeks fight and wage war with barbarians, and barbarians with Greeks, and are enemies by nature, and that war is the fit name for this enmity and hatred. Greeks, however, we shall say, are still by nature the friends of Greeks when they act in this way, but that Greece is sick in that case and divided by faction, and faction is the name we must give to that enmity.

I will allow you that habit of speech, he said.

Then observe, said I, that when anything of this sort occurs in faction, as the word is now used, and a state is divided against itself, if either party devastates the land and burns the houses of the other such factional strife is thought to be an accursed thing and neither party to be true patriots. Otherwise, they would never have endured thus to outrage their nurse and mother. But the moderate and reasonable thing is thought to be that the victors shall take away the crops of the vanquished, but that their temper shall be that of men who expect to be reconciled and not always to wage war.

That way of feeling, he said, is far less savage than the other.

Well, then, said I, is not the city that you are founding to be a Greek city?

It must be, he said.

Will they then not be good and gentle?

Indeed they will.

And won't they be philhellenes, lovers of Greeks, and will they not regard all Greece as their own and not renounce their part in the holy places common to all Greeks?

Most certainly.

Will they not then regard any difference with Greeks who are their own people as a form of faction and refuse even to speak of it as war?

Most certainly.

And they will conduct their quarrels always looking forward to a reconciliation?

By all means.

They will correct them, then, for their own good, not chastising them with a view to their enslavement or their destruction, but acting as correctors, not as enemies.

They will, he said.

They will not, being Greeks, ravage Greek territory nor burn habitations, and they will not admit that in any city all the population are their enemies, men, women, and children, but will say that only a few at any time are their foes, those, namely, who are to blame for the quarrel. And on all these considerations they will not be willing to lay waste the soil, since the majority are their friends, nor to destroy the houses, but will carry the conflict only to the point of compelling the guilty to do justice by the pressure of the suffering of the innocent.

I, he said, agree that our citizens ought to deal with their Greek opponents on this wise, while treating barbarians as Greeks now treat Greeks.

Shall we lay down this law also, then, for our guardians, that they are not to lay waste the land or burn the houses?

Let us so decree, he said, and assume that this and our preceding prescriptions are right. But I fear, Socrates, that, if you are allowed to go on in this fashion, you will never get to speak of the matter you put aside in order to say all this, namely, the possibility of such a polity coming into existence, and the way in which it could be brought to pass. I too am ready to admit that if it could be realized everything would be lovely for the state that had it, and I will add what you passed by, that they would also be most successful in war because they would be least likely to desert one another, knowing and addressing each other by the names of brothers, fathers, sons. And if the females should also join in their campaigns, whether in the ranks or marshaled behind to intimidate the enemy, or as reserves in case of need, I recognize that all this too would make them irresistible. And at home, also, I observe all the benefits that you omit to mention. But, taking it for granted that I concede these and countless other advantages, consequent on the realization of this polity, don't labor that point further, but let us at once proceed to try to convince ourselves of just this, that it is possible and how it is possible, dismissing everything else.

This is a sudden assault, indeed, said I, that you have made on my theory, without any regard for my natural hesitation. Perhaps you don't realize that when I have hardly escaped the first two waves, you are now rolling up against me the 'great third wave' of paradox, the worst of all. When you have seen and heard that, you will be very ready to be lenient, recognizing that I had good reason after all for shrinking and fearing to enter upon the discussion of so paradoxical a notion.

The more such excuses you offer, he said, the less you will be released by us from telling in what way the realization of this polity is possible. Speak on, then, and do not put us off.

The first thing to recall, then, I said, is that it was the inquiry in to the nature of justice and injustice that brought us to this pass.

Yes, but what of it? he said.

Oh, nothing, I replied, only this. If we do discover what justice is, are we to demand that the just man shall differ from it in no respect, but shall conform in every way to the ideal? Or will it suffice us if he approximate to it as nearly as possible and partake of it more than others?

That will content us, he said.

A pattern, then, said I, was what we wanted when we were inquiring into the nature of ideal justice and asking what would be the character of the perfectly just man, supposing him to exist, and, likewise, in regard to injustice and the completely unjust man. We wished to fix our eyes upon them as types and models, so that whatever we discerned in them of happiness or the reverse would necessarily apply to ourselves in the sense that whosoever is likest them will have the allotment most like to theirs. Our purpose was not to demonstrate the possibility of the realization of these ideals.

In that, he said, you speak truly.

Do you think, then, that he would be any the less a good painter, who, after portraying a pattern of the ideally beautiful man and omitting no touch required for the perfection of the picture, should not be able to prove that it is actually possible for such a man to exist?

Not I, by Zeus, he said.

Then were not we, as we say, trying to create in words the pattern of a good state?

Certainly.

Do you think, then, that our words are any the less well spoken if we find ourselves unable to prove that it is possible for a state to be governed in accordance with our words?

Of course not, he said.

That, then, said I, is the truth of the matter. But if, to please you, we must do our best to show how most probably and in what respect these things would be most nearly realized, again, with a view to such a demonstration, grant me the same point.

What?

Is it possible for anything to be realized in deed as it is spoken in word, or is it the nature of things that action should partake of exact truth less than speech, even if some deny it? Do you admit it or not?

I do, he said.

Then don't insist, said I, that I must exhibit as realized in action precisely what we expounded in words. But if we can discover how a state might be constituted most nearly answering to our description, you must say that we have discovered that possibility of realization which you demanded. Will you not be content if you get this? I for my part would.

And I too, he said.

Next, it seems, we must try to discover and point out what it is that is now badly managed in our cities, and that prevents them from being so governed, and what is the smallest change that would bring a state to this manner of government, preferably a change in one thing, if not, then in two, and, failing that, the fewest possible in number and the slightest in potency.

By all means, he said.

There is one change, then, said I, which I think that we can show would bring about the desired transformation. It is not a slight or an easy thing but it is possible.

What is that? said he.

I am on the very verge, said I, of what we likened to the greatest wave of paradox. But say it I will, even if, to keep the figure, it is likely to wash us away on billows of laughter and scorn. Listen.

I am all attention, he said.

Unless, said I, either philosophers become kings in our states or those whom we now call our kings and rulers take to the pursuit of philosophy seriously and adequately, and there is a conjunction of these two things, political power and philosophical intelligence, while the motley horde of the natures who at present pursue either apart from the other are compulsorily excluded, there can be no cessation of troubles, dear Glaucon, for our states, nor, I fancy, for the human race either. Nor, until this happens, will this constitution which we have been expounding in theory ever be put into practice within the limits of possibility and see the light of the sun. But this is the thing that has made me so long shrink from speaking out, because I saw that it would be a very paradoxical saying. For it is not easy to see that there is no other way of happiness either for private or public life.

Whereupon he said, Socrates, after hurling at us such an utterance and statement as that, you must expect to be attacked by a great multitude of our men of light and leading, who forthwith will, so to speak, cast off their garments and strip and, snatching the first weapon that comes to hand, rush at you with might and main, prepared to do dreadful deeds. And if you don't find words to defend yourself against them, and escape their assault, then to be scorned and flouted will in very truth be the penalty you will have to pay.

And isn't it you, said I, that have brought this upon me and are to blame?

And a good thing, too, said he, but I won't let you down, and will defend you with what I can. I can do so with my good will and my encouragement, and perhaps I might answer your questions more suitably than another. So, with such an aid to back you, try to make itplain to the doubters that the truth is as you say.

I must try, I replied, since you proffer so strong an alliance. I think it requisite, then, if we are to escape the assailants you speak of, that we should define for them whom we mean by the philosophers, who we dare to say ought to be our rulers. When these are clearly discriminated it will be possible to defend ourselves by showing that to them by their very nature belong the study of philosophy and political leadership, while it befits the other sort to let philosophy alone and to follow their leader.

It is high time, he said, to produce your definition.

Come, then, follow me on this line, if we may in some fashion or other explain our meaning.

Proceed, he said.

Must I remind you, then, said I, or do you remember, that when we affirm that a man is a lover of something, it must be apparent that he is fond of all of it? It will not do to say that some of it he likes and some does not.

I think you will have to remind me, he said, for I don't apprehend at all.

That reply, Glaucon, said I, befitted another rather than you. It does not become a lover to forget that all adolescents in some sort sting and stir the amorous lover of youth and appear to him deserving of his attention and desirable. Is not that your 'reaction' to the fair? One, because his nose is tiptilted, you will praise as piquant, the beak of another you pronounce right royal, the intermediate type you say strikes the harmonious mean, the swarthy are of manly aspect, the white are children of the gods divinely fair, and as for honey-hued, do you suppose the very word is anything but the euphemistic invention of some lover who can feel no distaste for sallowness when it accompanies the blooming time of youth? And, in short, there is no pretext you do not allege and there is nothing you shrink from saying to justify you in not rejecting any who are in the bloom of their prime.

If it is your pleasure, he said, to take me as your example of this trait in lovers, I admit it for the sake of the argument.

Again, said I, do you not observe the same thing in the lovers of wine? They welcome every wine on any pretext.

They do, indeed.

And so I take it you have observed that men who are covetous of honor, if they can't get themselves elected generals, are captains of a company. And if they can't be honored by great men and dignitaries, are satisfied with honor from little men and nobodies. But honor they desire and must have.

Yes, indeed.

Admit, then, or reject my proposition. When we say a man is keen about something, shall we say that he has an appetite for the whole class or that he desires only a part and a part not?

The whole, he said.

Then the lover of wisdom, too, we shall affirm, desires all wisdom, not a part and a part not.

Certainly.

The student, then, who is finical about his studies, especially when he is young and cannot yet know by reason what is useful and what is not, we shall say is not a lover of learning or a lover of wisdom, just as we say that one who is dainty about his food is not really hungry, has not an appetite for food, and is not a lover of food, but a poor feeder.

We shall rightly say so.

But the one who feels no distaste in sampling every study, and who attacks his task of learning gladly and cannot get enough of it, him we shall justly pronounce the lover of wisdom, the philosopher, shall we not?

To which Glaucon replied, You will then be giving the name to a numerous and strange band, for all the lovers of spectacles are what they are, I fancy, by virtue of their delight in learning something.. And those who always want to hear some new thing are a very queer lot to be reckoned among philosophers. You couldn't induce them to attend a serious debate or any such entertainment, but as if they had farmed out their ears to listen to every chorus in the land, they run about to all the Dionysiac festivals, never missing one, either in the towns or in the country villages. Are we to designate all these, then, and similar folk and all the practitioners of the minor arts as philosophers?

Not at all, I said, but they do bear a certain likeness to philosophers.

Whom do you mean, then, by the true philosophers?

Those for whom the truth is the spectacle of which they are enamored, said I.

Right again, said he, but in what sense do you mean it?

It would be by no means easy to explain it to another, I said, but I think that you will grant me this.

What?

That since the fair and honorable is the opposite of the base and ugly, they are two.

Of course.

And since they are two, each is one.

That also.

And in respect of the just and the unjust, the good and the bad, and all the ideas or forms, the same statement holds, that in itself each is one, but that by virtue of their communion with actions and bodies and with one another they present themselves everywhere, each as a multiplicity of aspects.

Right, he said.

This, then, said I, is my division. I set apart and distinguish those of whom you were just speaking, the lovers of spectacles and the arts, and men of action, and separate from them again those with whom our argument is concerned and who alone deserve the appellation of philosophers or lovers of wisdom.

What do you mean? he said.

The lovers of sounds and sights, I said, delight in beautiful tones and colors and shapes and in everything that art fashions out of these, but their thought is incapable of apprehending and taking delight in the nature of the beautiful in itself.

Why, yes, he said, that is so.

And on the other hand, will not those be few who would be able to approach beauty itself and contemplate it in and by itself?

They would, indeed.

He, then, who believes in beautiful things, but neither believes in beauty itself nor is able to follow when someone tries to guide him to the knowledge of it—do you think that his life is a dream or a waking? Just consider. Is not the dream state, whether the man is asleep or awake, just this—the mistaking of resemblance for identity?

I should certainly call that dreaming, he said.

Well, then, take the opposite case, the man whose thought recognizes a beauty in itself, and is able to distinguish that self-beautiful and the things that participate in it, and neither supposes the participants to be it nor it the participants—is his life, in your opinion, a waking or a dream state?

He is very much awake, he replied.

Could we not rightly, then, call the mental state of the one as knowing, knowledge, and that of the other as opining, opinion?

Assuredly.

Suppose, now, he who we say opines but does not know should be angry and challenge our statement as not true—can we find any way of soothing him and gently winning him over, without telling him too plainly that he is not in his right mind?

We must try, he said.

Come, then, consider what we are to say to him, or would you have us question him in this fashion—premising that if he knows anything, nobody grudges it him, but we should be very glad to see him knowing something—but tell us this, Does he who knows know something or nothing? Do you reply in his behalf.

I will reply, he said, that he knows something.

Is it something that is or is not?

That is. How could that which is not be known?

We are sufficiently assured of this, then, even if we should examine it from every point of view, that that which entirely is is entirely knowable, and that which in no way is is in every way unknowable?

Most sufficiently.

Good. If a thing, then, is so conditioned as both to be and not to be, would it not lie between that which absolutely and unqualifiedly is and that which in no way is?

Between.

Then since knowledge pertains to that which is and ignorance of necessity to that which is not, for that which lies between we must seek for something between nescience and science, if such a thing there be.

By all means.

Is there a thing which we call opinion?

Surely.

Is it a different faculty from science or the same?

A different.

Then opinion is set over one thing and science over another, each by virtue of its own distinctive power or faculty.

That is so.

May we say, then, that science is naturally related to that which is, to know that and how that which is is? But rather, before we proceed, I think we must draw the following distinctions.

What ones?

Shall we say that faculties, powers, abilities are a class of entities by virtue of which we and all other things are able to do what we or they are able to do? I mean that sight and hearing, for example, are faculties, if so be that you understand the class or type that I am trying to describe.

I understand, he said.

Hear, then, my notion about them. In a faculty I cannot see any color or shape or similar mark such as those on which in many other cases I fix my eyes in discriminating in my thought one thing from another. But in the case of a faculty I look to one thing only—that to which it is related and what it effects, and it is in this way that I come to call each one of them a faculty, and that which is related to the same thing and accomplishes the same thing I call the same faculty, and that to another I call other. How about you, what is your practice?

The same, he said.

To return, then, my friend, said I, to science or true knowledge, do you say that it is a faculty and a power, or in what class do you put it?

Into this, he said, the most potent of all faculties.

And opinion—shall we assign it to some other class than faculty?

By no means, he said, for that by which we are able to opine is nothing else than the faculty of opinion.

But not long ago you agreed that science and opinion are not identical.

How could any rational man affirm the identity of the infallible with the fallible?

Excellent, said I, and we are plainly agreed that opinion is a different thing from scientific knowledge.

Yes, different.

Each of them, then, since it has a different power, is related to a different object.

Of necessity.

Science, I presume, to that which is, to know the condition of that which is?

Yes.

But opinion, we say, opines.

Yes.

Does it opine the same thing that science knows, and will the knowable and the opinable be identical, or is that impossible?

Impossible by our admissions, he said. If different faculties are naturally related to different objects and both opinion and science are faculties, but each different from, the other, as we say—these admission do not leave place for the identity of the knowable and the opinable.

Then, if that which is a knowable, something other than that which is would be the opinable.

Something else.

Does it opine that which is not, or is it impossible even to opine that which is not? Reflect. Does not he who opines bring his opinion to bear upon something or shall we reverse ourselves and say that it is possible to opine, yet opine nothing?

That is impossible.

Then he who opines opines some one thing?

Yes.

But surely that which is not could not be designated as some one thing, but most rightly as nothing at all.

Yes.

To that which is not we of necessity assigned nescience, and to that which is, knowledge.

Rightly, he said.

Then neither that which is nor that which is not is the object of opinion.

It seems not.

Then opinion would be neither nescience nor knowledge.

So it seems.

Is it then a faculty outside of these, exceeding either knowledge in lucidity or ignorance in obscurity?

It is neither.

But do you deem opinion something darker than knowledge but brighter than ignorance?

Much so, he said.

And does it lie within the boundaries of the two?

Yes.

Then opinion would be between the two.

Most assuredly.

Were we not saying a little while ago that if anything should turn up such that it both is and is not, that sort of thing would lie between that which purely and absolutely is and that which wholly is not, and that the faculty correlated with it would be neither science nor nescience, but that which should appear to hold a place correspondingly between nescience and science.

Right.

And now there has turned up between these two the thing that we call opinion.

There has.

It would remain, then, as it seems, for us to discover that which partakes of both, of to be and not to be, and that could not be rightly designated either in its exclusive purity, so that, if it shall be discovered, we may justly pronounce it to be the opinable, thus assigning extremes to extremes and the intermediate to the intermediate. Is not that so?

It is.

This much premised, let him tell me, I will say, let him answer me, that good fellow who does not think there is a beautiful in itself or any idea of beauty in itself always remaining the same and unchanged, but who does believe in many beautiful things—the lover of spectacles, I mean, who cannot endure to hear anybody say that the beautiful is one and the just one, and so of other things—and this will be our question. My good fellow, is there any one of these many fair and honorable things that will not sometimes appear ugly and base? And of the just things, that will not seem unjust? And of the pious things, that will not seem impious?

No, it is inevitable, he said, that they would appear to be both beautiful in a way and ugly, and so with all the other things you asked about.

And again, do the many double things appear any the less halves than doubles?

None the less.

And likewise of the great and the small things, the light and the heavy things—will they admit these predicates any more than their opposites?

No, he said, each of them will always hold of, partake of, both.

Then is each of these multiples rather than it is not that which one affirms it to be?

They are like those jesters who palter with us in a double sense at banquets, he replied, and resemble the children's riddle about the eunuch and his hitting of the bat—with what and as it sat on what they signify that he struck it. For these things too equivocate, and it is impossible to conceive firmly any one of them to be or not to be or both or neither.

Do you know what to do with them, then? said I. And can you find a better place to put them than that midway between existence or essence and the not to be? For we shall surely not discover a darker region than not-being that they should still more not be, nor a brighter than being that they should still more be.

Most true, he said.

We would seem to have found, then, that the many conventions of the many about the fair and honorable and other things are tumbled about in the mid-region between that which is not and that which is in the true and absolute sense.

We have so found it.

But we agreed in advance that if anything of that sort should be discovered, it must be denominated opinable, not knowable, the wanderer between being caught by the faculty that is betwixt and between.

We did.

We shall affirm, then, that those who view many beautiful things but do not see the beautiful itself and are unable to follow another's guidance to it, and many just things, but not justice itself, and so in all cases-we shall say that such men have opinions about all things, (but know nothing of the things they opine.

Of necessity.

And, on the other hand, what of those who contemplate the very things themselves in each case, ever remaining the same and unchanged—shall we not say that they know and do not merely opine?

That, too, necessarily follows.

Shall we not also say that the one welcomes to his thought and loves the things subject to knowledge and the other those to opinion?

Do we not remember that we said that those loved and regarded tones and beautiful colors and the like, but they could not endure the notion of the reality of the beautiful itself?

We do remember.

Shall we then offend their ears if we call them doxophilists rather than philosophers and will they be very angry if we so speak?

Not if they heed my counsel, he said, for to be angry with truth is not lawful.

Then to those who in each and every kind welcome the true being, lovers of wisdom and not lovers of opinion is the name we must give.

By all means.

THE REPUBLIC OF PLATO
Book VI

Translated by Paul Shorey

So now, Glaucon, I said, our argument after winding a long and weary way has at last made clear to us who are the philosophers or lovers of wisdom and who are not.

Yes, he said, a shorter way is perhaps not feasible. Apparently not, I said. I, at any rate, think that the matter would have been made still plainer if we had had nothing but this to speak of, and if there were not so many things left which our purpose of discerning the difference between the just and the unjust life requires us to discuss.

What, then, he said, comes next?

What else, said I, but the next in order? Since the philosophers are those who are capable of apprehending that which is eternal and unchanging, while those who are capable of this, but lose themselves and wander amid the multiplicities of multifarious things, are not philosophers, which of the two kinds ought to be the leaders in a state?

What, then, he said, would be a fair statement of the matter?

Whichever, I said, appear competent to guard the laws and pursuits of society, these we should establish as guardians.

Right, he said.

Is this, then, said I, clear, whether the guardian who is to keep watch over anything ought to be blind or keen of sight?

Of course it is clear, he said.

Do you think, then, that there is any appreciable difference between the blind and those who are veritably deprived of the knowledge of the veritable being of things, those who have no vivid pattern in their souls and so cannot, as painters look to their models, fix their eyes on the absolute truth, and always with reference to that ideal and in the exactest possible contemplation of it establish in this world also the laws of the beautiful, the just, and the good, when that is needful, or guard and preserve those that are established?

No, by heaven, he said, there is not much difference.

Shall we, then, appoint these blind souls as our guardians, rather than those who have learned to know the ideal reality of things and who do not fall short of the others in experience and are not second to them in any part of virtue?

It would be strange indeed, he said, to choose others than the philosophers, provided they were not deficient in those other respects, for this very knowledge of the ideal would perhaps be the greatest of superiorities.

Then what we have to say is how it would be possible for the same persons to have both qualifications, is it not?

Quite so.

Then, as we were saying at the beginning of this discussion, the first thing to understand is the nature that they must have from birth, and I think that if we sufficiently agree on this we shall also agree that the combination of qualities that we seek belongs to the same persons, and that we need no others for guardians of states than these.

How so?

We must accept as agreed this trait of the philosophical nature, that it is ever enamored of the kind of knowledge which reveals to them something of that essence which is eternal, and is not wandering between the two poles of generation and decay.

Let us take that as agreed.

And, further, said I, that their desire is for the whole of it and that they do not willingly renounce a small or a great, a more precious or a less honored, part of it. That was the point of our former illustration drawn from lovers and men covetous of honor.

You are right, he said.

Consider, then, next whether the men who are to meet our requirements must not have this further quality in their natures.

What quality?

The spirit of truthfulness, reluctance to admit falsehood in any form, the hatred of it and the love of truth.

It is likely, he said.

It is not only likely, my friend, but there is every necessity that he who is by nature enamored of anything should cherish all that is akin and pertaining to the object of his love.

Right, he said.

Could you find anything more akin to wisdom than truth?

Impossible, he said,

Then can the same nature be a lover of wisdom and of falsehood?

By no means.

Then the true lover of knowledge must, from childhood up, be most of all a striver after truth in every form.

By all means.

But, again, we surely are aware that when in a man the desires incline strongly to any one thing, they are weakened for other things. It is as if the stream had been diverted into another channel.

Surely.

So, when a man's desires have been taught to flow in the channel of learning and all that sort of thing, they will be concerned, I presume, with the pleasures of the soul in itself, and will be indifferent to those of which the body is the instrument, if the man is a true and not a sham philosopher.

That is quite necessary.

Such a man will be temperate and by no means greedy for wealth, for the things for the sake of which money and great expenditure are eagerly sought others may take seriously, but not he.

It is so.

And there is this further point to be considered in distinguishing the philosophical from the unphilosophical nature.

What point?

You must not overlook any touch of illiberality. For nothing can be more contrary than such pettiness to the quality of a soul that is ever to seek integrity and wholeness in all things human and divine.

Most true, he said.

Do you think that a mind habituated to thoughts of grandeur and the contemplation of all time and all existence can deem this life of man a thing of great concern?

Impossible, said he.

Hence such a man will not suppose death to be terrible?

Least of all.

Then a cowardly and illiberal spirit, it seems, could have no part in genuine philosophy.

I think not.

What then? Could a man of orderly spirit, not a lover of money, not illiberal, nor a braggart nor a coward, ever prove unjust, or a driver of hard bargains?

Impossible.

This too, then, is a point that in your discrimination of the philosophical and unphilosophical soul you will observe—whether the man is from youth up just and gentle or unsocial and savage.

Assuredly.

Nor will you overlook this, I fancy.

What?

Whether he is quick or slow to learn. Or do you suppose that anyone could properly love a task which he performed painfully and with little result from much toil?

That could not be.

And if he could not keep what he learned, being steeped in oblivion, could he fail to be void of knowledge?

How could he?

And so, having all his labor for nought, will he not finally be constrained to loathe himself and that occupation?

Of course.

The forgetful soul, then, we must not list in the roll of competent lovers of wisdom, but we require a good memory.

By all means.

But assuredly we should not say that the want of harmony and seemliness in a nature conduces to anything else than the want of measure and proportion.

Certainly.

And do you think that truth is akin to measure and proportion or to disproportion?

To proportion.

Then in addition to our other requirements we look for a mind endowed with measure and grace, whose native disposition will make it easily guided to the aspect of the ideal reality in all things.

Assuredly.

Tell me, then, is there any flaw in the argument? Have we not proved the qualities enumerated to be necessary and compatible with one another for the soul that is to have a sufficient and perfect apprehension of reality?

Nay, most necessary, he said.

Is there any fault, then, that you can find with a pursuit which a man could not properly practice unless he were by nature of good memory, quick apprehension, magnificent, gracious, friendly, and akin to truth, justice, bravery, and sobriety?

Momus himself, he said, could not find fault with such a combination.

Well, then, said I, when men of this sort are perfected by education and maturity of age, would you not entrust the state solely to them?

And Adimantus said, No one, Socrates, would be able to controvert these statements of yours. But, all the same, those who occasionally hear you argue thus feel in this way. They think that owing to their inexperience in the game of question and answer they are at every question led astray a little bit by the argument, and when these bits are accumulated at the conclusion of the discussion mighty is their fall, and the apparent contradiction of what they at first said, and that just as by expert draughts players the unskilled are finally shut in and cannot make a move, so they are finally blocked and have their mouths stopped by this other game of draughts played not with counters but with words; yet the truth is not affected by that outcome. I say this with reference to the present case, for in this instance one might say that he is unable in words to contend against you at each question, but that when it comes to facts he sees that of those who turn to philosophy, not merely touching upon it to complete their education and dropping it while still young, but lingering too long in the study of it, likeness for the majority become cranks, not to say rascals, and those accounted the finest spirits among them are still rendered useless to society by the pursuit which you commend.

And I, on hearing this, said, Do you think that they are mistaken in saying so?

I don't know, said he, but I would gladly hear your opinion.

You may hear, then, that I think that what they say is true.

How, then, he replied, can it be right to say that our cities will never be freed from their evils until the philosophers, whom we admit to be useless to them, become their rulers?

Your question, I said, requires an answer expressed in a comparison or parable.

And you, he said, of course, are not accustomed to speak in comparisons!

So, said I, you are making fun of me after driving me into such an impasse of argument. But, all the same, hear my comparison so that you may still better see how I strain after imagery. For so cruel is the condition of the better sort in relation to the state that there is no single thing like it in nature. But to find a it and a defense for them one must bring together many things in such a combination as painters mix when they portray goat stags and similar creatures. Conceive this sort of thing happening either on many ships or on one. Picture a shipmaster in height and strength surpassing all others on-the ship, but who is slightly deaf and of similarly impaired vision, and whose knowledge of navigation is on a par with his sight and hearing. Conceive the sailors to be wrangling with one another for control of the helm, each claiming that it is his right to steer though he has never learned the art and cannot point out his teacher or any time when he studied it. And what is more, they affirm that it cannot be taught at all, but they are ready to make mincemeat of anyone who says that it can be taught, and meanwhile they are always clustered about the shipmaster importuning him and sticking at nothing to induce him to turn over the helm to them. And sometimes, if they fail and others get his ear, they put the others to death or cast them out from the ship, and then, after binding and stupefying the worthy shipmaster with mandragora or intoxication or otherwise, they take command of the ship, consume its stores and, drinking and feasting, make such a voyage of it as is to be expected from such, and as if that were not enough, they praise and celebrate as a navigator, a pilot, a master of shipcraft, the man who is most cunning to lend a hand in persuading or constraining the shipmaster to let them rule, while the man who lacks this craft they censure as useless. They have no suspicion that the true pilot must give his attention to the time of the year, the seasons, the sky, the winds, the stars, and all that pertains to his art if he is to be a true ruler of a ship, and that he does not believe that there is any art or science of seizing the helm with or without the consent of others, or any possibility of mastering this alleged art and the practice of it at the same time with the science of navigation. With such goings on aboard ship do you not think that the real pilot would in very deed be called a stargazer, an idle babbler, a useless fellow, by the sailors in ships managed after this fashion?

Quite so, said Adimantus.

You take my meaning, I presume, and do not require us to put the comparison to the proof and show that the condition we have described is the exact counterpart of the relation of the state to the true philosophers.

It is indeed, he said.

To begin with, then, teach this parable to the man who is surprised that philosophers are not honored in our cities, and try to convince him that it would be far more surprising if they were honored.

I will teach him, he said.

And say to him further. You are right in affirming that the finest spirits among the philosophers are of no service to the multitude. But bid him blame for this uselessness, not the finer spirits, but those who do not know how to make use of them. For it is not the natural course of things that the pilot should beg the sailors to be ruled by him or that wise men should go to the doors of the rich. The author of that epigram was a liar. But the true nature of things is that whether the sick man be rich or poor he must needs go to the door of the physician, and everyone who needs to be governed to the door of the man who knows how to govern, not that the ruler should implore his natural subjects to let themselves be ruled, if he is really good for anything. But you will make no mistake in likening our present political rulers to the sort of sailors we were just describing, and those whom these call useless and stargazing ideologists to the true pilots.

Just so, he said.

Hence, and under these conditions, we cannot expect that the noblest pursuit should be highly esteemed by those whose way of life is quite the contrary. But far the greatest and chief disparagement of philosophy is brought upon it by the pretenders to that way of life, those whom you had in mind when you affirmed that the accuser of philosophy says that the majority of her followers are rascals and the better sort useless, while I admitted that what you said was true. Is not that so?

Yes.

Have we not, then, explained the cause of the uselessness of the better sort?

We have.

Shall we next set forth the inevitableness of the degeneracy of the majority, and try to show if we can that philosophy is not to be blamed for this either?

By all means.

Let us begin, then, what we have to say and hear by recalling the starting point of our description of the nature which he who is to be a scholar and gentleman must have from birth. The leader of the choir for him, if you recollect, was truth. That he was to seek always and altogether, on pain of being an impostor without part or lot in true philosophy.

Yes, that was said.

Is not this one point quite contrary to the prevailing opinion about him?

It is indeed, he said.

Will it not be a fair plea in his defense to say that it was the nature of the real lover of knowledge to strive emulously for true being and that he would not linger over the many particulars that are opined to be real, but would hold on his way, and the edge of his passion would not be blunted nor would his desire fail till he came into touch with the nature of each thing in itself by that part of his soul to which it belongs to lay hold on that kind of reality—the part akin to it, namely—and through that approaching it, and consorting with reality really, he would beget intelligence and truth, attain to knowledge, and truly live and grow, and so find surcease from his travail of soul, but not before?

No plea could be fairer.

Well, then, will such a man love falsehood, or, quite the contrary, hate it?

I hate it, he said.

When truth led the way, no choir of evils, we, I fancy, would say, could ever follow in its train.

How could it?

But rather a sound and just character, which is accompanied by temperance.

Right, he said.

What need, then, of repeating from the beginning our proof of the necessary order of the choir that attends on the philosophical nature? You surely remember that we found pertaining to such a nature courage, grandeur of soul, aptness to learn, memory. And when you interposed the objection that though everybody will be compelled to admit our statements, yet, if we abandoned mere words and fixed our eyes on the persons to whom the words referred, everyone would say that he actually saw some of them to be useless and most of them base with all baseness—it was in our search for the cause of this ill repute that we came to the present question. Why is it that the majority are bad? And, for the sake of this, we took up again the nature of the true philosophers and defined what it must necessarily be?

That is so, he said.

We have, then, I said, to contemplate the causes of the corruption of this nature in the majority, while a small part escapes, even those whom men call not bad but useless. And after that in turn we are to observe those who imitate this nature and usurp its pursuits, and see what types of souls they are that thus entering upon a way of life which is too high for them and exceeds their powers, by the many discords and disharmonies of their conduct everywhere and among all men, bring upon philosophy the repute of which you speak.

Of what corruptions are you speaking?

I will try, I said, to explain them to you if I can. I think everyone will grant us this point, that a nature such as we just now postulated for the perfect philosopher is a rare growth among men and is found in only a few. Don't you think so?

Most emphatically.

Observe, then, the number and magnitude of the things that operate to destroy these few.

What are they?

The most surprising fact of all is that each of the gifts of nature which we praise tends to corrupt the soul possessor and divert it from philosophy. I am speaking of bravery, sobriety, and the entire list.

That does sound like a paradox, said he.

Furthermore, said I, all the so-called goods corrupt and divert, beauty and wealth and strength of body and powerful family connections in the city and all things akin to them—you get my general meaning?

I do, he said, and I would gladly hear a more precise statement of it.

Well, said I, grasp it rightly as a general proposition and the matter will be clear and the preceding statement will not seem to you so strange.

How do you bid me proceed? he said.

We know it to be universally true of every seed and growth, whether vegetable or animal, that the more vigorous it is the more it falls short of its proper perfection when deprived of the food, the season, the place that suits it. For evil is more opposed to the good than to the not-good.

Of course.

So it is, I take it, natural that the best nature should fare worse than the inferior under conditions of nurture unsuited to it.

It is.

Then, said I, Adimantus, shall we not similarly affirm that the best endowed souls become worse than the others under a bad education? Or do you suppose that great crimes and unmixed wickedness spring from a slight nature and not from a vigorous one corrupted by its nurture, while a weak nature will never be the cause of anything great, either for good or evil?

No, he said, that is the case.

Then the nature which we assumed in the philosopher, if it receives the proper teaching, must needs grow and attain to consummate excellence, but, if it be sown and planted and grown in the wrong environment, the outcome will be quite the contrary unless some god comes to the rescue. Or are you too one of the multitude who believe that there are young men who are corrupted by the Sophists, and that there are Sophists in private life who corrupt to any extent worth mentioning, and that it is not rather the very men who talk in this strain who are the chief Sophists and educate most effectively and mold to their own heart's desire young and old, men and women?

When? said he.

Why, when, I said, the multitude are seated together in assemblies or in courtrooms or theaters or camps or any other public gathering of a crowd, and with loud uproar censure some of the things that are said and done and approve others, both in excess, with full-throated clamor and clapping of hands, and thereto the rocks and the region round about re-echoing redouble the din of the censure and the praise. In such case how do you think the young man's heart, as the saying is, is moved within him? What private teaching do you think will hold out and not rather be swept away by the torrent of censure and applause, and borne off on its current, so that he will affirm the same things that they do to be honorable and base, and will do as they do, and be even such as they?

That is quite inevitable, Socrates, he said.

And, moreover, I said, we have not yet mentioned the chief necessity and compulsion.

What is it? said he.

That which these educators and Sophists impose by action when their words fail to convince. Don't you know that they chastise the recalcitrant with loss of civic rights and fines and death?

They most emphatically do, he said.

What other Sophist, then, or what private teaching do you think will prevail in opposition to these?

None, I fancy, said he.

No, said I, the very attempt is the height of folly. For there is not, never has been, and never will be a divergent type of character and virtue created by an education running counter to theirs—humanly speaking, I mean, my friend. For the divine, as the proverb says, all rules fail. And you may be sure that, if anything is saved and turns out well in the present condition of society and government, in saying that the providence of God preserves it you will not be speaking ill.

Neither do I think otherwise, he said.

Then, said I, think this also in addition.

What?

Each of these private teachers who work for pay, whom the politicians call Sophists and regard as their rivals, inculcates nothing else than these opinions of the multitude which they opine when they are assembled and calls this knowledge wisdom. It is as if a man were acquiring the knowledge of the humors and desires of a great strong beast which he had in his keeping, how it is to be approached and touched, and when and by what things it is made most savage or gentle, yes, and the several sounds it is wont to utter on the occasion of each, and again what sounds uttered by another make it tame or fierce, and after mastering this knowledge by living with the creature and by lapse of time should call it wisdom, and should construct thereof a system and art and turn to the teaching of it, knowing nothing in reality about which of these opinions and desires is honorable or base, good or evil, just or unjust, but should apply all these terms to the judgments of the great beast, calling the things that pleased it good, and the things that vexed it bad, having no other account to render of them, but should call what is necessary just and honorable, never having observed how great is the real difference between the necessary and the good, and being incapable of explaining it to another. Do you not think, by heaven, that such a one would be a strange educator?

I do, he said.

Do you suppose that there is any difference between such a one and the man who thinks that it is wisdom to have learned to know the moods and the pleasures of the motley multitude in their assembly, whether about painting or music or, for that matter, politics? For if a man associates with these and offers and exhibits to them his poetry or any other product of his craft or any political service, and grants the mob authority over himself more than is unavoidable, the proverbial necessity of Diomedes will compel him to give the public what it likes, but that what it likes is really good and honorable, have you ever heard an attempted proof of this that is not simply ridiculous?

No, he said, and I fancy I never shall hear it either.

Bearing all this in mind, recall our former question. Can the multitude possibly tolerate or believe in the reality of the beautiful in itself as opposed to the multiplicity of beautiful things, or can they believe in anything conceived in its essence as opposed to the many particulars?

Not in the least, he said.

Philosophy, then, the love of wisdom, is impossible for the multitude.

Impossible.

It is inevitable, then, that those who philosophize should be censured by them.

Inevitable.

And so likewise by those laymen who, associating with the mob, desire to curry favor with it.

Obviously.

From this point of view do you see any salvation that will suffer the born philosopher to abide in the pursuit and persevere to the end? Consider it in the light of what we said before. We agreed that quickness in learning, memory, courage, and magnificence were the traits of this nature.

Yes.

Then even as a boy among boys such a one will take the lead in all things, especially if the nature of his body matches the soul.

How could he fail to do so? he said.

His kinsmen and fellow citizens, then, will desire, I presume, to make use of him when he is older for their own affairs.

Of course.

Then they will fawn upon him with petitions and honors, anticipating and flattering the power that will be his.

That certainly is the usual way.

How, then, do you think such a youth will behave in such conditions, especially if it happen that he belongs to a great city and is rich and wellborn therein, and thereto handsome and tall? Will his soul not be filled with unbounded ambitious hopes, and will he not think himself capable of managing the affairs of both Greeks and barbarians, and thereupon exalt himself, haughty of mien and stuffed with empty pride and void of sense?

He surely will, he said.

And if to a man in this state of mind someone gently comes and tells him what is the truth, that he has no sense and sorely needs it, and that the only way to get it is to work like a slave to win it, do you think it will be easy for him to lend an ear to the quiet voice in the midst of and in spite of these evil surroundings?

Far from it, said he.

And even supposing, said I, that owing to a fortunate disposition and his affinity for the words of admonition one such youth apprehends something and is moved and drawn toward philosophy, what do we suppose will be the conduct of those who think that they are losing his service and fellowship? Is there any word or deed that they will stick at to keep him from being persuaded and to incapacitate anyone who attempts it, both by private intrigue and public prosecution in the court?

That is inevitable, he said.

Is there any possibility of such a one continuing to philosophize?

None at all, he said.

Do you see, then, said I, that we were not wrong in saying that the very qualities that make up the philosophical nature do, in fact, become, when the environment and nurture are bad, in some sort the cause of its backsliding, and so do the so-called goods—riches and all such instrumentalities?

No, he replied, it was rightly said.

Such, my good friend, and so great as regards the noblest pursuit, is the destruction and corruption of the most excellent nature, which is rare enough in any case, as we affirm. And it is from men of this type that those spring who do the greatest harm to communities and individuals, and the greatest good when the stream chances to be turned into that channel, but a small nature never does anything great to a man or a city.

Most true, said he.

Those, then, to whom she properly belongs, thus falling away and leaving philosophy forlorn and unwed, themselves live an unreal and alien life, while other unworthy wooers rush in and defile her as an orphan bereft of her kin, and attach to her such reproaches as you say her revilers taunt her with, declaring that some of her consorts are of no account and the many accountable for many evils.

Why, yes, he replied, that is what they do say.

And plausibly, said I, for other manikins, observing that the place is unoccupied and full of fine terms and pretensions, just as men escape from prison to take sanctuary in temples, so these gentlemen joyously bound away from the mechanical arts to philosophy, those that are most cunning in their little craft. For in comparison with the other arts the prestige of philosophy even in her present low estate retains a superior dignity, and this is the ambition and aspiration of that multitude of pretenders unfit by nature, whose souls are bowed and mutilated by their vulgar occupations even as their bodies are marred by their arts and crafts. Is not that inevitable?

Quite so, he said.

Is not the picture which they present, I said, precisely that of a little bald-headed tinker who has made money and just been freed from bonds and had a bath and is wearing a new garment and has got himself up like a bridegroom and is about to marry his master's daughter who has fallen into poverty and abandonment?

There is no difference at all, he said.

Of what sort will probably be the offspring of such parents? Will they not be bastard and base?

Inevitably.

And so when men unfit for culture approach philosophy and consort with her unworthily, what sort of ideas and opinions shall we say they beget? Will they not produce what may in very deed be fairly called sophisms, and nothing that is genuine or that partakes of true intelligence?

Quite so, he said.

There is a very small remnant, then, Adimantus, I said, of those who consort worthily with philosophy, some wellborn and well-bred nature, it may be, held in check by exile, and so in the absence of corrupters remaining true to philosophy, as its quality bids, or it may happen that a great soul born in a little town scorns and disregards its parochial affairs, and a small group perhaps might by natural affinity be drawn to it from other arts which they justly disdain, and the bridle of our companion Theages also might operate as a restraint. For in the case of Theages all other conditions were at hand for his backsliding from philosophy, but his sickly habit of body keeping him out of politics holds him back. My own case, the divine sign, is hardly worth mentioning—for I suppose it has happened to few or none before me. And those who have been of this little company and have tasted the sweetness and blessedness of this possession and who have also come to understand the madness of the multitude sufficiently and have seen that there is nothing, if I may say so, sound or right in any present politics, and that there is no ally with whose aid the champion of justice could escape destruction, but that he would be as a man who has fallen among wild beasts, unwilling to share their misdeeds and unable to hold out singly against the savagery of all, and that he would thus, before he could in any way benefit his friends or the state, come to an untimely end without doing any good to himself or others—for all these reasons I say the philosopher remains quiet, minds his own affair, and, as it were, standing aside under shelter of a wall in a storm and blast of dust and sleet and seeing others filled full of lawlessness, is content if in any way he may keep himself free from iniquity and unholy deeds through this life and take his departure with fair hope, serene and well content when the end comes.

Well, he said, that is no very slight thing to have achieved before taking his departure.

He would not have accomplished any very great thing either, I replied, if it were not his fortune to live in a state adapted to his nature. In such a state only will he himself rather attain his full stature and together with his own preserve the commonweal. The causes and the injustice of the calumniation of philosophy, I think, have been fairly set forth, unless you have something to add.

No, he said, I have nothing further to offer on that point. But which of our present governments do you think is suitable for philosophy?

None whatever, I said, but the very ground of my complaint is that no polity of today is worthy of the philosophical nature. This is just the cause of its perversion and alteration; as a foreign seed sown in an alien soil is wont to be overcome and die out into the native growth, so this kind does not preserve its own quality but falls away and degenerates into an alien type. But if ever it finds the best polity as it itself is the best, then will it be apparent that this was in truth divine and all the others human in their natures and practices. Obviously then you are next going to ask what is this best form of government.

Wrong, he said. I was going to ask not that but whether it is this one that we have described in our establishment of a state or another.

In other respects it is this one, said I, but there is one special further point that we mentioned even then, namely, that there would always have to be resident in such a state an element having the same conception of its constitution that you the lawgiver had in framing its laws.

That was said, he replied.

But it was not sufficiently explained, I said, from fear of those objections on your part which have shown that the demonstration of it is long and difficult. And apart from that the remainder of the exposition is by no means easy.

Just what do you mean?

The manner in which a state that occupies itself with philosophy can escape destruction. For all great things are precarious and, as the proverb truly says, 'fine things are hard.'

All the same, he said, our exposition must be completed by making this plain.

It will be no lack of will, I said, but if anything, a lack of ability, that would prevent that. But you shall observe for yourself my zeal. And note again how zealously and recklessly I am prepared to say that the state ought to take up this pursuit in just the reverse of our present fashion.

In what way?

At present, said I, those who do take it up are youths, just out of boyhood, who in the interval before they engage in business and money-making approach the most difficult part of it, and then drop it—and these are regarded forsooth as the best exemplars of philosophy. By the most difficult part I mean discussion. In later life they think they have done much if, when invited, they deign to listen to the philosophical discussions of others. That sort of thing they think should be bywork. And toward old age, with few exceptions, their light is quenched more completely than the sun of Heraclitus, inasmuch as it is never rekindled.

And what should they do? he said.

Just the reverse. While they are lads and boys they should occupy themselves with an education and a culture suitable to youth, and while their bodies are growing to manhood take right good care of them, thus securing a basis and a support for the intellectual life. But with the advance of age, when the soul begins to attain its maturity, they should make its exercises more severe, and when the bodily strength declines and they are past the age of political and military service, then at last they should be given free range of the pasture and do nothing but philosophize, except incidentally, if they are to live happily, and, when the end has come, crown the life they have lived with a consonant destiny in that other world.

You really seem to be very much in earnest, Socrates, he said. Yet I think most of your hearers are even more earnest in their opposition and will not be in the least convinced, beginning with Thrasymachus.

Do not try to breed a quarrel between me and Thrasymachus, who have just become friends and were not enemies before either. For we will spare no effort until we either convince him and the rest or achieve something that will profit them when they come to that life in which they will be born again and meet with such discussions as these.

A brief time your forecast contemplates, he said.

Nay, nothing at all, I replied, as compared with eternity. However, the unwillingness of the multitude to believe what you say is nothing surprising. For of the thing here spoken they have never beheld a token, but only the forced and artificial chiming of word and phrase, not spontaneous and accidental as has happened here. But the figure of a man 'equilibrated' and 'assimilated' to virtue's self perfectly, so far as may be, in word and deed, and holding rule in a city of like quality, that is a thing they have never seen in one case or in many. Do you think they have?

By no means.

Neither, my dear fellow, have they ever seriously inclined to hearken to fair and free discussions whose sole endeavor was to search out the truth at any cost for knowledge's sake, and which dwell apart and salute from afar all the subtleties and cavils that lead to nought but opinion and strife in courtroom and in private talk.

They have not, he said.

For this cause and foreseeing this, we then despite our fears declared under compulsion of the truth that neither city nor polity nor man either will ever be perfected until some chance compels this uncorrupted remnant of philosophers, who now bear the stigma of uselessness, to take charge of the state whether they wish it or not, and constrains the citizens to obey them, or else until by some divine inspiration a genuine passion for true philosophy takes possession either of the sons of the men now in power and sovereignty or of themselves. To affirm that either or both of these things cannot possibly come to pass is, I say, quite unreasonable. Only in that case could we be justly ridiculed as uttering things as futile as daydreams are. Is not that so?

It is.

If, then, the best philosophical natures have ever been constrained to take charge of the state in infinite time past, or now are in some barbaric region far beyond our ken, or shall hereafter be, we are prepared to maintain our contention that the constitution we have described has been, is, or will be realized when this philosophical Muse has taken control of the state. It is not a thing impossible to happen, nor are we speaking of impossibilities. That it is difficult we too admit.

I also think so, he said.

But the multitude—are you going to say?—does not think so, said I.

That may be, he said.

My dear fellow, said I, do not thus absolutely condemn the multitude. They will surely be of another mind if in no spirit of contention but soothingly and endeavoring to do away with the dispraise of learning you point out to them whom you mean by philosophers, and define as we recently did their nature and their pursuits so that the people may not suppose you to mean those of whom they are thinking. Or even if they do look at them in that way, are you still going to deny that they will change their opinion and answer differently? Or do you think that anyone is ungentle to the gentle or grudging to the ungrudging if he himself is ungrudging and mild? I will anticipate you and reply that I think that only in some few and not in the mass of mankind is so ungentle or harsh a temper to be found.

And I, you may be assured, he said, concur.

And do you not also concur in this very point that the blame for this harsh attitude of the many toward philosophy falls on that riotous crew who have burst in where they do not belong, wrangling with one another, filled with spite, and always talking about persons, a thing least befitting philosophy?

Least of all, indeed, he said.

For surely, Adimantus, the man whose mind is truly fixed on eternal realities has no leisure to turn his eyes downward upon the petty affairs of men, and so engaging in strife with them to be filled with envy and hate, but he fixes his gaze upon the things of the eternal and unchanging order, and seeing that they neither wrong nor are wronged by one another, but all abide in harmony as reason bids, he will endeavor to imitate them and, as far as may be, to fashion himself in their likeness and assimilate himself to them. Or do you think it possible not to imitate the things to which anyone attaches himself with admiration?

Impossible, he said.

Then the lover of wisdom associating with the divine order will himself become orderly and divine in the measure permitted to man. But calumny is plentiful everywhere.

Yes, truly.

If, then, I said, some compulsion is laid upon him to practice stamping on the plastic matter of human nature in public and private the patterns that he visions there, and not merely to mold and fashion himself, do you think he will prove a poor craftsman of sobriety and justice and all forms of ordinary civic virtue?

By no means, he said.

But if the multitude become aware that what we are saying of the philosopher is true, will they still be harsh with philosophers, and will they distrust our statement that no city could ever be blessed unless its lineaments were traced by artists who used the heavenly model?

They will not be harsh, he said, if they perceive that. But tell me, what is the manner of that sketch you have in mind?

They will take the city and the characters of men, as they might a tablet, and first wipe it clean—no easy task. But at any rate you know that this would be their first point of difference from ordinary reformers, that they would refuse to take in hand either individual or state or to legislate before they either received a clean slate or themselves made it clean.

And they would be right, he said.

And thereafter, do you not think that they would sketch the figure of the constitution?

Surely.

And then, I take it, in the course of the work they would glance frequently in either direction, at justice, beauty, sobriety and the like as they are in the nature of things, and alternately at that which they were trying to reproduce in mankind, mingling and blending from various pursuits that hue of the flesh, so to speak, deriving their judgment from that likeness of humanity which Homer too called, when it appeared in men, the image and likeness of God.

Right, he said.

And they would erase one touch or stroke and paint it another until in the measure of the possible they had made the characters of men pleasing and dear to God as may be.

That at any rate would be the fairest painting. Are we then making any impression on those who you said were advancing to attack us with might and main? Can we convince them that such a political artist of character and such a painter exists as the one we then were praising when our proposal to entrust the state to him angered them, and are they now in a gentler mood when they hear what we are now saying?

Much gentler, he said, if they are reasonable.

How can they controvert it? Will they deny that the lovers of wisdom are lovers of reality and truth?

That would be monstrous, he said.

Or that their nature as we have portrayed it is akin to the highest and best?

Not that either.

Well, then, can they deny that such a nature bred in the pursuits that befit it will be perfectly good and philosophical so far as that can be said of anyone? Or will they rather say it of those whom we have excluded?

Surely not.

Will they, then, any longer be fierce with us when we declare that, until the philosophical class wins control, there will be no surcease of trouble for city or citizens nor will the polity which we fable in words be brought to pass in deed?

They will perhaps be less so, he said.

Instead of less so, may we not say that they have been altogether tamed and convinced, so that for very shame, if for no other reason, they may assent?

Certainly, said he.

Let us assume, then, said I, that they are won over to this view. Will anyone contend that there is no chance that the offspring of kings and rulers should be born with the philosophical nature?

Not one, he said.

And can anyone prove that if so born they must necessarily be corrupted? The difficulty of their salvation we too concede, but that in all the course of time not one of all could be saved, will anyone maintain that?

How could he?

But surely, said I, the occurrence of one such is enough, if he has a state which obeys him, to realize all that now seems so incredible.

Yes, one is enough, he said.

For if such a ruler, I said, ordains the laws and institutions that we have described it is surely not impossible that the citizens should be content to carry them out.

By no means.

Would it, then, be at all strange or impossible for others to come to the opinion to which we have come?

I think not, said he.

And further that these things are best, if possible, has already, I take it, been sufficiently shown.

Yes, sufficiently.

Our present opinion, then, about this legislation is that our plan would be best if it could be realized and that this realization is difficult yet not impossible.

That is the conclusion, he said.

This difficulty disposed of, we have next to speak of what remains, in what way, namely, and as a result of what studies and pursuits, these preservers of the constitution will form a part of our state, and at what ages they will severally take up each study.

Yes, we have to speak of that, he said.

I gained nothing, I said, by my cunning in omitting heretofore the distasteful topic of the possession of women and procreation of children and the appointment of rulers—because I knew that the absolutely true and right way would provoke censure and is difficult of realization—for now I am nonetheless compelled to discuss them. The matter of the women and children has been disposed of, but the education of the rulers has to be examined again, I may say, from the starting point. We were saying, if you recollect, that they must approve themselves lovers of the state when tested in pleasures and pains, and make it apparent that they do not abandon this fixed faith under stress of labors or fears or any other vicissitude, and that anyone who could not keep that faith must be rejected, while he who always issued from the test pure and intact, like gold tried in the fire, is to be established as ruler and to receive honors in life and after death and prizes as well. Something of this sort we said while the argument slipped by with veiled face in fear of starting our present debate.

Most true, he said. I remember.

We shrank, my friend, I said, from uttering the audacities which have now been hazarded. But now let us find courage for the definitive pronouncement that as the most perfect guardians we must establish philosophers.

Yes, assume it to have been said, said he.

Note, then, that they will naturally be few, for the different components of the nature which we said their education presupposed rarely consent to grow in one, but for the most part these qualities are found apart.

What do you mean? he said.

Facility in learning, memory, sagacity, quickness of apprehension, and their accompaniments, and youthful spirit and magnificence in soul are qualities, you know, that are rarely combined in human nature with a disposition to live orderly, quiet, and stable lives, but such men, by reason of their quickness, are driven about just as chance directs, and all steadfastness is gone out of them.

You speak truly, he said.

And on the other hand, the steadfast and stable temperaments, whom one could rather trust in use, and who in war are not easily moved and aroused to fear, are apt to act in the same way when confronted with studies. They are not easily aroused, learn with difficulty, as if benumbed, and are filled with sleep and yawning when an intellectual task is set them.

It is so, he said.

But we affirmed that a man must partake of both temperaments in due and fair combination or else participate in neither the highest education nor in honors nor in rule.

And rightly, he said.

Do you not think, then, that such a blend will be a rare thing?

Of course.

They must, then, be tested in the toils and fears and pleasures of which we then spoke, and we have also now to speak of a point we then passed by, that we must exercise them in many studies, watching them to see whether their nature is capable of enduring the greatest and most difficult studies or whether it will faint and flinch as men flinch in the trials and contests of the body.

That is certainly the right way of looking at it, he said. But what do you understand by the greatest studies?

You remember, I presume, said I, that after distinguishing three kinds in the soul, we established definitions of justice, sobriety, bravery, and wisdom severally.

If I did not remember, he said, I should not deserve to hear the rest.

Do you also remember what was said before this?

What?

We were saying, I believe, that for the most perfect discernment of these things another longer way was requisite which would make them plain to one who took it, but that it was possible to add proofs on a par with the preceding discussion. And you said that that was sufficient, and it was on this understanding that what we then said was said, falling short of ultimate precision as it appeared to me, but if it contented you it is for you to say.

Well, he said, it was measurably satisfactory to me, and apparently to the rest of the company.

Nay, my friend, said I, a measure of such things that in the least degree falls short of reality proves no measure at all. For nothing that is imperfect is the measure of anything, though some people sometimes think that they have already done enough and that there is no need of further inquiry.

Yes, indeed, he said, many experience this because of their sloth.

An experience, said I, that least of all befits the guardians of a state and of its laws.

That seems likely, he said.

Then, said I, such a one must go around the longer way and must labor no less in studies than in the exercises of the body, or else, as we were just saying, he will never come to the end of the greatest study and that which most properly belongs to him.

Why, are not these things the greatest? said he. But is there still something greater than justice and the other virtues we described?

There is not only something greater, I said, but of these very things we need not merely to contemplate an outline as now, but we must omit nothing of their most exact elaboration. Or would it not be absurd to strain every nerve to attain to the utmost precision and clarity of knowledge about other things of trifling moment and not to demand the greatest precision for the greatest matters?

It would indeed, he said, but do you suppose that anyone will let you go without asking what is the greatest study and with what you think it is concerned?

By no means, said I, but do you ask the question. You certainly have heard it often, but now you either do not apprehend or again you are minded to make trouble for me by attacking the argument. I suspect it is rather the latter. For you have often heard that the greatest thing to learn is the idea of good by reference to which just things and all the rest become useful and beneficial. And now I am almost sure you know that this is what I am going to speak of and to say further that we have no adequate knowledge of it. And if we do not know it, then, even if without the knowledge of this we should know all other things never so well, you are aware that it would avail us nothing, just as no possession either is of any avail without the possession of the good. Or do you think there is any profit in possessing everything except that which is good, or in understanding all things else apart from the good while understanding and knowing nothing that is fair and good?

No, by Zeus, I do not, he said.

But, furthermore, you know this too, that the multitude believe pleasure to be the good, and the finer spirits intelligence or knowledge.

Certainly.

And you are also aware, my friend, that those who hold this latter view are not able to point out what knowledge it is but are finally compelled to say that it is the knowledge of the good.

Most absurdly, he said.

Is it not absurd, said I, if while taunting us with our ignorance of good they turn about and talk to us as if we knew it? For they say it is the knowledge of the good, as if we understood their meaning when they utter the word 'good.'

Most true, he said.

Well, are those who define the good as pleasure infected with any less confusion of thought than the others? Or are not they in like manner compelled to admit that there are bad pleasures?

Most assuredly.

The outcome is, I take it, that they are admitting the same things to be both good and bad, are they not?

Certainly.

Then is it not apparent that there are many and violent disputes about it?

Of course.

And again, is it not apparent that while in the case of the just and the honorable many would prefer the semblance without the reality in action, possession, and opinion, yet when it comes to the good nobody is content with the possession of the appearance but all men seek the reality, and the semblance satisfies nobody here?

Quite so, he said.

That, then, which every soul pursues and for its sake does all that it does, with an intuition of its reality, but yet baffled and unable to apprehend its nature adequately, or to attain to any stable belief about it as about other things, and for that reason failing of any possible benefit from other things—in a matter of this quality and moment, can we, I ask you, allow a like blindness and obscurity in those best citizens to whose hands we are to entrust all things?

Least of all, he said.

I fancy, at any rate, said I, that the just and the honorable, if their relation and reference to the good is not known will not have secured a guardian of much worth in the man thus ignorant, and my surmise is that no one will understand them adequately before he knows this.

You surmise well, he said.

Then our constitution will have its perfect and definitive organization only when such a guardian, who knows these things, oversees it.

Necessarily, he said. But you yourself, Socrates, do you think that knowledge is the good or pleasure or something else and different?

What a man it is, said I. You made it very plain long ago that you would not be satisfied with what others think about it.

Why, it does not seem right to me either, Socrates, he said, to be ready to state the opinions of others but not one's own when one has occupied himself with the matter so long.

But then, said I, do you think it right to speak as having knowledge about things one does not know?

By no means, he said, as having knowledge, but one ought to be willing to tell as his opinion what he opines.

Nay, said I, have you not observed that opinions divorced from knowledge are ugly things? The best of them are blind. Or do you think that those who hold some true opinion without intelligence differ appreciably from blind men who go the right way?

They do not differ at all, he said.

Is it, then, ugly things that you prefer to contemplate, things blind and crooked, when you might hear from others what is luminous and fair?

Nay, in heaven's name, Socrates, said Glaucon, do not draw back, as it were, at the very goal. For it will content us if you explain the good even as you set forth the nature of justice, sobriety, and the other virtues.

It will right well content me, my dear fellow, I said, but I fear that my powers may fail and that in my eagerness I may cut a sorry figure and become a laughingstock. Nay, my beloved, let us dismiss for the time being the nature of the good in itself, for to attain to my present surmise of that seems a pitch above the impulse that wings my flight today. But of what seems to be the offspring of the good and most nearly made in its likeness I am willing to speak if you too wish it, and otherwise to let the matter drop.

Well, speak on, he said, for you will duly pay me the tale of the parent another time.

I could wish, I said, that I were able to make and you to receive the payment and not merely as now the interest. But at any rate receive this interest and the offspring of the good. Have a care, however, lest I deceive you unintentionally with a false reckoning of the interest.

We will do our best, he said, to be on our guard. Only speak on.

Yes, I said, after first coming to an understanding with you and reminding you of what has been said here before and often on other occasions.

What? said he.

We predicate 'to be' of many beautiful things and many good things, saying of them severally that they are, and so define them in our speech.

We do.

And again, we speak of a self-beautiful and of a good that is only and merely good, and so, in the case of all the things that we then posited as many, we turn about and posit each as a single idea or aspect, assuming it to be a unity and call it that which each really is.

It is so.

And the one class of things we say can be seen but not thought, while the ideas can be thought but not seen.

By all means.

With which of the parts of ourselves, with which of our faculties, then, do we see visible things?

With sight, he said.

And do we not, I said, hear audibles with hearing, and perceive all sensibles with the other senses?

Surely.

Have you ever observed, said I, how much the greatest expenditure the creator of the senses has lavished on the faculty of seeing and being seen?

Why, no, I have not, he said.

Well, look at it thus. Do hearing and voice stand in need of another medium so that the one may hear and the other be heard, in the absence of which third element the one will not hear and the other not be heard?

They need nothing, he said.

Neither, I fancy, said I, do many others, not to say that none require anything of the sort. Or do you know of any?

Not I, he said.

But do you not observe that, vision and the visible do have this further need?

How?

Though vision may be in the eyes and its possessor may try to use it, and though color be present, yet without the presence of a third thing specifically and naturally adapted to this purpose, you are aware that vision will see nothing and the colors will remain invisible.

What is this thing of which you speak? he said.

The thing. I said that you call light.

You say truly, he replied.

The bond, then, that yokes together visibility and the faculty of sight is more precious by no slight form than that which unites the other pairs, if light is not without honor.

It surely is far from being so, he said.

Which one can you name of the divinities in heaven as the author and because of this, whose light makes our vision see best and visible things to be seen?

Why, the one that you too and other people mean, he said, for your question evidently refers to the sun.

Is not this, then, the relation of vision to that divinity?

What?

Neither vision itself nor its vehicle, which we call the eye, is identical with the sun.

Why, no.

But it is, I think, the most sunlike of all the instruments of sense.

By far the most.

And does it not receive the power which it possesses as an influx, as it were, dispensed from the sun?

Certainly.

Is it not also true that the sun is not vision, yet as being the cause thereof is beheld by vision itself?

That is so, he said.

This, then, you must understand that I meant by the offspring of the good which the good begot to stand in a proportion with itself. As the good is in the intelligible region to reason and the objects of reason, so is this in the visible world to vision and the objects of vision.

How is that? he said. Explain further.

You are aware, I said, that when the eyes are no longer turned upon objects upon whose colors the light of day falls but that of the dim luminaries of night, their edge is blunted and they appear almost blind, as if pure vision did not dwell in them.

Yes, indeed, he said.

But when, I take it, they are directed upon objects illumined by the sun, they, see clearly, and vision appears to reside in these same eyes.

Certainly.

Apply this comparison to the soul also in this way. When it is firmly fixed on the domain where truth and reality shine resplendent it apprehends and knows them and appears to possess reason, But when it inclines to that region which is mingled with darkness, the world of becoming and passing away it opines only and its edge is blunted, and it shifts its opinions hither and thither, and again seems as if it lacked reason.

Yes, it does.

This reality, then that gives their truth to the objects of knowledge and the power of knowing to the knower, you must say is the idea of good, and you must conceive it as being the cause of knowledge, and of truth in so far as known. Yet fair as they both are, knowledge and truth, in supposing it to be something fairer still than these you will think rightly of it. But as for knowledge and truth, even as in our illustration it is right to deem light and vision sunlike, but never to think that they are the sun, so here it is right to consider these two their counterparts, as being like the good or boniform, but to think that either of them is the good is not right. Still higher honor belongs to the possession and habit of the good.

An inconceivable beauty you speak of, he said, if it is the source of knowledge and truth, and yet itself surpasses them in beauty. For you surely cannot mean that it is pleasure.

Hush, said I, but examine the similitude of it still further in this way.

How?

The sun, I presume you will say, not only furnishes to visibles the power of visibility but it also provides for their generation and growth and nurture though it is not itself generation.

Of course not.

In like manner, then, you are to say that the objects of knowledge not only receive from the presence of the good their being known, but their very existence and essence is derived to them from it, though the good itself is not essence but still transcends essence in dignity and surpassing power.

And Glaucon very ludicrously said, Heaven save us, hyperbole can no further go.

The fault is yours, I said, for compelling me to utter my thoughts about it.

And don't desist, he said, but at least expound the similitude of the sun, if there is anything that you are omitting.

Why, certainly, I said, I am omitting a great deal.

Well, don't omit the least bit, he said.

I fancy, I said, that I shall have to pass over much, but nevertheless so far as it is at present practicable I shall not willingly leave anything out.

Do not, he said.

Conceive then, said I, as we were saying, that there are these two entities, and that one of them is sovereign over the intelligible order and region and the other over the world of the eyeball, not to say the sky-ball, but let that pass. You surely apprehend the two types, the visible and the intelligible.

I do.

Represent them then, as it were, by a line divided into two unequal sections and cut each section again in the same ratio—the section, that is, of the visible and that of the intelligible order—and then as an expression of the ratio of their comparative clearness and obscurity you will have, as one of the sections of the visible world, images. By images I mean, first, shadows, and then reflections in water and on surfaces of dense, smooth, and bright texture, and everything of that kind, if you apprehend.

I do.

As the second section assume that of which this is a likeness or an image, that is, the animals about us and all plants and the whole class of objects made by man.

I so assume it, he said.

Would you be willing to say, said I, that the division in respect of reality and truth or the opposite is expressed by the proportion—as is the opinable to the knowable so is the likeness to that of which it is a likeness?

I certainly would.

Consider then again the way in which we are to make the division of the intelligible section.

In what way?

By the distinction that there is one section of it which the soul is compelled to investigate by treating as images the things imitated in the former division, and by means of assumptions from which it proceeds not up to a first principle but down to a conclusion, while there is another section in which it advances from its assumption to a beginning or principle that transcends assumption, and in which it makes no use of the images employed by the other section, relying on ideas only and progressing systematically through ideas.

I don't fully understand what you mean by this, he said.

Well, I will try again, said I, for you will better understand after this preamble. For I think you are aware that students of geometry and reckoning and such subjects first postulate the odd and the even and the various figures and three kinds of angles and other things akin to these in each branch of science, regard them as known, and, treating them as absolute assumptions, do not deign to render any further account of them to themselves or others, taking it for granted that they are obvious to everybody. They take their start from these, and d pursuing the inquiry from this point on consistently, conclude with that for the investigation of which they set out. Certainly, he said, I know that.

And do you not also know that they further make use of the visible forms and talk about them, though they are not thinking of them but of those things of which they are a likeness, pursuing their inquiry for the sake of the square as such and the diagonal as such, and not for the sake of the image of it which they draw? And so in all cases. The very things which they mold and draw, which have shadows and images of themselves in water, these things they treat in their turn as only images, but what they really seek is to get sight of those realities which can be seen only by the mind.

True, he said.

This then is the class that I described as intelligible, it is true, but with the reservation first that the soul is compelled to employ assumptions in the investigation of it, not proceeding to a first principle because of its inability to extricate itself from and rise above its assumptions, and second, that it uses as images or likenesses the very objects that are themselves copied and adumbrated by the class below them, and that in comparison with these latter are esteemed as clear and held in honor.

I understand, said he, that you are speaking of what falls under geometry and the kindred arts.

Understand then, said I, that by the other section of the intelligible I mean that which the reason itself lays hold of by the power of dialectic, treating its assumptions not as absolute beginnings but literally as hypotheses, underpinnings, footings, and springboards so to speak, to enable it to rise to that which requires no assumption and is the starting point of all, and after attaining to that again taking I hold of the first dependencies from it, so to proceed downward to the conclusion, making no use whatever of any object of sense but only of pure ideas moving on through ideas to ideas and ending with ideas. I understand, he said, not fully, for it is no slight task that you appear to have in mind, but I do understand that you mean to distinguish the aspect of reality and the intelligible, which is contemplated by the power of dialectic, as something truer and more exact than the object of the so-called arts and sciences whose assumptions are arbitrary starting points. And though it is true that those who contemplate them are compelled to use their understanding and not their senses, yet because they do not go back to the beginning in the study of them but start from assumptions you do not think they possess true intelligence about them although the things themselves are intelligibles when apprehended in conjunction with a first principle. And I think you call the mental habit of geometers and their like mind or understanding and not reason because you regard understanding as something intermediate between opinion and reason.

Your interpretation is quite sufficient, I said. And now, answering to these four sections, assume these four affections occurring in the soul—intellection or reason for the highest, understanding for the second, belief for the third, and for the last, picture thinking or

conjecture—and arrange them in a proportion, considering that they participate in clearness and precision in the same degree as their objects partake of truth and reality.

I understand; he said. I concur and arrange them as you bid.

SPARTAN PLEASURES

From Tony Perrottet, *Pagan Holiday*

From Delphi, Roman tourists would head to the Peloponnesus—a virtual island, shaped like an arthritic claw, connected only by a narrow isthmus to the rest of Greece. The Roman highway along this umbilical cord was cut into precarious cliffs, with endless views across the Aegean. Today, the route is still a humbling introduction: You can see why Henry Miller compared his first view of this rugged peninsula to "a short, sharp stab to the heart."

As the ancient travel map, the Peutinger Table, shows, the Roman highway hung like a noose around the entire Peloponnesus, linking the towns where many of the tourist attractions lay. The modern Greek highway was built above the ancient, so we were following the same basis route (in fact, the Peutinger sometimes seemed easier to use than contemporary road maps, which are dense with Greek lettering that bears no correspondence to any road signs).

As I ground the Donko's rusty gears up and down the bare mountainsides—we'd taped a sheet of plastic over the broken window, and tied coat-hanger wire around my door so it wouldn't pop open whenever the car stopped—it was easy to picture those roving Roman tourists clattering along in their squeaky wagons, trying to read their papyrus guide books as they reclined on their down pillows, or idly watching the countryside roll by. In between the urban centers, Roman Greece was beautiful but impoverished: The relative prosperity of the "Indian summer that the Empire had brought to the province did not extend to the countryside. Visitors were surprised to find a hand-to-mouth peasant world, roamed by shepherds and goatherds. Just off the roadway lay towns that had fallen into destitution: the orator Dio the Golden-Tongued described plazas that had been turned into plowed fields, while just beyond their broken gates, the land was completely overgrown—"as though this were the depths of a wilderness and not the outskirts of a city."

Not surprisingly, the tourist facilities between major attractions could be quite basic. A certain Apollinarius Sidonius was appalled by a "greasy tavern" in rural Greece, whose halls were black with smoke from all the thyme-herbed sausages forever burning on the kitchen grill. His hard-reed bed was hopping with lice all night, lizards and

411

spiders fell from the ceiling. Aristides preferred to sit up all night covered in dust from the road rather than climb between a country inn's filthy sheets: hotel rooms leaked during winter storms, in summer they were full of insects. (He notes dryly of one rustic establishment: It became clear through the multitude of mosquitoes that I would have to forego sleep.") Apuleius was given a "worm-eaten old army bunk" with a broken leg—although this rather pales beside the testimony of one character in his novel, The Golden Ass, who woke up to see his roommate being attacked by the innkeeper-witch: She breaks down the door with a magical spell, tears out the man's heart, and then strings his corpse to the rafters by the genitals. Rural hotel porters were notoriously surly characters, perched in the courtyards, always watching out for any suspicious activity from guests after dark.

The backwoods clientele was also more rough-and-ready than in the cities: Plutarch advises travelers not to be intimidated by the taunts of sailors or muleteers at dinner. Instead, he says, one should chant loudly to oneself to block out the noise. Drunks would play music and demand money. Apollonius of Tyana was accosted by one musician who sang Nero's poetry—"drawling out the verses which the Emperor was in the habit of murdering by his miserable modulations." When the guests said they were bored, the drunk accused them of treason.

But it was best to keep an open mind in these humble inns. Guests could meet fellow travelers and stay awake into the small hours, exchanging arcane travel stories and drinking honeyed wine by the fire. Apuleius mentions being challenged by a roomful of friendly locals to an eating race one might—although he swallowed too large a piece of polenta and nearly choked to death.

As ever, the discomforts of the journey were worth it: the Peloponnesus contained Greece's greatest sites. Like those roving Romans, we slipped into Corinth, official capital of the ancient province, famous for its sacred prostitutes of Aphrodite; tested the acoustics in the amphitheater at Epidaurus; paused at the mountain citadel of Mycenae, where, behind the Lion Gate, ancient tourists would pay their respects at the grave of King Agamemnon, leader of the Greeks in Troy.

But the true goal lay south, in a city whose very lifestyle was the staff of violent legend.

THE ALTAR TO MACHISMO

Navigating down the hairpin bends to Sparta inspired a certain trepidation—and not just because of the grinding Russian brakes. Maybe it was the news that we were going to have a son, but the image of that warlike city seemed even less palatable than usual.

The Spartans have been awarded the prize as the testosterone-fueled fascists of ancient history. Mortal enemies of the artsy, philosophy-loving Atheruans, they ran a sadistic, totalitarian regime throughout the classical age, whose heartless social code was geared exclusively to creating invincible armies. Newborn babies were inspected by an all-male council, and the physically inferior tossed into a ravine. Boys were taken from their families at age seven, raised by the state in thuggish boot camps, and toughened up by being forced to sleep in the fields and steal their food to survive. As adults, males could look forward to a jolly lifetime of bullying, bludgeoning, sparring and silently eating gruel in crowded communal barracks. Spartan girls, meanwhile, were born only to breed: Their education consisted of running, wrestling naked, and learning domestic chores, while celibacy was a crime punishable by exile. This inhuman system, where mindless discipline was elevated to a religious principle, was much admired by European thinkers in the eighteenth century, but ever since the Romantic era the Spartans have been disdained as philistine lowlifes—antiquity's sullen skinheads. It's not surprising to learn that the Nazis adored then, celebrating Sparta as the most "Nordic" state in Greece. Hitler entertained fantasies about the superclass of male hunters and fighters, who through their inherent superiority exercised raw power over a vast population of Helots. He saw the staunch, fight-to-the-death spirit of the battle of Thermopylae in Stalingrad, and even declared that the peasant soup of the German province Schleswig-Holstein was descended from Spartan broth.

The Roman tourists who converged on the city in the first and second centuries A.D. were also inveterate Sparta fans: They were fascinated with the grim. "Lycurgan code," which reminded them of the tough, simple, disciplined Romans of earliest antiquity, the men and women who had built the Empire. They eagerly inspected the military trophies on display in the city center, but the real attraction was Sparta's austere lifestyle options. Special local guides called "interpreters of the Lycurgan customs" proudly showed visitors around local institutions explained the brutal system of education and arranged introductions to charming Spartan officials like the "Controllers of the Women." Many tourists dined on grisly black broth with the men in the communal barracks, noting with approval how they still wore their hair long over traditional vermilion cloaks. The more valiant liked to spar with them. There is a record of one Roman tourist by the name of Palfurius Sura—a senator no less—electing to wrestle a muscular Spartan girl in the ring. The sex-starved poet Propertius, meanwhile, preferred to watch, going into paroxysms of delight at the naked grapplings.

Above all, there were the sadistic rituals: Every tourist tried to have his visit coincide with the annual scourging of the youths at the festival of Artemis. That was when the adolescent boys of Sparta were forced to run a merciless gauntlet through the streets, while the city's grown men flogged them savagely with sticks and whips. At the end of the ordeal, the boys prostrated themselves at the altar of the goddess, the savage huntress Artemis, whose primitive wooden idol ran crimson with splattered blood. In this prototype boarding-school ritual, it was crucial that youngsters never wince or cry out in pain. Pausanias, who attended one year, notes that the priestesses of Artemis eagerly urged Spartan men to whip the boys harder, abusing them roundly if they held back their strokes "because of a boy's good looks or social rank." Several of the frailer urchins inevitably died from their wounds: the survivors had their backs scarred for life. As a consolation, the bravest victims were honored with the title Conquerors of the Altar.

The scourging was as popular among voyeuristic Romans as the running of the bulls at Pamplona is for tourists today: raised on a diet of gladiatorial fights, they were hardly squeamish about the bloodshed. Even otherwise humane figures like Cicero reveled in the Old World tradition. The pagan holy man Apollonius was less impressed: "[Crowds] flock to see the spectacle with unbridled enthusiasm, as if it was the annual hyacinth festival." But the majority lapped up the agonies of the young, and made sure to patronize other violent Spartan events like the sphaireis—a bone-crunching ball game between five teams, which one historian likened to a no-holds-barred version of American football, played without helmets or padding.

All very macho, no doubt. But the secret—and rather embarrassing—truth is that these Spartan rituals only survived thanks to the ancient tourist industry. In fact, modern semiotic theorists could have a field day with Sparta: Their most famous habits were examples of what today's anthropologists call "staged authenticity"—a tradition kept alive self-consciously for profit.

Actually, the city's toughest laws and customs had lapsed long before the Roman conquest of Greece. Although the old code was given lip service, it seemed the Spartans had gone soft. But after the occupation, the Romans encouraged the revival of the harsh way of life they admired so much. In the first century A.D. the emperors began giving Spartans special treatment for their noble traditions. Increasing numbers of tourists from around the Empire arrived in search of "the real Sparta" they had read about back home, creating a lucrative trade.

It's tempting to be cynical about Sparta, putting its rituals on a par with modern tourist shows like the "native dances" held every night in Caribbean hotels. But cultural revivals are rarely so simple. Spartan families eagerly sent their sons forward every year to their thrashing for reasons that were far from mercenary. Keeping up tradition won Sparta respect throughout the Empire—ensuring that an otherwise tiny and not particularly remarkable provincial city could maintain its status in the world. To be a Spartan was to be unique, the inheritor of prestige that ran back to king Leonidas. You can almost feel sorry for the Spartans: Like old gunslingers in Wild West movies who because of their reputations are forever challenged by young bucks to shoot-outs, the Spartans were trapped by their past, doomed to repeat the bloodstained rites of their code. If ever they failed to live up to their image, Greeks and Romans were furious: Aristides devoted a whole oration to denouncing the Spartans for taking a fancy to pantomime.

I ♥ SPARTA

Descending through that ring of mountain peaks around Sparta—which pressed so tightly that the ancient city never needed defensive walls—I hardly expected its modern citizens to wear their badge of severity today. But somehow I couldn't hold out much hope for the city itself. It would be an industrial wasteland at best, full of sullen shadows of its unpleasant forebears.

This image slowly withered as we passed through the luscious groves of orange trees, past the flourishing flower gardens, and took a sent in the main plaza, past the flourishing flower gardens and took a sent in the main plaza, filled with fresh-faced young families to discover that once fearsome Sparta has become one of the most docile towns in Greece. And because its historical ruins are notoriously this, it sees hardly any visitors.

His name was Kosta. He had thick black-framed glasses and a Trotsky goatee. Like so many Greeks, he'd done a tour of duty overseas to make his money without ever forgetting his plans to come home to the impoverished plot of land where he grew up. After pumping our hands, he yelled out to his waitress daughter. "Hey, Alexia! C'mere. These guys are from New York!"

"Oh yeah? Manhattan? She was in her twenties. With heavily made up almond eyes, like a princess in a Minoan painting. "I liked growing up there in America, sure I did. But you can't beat Sparta."

"Best little town in Greece," her pop agreed.

I asked this Spartan Chamber of Commerce what was so great about it.

"You've been to Athens, right?" Alexia said. "Everyone's just in a bad mood. They're rude and pushy. They want to take your money then they want you out. You try to live in the countryside, it's full of sad old people. Young people, they just have to leave."

I thought of the last six villages we'd driven through, and took her point. Sparta was a boomtown by comparison. And then, to eradicate any doubt, Alexia insisted on taking us to something called the Hellas Cultural Association.

It was a Saturday afternoon—party time in the Peloponnesus—and from an unassuming back street we caught the semihysterical strains of bouzouki music wafting from a window. For once, it wasn't the ubiquitous "Zorba" on a perpetual loop—but actual live music, boisterous and loud.

Dark stairs led up to a bar, where an impromptu jam session was in progress. Littered throughout the tightly packed tables, a half-dozen customers, faces sweating out pure alcohol, were beating on battered guitars and tambourines, while the rest of the patrons—the most bohemian Greeks I'd ever seen—were quaffing vials of ouzo, all the while hypnotized by the music. The place felt private and intimidatingly insular, like some mystical cabal, but the owner saw Alexia and waved us over. When he saw the silver worry beads in my hand, he mistook us for Greeks, too: With great enthusiasm he grabbed our arms and dragged us over to the only empty table.

"Retsina," I mumbled to the waitress in my thickest accent.

And then the whole room erupted into song shifting easily from a mournful ballad to full-throated anthem. One by one, ouzo-addled guests stood up and clapped or sang, tears in their eyes, to signify their approval. An enormous gypsy lady suddenly swayed to her feet to dance. She spun slowly on her heels, gliding easily from one table to the next, like a great soft pinball, leaving a trail of admirers in her wake. The audience guided her around the room with their open palms slipping hundred-drachma notes into her belt as tokens of appreciation; several threw their glasses onto the floor in musical punctuation. Through the window the fortress hill of Sparta turned golden in the dusk.

"You see!" Alexia announced jubilantly. "This is when Greeks are really themselves! The rest is just an act."

That night, as we wandered back to our hotel through the empty provincial plaza, I was more than ready to sign on to the new Spartan code. The physical remains of ancient Sparta didn't add up to much—in fact, as the historian Thucydides once wrote, future generations would find it difficult to believe the great power Sparta had once wielded. But I looked at it this way: In the last two thousand years, Spartans had certainly learned to chill out.

And yet ... I couldn't help wondering, a little illogically, I admit, what had happened to those feral Spartans and all those savage warriors in their brilliant vermilion cloaks and hair hanging down to their shoulders, the men who would fight to the death or commit hara-kiri in shame. Could the cultural DNA of Sparta have so completely dissolved?

I was as bad as an ancient Roman: I wanted a sign from the past.

HIGHWAY TO THE UNDERWORLD

It was only a couple of days later when I understood: the austere military code had migrated about one hundred miles south of the city, to a remote finger of harsh (and yes, Spartan) desert known simply as the Mani. It's a scorched, inhuman domain of rocks and thorns—and a logical setting, at its farthest tip, for Cape Taenarus, the entrance to the underworld that Hercules used when he went to capture the three-headed dog of Hades, Cerberus. (Pausanias made the journey there to pay his respects, but was disappointed to find that the cave actually led nowhere; today, even the cave has disappeared, although the windswept, uninhabited promontory, surrounded by sheer cliffs and patrolled by the occasional quail hunter, feels like the remotest and loneliest place in the Mediterranean). The inhospitable wasteland of the Mani was where the bravest Spartan warriors were said to have retreated after the Roman invasion of Greece. In the Middle Ages, it was the last holdout of die-hard pagans against Christians; later, of Byzantine knights against Turks.

Even today, the Maniots try to uphold the military ethic of Sparta—especially in the fortress-hotels of Aeropolis, a town named after the ancient god of war, Ares.

"I am partisan! Boom boom!" our elderly host, George Versakos, announced at the breakfast table on the first morning, waving a bayonet with a derringer attached to it. He gestured to a tinted photograph of himself as a partisan soldier, taken fifty-five years ago.

"Germans afraid! Boom boom!"

"Nescafe?" his wife asked, ignoring the man completely as she offered a lone sachet of instant on a saucer like an after-dinner mint.

Mr. Versakos snorted in disgust at this domestic interruption, and continued to show off his private war museum, a rusty collection of Turkish scabbards, cowboy Colt pistols, and antique machine guns. Now in his seventies, he was spiffily dressed, with a trimmed white mustache and a buffed Greek naval cap. His house, a three-hundred-year-old family heirloom, was actually a stone defensive tower with slits for windows. Mr. Versakos and his wife kept their paying guests in the two spare rooms—or at least tried to. When they weren't throwing things at each other or screaming abuse at the top of their voices, for their mutual hatred was implacable.

It turns out that the Spartan traditions have never quite died in the Mani. As late as the early 1900s, its scowling, illiterate peasants lived completely isolated from the rest of Greece in a primitive feudal society that was consumed by rabid blood feuds. According to one Greek poem recorded by the travel writer Patrick Leigh Fermor, Maniots went about "armed to the teeth wilder than vampires," slaughtering one another gleefully. Women's work was to breed large families; male children were called literally, "guns," and tutored in brutality. To further their endless and meaningless wars, the Maniots built hundreds of these stolid stone towers, so that enemy families could pick one another off with rusty antique muskets and cannons. Recently, some of these box relics have been turned into small and uneconomical bed-and-breakfasts.

In Aeropolis, Mr. Versakos continues to upset his guests' digestion every morning by leaping up from the breakfast table, waving a scimitar, and denouncing all Turks as barnyard animals.

"Greek soldier? Bravo! Turkish soldier? Baa-baa."

Not sure what to say to George, I tried a little light conversation with Mrs. Versakos "Ah … so your husband was a partisan in the war?"

She just rolled her eyes and pushed forward a plate of dried olives, the inexplicable core of any Greek breakfast.

"Boom boom!" Mr. Versakos repeated more loudly.

Portraits of Greek independence heroes with huge mustaches covered the walls—Mr. Versakos claimed they had all slept here in the fortress, back in the 1800s—as well as a framed photo of the Versakoses' son Nick in military uniform. Nick was carrying on the great tradition of King Leonidas as a Greek air force pilot. From behind enormous mirrored glasses, he stared back at the young colonel Gadhafi.

"My hero son," Mrs. Versakos said enigmatically "You will meet him."

The next morning, we did have the pleasure, when we came across Nick sprawled out on the living room floor. Compared to the photograph, he was looking somewhat the worse for wear. He was wearing a sweat-stained undershirt and was disheveled and unshaven, with a burned-out cigarette hanging from one lip. Mr. Versakos, whose outfit was as crisp as Bertie Wooster's gazed on appalled as his offspring stretched himself, rearranged his inside trouser leg, and lit another rancid cigarette. The son, for his part, groaned every time George went "boom boom," and muttered curses under his breath. Mrs. Versakos looked at them both with open contempt, then limped off to the laundry to do the actual work of running a guest house.

Later I asked the locals about the Versakos clan and their military fables. They were decidedly exaggerated, apparently. There were no records of independence heroes staying in the house. Even the Greek navy cap was an affectation, they opined. Since Mr. Versakos had certainly never been to sea—not even on a ferry to the islands.

But, I asked, he must have been with the partisans in the war: The portrait of him proved it. Or was that all an elaborate fantasy as well?

"Oh, I'm sure he joined the partisans," a neighbor snorted. "But only to wear the uniform."

PAUSANIAS' GUIDE TO GREECE
Book III: Lakonia

Translated by Peter Levi

[I] Beyond Thornax you come to the city originally called SPARTA which in the course of time came also to be called Lakedaimon, the old territorial name. Before I speak about the Spartans I must make the same clarification that I made in my essay on Attica: I am not going through everything in order, but selecting and discussing the really memorable things. It has been the intention of this book from the beginning to discriminate what truly merited discussion from the mass of worthless stories which every people will tell you about themselves. Since my plan has been a good one there is no change I can make in it.

[2] The Lakonians of Sparta have a MARKET-PLACE worth seeing, and the council-house of the Elders and the government chambers of the Governors and the protectors of laws and of the Bidiaioi are in the market-place.[1] The Elders are the principal political committee of Lakonia, and the rest are government officers. There are five Governors and five Bidiaioi; the Governors control the most important arrangements and years are

---

1   The site of Sparta lies almost in the shadow of the great Byzantine fortress of mistra; it was called palaiokastro, the old castle, and was never entirely abandoned. Its site became known to the west through Gemistos Plethon of *mistra*, which was also called *spartovouno*. Cyriaco of Ancona visited it in September 1437. The area of ancient Sparta was then still littered with fragments of antiquity, including inscriptions, though a great part of it seems to have been deliberately destroyed by the Abbé Fourmont in the eighteenth century, who ravaged Sparta with from forty to sixty workmen for thirty days, in order to increase by rarity the value of the notes he took. Much of what was left was taken by the villagers of another village for building materials. The first building to be positively identified was the theatre, which was discovered by the Russian military expedition of 1770 under Count Orlov, while they were digging themselves in against the Turks. In the 1840s Ernst Curtius discovered the ruins of the Eurotas bridge by which I suppose Pausanias entered the city. There is an interesting archaeological guide to Sparta in modern Greek by C. A. Christou. The *agora*, the chief public square of Pausanias's Sparta, seems to have been the level ground south-east of the akropolis and the theatre. We know from Thukydides (1, 10) that classical Sparta was not physically impressive; Roman Sparta was certainly more elaborate, but very little of the agora is to be seen. Cf B.S.A., 12, 1905–6, pp. 432–5 and the general map in B.S.A., 13.

named after them, just as one of the nine at Athens is eponymous officer; the Bidiaioi hold the games at the Planes and the other traditional games for lads past adolescence. [3] The most striking monument in the marketplace is called the PERSIAN COLONNADE, built from the spoils of the Persian Wars.[2] It was altered in the course of time until it reached the size and the decorative splendour you now see. One of the Persians carved in marble on the pillars is Mardonios. There is also a sculpture of Artemisia, daughter of Lygdamis and queen of Halikarnassos. She is supposed to have volunteered to fight for Xerxes against Greece, and done great deeds in the sea-fight at Salamis.[3] [4] The TEMPLES on the market-place are consecrated to Caesar, the first Roman to set his heart on supreme sovereignty and the first founder of the established empire, and to Caesar's son Augustus, who established the empire more solidly and outdid his father in dignity and in power. His name was Augustus; in Greek it means 'august'. [5] By Augustus's altar they show you a bronze portrait of Agias. They say this Agias by his prophetic advice to Lysander took the whole Athenian fleet at Aigospotamoi except for ten warships that fled to Cyprus.[4] All the rest were caught by the Lakonians, ships and men. Agias was the son of Agelochos, whose father Tisamenos belonged to the Elean clan of the Iamidai.[5] [6] There was a prophecy that Tisamenos was going to carry off five very famous contests, so he trained for the Olympic pentathlon but he was beaten, though he came first in two events. He beat Hieronymos of Andros in the running and the jumping, but he was beaten in the wrestling and lost his victory, so then he understood the oracle: the god was going to give him prophecy and victory in five battles. [7] The Lakonians had heard what the Pythian priestess had predicted for Tisamenos, and they persuaded him to move from Elis to prophesy for the Spartan people. Tisamenos won his five battles, first against the Persians at Plataia, second at Tegea in a battle the Lakonians fought against Tegeans and Argives, then at Dipaia, which is an Arkadian town in the region of Mainalos, against all Arkadia except for Mantineia; [8] the fourth time he fought against the rebel serfs from the isthmus[6] at Ithome—it was not all the serfs who rebelled, but the Messenians who split off from the old serfs, as I shall explain presently. Lakonia was persuaded by Tisamenos and the Delphic oracle to let the rebels get away under a truce. Finally Tisamenos prophesied for the Lakonians when they met the Athenians and the Argives at Tanagra.

---

2   The statues of the enemy held up the roof. Cf. Vitruvius, 1, 1, 6.

3   This history is told more fully by Herodotos (7, 99, and 8, 87f.); Pausanias combines as well as abbreviates the two passages and adds a seed of uncertainty. Herodotos, whom he trusts, is very likely not his direct source here.

4   The decisive battle of the Peloponnesian War.

5   They had prophetic powers; cf. Bk IV, 16 (1), etc. This story comes from Herodotos (1, 33–6).

6   This peculiar phrase comes from Herodotos (9, 35). Perhaps Herodotos thought Messenia was an isthmus. There was a legendary Messenian King Isthmios (Bk IV, 3 (10)).

[9] This was what I discovered about Tisamenos. The Spartans have statues in their market-place of Pythaian Apollo and Artemis and Leto.[7] This whole area is called the dancing floor, because on the feast of the naked boys, which is the most solemn of all Lakonian festivals, this is where the boys of fighting age dance to Apollo. Not far from here is a sanctuary of Earth and of Market Zeus,[8] and one of Market Athene and the Poseidon called Safe Poseidon, and one of Apollo and Hera. There is a large statue of the People of Sparta. [10] The Lakonians have a sanctuary of the Fates as well, with the grave of Agamemnon's son Orestes beside it; when his bones were brought from Tegea through the oracle this is where they buried him.[9] Beside his grave is a portrait of Polydoros son of Alkamenes, a king so honoured that the officers of state seal every sealed document with his portrait.[10] [11] There is a Market Hermes holding the boy Dionysos, and the ancient sanctuary of the Governors as it was called, with the monuments of Epimenides the Cretan and Aphareus son of Perieres. I think that the Lakonian story about Epimenides is a more likely one than the Argos story.[11] The Lakonian Hearth goddess and Zeus of Strangers and Athene of Strangers are in the same place as the Fates.

[1] As you leave the market-place by LEAVING STREET you come to what they call the CATTLEPRICE; but I must deal first with the name of the street. They say Ikarios held a race for Penelope's lovers, and obviously Odysseus won, but the others were left

---

7   'Pythaian' is a variant of 'Pythian' Apollo. 'Python' is usually the name for Apollo's original enemy, the monster that he killed; its etymology has to do with corruption (cf. Bk X, 6 (5)). Apollo is a god of institutional and ritual purity and its benefits; Apollo and Artemis were Leto's children. For the unconvincing figure of 'Pythaieus son of Apollo', cf. Bk II, 35 (2).

8   The *agora* is not simply a market: the word means the meeting-place and in Homer the assembly of the whole people. It is impossible to convey all the nuances of such a word by blunt translation; in fact it is often difficult to determine them.

9   Cf. Bk III, 3 (6).

10   Polydoros is an early king (cf. Bk III, 3 (1)). His house was also preserved (Bk III, 12 (3)). Since he is supposed to have been murdered, these traces of cult may have been originally a placation of his dangerous ghost; at any rate one should note his association with the magic bones of Orestes, and with the sanctuary of the Fates, who are closely related to the Furies. The seal, if it was not a modern 'portrait,' may possibly have been a Minoan seal-stone; these seals survived in use, or were rediscovered, and one was found for example in the context of an archaic Lakonian sanctuary at Tocra in Libya.

11   11.This Hermes appears on the Roman coinage of Sparta. Epimenides the Cretan was a legendary holy man and prophet whom the Lakonians were supposed to have murdered after a war with Knossos; they claimed to possess his relics in this monument, but he had another grave at Argos; the Argives claimed to have taken home his dead body and buried it at a temple of Athene (cf. Bk II, 21 (3)). Aphareus was a legendary king of Messenia, where he was associated with the cult of the Great goddesses (cf. Bk III, 1 (4), and Bk IV, 2 (7)). No legends have survived about his death or his burial at Sparta, but his two sons were killed by the Dioskouroi.

behind in Leaving Street. [2] I imagine Ikarios got the idea of a race from Danaos, who did the same thing for his daughters.[12] No one would marry them because they were criminals, so he announced he would give them away without a bride-price to anyone who thought they were beautiful; some men did turn up though not many, so he held a race for them, and the first home had first choice and the second home had second choice and so on down to the last. The girls left over had to wait for more lovers to arrive and another race. [3] On this road as I said before lies the Cattleprice, which was once King Polydoros's house; when he died they bought it with cattle from his widow. There was no silver or gold money in those days, and they still used to pay in the old-fashioned way with cattle and slaves and un-minted silver and gold. [4] The sailors on the ships that go to India say the Indians will give produce in exchange for a Greek cargo, but coins are meaningless to them, even though they have an enormous amount of gold and bronze.

Beyond the government chambers of the Bidiaioi there is a SANCTUARY OF ATHENE.[13] Odysseus is supposed to have installed the statue and called it Athene of the Road when he beat Penelope's lovers in the race. He installed three separate sanctuaries of Athene of the Road separately placed. [5] Farther along Leaving Street there are the shrines of the divine heroes Iops, who is thought to have lived in the time of Lelex or Myles, and Amphiaraos son of Oikles. They think this last was built for Amphiaraos by the sons of Tyndareos because he was their cousin.[14] There is another shrine to the divine hero Lelex himself, and not far off a sacred enclosure of Poseidon with the title Poseidon of Tainaron, with a statue of Athene quite close to it which they say was dedicated by Taras and the colonial expedition that went to settle in Italy.[15] [6] The story about the place called HELLENION is that when Xerxes crossed into Europe and they were getting

12   There was a religious cult of Penelope in eastern Arkadia, where she was supposed to have died (cf. Bk VIII, 12 (3)). There was a legend that she was the mother of the Arkadian god Pan (Herodotos, 2, 145). The story of Danaos and his daughters, who were all married off before lunch, is told in perhaps the most sparkling of all Pindar's odes, the ninth Pythian (193f.). Their crime was murdering the fifty sons of Aigyptos, who were their first husbands, on their wedding night.

13   For the Bidiaioi cf. Bk III, 11 (2), above.

14   No one knows anything at all about Iops; but there are local divine heroes of whom the same can be said everywhere in Greece. The prophet Amphiaraos was a cousin of the sons of Tyndareos, that is of Kastor and Polydeukes, the Dioskouroi, because Amphiaraos's mother Hypermnestra was their mother Leda's sister.

15   For Lelex cf. Bk III, 1 (1), above. Tainaron is Cape MATAPAN, the southernmost point of the MANI, which is the central prong of southern Greece (cf. Bk III, 25 (4–8), and Bk IV, 24 (5)). Poseidon of Tainaron was the god of a rich and elaborate guild at Sparta which recorded its membership in three inscriptions now in the Sparta museum (n. 205–7, = 1G. V (i) 210–12). They were found in June 1857 when a house was being built for Loukas Rallis 'in the lowest part of the city towards the Eurotas'. Mr Rallis in the old Greek tradition built them into his walls above his front door 'come un piccolo museo di statue ed inscrizioni' (cf. Conze and Michaelis in *Annuali dell' Instituto di Correspondenza Archaeologica* for 1861, pp. 41f.).

ready to fight for Greece, this was where they planned their method of defence. The other story is that the men who fought the Trojan War for Menelaos made their plan here to sail to Troy and punish Paris for the rape of Helen.

[7] Close to the Hellenion they point out Talthybios's tomb. But the Achaians of Aigion show you what they, just like the Lakonians, call Talthybios's tomb in their own market-place. Talthybios's revenge for the murder of the heralds who were sent to Greece to demand earth and water for King Darius fell in Lakonia on the whole people, but in Athens it struck privately at the family of one man, Miltiades son of Kimon, because he was responsible for the heralds who came to Attica being killed by the Athenians.[16]

[8] The Lakonians have an ALTAR OF APOLLO of the Peak, and a sanctuary of Earth called GASEPTON, above which is Apollo Maleates.[17] At the end of Leaving Street and very close to the ramparts there is a SANCTUARY OF DIKTYNNA, and the royal GRAVES OF THE EURYPONTIDAI are here. By the Hellenion is a sanctuary of Arsinoe, Leukippos's daughter, whose sisters were the wives of Kastor and Polydeukes. Near the Forts as they call them there is a TEMPLE OF ARTEMIS, and a little farther on you come to the monument of the prophets from Elis called the Iamidai.[18] [9] There is also a sanctuary of Maro and of Alpheios, who, it seems, fought best after Leonidas himself in the battle of Thermopylai. The SANCTUARY OF ZEUS of the Trophy was built by the Dorians after winning a war against the Amyklaians and against all those other Achaians who in those days held Lakonia.[19] The honours given to the SANCTUARY OF THE GREAT MOTHER are really extraordinary. Beyond it lie the shrines of the divine heroes, Theseus's son

---

Presumably all this rich material marked the sanctuary of Poseidon and the direction of Pausanias's road, but the place where it was found cannot now be pinpointed.

16 Talthybios is Agamemnon's herald in the *Iliad*. He was an important divine hero, and legendary founder of the clan of Talthybiadai, the hereditary heralds of Sparta (cf. Herodotos 7, 134). Pausanias records several instances of religious cult attaching to the sacred statues of heralds. Since it was the function of heralds to ask a truce for the burial of the dead, and since Hermes is a herald as well as an underworld messenger, there may be a connexion with the cult of Hermes.

17 Apollo Maleates had a sanctuary on the hill above the Asklepieion at Epidauros; he is also associated with Asklepios's cave at Trikka in Thessaly; cf. Bk II, 27 (7).

18 For Artemis's nymph Diktynna, patron of the great temple on Aigina, cf. Bk II, 30 (3). The topography of all these Spartan sanctuaries lacks a fixed point. For the Iamidai, cf. Book VI, 2 (5).

19 Pausanias presents a version of early Spartan history in which expansion towards the south came comparatively late, presumably because it was blocked by Amyklai only a few miles away. By Achaians he means non-Dorians, that is the inhabitants of southern Greece before the 'Dorian invasion', which he identifies with the 'return of the children of Herakles'. Historically this theory is of course worthless, but it is only by understanding how most of his views of early history arose from general principles that one can distinguish grains of specific fact and tradition like this one.

Hippolytos and Aulo the Arkadian who was a son of Tlesimenes. They say Tlesimenes was a brother of Parthenopaios son of Melanion, and Aulo's father.[20]

[10] There is another road out of the market-square; what they call the CANOPY stands on it; political assemblies take place there to this day.[21] They say the Canopy was built by Theodoros of Samos; he was the first man to forge iron and make statues from it.[22] Here the Lakonians hung up the guitar played by Timotheos of Miletos, when they condemned him for adding four new strings to the old seven-stringed guitar.[23] [11] Beside the Canopy is a rotunda with statues of Olympian Zeus and Olympian Aphrodite. They say it was erected by Epimenides; they disagree with the Argives about Epimenides, and deny that they ever fought a war against Knossos.[24]

[1] Near by is the grave of Kynortas the son of Amyklas; KASTOR'S TOMB is there, and he has a sanctuary as well as a tomb. They reckon it was not until forty years after their fight with Idas and Lynkeus that the sons of Tyndareos were accepted for gods. They show you the grave of Idas and Lynkeus near the Canopy.[25] According to probability Idas and Lynkeus were buried in Messenia, and not buried here; [2] but the calamities of history and the period of the Messenian exile from the Peloponnese have obliterated a great part of Messenian antiquity, even if you go down there; and since the Messenians have no real information, anyone who wants can contradict them.

Opposite Olympian Aphrodite stands the TEMPLE OF THE MAID of Salvation., supposed to have been built by Thracian Orpheus, though some say Abaris came from the fabulous North to build it. [3] Karneios, whose title is Household Karneios, was worshipped at Sparta even before the return of the children of Herakles; his sanctuary was in the house of Krios son of Theokles, who was a prophet. One day some Dorian spies met Krios's daughter fetching water, and by talking to her they got to see Krios,

---

20 Aulo is quite unknown except for this passage. His name is a place-name, and there was an Aulonian Asklepios in Messenia (Bk IV, 36 (7); cf. Xenophon, *Hellenika*, 3, 2, 25).

21 The word is hard to translate; it means a building with a roof like a sunhat or a parasol. The *Etymologicon Magnum* says this building was a music-hall, an *Odeion*.

22 Elsewhere he says this master worked in bronze (Bk VIII, 14 (8)). He also remarks (Bk X, 38 (6)) that he has never seen any of Theodoros's works, at least his bronze works. Theodoros lived in the mid sixth century.

23 This was a famous piece of Spartan austerity. Timotheos was born about 450 B.C. and seems to have lived to be ninety. Fragments of a rhetorical and grotesquely pretentious poem by him have survived on a papyrus of the fourth century B.C. He regarded himself as a revolutionary musician, which no doubt he was.

24 Cf. Note 82 above.

25 For Kynortas, cf. Bk III, 1 (3). Kastor and Polydeukes are the Dioskouroi, the legendary twin sons of Tyndareos, who came to be thought of as sons of Zeus. In the *Iliad* they are simple human beings and in fact dead and buried in Sparta (3, 237f.). but in the *Odyssey* they take it in turns to be dead or alive (11, 300f). The fight was when the Dioskouroi carried off two girls, Leukippos's daughters; Leukippos's nephews Idas and Lynkeus were killed, but so was Kastor. The legend is that Kastor was human and Polydeukes was a god, but after Kastor's death they used Polydeukes' immortality on alternate days.

who told them about the taking of Sparta. [4] All the Dorians have a tradition of the worship of Karnean Apollo, because of Karnos who was by blood an Akarnanian, and a prophet of Apollo. When Hippotes the son of Phylas killed Karnos, the vengeance of Apollo fell on the Dorian camp; Hippotes went into exile for the murder, and since that time the Dorians have had the tradition of placating the Akarnanian prophet. But the Lakonian Household Karneios is different; he is the god who was worshipped in the house of Krios the prophet when the Achaians still owned Sparta.[26] [5] Praxilla has written that Karneios was the son of Europa and Zeus, brought up by Apollo and Leto; and there is another story about him, saying that to make the wooden horse the Greeks cut down wild cherry-trees growing in Apollo's wood on the Trojan mount Ida; when they heard the god was angry with them they placated him with sacrifices and named him Karneian Apollo after the word kraneia (a wild cherry-tree), changing the position of the letter R in what is apparently an ancient way.[27]

[6] Not far from Karneios is what they call the statue of the Starting god. This is where they say the race for Penelope's lovers began. There is a kind of square with colonnades which in the old days used to be the place for small trading. Beside it is an altar of Zeus of Counsel and Athene of Counsel and even the Dioskouroi of Counsel. [7] Opposite all this stands KOLONA with the temple of Dionysos of Kolona, with the sacred enclosure of a divine hero who is supposed to have shown Dionysos the way to Sparta. The daughters of Dionysos and of Leukippos sacrifice to this hero before sacrificing to the god. The other eleven who are also called daughters of Dionysos have a race in which they run; they took the tradition from Delphi.[28] [8] Not far from Dionysos's temple is a SANCTUARY OF ZEUS of good winds, on the right of which is a shrine of the divine hero Pleuro, ancestor of the sons of Tyndareos on their mother's side, because Asios says in his poetry that Leda's father Thestios was the son of Pluero's son Agenor.[29] Not far from his shrine a TEMPLE OF ARGIVE HERA stands on the top of a slope. It is supposed to have been founded by Lakedaimon's daughter Eurydike, who

---

26   The family of a hereditary priestess of Karneios in the Roman imperial period has been elaborated and charted on the evidence of inscriptions (I.G., V, p. 131). The word karnos means a ram; so does the word *krios*, and rams were slaughtered at the Karneian festival.

27   Praxilla of Sikyon was a fifth-century poetess. The story about the wild cherry may not be as old as it looks; the etymology could easily be Alexandrian. (But cf. also Vergil, *Aeneid*, 3, 22f. and Plutarch, *Romulus*, 20.)

28   These 'daughters' are religious guilds. There is perhaps a remote analogy with the festival being celebrated in Alkman's Partheneion. If the Dionysos of Kolona of Pausanias and of his predecessor Polemo (cf. Athenaios 13, 574 c–d) is the same as Strabo's Dionysos in the Marshes (8, 5, 1; 363), then Kolona is presumably the hill between Artemis Orthia and the akropolis.

29   The manuscripts of Pausanias say this poet was called *Areios*; if they are right he seems to be a writer of genealogical hexameters of whom absolutely nothing is known. On the other hand we know that Pausanias quotes Asios elsewhere, and we know that Asios did write a genealogical poem (Bk IV, 2 (1)).

was Akrisios's wife. The sanctuary of Hera of the Raised Hands was built because of an oracle when the Eurotas was flooding badly.

[9] The ancient wooden idol is called Aphrodite Hera; the custom is for mothers to sacrifice to this goddess when a daughter marries.[30] On this same hillside along the road to the right there is a portrait of Hetoimokles; he and his father Hipposthenes won the wrestling at Olympia eleven times between them; Hipposthenes won one more time than his son.[31]

[1] As you go from the market-place towards the setting sun, you come to the empty monument of Brasidas the son of Tellis.[32] Not far away lies the THEATRE, which is marble and worth seeing. Opposite the theatre stands the MONUMENT OF PAUSANIAS who commanded at Plataia, and the MONUMENT OF LEONIDAS; Pausanias brought his bones home from Thermopylai forty years after the battle.[33] Every year they make speeches about them, and hold games in which only Spartans can enter. There is a stone tablet here with the names of all the men who fought out that battle, and their father's names.

[2] There is a place at Sparta called THEOMELIDA; the royal tombs of the Agiadai are in this part of the city, the Krotanian club is near the tombs, and the Krotanians belong to the Pitanatai; there is a sanctuary of Asklepios near the club called the sanctuary of Asklepios at the Agiadai.[34] Farther on you come to the MONUMENT OF TAINAROS, after whom the cape jutting out into the sea is supposed to have been named, and there are SANCTUARIES of Horse-breeding Poseidon and Artemis of the Goats. On the way back to the club you come to a sanctuary of Issorian Artemis; she also has the title of the Lake-goddess; she is not really Artemis, but Cretan Britomartis, whom I discussed in my description of Aigina.[35] [3] Very close to the monuments of the Agiadai you will

---

30 Plotinos (3, 5, 8) points out that the planet Venus (Aphrodite) is also Hera's star. The problem of a compound goddess Aphrodite Hera is best discussed by Hitzig and Blümner in their commentary on Pausanias, I (2), p. 782.

31 Cf. Bk V, 8 (9).

32 The fifth-century Brasidas, the greatest Spartan commander in the war with Athens. He was buried at Amphipolis. The Hellenistic theatre has been disengaged but its marble has not survived.

33 The traditional 'tomb of Leonidas' identified by early travellers is some distance from the theatre and the akropolis, just on the edge of the modern town. It is a small, massively built Hellenistic temple. These two tombs must have been close to the theatre; they have not been found.

34 The Pitanatai are the villagers of Pitane. The villages of which the city of Sparta, like old London, consisted were never completely integrated; these districts can be more or less accurately identified through a combined use of Pausanias and of the evidence of inscriptions (cf. Christou, *Archaia Sparte*, pp. 47–52). Two stamped tiles belonging to the Pitanatai have been recovered from a wall on KOKKINOKI; the area is now called magoula.

35 Cf. Bk II, 30 (3). This sanctuary was a strongpoint and stood on a hill (Plutarch, *Agesilaos*, 32). Issorion was the name of the hill, though 'Issorian Artemis' was also worshipped at Teuthrone (cf. Bk III, 25 (4)), and

see a tablet engraved with the races won by a Lakonian called Chionis, some of them at Olympia. He won seven times at Olympia, four times over one length and three times over two; the race with the shield at the end of the games did not yet exist. They say Chionis took part in the expedition with Battos of Thera and helped him found Kyrene and subdue the neighbouring Libyans.[36]

[4] This is the origin they give for the foundation of the SANCTUARY OF THETIS. In the war against the Messenian rebellion King Anaxander had invaded Messenia and taken some women prisoners; one of these was Kleo, who was a priestess of Thetis. Anaxander's wife asked him for Kleo, and discovered that she had the wooden idol of Thetis, so she and Kleo made a temple for the goddess. Leandris did this because of what she saw in a dream.[37] [5] The wooden idol of Thetis is kept hidden. The Lakonians claim they were taught to worship Underground Demeter by Orpheus, but in my opinion it was through the sanctuary at Hermione that the tradition of Demeter as Underground goddess spread to Lakonia.[38] There is also a Spartan SANCTUARY OF SARAPIS, which is extremely new, and of Zeus under the title of Olympian.

[6] There is a place they call the RACE-COURSE, where the young Lakonians practise running to this day.[39] If you proceed to the Race-course from the tomb of the Agiadai, the monument of Eumedes will be on your left. This Eumedes was another of the sons of Hippokoon. There is a statue of Herakles where sacrifices are offered by the Ball-players, adolescent boys just on the point of complete manhood. There are also gymnasia built on the Race-course, one of them dedicated by Eurykles the Spartan.[40] Outside the Race-course by Herakles' statue stands a house which in our own times is in private hands, but in antiquity it belonged to Menelaos As you go on from the Race-course you come to a SANCTUARY of Dioskouroi and Graces, and one of Eileithuia and Karneian Apollo and Artemis the Guide. [7] The SANCTUARY OF AGNITES stands on the right of the Race-course. Agnites is a title of Asklepios, because the god had a wooden idol made of agnus castus; this is a kind of vitex, in the same way as buckthorn. Not far from Asklepios stands a trophy; the story is that Polydeukes put it up after beating Lynkeus, which seems to me another demonstration of how likely it is that the sons of

---

there was a festival called the Issoria. The hill may be klaraki, north-west of the akropolis.

36 Pausanias says he first won in 668 (cf. Bk IV, 23 (4), and Bk VI, 13 (2)). This just fits the traditional foundation date of Kyrene at about 630 B.C. Herodotos tells the story (4, 150 f.).

37 Thetis is an unusual goddess, but the Spartans were particularly enthusiastic about sea-goddesses, and at least in southern Sparta people are still interested in mermaids. There is a fascinating account of this phenomenon in Patrick Leigh Fermor's classic work on southern Greece (*Mani*, p. 50, and pp. 169–70).

38 Cf Bk II, 35 (4f.).

39 This has not been found, and no one knows where it was. N. D. Papahadzis in his commentary on Pausanias (1963) argues persuasively that it lay to the west of the ancient city.

40 Perhaps the rich Augustan Spartan Eurykles (cf. Bk II, 3 (5)) who has a curious niche in history as having been a bad influence in the court of Herod the Great.

Aphareus were not buried at Sparta.[41] By the beginning of the Race-course there are the Dioskouroi as Starting gods, and a little farther on you come to the shrine of the divine hero Alkon; they say he was a son of Hippokoon. By Alkon's shrine is a SANCTUARY OF POSEIDON under the title of House-god.[42]

[8] The place called THE PLANES is named after the plane-trees growing tall and dense all round it. This place, which is the traditional ground for the fight between adolescent boys, is encircled by a moat as if it were an island in the sea; the entrances are bridges. On one of the bridges is a statue of Herakles, on the other a portrait of Lykourgos: among his other constitutional laws Lykourgos legislated for this fight between adolescent boys. They have these other rituals to go through as well: [9] before the fight they sacrifice in the PHOIBAION which is outside the city, not far from Therapne;[43] each side sacrifices a puppy there to Enyalios, with the idea that the most aggressive tame animal will be the right victim for the most aggressive god. I know of no other Greeks who believe in sacrificing puppies except at Kolophon,[44] where they sacrifice a black bitch to Hekate. The sacrifice at Kolophon takes place at night, and so does the boys' sacrifice in Lakonia. [10] After the sacrifice the boys put down hand-reared fighting boars. The side whose boar wins is generally the one that wins at the Planes. That is all done at the Phoibaion; on the next day a little before mid-day they enter the ground I described over the bridges: the entrance each side comes in by was decided by picking straws during the night. They fight hand to hand and with running kicks, they bite and they gouge, man to man; one side flings itself at the other in general charges and they push one another into the water.[45]

[1] Kyniska the daughter of King Archidamos of Sparta has a divine hero's shrine by the Planes. She was the first woman to raise horses and the first woman to win with a team at Olympia.[46] There are some shrines of divine heroes behind the COLONNADE which runs beside the Planes: one of Alkimos, one of Enaraiphoros, one of Dorkeus not far off, with one of Sebros.[47] [2] The spring nearby is called the Dorkeian spring

---

41 I suppose he means that if the fight was here Lynkeus would have been buried here? Cf. Note 96 above.

42 The hereditary priestess Damosthenia (cf. Note 98 above) was also a priestess of Poseidon the House-god.

43 Therapne was south-east of Sparta, on or behind the high cliffs of the Eurotas; cf. Bk III, 19 (7). The Phoibaion has not been discovered, perhaps because there is an *embarras de richesses* of antiquities in this area, and scholars have been confused by inadequate literary sources.

44 Kolophon is in Asia Minor south of Izmir, north-west of Ephesos, and north-east of Samos. Cf. Bk VIII, 3 (1–4).

45 This is the object of the exercise. Cicero's jaundiced account of the violence of this game, which he once saw, is apparently heavily coloured by a context of philosophic argument. The principle is more or less that of the Eton wall game, only with more action.

46 Cf. Bk III, Note 45.

47 Alkimos and his uncouth-sounding brethren are more of the sons of Hippokoon. The spelling of some of their names is uncertain and probably ought not to be regularized. The fragmentary papyrus of Alkman's

after Dorkeus's shrine, and the whole area is called the Sebrion after Sebros. On the right of the Sebrion is ALKMAN'S MONUMENT; the pleasure of the songs he composed is not at all spoilt by their being written in Lakonian, the least musical of languages.

[3] HELEN'S SANCTUARY is near Alkman's grave; HERAKLES' SANCTUARY is very close to the ramparts. It has an armed statue of Herakles; the story is that Herakles' statue is like this because of his battle with Hippokoon and his sons. Herakles is supposed to have been an enemy of Hippokoon and his family because of when he came to Sparta for purification after killing Iphitos, and they refused to let him be purified.[48] [4] There was another cause that contributed to the outbreak of this war: Herakles' nephew Oionos who was a boy at the time came to Sparta with his uncle. He was the son of Alkmene's brother Likymnios. Oionos was wandering about investigating the city and arrived at Hippokoon's house. Hippokoon's guard-dog attacked him, so he flung a stone and knocked the bitch over; Hippokoon's sons came rushing out of the house and beat him to death with their wooden staves. [5] This made Herakles absolutely infuriated with Hippokoon and his sons, and he came and fought them there and then with the anger still in him. On that occasion he was wounded and had to get away quietly, but later on he fought a war against Sparta and took vengeance for the murder of Oionos from Hippokoon and Hippokoon's sons. Oionos's monument stands beside the Herakleion.

[6] Going dead east from the Race-course you come to a path on your right leading to the SANCTUARY OF ATHENE of Vengeance Deserved, because when Herakles came back from giving Hippokoon and his sons what they had been asking for he founded a sanctuary of Athene with the title of Vengeance Deserved, vengeance being the old word for punishment. If you leave the Race-course by the road, you come to a different SANCTUARY OF ATHENE, which they say was founded by Theras son of Autesion, grandson of Tisamenos and great-grandson of Thersander, when he sent off his expedition of colonists to the island which still carries his name, though in ancient times it was called Kalliste.[49] [9] Near this is a shrine of Hipposthenes, the Hipposthenes who won so many wrestling matches. They worship Hipposthenes in honour of Poseidon; the cult was established by an oracle.[50] Just opposite this temple is an antique statue of Enyalios in chains. The Lakonians have the same idea about this statue as the Athenians have about Wingless Victory: in Lakonia they think the god of war will never desert them

---

Partheneion opens with a list of Hippokoon's sons; there is an attempt at a complete list in Apollodoros (3, 10, 5).

48   According to Homer, Herakles had treacherously murdered Iphitos in order to steal some mares and some mules (*Odyssey*, 21, 22f.).

49   Cf. Bk III, Note 7.

50   Cf. Bk III, 13 (9). It has been suggested that this Hipposthenes was simply a projection of Poseidon of Horses. His connexion with the god is certain at least after his death; but he must surely have been a human being.

if they keep him in chains; in Athens they believe Victory will stay with them forever because she has no wings.[51]

[8] That is the kind of cult-statue these cities have erected and that was the kind of belief in which they did so. At Sparta there is also the Painted MEETING-HOUSE with shrines beside it of the divine hero Kadmos son of Agenor and two of his descendants, Oiolykos the son of Theras and Aigeus the son of Oiolykos. The story is that these shrines were built by Maisis, Laias and Europas, the sons of Aigeus's son Hyraios. They built the one for Amphilochos too, because Amphilochos's sister Demonasse was the mother of their ancestor Tisamenos.[52]

[9] The Lakonians are the only people in Greece who have the custom of calling Hera the Goat-eater and sacrificing goats to her. They say Herakles founded the sanctuary and was the first to sacrifice goats, because when he fought Hippokoon and his sons Hera made no trouble for him in the way he felt she opposed him on other occasions. They maintain that he sacrificed goats because he had no other victims.

[10] Not far from the theatre there is a SANCTUARY OF FAMILY POSEIDON, and there are shrines of the divine heroes Kleodaios son of Hyllos and Oibalos.[53] The grandest SANCTUARY OF ASKLEPIOS is at the Cattleprice, and to the left of it lies the shrine of the divine hero Teleklos, whom I shall be mentioning again in my treatment of Messenia.[54] Not far from here you will come to a hill, not very high, on which there is an ancient TEMPLE and an armed cult-statue of Aphrodite. This temple is unique so far as I know in having an upper storey consecrated to the Beautiful goddess. [11] The Beautiful goddess is a title of Aphrodite;[55] she is enthroned and veiled, with fetters on her feet. They say it was Tyndareos who put fetters on her, meaning that the relationship of women to their husbands was as absolute as fetters. As for the story that Tyndareos was

---

51 There was an Aktaion in chains at Orchomenos (Bk IX, 38 (5)) and a chained Aphrodite at Sparta. Frazer in his commentary on Pausanias gives a long and persuasive list of ancient and modern analogies, but it is not clear that the chains were not simply dedications, like perhaps those on Oinomaos's pillar at Olympia.

52 This genealogy is systematic (cf. also Bk V, 17 (7), and Bk IX, 5 (15)). The facts were already entangled with myth and religion in the time of Pindar (*Pythian Odes*, 5, 69–85). It has been plausibly suggested (Immerwahr, *Lakonika*, pp. 79–80) that Pausanias's doctrine had already been systematized by Ephoros in the fourth century. The personal name Damonassa was still in use on Thera until the Hellenistic period (on three inscriptions). Amphilochos and Demonasse (or Damonassa) were the son and daughter of the prophet Amphiaraos. Amphilochos inherited his father's powers; Pausanias mentions (Bk I, 34 (2)) that he had an altar at Athens and an oracle in Asia and that his children shared their grandfather's great altar at Oropos.

53 These are both members of the earliest generations of the Dorian invaders.

54 Cf. Bk IV, 4 (2). He was a Spartan king.

55 That is, *Morpho*; the form of the word indicates a noun and not an adjective. An archaic temple of Aphrodite recently discovered in the Mani by Mr Delivorias (cf. Bk III, Note 255) was inscribed *Iostephano*, the goddess of the violet wreath, a title which occurs as an epithet in the Homeric hymns; it seems to have the same relation to Aphrodite as *Morpho* at Sparta.

taking vengeance on the goddess because he thought it was Aphrodite who disgraced his daughters, I shall not even discuss it.[56] It would have been utterly idiotic to make a doll of cedar-wood and call it Aphrodite, and then imagine he was striking a blow at the goddess.

[1] Near here there is a SANCTUARY OF HILAEIRA AND PHOIBE; the poet of the Kypria says they were Apollo's daughters. Their priestesses are virgin girls, who are called by the same name as the goddesses, Leukippides.[57] One of the statues was ornamented by a Leukippis who had served as a priestess. She gave it a face of contemporary artistry instead of its ancient one, but a dream forbade her to do the same for the other statue. There is an egg here hanging from the roof tied with ribbons; they say this is the legendary egg which was laid by Leda.[58]

[2] Every year the women weave a tunic for the Apollo at Amyklai, and they call the room where they weave it the TUNIC-HOUSE. There is a house near it which they say was first built by Tyndareos's sons, and later came into the possession of a Spartan called Phormion. The Dioskouroi came to visit him disguised as foreigners; they told him they had come from Kyrene and asked him to take them in and let them have the room they had loved most when they were among mankind. [3] He told them they could live wherever they liked in the rest of his house, but not in that room, because his daughter was a young virgin girl and she was living in it. The next morning the young girl and all her attendants vanished; and statues of the Dioskouroi were found in the room, and also a table with sylphium on it.[59]

[4] That is how they say it happened. On the way to the gates from the Tunic-house is a shrine to the divine heroes Chilon who had a reputation for wisdom and Athenodoros who was a member of the Sicilian expedition with Dorieus son of Anaxandridas.[60] This expedition sailed in the belief that the Erykinian territories belonged to Herakles'

---

56 Klytaimnestra murdered her husband Agamemnon, and Helen caused the Trojan war.

57 Leukippos's two daughters who were stolen by the Dioskouroi. The Kypria was an epic poem from which Herodotos, Pausanias and Athenaios have quoted a few fragments, and of which Proklos preserves the skeleton of the plot (Kinkel, *Epic. Gr. Frag.*, pp. 15–31).

58 It was double-yoked and contained the heavenly twins, the Dioskouroi. To mate with Leda Zeus had taken the form of a swan.

59 The sons of Tyndareos are the Dioskouroi; Kyrene was a Lakonian colony, and silphium was the foundation of its wealth. Although silphium is clearly represented on the coinage of Kyrene, it has never been identified in modern times. We know that it was precious and medically powerful, and that it had magic properties.

60 Chilon was an influential mid-sixth-century Governor of Sparta and one of the proverbial Seven Wise Men of the ancient world. He seems to have been responsible for bringing home Orestes' bones. 'Athenodoros' was invented by Madvig to cover a confused and corrupt phrase in the manuscripts. Although Dorieus's expedition (cf. Bk III, 3 (10), and 4 (1)) is described by Herodotos (5, 42–8), 'Athenodoros' is not mentioned. This expedition ended very badly, and it is hard to see how he alone came to be buried at home. Perhaps there was really a shrine of all the Spartan dead whose bones were brought back.

descendants and not to the barbarians who lived there. The story is that Herakles wrestled with Eryx on terms that if Herakles won he should have Eryx's land, and if he was beaten Eryx should take Geryon's cows, which Herakles was driving away at the time; [5] the cows had swum over to Sicily and Herakles had come across to find them at the crooked olive-tree. The gods did not favour Dorieus as they favoured Herakles: Herakles killed Eryx, but Dorieus and most of his army were massacred by the people of Egesta.

[6] The Lakonians have also made a god's SANCTUARY FOR LYKOURGOS the Law-giver.[61] Behind the temple lies the grave of his son Eukosmos, and beside the altar the graves of Lathria and Anaxandra, the twin sisters who were married to Aristodemos's twin sons. They were Thersander's daughters; Thersander's father was Agamedidas king of Kleonai, who was the fourth in line of descent from Herakles' son Ktesippos.[62] Opposite this temple are the memorials of Theopompos son of Nikander, and of Euribiadas who commanded the Lakonian battle fleet against the Persians at Artemision and at Salamis, and nearby is what they call the hero's shrine of Astrabakos.[63]

[7] The place called the LAKE SANCTUARY is sacred to Standing Artemis.[64] They claim this as the idol that Orestes and Iphigeneia stole from the Taurians. The Lakonian

---

61 This sanctuary already existed in the time of Herodotos (1, 66). The most fundamental Spartan laws were attributed to him; he is a shadowy, perhaps a legendary figure, and we know from many inscriptions he was not a divine hero but a god, like Herakles, although, a generation before Pausanias, Plutarch had written his biography. What might possibly be Lykourgos's altar was found by British archaeologists in the bed of the Eurotas in 1906 (B.S.A., 12, pp. 301–2). We depend for the laws on a lost work of Aristotle quoted by Plutarch; they have been much discussed (lucidly and I think most recently by W. G. Forrest in his *History of Sparta*, 1968); their language is so strange as to be suspicious (cf. Jeffery in *Historia*, 1961, and Hammond in *Journal of Hellenic Studies*, 1950, p. 43, n. 8: *horas ex horas* is a phrase for prayers and holy blessings and belongs to the liturgical language of annual festivals).

62 For Aristodemos and his twin sons cf. Bk III, 1 (5f.). Kleonai was a city on high ground between Corinth and Argos, not far from hagios basilios.

63 King Theopompos is associated with the first Messenian War (cf. Bk IV, 4 (4)), which was probably in the late eighth century; this makes him more or less a contemporary of Homer. We know from Section 9 below that Astrabakos was a dead ancestor once driven mad by Artemis; his shrine was at the gate of King Ariston's house, and the dead hero is supposed to have slept with Ariston's wife and generated Demaratos (Herodotos, 6, 69).

64 East of the akropolis and left of the Eurotas bridge as you enter Sparta from Tripolis. This SANCTUARY was excavated by British archaeologists in the 1900s; a small amphitheatre had been noticed there ever since the eighteenth century; its significance emerged in 1906 through the appearance of some archaic lead figurines below the ruins where the Eurotas was eating away its banks. This theatre was in fact built in the third century A.D. to face the east end of a temple which had survived on the same foundations since about 600 B.C. The earliest deposits (corroded bronze and geometric pottery) were in the central and lowest area of a natural hollow; altar succeeded altar in the same position. The characteristic flat lead figurines from

story is that it was brought to Lakonia when Orestes was king here, and this seems to me more probable than the Athenian version, because why should Iphigeneia leave the statue behind at Brauron? And how is it that when the Athenians were getting ready to abandon their country they failed to load this statue on to a ship?[65] [8] To this day the Taurian goddess has so great a name that Cappadocians and the people on the shores of the Euxine claim to possess the same statue, the Lydians claim it at the sanctuary of Artemis Anaiitis, and the Athenians if you please are supposed casually to have watched it disappear as Persian loot: the statue from Brauron was taken to Sousa; later it was given as a gift by Seleukos; and the Syrians of Laodikea have it today.[66] [9] There is another piece of evidence that the Standing goddess of the Lakonians is the old barbarian idol: Astrabakos and Alopekos, the sons of Irbos and the descendants of Agis through Amphikles and Amphisthenes, suddenly went mad when they found this statue, and when the Spartans of Limnai, Kynosouria, Mesoa and Pitane sacrificed to Artemis she cursed them through this statue with quarrels and then with murders; many of them died at her altar and disease devoured the rest.[67] [10] This is the reason why they bloody the altar with human blood. They used to slaughter a human sacrifice chosen by drawing lots; Lykourgos substituted the whipping of fully grown boys, and the altar still gets its fill of human blood.[68] The priestess with the idol stands beside them; the idol is small and light, [11] except that if ever the scourgers pull their strokes because of a boy's beauty or his rank, then the woman finds the idol heavy and hard to carry; she blames the scourgers and says they are hurting her: such a taste for human blood has survived in that statue from the time of the Taurian sacrifices. She is called

---

this sanctuary were recovered in huge numbers and are in many museums, but the principal finds are in the Sparta museum. For a fourth-century sacred building just north of the sanctuary, c.f. *Arch. Reports.* 1968–9, p. 17.

65   Cf. Bk I, 33 (1). The Athenians claimed to have lost it in the Persian wars (cf. Bk VIII, 46 (3)).

66   Strabo said it was at Komana in Cappadocia (12, 2, 3); the claimants on the Euxine are unknown. There seem to have been several cult-places of Artemis Anaiitis in Lydia, and others in Phrygia (B.C.H., 4, 1880, p. 120). She was worshipped at Balkh in Bactria and by Parthians and Sakai as well as Greeks. She was the local water goddess of central Asia (Anahita: the Undefiled) with a thousand arms and a thousand canals, identical with the river Oxus (Amu Darya), cf. Tarn, *Greeks in Bactria and India* (1966), p. 102. For Sousa, cf. Bk III, Note 55. The Laodikean Artemis is represented on coins. Seleukos was one of Alexander's generals who became king of Syria.

67   The people of the four districts or villages of which Sparta was composed.

68   What Pausanias says here about human sacrifice is nonsense based on Euripides. This primitive ritual beating had in the classical period the character of a kind of very rough initiation; in the Roman period the ancient disciplines of Sparta were not only revived but exaggerated to a horrifying degree. The disgusting third-century-A.D. addition of an amphitheatre for tourists to watch boys being savagely beaten can reasonably be related to the other entertainments of that age.

not only the Standing one, but also Withy-tied, because she was found in a thick tangle of withies, with the withy-tree winding round the statue and keeping it standing.

[1] Not far from the Standing one is a SANCTUARY OF EILEITHUIA; they say they built it and recognized Eileithuia as a goddess by order of the Delphic oracle.[69]

The Lakonian AKROPOLIS is not so high as to be a landmark, like Theban Kadmeia and Argive Larisa, nor is it the only hill in the city, but the hill that rises highest into the air is called the akropolis. [2] There is a sanctuary built here of Athene of the City, who is also called BRONZEHOUSE ATHENE.[70] According to the story it was Tyndareos who started the building of this sanctuary, and when he died his sons wanted to finish the building from the spoils of Aphidna, but like their father they died too soon, and it was the Lakonians many years afterwards who erected the temple and the bronze statue, which was made by a local man, Gitiadas.[71] Gitiadas also composed Dorian songs, including a hymn to the goddess. [3] The bronze is worked with numerous labours of Herakles, and numerous good deeds he did of his own free will, and the deeds of the sons of Tyndareos, including the carrying-off of Leukippos's daughters; there is also Hephaistos freeing his mother from the fetters: a story I have explained before in my records of Athens.[72] There is Perseus setting out for Libya to meet Medusa, with the nymphs giving him his cap and the sandals to travel through the air. And the story of Athene's birth is represented, with Amphitrite and Poseidon, in my opinion the most rewarding and the greatest figures of all. [4] There is also another sanctuary here to Athene of Work. If you go into the colonnade to the south you come to a shrine of Zeus the Marshal, in front of which is Tyndareos's memorial. The western colonnade has two eagles carrying two Victories: they were dedicated by Lysander in memory of both his victories, the one at Ephesos when he beat the Athenian warships under Alkibiades' captain Antiochos, and the later one at Aigospotamoi when he destroyed the Athenian fleet.

---

69 Eileithuia is the birth goddess. Perhaps cf. *Arch. Reports,* 1968–9, p. 17.

70 It was found by British archaeologists early in 1907 at the west end of the akropolis, and excavated. The title Athene of the City occurs in a mid-fifth-century inscription, half of which was found here (I.G., V, 1, 213), and the title Bronzehouse Athene is at least as early as Thukydides (1, 134f.). The excavators recovered a few splendid archaic bronzes; below the early or mid sixth-century sanctuary there was a rich level of geometric pottery which may perhaps indicate the earliest date of the cult. (In the whole of Sparta only the most insignificant traces of Mycenaean antiquities have been found, and it is unlikely that Sparta itself existed as a significant settlement in Mycenaean times.)

71 This statue perhaps appears on bronze Spartan coins of the third century a.d. Gitiadas would seem to have worked in the middle of the sixth century (cf. Note 158 below). For the spoils of Aphidna, cf. Bk I, 17 (5).

72 Bronze plates and nails (from the walls?) were found in the excavation, but all the bronze that survived was terribly corroded and was undecorated. For the myth (which figures in the first book of the *Iliad* and the first book of *Paradise Lost*), cf. Bk I, 20 (3). For the sons of Tyndareos, cf. Bk III, Note 96. The decoration of an archaic temple did not necessarily have anything to do with its cult.

[5] On the left of Bronzehouse Athene they have erected a sanctuary of the Muses, because the Lakonians used to march out to battle not to the tune of trumpets, but with the music of flutes and the striking of harp-strings and guitars.[73] Behind Bronzehouse Athene is a TEMPLE OF APHRODITE of War; the cult-statues are as ancient as any in Greece.[74] [6] On the right of Bronzehouse Athene is a statue of Zeus the Highest, the oldest of all bronze statues, not cast in bronze in one piece, but each part made of beaten bronze and then fitted together and all held in place with bolts. They say this statue was made by Klearchos of Region, who is supposed to have been a pupil of Dipoinos and Skyllis, or some people say of Daidalos himself.[75] By the Tabernacle as they call it is the portrait of a woman the Lakonians call Euryleon's daughter, who won an Olympic race with a chariot and pair.

[7] Beside the altar of Bronzehouse Athene stand two portraits of Pausanias who commanded at Plataia. I shall not tell his story because people know it already; what earlier writers have written is quite accurate enough.[76] For myself, I shall simply add what I heard from a Byzantine: the only reason Pausanias's purposes were discovered, and that he alone could not obtain forgiveness by ritual application from Bronzehouse Athene, was a murderous stain that nothing could wash out. [8] When he was in the Hellespont with the Lakonian and all the Greek ships, he lusted for a virgin girl from Byzantion; as soon as night fell Kleonike, as she was called, was brought to him by his orders, but meanwhile Pausanias had been asleep and the noise woke him: as she came to him she accidentally upset the burning lamp. Pausanias, who was conscious of having betrayed Greece, and was troubled and panic-stricken at all times, leapt up and struck at the girl with his short sword. [9] Pausanias went through every kind of purification, he supplicated to Zeus of Escape and he even went to visit the necromantic priests at

---

73   No one but Pausanias mentions lyres and guitars ('lyre' and 'kithara'). A few lines of certain Spartan battle-songs have survived (cf. Page, P.M.G., n. 856–7), and there is a boy flute-player in a black tunic between two ranks of advancing soldiers among the magnificent decorations of the Chigi vase (cf. Arias-Hirmer, *Greek Vase-painting*, n. 16). The painting is Corinthian, but the custom survived longer in Sparta (cf. Thukydides, 5, 70, etc.).

74   Aphrodite of War is perhaps a Fury (cf. Wide, Lakonische Kulte, pp. 141–2). One would rationally expect any Spartan goddess of young people to to be identified with their warlike pursuits, but the origins of cults are not so easily categorized.

75   Klearchos is known only through Pausanias (cf. also Bk VI, 4 (4)). It seems obvious that he really existed, but his apprenticeship is a fabrication, since Daidalos is a creature of legend; for Dipoinos and Skyllis, in whom Pausanias was interested, cf. Bk II, 15 (1). The technique of this Zeus certainly sounds primitive and nothing like it has been found, though there are occasional sixth-century figures cut from thin sheet-bronze, which is then doubled to give two profiles (cf. W. Lamb, *Greek and Roman Bronzes*, pp. 99–100). Fragmentary inscriptions to Zeus the Highest have been found in more than one part of the akropolis.

76   Thukydides, 1, 128–34. King Pausanias of Sparta was stoned to death with roof-tiles in this sanctuary in about 470 B.C.

Phigalia in Arkadia,[77] but he could never get rid of the stain of this guilt. So he paid the penalty of justice to Kleonike and to the goddess. In fulfilment of a command from Delphi, the Lakonians erected these bronze portraits and honour the daemonic power of the Generous god, who they say turned away the curse of Zeus of Suppliants which fell on them because of Pausanias.

[1] Near the figures of Pausanias is a statue of Aphrodite the Turner-away-of-old-age, which was erected through an oracle, and statues of Sleep and Death, whom they believe to be brothers as the Iliad says.[78] [2] On the way to the ALPEION is a SHRINE OF ATHENE of Eyes;[79] the story is that Lykourgos dedicated it, because one of his eyes had been put out by Alkander, who disliked the laws he made. He escaped to this place, where the Lakonians protected him from losing the other eye, and so he built a shrine of Athene of Eyes. [3] Farther on you come to a SANCTUARY OF AMMON; the Lakonians seem to have used the Libyan oracle more than anyone else in Greece from the beginning. Also they say, when Lysander was besieging Aphytis in Pallene,[80] Ammon appeared to him in the night to warn him it would be better for himself and better for Lakonia to give up their war with Aphytis; so Lysander broke up the siege and made the Lakonians offer more worship to this god; Ammon is not more honoured by the Lybian Ammonians than he is at Aphytis.

---

77 Plutarch says it was at Herakleia (*Kimon*, 6). The standard commentaries on Pausanias give lists of necro-mantic shrines all over the Greek world, but nothing is known about one at Phigalia. It seems likely that it centred on the formidably deep and dark hole into which the river Neda disappears; as late as 1963 it was still the custom to throw things into this hole from the high cliffs of the Neda gorge on a certain day in the year. It is an impressive and snake-haunted spot.

78 Plutarch quotes a line or two of a prayer to this Aphrodite (Page, P.M.G., n. 872). Sleep and Death are the twin brothers who carry away Zeus's dead son Sarpedon in the sixteenth book of the *Iliad* (672). Sleep is identified with the Generous god at the Sikyonian Asklepieion (Bk II, 10 (2)).

79 Alpeion seems to have been the land north-west of the akropolis but south of the small river mousga. Some tiles have been found there stamped for the colonnade in Alpeion.

80 The oracle of Zeus Ammon at the Siwa oasis in the Libyan desert has never been excavated. Zeus Ammon was a projection of the god of Egyptian Thebes, Amon Ra, who was originally the Libyan god Ammun. The oracle is treated in Parke's *Oracles of Zeus* (1967), p.p 194f, and by Oric Bates in *The Eastern Libyans*. Lysander seems to have had an inherited family friendship with the king of the Ammonites, aphytis was near Potidaia on the east side of the Pallene peninsula in Macedonia.

POLITICS:
THE CLOSING OF DEMOCRACY

From Oliver Taplin, *Greek Fire*

This is true Liberty when free born men
Having to advise the public may speak free ...
(Euripides translated by Milton)

What kind of democracy will survive into the twenty-first century? We live in a world where over half the people are governed by dictators, oligarchies and military regimes; yet everyone or nearly everyone agrees that democracy is the distinguishing mark of a civilised modern society. East Germany, the Deutsche Demokratische Republik, proclaims its democracy more overtly than West Germany. Marxists expose the ways in which Western democracy is a charade: the West, in the name of democracy, re- sists Russian infiltration of the Third World. The word is used without asking the open questions: who rules? within what limits? for what ends? directly or indirectly? Implicit, and different, answers underlay the democratic claims of the inaugural speech of President Bush on 20 January 1989 and Mikhail Gorbachev's speech to the special Party Congress on 27 June 1988.

In those Western countries which regard themselves as the true democracies the citizens vote sporadically and carelessly. There are mighty forces militating against really concentrated participation in the state by ordinary citizens: the professionalisa- tion of politicians, the growth of bureaucracy, the relentlessly swelling power of the multinationals, and the narcotic effect of the mass media. In Britain 'Charter 88', the call for a new constitutional settlement published in autumn 1988, has some harsh things to say of the British brand of democracy. It speaks of the breakdown of Britain's 'convention of compromise and tolerance: essential components of a free society. Instead, the inbuilt powers of the 1688 settlement have enabled the government to discipline British society to its ends, to impose its values on the civil service; to menace the independence of broadcasting; to threaten academic freedom in the universities and schools; to tolerate abuses committed in the name of national security. The break with the immediate past shows how vulnerable Britain has always been to elective dictatorship.' When does a democracy become an elective dictatorship?

BLOOM V. STONE

In the United States of America, if anywhere, democracy is held to be firmly and conclusively incorporate. Every immigrant must be able to answer some basic questions about democracy to qualify for entry. Yet two recent books have revealed, I suspect, the anxiety of the American educated public on this allegedly secure topic. Ancient Athenian democracy is central to both these best-sellers. In 1987 Allan Bloom published *The Closing of the American Mind*, subtitled *How higher education has failed democracy and impoverished the souls of today's students*. The first printing was presumably small, yet within a year it had sold half a million copies: Bloom's mission, with Socrates and Plato as his standard-bearers, is to restore sure values and standards in a society which has slipped into aimless and careless self-indulgence under the pretext of being liberal and tolerant. He claims that the intelligentsia, seen at its worst in the 'hippy' era, has encouraged the mass of people to believe that in a democracy anything goes; and that this has led to a general enslavement to the whims and desires of the lowest common denominator in society. He calls for some sort of maturity to resist this 'undemocratic and irrational mystique': 'some kind of authority is often necessary for most men and is necessary, at least sometimes, for all men'. Inspired by de Tocqueville's *La Démocratie en Amérique* (1835–40), he calls on the universities to turn to Socrates and to supply that lead.

Completely independently I. F. Stone was writing *The Trial of Socrates*, which takes a quite opposite point of view on many issues, all the way from the relative rights and wrongs of Socrates versus Athenian democracy down to the issues of contemporary liberty. Stone, whose broadsheet *I. K Stone's Weekly* (sometimes *Bi-Weekly*) was highly influential between 1953 and 1971, especially against McCarthyism, taught himself Greek in retirement to prepare for the task. His study is detailed and scholarly; published six months before I wrote this, it has been in the best-seller lists on both sides of the Atlantic. His thesis—while not, of course, endorsing the death penalty like President Bush—is that the Athenians were justified in regarding Socrates as fundamentally undermining their democracy. For Stone the key principle of democracy is the equal right of *any* citizen, however poor, however untrained, to speak out in the parliament without fear of prosecution. This was the case in the Athenian assembly; and Section 6 Article 1 of the American Constitution declares that no member of the Congress can be prosecuted for anything said in any speech or debate in either House'. For Stone the great threat to democracy comes from people such as Socrates, and indeed Allan Bloom, who set themselves up as having special access to some higher, absolute values, to certainties which override the independence of mind of ordinary citizens. Bloom proudly equates himself with Socrates: Stone with Athenian democracy.

THE SELF AND SOCIETY

For all their antipathies, these two have something vital in common. Both Bloom and Stone think of the individual as a member of the 'democracy'. They do not set up the self in opposition to society—the individual against the machine—but as an entity which can only fully be an entity in relation to other people. 'The self' only makes sense in relation, not just to immediate family or friends, but to other people in the community as a whole. The classic statement of this priority is Aristotle's 'Man is by nature a political animal'

This statement needs some expansion. First, the word for 'man' means 'human being' (it is not male). Second, Aristotle is making a quasi-zoological point: as some creatures go round in pairs and some in flocks and so on, so the human animal lives according to nature politically. Finally, political means 'in a *polis*'. *Polis*, often translated as 'city', does not mean 'conurbation', but an entire independent community—the town, sanctuaries, fields, hills, harbours, and everyone who lives there. The usual Greek *polis* was very small, with a population in thousands. Aristotle recommends as a criterion of the optimum size that it should be possible for all the citizens to be addressed by a single herald (without microphone!). Athens, the largest city in classical times (before being overtaken first by Alexandria, then Rome), had in the middle of the fifth century B.C. about 250,000 inhabitants in all, with perhaps 75,000 of them in the conurbation—about one fortieth of the population of New York City today. It is important to bear in mind this vast difference in human numbers.

The citizens, *politai*, were, as a rule, only the adult males whose fathers were citizens—at Athens (or rather Attica, the whole area of *the polis*, about 2,400 square km.) they are reckoned to have been about 40,000 out of the 250,000. It was their privilege to administer their own city, and to fight for her in war, if called for by the majority. It was their citizenship which made them fully human. According to the 'Funeral Speech' of Pericles, which, as given to us by Thucydides, is the finest eulogy of Athenian democracy, if a man does not participate in the *polis*, then, far from being unobtrusive, he is useless. To withdraw yourself from political life in this view—a view endorsed by Aristotle—was to withdraw yourself from being fully human. I.F. Stone says, 'I share the Athenian view that a citizen has a duty to take part in the life of the city.' (We shall come back to women, immigrants and slaves who had no opportunity to be 'fully human' in this sense.)

This Greek view of the place of the citizen in society—of politics—is by no means the standard modern perspective. Moderns tend to define their selves in terms of their own inner beings and perhaps of a small circle of family and friends. Society, the state, is something imposed from outside, something which does not include 'us', which may actually be against us. The starting point of John Stuart Mill's *On Liberty* is a search to find the *minimum* that the state should be allowed to interfere with the private individual. George Steiner puts the contrast with the Greek perspective provocatively: 'we have swung into a very private ideal ... the belief that the good life is the one which we live in our marriages ... in our small circles of friendship, that the debts we owe are primarily to those circles and bonds ... the feeling that the best of us is behind closed doors. This, the Greeks thought, would have been a scandalous failure of human maturity. They clearly foretold our own fate, which is that, when you do this, the mafiosi, the thugs and the third-rate move into the seats of power. And we have very little right, then, to complain.'

The mafiosi, the thugs and the third-rate are presumably the bosses of the multi-nationals and the people who come under the rough heading 'politicians'. In Athens every citizen was a politician. Plato criticised the amateurism and said that government should be handed over to experts. We have done just that, and relinquished the role to a small number of professionals who are overtly in power and to other small groups who operate behind the scenes. We have thus come to a much more narrow sense of 'political' than in 'man is by nature a political animal'. When a figure such as the Bishop of Durham speaks out, he is told to keep politics out of religion; when sports-men who have participated in South Africa are threatened with disqualification, we are told that this is muddling sport up with politics. The very idea of religion or sport being divisible from politics would have been incomprehensible to an ancient Greek, whether or not a democrat.

The professional politicians wish to mark off an area as their terrain. This is true of all modern 'democracies', east, west, far east, capitalist and socialist alike. Election is the key to power. But in ancient Greece election was generally regarded as an undemo-cratic procedure, promoting rule by a few. In ancient Athens *all* qualified citizens were encouraged to participate in the decision-making process in the parliament, indeed they were sometimes literally roped in.

All those touched by a red-dyed rope swung around by an official in the civic centre were obliged to attend. The non-politician citizens of modern democracies are not positively encouraged towards open political expression, and have no occasion (like the Athenian assembly) where they can say anything they want without fear of redress. The nearest experience to this now is serving on a jury, perhaps the most truly demo-cratic of our institutions. In British democracy, at least, there is, as Charter 88 points out, discouragement. How often, after all, do we actually participate in a substantive political *decision*? In a representative democracy there are a few seconds every four or five years when the citizens have power over the politicians; and even then we are not voting directly on the issues. Hardly any government in Britain since the war has been put into power by over fifty per cent of those voting (let alone of those qualified to vote), and forty-two per cent is constantly called 'an overwhelming popular mandate'. In the last election seventy-five per cent of the electorate voted; in the U.S. Presidential election of 1988 the proportion was forty-eight per cent. An ancient Athenian would be totally baffled to hear this called democracy.

THE MIXED REPUBLIC OF THE FOUNDING FATHERS

It is the Greek legacy of *political theory* rather than actual practice which gave birth to the modern kind of democracy. Much Greek political theory was based on the observation that in practice almost all Greek societies from earliest times had three levels of power: a very small number of kings or magistrates; a council of the most powerful men, which generally meant the big landowners; and then a gathering or assembly of all the other citizens. In most places at most times, in ancient Greece power lay with the first of these two groups, sometimes in collaboration and sometimes in rivalry, while the third level, the masses, merely rubber-stamped by acclamation. This tripartite analysis is already found in the fifth-century historian Herodotus. In the next century it was more fully explored and theorised by Plato, especially in his *Republic*, and then by Aristotle in his *Politics*, the two foundation works of political science. In their terms, if the 'kings' were dominant you had 'monarchy' or 'tyranny' (the word was not originally derogatory); if the 'knights' dominated, you had 'aristocracy' or 'oligarchy'; if the popular assembly, the many—*hoi polloi*—managed to appropriate the power, then that was 'democracy'. The Greek word actually means 'power in the hands of the common people' (*dēmos*). Different cities came up with different combinations and emphases. Aristotle's school of political science compiled accounts of 158 different constitutions from all over the Greek world.

Aristotle regarded rule by the many (i.e. democracy) as irresponsibly self-interested and unstable. Characteristically he advocated a compromise, an attempt to have the best of all three types of political system, in other words a *mixed* constitution. When the Greek Polybius was held under house-arrest in Rome for 20 years in the middle of the second century B.C., he analysed the Roman constitution in Greek terms and praised the resilience of its mixture. The three levels—consuls, senate and people—regulated each other by having control of certain crucial spheres of influence (though in fact the popular meetings had little power).

There has been much study of how far this Greek political theory actually influenced the Founding Fathers in the United States, who in 1787 drew up the Constitution which has lasted so remarkably well and been so influential in the rest of the world. There can be no doubt of the recourse to ancient precedent; Richard R. Johnson finds that 'in retrospect, and judging simply by the frequency of citations made and parallels drawn, the influence of the Greek past reached an unprecedented peak in American political discourse around 1787'. John Corbin said, for example, 'The theory of our constitution derives from Aristotle, and was put into successful practice in Rome ...' and John Adams that 'it is manifest that the best form of government is that which is compounded of all three forms'.

So the Founding Fathers thought of themselves as establishing a Republic, as in Rome, not a Democracy as in fifth-century Athens. Indeed Athens was a negative model. As Meyer Reinhold says, 'One of the prime lessons adduced from antiquity by the Founding Fathers was the unsuitability of direct assembly government, because of the instances known of instability and capriciousness of decisions in ancient republics.' The shift to the positive model of Athens was a late nineteenth-century phenomenon. Earlier in the century the great theorists de Tocqueville and Mill thought that ever-increasing popular participation in the United States would come closer and closer to ancient Athens. The irony is that in our times, when the paradigm of Athens is universally paid lip-service, democracy has moved away from, rather than towards, real participation by the many. The nearest that the *dēmos* of our era gets to power is a television screen.

'WHO WISHES TO SPEAK?'

Everyone may know that 'the Greeks invented democracy' and that 'Athens was the cradle of democracy', but few have any notion how very different Athenian democracy was from democracy as we know it, or realise that most Greeks, including Plato and Aristotle, strongly disapproved of it. Though many have maintained that it was un-stable and short-lived, there was, in fact, democracy at Athens from the great reforms of Cleisthenes in 508 B.C., which set up a political organisation that cut across the old clan and local groupings, until 338 B.C. when Philip of Macedon took over. That timespan is not far short of the time that the American Constitution has lasted. Indeed democratic structures and procedures continued at Athens down into the Roman pe-riod, though in a rather empty way. The golden age, however, during which many other Greek cities became democracies under the influence of Athens, lasted roughly from the 460s to the 420s, the period when Pericles was the most influential individual. And this golden age of democracy was also a golden age in many other spheres of activity.

There were, as ever, the three centres of power. There was a small number of state officers, the most important of these being the ten military commanders-in-chief who were elected annually by the citizens. Election was not really a democratic method of choice, but they were subject to a rigorous scrutiny after their period in office. The ele-ment of the council was supplied by a body of 500. They were appointed for one year from volunteers spread among the groups of community, and the final selection was by an elaborate system of lot. No-one was allowed to serve more than twice in a lifetime, so a large proportion of citizens would serve on the council at some time. It met in a special building on the west side of the Agora, where it prepared all the business for the popular assembly, and was the day-to-day executive government. Every month (there were 10 in a year) 50 of the 500 lived at public expense in the round *tholos* next door, and were on emergency call to deal with urgent business. Their chairman was chosen daily by lot—so the person whose role was nearest to that of the President or the Prime Minister changed *every day*.

Sovereign, finally, was the people's assembly, the *ekklesia*. All matters of principle or substance were settled here by majority vote. Its decisions were final, and there was in effect no party system or opposition. The assembly met in the morning four times a month on the hill called the Pnyx, which was artificially banked to make an auditorium large enough to hold getting on for 10,000 people. The Herald would ask, 'Who wishes to speak?' No doubt a limited number of individuals tended to dominate business, but the fact remains that in principle any citizen whosoever could respond to this call. It has been calculated that at a normal meeting of the *ekklesia* 4,000–5,000, or ten per cent of the citizen body, used to attend, and there was hardly ever more than twenty per cent present. Before taking this to undermine the claims of Athenian democracy, it is worth asking how often ten per cent of a modern community gathers in one place for any occasion, let alone a serious one, let alone forty times a year. Ten per cent of the adult population of New York City would amount to more than half a million people. Do ten thousand New Yorkers know what is going on in Congress in any given month? Only fifty per cent of the electorate turns out for the one opportunity they have every four years to choose their chief executive.

Athenian democracy actually involved an extraordinarily high proportion of all those qualified in its government. It was truly participatory. Fortunately, the historian Thucydides decided to write out the speech, or his version of the speech, which Pericles delivered in the winter of 430 B.C. in honour of the Athenians killed in the first year of the Peloponnesian War. Thucydides, writing 15 or 20 years later, was aware that this marked the beginning of the end of the golden age, and that Pericles was himself soon to die of the terrible plague. His 'Funeral Speech' was revolutionary then, and in many ways still is. Students have been arrested in Greece under modern dictatorships for distributing it.

> We are called a democracy, for the administration is in the hands of the many and not of the few. But while the law secures equal justice for all alike in their private disputes, the claim of excellence is also recognised; and when a citizen is in any way distinguished he is preferred to the public service, not as a matter of privilege, but as the reward of merit. Neither is poverty a bar, but a man may benefit his country whatever be the obscurity of his condition. There is no exclusiveness in our public life …

Does any modern democracy genuinely aspire to this manifesto?

LIBERTY FOR THE PEOPLE OR TYRANNY BY THE PEOPLE?

Another proud declaration of the ideals of democratic Athens is put in the mouth of the legendary King Theseus in Euripides' play *Suppliants* (420s). John Milton translated some lines on the title-page of *Areopagitica*, his rousing call to parliament for freedom of expression in print in 1644 (named after the Areopagus rock near the Acropolis in Athens):

> This is true Liberty when free born men
> Having to advise the public may speak free,
> Which he who can, and will, deserv's high praise,
> Who neither can nor will, may hold his peace;
> What can be juster in a State than this?

Some Levellers in the 1640s also pointed to ancient Athens for popular participation in power, but they were long before their time. Marchamont Nedham changed his views with the times, but in the *Excellencie of a Free State* (1656) he is full of favour for Athens. During the sixteenth, seventeenth and eighteenth centuries democracy was normally regarded as unstable mob rule, as Plato and Aristotle taught. The great political theorists, such as Machiavelli, Harrington and Montesquieu, even Rousseau, looked upon democracy as acceptable only if incorporated into a mixed constitution. Montesquieu (*De l'esprit des lois* 1748) put Athens back on the map as a live force in political thought, but the revolutions in France and America still did not, as a rule, use 'Athens' or 'democracy' as positive terms in their rhetoric.

In a Britain alarmed by events across the Channel and across the Atlantic, the Tory landowner William Mitford wrote a highly influential history of Greece (published between 1784 and 1810) which utterly condemned Athenian democracy as nothing less than 'a tyranny in the hands of the people'. This remained the standard view for 50 years, and was not properly challenged until George Grote, the reforming radical and former MP, went to the other extreme in his *History of Greece* (1846–56) and made Athens sound much more stable and British than it really was. Frank M. Turner's account sums up the issue well:

> Grote's strategy [was to make] Athens an object lesson in the dangers posed
> by conservative forces in a democracy. Previous anti-democratic writers, such
> as Mitford, had argued that a modern liberal democratic state would resemble
> lawless Athens. Reversing the analogy, Grote presented ancient democratic
> Athens as almost a mirror image of the stable, liberal mid-Victorian polity.

Athens now became idealized. John Stuart Mill had maintained that the Athenian system 'raised the intellectual standard of an average Athenian citizen far beyond anything of which there is yet an example in any other age of men, ancient or modern ...' E. A. Freeman, Professor of History at Oxford, went further: 'The average Athenian citizen was, in political intelligence, above the average English member of Parliament'! In fifty years Athens shifted from an awful example to an inspiration. In 1915 extracts from Pericles' *Funeral Speech* were put up in London buses as part of the recruiting campaign, for the armed forces against the enemy which threatened freedom and democracy. There was a similar shift in France, traced by Pierre Vidal-Naquet and Nicole Loreaux, by which Athens was transformed from a terrible warning to a shining model during the course of the nineteenth century, above all by the *Histoire Grecque* of Victor Duruy (1851).

WOMEN, SLAVES AND SELF-RIGHTEOUSNESS

So democracy won the nineteenth-century debate, though it was not the participatory democracy of Athens. In practice it was the representative democracy of the United States and of de Tocqueville. Indeed during the twentieth century any allusion to Athenian participatory democracy has, as often as not, been accompanied by qualification, disclaimer and even scorn. The modern reservation has not been the old horror of mob rule, but the complaint that Athenian democracy *excluded* so many people from its privileged circle of citizens. 'How can it be called democracy when women and slaves were without political rights?' There may be a hint of self-righteousness and even of resentment in the standard depreciation. What hides behind this?

First some approximate facts about Athens. Within the round-figure calculation of 250,000 inhabitants of Attica, there would have been some 40,000 *politai*, i.e., participant citizens comprised about sixteen per cent of the total This reckoning supposes 100,000 women and children of citizen families. There were also some 20,000 or so resident immigrants, called 'metics', who were free but without citizen rights, and up to 100,000 slaves, who were owned by citizens and who had virtually no rights, not even the right to have a family. Some led quite pleasant lives, but many, especially those who worked in the silver mines of Laurion in the south of Attica, lived and died under horrific conditions. Surely this justifies the twentieth-century self-righteousness? There is something hypocritical in treating the exclusion of women from politics let alone suffrage as a primitive inhumanity. Women got the vote in the United States in 1918, in Britain in 1919 (with limitations), in Italy and France in 1945. In Quebec and Switzerland they had to wait until 1971. In some respects the mass meetings of the small Swiss canton are the nearest modern analogy to the Athenian *ekklesia*. It is amusing, then, to find that in the canton of Appenzell, not only must men wear their swords to a meeting but women still do not have the vote at that level of government. The treatment of women in enlightened fifth-century Athens is a disturbing story but we are hardly in a position to be too superior about it. In the British parliament there are at present 41 women MPs in a total of 650; and in the United States House of Representatives the proportion is even smaller.

Slavery is now of course an abhorred institution; these days we have machines instead. Yet a number of those who signed the Declaration of Independence in 1776 owned slaves, and there are still many countries throughout the world where sections of the labour force are so constrained as to be in a condition very close to slavery—*Gastarbeiter* for instance. The gold mines of South Africa have much in common with the silver mines of Laurion.

All the same, the standard indictment of Athenian democracy is not so much that it excluded slaves as that it *depended on* slave labour. It was only the economic exploitation, it is claimed, that freed ordinary Athenians for politics. The Tory Mitford was the first to put forward this argument in the 1790s, as he warned Britain of the dangers: democracy means that the workers will stop working and devote themselves to power-seeking instead. Ironically, the doctrine has since then been taken over by very different political ideologies. Engels wrote in 1884: 'the downfall of Athens was not caused by democracy, as the European lickspittle historians assert to flatter their princes, but by slavery, which banned the labour of free citizens'. Either way, recent research, for example by Ellen Meiskins Wood in her *Peasant, Citizen and Slave*, suggests that this is a myth, and that the great majority of Athenian citizens did work most of the time, especially on the land. Wealthier citizens, who could afford a suit of bronze armour and who constituted the land army, did not need to work. The larger number who manned the ships in time of war were neither wealthy nor idle, and they constituted the backbone of a peasant democracy.

It is curious that in the first century which has ever taken 'democracy' to be by definition a word of approval, the twentieth century A.D., there has also been a widespread tendency to run down the Athenian achievement. There are, I suggest, reasons why modern democracies, communist and capitalist alike, might wish to divert admiration away from ancient Athens. The elected powers do not want their citizens to participate too actively, not even the middle-class men, let alone the women and the menial labourers.

THE SPARTAN ANTITHESIS

Democracy is by no means the only Greek model which has been evoked over the centuries. Plato and Aristotle both deplored it. The influence of Aristotle's *Politics* has been immense: Karl Marx, among his admirers, called him 'a giant thinker'. It is not surprising that Aristotle, who based his theories on the observation of practice, disapproved of democracy as unbalanced and unstable. He was not an Athenian, after all, and by the time he arrived in Athens the golden age was over half a century in the past. Plato, on the other hand, was an Athenian and so subject to the law which said, 'If any man overthrow the democracy at Athens … he shall be held an enemy of the Athenians and may be killed without penalty to his killer.' Yet Plato went much further than Aristotle in his rejection of the system which condemned Socrates. He equated the people (*dēmos*) with the lowest, emotional, unthinking part of man's three-level soul. The city should be run by the 'guardians', the 'philosopher-kings', who have perfected the highest, rational level of their souls. That is according to his utopian *Republic*. Later in life he worked out a 'second-best state' in the *Laws* which is so repressive and conservative that even children's games are to be stabilised and regulated. All the work is to be done by slaves and disenfranchised people, since the citizens are to concentrate, not on politics, but on military training. Ultimate power lies with an exclusive and sinister body, the Nocturnal Council.

Plato was one of a group of Athenians who thought that Sparta was great. Much in the *Laws* is Plato's own brainchild, but he was clearly influenced by the practice of the city whose politics he so much admired. Sparta (the whole area was called Lacedaemon), well inland in the southern Peloponnese, was Athens' great enemy, and was in many ways about as unlike Athens as could be. The contrast is still apparent to the modern visitor. Thucydides made a remarkable prediction: 'Suppose the city of Sparta to be deserted, and nothing left but the temples and the ground plan, distant ages would be very unwilling to believe that the power of the Lacedaemonians was at all equal to their fame ... whereas, if the same fate befell the Athenians, the ruins of Athens would strike the eye, and we should infer their power to have been twice as great as it really is.' The grand monuments of Athens are gathered round the majestic Acropolis: the site of ancient Sparta, which was in effect a group of villages without a defensive wall, is now a group of hillocks covered in olive trees, surrounded by the fertile valley of the river Eurotas.

The political system at Sparta was attributed to the semi-legendary legislator Lycurgus. As everywhere there were the three levels of power among the citizens; but the relative distribution could hardly have been more different from that at Athens. At the top were two hereditary kings, and five annually elected magistrates called *ephors*, who had substantial executive powers. Next, the council, called the *gerousia*, had 28 members, all aged over sixty and all appointed for life. The *gerousia* made decisions of war and peace, and was the centre of legislation and judicial power. Finally, there was the popular meeting (*apella*) of all citizens over thirty, known as the *Spartiates*. They numbered fewer than 10,000, met rarely and irregularly, and even then did little more than rubber-stamp the proposals which emanated from the 35 people with the real power. Non-citizens were divided into the freedom inhabitants of the villages, and the *helots*, Greeks who were in effect serfs. The whole Spartan system depended on this large subject population which provided for the elite.

The life of the Spartiate was devoted to military fitness. All weak babies were exposed in the gorges of Mount Taygetus, a practice applauded by Hitler. From the age of seven until thirty every young male lived a life of harsh military training, first as a cub then as a pack-leader. A folk-lore about their way of life had already grown up in ancient times. It claimed, for instance, that every boy was allowed one cloak a year, and slept on rushes which he gathered for himself from the river. Drill exercises and violent competitive games were kept on the move by the whip; there were competitions to endure the lash without crying out. On special occasions they were let loose and allowed to lynch a few helots. At the age of thirty the new Spartiates were expected to marry and were allotted land, though they did not farm it themselves—that was what the helots were for. They spent their days not at home but in messes, where they ate together with the members of their 'battalion' (the black broth was famous). Their purpose in life was to be one of ten thousand identical component parts in a war machine.

However repulsive this may sound, a myth was built up over the centuries of Sparta as the model of a stable, patriotic society—the 'Spartan Mirage' as it is sometimes known. Plato's admiration was significant, but the most important idealisation was that of the biographer Plutarch (about 100 A.D.), especially in his *Life of Lycurgus*. Plutarch was taken very seriously during the Renaissance, and there was a fine sixteenth-century translation into French by Amyot. In the nineteenth century Mary Garth, we are told in the finale of *Middlemarch*, 'wrote a little book for her boys, called *Stories of Great Men taken from Plutarch*'. So it is that many towns in the United States are called Sparta; and this is why in 1834, very soon after Greek independence, a new *Sparti* was laid out on the edge of the ancient site. This rectangular symbol of the rebirth of Greece went inextricably hand in hand with the end of the town of Mistra, some 8 kilometres away. Mistra was founded by the Francs in 1247, and was one of the great cities of late Byzantine Greece—indeed Gemistos Plethon even established a Platonic academy there during 1400–42. Yet this centre of orthodox religion and learning was deserted to refound militaristic and patriotic Sparta. (Comparably the last Christian service to be held in the temple of Hephaestus at Athens—a church for over 1,000 years—was to welcome King Otto on his arrival in Athens on 13 December 1834.)

The story of Sparta in later ages has been well studied by Elizabeth Rawson in *The Spartan Tradition in European Thought*. Those who have nominated Sparta and Lycurgus with enthusiastic approval include most of the great names of political science, even Machiavelli and Montesquieu. James Harrington in *The Commonwealth of Oceana* (1656) urged Cromwell to imitate Lycurgus, and cited Sparta's stability as second only to Venice. Rousseau, often seen as the founder of the Western democratic tradition, praised the Spartan system (as given by Plutarch) unreservedly in *Du contrat social* (1762). 'American leaders', writes Meyer Reinhold, 'judged Sparta [as opposed to Athens] as a model of freedom and order, a stable, long-lived commonwealth, its people distinguished by virtue, simple life-style, patriotism, vigour.' John Dickson in 1769 reckoned the Spartans 'as brave and as free a people as ever existed', and Samuel Adams looked forward to Boston becoming 'a Christian Sparta'.

It is hard to pin down a turning-point, but the reflections of the great French romantic Chateaubriand on 18 August 1806 are on the dividing line. On that day he visited the site of Sparta (no new town as yet) and wrote: 'even if I loathe the manners of the ancient Spartans, I am not blind to the greatness of a free people, and it was not without emotion that I trampled on their noble dust'. In the course of the nineteenth century, as Athens took over as the model to be admired, Sparta was forgotten more than actively condemned. I am aware of only one outburst of enthusiasm for Sparta in the second half of the century: Walter Pater's essay 'Lacedaemon'. He muses on the 'half-military, half-monastic spirit which prevailed in this gravely beautiful place', and he compares ancient Sparta explicitly, and with sentimental affection, with the English public schools. There were indeed similarities, not least the dormitory homosexuality and the obsessive fascination with beating. Richard Jenkyns has found a poignant pendant to this parallel. The Baron de Charlus in Proust is led by the struggles of the First World War to muse: 'Those English soldiers who at the beginning I dismissed as mere football-players ... well, they are the young men of Plato, or rather they are Spartiates.'

PLATE, LENIN, HITLER

The fire of Plato and of Sparta has continued to flare even in the twentieth century—perhaps at its most dangerous. The resemblances between the education of Spartan boys and the *Gioventù fascista* or the *Hitlerjugend* are no coincidence. As early as 1933 there was a book *Hitlers Kampf und Platons Staat* by Joachim Bannes. An education committee set up to oversee the Adolf Hitler-Schule compiled a textbook about Sparta, emphasising its communal training. Its toughness and spirit of *Kameradschaft*. 'Many of the plans and ground rules which the Spartans had about how to build a state and how to train its ruling class are of relevance to us ... we want to help the Führer to build a great Reich. Sparta should be a rousing example to us.' One Hans Bogner, in a book on education published in 1937, recommends that German teachers should pay special attention to Plato's 'Guardians'. 'Germany of the New Spirit has the special destiny, on account of its historical situation, to acknowledge Plato as a living force.' Plato is cited in support of the censorship of the theatre, the promotion of gymnastics, and of the doctrine that a democracy ceases to be a democracy when it fails to pick the right leaders. (And who decides who is right?) Hitler himself, according to his *Table Talk*, often praised the Spartans, and their subjugation of the helots. He even claimed that the peasant soup in Schleswig-Holstein bore a significant resemblance to black broth!

In 1937 Richard Crossman, a future Labour minister, then an Oxford don, published a series of talks he had been giving on BBC Radio as *Plato Today*. He attacked Plato as the greatest ever enemy of liberal ideas and as an inspirer of fascism. Arnold Toynbee voiced similar sentiments, and so did Bertrand Russell, who described Lenin and Hitler as Plato's greatest disciples. The heaviest attack on Plato came later, in 1945, from Karl Popper, who had fled his native Austria when in his mid-thirties, and who established himself at the London School of Economics after the Second World War. Volume I of *The Open Society and its Enemies* is directed against Plato, volume II against Hegel and Marx. Popper's central point is that in politics (as in science) it is a fundamental error to ask 'How can we be certain?' and 'How can we secure perfect rulers?': what we must ask is 'How can we detect and remedy our mistakes as quickly as possible?' and 'How can we minimise the damage that our rulers may do?' It is curious to find no mention of Popper in *The Closing of the American Mind*, nor any kind of defence against Popper's far from lightweight attack. In fact Bloom does not allude at all to Sparta, or to Plato's admiration for that impersonally patriotic regime. It is an intriguing, and perhaps frightening, twist of Greek Fire that in 1987 Plato can be offered as a champion of American Democracy. When does democracy become an elective dictatorship?

THERMOPYLAE

By Constantine P. Cavafy

Honor to those who in their lives
have defined and guard their Thermopylae.
Never stirring from duty;
just and upright in all their deeds,
yet with pity and compassion too;
generous when they are rich, and when
they are poor, again a little generous,
again helping as much as they can;
always speaking the truth,
yet without hatred for those who lie.

And more honor is due to them
when they foresee (and many do foresee)
that Ephialtes will finally appear,
and that the Medes in the end will go through.

Constantine P. Cavafy (1903)

Notes:

In 480 BC, Xerxes led the Persians (*Medes*) and invaded Greece. The Spartan king Leonidas, in charge of 7000 Greeks, was ordered to cut the advance of the Persian army at *Thermopylae* (in central Greece), a narrow strip of land between the sea and impassable mountains. The Persian army, 250,000 strong, attacked twice and was forced to retreat, due to the fact that the passage was so narrow that they could not fully deploy their force. However, an avaricious local farmer, *Ephialtes*, led a force of Persian infantry through a mountain passage and next morning they appeared behind the Greek lines. Leonidas ordered the rest of the army withdraw, and held the passage with 300 Spartans. As a true Spartan, he chose death over retreat; all 300 Spartans, including Leonidas, died, but held the Persians long enough to ensure the safe withdrawal of the rest of the Greek army.

LaVergne, TN USA
03 January 2009
168617LV00001BA/2/P